Genesis of the Mormon Canon

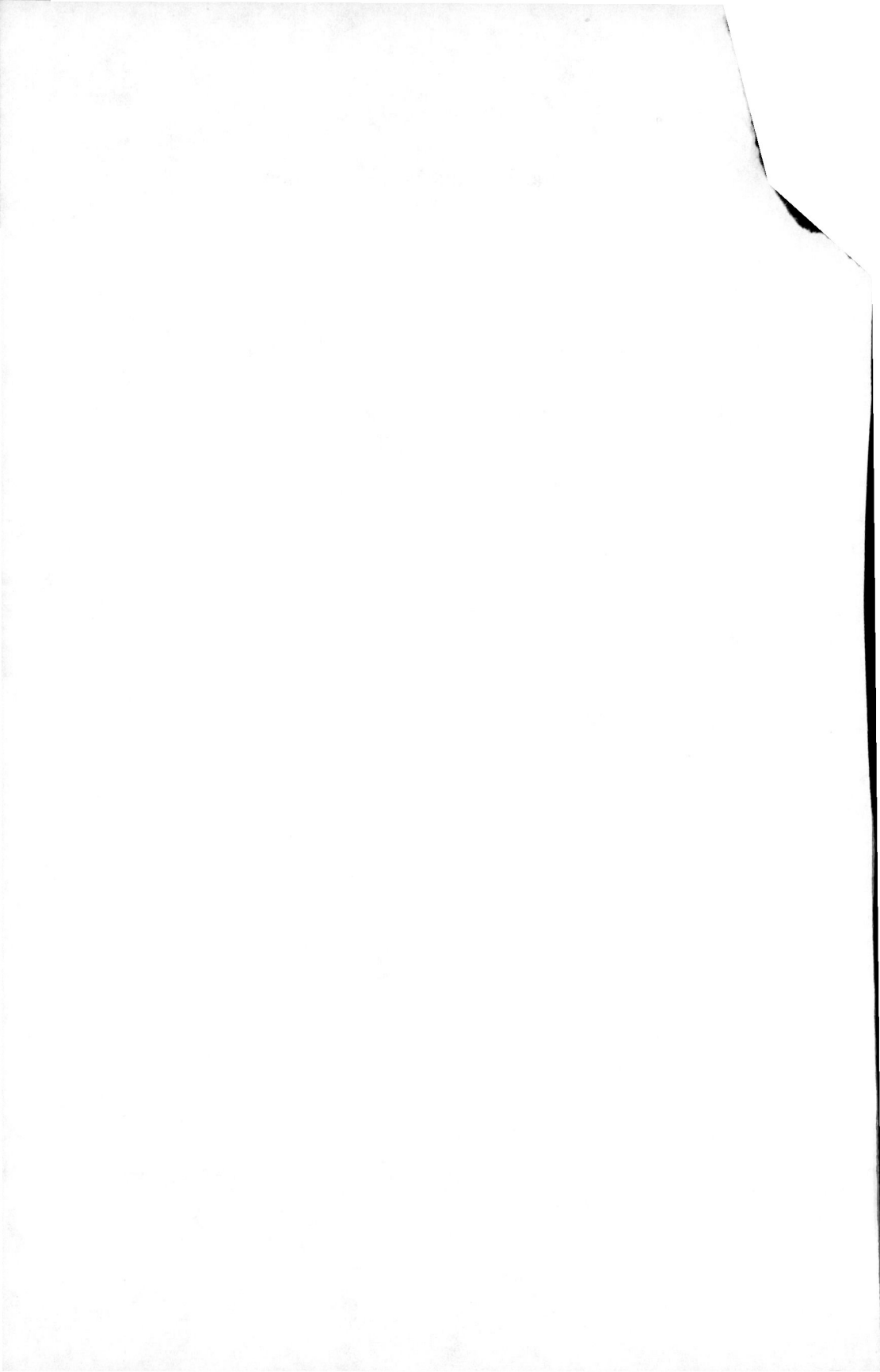

Genesis

of the

Mormon Canon

Arthur Chris Eccel

GP
Touchstone

2023

Genesis of the Mormon Canon by Arthur Chris Eccel

@ 2023 by Arthur Chris Eccel

ISBN 979-8-218-25042-3

sembase.org; gptouchstone.org (Hilo, Hawaii)
GP Touchstone is an imprint of Arthur Chris Eccel, publisher.

Hilo, Hawaii

Printed by IngramSpark.

𝕲𝕻
𝕿𝖔𝖚𝖈𝖍𝖘𝖙𝖔𝖓𝖊

VERITAS

About the Author

Dr. Eccel completed a mission in the French East Mission of the Church of Jesus Christ of Latter-day Saints (1961-64) after graduating from East High in Salt Lake City, Utah. After his return, he received his BA in 1967 from the University of Utah in classics (Greek and Latin). Graduating number one in the language department, he received the coveted Woodrow Wilson scholarship. In 1970 he received his MA from Harvard in Near Eastern Languages and Literatures, with concentrations in Arabic and Hebrew, while at the same time studying Aramaic and Ge'ez (old Ethiopic). At Harvard, he studied under the renowned Hebrew scholar, Frank Cross. After declining the Emma da Garmo grant for second-year law at UCLA Law School, he received his MA in sociology from the University of Utah, and went on to get his PhD from the University of Chicago, from the Department of Sociology in collaboration with its famous Oriental Institute,where his postgraduate focus was Islamic mocernism under Fazlur Rahman.

He has taught at the university level at several universities, including criminology at Elmhurst University, and three years as assistant professor of sociology at the American University of Beirut (AUB), 1978-81. He has worked as a professional researcher, first for eighteen months at the American University in Cairo (AUC) with full Ford Foundation funding, and then two postdoctoral years at the American Research Center in Egypt (ARCE). This culminated in his book, *Egypt, Islam and Social Change: Al-Azhar in Conflict and Accommodation* (Berlin, 1984). Other scholarly publications are mostly in Islamic studies. He also served as a project ethnographer in an ethnoarchaeological project directed by Helga Seeden in Busra eski Sham, Syria. His research interests have been in the sociohistory of religion, using comparative and historical methodologies, and in Semitic lexicography. His languages include Hebrew, Arabic, Aramaic, Ge'ez, Sabaic and Akkadian (the latter in transliterated texts), as well as Greek, Latin, French and German. His ability in these languages ranges from full fluency to adequate research competency.

In 1986, he joined the U.S. Diplomatic Corps and served for 21 years in Iraq, Saudi Arabia, Bahrain, Yemen, Algeria and Syria, retiring as Counselor of Embassy for Public Relations and Director of the American Cultural Center in Damascus, Syria. At the Department of State he was webmaster (1997-98) of a website that he created in Arabic to give citizens of Arabic-speaking countries access to information and principal documents regarding US foreign policy in the Middle East.

After retirement he was able to dedicate more time to researching various issues in Mormon Studies, and published *Mormon Genesis* in 2018.

Chris met his wife, Kozue (Kay) Abe Nagata, in Baghdad, Iraq, during the Iran-Iraq war. Having served for thirty years as a UN official, she retired as the Director of the UNESCO office in Islamabad, and is now a professor of international relations in Nagoya, Japan.

Table of Contents

Genesis of the Mormon Canon

Genesis of the Mormon Canon

Genesis of the Mormon Canon

Genesis of the Mormon Canon

Figures

Genesis of the Mormon Canon

Abbreviations

ALJ	after leaving Jerusalem
BCE	before the Common Era (i.e. BC)
BoA	Book of Abraham
BoC	Book of Commandments
BoE	Book of Ether
BoM	Book of Mormon
CE	Common Era (i.e. AD)
D&C	Doctrine and Covenants
JSP	Joseph Smith Papers
KJV	King James Version
ms$\mathcal{O}$	"original » manuscript
ms$\mathcal{P}$	printer's manuscript
ms$\mathcal{U}$	urtext manuscript

PROLOGUE

In 2030, the Church of Jesus Christ of Latter-day Saints will celebrate the bicentennial of its keystone scripture, its sacred New World bible, the *Book of Mormon*. By the time of the murder of its founder in 1844, Joseph Smith, additional works had been added to the Mormon canon, including the (LDS) *Book of Moses*, the *Book of Abraham,* the collected revelations issued by Joseph Smith in the *Doctrine and Covenants*, and "Joseph Smith" (his history).

Keenly aware that the Christian world would attack this new bible and a latter-day prophet, the *Book of Mormon* adopted the policy that the best defense is a good offense. The message of the apostasy of early church fathers was first ramped up in the *Book of Mormon* where an angel shows Nephi the "great and abominable church" and declares that there are but two churches, the church of God and the church of the devil (1 Nephi 14:9-10). "The Gentiles do stumble exceedingly, because of the most plain and precious parts of the gospel of the Lamb which have been kept back by that abominable church, which is the mother of harlots, saith the Lamb" (1 Nephi 13:34). Even the Jews were not overlooked: "there is none other nation on earth that would crucify their God" (2 Nephi 10:3).

Although the BoM took first blood, the critics responded in kind. Over a period of nearly two hundred years, there has developed a rich literature of LDS apologetics, and the efforts of critics (including some outright anti-Mormons). To some extent, this book revisits the more important issues argued in the past, but with new data or approaches. Along the way, new studies suggested themselves, even some serendipity that could be developed into original studies. Overall, what emerged is a roundup of individual and largely independent research projects. In most cases, each chapter is a standalone study. A detailed table of contents enables the reader to pick and choose what to read next.

This research is based as much as possible on contemporary material. For example, for studies of the *Book o Mormon*, the key material is the so-called original manuscript (ms𝒪, only 30% extant) along with the printer's manuscript (ms𝒫). These are by far the principal primary sources. As for the statements of those involved in the production of the canon, every effort has been made to avoid convenient interpretations in support of this or that theory. Finally, the studies are clearly stated and presented in a manner to facilitate replication.

Genesis of the Mormon Canon

< Chapter 1 >

Precursors Incorporated in the *Book of Mormon* Thesis

For decades, Mormon studies scholars have contended that the preachers and writers of the Second Great Awakening provided Joseph Smith with foundational elements for his Pre-Columbian New World bible.

The Sons of Noah

In the early 19th century New England, even many educated people held to some concept of a racial ranking of the nations. In the early centuries of the Common Era (CE, rather than AD), two scriptural communities, the Jews and the Christians, overlapped in their belief in certain books later incorporated into what the Christians came to call the Old Testament. Even some of their most erudite scholars believed that Noah's flood had actually happened, and that a wrathful deity had destroyed every man, woman and child from the face of the earth, with the exception of the family of Noah in the Ark. Partly to define how they should relate to the peoples of the earth, but also to make their belief in this tale more credible, they set about constructing a global family tree. They had become aware of the existence of numerous large, well-peopled and even ancient civilizations in Europe, Africa and Asia, all of which had somehow been descended from the family of Noah. Various branches of the tree were more favored by God, and others even cursed.

The earliest and most influential effort to define the global family tree was that of Flavius Josephus (1st century CE), in his book *Antiquities of the Jews*. Christian efforts built on the work of Josephus, and the works of Hippolytus of Rome (c. 234 CE), Saint Jerome (c. 390 CE) in his work *Hebrew Questions on Genesis*, and Isidore of Seville (c. 600 CE) in his *Etymologiæ*. As Christians became more aware of other civilizations than their own, and even some other significant civilizations, it became necessary to rethink the family tree. The entire enterprise suffered a major shock, when in 1492, Columbus discovered the New World, replete with yet other extensive, developed and even rich civilizations.

Who Are the Indians?

Although most Europeans who actually went to the Americas spontaneously recognized that the inhabitants native to these new lands were actually human beings, strange views of these peoples began to circulate back home. Europe already had many tales of wild men, monstrous races and fabulous creatures. Lewis Hanke, in his work *Aristotle and the American Indians*, provides many details of Europe's first theories to explain these peoples. "A 1498 edition of John of Holywood's *Sphaera Mundi* describes the inhabitants of the New World as being 'blue in colour and with square heads'."[1] In Wilberforce Eames' "Description of a Wood Engraving, Illustrating the South American Indians (1505)," we read:

> They go naked, both men and women; they have well-shaped bodies, and in colour nearly red; they bore holes in their cheeks, lips, noses and ears, and stuff these holes with blue stones, crystals, marble and alabaster, very fine and beautiful. This custom is followed alone by the men. They have no personal property, but all things are in common...They take for wives whom they first meet, and in all this they have no rule. And they eat one another, and those they slay are eaten, for human flesh is a common food. ... They live to be a hundred and fifty years old, and are seldom sick.[2]

Already in the sixteenth century, we find notions that the Americas had become the home of giants, of Gog and Magog, and yes, even of remnants of the Lost Tribes of Israel.

Who Discovered America: the Welsh, Romans or Central Asians?

Today it seems that everyone wants to lay claim to getting to the Americas before Columbus. One begins to wonder, "Who didn't discover America?" The two claims that seem to have real evidence are those for the Vikings and for the Polynesians. Prior to 1825 the list was much shorter, and sometimes literary rather than literal.

According to Welsh folklore, Madoc, or Madog ab Owain Gwynedd, sailed to America in 1170. In Robert Southey's (1807) treatment of the legend, Madoc makes a dangerous voyage to the west, and at long last he "stood triumphant on another world!" He witnesses Aztec human sacrifice and recruits the assistance of a local tribe to subdue the Aztecs and put an end to this practice. On a return voyage, he finds that the Aztecs had reverted to their traditions.

---

[1] Lewis Hanke, *Aristotle and the American Indians. A Study in Race Prejudice in the Modern World* (Mishawaka, IN: Better World Books, 1970).
[2] *Ibid*, 5.

A more prominent work in Mormon studies is the historical romance of Solomon Spalding (Spaulding), who died in 1816. His work was based on a landing of Romans headed to England, but blown off course. We will examine this work in greater detail within the context of the Spalding-Rigdon theory of *Book of Mormon* (BoM) origins.

Constantine Samuel Rafinesque championed a less theological approach. This polymath professor was an indefatigable reader and field worker, who identified and published quite a number of American species, some of which still bear the names he gave them. Natural history was his main field, but he included human history in that rubric. He assembled a huge collection of actual and legendary names of people, peoples and clans, worldwide, and attempted to arrive at a history of the dispersion of the postdiluvian peoples across Eurasia and Africa, and then the Americas. The earliest arrivals included migrations and more casual contacts from Europe to North America, including from the little-known Atlantans of Plato. A second migration came from Central Asia and Siberia, across the Behring Straits.[3] The migration from Asia is now well established, and the migration from Europe is not yet a dead theory, although very skimpily evidenced. Along the way, he presented a description of the evolution of the species, without any knowledge of the mechanisms supplied by Darwin.[4] Mayanists respect him for identifying the elementary principles of how the Mayans represented their counting system, generally considered to be the first correct step anyone every made towards deciphering Mayan texts.[5] It is notable that, unlike so many others, when giving the names of so many peoples and clans that figured in the settlement of the Americas, he wrote "that many nations came to America before and after the flood; but no Jews ever came there before Columbus."[6]

---

[3] C. S. Rafinesque, *Ancient History, or Annals of Kentucky; with a Survey of the Ancient Monuments of North America; and a Tabular View of the Principal Languages and Primitive Nations of the Whole Earth* (Frankfort, KY: printed by the author, 1824); see also *Atlantic Journal and Friend of Knowledge* (1832-33).
[4] C. S. Rafinesque, "Extract of a letter to Dr. J. Torrey of New York dated 1st Dec. 1832," in Charles Boewe, ed., *Rafinesque Anthology* (Jefferson, NC: McFarland & Company, 2005), 242-48.
[5] This was published in a letter to the editor of the *Saturday Evening Post*.
[6] C. S. Rafinesque, "Letter of Professor Rafinesque, of Philadelphia, to Mr. Josiah Priest, of Albany, on *American Antiquities*," dated 5 January 1835, in Boewe, *Rafinesque Anthology*, 16.

Europe and the Indians

At the same time that most Spaniards in the Americas were mostly devoted to Gold, Glory and God (often in that order), in 1550, Charles V summoned the Council of the Fourteen to sit in Valladolid (Spain), to judge the issues regarding what the relationship should be between the Spanish crown and the Indians, to wit: "is it lawful for the king of Spain to wage war on the Indians before preaching the faith to them in order to subject them to his rule, so that afterwards they may be more easily instructed in the faith?"[7] Sepulveda argued that the use of force was both lawful and expedient as a preliminary to conversion, while Las Casas took the opposite view. Urging the colonization of Virginia, Samuel Purchas (1577?-1626) wrote: "God in wisdom having enriched the Savage Countries, that these riches might be attractives for Christian suters, which there may sowe spirituals and reape temporals."[8]

Cromwell and Manasseh ben Israel

The Jews had not had any significant presence in England prior to William the Conqueror, and were expulsed from England at the time of the defeat of the Normand occupation. Oliver Cromwell (1599-1658), who ruled England as Lord Protector (1653-58), undertook an economic policy of mercantilism, to promote the expansion of British trade abroad. He clearly understood that readmitting the Jews, and allowing the establishment of a Jewish commercial presence in England, would give England access to an international commercial network, almost with the stroke of a pen. To do this, he would have to overcome opposition in Parliament, where deep prejudices existed against Jews, based on the religious prejudice that branded them as "Christ killers."

Manasseh ben Israel (1604-1657), a leading rabbi in Amsterdam, undertook a mission of Christian-Jewish reconciliation, and worked to secure the resettlement of Jews in England. Manasseh knew well that Cromwell had other than religious interests in this issue. He wrote a booklet to the Lord Protector titled *How Profitable the Nations of the Jewes Are*. When he arrived at Whitehall in the fall of 1655, his petition in hand, he was not admitted to the Council of State. Cromwell had taken the matter in hand personally, and had met with fierce opposition. Even

---

[7] Hanke, *Aristotle and the Indians*, 38.
[8] Samuel Purchas, *Hakluytus Posthumus, or, Purchas his Pilgrimes (a Discourse on Virginia)* (Glasgow: James MacLehose & Sons, 1905), XIX, 232-233).

though the petition was never actually accepted, Manasseh's efforts are deemed a success, as the presence and commercial activities of the Jews in England soon began to prosper, and some already there took off their Christian masks. His theological argument has remained important as well. "The 'Hope of Israel'–the Messiah–could not come until the Jews were dispersed to the ends of the Earth. Since they had been found even in America [he claimed], and since the oppressions accompanying the 'Coming' were apparent, it became more and more vital to return the Jews to England."[9] England was holding up the Second Coming.

Thomas Thorowgood: *Jews in America*

In the same year that Manasseh published *Spes Israelis* (*The Hope of Israel*), Thomas Thorowgood (1600-1669) published in England his *Jews in America, or Probabilities That the Americans Are of That Race*, in which he quotes from *Spes Israelis*. His work is an investigation into the evidence that the native Americans are descended from the Israelites, a condemnation of the treatment that the Indians have suffered at the hands of the Conquistadors, and, at the same time, concern regarding the religious neglect they have suffered at the hands of the English. Although he began his career as a priest in the Anglican Church, he joined the Puritans in 1640.

Thorowgood echoes the Sepulveda/Las Casas debate when he writes: "Athanasius never committed any man to a Gaoler, saith hee himselfe in his Apology; and againe, the truth is not preached with swords, and darts and Armies, but by reason and Arguments..." The first of the four requirements he lists to this end is language, the need to approach the Indians in their own tongue, and, presumably, to translate the scriptures. He urges that

> a stock of money must be remembered, which in some sense, is as it were the soule of this worke ...If we meane the Indians shall be Gospellized, they must first be civilized... The Spanish books relate strange things of their zeale in this kinde, and one whom we may credit tells us, that America hath

---

[9] Lee Eldridge Huddleston, *Origins of the American Indians. European Concepts, 1492-1729* (Austin: The University of Texas Press, 1967), 132. The Hebrew original of *Spes Israelis* apparently claimed that the Indians did not descend from the Ten Tribes, although Israelites had gone to America. See Henry Méchoulan & Gérard Nahon, "Introduction," in Menasseh ben Israel, *The Hope of Israel. The English Translation by Moses Wall, 1652* (Oxford: Oxford University Press, 1987), 63 & 89.

foure Arch-Bishops, thirty Bishops, and many other houses as they call them of Religion, and if it be said their lot fell into the golden part of that world, and out of their superfluities they might well spare vey much, tis very much indeed, and yet tis somewhat more that the same writer observeth how the King of Spain maintaines the lists and bonds of Missionaries, Priests, Fryers and Jesuits, that are continually transported into America, hee provides for every of them ten yeeres, and that to this day.[10]

Since reports back to England on the progress of "gospellizing" the Indians are urged, it is noteworthy that his book contains just such a report, published anonymously (by Thomas Shepard?), titled *The Day-Breaking, if not the Sun-rising of the Gospell* (sic) *with the Indians in New England* (London, 1647; usually included as one of the Eliot tracts).

There was of course some awareness that there were many Indian languages, although people tended to refer to the language of the Indians. The need to be able to communicate with these people was felt also by Roger Williams, founder of Providence, who published *A Key into the Language of America* in 1643. His was the first book on an Indian language in English. He made some reference to a comparison with the Hebrews, and though he found some words similar to Hebrew, he wrote, "Yet againe, I have found a greater Affinity of their Language with the Greek Tongue."[11]

John Eliot, "Apostle to the Indians"

John Eliot, a Puritan minister at the church in Roxbury (Massachusetts Bay Colony), immigrated to New England in 1631. Although he held no high position in the colony, or in the church, his influence was considerable, to the point that he was considered by his contemporaries (and ever since) as the Apostle to the Indians, a sort of New England Paul. Already in the colonies there were not only the Native Americans who were not Christian, but also a growing number of settlers, born in frontier areas, who had no church affiliation, and had never been baptized. This situation gave rise to The Great Awakening (or The First Great Awakening), oriented both to the conversion of the Indians, and relatively heathen Gentiles alike. Eliot authored various tracts, mostly to raise funds in England for the missions to the Indians, and his key role in this regard

---

[10] Thomas Thorowgood, *Jews in America, or Probabilities That the Americans Are of That Race* (London: W.H. for Thomas Slater, 1650), 70, 94-95.

[11] Roger Williams, "To the Reader," in *A Key into the Language of America* (Bedford MA: Applewood Books reprint, 1936). First published in 1643.

made him, posthumously, a central figure in the Second Great Awakening, in the first few decades of the nineteenth century. His view, that the Indians were descended from the Israelites, continued to attract attention in the revival movements in New England. In pursuit of his mission, he published in 1666 *The Indian Grammar Begun, or an Essay to bring the Indian Language into Rules*. He set up the Christian Indian town of Natick for the Nonantum, Neponset, and Musketaquid Indians, in an effort to prepare them for the reign of Christ. "The Lord Jesus is about to set up his blessed kingdom among these poor Indians" (first letter to Winslow). "In September 1651, he installed the millennial civil polity at Natick up through a single ruler of one hundred," [12] and in that same year he published his translation of the New Testament into the Indian tongue, and his translation of the Old Testament two years later. This was the first Bible printed in America. Eliot remained almost a revivalist rock-star; in 1822, Martin Moore published the *Memoirs of the Life and Character of Rev. John Eliot* (Boston), and a steady flow of books and pamphlets about John Eliot has continued to this day.

The Hebrew Diaspora in Pre-Columbian America

> And the Lord shall scatter thee among all people, from the one end of the earth even unto the other; and there thou shalt serve other gods, which neither thou nor thy fathers have known, even wood and stone. (Deuteronomy 28:64)

Another writer speculating on the origin of the American Indians was Daniel Gookin, who had ties to Rev. John Eliot Sr., Apostle to the Indians, by the marriage of his daughter to Eliot's son. In his *Historical Collections of the Indians in New England* (1674), he presented various theories, including that of derivation from the Israelites. He refers to "those inhabiting Peru and Mexico, who were most populous, and had great cities and wealth..." Of the Israelite theory, he says it is "perhaps not so improbable, as many learned men think."[13]

In 1775, James Adair, "A Trader with the Indians, and Resident in their country for Forty Years," published *The History of the American Indians*, which is largely a marshaling of what he considered to be

---

[12] Richard W. Cogley, *John Eliot's Mission to the Indians before King Philip's War* (Cambridge: Harvard University Press, 1999), 92.

[13] Daniel Gookin, *Historical Collections of the Indians in New England* (Boston: At the Apollo Press, by Belknan & Hall, 1792 [complete in 1674]), 145. The copy cited is an exact replica from Book Renaissance.

evidence for a Hebrew origin of the Indians. He wrote, "From the most exact observations I could make in the long time I traded among the Indian Americans, I was forced to believe them lineally descended from the Israelites, either while they were a maritime power, or soon after the general captivity; the latter however being the most probable."[14]

Foundations Already in Place for the Smiths' Enterprise

In 1801, Charles Crawford published the second edition of *An Essay on the Propagation of the Gospel; in which there are numerous facts and arguments adduced to prove that many of the Indians in America are descended from the Ten Tribes.* He refers to the work of Adair, among others, to make his arguments, and writes that William Penn (*General Description of Pennsylvania*) said of the natives of Pennsylvania, "For their original I am ready to believe them of the Jewish race, I mean of the stock of the Ten Tribes; and that for the following reasons: First, they were to go to a land not planted or known, which to be sure Asia and Africa were, if not Europe."[15]

In 1824, John V. Yates and Joseph W. Moulton listed many prominent finds of the early inhabitants of the Americas, in their *History of the State of New York.* They wondered at the remains:

> In the valley of the Mississippi, the monuments of buried nations are unsurpassed in magnitude and melancholy grandeur by any in North America. Here cities have been traced similar to those of ancient Mexico, once containing hundreds of thousands of souls. Here are to be seen thousands of tumuli, some a hundred feet high, others many hundred feet in circumference, the place of their sepulchers, their worship, and perhaps of their defence [sic]. [16]

---

[14] James Adair, *The History of the American Indians*, edited and with an introduction and annotations by Kathryn E. Holland Braund (Tuscaloosa: University of Alabama Press, 2005), 74; first published in 1775. Contrary to his information, Israel had never been a maritime power. The Hebrews had generally not inhabited the coastal regions of the Land of Canaan. Hiram, King of the Canaanites (Phoenicians), built the fleet of Solomon at Tyre/Sidon.

[15] Charles Crawford, *An Essay on the Propagation of the Gospel in Which There Are Numerous Facts and Arguments Adduced to Prove That Many of the Indians in America Are Descended from the Ten Tribes* (Philadelphia: James Humphreys, 1801), 12.

[16] John V. N. Yates and Joseph W. Moulton, *History of the State of New York*, vol. I, part I (New York: A. T. Goodrich, 1824), 20.

Their work sounds very modern, although lacking the information available today. After stating that "not one authentic record remains of even the name of any of these populous and powerful nations,"[17] they review many writers, with as many theories, including the possibility that the Indians descend from the Tartars, and that they in turn descend from the lost tribes of Israel. They also suggest that a number of Old World nations might have made contact with the New World prior to Columbus.

In 1826, Josiah Priest published *The Wonders of Nature and Providence Displayed*, a collection of very disparate accounts of natural and human phenomena. It includes two accounts of North American Indians, including "Proofs that the Indians of North America are lineally descended from the ancient Hebrews."[18] In 1833, he published three editions of his *American Antiquities*.[19] The fifth edition of this work advertises that 22,000 copies had been sold to subscribers only.

In 1828, Israel Worsley published *A View of the American Indians, their General Character, Customs, Language, Public Festivals, Religious Rites and Traditions: Shewing them to be the Descendants of the Ten Tribes of Israel. The Language of Prophecy concerning them, and the course by which they travelled from Media into America.* He quotes from 2 Ezra, (quoted by Ethan Smith as well). By his estimation, they crossed by "Bhering's Straits" near a copper island, and reached this continent through the Northeast Passage.[20]

In 1829, Barbara Anne Simon published *Hope of Israel. Presumptive Evidence that the Aborigines of the Western Hemisphere are Descended*

---

[17] *Ibid*, 22.

[18] Josiah Priest, *The Wonders of Nature and Providence Displayed* (Albany: published by the author, 1826). It includes "Proofs that the Indians of North America Are Lineally Descended from the Ancient Hebrews," 372; "An Account of Festivals in Honour of Idols among the Ancient Mexicans," illustrated with a lithograph, 173; and "Narrative of the Travels and Adventures of Mr. Ker, through the Wilderness from New-Orleans, toward New-Mexico, as far as the Macedus, or Welch Indians—Also his account of several other Tribes, of Mines, Wild Bests, &c.," 472.

[19] Josiah Priest, *American Antiquities and Discoveries in the West being an Exhibition of the Evidence that an ancient population of partially civilized nations, differing entirely from those of the present Indians, peopled America, many centuries before its discovery by Columbus, and inquiries into their origin* (Albany, NY: Hoffman and White, 1833)

[20] Israel Worsley, *A View of the American Indians* (Plymouth: W. W. Arliss, 1828); edition cited (New York: Arno Press reprint, 1971), 132-34.

from the Ten Missing Tribes of Israel.[21] After 1830, some authors sought to buttress this view by referencing *Antiquities of America* by Edward King.[22] By 1836 Simon's sequel bore a more assertive title.[23]

Many of these accounts attempt the precarious task of describing the Hebraic character of the American Indians, while admitting that they are now in a savage or degraded condition.

The American Jewish community had their own vision of the near future, which grew into the Zionist movement. A prominent example almost in Joseph Smith's backyard was the effort of Mordecai Manuel Noah (1785-1851). "In 1825, Noah helped purchase a tract of land on Grand Island in the Niagara River near Buffalo, where he envisioned a Jewish colony to be called Ararat."[24] "Noah's city of refuge became a nationwide *cause célèbre* in the weeks and months that followed his 'Proclamation for the Jews' at the dedication and the elaborate speech he gave the following day."[25] "To accommodate the large inaugural crowd, Noah rented a Buffalo church. Cannoneers fired a salute and Seneca Chief Red Jacket arrived by boat (Noah was convinced that America's Indians were the Ten Lost Tribes of Israel)."[26] The Smiths, and their collaborators, Cowdery and the Whitmers, could hardly have been unaware of this extravaganza.

Ancient Christian Indians

One might think that the Americans in the first half of the nineteenth century would be surprised to read in the *Book of Mormon* that pre-Columbian America had been Christianized in antiquity. But some already considered this obvious. Note, for example, the argument of Samuel

---

[21] Barbara Anne Simon, *Hope of Israel. Presumptive Evidence that the Aborigines of the Western Hemisphere are Descended from the Ten Missing Tribes of Israel* (London: R. B. Seeley, 1829).
[22] Edward King (Lord Kingsborough), *Antiquities of Mexico* (London: A. Aglio, 1830-48).
[23] Barbara Anne Simon, *The Ten Tribes of Israel Historically Identified with the Aborigines of the Western Hemisphere* (London: R. B. Seeley, 1836).

[24] "Mordecai Manuel Noah," in the Jewish Virtual Library, accessed 24/03/2017.
[25] Eran Shalev , "'Revive, Renew, and Reestablish': Mordecai Noah's Ararat and the Limits of Biblical Imagination in the Early American Republic," posted on http//:www.americanjewisharchives.org (downloaded 25/03/2017).
[26] "Mordecai Manuel Noah," http//:www.myjewishlearning.com (downloaded 25/03/2007).

Mather published in 1773. "Then there must be above two hundred and fifty Brethren, besides the twelve Apostles and the Seventy Disciples, who had seen CHRIST, and could attest to the Truth and Certainty of his Resurrection, and so to the Divinity of his Religion: And a considerable Number of these might come to our Western World. And so America must have been filled up with the Gospel, according to our Apostle's Expression."[27] In the minds of the BoM authors, the visit of Jesus himself to the new world would be an equally obvious deduction from the verse "And other sheep I have, which are not of this fold: them also I must bring, and they shall hear my voice; and there shall be one fold, and one shepherd." (John 10:16)

Although Thorowgood ultimately rejected the assertion that the Indians had been Christianized c. 150 CE, he wrote:

> ...all are not of the mind that the Indians have not heard of the Gospell: for Osiander speaking of Vilagagno, and his planting there in Brasil, writes confidently, without doubt those people received the Gospel of Christ by the preaching of the Apostles 1500 years since, but they lost it againe by their unthankfulnesse; and Malvenda allegeth some conjectures that Christianity might have been among them..[28]

The Latter Days and the Second Coming

A central rationale of the *Book of Mormon* is that the gold plates would be dug up as part of the restoration of all things, and to gather the part of Israel in the New World in the Last Days. This is stressed early in the text (1 Nephi 25-27), and near the end. In Mormon 5:15 we find that "this people shall be scattered, and shall become a dark, a filthy, and a loathsome people." But "out of the earth shall they [the plates] come in a day when it shall be said that miracles are done away..." (Mormon 8:26) "Behold, the Lord hath shown unto me great and marvelous things concerning that which must shortly come, at the day when these things shall come forth among you." (Mormon 8:35)

This reflects the belief among many during much of the nineteenth century, that the Second Coming was imminent. Heightened expectations of millennialism and adventism, began in the First Great Awakening of the eighteenth century, were revived in the Second Great Awakening, and produced a number of notable movements in the nineteenth century. In

---

[27] Samuel Mather, *An Attempt to Shew that America Must Be Known to the Ancients* (Boston: J. Kneeland, 1773), 23-24.

[28] Thorowgood, *Jews in America*, 24.

1758, millennialism was spelled out in Joseph Bellamy's *The Millennium*, his "immensely popular sermon."[29] He said:

> But when shall the son of David reign, and the church have rest? ... Perhaps the very time was designed to be shadowed forth in the law of Moses, in the institution of their holy days. The *seventh day*, said God, who always had this glorious season of rest in view, 'the seventh day shall be a Sabbath of rest, the seventh month shall be full of holy days, the seventh year shall be a year of rest' so, perhaps, after *six thousand* years are spent in labour and sorrow by the church of God, the *seven thousandth* shall be a season of spiritual rest and joy, an holy Sabbath to the Lord.[30]

> Surely it is infinitely unbecoming the followers of Him who is King of kings and Lord of lords, to turn aside to earthly pursuits, or to sink down into unmanly discouragements, or to give way to sloth and effeminacy, when there is so much to be done, and the glorious day is coming on.[31]

In Pennsylvania, communal millennialism was promoted by the Rappists (Harmonites), and the Harmony Society founded by Johann Georg Rapp. Their center was at first at Harmony, Butler Co., Pennsylvania, then Harmony, Indiana, and at the time of the Second Great Awakening at Economy (Ambridge), Pennsylvania. The Shakers (originally, the United Society of Believers in Christ's Second Appearing) also formed millennialist communal settlements, centered in New Lebanon, New York (southeast of Albany). The popularity of the millennialist doctrine is seen in Josiah Priest's 1828 work, *A View of the expected Christian Millenium* (sic), *which is promised in the Holy Scriptures, and is believed to be nigh; its commencement, and must transpire before the Conflagration of the Heavens and the Earth, Embellished with a chart, of the Dispensations from Abraham to the end of time.* (Albany: Published for subscribers by Loomis' Press, 1828).

God Made America, a Special Place Insulated from the Nations

The *Book of Mormon* asserts that Israelites were brought to a land kept empty to be their own inheritance. In 1823, Ethan Smith (no relation to Joseph Smith), a Congregational pastor in Poultney, Vermont, published *View of the Hebrews* asserting that the Indians are the descendants of

---

[29] Alan Heimert and Perry Miller, eds., *The Great Awakening* (Indianapolis and New York: The Bobbs-Merrill Company, Inc., 1967), 610.

[30] Heimert and Miller, *The Great Awakening*, 617.

[31] Heimert and Miller, *The Great Awakening*, 634.

Israel, and in 1825, he published an expanded edition, *View of the Hebrews; or The Tribes of Israel in America*. He wrote

> It inevitably follows, that the ten tribes of Israel must now have, somewhere on earth, a distinct existence in an *outcast* state. And we justly infer, that God *would* in his holy providence provide some suitable place for their safe keeping, *as his outcast tribes*, though long unknown to men as such…If God will restore them at last as his Israel, and as having been '*outcast*' from the nations of the civilized world for 2500 years; he surely must have provided a place for their safe keeping, as a distinct people, in some part of the world during that long period.[32]

Quoting from 2 Ezra (13:40-44, called the Fourth Book of Ezra, an apocryphal work, in a Latin text, thought to be originally in Greek, composed c. 100 CE), he writes:

> Those are the ten tribes which were carried away prisoners out of their own land, in the time of Osea, the king, whom Salmanezer, the king of Assyria, led away captive; and he carried them over the waters, and so came they into another land…But they took this counsel among themselves, that they would leave the multitude of the heathen, and go forth into a further country, where never man dwelt; that they might there keep their statues (sic) which they never kept in their own land.—There was a great way to go, namely, of a year and a half.[33]

The work of Ethan Smith is significant, not just that it asserts an Israelite origin of the Indians, but that it argues that the land had been set aside for the lost tribes to be kept distinct and apart. This is also the view in the *Book of Mormon*, 2 Nephi 1:8, "And behold, it is wisdom that this land should be kept as yet from the knowledge of other nations; for behold, many nations would overrun the land, that there would be no place for an inheritance."

---

[32] Ethan Smith, *View of the Hebrews, Exhibiting the Destruction of Jerusalem…* (Poultney, VT: Smith & Shute, 1823). Ethan Smith, *View of the Hebrews; or the Tribes of Israel in America. Second edition, improved and enlarged* (Poultney, VT: Smith & Shute, 1825). The edition cited is: (Salt Lake City: Bookcraft for the Religious Studies Center at Brigham Young University, 1996), 50.
[33] See Ethan Smith, *View of the Hebrews* (1825), 51.

God Destroys One People to Make Room for His Chosen People

A New England assembly defined relations with the indigenous people of North America in the following decisions:

> The earth is the Lord's and the fullness thereof. Voted
> The Lord may give the earth or any part of it to His chosen people. Voted
> We are His chosen people. Voted[34]

In the justification of prominent Quaker John Archdale (1707), we find, "the hand of God was eminently found seen in *thinning the Indians, to make room for the English* (emphasis added)...it at other times pleases Almighty God to send unusual Sickness amongst them, as the Smallpox, to lessen their numbers, so that the English in Comparison to the *Spanish*, have but little *Indian* Blood to answer for." "Example of God's more immediate hand, in making a Consumption upon some *Indian* nations in North Carolina."[35]

Jonathan Edwards: America and the Isles of the Sea

"*The Latter-day Glory Is Probably to Begin in America*"

Perhaps no American writer on religion was as influential as Jonathan Edwards. He is often considered to be the greatest American theologian. When he fell out of favor with the religious establishment in his district, he became pastor of the church in Stockbridge, Massachusetts and a missionary to the Housatonic Indians. He boldly defended their interests, successfully attacking the Whites who were using their official positions among them for self enrichment. His view that the work of God in the Latter-day glory will most likely begin in America is consistent with the rise of the view of America as the modern Zion. He writes:

> And there are many things that make it probable that this work will begin in America.—It is signified that it shall begin in some very remote part of the

---

[34] Garrett Mattingly, *Renaissance Diplomacy* (Boston, 1955, 290, in Hanke, *Aristotle and the American Indians,* 100.

[35] John Archdale, "A New Description of the Fertile and Pleasant Province of Carolina...(1707)," in B. B. Carroll, *Historical Collections of South Carolina*, II (2 vols., New York, 1836), 88-89. This is found in Hanke, *Aristotle and the American Indians*, 100.

world, with which other parts have no communication but by navigation, in Isa. Lx. 9. "Surely the isles shall wait for me, and the ships of Tarshish first, to bring my sons from far." It is exceeding manifest that this chapter is a prophecy of the prosperity of the church, in its most glorious state on earth, in the latter days; and I cannot think that any thing else can be here intended but America by the isles that are far off, from whence the first-born sons of that glorious day shall be brought.[36]

In 1816, Elias Boudinot published his *Star in the West; or, a Humble Attempt to Discover the Long Lost Ten Tribes of Israel, Preparatory to Their Return to Their Beloved City, Jerusalem.* In this work, a sense of national mission emerges. "Who knows but God has raised up these United States in these latter days, for the very purpose of accomplishing his will in bringing his beloved people to their own land."[37]

Precursors Incorporated in the *Book of Mormon* Thesis

Key claims that would be incorporated into the *Book of Mormon* had already become common fare in the Second Great Awakening, and available to the preachers of the open-air and tent revivals. They include:

§ The native Americans are of Israelite origin.

> Menasseh ben Israel, Thomas Thorowgood, John Eliot, Daniel Gookin, James Adair, Charles Crawford, William Penn, Elias Boudinot, Ethan Smith, Josiah Priest, Israel Worsley, Barbara Anne Simon and Mordecai Manuel Noah

§ The remnant of Israel must be kept pure and apart from other nations:

> Ethan Smith, Charles Crawford, (and William Penn?)

§ Christians had (may have) come to preach in Pre-Columbian America:

---

[36] Jonathan Edwards, "The latter-day glory, is probably to begin in America," in *Some Thoughts Concerning the Revival of Religion in New England*, Part II, Sect. II, (Boston: Printed and sold by S. Kneeland and T. Green in Queen-street, 1742). The edition cited is in *The Works of Jonathan Edwards* (Edinburgh: The Banner of Truth Trust, 1990), 381.

[37] Elias Boudinot, *Star in the West or a Humble Attempt to Discover the Long Lost Ten Tribes of Israel Preparatory to Their Return to Their Beloved City Jerusalem* (Trenton, NJ: George Sherman, Printer, for D. Fenton, S. Hutchinson and J. Dunham, 1816), 297.

Samuel Mather, Thomas Thorowgood

§ Millennial Expectations:

Joseph Bellamy, Josiah Priest

§ God "thins" one people to make room for his chosen people.

John Archdale

§ God's great work to gather his beloved people will begin in America, which is the Isles of the Sea in the Bible:

Jonathan Edwards, Elias Boudinot

In the *Book of Mormon*, the Hebraic origin of the Indians, their degraded state and potential restoration to their promise, and the coming forth of the gold plates, are all part of the millennial hope in an American Zion, and the Second Coming. This popular view of the Hebrews had swelled to become a significant wave, and the *Book of Mormon* would prove that it could ride it well. This is the

Precursor Reality

< Chapter 2 >

The Anachronistic Saga of Lehi, re the Sack of Jerusalem

The *Book of Mormon* account of the events leading up to the arrival of an Israelite population in the New World begins "in the <u>commencement</u> of the first year of the reign of Zedekiah, king of Judah" (1 Nephi 1:4). In a vision, Lehi, a BoM Prophet, reads the words, "Wo, wo, unto Jerusalem, for I have seen thine abominations!" He learned "that it should be destroyed, and the inhabitants thereof; many should perish by the sword, and many should be carried away captive into Babylon." (1 Nephi 1:13)

Nephi makes the sequence of events clear, speaking of "the destruction which should come upon them, *immediately after my father left Jerusalem.*" (2 Nephi 25:10; emphasis added) Lehi went out to prophesy to the inhabitants of Jerusalem, and call them to repentance. The Jews [Judeans] became angry with him, mocked him and sought his life. After he had returned home, God commanded him "that he should take his family and depart into the wilderness." (1 Nephi 2:2) Obeying, he "left his house, and the land of his inheritance, *and his gold, and his silver, and his precious things.* (emphasis added)" Clearly, he was prosperous.

The party leaving Jerusalem is eventually made up of Lehi, his wife Sariah, their sons Laman, Lemuel, Sam and Nephi, plus Ishmael, his wife, two sons and five daughters. A servant is included, Zoram, and after the birth to Lehi of Jacob and Joseph in the desert, and death of Ishmael, the number boarding their ship on the Arabian coast of the Indian Ocean is at least seventeen. Lehi (and possibly Ishmael as well?) is a descendant of Joseph of Egypt, making this group a branch of the tribe of Joseph. *Book of Mormon* dating is largely based on their departure from Jerusalem, or the number of years after that signal event. In several places, it is made clear that the birth of Jesus is 600 years <u>a</u>fter <u>l</u>eaving <u>J</u>erusalem (ALJ), which makes this event 600 BCE by the Gregorian calendar (1 Nephi 10:4, 19:8, 2 Nephi 25:19 & 3 Nephi 1:1). After eight years in the wilderness, they set sail for the New World.

This Israelite departure happens in three stages. First, the family of Lehi travel into the wilderness and eventually camp near the Red Sea in Arabia. Then Nephi and his elder brothers are sent back again, this time to get some brass plates found in the possession of Laban, a military commander (and presumably a kinsman). These, often called the Brass Plates of Laban, contain the Bible, translated into ancient Egyptian, up to and including the first part of Jeremiah. To succeed in this task, Nephi

17

beheads Laban with his own sword. A servant of Laban, Zoram, is persuaded to join Lehi's party. Finally, Nephi with his two elder brothers is sent back to get the family of Ishmael, primarily to provide daughters to marry Lehi's sons. All of these people, and the sword and Brass Plates of Laban, are essential components of the account in First Nephi of the Israelite departure to their very own promised land in the New World.

Sources

We are fortunate to have interlocking historical information for the important events pertinent to the period from just before Lehi's call to his departure from Jerusalem. These are from both Biblical and Babylonian sources. The former is First and Second Kings (originally a single work), First and Second Chronicles (also originally a single work), Jeremiah and Ezekiel. The Babylonian sources are the *Babylonian Chronicle* and the *Jehoiachin Ration Tablets*.

The Books of the Kings give an account that tends to resemble our concept of a history. We do not know the author(s), and it certainly had its own redaction history. But it does make reference to earlier sources, including a *Book of the Acts of Solomon* (11.41), *The Chronicles of the Kings of Judah* (14:29) and *The Chronicles of the Kings of Israel* (14:19). Unfortunately, all three are lost works.

Chronicles is largely drawn from other books of the Bible. It very probably had additional sources.

Jeremiah should, in theory, be reliable, since he was present for all of the events we shall discuss. Unfortunately, opinions vary considerably regarding its redaction history. As in the case of Isaiah, scholars have found evidence to indicate that this work has, as its core, various materials from Jeremiah himself, other, often linking materials to tie these all together into a flowing history, and yet more material edited into the text somewhat later. The most telling evidence is the fact that the text of the Greek Septuagint translation is around one eighth shorter than the Hebrew Masoretic text. Yet both versions have been evidenced in Hebrew texts among the Dead Sea Scrolls. Most scholars believe that the shorter Hebrew text that was translated into Greek is older than the longer and much later Masoretic text, which was expanded with later additions.

Ezekiel was exiled to Babylon with thousands of others along with the boy king Jehoiachin in 597 BCE. His book was entirely written in Babylon. He is important here as a Judean source in Babylon who can testify to the exile of Jehoiachin: "In the fifth day of the month, which was the fifth year of king Jehoiachin's captivity, The word of the LORD came expressly unto Ezekiel the priest" (1:2-3). He refers to Jehoiachin as *melek* (king), but to Zedekiah as *nāšî'* (headman, chief), possibly because this latter was installed by Babylon to be its client king in Jerusalem (i.e. Nebuchadnezzar's tribute-collector-in-chief).[38]

The *Babylonian Chronicles* are a series of tablets that contain the more important events of each previous year. The *Jehoiachin Ration Tablets* contain decrees establishing the grain and oil rations for the exiled Judean boy king, Jehoiachin. These sources are primarily of great importance because they corroborate pertinent Biblical material.

Historical Jerusalem

By 600 BCE, war and other geopolitical competition had been going on between Babylon and Egypt for control of Palestine and parts of Syria, and Babylon had gotten effective control over all the land from "the river of Egypt unto the river Euphrates." (2 Kings 24:7) Even so, some Judean rebels unwisely hoped that they could use an alliance with Egypt as leverage against Babylon.

In 609 BCE, the pharaoh Necho II deposed the king of Judah, Jehoahaz and placed Eliakim on the throne. His name was changed to Jehoiakim. In 605 BCE Babylon defeated the Egyptians at the battle of Carchemish. In the same year Nebuchadnezzar II ascended to the throne, and besieged Jerusalem. Jehoiakim changed his allegiance to Babylon to avoid bloodshed, but changed his allegiance back to Egypt in 601 BCE. The Babylonian army besieged Jerusalem for three months, during which time Jehoiakim died. He was succeeded by his son Jehoiachin, also known by a name variant, Jeconiah. Second Chronicles gives his age as eight when ascending to the throne, but Second Kings gives it as eighteen. This is probably a copy error. After only three months on the throne, he, his mother and the entire palace staff went out and surrendered to Nebuchadnezzar, who promptly exiled them to Babylon.

The fact of the exile of Jehoiachin is clear first from the account of Ezekiel (1:1), and from a Babylonian decree to establish Jehoiachin's rations. Being recorded in the Babylonian Chronicles, the historicity of the Sack of Jerusalem is beyond any doubt, as is the accompanying exile, by far the largest in the series of three exiles to Babylon.

---

[38] Iain Duguid, *Ezekiel and the Leaders of Israel* (Leiden: Brill, 1994), 18-25.

The Babylonian Chronicle gives the date of the surrender as March 16, 597,[39] stating that Nebuchadnezzar appointed a king of his own choice. "the king of Babylon made Mattaniah his [Jehoiachin's] father's brother king in his stead, and changed his name to Zedekiah." (2 Kings 24:17) "And [the king of Babylon] hath taken of the king's seed, and made a covenant with him [Mattaniah/Zedekiah], and hath taken an oath of him: he hath also taken the mighty of the land." (Ezekiel 17:13-18)

At some point late in Zedekiah's eleven-year reign, he too fell in with the Judean rebels and, in spite of the strong remonstrances of Jeremiah, Baruch and Neriah, as well of some advisers and family, he entered into alliance with Egypt and withheld tribute. Nebuchadnezzar laid siege to Jerusalem for about thirty months, when, in the eleventh year of his reign, Zedekiah and his followers attempted to flee, but were captured on the plains of Jericho. He and his family were taken to Riblah in the district of Hamath, north of Damascus, where he was forced to witness the execution of his sons. His eyes were then gouged out and he was taken captive to Babylon. The status of a captive in Babylon was far worse than that of the exiles. *And so*, the Lehi saga anachronism: *First Nephi mistakenly lumped the Sack of Jerusalem of 597 BCE into this later Babylonian conquest.*

Table 1. Babylonian Documents re the Sack of Jerusalem[40]

The Babylonian Chronicle
He [Nebuchadnezzar] camped against the city of Judah [Jerusalem] and on the second day of the month of Adar [March 16, 597 BCE] he took the city and captured the king [Jehoiachin]. He appointed a king of his own choice there [Zedekiah], took its heavy tribute and brought them to Babylon.
Two of Several Jehoiachin Ration Tablets
1. "10 (sila of oil) to the king of Judah, Iaukin [Jehoiachin]; 2 ½ sila (oil) to the offspring of Judah's king; 4 sila to eight men from Judea." 2. "1 ½ sila (oil) for three carpenters from Arwad, ½ apiece; 11 ½ sila for eight wood workers from Byblos. . .; 3 ½ sila for seven Greek craftsman, ½ sila apiece; ½ sila to the carpenter, Nabuetir; 10 sila to Ia-ku-u-ki-nu [Jehoiachin], the son of the king [Jehoiakim] of Ia-ku-du [Judah, Heb. *Yehûdâ*] ; 2 ½ sila for the five sons of the Judean king." [Hebrew sounds "h" & "y", were lost in Babylonian (Akkadian). See John Huehnergard *A Grammar of Akkadian* (Lake Winona IN: Eisenbrauns, 2011), p. 38. Jehoiachin, in 7th c. BCE Hebrew, was Yehoyakin. So

---

[39] Parker, Richard A., and Waldo H Dubberstein, *Babylonian Chronology: 626 B.C. - A.D. 75* (Providence, RI: Brown University Press, 1956). See also Antti Laato, *Guide to Biblical Chronology* (Sheffield: Sheffield Phoenix Press, 2015).

[40] L. E. Pearce and C. Wunsch, *Documents of Judean Exiles and West Semites in Babylonia in the Collection of David Sofer* (Bethesda, MD: Cornell Univ. Studies in Assyriology and Sumerology 28, 2014).

accordingly, note that in Babylonian transcription, "k" could be used for Hebrew "h" & "l" for "Y" (e.g., Judah {Heb. *Yehûdâ*}: *Ia-ku-du*).]

We thus have two major events, the Sack of Jerusalem just before Zedekiah's ascension to the throne, and the destruction of the temple, palace and walls of Jerusalem at the end of Zedekiah's rule. In the Sack of Jerusalem, the city was thoroughly plundered of all precious moveable items, including the vessels of the temple, and other gold, silver and brass items in the temple and palace. Thousands were exiled to Babylon.

The Exiles: Who and How Many?

The Sack of Jerusalem was devastating. Note 2 Kings 24:13-16:

13. And he carried out thence all the treasures of the house of the LORD, and the treasures of the king's house, and cut in pieces all the vessels of gold which Solomon king of Israel had made in the temple of the LORD, as the LORD had said.
14. And he carried away all Jerusalem, and all the princes, and all the mighty men of valour, even ten thousand captives, and all the craftsmen and smiths: none remained, save the poorest sort of the people of the land.
15. And he carried away Jehoiachin to Babylon, and the king's mother, and the king's wives, and his officers, and the mighty of the land, [those] carried he into captivity from Jerusalem to Babylon.
16. And all the men of might, even seven thousand, and craftsmen and smiths a thousand, all that were strong and apt for war, even them the king of Babylon brought captive to Babylon.

Some consider verse 14 to be an addition, and give preference to the figures in verse 16 (eight thousand exiles). By contrast, the Masoretic version of Jeremiah (52:28) gives us a much smaller number. "This is the people whom Nebuchadnezzar carried away captive: in the seventh year three thousand Jews and three and twenty" [i.e. in the 597 exile]. But we have to consider the fact that in the Septuagint Jeremiah 52:28-30 is absent, and so these verses may have been added in a later redaction that eventually resulted in the Masoretic text, of which the KJV is a translation. If so, added by whom, and when? Even so, 3,023 exiles is large by contrast with the number this version of Jeremiah gives for the two following exiles: 832 at the end of Zedekiah's reign, and 745 in the 23rd year of Nebuchadnezzar's reign, in 582-81 BCE (Jeremiah 52:29-30).

Since the numbers given in Second Kings are rounded off in thousands, they cannot be the actual numbers. Some scholars prefer to use the figure given in Jeremiah. Others base their estimates on the categories included in the exile, and arrive at more mid-range estimates.

As for these categories, in addition to those found in 2 Kings 24:14 ("the princes, and all the mighty men of valour...the craftsmen and smiths"), more information regarding "who" is found in a letter from Jeremiah to the exiles before the fall of Zedekiah (Jeremiah KJV 29:1-2; Septuagint 36:1):

> 1. Now these [are] the words of the letter that Jeremiah the prophet sent from Jerusalem unto the residue of the elders which were carried away captives, and to the priests, and to the prophets, and to all the people whom Nebuchadnezzar had carried away captive from Jerusalem to Babylon.
> 2. (After that Jeconiah [Jehoiachin] the king, and the queen, and the eunuchs, the princes of Judah and Jerusalem, and the carpenters, and the smiths, were departed from Jerusalem). (parentheses are original)

So, the exile included elders and priests as well. Here, "residue of the elders" is understood to mean those that were still alive at the time of the letter. Scholars study every passage in the OT where these terms occur (elders, princes, mighty men of valor) to determine what sort of status is involved in each case. Collectively, they refer to "persons of high status, wealth, power and honor."[41] As for the total number in the 597 exile, in view of the general reliability of Second Kings, the dubious redaction history of Jeremiah, and the absence of any numbers in the Septuagint version of Jeremiah, it seems reasonable to opt for some mid-range total.

Moreover, the *Jewish Encyclopedia*[42] states that these are only the men, and the total number of exiled persons has to be three to four times these numbers, or, in 597 BCE, a minimum of 9,000 persons, based on Jeremiah, or 24,000 based on 2 Kings 24:16. So then, if we use the figure of 9,000 from Jeremiah, and a Jerusalem population of 80,000, then the exiles would minimally constitute eleven percent, or most of those in the upper echelons. By any estimate, this was by far the largest Judean captivity, and truly one that must have totally disrupted all social, religious and economic life in Jerusalem.

We need to know what this is as compared to the total population of Jerusalem. This should not be confused with the total for Judea, the entire

---

[41] Oded Lipschits, *The Fall and Rise of Jerusalem. Judah under Babylonian Rule* (Winona Lake, IN: Eisenbrauns, 2005), 58, notes 81 & 82.
[42] "Babylonian Captivity," (*Jewish Encyclopedia* online, 2002; accessed 18 June 2019).

kingdom. Estimating this population in 597 BCE is not a simple matter. The maximalist view places it around 100,000. The minimalist view places it at about 20,000. Some scholars go once again for a mid-range figure, between 60,000 and 80,000. As in other early populations, there was no middle class. A relatively small proportion was in the upper end of the socio-economic continuum, while most might have qualified as "the poorest sort of the people of the land." Clearly, the removal to Babylon of those of this upper group would have had a devastating effect on the city.

It is interesting to note the different perspectives of the OT prophets and of Babylon. In the view of the former, the major onus for this disaster is placed on the Judeans themselves, for having violated the covenant Yahweh had made with the chosen people. Babylon is just God's instrument to chastise them. By contrast, Babylon wants to keep Judea as a functioning economy capable of meeting its tribute obligations. It is interesting to note that Ezekiel was exiled to Babylon, while Jeremiah was not. Jeremiah's exemption might be explained by the fact that he was an adamant opponent to the Judean rebels. He urged accepting the Babylonian yoke. For example, in Jeremiah 27:

> 8. And it shall come to pass, that the nation and kingdom which will not serve the same Nebuchadnezzar the king of Babylon, and that will not put their neck under the yoke of the king of Babylon, that nation will I punish, saith the LORD, with the sword, and with the famine, and with the pestilence, until I have consumed them by his hand.
> 11. But the nations that bring their neck under the yoke of the king of Babylon, and serve him, those will I let remain still in their own land, saith the LORD; and they shall till it, and dwell therein.
> 12. I spake also to Zedekiah king of Judah according to all these words, saying, Bring your necks under the yoke of the king of Babylon, and serve him and his people, and live.

Clearly, Jeremiah was of greater use to Nebuchadnezzar in Jerusalem than in exile. Ezekiel, on the other hand, identifies himself as a priest. In 597 he seems to be around 25 years old, and may have been officiating in the temple. His inclusion among the exiles may be solely due to this status (Jeremiah 29:1; Ezekiel 1:3)).

The exile of the men of valor (military men) is intended to keep Jerusalem defenseless. It may also have included "all that were strong and apt for war" (2 Kings 24:16; young strong men who potentially could be recruited or pressured to join a future rebellion against Babylon). This would include the sons of Lehi.

The exile of the craftsmen is a standard way to acquire skilled personnel to maximize the glory of Babylon. For example, Timur the Lame (Tamerlane) routinely exiled all the artisans and builders to his capital Samarkand and made it into a magnificent garden city. A historian contemporary to the Ottoman conquest of Egypt, Ibn Iyas, described the wholesale exile of Egyptian craftsmen to Istanbul (c. 1517).

Lehi's Jerusalem

The author of 1 Nephi, working in the late 1820s, must have been totally focused on the destruction of the temple. This could explain how he could have merged the events of the 597 Sack of Jerusalem into the destruction of the walls, palace and temple of Jerusalem in the eleventh year of Zedekiah's reign, thereby creating a historically impossible scenario for the *Book of Mormon*. On the other hand, we should not be too hard on him. As far as I can determine, this fatal anachronism was not detected until attention was drawn to it in *Mormon Genesis*.[43]

The Sack of Jerusalem befell the sacred city shortly before the *commencement* of Zedekiah's rule. For at least one year, Jerusalem must have been in total turmoil. Yet, 1 Nephi is totally unaware of this devastating cataclysm and warns regarding it as a disaster threatened by God, that had yet to happen. It depicts the first year of the reign of Zedekiah as a period of warning: "and in that same year there came many prophets, prophesying unto the people that they must repent, or the great city Jerusalem must be destroyed." Nephi says of his older brothers, "Neither did they believe that Jerusalem, that great city, could be destroyed according to the words of the prophets" (1 Nephi 2:13). After eight years in the wilderness, Nephi says "I know not but they are at this day about to be destroyed…save a few only who shall be led into captivity." (I Nephi 17:43) In the many passages that refer to the future destruction of Jerusalem, there is no mention of the Sack of Jerusalem that happened just days or weeks before they set out for their promised land.

Worse yet, principal characters in 1 Nephi would have been swept up in the exile, along with Ezekiel and thousands of others. Much or all of the cast would not have been available to enact the departure drama. The Babylonian exile would have targeted the following:

1. The BoM describes Lehi as being quite prosperous. When he left Jerusalem, "he left his house, and the land of his inheritance, and his gold,

---

[43] Arthur Chris Eccel, *Mormon Genesis* (Hilo, HI: GPTouchstone, 2018), 91-94.

and his silver, and his precious things" (1 Nephi 2:4). Certainly he was not one of the poorest of the land. Furthermore, also as a prophet, then so active that the Judeans had sought to kill him, Lehi would be among the exiles. The exile of prophets at this time is documented among the addressees in Jeremiah's letter to the exiles in Babylon (Jeremiah 29:1).

2. Nephi describes himself as "being a man large in stature, and also having received much strength of the Lord" (1 Nephi 4:31). He was armed with a unique steel bow (1 Nephi 16:18). Certainly he fits the bill as being "strong and apt for war." Laman and Lemuel also had special bows, which later "lost their springs" (1 Nephi 16:21). Lehi and his family would have been getting situated in their Babylonian exile, rather than trekking across Arabia to the Indian Ocean and their promised land.

3. We are told little about the background of Ishmael. He and his family most probably were not among the poorest of the land.

4. Laban was a major military leader. Laman and Lemuel murmured, "Behold, he [Laban] is a mighty man, and he can command fifty, yea, even he can slay fifty; then why not us?" (Nephi 3:31) When Nephi slays and beheads him, he finds him in a breastplate, and bearing an amazing sword: "the hilt thereof was of pure gold, and the workmanship thereof was exceedingly fine, and I saw that the blade thereof was of the most precious steel" (1 Nephi 4:9). His possession of brass plates written in Egyptian, which the Babylonian military could not read, may have incriminated him as a conspirator with the Egyptians. Clearly Laban would either have been executed by the Babylonians, or exiled. Such a warrior would not have escaped the exile dragnet, nor his precious military equipment. His sword and the bows of Nephi, Laman and Lemuel, would have been seized by Babylonian troops to grace the collections in the royal armory.

5. According to the servant of Laban, his master had been out with the elders of the Jews. The elders possessed secular rather than priesthood authority. In *Eerdmans Dictionary of the Bible*, David Rensberger[44] rehearses the functions found in their connection in various passages of the Old Testament: "groups called elders serve a variety of functions in various contexts throughout the OT. Elders sometimes represent the whole people or individual cities (Exodus, Deuteronomy, Judges); sometimes they serve as a governing authority (Joshua, Kings, Ezra); sometimes as judges (Deuteronomy, Ruth, Kings) and sometimes as advisers (Samuel, Kings)." The exile of the elders of the Jews is documented. They are

---

[44] David Rensberger, "Elder," in *Eerdmans Dictionary of the Bible* (Grand Rapids: 2000), 388. See this source for the specific Biblical references.

among those mentioned in the Babylonian exile to whom Jeremiah sent his letter (Jeremiah 29:1). If a Commander Laban were drinking with the elders of the Jews in *the commencement of the first year of the reign of Zedekiah*, they would be quaffing Babylonian beers in the balmy breezes somewhere between the Tigris and Euphrates.

6. Babylon had to import both copper and tin to make brass and bronze. Jeremiah (52:17-22) records that when the temple was pulled down in the eleventh year of Zedekiah, it was stripped of the brass accoutrements that had been used to make decorative and ritual components.

> 17. Also the pillars of brass that were in the house of the LORD, and the bases, and the brazen sea that was in the house of the LORD, the Chaldeans brake, and carried all the brass of them to Babylon. 18. The caldrons also, and the shovels, and the snuffers, and the bowls, and the spoons, and all the vessels of brass wherewith they ministered, took they away. 19. And the basons, and the firepans, and the bowls, and the caldrons, and the candlesticks, and the spoons, and the cups; that which was of gold [in] gold, and that which was of silver in silver, took the captain of the guard away. 20. The two pillars, one sea, and twelve brasen bulls that were under the bases, which king Solomon had made in the house of the LORD: the brass of all these vessels was without weight [beyond weighing]. 21. And concerning the pillars, the height of one pillar was eighteen cubits; and a fillet of twelve cubits did compass it; and the thickness thereof was four fingers: it was hollow. 22. And a chapiter of brass was upon it; and the height of one chapiter was five cubits, with network and pomegranates upon the chapiters round about, all of brass. The second pillar also and the pomegranates were like unto these. 23. And there were ninety and six pomegranates on a side; and all the pomegranates upon the network were an hundred round about.

This passage shows the huge value that the Babylonians put on brass. Although they spared the temple and palace in 597, they plundered them as well as private estates and buildings, and could not have missed the treasury of Laban, and the brass plates. These would certainly have been included in the booty collected on the eve of the ascension of Zedekiah to the throne, and would not be present at the commencement of his reign. They would have been melted down and made into luxury or utilitarian articles in Babylon.

The authors were keen to report on the Babylonian exile. Unaware of the Sack of Jerusalem, and so in the commencement of the reign of Zedekiah, speaking of the future, in 1 Nephi 1:13 (cf. 10:3), Lehi read in vision that "many should be carried away into Babylon." After eight years in the wilderness, once in the New World Lehi received a vision that

Jerusalem had been destroyed, and later Jacob stated that, "those who were at Jerusalem…have been slain and carried away captive." (2 Nephi 6:8) These statements are subsequent to the second Babylonian attack in the eleventh year of Zedekiah, when a far smaller exile was carried out. The Nephi narrative is totally unaware that a by far greater exile had already happened, shortly before Lehi in Jerusalem was sent to warn its residents that lest they repent they would face conquest, death by the sword and exile.

◆ Moreover, Lehi was in need of provisions and tents (1 Nephi 2:4). They would have had a difficult if not impossible time to acquire the essentials needed to survive in the wilderness and across Arabia. Nebuchadnezzar's army would have requisitioned all riding and transport animals, as well as all foodstuffs for the troops and to feed the thousands of exiles during an arduous trip to Babylon.

Figure 1. The Sack of Jerusalem Anachronism: Nephi vs History

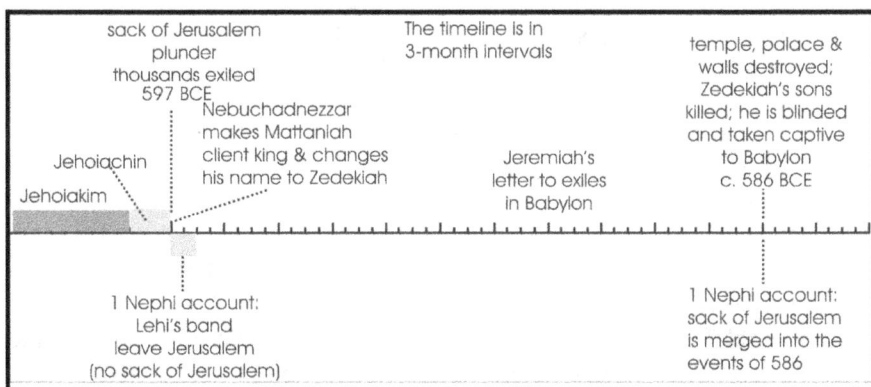

◆ The events of 1 Nephi could not have taken place on the heels of the Sack of Jerusalem, with no awareness of it, no awareness of many killed and the thousands exiled to Babylon, including priests (such as Ezekiel) and prophets, the political and social elites, the artisans and craftsmen. First Nephi is impossible, with Lehi and his family carried off to Babylon, with Laban and the elders of the Jews killed or exiled to Babylon, with the Brass Plates melted down and repurposed in Babylon, and possibly with Ishmael and his family in Babylon as well. This is the

Historical Issue

< Chapter 3 >

Joseph Smith's Palmyra: A Center of the Occult

Even though the production of the *Book of Mormon*, and the initial founding of the Church of Christ, as it was called in 1830, were largely collaborative projects, there is no doubt that Joseph Smith Jr. was the pivotal founder. This was done within an environment that was comfortably familiar with the occult.

Occult Beliefs and Practices in Palmyra & Manchester, NY

A study by a former professor at Brigham Young University, D. Michael Quinn,[45] has presented an exhaustive and well-documented analysis of these predispositions. They include a culture in which many claimed to have received visions of angels or God and Jesus Christ. Many also believed in witchcraft. As we saw in Chapter 1, a belief was alive and well among many that the Indians were of Hebrew origin and were to be gathered to the fold of the Lord imminently in "these" latter days.

      Perhaps as early as his late teens, Smith was deeply into the occult. He came by it naturally. The belief in witchcraft in New England immediately brings to mind the Salem witch trials. A Samuel Smith of Boxford gave evidence of witchcraft against Mary Easty at Topsfield, and a John Gould gave evidence of witchcraft against Sarah Wilds. Both women were hanged as witches at Salem partly based on their testimony. This Samuel Smith was Joseph Smith's great-grandfather Samuel, and John Gould was Samuel's father-in-law. [46] There are contemporary accounts that state that both Joseph Smith, and his father, Joseph Smith Sr., believed in witchcraft.[47] This belief is recorded in Mormon scripture: *Book of Mormon* (Alma 1:32, 3 Nephi 21:16 & 24:5, Mormon 1:19 & 2:10); and *Doctrine and Covenants* (63:17 & 76:103). Smith's own specialization was as a seerstone scryer (cf. crystal scryer or gazer). At least when outsiders were present, he typically placed his seerstone in his hat and sat with his face burrowed into it to read out what he claimed to be a revealed text. Smith also claimed to have engaged in necromancy, i.e.

---

[45] D. Michael Quinn, *Early Mormonism and the Magic World View*, 2nd ed. (Salt Lake City: Signature Books, 1998).
[46] D. Michael Quinn, *Early Mormonism and the Magic World View*, 31.
[47] *Ibid*, 291.

to have gotten ancient gold plates by meeting the demands of the guardian spirit of the deceased person who had hid them up.

Claims of such experiences were not rare in the early 19th century. We note the conversion experience of David Brainerd, active in the Second Great Awakening, and also considered by some to be an apostle to the Indians. His account was published in twenty-five editions from 1745 to 1835: "My soul rejoiced with joy unspeakable to see such a God, such a glorious divine Being."[48] Elias Smith recounted a vision he had in the woods, published in New Hampshire in 1816: "While in this situation, a light appeared to shine from heaven. ... My mind seemed to rise in that light to the throne of God and the Lamb."[49] The *Wayne Sentinel* of Palmyra (22 October 1823) published an article titled "Remarkable VISION and REVELATION, as seen and received by Asa Wild of Amsterdam [NY]." Wild said, "I dreamed Christ descended from the firmament, in a glare of brightness exceeding ten fold the brilliancy of the meridian Sun, and that he came to me, saying: 'I commission you to go and tell mankind that I am come; and bid every man to shout victory.'" From January to March of 1825, Wild, a Universalist minister, preached in Palmyra. Joseph Smith Sr. was at one time attending Universalist meetings. In the 1790s, a Billy Hibbard in Norway, New York, claimed a vision, saying, "as I looked up I saw heaven open, and Jesus at the right hand of God, and the Heavenly hosts surrounding the throne, adoring the Father and Son in the most sublime strains."[50] Benjamin Abbott published a narrative that went through thirteen printings, including New York editions in 1805 and 1813, in which he remembered "and at that instant I awoke , and saw, by faith, the Lord Jesus Christ standing by me, with his arms extended wide, saying to me, 'I died for you.'"[51] In 1815, Norris Stearns published a vision in which he saw "a small gleam of light in the room, above the brightness of the sun," and two personages; "One was God, my Maker, almost in bodily shape like a man. His face was, as it were a flame of fire ... Below him stood Jesus Christ my redeemer, in perfect shape like a man—His face was not ablaze, but had the countenance of fire, being bright and shining."[52]

---

[48] *ibid*, 14.

[49] *ibid*, 14.

[50] B[illy] Hibbard, *Memoirs* ... (New York: 1825), in Quinn, *ibid*, 15.

[51] Benjamin Abbott, *The experience and gospel labours of the Rev. Benjamin Abbott: to which is annexed a narrative of his life and death, by John Ffirth*, (Philadelphia: pr. by Solomon 1801, W. Conrad, for Ezekiel Cooper, 1801). Benjamin Abbott was an itinerant minister of the Methodist Episcopal Church in New Jersey, 1732-1796. For the quote here, v. Quinn, *ibid*, 15.

[52] Quinn, *Early Mormonism and the Magic World View*, 15.

These are just examples, just experiences that managed to get into print. The many editions of these publications indicate the great interest at the time. Even if believers read none of these reports, it is certain that faith-building mentions were made of visionary experiences by the preachers of the ongoing popular religious awakening.

The Smiths had been exposed to the idea that the Indians were of Israelite origin. H. Michael Marquardt notes, "After they moved to their Manchester farm, the Smith family received the *Wayne Sentinel*." On one occasion, Joseph Sr. placed an advertisement in this paper. [53] The newspaper ran a series by Mordecai M. Noah on the Hebrew origins of the Indians. He wrote, "If the tribes could be brought together, could be made sensible of their origin, could be civilized, and restored to their long lost brethren, what joy to our people, what glory to our God, how clearly have the prophecies been fulfilled, how certain our dispersion, how miraculous our preservation, how providential our deliverance."[54]

Curses were a large part of the BoM world view. "Curse" (with conjugation variants: *curse, cursed, curseth*) occurs seventy times. Chief among these are those relating to the divine curse that gave the Lamanites (the ancestors of the native Americans) a "dark" and "loathsome" skin. Peoples and individuals violating God's law suffer sore curses. This comes straight out of the world view of the Mormon project. When Harris lost the purloined pages of Smith's first manuscript effort, his mother claimed that a blight was sent upon his field, while his neighbor's just across the road was spared. Reportedly, Joe Sr. put a curse on the rifles at a turkey shoot so that they would miss the turkeys.[55] A range of occult practices were used by the BoM team, and several were given prominence in the new bible's narrative.

To be fair, we must bear in mind that for many Euro-Americans of the day, curses were not a matter of belief. They were empirically true. They remembered that the European Christians arrived and prospered in he New World, while the local heathens were "stricken" terribly sick and died in their thousands. For many, their curse was clear and providential.

---

[53] H. Michael Marquardt, *The Rise of Mormonism: 1816-1844, Second Edition, Revised and Enlarged* (Maitland, FL: Xulon Press, 2013), 22-23.
[54] *Wayne Sentinel*, 11 October, 1825. See supra, p. 10.
[55] Quinn, *Early Mormonism and the Magic World View*, 31.

Perspective: Pseudepigrapha and Other Deceptions

Pseudepigrapha are works composed by one person, but ascribed by the author to another (cf. pseudonymous). This is usually done because the author absolutely knows that he has some important knowledge that needs to be taught to those who are able to understand it, but also knows that if issued to the world under his own name, it would not be accepted or read, and even in some cases, the author may fear persecution. There are over forty works of Old Testament pseudepigrapha. There are also a number of works of New Testament pseudepigrapha, such as the *Gospel according to Mary* and the *Gospel according to Judas*. A late work, the *Gospel according to Barnabas*, apparently by a convert to Islam in Italy, was written to prefigure the coming of Muhammad. Presumably, the author labored to bring Catholics into the true faith of Islam. Some pseudepigrapha made it into the Bible. Most scholars divide Isaiah into two, and even three parts (1st, 2nd & 3rd Isaiah), only the first being accepted as mostly the work of Isaiah himself. Many scholars accept that several of the epistles of Paul were not written by the man himself. The four canonical gospels do not fall into this category, for although they were not written by Matthew, Mark, Luke and John, they do not claim to have been, the titles saying the Gospel *according to* (Matthew, etc.), the probable author being a student of the apostle. There are also pseudepigrapha posing as classical, nonreligious works.

Pseudepigrapha may be written to influence the theology of an established religion, but they are not generally written for personal gain (no large print runs or best sellers back then, and the author must remain unknown), or to establish a new religion. In this sense, the Smith pseudepigrapha are unusually ambitious.

Some more recent pseudepigrapha, and similar impostures, have been exposed and studied. One such work is a presumed epic by Ossian, a Gaelic bard contrived by Scott James Macpherson in the 1770s, a legend with Irish heroes that Macpherson said were part of Scottish heritage, angering the Irish. He even developed a sufficiently credible old Gaelic text that many experts were fooled for years, and even today there are a few die-hards who adhere to this Gaelic Homer.

A non-textual work is the infamous Piltdown man. It was fabricated from a medieval human skull, a 500-year-old lower jaw of a Sarawak orangutan and fossilized chimpanzee teeth. The identity of the author of this hoax has not been identified, although there are some interesting candidates. It is thought that it was done by someone who wanted to provide the missing link for the evidence for human evolution. He was a bit too impatient. Little did he know that not just one, but a whole series of fossil links would be discovered legitimately.

A fascinating literary example is the works claimed to be by a Patience Worth, allegedly a spirit contacted by Pearl Lenore Curran (1883–1937). This otherworldly symbiotic relationship produced several novels and works of poetry and prose that Pearl Curran affirmed were delivered to her through channeling the spirit, Patience Worth. Literary critic William Marion Reedy considered *The Sorry Tale* to be a new classic of world literature. The Joint Committee of Literary Arts of New York listed Patience Worth as one of the outstanding authors of 1918. That year's edition of *The Anthology of Magazine Verse and Year Book of American Poetry* honored her by printing the complete text of five of her poems, along with other leading poets of the day. Some used her example as evidence for life after death. Eventually the enthusiasm for her work abated, and she slid into oblivion. Curan's supporters typically exaggerated her humble origins as proof that she could not have done this work herself (as in the case of Jesus, Muhammad and Joseph Smith).

A work more closely paralleling that of the BoM authors is *Walam Olum* of Samuel Constantine Rafinesque. A fascinating polymath, born in the outskirts of Constantinople (Istanbul), and self-educated in Paris, he pursued a distinguished and productive career in US academia in the first half of the 19th century, identifying various species of the Americas, and surveying pre-Columbian earthworks of North America. He claimed that a medical doctor, Dr. Ward, had received an Indian document written on strips of birch bark. Rafinesque obtained the strips and claimed to translate them, rendering a single character into a whole phrase or sentence. He claimed to have lost the strips, but fortunately had made a complete transcription of the original texts. Made up of 183 verses, it is supposed to be the tribal chronicle of the Lenni Lenape (Delaware Indians), reporting their migration from Asia to Alaska, and then on down to the eastern United States. The work was taken very seriously by scholars of the 19th century. During the 20th century it has been critically analyzed and the overwhelming consensus now rejects it, although it remains unclear whether the otherwise distinguished Rafinesque created a hoax, or was himself the victim of a fraud, or, perhaps, sincerely fabricated a text and translation to evidence what he was so sure must really have happened.[56]

---

[56] *Walam Olum, or Red Score. The Migration Legend of the Lenni Lenape or Delaware Indians*, including a transcription and ostensible translation of *Walam Olum* by C. (Constantine) S. (Samuel) Rafinesque, with studies by various authors, (Indianapolis: Indiana Historical Society, 1954).

The Necromancer's Magic Book and the Rodsman's Hazel

During much of the 1820s, an able and very active necromancer, Luman Walters (c. 1788-1860), who apparently had lived a bit in Europe, plied his trade in the region of Palmyra and Manchester. He had an itinerant lifestyle, going about with all of "the trappings of a medieval magician— 'magic stone,' 'stuffed toad,' 'rusty sword' used for drawing magic circles on the ground [i.e. where to dig], esoteric books written in Latin from which he read various incantations, and a flair for the dramatic."[57] In 1818 he escaped from jail in Hopkinton, New Hampshire, where he had been sentenced for breaking a hundred-year-old law against the occult practices of his occupation. Subsequently he moved to Pultneyville/Sodus, a town only about seventeen miles from Palmyra, which Vogel estimates to have been several hours on horseback. His activities are rather well recorded in local papers and by witnesses, including a colorful description by Brigham Young who had known him.[58] Lorenzo Saunders reported, albeit decades after the fact, that Willard Chase told him that he and Alvin Smith had dug for treasure under Walters' direction, once on the Chase property, and again on that of justice of the peace Abner Cole.[59] Some accounts indicate that Walters had a relationship with both Joseph Sr. and Jr.[60] Additionally, Vogel suggests that it was after he left the area that Joseph Smith Jr. undertook to fill the necromantic void left in his wake,[61] a view also expressed in an 1830 newspaper.[62]

Apart from treasure hunting, there are some parallels between his practices and the early history of Joseph Smith. Walters' use of a magic book could have suggested finding treasure in the form of a book. The use of a sword to mark off a magic circle has a parallel in the relic of the sword of Laban. The role of necromancy, charming a custodian spirit, which was part of Walters' routine, may have led to the idea that a spirit guarded the gold plates, and that the custodian spirit of an ancient American would appear to guide the chosen one to find them. Even early Mormons sometimes referred to the plates as a treasure.[63]

---

[57] Vogel, *Joseph Smith, The Making of a Prophet* (Salt Lake City: Signature Books, 2004), 37 & 583, note 14.

[58] Quinn, *Early Mormonism and the Magic World View*, 120. See 119-32.

[59] Vogel, *Joseph Smith*, 37.

[60] Quinn, *Early Mormonism and the Magic World View*, 118.

[61] Vogel, *Joseph Smith*, 38.

[62] Quinn, *Early Mormonism and the Magic World View*, 118.

[63] Vogel, *Joseph Smith*, 139, 160-64 & 168.

In the same timeframe that this necromancer was active in the Smiths' neighborhood, a prominent rodsman, Justus Winchell, kept his hazel divining rod in good practice. One can be forgiven for thinking of a magic wand in this connection, since in one common rodsman role he would have been known as a water witch. Martin Quinn has investigated in detail his connections and possible mentor relationship with both Joseph Smith Sr. and William Cowdery.[64] Joseph Smith's use of a seerstone was never hidden, so this practice has generally not been a problem for LDS scholars, even in extension to others involved in the BoM project.

The early nineteenth-century religious scene was not monolithic. There were many who opposed practices related to magic or the occult, among the clergy of the more established religions, and in various social circles associated with the sciences. In the 1830s the emergent Church doctrine wrote the use of a divining rod out of its history, as we shall see.

Table 2. The Birth Family of Joseph Smith Jr.

1771	Joseph Smith Sr. was born in Topsfield, MA.
1775	Lucy Mack (Smith) was born in Gilsum, NH.
1779	Apparently residing in Derryfield (Manchester), NH, since his father served as town clerk of Derryfield during this period.
1796	Joseph Sr. and Lucy married in Tunbridge, VT.
1797	He, along with his father Asael Smith and brother Jesse Smith, joined with others to state that they had formed a society and "wish to be known by the Name or forme of universalists." (Tunbridge, VT)
1797	An infant son was born to Lucy and Joseph Sr., but did not survive.
1798	Alvin was born, first child of Joseph & Lucy. (Tunbridge, VT)
1800	Hyrum was born, their second child. (Tunbridge, VT)
1803	Sophronia was born (Tunbridge, VT). About this time Lucy attended church at several denominations, including the Methodists. Her husband attended at her request, seriously angering his father Asael, who insisted that he read the *Age of Reason* by Thomas Paine.
1805	Joseph Smith Jr. was born, 23 December, in Sharon, VT. The Smiths moved back to Tunbridge, Vermont, having lived previously in Tunbridge, Royalton and Sharon, where Joseph Sr. farmed summers and taught school winters.
1808	Samuel was born in Tunbridge. Soon after the Smiths moved to Royalton, Vermont. There, Joseph Sr. went to school on Dewey Hill and was taught by Deacon Jonathan Rinney.
1810	Ephraim was born, but died 11 days after his birth. (Royalton, VT)
1811	William was born in Royalton, VT. The family moved to Lebanon, New Hampshire. Hyrum was sent to Moore's Academy in Hanover,

---

[64] Quinn, *Early Mormonism and the Magic World View*, 119-133.

	and the others to a common school nearby. Joseph Smith Sr. had what Lucy called his first vision.
1812	Catherine was born. (Lebanon, NH)
1813	In the winter of 1812-13 the children were afflicted with typhoid fever. All survived, but Joseph Jr. suffered an abscess in his leg. Hyrum cared for him, and braced his afflicted leg, one of the events in a lifelong devotion to his younger brother. Eventually, an operation was performed to remove afflicted parts of the bone without anesthesia. Joseph was on crutches for about three years, and had a slight limp for life.
1814	Having become essentially penniless, the Smiths moved to Norwich, Vermont, farming perhaps as squatters. Due to a series of cold winters, their crops failed.
1816	Don Carlos was born in Norwich, VT. The Smith family moved to Palmyra in northwest New York.
1820	Joseph Smith Sr. had his seventh and last vision in 1819 or 1820, according to his wife.
1821	Lucy was born in Palmyra, NY.
1823	Alvin Smith died of mercury poisoning from a calomel treatment for bilious colic.
1824?	1824-25: The possible time when Lucy, Hyrum, Samuel and Sophronia joined the Presbyterian Church. Joseph Sr. & Jr. did not.
1825	November 1, Joseph Smith Sr. & Jr. sign the "Articles of Agreement" with Josiah Stowell and others to share in any gold or silver mine found "at a certain place in Pennsylvania near a Wm. Hale's."
1826	Hyrum married Jerusha Barden.
1828	Since about September of this year, Lucy, Hyrum and Samuel stopped attending the Presbyterian Church. Concerned, on March 3, 1830, a Presbyterian committee was assigned to visit them and report. (Milton V. Backman & James B. Allen, *BYU Studies* 10:4, p. 483)
1831	Samuel went on a mission to Kirtland, Ohio. This was followed by proselytism in Missouri, Indiana, Connecticut, Massachusetts, Rhode Island, Maine and New York.
1834	Samuel married Mary Bailey. He was appointed as one of 12 members of the High Council of the Church.

Joseph Smith's 1826 Pretrial Examination

According to Smith's account, he stayed on the Stowell farm and worked for about a month. According to his mother's account, he worked for him "by the month," while the account of Oliver Cowdery reports the period as having been "a few months."[65] Smith admitted that he failed. Josiah

---

[65] *Ibid*, 38-39.

Stowell was apparently not unhappy with the situation. The original legal proceeding (20 March 1826), a pretrial examination, was for disorderly conduct, which included pretending to find lost goods.[66] It appears that this proceeding did not lead to an actual trial. After the publication of the *Book of Mormon*, there was a new attempt to try him on the same charge. The constable's bill is dated 4 July 1830.

Smith was apparently acquitted. He was subsequently arraigned on similar charges before another judge and in a different jurisdiction for his activities, but it appears he was acquitted or charges were dismissed. In the case of farmer Stowell, the person who might have standing was not complaining. In another case, apparently the statute of limitations had run out.[67] In any case, he was only doing what so many other seerstone scryers and rodsmen were doing. One assumes that it was even difficult to find a statute that specifically applied. *Nullum crimen sine lege*. The details of the trials are not important here. The cases indicate the extent to which Joseph Smith Jr. was involved in gold hunting with his seerstone.

Gold Fever

New England settlers were sorely aware of the fact that while the English were farming the stubborn stony New England ground, Spanish ships were carrying tons of gold back to their homeland. They can be forgiven for thinking that certainly there must also be gold to be found in their vicinity, and possibly on their own farm. On 1 February 1831, a Palmyra newspaper, *The Reflector*, taking a critical look at Smith's "GOLDEN BIBLE,' can be quoted here as a reflection of the atmosphere in Palmyra in the 1820s:

> It may not be amiss in this place to mention that the MANIA of money-digging soon began rapidly to diffuse itself through many parts of the country; men and women without distinction of age or sex became marvelous wise in the occult sciences, many dreamed, and others saw visions disclosing to them deep in the bowels of the earth, rich and shining treasures and to facilitate those *mighty* mining operations, (money was usually if not always sought after in the night time,) divers devices and implements were invented, and although the *SPIRIT* was always able to retain his precious charge, these discomfited as well as deluded beings, would on a succeeding night return to their toil, not in the least doubting that success would eventually attend their labors.

---

[66] *Ibid*, 40-45.
[67] For a detailed discussion, see Marquardt, *Rise of Mormonism*, 140-47.

Mineral rods and balls, (as they were called by the impostor who made use of them,) were supposed to be infallible guides to these sources of wealth— "*PEEP STONES*" or pebbles taken promiscuously from the brook or field, were placed in a hat or other situation excluded from the light, when some WIZARD or WITCH (for these preformances [sic] were not confined to either sex) applied their eyes and nearly starting their balls from their sockets, declared they saw all the wonders of nature, including of course, ample stores of silver and gold.[68]

Edward Augustus Kendall observed in his *Travels Through the Northern Parts of the United States in the Years 1807 and 1808*, "The settlers of Maine, like all the other settlers in New England, indulge an unconquerable expectation of finding money buried in the earth," a passion encouraged by the fact that money chests "have been dug for in all parts of the United States; and, as the history further goes, they have not unfrequently been found."[69]

Early nineteenth-century New England had a large number of rodsmen, practitioners of the art of divining rods, used to find water, gold and hidden information. The *Palmyra Herald and Canal Advertiser* carried an article on 24 July 1822, titled "MONEY DIGGERS," claiming "Much, however depends on the skillful use of the genuine mineral rod," and recounts that one Vermont man "after digging with sufficient unyielding confidence and unabating diligence for ten or twelve years, found a sufficient quantity of money to build him a commodious home for his own convenience, and to fill it with comforts for weary travelers." Another person dug up treasure worth "the enormous sum of fifty thousand dollars!"

The use of the seerstone by Joseph Smith is reflected in the standard title of the President of the LDS Church: Prophet, Seer and Revelator. A seerstone that belonged to Smith is currently in the office of the Church Historian.

---

[68] Reprinted in Francis W. Kirkham, *A New Witness for Christ in America, "The Book of Mormon"* (Independence, MO: Press of Zion's Publishing Company, 1951), vol. 2, 69.

[69] Edward Augustus Kendall, *Travels Through the Northern Parts of the United States in the Years 1807 and 1808*, 3 vols. (New York: I. Riley: 1809), 3:84, 87-88.

Necromancy: A Guardian Spirit by Any Other Name...

Necromancy is the practice of communicating with the spirit of a dead person to get information. The Biblical example is Saul's visit to the Witch of Endor (*ba'alat 'ôb* at *'ayn dôr*) to call up Samuel from the grave regarding Saul's prospects vis à vis David and the Philistines, before the battle at Mount Gilboa. Similarly, Smith's communion with the spirit guarding the gold plates, and meeting his demands to get them with the information inscribed thereupon, is necromancy, pure and simple.

From his first use of a seerstone, Joseph Smith began to believe he had a special power. The scryer is able to do what others cannot. He or she is claiming to be assisted by some divine or spiritual source. The whereabouts of a treasure was believed to be revealed, at times, by a dream or vision. The situation of the rodsman is similar. A revelation tells rodsman Oliver Cowdery, "there is no other power save God, that can cause this rod of nature, to work in your hands." (BoC 7)

What came to be called the second vision, involving the visit of the angel that revealed the gold plates, also underwent some evolution.[70] Buried treasure was often said to be secured by guardian spirits. "Typically the treasure 'moved off' through the earth when guardian spirits were not securely bound by proper ceremony or were offended when the diggers breached the necessary silence."[71] The belief in guardian spirits, and that the location of treasure could be learned by revelation, readily becomes a story that a guardian spirit had hidden his people's history engraved on gold plates, a spirit that revealed the location of this treasure to Joseph Smith.

It is significant to note that a messenger or an angel visited Smith in the earlier accounts, but specifically the angel Moroni visited him in the later and now official account. It was not possible to call him the angel Moroni before the character had been named, or even created in the BoM text. An interesting evidence of this evolution is the fact that in the 1838 version of the vision, Smith gave the name as Nephi. This was edited, writing Moroni above Nephi.

> He called me by name and said unto me that he was a messenger sent from the presence of God to me and that his name was ~~Nephi~~ ‹Moroni›.

---

[70] Marquardt, *Rise of Mormonism*, 47.

[71] Quinn, *Early Mormonism and the Magic World View*, 60.

Joseph Smith himself dictated this text to a scribe, James Mulholland. Much later, B. H. Roberts made the correction, Nephi to Moroni, at the turn of the century, when he was preparing the *History* for publication. Today, no eighteen-year-old missionary, or lay Sunday school teacher would make such a slip of the tongue. It is possible that Nephi had been a candidate for the messenger, and so was still stuck in Smith's mind, giving rise to the error.[72]

Even though we read in the current LDS D&C 28:5 (section 28, at some point dated August, 1830), "Moroni, whom I have sent unto you to reveal the *Book of Mormon*," this text was not found in the 1830 section 28 of the *Book of Commandments* (precursor to the D&C), and was added into the 1835 D&C text of section 28.[73]

The currently official account of receiving the gold plates is:

51. Convenient to the village of Manchester, Ontario county, New York, stands a hill of considerable size, and the most elevated of any in the neighborhood [later called the Hill Cumorah]. On the west side of this hill, not far from the top, under a stone of considerable size, lay the plates, deposited in a stone box. This stone was thick and rounding in the middle on the upper side, and thinner towards the edges, so that the middle part of it was visible above the ground, but the edge all around was covered with earth.

52. Having removed the earth, I obtained a lever, which I got fixed under the edge of the stone and with a little exertion raised it up. I looked in, and there indeed did I behold the plates, the Urim and Thummim, and the breastplate, as stated by the messenger. The box in which they lay was formed by laying stones together in some kind of cement. In the bottom of the box were laid two stones crossways of the box, and on these stones lay the plates and the other things with them.

53. I made an attempt to take them out, but was forbidden by the messenger, and was again informed that the time for bringing them forth had not yet arrived, neither would it, until four years from that time; but he told me that I should come to that place precisely in one year from that time, and that he would there meet with me, and that I should continue to do so until the time should come for obtaining the plates.

54. Accordingly, as I had been commanded, I went at the end of each year, and at each time I found the same messenger there, and received instruction and intelligence from him at each of our interviews, respecting what the Lord

---

[72] Jessee, The *Personal Writings of Joseph Smith* (Salt Lake City: Deseret Book Company, 1984), 203 & 667, note 12.

[73] H. Michael Marquardt, *The Joseph Smith Revelations, Text & Commentary* (Salt Lake City: Signature Books, 1999), 72-73.

was going to do, and how and in what manner his kingdom was to be conducted in the last days.

55-58. [an account of events in his family, and of persecution]

59. At length the time arrived for obtaining the plates, the Urim and Thummim, and the breastplates. On the twenty-second day of September, one thousand eight hundred and twenty-seven, having gone as usual at the end of another year to the place where they were deposited, the same heavenly messenger delivered them up to me with this charge: that I should be responsible for them; that if I should let them go carelessly, or through any neglect of mine, I should be cut off; but that if I would use all my endeavors to preserve them, until he, the messenger, should call for them, they should be protected.[74]

Another observation is presently more pertinent, and possibly more important. Since the earlier "messenger" designation predates the BoM, i.e. the new bible, it was appropriate for a period when a gold record engraved with curious characters was to be translated as a more secular history. The treasure aspect lay in the expected book sales.

The Ordeal of Getting the Plates

There are other, earlier, accounts.[75] In one account, Joseph Smith Sr. reportedly told a neighbor, Willard Chase, that "On the 22d of September, he [Joe Jr.] must repair to the place where was deposited this manuscript, dressed in black clothes, and riding a black horse with a switch tail, and demand the book in a certain name, and after obtaining it, he must go directly away, and neither lay it down nor look behind him. They accordingly fitted out Joseph with a suit of black clothes and borrowed a black horse."[76] Smith's own earliest account (1832) reads:

> and it was on the 22d day of Sept. AD 1822 [1823] and thus he [the messenger] appeared unto me three times in one night and once on the next day and then I immediately went to the place and found where the plates was (sic) deposited as the angel of the Lord had commanded me and straightway made three attempts to get them and then being exceedingly frightened I supposed it had been a dream of Vision but when I considered I knew that it was not therefore I cried unto the Lord in the agony of my soul why can I

---

[74] *The Pearl of Great Price*, Joseph Smith 2:51-59.

[75] Marquardt, *Rise of Mormonism*, 47-48; Joseph Smith's history of 1838, in Jessee, *Personal Writings of Joseph Smith*, 202-208. Lamar Petersen, *Problems in Mormon Text* (Concord, CA: Pacific Publishing Company, no date), 63-69.

[76] Marquardt, *Rise of Mormonism*, 48.

not obtain them behold the angel appeared unto me again and said unto me you have not kept the commandments of the Lord which I gave unto you therefore you cannot now obtain them for the time is not yet fulfilled therefore thou was left unto temptation that thou mightest be made acquainted with the power of the advisary [adversary] therefore repent and call on the Lord thou shalt be forgiven and in his own due time thou shalt obtain them for now *I had been tempted of the advisary and sought the Plates to obtain riches* and kept not the commandment that I should have an eye single to the glory of God.[77] (emphasis added)

In this account, Smith himself states that his original desire was to get riches from the plates (or possibly a claimed translation of them).

A curious account of a statement that Willard Chase attributed to Joseph Smith Sr. reads:

but fearing some one might discover where he got it, he laid it down to place back the top stone, as he found it; and turning around, to his surprise there was no book in sight. He again opened the box, and in it saw the book, and attempted to take it out, but was hindered. He saw in the box something like a toad, which soon assumed the appearance of a man, and struck him on the side of his head.[78]

After trying again, and being struck again, he was told:

come one year from this day, and bring with you your oldest brother, and you shall have them. This spirit, he said, was the spirit of the prophet who wrote the book, who was sent to Joseph Smith, to make known these things to him.[79]

In this account, "the [nameless] prophet who wrote the book" is a strange expression, since that would presumably be Mormon, perhaps also an early candidate for the messenger. Or perhaps here again we have Nephi as the messenger (i.e., author of the Book of Nephi).

Smith was commanded to return in a year with his oldest brother. Since that brother had died during the year, Smith returned without him, and showing up without his oldest brother, he was ordered to return again a year later, and bring a man with him. On asking who might be the man, he was answered that he would know him when he saw him. Marquardt[80]

---

[77] Jessee, *Papers of Joseph Smith*, I:7-8.

[78] Marquardt, *Rise of Mormonism*, 48.

[79] Marquardt, *idem.*

[80] Marquardt, *ibid*, 51-53.

reports several other accounts, including accounts by Joseph's mother Lucy, his sister Catherine, his brother William and a joint account by two cousins of Joseph's wife, Emma Hale Smith. Accounts by non-Mormons can be challenged, secondhand reports by close relatives were memories later in life, and the official account is just that. The earliest account, by Smith himself, differs from the official account; but it too is probably already an effort to spin an official account. Smith's mea culpa that he had wanted to get gain from the plates probably would assuage the concerns of some who had known him in the early days, when he sought gold treasure, or later on, when his more secular claims spoke of gold plates and a forthcoming translation from which he and Harris would make a lot of money. Also, it may be that this long period of attempting to get the plates is nothing more than a period of claiming to have found gold plates prior to coming up with the plan to turn his claim into profit by publishing a translation. Harris' enduring focus on profit would be a continuation of what had initially been a shared Smith-Harris motivation.

Once he claimed to have obtained the plates in late September of 1827, he soon began to assert that persons who had learned of his gold plates were attempting to steal them. This is possible. Josiah Stowell engaged Joseph Smith (Jr. & Sr.) to hunt for Spanish treasure at Harmony, Susquehanna Co, PA. After their arrival in Harmony and with great expectations, Joseph signed the "Articles of Agreement" (1/11/1825), also signed by his father and seven others, to share their finds.[81] In 1881, David Whitmer stated, 'I had conversations with several young men who said that Joseph Smith had certainly golden plates, and that before he obtained them he had promised to share with them, but had not done so, and they were very much incensed with him.'"[82] Accordingly, Smith began to claim to have hidden them in various locations, in a hollow log, in an old black oak tree, beneath the family hearth, in his father's cooper shop and in a barrel of beans.

It would appear that after his experience with the 1826 pretrial investigation, Smith sought a better way to profit from seeking the gold that he had simply not been able to find. The claim that he had found gold plates could not be challenged, since he had been commanded by their guardian, the messenger, to not show them to anyone. His prior reputation, and the "Articles of Agreement" prompted many to assume that he had

---

[81] Dan Vogel, Early *Mormon Documents* (Salt Lake City: Signature Books, 2002), IV:407-13.
[82] Petersen, *Problems in Mormon* Text, p. 65.

indeed found the plates, and was claiming he could not show them to avoid sharing his treasure.

The Weighty Issue of a Gold Record

Since many involved stated that they had hefted the plates, it is clear that no one really had any idea how heavy gold is.

The table below reviews the options, with different metals. The accounts of hefting the plates need to be evaluated in the light of the weighty facts: if they were gold, they would weigh 161 pounds, calculated with a very generous estimate that the air between the plates could account for 20% of the volume. In fact, 10% is more likely. On the other hand, the plates may have been only 80% gold, and 20% copper, an alloy called tumbaga actually used in South America in *Book of Mormon* times. Tumbaga plates with these proportions would weigh 143 pounds, again with the same generous allowance for air between them. It seems clear that very few witnesses would be able to heft 161 pounds. The testimonies would read more in the vein of attempts: "I tried to heft them, but could not lift them."

In the table below, the assumption that the volume occupied by the plates could have been 20% air seems more than generous. There are various estimates of plate thickness, from 1/8″ to the thickness of common tin plate, perhaps 1/16″. Taking the latter, there would have been 96 plates (6″ X 8″, stacked 6″ high). Inscribed on both sides, they could have lain somewhat less than flat, although the serious weight of the gold would have served to press the lower plates in the stack relatively flat and tight. Gold is a very soft metal.

Table 3. Weight of the Plates (Various Metals Compared)

Weight in pounds of Each Option Adjusted for the Percent Air (20%)							
Solid block is 6″x8″x6″ or 288 cubic inches. Plates weight = 80% of solid block weight.							
Plate option by substance	lbs. gold/ cubic inch	lbs. copper/ cubic inch	lbs. brass[4/] cubic inch	G gold C copper	solid block weight	w/o air	TOTAL: solid block x .8
Gold	.7				201.6	80%	**161.3**
Copper		.32			92.16	80%	73.7
Brass			.3		86.4	80%	**69.1**
Tumbaga A	.56	.256		G80% C 20%	179.14	80%	**143.8**
Tumbaga B	.525	.078		G 75% C 25%	156.67	80%	**147.5**

1. The weights per cubic inch of gold, copper and brass are multiplied by 288 to get the weight of a solid block. The weight of the plates for each metal is this times .8 (adjusting for air).
2. A solid block of gold equals 288x.7=201.6. If air is 20%, then the gold is 201.6x.8=**161.28 lbs.**
3. The tumbaga option A is rated here as being 80% gold & 20% copper. Since copper is .32 lbs. per cubic inch, 20% of that is .32 lbs.x.20, or .064 lbs. The gold is 80% of the cube, so its weight is .7 X

.8 = .56 lbs. The weight of a one cubic inch cube is the sum of the two metals, i.e. .064+.56=.624.
Since the number of cubic inches is 288, the plates equal 288x.624xx.8 [for air] = **143.8** lbs.
4. The tumbaga B is rated here as being 75% gold & 25% copper. Since copper is .32 lbs. per cubic
inch, 25% of that is .32 lbs. x .25, or .08 lbs. The gold is 80% of the cube, so its weight is .7 X .8 =
.56 lbs. The weight of a one cubic inch cube is the sum of the two metals, i.e. .08+.56=.64. Since the
number of cubic inches is 288, the plates equal 288x.64x.8 [for air] = **147.456** lbs.
5. The weight of brass varies according to the amount of tin it contains. A review of converters online
gives us a medial value of .3 lbs. per cubic inch. So, .3 X 288 = 86.4 and 86.4 X.8 = **69.12** lbs.

In the case of tumbaga, although the ratio was as high as 80% gold, more usually it was only 75%, but could be even lower. It has higher tensile strength and a lower melting point than either metal alone, and can be gilded by applying a mild vegetable acid. This dissolves away the surface copper, leaving a pure gold surface film, and this process can be repeated when wear occurs. However, tumbaga does corrode:

> Non-gilded archaeological metals having a high percentage of copper are known to survive in better condition than gilded tumbaga objects primarily due to galvanic forces and preferential corrosion between gilded layers and the underlying alloy in a burial environment. The less noble copper will eventually corrode, the resulting corrosion products will undermine the gilding, and the thin gilded layer may eventually become detached from the heavily mineralized base alloy.[83]

Alloys must be above fifty *atomic percent* (At.%) gold to be corrosion resistant.[84] Atomic percentage is the percent of the atoms in the alloy that are a particular metal. To the extent that the copper atoms outnumber the gold atoms, they will be more susceptible to oxidation, producing serious deterioration. The following formula calculates the weight percentage when the atomic weights and atomic percentages of two metals in an alloy are known. I am using x for gold and y for copper. This example has 50 At.% (.5) for each metal.

$$\text{Wt. \% x} = \frac{(\text{At. \% x})(\text{At. Wt. x})}{(\text{At. \% x})(\text{At. Wt. x}) + (\text{At. \% y})(\text{At. Wt. y})} \times 100$$

$$= (.5 \times 196.966)/[(.5 \times 196.966)+(.5 \times 63.546)] \times 100 = 75.6\%$$

---

[83] Scott Fulton and Sylvia Keochakian, "The conservation of tumbaga metals from Panama at the Peabody Museum, Harvard University," *Objects Specialty Group Postprints*, Volume Twelve (2005), 76-90.

[84] Lyndsie Selwyn, "Corrosion Chemistry of Gilded Silver and Copper," in Terry Drayman-Weisser, *Gilded Metals, History, Technology & Conservation* (London: Archetype Publications, 2000), 21-47.

Therefore, more than 76% gold, by scale weight, is needed for the plates to be relatively corrosion resistant. If the gold is 67% by scale weight, the atomic weight percent falls to 40%. Over a period of 1500 years, serious corrosion would occur. Presumably, corroded plates with the ultra thin gilding scaling off, are no one's image of Smith's gold plates.

So bearing in mind that gold plates would weigh at least 161 pounds, and even tumbaga plates would weigh from 143 to 147 pounds to survive relatively free of corrosion, we read his mother's account of how he got them out of their hiding place in a log in the woods and home:

> Joseph…wrapping them in his linen frock, placed them under his arm and started for home…travelling some distance after he left the road, he came to a large windfall, and as he was jumping over a log, a man sprang up from behind it, and gave him a heavy blow with a gun. Joseph turned around and knocked him down, then ran at the top of his speed. About half a mile further he was attacked again in the same manner as before; he knocked the man down in like manner as the former and ran on again; and before he reached home he was assaulted the third time. In striking the last one he dislocated his thumb…he threw himself down in the corner of the fence in order to recover his breath.[85]

Joseph runs more than a mile with a weight of at least 143 pounds. He carries it under his arm, like a schoolbook. With it, he jumps over a log. And during this whole time, carrying it from place to place, there is no mention that he can hardly even lift it. Moreover, he was still suffering the effects of the removal of a large abscess in a leg. Smith's mother also reportedly said that she had herself handled and hefted the plates. [86]

Martin Harris had spent his life working on his farm, and was no stranger to hefting heavy objects. Reportedly he claimed to have hefted the plates, and said that they weighed forty or fifty pounds.[87] William Smith recounted that when Joseph first got the plates home, although he did not see them uncovered "I handled them and hefted them while wrapped in a tow frock;" and that "Father and my brother Samuel saw

---

[85] Lucy Mack Smith in Levina Fielding Anderson, ed., *Lucy's Book, a Critical Edition of Lucy Mack Smith's Family Memoir* (Salt Lake City: Signature Books, 2001), 385-86.

[86] Sally Parker to John Kempton, 26 August 1838, in Vogel, *Early Mormon Documents*, I:218-19.

[87] Martin Harris as quoted in Joel Tiffany, "Mormonism—No. II," Tiffany Monthly (August 1859, in Vogel, *Early Mormon Documents*, II:306.

them as I did while in the frock. So did Hyrum and others of the family."[88]
Lucy Smith wrote that she invited Mrs. Harris over to see them. In an
interview to Edward Stevenson, Martin Harris stated that his wife and
daughter had hefted the plates and felt them under cover; he said, "My
daughter said, they were about as much as she could lift. They were now
in the glass-box [a wood box for window panes], and my wife said they
were very heavy. They both lifted them."[89]

In summary, whether we consider those who claimed to have hefted
the plates (even Mother Smith), Martin Harris' estimate of their weight, or
the adventures of Joseph running through the woods, the bottom line is
that the sheer weight of even tumbaga plates cannot be reconciled with the
stories. And the weight of even these hypothetical tumbaga plates was
generously underestimated.

The writing area is also a problem. The following data reveal the
extent of the issue:

height of the stack of gold plates	6"
thickness of the plates (at the low end of estimates)	1/16"
number of plates (16 per inch = 6X16)	96
number of unsealed plates (using the high-end estimate, i.e. 50%)	48
number of engraving spaces with the plates engraved on both sides	96
number of BoM printed pages in the customary LDS edition	520
Skousen's estimate of ms𝒪 pages for Nephi thru Words of Mormon[90]	124
number of BoM printed pages to cover Nephi thru Words of Mormon	133
estimated printed pages to cover the 116 pages of the lost Book of Lehi	100
number of printed pages for the BoM with the lost book of Lehi	620
number of English printed pages per gold-plate writing space	**6.46**

The number of plates would be less if they did not lie perfectly flat. There
must have been a margin, and a wider gutter to accommodate the binding
rings. Using figures at the end of the range of estimates most favorable to
the gold-plate story, the plates would have had to have the equivalent of
6.46 pages in English per side, in largely reformed Egyptian, but partly in

---

[88] William B. Smith, "Wm. B. Smith's last Statement," *Zion's Ensign* 5: Jan. 13,
1894, in Marquardt, *Rise of Mormonism*, 72.
[89] Martin Harris as quoted by Joel Tiffany in "Mormonism—No. II," Tiffany
Monthly (August 1859, in Vogel, *Early Mormon Documents*, II:309.
[90] Royal Skousen, *The Original Manuscript of the Book of Mormon: Typographical Facsimile of the Extant Text* (Provo, UT: Foundation for Ancient
Research and Mormon Studies, 2001), 21.

7th century BCE Egyptian (Lehi and its Nephi replacement text). It is hard to imagine compressing any real script to this extent.

How about Brass Plates?

To cover other possibilities, it is instructive to have knowledge of metallurgy in the early Americas, as well as in early nineteenth-century New England. Smelting gold, silver and copper began in South America, where alloying also emerged. Well before the Common Era, bronze and tumbaga were produced. The Moche culture was especially advanced, and South American trading ships carried on an active trade with Mesoamerica, resulting in local metallurgy among the Maya in their classic period (c. 250-900 CE).

In colonial America, the British tried to prevent the local development of the metal industries. Still, a substantial percentage of the world's identified lead deposits is in Missouri's lead belt, and it was being mined as early as 1720. Frontiersmen needed it to cast balls for their muskets. Prior to 1800, brass was mostly used in the button industry. Buttons were formed from sheet brass, and these craftsmen got their brass rolled in early steel rolling mills. The center of the New England brass industry came to be in Waterbury, Connecticut, the self-dubbed "Brass Town." Aaron Benedict began rolling sheet brass in 1824, and quickly found a market for his product. Joseph Smith came from a cooper family. His grandfather was a cooper, he was a cooper's son, and his family had a cooper shop. It is interesting to observe that this shop was one of the first places where he claimed he was hiding the plates.

The weight of brass plates would be at least 69 pounds, more than the upper end of Martin Harris' estimate for the weight of the gold plates. The unsealed portion of brass plates could have been easily inscribed with Smith's character set using an awl, or even an ice pick. But does this mean that the Smiths had actually produced this sort of prop for their project? Not necessarily. Everyone who claimed to have hefted or otherwise examined the plates may have been a confederate. But having a brass-plate prop would have been effective, even just for feeling it through a cloth and hefting it. After all, we do not know that all those who had this privilege got their experience into print.

Conclusions

§ In the region of Palmyra (upstate New York), the practitioners of the occult and printed accounts of their activities included seerstone scryers, rodsmen, necromancers and prophets (i.e. persons who speak words given them by a deity). Joseph Smith had become a credible scryer and necromancer among their ranks.

§ The ancient Nephite gold plates were claimed to have lain secure in the care of the spirit of the ancient that had hidden them up, and Smith obtained them only after meeting the demands of their guardian spirit.

§ The weight of the claimed plates, if gold, is completely inconsistent with the stories told about their being carried and hefted.

§ Corrosion-resistant tumbaga plates could look like gold, but are still too heavy. More than 76% gold by scale weight is needed to be corrosion resistant. Otherwise, the gold outer skin will separate and peel off if the copper proportion is too great.

§ It was possible in the mid 1820s for a cooper's son to fabricate a brass-plate prop, although there is no need to assume that this happened.

§ By comparison with known writing systems, it is highly unlikely that the writing area of the unsealed plates as described could have held the entire text of the *Book of Mormon* (including the *Book of Lehi* and *Book of Ether*).

This is the

Gold Plates Issue

< Chapter 4 >

Father Smith, His Visionary Family & the Occult

Joseph Smith Jr. was introduced to various occult practices by family members, and also others in upstate New York, who were active in the occult, particularly seers, rodsmen and necromancers.

The Heritage and Family of Joseph Smith, Jr.

The Smiths, Whitmers and Cowdery were not highly unusual in their milieu. The negative image of the Smiths in Eber D. Howe's *Mormonism Unvailed* is exaggerated. [91] They were descended from relatively prosperous progenitors occasionally active in civic affairs, but who rather recently had fallen on hard times. This can be seen in the paternal lines of both Joseph Smith Sr. and Lucy Mack (Smith).

Table 4. The Paternal Line of Joseph Smith Jr.

c. 1626	Robert Smith was born in England (possibly Kirton, Lincolnshire).
1638	He came to Massachusetts at about age 12.
1656	He married the daughter of Thomas French, & later bought 280 acres in Rowley (aka Boxford, MA).
1666	Samuel Smith was born, son of Robert Smith (Rowley, Essex, MA). He came to hold public office, and is listed with the title of "Gentleman."
c. 1692	Mary Easty was executed on 09/22/1692, partly as a result of the deposition of Samuel Smith against her in the Salem witch trials.
1673	Active in civic affairs, he signed a petition to the General Court.
1693	He died leaving an estate valued at 189 pounds.
1707	He married Rebecca Curtis.
1714	Samuel Jr. was born in Topsfield, MA, son of Samuel Smith. He was active in public affairs, served six terms in the legislature, and twelve terms as selectman.
1744	Asael (Asahel; the grandfather of Joseph Smith Jr.) was born in Topsfield, Essex, MA.
1768	Jesse Smith was born in Topsfield, Essex, MA.
1771	July 12, 1771, Joseph Smith Sr. was born.
1772	March 8, 1772, Jesse, Priscilla and Joseph were baptized in the Topsfield Congregational Church.

---

[91] Eber Dudley Howe, *Mormonism Unvailed* (Salt Lake City: Signature Books, 2015; first published: Painesville, OH: Telegraph Press, 1834).

1773	Asael was chairman of the Tea Committee at Topsfield, which sustained the action of the Boston Tea Party.
1774	He was elected to the Ipswich Convention and the First Provincial Congress in Massachusetts.
1775	Captain Asael Smith, marched on the Alarm, April 19.
1776	He enlisted in Colonel Joshua Wingate's Regiment for service in the Revolutionary War.
1779	1779-1786, he served as town clerk of Derryfield (Manchester, NH). His son Silas Smith was born.
1781	John Smith was born.
1786	Asael was listed as a cooper.
1791	Asael sold his lands to settle his father's debts incurred partly due to neglect of private affairs and partly due to economic crisis associated with the Revolutionary War. He rented a dairy farm.
1791	He acquired land in Tunbridge, VT.
1792	Jesse married Hannah Peabody in Middleton, Essex, MA.
1793	Asael began to serve frequently as a selectman of Tunbridge, VT.
1797	He moderated a meeting to establish one of the early Universalist Societies in Vermont. (submitted in Tunbridge, VT)
18??	Sometime between 1811 & 1820 Asael moved to Stockholm, NY.
1829	Jesse Smith was residing in Stockholm, St. Lawrence, NY.
1830	Asael died in Stockholm, St. Lawrence, NY.

Joseph Smith Jr.'s maternal forebears had suffered a gradual decline in fortune. Still, we note that his grandmother Lydia taught school. His father learned to read and write and was active in the school district. All were hardworking.

Table 5. The Maternal Line of Joseph Smith Jr.

1669	John Mack came to Massachusetts and settled in Salisbury. He was born in Inverness, Scotland, and descended from a line of clergymen.
1697	Ebenezer Mack was born. He inherited his father's large property in Lyme, Connecticut. He married Hannah Huntley, a teacher for thirty years. He suffered financial misfortunes.
1732	Solomon Mack was born in Lyme, Connecticut. Due to his father's financial problems, he was indentured.
1755	Enlisted in the French and Indian War, he fought in the battle of Halfway Brook.
1756	Solomon bought a farm in Connecticut and added to it in 1758.
1759	Solomon married Lydia Gates, schoolteacher and member of the Congregational Church. She taught him to read and write along with their children, but he resisted her religious instruction.
1761	He and Lydia acquire 100 acres in a wilderness at Marlow, New Hampshire.

1767	He was elected deer reeve (game warden).
1775	Lucy Mack, born in Gilsum, Cheshire, NH.
1796	Solomon's daughter Lucy married Joseph Smith Sr.
1810	At age 77 & seriously ill, he became religious.
1820	Solomon died nearly 88 years old.
1856	Lucy Mack Smith, died 14 May in Nauvoo, Il.

Joseph Smith Sr.'s children had fewer opportunities for education as the family fortunes declined. Hyrum was the best off in this regard, being sent to Moore's Academy (est., 1755), which had been moved to Hanover, and re-established as Dartmouth College (1817). Even so, current research indicates that Joe Jr.'s education, as irregular as it may have been, was better than formerly characterized.[92]

Joseph Smith Sr. (1771-1840)

Born in Topsfield, Massachusetts, he moved with his parents to Tunbridge, Vermont, where he met his wife, Lucy Mack Smith. They were married there in 1796. After a failed business venture, and being forced to sell their farm and become tenant farmers, they moved from Norwich (in the Tunbridge area) to Palmyra in upstate New York (Joseph Smith Sr. in late 1816, and his family in early 1817). Apart from farming and small business, he was also a cooper like his father, a schoolteacher, a seerstone scryer and rodsman. Rural coopers often made their own hoops. Unlike his wife, Lucy, who was searching for a church for her family, he was not comfortable with organized religion. The principal exception to this was his interest in Universalism. Nonetheless, he claimed seven visions, five of which were recounted by his wife in some detail, showing the degree to which his visions were taken seriously, at least at home. In Royalton, Vermont he went to school on Dewey Hill and was taught by Deacon Jonathan Rinney.

Joseph Smith Sr. had become well equipped for his occult activities. The paraphernalia for occult practices in the Smith home must have been among his possessions. In addition to seerstones and hazel rods (at least in the case of Oliver, Joseph Smith Sr. and William Cowdery), other paraphernalia of the Smiths in the 1820s included lamens (magic parchments), an engraved silver magic talisman and a family dagger "inscribed with the astrological symbol of Mars, the magic 'sigil' (or 'seal') for the 'intelligence' of Mars" and a name of the OT deity in

---

[92] William Davis, "Reassessing Joseph Smith Jr.'s Formal Education," published in *Dialogue: A Journal of Mormon Thought* 49, no. 4 (Winter 2016):1-58.

Hebrew letters: *Adonay*."[93] The dagger was used like Winchell's sword to draw magic circles in treasure hunting. Note that the hazel divining rod was used to get information, as well as for treasure hunting.

It is clear that Joseph Smith Jr. was influenced by his father in these regards. One important question is the extent to which the father played a leading or even seminal role in his son's efforts to produce a new scripture and church. The *Book of Mormon* begins with the divine command to emigrate from Jerusalem, coming to the family patriarch, Lehi, although his son Nephi is by far the chief protagonist. Lehi descends from Joseph; Smith Sr. and Jr. are both named Joseph. How autobiographical is this?[94]

Another important issue concerns the family relations between William Cowdery, father of Oliver Cowdery, and Joseph Smith Sr. His son and Oliver Cowdery were third cousins. The two families lived for over a decade not much more than fifty miles apart. There are reports that for a time Joseph Smith Sr. resided in Poultney, Vermont, and that both he and William Cowdery were involved in the rodsmen religious movement of Nathaniel Wood in Middletown. This came to a head in an infamous incident called the Wood scrape. Whether they, either one or both, were involved in this cannot be proved; orthodox LDS scholars have challenged the assertion.[95] The fact that William's son, Oliver, was a rodsman raises the possibility that his father was as well. Family relations between the Smiths and Cowderys are also rendered probable by the fact that in the late 1820s, Hyrum Smith got Oliver Cowdery appointed as a teacher, and the latter took up residence in the home of Joseph Sr. This does not happen casually.[96]

Hyrum, a son of Smith Sr., was a member of the Masonic Lodge in Palmyra, being listed as a member of the Mount Moriah Masonic Lodge No. 112 for the period June 1827 to June 1828. Joseph Smith Jr. later became a Freemason. About 1830, Joseph Smith Sr. with his son Don Carlos, visited Smith family relatives in Stockholm and Potsdam, St. Lawrence, NY, to announce the message of Mormonism. In 1833 he was ordained the first Church Patriarch, and in 1836 he and his brother John Smith went on a mission for three months to the branches of the Eastern States.[97] John became Presiding Patriarch under Brigham Young.

---

[93] Quinn, *Early Mormonism and the Magic World View*, 66-7, 70, 102-05.

[94] For insight into this issue, see Dan Vogel, *Joseph Smith*, 2004), 698.

[95] Quinn, *Early Mormonism and the Magic World View*,1 21 (see 121-30).

[96] ibid, 34-39.

[97] *History of the Church*, 2:446.

The Family: Joseph Smith Jr. Begins His Mission

Joseph Smith's education was sporadic due to demands made on him to help support his birth family. His account is that he studied reading, writing and arithmetic. We know that he owned a book titled *First Lines in Arithmetic, For the Use of Young Scholars*, and the *Sacred Geography or a Description of the Places Mentioned in the Old and New Testament* (1824) by Thomas T. Smiley. It is safe to assume that he had access to other books in the Smith household. Although he initially started off slowly, his progress improved greatly once his father began teaching his children at home.[98] William Davis has taken a new look at Joseph Jr.'s education, and concluded regarding his school attendance during his family's time in Royalton, VT, that, "prior to Joseph's departure from Royalton, he may well have obtained as much formal education as historians tend to attribute to his entire lifetime, if not more."[99]

After moving to West Lebanon, VT, Joseph Jr. suffered a serious illness requiring surgery to remove a large abscess on a leg. Although this clearly had an impact on his formal education, it was not without some possible positive consequence. Smith's mother wrote that his uncle Jesse Smith took him to convalesce for a bit at his home in Salem. This is not proven, but it seems unlikely that she would have written this if at least some trip to Salem had not happened.[100] Even so, H. Michael Marquardt points out that there is nothing in Jesse's ledger book to evidence such a visit.[101] William Davis, in his study of Joseph's education, writes,

> Joseph's trip to Salem, of whatever length and whenever it actually took place, would have offered its own form of practical education. Salem was a major port city of trade: merchant ships brought exotic cargo from all over the world, and its bustling shops were packed with a rich panoply of merchandise and patrons. Yet, such excitement would have been counterbalanced by a hostile British navy patrolling along the seacoast, seizing ships, impressing sailors, and threatening invasion.

Regarding this possible visit, see also Vogel and Hill.[102] Davis further suggests that in the last part of the family's time in West Lebanon, while

---

[98] Marquardt, *Rise of Mormonism*, 21.
[99] Davis, "Reassessing Joseph Smith Jr.'s Formal Education," 17.
[100] Lucy Smith, in Anderson, *Lucy's Book*, 310.
[101] H. Michael Marquardt, personal communication.
[102] Vogel, *Joseph Smith*, 18. Donna Hill, *Joseph Smith, the First Mormon* (Salt Lake City: Signature Books, 1999 [1977]), 36.

recuperating on crutches from his illness, he might have attended school, since he would not have been able to engage in heavy labor.[103] He argues that the lack of specific documentary evidence should not outweigh Lucy Smith's declared commitment to education. After the arrival of the Smith's in Palmyra, and then in Manchester, there is more evidence of at least some school attendance. Jacob E. Terry of East Palmyra was a classmate with Joseph. In the Parshall Terry family history, reviewing dates in her memory, Jacob's sister wrote, "this would indicate that Joseph Smith attended school immediately after his arrival at Palmyra sometime during the winter of 1816–1817."[104] Marquardt adds to the picture, stating that "Smith, though almost twenty years old, enrolled in school in the Bainbridge, New York area while he was working for Josiah Stowell during the winter of 1825-26. While being examined before Justice Albert Neely on March 20, 1826, Smith testified that he had been 'going to school.'"[105]

Another source of education in the Smith home was the *Palmyra Register and Herald*, and later the *Wayne Sentinel*. In these sources the Smiths had available the article on the Hebrew origins of the Indians by Mordecai M. Noah, and the visions of Asa Wild, who claimed that the existing churches were in error, as well as coverage of other religious events in the area. The above evidence must be considered in the context of anti-Mormon efforts to demean Joseph Jr. as an illiterate country bumpkin, plus a concerted Smith-Cowdery effort to control the early history of the Church, which also involved depicting the founding prophet as being decidedly unable to produce the *Book of Mormon*.

Although we cannot take the sequencing as proven, Lucy Mack Smith, Joseph's mother, wrote that after her son had started talking about the visit of an angel, but before he claimed to have gotten the gold plates, he was a great story teller:

> During our evening conversations, Joseph would occasionally give us some of the most amusing recitals that could be imagined. He would describe the ancient inhabitants of this continent, their dress, mode of travelling, and the animals upon which they rode; their cities, their buildings, with every particular; their mode of warfare; and also their religious worship. This he would do with as much ease, seemingly, as if he had spent his whole life with them.[106]

---

[103] *Ibid*, 17-22.
[104] Davis, "Reassessing Joseph Smith Jr.'s Formal Education," 24.
[105] *Ibid*, 22.
[106] Lucy Smith, in Anderson, ed., *Lucy's Book*, 345.

Not only did Smith seek opportunities for conventional schooling, but also for religious learning and training. He attended Methodist training to be an exhorter (in Palmyra, and again in Harmony, Pennsylvania). Orsamus Turner, a Palmyra *Register* newspaper apprentice, reported, "after catching a spark of Methodism in the camp meeting, away down in the woods, on the Vienna road, he was a very passable exhorter in evening meetings."[107] The importance of this effort goes beyond the training received; becoming an exhorter was the first step to becoming a Methodist minister. At least the possibility of a career in religion was on the table. He also attended a debating club in Palmyra, where he made positive impressions.[108] We do not know if Joseph Smith's considerable ability at extemporaneous speaking was totally natural, or if it was at least partly acquired in these two training experiences. Itinerant preachers often used the extemporaneous style, which became highly prized in the second half of the nineteenth century, and used on occasion even by the renowned Reverend C. H. Spurgeon, whose massive sermon collection is still studied today. Finally, like the rest of Joseph's family, he was able to make use of the family Bible, which he was apparently quite fond of studying.

As early as July 1828, he began receiving regular revelations worded in the divine first person, i.e., that of the Lord (D&C 5:1). After 1830, it was not uncommon for these to be received in the presence of his scribe, who wrote down the Lord's words issuing from Smith's mouth. Two of his scribes have left us a description of Smith's ability to perform extemporaneously (although considerable memorized preparation may have gone into each session). Scribe William E. McLellin wrote:

> I, as scribe, have written revelations from the mouth of both the Revelators, Joseph Smith and David Whitmer. And I have been present many times when others wrote for Joseph; therefore I speak as one having experience. The scribe seats himself at a desk or table, with pen, ink and paper. The subject of enquiry being understood, the Prophet and Revelator enquires of God. He spiritually sees, hears and feels, and then speaks as he is moved upon by the Holy Ghost, the 'thus saith the Lord,' sentence after sentence, and waits for his amanuenses to write and then read aloud each sentence. Thus they proceed until the revelator says Amen, at the close of what is then communicated.[109]

---

[107] O[rsamus] Turner, *History of the Pioneer Settlement*, 214, 400; quoted here from Marquardt, *Rise of Mormonism*, 30.

[108] Marquardt, *Rise of Mormonism*, 31.

[109] William E. McLellin, ed., *The Ensign of Liberty* (1, August, 1849), 98.

Parley P. Pratt gave virtually the same account, and said, "…I was present to witness the dictation of several communications of several pages each."[110] This said, let us bear in mind that Smith's dictation was done in small bits. He dictated, then waited (reflected) while his scribe finished writing, and then dictated again. These texts were later edited.

Smith received more education than has usually been thought, was fascinated from the start with the American Indians, capable of extemporaneously entertaining his family as a young man with detailed stories about them, capable of articulating extemporaneous revelations several paragraphs in length, and articulate enough to impress as a Methodist exhorter, although at a neophyte level.

In the mid-18th century, Jonathan Edwards became concerned regarding the activities of exhorters. On the issue of reversals in church progress, he assigned blame:

> far more to the unrestrained zeal of a considerable number of misguided men—some of them preachers of the gospel, and others lay exhorters—who, intending to take Mr. Whitefield as the model, travelled from place to place, preaching and exhorting wheresoever they could collect an audience…and whenever they judged a minister, or a majority of the church, destitute of piety—which they usually did, not on account of their false principles or their irreligious life, but for the want of an ardour and zeal equal to their own—advised, in one case, the whole church to withdraw from the minister…[111]

England had similar problems. By 1746, the status of "exhorter" was formalized. The Minutes of the 1746 Methodist Conference contain the following resolution:

> 1. Let none exhort in any of our Societies, without a note of recommendation from the Assistant. 2. Let every exhorter see that this is renewed yearly. 3. Let every Assistant rigorously insist upon this[112]

In New England this note came to be known as an exhorter's license.

---

[110] Parley P. Pratt, *Autobiography of Parley P. Pratt*, edited by his son, Parley P. Pratt (Salt Lake City: Deseret Book Company, 1934), 48. Edition quoted, 1994.

[111] Sereno E. Dwight, "Memoirs of Jonathan Edwards," in *Works of Jonathan Edwards*, I:lxxi.

[112] *Minutes of the Methodist Conferences from the first held in London by the late Rev. John Wesley, A.M. in the Year 1744* (London: Methodist Conference Office, 1812), 1: 30.

By 1778 the term exhorter appeared often without explanation. We can assume that the office of exhorter was a commonly known part of the Methodist working system by this time and no explanation was needed. At the Conference held at Kent County, Delaware, beginning April 28, 1779, a rule recorded in the Minutes states that "every exhorter and local preacher go by the directions of the assistants where, and only where, they shall appoint." On April 24, 1780, when the northern Conference met in Lovely Lane Chapel in Baltimore, Question 10 noted that every local preacher and exhorter should have a license, to be renewed quarterly, after examination, and that none should "presume to speak in public without taking a note."[113]

Smith had not gotten a license, and had not even become a Methodist. Any action on his part in the role of exhorter would have drawn fire form the clergy. Rather than knuckle under to Methodist rules and theology, he went his own way, determined to preach on his own terms. Later in his life, the view of Smith's authority that he wished others to accept is expressed in one of his revelations: "…my [the Lord's] word…whether by my own voice, or by the voice of my servants, it is the same." (D&C 1:38) Even so, once received, Smith's sacred texts were not set in concrete. They were subject to being edited, not just for typos, but at times for substantive content.

Smith could be somewhat cavalier regarding his relationship to God. In a letter seeking to ingratiate himself to General Smith, Major-General James Arlington Bennet wrote, "You know, Mahomet had his '*right-hand man.*" Smith's reply did not mince words, saying, "I combat the errors of ages; I meet the violence of mobs; I cope with illegal proceedings from executive authority; I cut the Gordian knot of powers; and I solve mathematical problems of Universities: WITH TRUTH, *diamond truth, and God is my 'right-hand man.*"[114] It is not always possible to know how seriously he took his own words. In a letter to Oliver Cowdery in October, 1829, he wrote, "two of our most formidable persacutors (*sic*) are now under censure and are cited to a triyal (*sic*) in the church for crimes which if true are worse than all the Gold Book business."[115]

---

[113] Rev. Robert A. Sisler, Newburg Charge, District Director on Lay Speaking "History of Lay Speaking" (http://www.angelfire.com/biz/SELLC/history.html, accessed 14/04/2017).

[114] Joseph Smith, letter to James Arlington Bennet dated 13 November 1843, *History of the Church*, 6:78. It was also published in Henry Mayhew & Charles MacKay, *The Mormons: or Latter-day Saints* (London: Office of the National Illustrated Library, 1851), 119.

[115] Joseph Smith, letter to Oliver Cowdery dated 22 October 1829, in Vogel, *Early Mormon Documents*, II:7.

Joseph Smith Sr. was also a visionary, a person who received dreams from the sacred. After he had experienced seven vivid dreams or visions, and apparently either at about the same time or shortly after the seventh in 1819, Joseph Smith Jr. claimed to also have had a vision, in some ways similar to those mentioned above. We will never know the actual year this happened, or the specific content. The first full account is found in Smith's 1832 history, about a decade after the event, and at a time when the concept of an official history was emerging. There was a need to tell the story of his early life in terms more religious than his reputation as a gold-seeking scryer, and foreshadowing the mission that would become his destiny. He claimed that he was sixteen at the time.[116] Giving this earliest account priority, and since he was born on 23 December 1805, 1821 is possible, but 1822 more probable. The text follows:

> while in ⟨the⟩ attitude of calling upon the Lord ⟨in the 16ᵗʰ year of my age⟩ a pillar of ~~fire~~ light above the brightness of sun at noon day come down from above and rested upon me and I was filled with the spirit of god and the ⟨Lord⟩ opened the heavens upon me and I saw the Lord and he spake unto me saying Joseph ⟨my son⟩ thy sins are forgiven thee. Go thy way walk in my statutes and keep my commandments behold I am the Lord of glory I was crucifyed (sic) for the world that all those who believe on my name may have Eternal life behold the world lieth in sin ~~and~~ at this time and none doeth good no not one they have turned aside from the gospel and keep not ⟨my⟩ commandments they draw near to me with their lips while their hearts are far from me and my anger is kindling against the inhabitants of the earth to visit them according to th[e]ir ungodliness ...[117]

In Joseph Smith's *History of the Church*, he wrote in 1838-39:

> Just at this moment of great alarm I saw a pillar ⟨of⟩ light exactly over my head above the brightness of the sun, which descended ~~gracefully~~ gradually until it fell upon me. It no sooner appeared than I found myself delivered from the enemy which held me bound. When the light rested upon me I saw two personages (whose brightness and glory defy all description) standing above me in the air. One of ⟨them⟩ spake unto me calling me by name and said "This is my beloved son. Hear him."... No sooner therefore did I get possession of myself as to be able to speak, than I asked the personages who stood above me in the light, which of all the sects was right... I was answered that I must join none of them, for they were all wrong, and the Personage who addressed me said that all their creeds were an abomination in his sight,

---

[116] Joseph Smith, "History, 1832," in Vogel, *Early Mormon Documents*, I:28.
[117] Dean C. Jessee, *The Personal Writings of Joseph Smith*, 6.

that those professors were all corrupt, that "they draw near to me with their lips but their hearts are far from me, They teach for doctrines the commandments of men, having a form of Godliness but they deny the power thereof."[118] [Cf. Isaiah 29:13; Matthew 15:8; and 2 Nephi 27:25.]

This is the third of Smith's accounts, and currently the official one.[119] All accounts were written a decade or more after the presumed event. Already we see an evolution in the story. The first account only mentions Jesus Christ, while the official version features God the Father and God the Son as two discrete anthropomorphic deities, presumably reflecting the move from a period of strict monotheism toward the emergence of LDS polytheism. It is God the Father who addresses Smith.

In the account of 1832 he states, "by searching the scriptures I found that mand ‹mankind› did not come unto the Lord but that they had apostatiseds [sic]." Christ's message that he reports does not mention the churches of the day. It was more far-reaching and severe, condemning all mankind: "the world lieth in sin and at this time and none doeth good no not one they have turned aside from the gospel..." Christ's "anger is kindling against the inhabitants of the earth." The absence of any order to not join any of the churches is consistent with Smith's entering into training as a Methodist exhorter, and even practicing as one on a neophyte level. Furthermore, four members of his family to whom he was close and over whom his religious persona held a certain sway, his mother, brothers Hyrum and Samuel Harrison and sister Sophronia, continued to be practicing Presbyterians up to c. September of 1828, possibly marking the approximate date when it was decided to establish a new church. By contrast, this is clearly inconsistent with the harsh language directed at the churches in the third dated version of his First Vision, and the admonition not to join any of them. It militates against a date for this portion of his experience prior to 1828. The message of apostasy was first ramped up in the *Book of Mormon* where an angel shows Nephi the "great and abominable church" and declares that there are but two churches, the

---

[118] Jessee, *Personal Writings of Joseph Smith*, 199-200. Jessee, *Papers of Joseph Smith*, I:265-66 & 272-73. Milton V. Backman, Jr., *Joseph Smith's First Vision; Confirming Evidences and Contemporary Accounts, Second Edition, Revised and Enlarged* (Salt Lake City: Bookcraft, 1980), 160-63. The text was possibly dictated in 1838, but the ms reporting it was begun in 1839.

[119] The 1838-39 account; for all three, and a study of them, see Backman, Jr., *Joseph Smith's First Vision*; & Dean C. Jessee, *The Early Accounts of Joseph Smith's First Vision* (Sandy, UT: Mormon Miscellaneous [reprint series],1984).

church of God and the church of the devil (1 Nephi 14:9-10). This message is closer to that of the 1838-39 account of the First Vision.

A strong disdain for the churches of his day was alive and well in the region, a view shared by Joseph Sr. This disdain, passed on to his son, was probably the first manifestation of this declaration. It was first made a revealed doctrine in the *Book of Mormon*, with God condemning all of the churches of his day, and ratcheted up considerably in the First Vision account of 1832, condemning all mankind. In the 1838-39 account it was walked back again to just a condemnation of the churches.

Just as a gold history became a gold bible, and a guardian messenger eventually became the angel Moroni, a vision of Christ became a vision of God the Father and God the Son in anthropomorphic form in the 1838-39 version, consistent with the emergence of LDS polytheism. Similarly, Smith's aversion to these churches, first acquired from his father, became expressed in terms of the "great and abominable church" in the *Book of Mormon* (1 Nephi 14:9), then a condemnation of all mankind in the 1832 recital of the First Vision, and then the declaration in the 1838-39 version just condemning the churches, declaring that "all their creeds were an abomination in his sight," coupled with a command to not join any of them. All of this shows the fluidity and development of Joseph Smith's assertions over time.[120]

The Family: Hyrum Smith—Brother, Confidant, Collaborator

Hyrum was five years older than Joseph. After the death of his eldest brother Alvin, Hyrum assumed an important place in the life of his younger brother. He was sent to Moore's Academy, or Moor's Charity School, which had been established by Eleazar Wheelock in 1754 to educate Native Americans to become preachers of the gospel to their own people. In 1770 it was moved to Hanover, New Hampshire, where it was re-established as Dartmouth College. Hyrum's experience there was possibly at the level of secondary education. There, he must have heard a great deal about missions to convert Native Americans, or, in those days, simply the Indians. He moved to Manchester, Ontario Co., New York in 1825 and was there when the entire Smith family was living in their log home after June 1829. He married Jerusha Barden on 2 November 1826 at Manchester. In 1827 he was initiated into Freemasonry (Mount Moriah Masonic Lodge No. 112).

---

[120] For perspective on this transition, see Brant Gardner, *The Gift and the Power* (Sandy, UT: Greg Kofford Books, 2011).

Hyrum's role in the BoM project began early. According to his mother Lucy, early in 1828 he accompanied Martin Harris to Harmony to begin his work as Joseph's scribe, before Martin's mission to show learned scholars, including Charles Anthon, some characters said to be from the gold plates.[121] In May of 1829, he visited Joseph and Oliver in Harmony ostensibly to check on how the translation was coming along.[122] During this visit he may already have informed them that David Whitmer would come. In a letter of 14/06/1829, Oliver Cowdery was already urging Hyrum, "Stir up the minds of our friends against the time we come unto you, that thus they may be willing to take upon them the name of Christ..."[123] On 17/06/1829 his uncle Jesse wrote him accusing that, "Uncle Jesse did, and still does think the whole pretended discovery, not a very deep, but a very clear and foolish deception, a very great wickedness..."[124] After they completed their stay at the home of Peter Whitmer Sr. to finish up the *Book of Mormon* (i.e. specifically Mormon's abridgment), Oliver resided with Hyrum Smith, apparently with the rest of the Smith family, while he worked on ms𝒫. He was one of the Eight Witnesses who claimed to have viewed, hefted and handled the gold plates. It was he who brought the first gathering (ms signature) of ms𝒫 to the printer for publication, and he brought other gatherings along with Cowdery and Harris. He was thus a collaborator as early as work on the *Book of Lehi*, was urged to engage in preparatory proselytism while Cowdery was in Fayette, and worked in a facilitator role all the way through to the publication of the *Book of Mormon*. If the Book of Mosiah is the product of a third drafter, he is a possible candidate.

Hyrum's rise in the Church was meteoric. On 3 September 1837, he was appointed Assistant Counselor in the First Presidency; on 7 November 1837 Second Counselor in the First Presidency; on 14 September Presiding Patriarch, following his father Joseph Sr.; and on 24 January 1841 Assistant President of the Church (and a Latter Day Saint Apostle?). For all of these appointments he was called by his brother Joseph Smith Jr. He and Joseph were murdered at Carthage Jail on 27 June, 1844, with the Church only fourteen years old.

---

[121] Lucy Smith, in Anderson, *Lucy's Book*, 402.

[122] Marquardt, *Rise of Mormonism*, 86.

[123] Oliver Cowdery, letter to Hyrum Smith dated 14 June 1829, in Vogel, *Early Mormon Documents*, II:403.

[124] Jesse Smith in a letter to Hyrum Smith dated 17 June 1829, in Vogel, *ibid*, I:552.

The Family: Samuel Harrison Smith

Regarded as the first missionary of Smith's Church of Christ (est. 1830; currently the LDS branch of the Mormon movement), he was born on March 13, 1808. In February of 1829, he accompanied his father to Harmony, and undertook scrivener duties for Joseph. In the first week of April he accompanied Cowdery to Smith Jr.'s residence in Harmony and introduced him to his brother Joseph. He continued to be a practicing Presbyterian up to c. September of 1828. According to his brother William, "I handled them [the plates] and hefted them while wrapped in a tow frock;" and that "Father and my brother Samuel saw them as I did while in the frock." On 17 February 1834, he was chosen as a member of the High Council in the incipient organization of what was then called the Church of Christ. Having moved west in 1838, he participated actively in the Missouri War and fled to relocate in Illinois. In 1844, he was attacked by a mob on his way to assist his brothers in Carthage, and only managed to arrive in time to retrieve their bodies. He died shortly after, on 30 July.

The Family: William Smith

Born on 13 March 1811, he was too young to play a major role in the pre-1830 history of the Smith project. Even so, he did claim that he had felt the gold plates through a tow frock. Although Phineas Young, brother of Brigham, had been designated one of the inaugural members of the Quorum of the Twelve on February 14, 1835, Joseph Smith insisted that William be designated instead. He was so ordained the next day. Oliver Cowdery and David Whitmer later reported that William's selection was "contrary to our feelings and judgment, and to our deep mortification ever since."[125] He and Orson Hyde were suspended from the Quorum of the Twelve by a vote of the church on May 4, 1839; however, William was readmitted to the Quorum on May 25. From April to December 1842, he was the editor of *The Wasp*, a secular but pro-Mormon newspaper. On May 24, 1845, William Smith succeeded his late brother Hyrum as the Presiding Patriarch of the church. On 12 October, 1845 he was excommunicated, and on 1 March 1846 he sustained James Jesse Strang as the successor to his brother Joseph. He associated briefly with Lyman Wight's movement (1849-50), initiated a new movement with Martin Harris and Chilton Daniels in Kirtland (c. 1855) and joined the

---

[125] Oliver Cowdery to Brigham Young, February 27, 1848; & Zenas H. Gurley Jr. interview of David Whitmer, 14 January 1885.

Reorganized Church of Jesus Christ of Latter Day Saints (now the Community of Christ) in 1878. On 13 November 1893 William died in Osterdock, Iowa.

Joseph Smith Sr. Seizes the Moment

We will never fully know the role of father Smith in the early history of the BoM project, prior to his son's and Cowdery's move to the Whitmer home to complete their translation of the Nephite narrative from the gold plates. For his son, he was a role model as a visionary, and their relationship was close in the business of scrying for gold. The problem with using the seerstone or the mineral rod to find gold is that one rarely found anything of much value. The virtue of finding the gold plates is that one can make the claim while being commanded to not show the find to detractors. Perhaps the father sat back and observed as his son's claims started to gain traction in their community. At some point, he may have begun to get a glimmer of how one could develop this emerging phenomenon into something much bigger than a history that might not even sell. Unfortunately, the transition from treasure hunting to gold plates to a gold bible is lost in a void of contemporary records, and a fog of official-account obfuscation.

As a result of his actions resulting in the loss of the 116 pages, Joseph Jr. claimed to have lost his gift for a spell (D&C 3):

> 12. And when thou deliveredst up that which God had given thee sight and power to translate, thou deliveredst up that which was sacred into the hands of a wicked man,
> 13. Who has set at naught the counsels of God, and has broken the most sacred promises which were made before God, and has depended upon his own judgment and boasted in his own wisdom.
> 14. And this is the reason that thou hast lost thy privileges for a season—

It is clear from this that there was a cessation of work on the BoM text for an unknown period of time in the fall of 1828. In his 1832 history, Smith wrote: [126]

> ... wherefore the plates was (sic) taken from me by the power of God and I was not able to obtain them for a season and it came to pass after much humility and affliction of soul I obtained them again when Lord appeared

---

[126] Joseph Smith, 1832 history, in *Papers of Joseph Smith*, I:10.

unto a young man by the name of Oliver Cowdery and showed unto him the plates in a vision.

We do not know when Cowdery had this vision, or even if we can reliably link these two events. But most probably it would be in the fall of 1828. In his 1838-39 history, Joseph Jr. claimed that in July of 1828 a heavenly messenger took "the plates and the Urim and Thummin (*sic*)" away, but gave them back after a few days.[127] After tarrying with his parents for a while, he repaired to Harmony, Pennsylvania, to work on his farm, out of necessity to support his family:

> I did not however go immediately to translating, but went to laboring with my hands upon a small farm which I had purchased of my wife's father, in order to provide for my family.[128]

This suspension of his gift decreed by his heavenly father may have actually been advice to suspend work for a while, advice from his biological father, whom he respected tremendously, to the point of making him the first patriarch of the Church, and the heir to what was to be claimed to be the highest priesthood, the Patriarchal Priesthood. His need to work his farm might reflect the strained relations with Harris and the very likely possibility that for a while Martin was not forthcoming with money. He and his parents had the opportunity to review their options and to arrive at a plan to replace the *Book of Lehi*, both prior to his return to Harmony, and during their visit in September of 1828. Achieving this was certainly not nearly as difficult as some would have us believe (v. p. 389).

When Joseph Smith arrived at the Smith home in Manchester in midsummer of 1828, he must have been justifiably proud of his work thus far. The loss of the 116 pages clearly came as a blow. But this loss did not necessarily mean abandoning his overall concept of what his project should be about. It is reasonable to assume that a radically new approach would probably not have come from him. In Harmony he was largely isolated from those who would become major players. The eventual cast of characters reads almost like a reunion of seerstone scryers. Joseph Sr., his son Joseph Jr., Oliver Cowdery, David Whitmer, Jacob Whitmer and Hiram Page were all scryers and/or rodsmen.[129] Since the next major steps took place in the Manchester-Palmyra area, it must have been father Smith

---

[127] *Ibid*, 1838-39 History, 1:287. Smith's comment regarding D&C 3.

[128] *Ibid*, 288.

[129] Jessee, *Papers of Joseph Smith*, I: 322–23; D. See also Michael Quinn, *Early Mormonism and the Magic World View*, 239–40, 247–48.

who stepped up to the challenge. His eldest son, Hyrum, was a trustee of the local school, and so responsible for hiring teachers. Lyman Cowdery applied, but after being accepted, he found he had to pursue some other option, and recommended his brother Oliver, who was hired. For an unknown period, he boarded in the Smith home in Manchester. During that period, in the fall of 1828, Joe Sr. and Hyrum were able to recruit Oliver to the project, perhaps as early as some point in October. Note that the stay of the Smith elders with the Whitmers on route to Harmony must have been as much as two months earlier. Both David (initially?), and then Oliver were recruited in the absence of Smith Jr., who was not less than a hundred miles to the southeast.

Table 6. Manchester-Harmony Timeline for the BoM Replacement Text

Date	Prior to 1828
1820	Many years later, Smith claimed his first vision was in 1820. Smith later assigned this year to his claimed vision re the gold plates.
1826	Smith's Pretrial Examination (Joseph Smith the Glass Looker).
1827	September, 22, Smith claimed he retrieved the gold plates.
Dec. 27	Joseph & Emma moved to Harmony, Susquehanna Co., PA, near her family.
	1828
February	Harris arrived to write for Smith & to take characters claimed to have been transcribed from the plates to scholars in New York.
Spring	Harris wrote for Joseph from April 12 to June 14 (see *supra*, p. 77).
June	Harris took 116 pages to show his wife and they disappeared.
July	Smith visited his parents & learned of the fate of the 116 pages.
August	Late July-early August, he remained with his parents for an unknown period. Father-and-son discussion regarding the way forward.
July	Smith issued a revelation asserting that God will prevail over Satan, and calling Martin Harris a wicked man.
Summer	David Whitmer stayed with Oliver Cowdery in Palmyra; they discussed rumors of the gold plates & resolved to investigate.
August	David Whitmer sought out Smith Sr., and was sufficiently impressed that he invited the Smith elders to overnight at his father's home in Fayette on their way to Harmony to visit their son.
Sept.	Early September, the Smith elders overnighted at the Whitmer home and instructed them regarding the gold plates and the BoM project.
Sept.	The Smith elders visited their son in Harmony. Father and son planned the way forward for the BoM project.
Sept.	C. September 10, the Smith elders return to Manchester to find Samuel Harrison sick. Entry in doctor Robinson's daybook for medicine for "boy Harrison" dated 11 September. (See p. 530)

Sept.	Lucy, Hyrum, Samuel and Sophronia quit attending Presbyterian services.
Fall	Smith farmed (plowed & sowed) due to lack of Harris' funding.
October	Late September or early October, Cowdery is hired by Hyrum Smith to teach school in Palmyra.
Fall	Cowdery resides with the Smiths in Manchester for an unknown period (extending into or through winter of 1829?).
Fall	Cowdery claimed to have had a vision of the gold plates.
Winter	By the first of winter, Smith had been working on the replacement text and received material assistance from Joseph Knight Jr.
1829	
Winter	From c. mid December to February, Emma wrote for her husband.
February	Smith was visited by his father and his brother Samuel H. Father-and-son discussion of plans to establish a new church. Joseph Jr. issued a revelation for his father, announcing a marvelous work about to come forth among the children of men.
Winter	C. mid February to mid March, Samuel wrote for Smith.
March	In need of funding to publish the BoM, in March Smith issued a revelation with a conditional promise for Harris to view the plates.
March	Sometime in March, Smith halted his work on ms𝒰.
May	On 5 April, Oliver Cowdery arrived in Harmony, with Samuel.
May 6	Cowdery drafted a contract for Isaac Hale to sell land to Smith; Cowdery began to write for Smith.
May	Oliver was made cotranslator (coauthor) of the BoM. At some point after this, he was demoted to scribe.
May 15	Aaronic priesthood was restored & Joseph & Oliver were baptized.
1830-44	
April 6	The Church of Christ was established on April 6, 1830.
April	The United Firm was established in Kirtland, April, 1832.
1834	(First) High Council (17 February; D&C 102).
1834	The United Firm was disbanded
1835	Members of the Quorum of the Twelve were announced, 14 Feb..
1835	In June Michael Chandler sold Egyptian papyri to the Church.
1836	Kirtland Safety Society Anti-Banking Company, organized on Jan. 2.
1839	LDS purchased Commerce, IL, and renamed it Nauvoo in 1840.
1843	On July 12, Smith revealed eternal marriage and plural marriage. On July 12, Smith revealed LDS polytheism.
1844	On June 27, Smith was murdered at Carthage Jail (Carthage, IL).

David Whitmer

David Whitmer's father moved to Waterloo, New York, in 1809, and then to Fayette, New York, after 1827. David is said to have had as many as two seerstones, with at least one in the archives of the Community of Christ. These are Indian gorgets, pendants (from French *gorge*, "throat"). They are oval nicely worked stones (slate, or possibly shell) with holes pierced for a cord (sinew). If David actually knew their origin, the fact that he had more than one may indicate that he had at least some interest in Indian lore. Perhaps he felt that this origin contributed to their power. At least two other members of the Whitmer family had a seerstone: Jacob Whitmer (a rectangular gorget) and Hiram Page.

Apart from Joseph Smith himself, the chief core group included the Smith elders, Oliver Cowdery and the Whitmers. Their emergence as a committed and cohesive group took place between the time of Joseph Smith's return to Harmony in the summer of 1828 and spring of 1829. Yet this period and its events are inadequately understood. Clearly Joseph Smith Sr. was already a fully committed player at the outset of this period.

But what was the sequencing of the burgeoning relationships between the Smith elders, Cowdery and David Whitmer? Lucy recounts how she and Joseph Sr. stayed overnight at the Whitmer home in Fayette, c. late August or early September, on their way to visit their son, his wife and in-laws in Harmony, "at which time we stopped with David over night, and gave him a brief history of the Record." [130] Her memory of this event is highly probable, as it involves major actions on the part of herself and Joseph Sr., actions so specific that one would not easily misremember their general tenor. The visit would require breaking their trip, probably at Lyons or Waterloo, getting a separate conveyance to the Whitmer farm, teaching the account of the record, eating dinner there, sleeping on a bedroll, eating breakfast also with the Whitmer family, and then continuing their trip. One point to note is that the visit could not have happened without an invitation and explicit instructions to find the Whitmer farm, undoubtedly from David. As a result, we have reason to believe that the Whitmers were instructed regarding the plates and some details of the BoM project more than a month before Cowdery was engaged to teach school, and before he began his residence with the Smiths in Manchester.

---

[130] Lucy Smith in Anderson, *Lucy's Book*, 449-50. This is not found in the 1845 text, but is inserted into the 1853 Coray revision.

Apparently, prior to this visit, while on a business trip to Palmyra, David Whitmer, Oliver Cowdery and others discussed rumors that Joseph Smith had found gold plates. Cowdery told Whitmer that he was acquainted with the Smiths, believed there must be some truth to it and intended to investigate the matter. In addition to Cowdery, Whitmer met treasure hunters who claimed that they knew Smith had found gold plates, that he had promised to share whatever gold he found and he was refusing to do so. He said that up to this point he had never met any member of he Smith family. "After thinking over the matter for a long time, and talking with Cowdery, who also gave me a history of the finding of the plates [i.e. presumably what he had gleaned from the treasure hunters], I went home..." [131] It would appear from these statements that Cowdery had acquired at least some knowledge from the rumors regarding the plates prior to the Smith elders' visit to the Whitmers, which he shared with David Whitmer. David then proceeded to seek more information and in the process invited the Smith elders to visit. Then, after moving in with the Smiths, Cowdery also received more detailed instruction.

David's father, Peter Whitmer Sr., and siblings, were not far behind. In just months, Whitmer Sr.'s sons, Jacob, Peter Jr. and John, as well as David's brother-in-law, Hiram Page, all followed suite, as indicated by the arrangements for David Whitmer to go to Harmony and get Joseph Jr. and Oliver to the home of Peter Whitmer Sr. in Fayette, NY, to complete the *Book of Mormon* (i.e. the nearly complete initial draft, urtext, or ms$\mathcal{U}$). This too might have been at father Smith's initiative. Smith Jr. had been in Harmony nine months, and Cowdery since April 5. Harmony-Manchester communications being what they were, certainly Smith Jr. did not recruit the Whitmers, and neither one could have arranged for the move to the Whitmer home. Joseph reported that the Whitmer family was very helpful from the moment they arrived. [132]

The date of the Smith elders' visit to harmony is evidenced by the fact that upon their return they found their son Samuel Harrison sick, and by an entry in doctor Robinson's daybook for medicine for "boy Harrison" dated 11 September.(See p. 529) Although we do not know the overall length of their visit, it is probable that they were there during the first week of September.

---

[131] *Kansas City Journal* (1 June 1881), "Mormonism. Authentic Account of the Origin of The Sect from One of the Patriarchs." A report of a statement from David Whitmer, proofed and corrected by Whitmer, in Vogel, V:72-73.

[132] Joseph Smith, "History, 1839," in Vogel, *Early Mormon Documents*, I:80.

Joseph went to work on his farm, doing the fall plowing and sowing, necessitated by expectations of his in-laws and in the absence of funding from Martin Harris, due to the gulf between them. Even so, we learn from a first-person account by Joseph Knight Sr. that he was back translating by the beginning of winter. (v. p. 397) This is what we might expect. During his stay with his parents after the theft of the 116 pages, and during Joseph Sr.'s September visit, there had been ample time to come up with the relatively simple solution. Due to the nature of the replacement text, it is probable that the project was already changed to the creation of a new bible, rather than simply a history of Israelites in America.

Circa September of 1828, Lucy, Hyrum, Samuel and Sophronia stopped attending the Presbyterian Church. (v. p. 382) Concerned, on March 3, 1830, a Presbyterian committee was assigned to visit them and report. Given Lucy's desire for herself and her children to attend a church, this total departure from the church she had chosen probably corresponds to a decision on the part of the Smiths to establish a new church. This must have been a major point of father-son discussion when Joseph Sr. visited in Harmony in February, 1829. Joseph Jr. responded in a revelation issued for his father, in which he announced that "a marvelous work is about to come forth among the children of men..." (BC 3; D&C 4:1)

Also at that time Joe Jr. may have been apprised of the addition of Cowdery and David Whitmer to the project. Clearly, he welcomed the addition of both. Oliver Cowdery and the Whitmers accounted for two of the three witnesses to the gold plates and five of the eight witnesses, essentially all in the absence of Joe Jr. The Whitmer addition is particularly noteworthy. They first met Joseph Smith in early June and progressed to being witnesses to the plates in little more than a week!

Two of Joseph Sr.'s sons, Hyrum and Samuel, were especially close to Joseph Jr. and present in the Manchester-Palmyra area for participation in the project. Like their brother, they were undoubtedly influenced by their father's views on religion. Their role was at times largely as facilitators. Hyrum accompanied Harris to Harmony to begin his scribal duties there, and visited Joseph and Oliver in May of 1829, ostensibly to check on how the translation was coming. Apart from their younger brother William, in one capacity or another, the whole Smith family was involved in the project.

These two founding families had a great deal in common. They were visionary families, largely disaffected with the organized churches of their day including what was being called priestcraft, and they were very motivated by an immutable sense of family loyalty. Consequently, it was essential for the family head, Peter Sr., to be mobilized as well. Smith promptly received revelations for David (D&C 14), John (D&C 15) and Peter Jr. (D&C 16). Clearly when Joseph Jr. arrived he did not disappoint. All of these Whitmers save Peter Sr. were chosen to be witnesses of the plates. David was baptized on 3 June 1829, about as soon as Cowdery and Smith had unpacked. His brother John Whitmer was also baptized in that June. But Peter Sr., Peter Jr., Christian, Jacob and Hiram Page were not baptized until April 1830, including four witnesses to the plates. Less than four weeks after meeting Joseph, six members of this family were comfortable with a testimony that they had viewed the plates, and five averring no accompanying visionary dimension. One cannot determine to what extent this arose from conversion, or from collusion (or both?).

Oliver Cowdery

The recruitment of Cowdery to the project was largely due to the efforts Joseph Smith Sr. Certainly he must have played a major role, but the issue is more complex, including probable interaction with Hyrum Smith.

Perhaps because Oliver Cowdery was deliberately kept in the background as scribe, his life was never the object of scrutiny to the extent that was the case of Joseph Smith, and so was never so well documented. Even though his paternal line goes back to impressive origins, once in the New World his forebears became less so.

Table 7. Heritage and Family of Oliver Cowdery

1602	Deacon William Cowdery was born in Weymouth, England, descendant of the family of Lord Cowdery, of Cowdery Castle at Midhurst, England.
1630	Deacon William Cowdery came to America & settled first in Essex, then Reading, Massachusetts.
1630?	Nathaniel Sr. was sired by Deacon William Cowdery (in England?).
1657	Samuel Sr. was sired by Nathaniel Sr. in Reading, Middlesex, MA
1691	Nathaniel Sr. was sired by Samuel Sr. in Reading, Middlesex, MA
1737	William Sr. was sired by Nathaniel Sr.
1765	William Jr. was born in East Haddam, Connecticut.
1768	Rebecca Fuller was born. She became the wife of William Jr.
1777	The Vermont Constitution enjoined the legislature the duty of establishing schools in each town at public expense, a factor that made it probable that Oliver received essential education.
1787	A Congregational Church was established and William Sr. became one of four deacons. In 1792 the pastor died and the deacons took turns for many years reading the sermons of Jonathan Edwards. Oliver was raised Congregationalist.

1788	Oliver's eldest brother Warren was born.
1792	William was appointed Surveyor of Highways (and again in 1803).
1802	Oliver's brother Lyman was born. He became a lawyer, served as a probate judge and served in the state legislature.
1806	Oliver Cowdery was born of William Jr. and Rebecca in Wells Township, Vermont. John Fuller was the grandfather of Rebecca and John Fuller's brother Shubael was the great-grandfather of Lucy Mack.
1816	Warren Cowdery moved to Freedom, New York
1818	Warren Cowdery became a commissioner of Ontario County, New York.
1824	Warren became the first postmaster in Freedom, New York
1825	In about 1825-1828 Oliver Cowdery clerked in a store (Jensen, LDS Biographical Encyclopedia, 1:246)
1828	Oliver taught school in the fall of 1828 and winter of 1829.
1829	On April 5 he arrived in Harmony; he was made cotranslator with Joseph Smith. Later in April, he was demoted to scribe (D&C 9)
1829	He wrote most of mss *U, O* and P, where we observe that his work was superior to the other scribes.
1831	He was appointed in a revelation to assist printer William W. Phelps in printing the revelations, "to copy, and to correct, and to select."

Oliver's birth family shows well above average accomplishment. Father William Cowdery was for a time Inspector of Roads (or Surveyor of Highways) at Wells, Vermont.[133] Like his son he was a rodsman.[134] His eldest brother studied to become a physician and became a commissioner of Ontario County, while his brother Lyman became a lawyer, served as a probate judge and a representative in the state legislature. Oliver Cowdery clerked in a store and taught school before 1829.[135] His literacy included tolerable scrivener skills. We do not know when he began reading law, but a day after arriving at the Smith residence in Harmony, Oliver drew up a contract for Joseph to purchase land from Isaac Hale, to the satisfaction of both, and after leaving the Church, he practiced law in Tiffin OH, where he joined the Methodist church for which he served as secretary. He edited the local *Democrat* newspaper and was nominated as this party's candidate for the state senate, before his connection to the *Book of Mormon* was discovered. Regarding his assistance to Gilbert in printing the *Book of*

---

[133] Larry E. Morris, "Oliver Cowdery's Vermont Years and the Origins of Mormonism," *BYU Studies* 39:1 (2000), 106-129.

[134] Quinn, *Early Mormonism and the Magic World View*, 35-36, 38, 121 & 127.

[135] Lucy Cowdery (Phineas) Young to Andrew Jenson, March 7, 1887, in Vogel II, 397.

Mormon, he wrote to Joseph Smith in December 1829, "it may look rather strange to you to find that I have so soon become a printer and you may cast in your mind what I shall become next." Following up by later assisting Church printer William W. Phelps, he acquired the printer's art sufficiently that in 1835 he could take on a nephew as an apprentice.[136]

Joe Smith Jr.'s father used a hazel rod and a seerstone to hunt treasure. Joe Jr. used a seerstone, as well as his mother, and his ill-fated eldest brother Alvin. Oliver Cowdery used a hazel rod (or dowsing rod, mineral rod) by which he claimed to have received knowledge revealed by divine power. Reportedly, his father did as well. The list of seerstone scryers also included David Whitmer, Jacob Whitmer and their brother-in-law Hiram Page. On another plane, some claimed to have received information or commands from a spirit, an angel, or even a deity. Martin Harris claimed to have received revelations, apparently without the aid of any seerstone or rod. Joseph Smith's visions involved the angel Moroni, Jesus and God the Father, while Joe Sr. claimed seven visions.

Joseph Smith senior, and his sons Joseph and Hyrum, along with a proficient rodsman Alva(h) Beman (Beaman), frequently went on treasure quests. In addition to using the mineral rod, the Smiths and many others used the seerstone, both for gold and for information.[137] There is even a report that Joseph Smith's mother, Lucy Mack Smith used a seerstone.[138] One account reports that the fee Joseph Smith charged E. W. Vanderhoof was 75 cents to use his seerstone to find a lost mare.[139]

Ground zero for this issue is none other than Smith Jr. and Cowdery. In a revelation in the *Book of Commandments*, the Lord says to Oliver Cowdery, "for you have another gift, which is the gift of working with the rod: behold, it has told you things: behold, there is no other power save God, that can cause this rod of nature to work in your hands..." (BC 7). God's words were revised for the D&C. Quinn notes that "The 1835 *Doctrine and Covenants* substituted the phrase 'the gift of Aaron' in place of 'working with the rod' and 'rod of nature' in the 1833 *Book of Commandments*,"[140] so that the gift became "the gift of Aaron," with other rewording to eliminate any reference to Cowdery's use of the rod, and

---

[136] Oliver Cowdery, letter to Joseph Smith dated 28 December 1829, in Vogel, *Early Mormon Documents*, II:408, *and* Oliver Cowdery, in a letter of Oliver to Warren Cowdery dated 15/10/1835, in Stanley R. Gunn, *Oliver Cowdery, Second Elder and Scribe* (Salt Lake City: Bookcraft, 1962), 17.

[137] *Ibid*, 41.

[138] *Ibid*, 42.

[139] *Ibid*, 43.

[140] Quinn, *Early Mormonism and the Magic World View*, 37.

especially any notion that it had divine approval. Since Smith's original revelation shows approval, then he too must have approved of the practice initially, even if he was not himself a rodsman. Evidence indicates that both Joseph Jr. and Oliver got their rodsman background from their father, with some influence from Justus Winchell.[141]

As stated above, in the fall of 1828, Hyrum Smith, a member of the School Board of Trustees of Manchester, Ontario, NY, hired Oliver as a teacher. Moving to the Manchester area, he took up residence at the Joseph Smith Sr. home. It is generally said that at this time, Cowdery learned of the gold plates. Knowing that his son's gold-plates project was at a standstill, it may be more accurate to say that Father Smith saw an opportunity to recruit sorely needed fresh and better educated talent, and to jump-start a resumption and redirection of the project. With the original manuscript out of the picture, there was the opportunity to start *de novo*, with a more grand objective.

The official version of this history states that on 5 April 1829, Samuel Harrison Smith and Oliver Cowdery showed up on the latter's distant cousin Joseph's doorstep, and the two met for the first time. Incredibly, already on April 7, Cowdery was made Joseph's scribe for the project, and then a cotranslator for a short while. Joseph the scryer and Oliver the rodsman were colleagues in the occult, and respected each other's gifts. It was later claimed that in mid May of 1829, Joseph and Oliver were ordained by John the Baptist to the Aaronic Priesthood. Then Joseph baptized Oliver, followed by Joseph's baptism at the hands of Oliver.[142] Referring to this messenger as John the Baptist, Smith wrote that he, "descended in a cloud of light, and having laid his hands upon us, he ordained us..."[143] Cowdery described this experience as being "while we were in the heavenly vision."[144] Prior to their ordination, he seems to describe some sort of theophany: "and we were rapt in the vision of the Almighty!" His description of the angel sent to ordain them uses deliberate wording that goes beyond a visionary experience:

> On a sudden, as from the midst of eternity, the voice of the Redeemer Spake peace to us, while the veil was parted and the angel of God came down clothed with glory...and while all men were resting upon uncertainty, as a

---

[141] *Ibid*, 121-32.

[142] Marquardt, Rise of Mormonism, 85, 221.

[143] Joseph Smith, "History, 1839," in Vogel, *Early Mormon Documents*, I:75.

[144] Oliver Cowdery in an introduction to blessings, 09/1835, in Vogel, Early Mormon Documents, II:453.

general mass, our eyes beheld—our ears heard…with what surprise we must have bowed…when we received under his hand the holy priesthood…"[145]

By 1835 it was claimed that a bit later they were visited by and communed with Peter, James and John (D&C 27:12-13). Apart from being favored by a vision of the Almighty, these events go beyond the language of being in vision: "our eyes beheld—our ears heard." This, and other concrete aspects of their claim, such as the laying on of the hands of John the Baptist, the Baptism by immersion and the apostolic visitation, make it clear that Oliver Cowdery was already a total confederate. His supposed sudden appearance on Smith's doorstep on April 5 indicates that he had been recruited, briefed and probably even already put to work by Joseph Smith Sr.

As will be seen, from this time on the work takes on a more organized and professional aspect. Oliver Cowdery had become a friend of the Whitmers. In December 1832, he married Elizabeth Ann Whitmer, whom he had baptized on 18 April 1830. Joseph Smith Sr. was also in contact with David Whitmer, whom he had quite possibly known for some time. At least the groundwork for the arrangement for Joseph Jr. and Oliver to complete the *Book of Mormon* in the extended-family home of Peter Whitmer Sr. must have been through the joint efforts of Cowdery and Smith Sr., although the latter may have secured it after Oliver's move to Harmony. We do not know what role Hyrum Smith played in this, if any. Near the beginning of June, David Whitmer arrived at Joseph Jr.'s home in Harmony, Pennsylvania, and took him and Oliver back to the Peter Whitmer Sr. farm in Fayette Township, Seneca County, New York, where they completed the translation draft, ms𝒰. Emma arranged affairs in Harmony and joined them later.

As remarkable as his immediate appointment as scribe was, it is nothing compared to Cowdery's further elevation a bit later (still in April) to cotranslator, along-side Joseph. "And, behold, I grant unto you a gift, if you desire of me, to translate, even as my servant Joseph." (D&C 6:25 & 8:3-4) A cotranslator was a coauthor. Bear in mind that the *Book of Mormon* had been begun all over again. So how is it that Smith would make Cowdery a coauthor? It makes sense if Oliver arrived in the company of Samuel with a draft text of some part of the BoM in hand that he had already produced, and so had expectations of being more than just a scribe, and had Smith family support for the same.

---

[145] Oliver Cowdery, a letter to W. W. Phelps dated 07/09/1834, in Vogel, *Early Mormon Documents*, II:420-21.

Even more curious is the wording of the revelation that reduced his role in producing the BoM to scribe rather than translator (D&C 9:1):

> Behold, I say unto you, my son, that because you did not translate according to that which you desired of me, and did commence again to write for my servant, Joseph Smith, Jun, even so I would that ye should continue until you have finished this record, which I have entrusted unto him.

Here again we have a statement that makes no sense, and leaves us wondering what the subtext might be. In this revelation he is promised that he may yet translate other records. But what was the reason for this demotion? How is this a meaningful justification: "because you did not translate according to that which you desired of me, and did commence again to write for my servant, Joseph…"? How does this rather brief service to his distant cousin make him ineligible to translate? As a justification, it is a lame excuse. But is that all it is?

At first blush, one might presume that Joseph realized that Oliver's elevation to his own level might nurture a future competitor. But the wording of the justification suggests a different, or perhaps additional reason. Especially in view of Cowdery's talents and experience, even as a schoolteacher, it was necessary to avoid the appearance that this duo was in fact in collaboration. The Smith family strategy had been to keep everyone else in the background to give credence to the claim that since the BoM could not have been written by Joseph Smith, it can only have come from a divinely assisted translation of the gold plates. Just issuing a revelation saying Cowdery did not contribute substantively would draw attention to what might appear to be a suspicious denial of what was really happening. A more clever approach was to make him a translator, and then revoke that status with a justification that asserts that he had not translated so far, and never would translate on this project. Otherwise, this justification for his demotion makes no sense.

We know that Emma and Samuel had been writing for Joseph before Cowdery's arrival, and that the portion of ms𝒪 that they would have written is not in their handwriting. Their scribal work is not in ms𝒪 because they were writing in ms𝒰, and the copying of 1 Nephi from it into ms𝒪 was begun by Cowdery and the scribes in Fayette.

Furthermore, Oliver was perfectly capable of finding his own way to Joseph's small farm in Harmony. It may be that father Smith sent his son Samuel along with him to assure a smooth transition to collaboration between the distant cousins. Samuel's role needs to be further investigated.

He also accompanied his father to visit Joseph Jr. in February 1829, when he wrote for him.

On the occasion of Smith Sr.'s visit in February, an imminent "marvelous work" was announced. Two months later, with Cowdery onboard, the project for a new bible was coupled with steps to establish a new church. Only about five weeks after his arrival at Harmony, he and Smith claimed to have received both the authority to baptize, and a valid baptism. The claim of a restored priesthood clearly indicates an intention to establish a true church. The role of a revelation claimed to have been received in June 1829 by Cowdery, and its church establishment passages, will be examined in the context of the somewhat belated addition of the Book of Moroni.

The possibility of drafting in Manchester is strongly supported by the time factor. The nearly edit-free condition of ms$O$ was possible by virtue of its being an improved version of an earlier draft, ms$U$ (v. Chapter 10). Between April 5 and even September, there just is not enough time to produce the work first in fully developed drafts, with considerable investigation into the scriptures and other issues, and then to produce ms$O$. Logistically, the timeline works much better if we assume drafting done in both Manchester and Harmony prior to April. The evidence, yet to be presented, of at least two, but possibly even three drafters indicates that in addition to Joseph Smith, one or two others were involved. One of these must certainly have been Oliver Cowdery. A third might well have been Hyrum Smith, although Joseph Sr. cannot be ruled out. Hyrum may have also played a role in the conversion of David and other Whitmers.

The Lehi text composed by Joseph Jr. was not designed to be a new bible. The plan to address the loss of Lehi by starting over and producing a New-world bible was complemented by plans to restore all things in preparation for the gathering of both branches of Israel, and therefore the restoration of the true church of Christ. If this far grander project, this departure from the Book of Lehi history of the Indians, was already formulated in Manchester, it may have been the brainchild of Joseph Smith Sr., born of collaboration with men he had recruited to the project.

< Chapter 5 >

BoM Funding, & the Language, Birth & Death of Lehi

According to Willard Chase, Joseph Smith worked for him in 1822 to help with digging a well. About twenty feet down, a stone was found that Smith claimed to be a seerstone. He took possession of it for his use.[146] At that point he would have been about seventeen years old. By 1825 he already had a reputation for this activity. Based on this renown, Josiah Stowell sought him out to assist in locating treasure on his property in the latter half of that year.[147] This is how it all began.

The Production of the Book of Lehi

In December of 1827, Joseph and Emma moved to Harmony (now Oakland, Susquehanna County, in northeast Pennsylvania, near the New York border). Initially he got more acquainted with her family, and set up their new living quarters. At some point, he began dictating his "translation" of the Book of Lehi to "scribes," his wife Emma, and her brother, Reuben Hale.[148] Later, Martin Harris took up the scrivener duty. In February, 1828, he traveled to Harmony, picked up a copy of characters claimed to be copied from the gold plates, and traveled to Utica, Albany and New York City to show them to learned scholars. After his return to Harmony, he went back to Palmyra in upstate New York to get his skeptical wife, Lucy Harris, attempting to change her mind about his financial participation in the project.

Upon her arrival she began to ransack their living quarters looking for the plates until she satisfied herself that they did not exist. She had rented a room in a nearby house, and began a campaign to defame Joseph Smith. Eventually this latter told Harris that he had to take her back to their Palmyra farm. After her return she began moving all of her furniture out of their house to be kept with friends. This was the first step of the process of ending their relationship.

---

[146] The statement of Willard Chase was printed in Howe, *Mormonism Unvailed,* 338. The first edition was in 1834. See also Marquardt, *Rise of Mormonism,* 33-46.

[147] Marquardt, *Rise of Mormonism,* 38.

[148] Marquardt, *Rise of Mormonism,* 75, 80-81.

Martin returned to Harmony in April to be Joseph's scribe. Picking up after Emma and her brother, the period of his scribal duty then was from April 12 to June 14, at which point at least 116 pages had been done.[149]

Martin Harris: A Doubting Thomas, or a Scout, or Both?

Translation was described as being by means of divine power, using the "spectacles" or "interpreter," early names for the Urim and Thummim. But this device and the gold plates had to be kept unseen. The latter were mostly hidden away, in the woods or elsewhere, presumably to be protected from thieves. Since translation was being done in their absence, it was more practical to simply use a seerstone. With his face in his hat, he could not see the plates anyway, and with the text coming by divine power, he needed neither the plates nor the spectacles (nor even the seerstone?).

The LDS account states that Smith translated with the use of a scribe. Even with this orthodox interpretation, the scribe could serve as an interface to improve on Smith's spelling deficiency, although even the scribes would never win any spelling bee. Like those who cannot write well, but who can compose very well by speaking verbally to a computer text processor enabled with speech recognition, Smith may have been a far better storyteller than writer.

His principal collaborator initially was a prosperous farmer, Martin Harris, for whom Joseph had worked from time to time. Although on occasion others also acted as scribes, for the *Book of Lehi* it was mostly Harris. He was also an absolutely essential member of the team as the financial backer without whom they would not have the funds to publish the book. The BoM is over 500 pages in the traditional edition, but a shorter text may have been originally planned as a history of the Jews in America. Shortly after Smith claimed to have the plates, Harris provided him with fifty dollars, a substantial sum at that time, to cover the Smiths' move to harmony and translation expenses. Perhaps it was to court this funder that Hyrum Smith escorted him for his first visit to Joseph's home in Harmony.[150]

According to the official account, at some point, Harris began having doubts about the existence of the plates and Smith's calling. To assuage this doubt, Smith copied characters from the plates to produce a transcript,

---

[149] Martin Harris as cited in an interview to William Pilkington, 1934/04/03, in Vogel II:353.

[150] Lucy Smith, in Anderson, *Lucy's Book*, 402.

a sample of the text found on the plates, so that Harris could show them to learned men for reassurance (February 1828). At first blush, this account seems totally suspect. If Harris were having doubts, sending him on such a mission, and exposing him to scholarly evaluation, would have been highly risky. A negative evaluation may have ended Harris' ability to believe in the gold plates. Alternatively, we note that one of the scholars, Professor Charles Anthon, reported that what he was shown was a mixture of known scripts arranged in columns, unlike the characters assembled later for exhibition to the curious, i.e. unknown characters in rows (Figure 2). Smith may have provided Harris with a first set of known characters expecting that the renowned professor would confirm that they were authentic, albeit an odd mixture. Smith may have calculated correctly that this would be enough to persuade Harris that his claim that they had come from an authentic source was true. Indeed, he may have shown Harris Isaiah 29:11, "the vision of all is become unto you as the words of a book that is sealed, which men deliver to one that is learned, saying, Read this, I pray thee: and he saith, I cannot; for it is sealed." Martin may have been delighted to observe that he had been chosen to be a man for the fulfillment of this prophecy. Unfortunately for our research, the only account of what Harris reported back to his partner has come from Smith.

Figure 2. "Caractors" — A Version of Smith's Gold Plates Characters

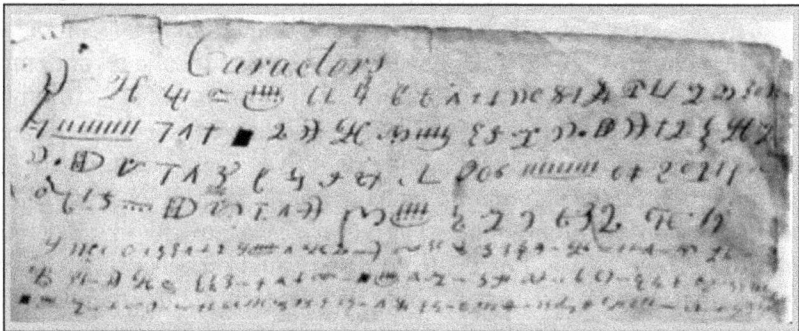

Others wanted to see the plates. Unhappy that they could not, at least some must have asked Smith to at least copy a sample of the writing from the plates to assuage their skepticism. This may have led to the idea that a transcription of characters said to be from the plates would facilitate acceptance of their book in the absence of a view of the actual gold plates. Perhaps they should even include it in the published book.

The possibility that the characters were also devised to promote the book becomes probable when we note that in fact just this tack was taken in a broadside (essentially a one-sheet newspaper) of the short-lived paper *The Prophet* established by William Smith and published in 1844 in New York, NY. It reads:

Figure 3. The Characters Broadside (*The Prophet*, NY, NY)

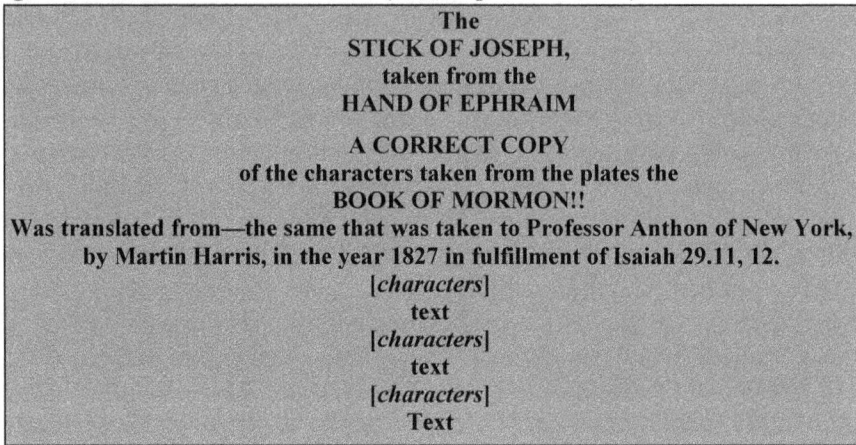

> The
> **STICK OF JOSEPH,**
> taken from the
> **HAND OF EPHRAIM**
>
> **A CORRECT COPY**
> of the characters taken from the plates the
> **BOOK OF MORMON!!**
> Was translated from—the same that was taken to Professor Anthon of New York,
> by Martin Harris, in the year 1827 in fulfillment of Isaiah 29.11, 12.
> [*characters*]
> text
> [*characters*]
> text
> [*characters*]
> Text

The first two lines of characters are virtually the same as the first two lines in Figure 2, but the third differs, especially the second half of it. We do not know what response this broadside got.

Harris went to show Smith's transcription document to Dr. Samuel L. Mitchill (Mitchell), Vice President of Rutgers Medical College, and, most notably, to Professor Charles Anthon (1797-1867) at Columbia University. The qualifications of the latter have at times been overstated. Although evidence indicates that a copy of Jean François Champollion's, *Précis du Système Hiéroglyphique des Anciens Égyptiens* eventually was added to Anthon's library, since Harris' trip was made in 1828, and Champollion's work was not even published in France until 1824, we cannot say that Anthon even knew about this breakthrough, much less that he had already acquired the book. Even the Library of Congress has only the second edition (1827-28).

We do not have a report from Harris himself. In 1837, he was excommunicated, and still in 1839 he was speaking out against Smith. This may have made it easier for Smith, in his 1839 history, to ascribe to Harris a report that says, in part:

> Professor Anthony stated that the translation was correct, more so than any he had before seen translated from the Egyptian.

I then showed him those which were not yet translated, and he said that they were Egyptian, Chaldeak, Assyriac and Arabac...He gave me a certificate certifying to the people of Palmyra that they were true characters and that the translation of such of them as had been translated was also correct. I took the Certificate and put it into my pocket, and was just leaving the house, when Mr Anthon called me back and asked me how the young man found out that there were gold plates where he found them. I answered that an Angel of God had revealed it unto him. He then said to me, let me see that certificate, I accordingly took it out of my pocket and gave it him when he took it and tore it to pieces saying that there was no such thing now as ministering of angels, and that if I would bring the plates to him, he would translate them.[151]

About five years earlier, Eber D. Howe informed Anthon regarding the claim the Mormons were making that he had stated that some translated characters from the gold plates were an accurate translation of Egyptian. Anthon sent the following reply:

This paper was in fact a singular scrawl. It consisted of all kinds of crooked characters disposed in columns, and had evidently been prepared by some person who had before him at the time a book containing various alphabets. Greek and Hebrew letters, crosses and flourishes, Roman letters inverted or placed sideways, were arranged in perpendicular columns, and the whole ended in a rude delineation of a circle divided into various compartments, decked with various strange marks...and [I] remember well that the paper contained anything else but "*Egyptian Hieroglyphics.*"[152]

Note that both Smith and Anthon list languages not found in the later "Charactors" document. Anthon makes his pointed denial regarding Egyptian in response to Howe's specific query regarding the Mormon claim that he had found Smith's translation of Egyptian to be correct. This claim is itself odd in that the *Book of Mormon* says that no one could read the reformed Egyptian text, presumably including Anthon. The professor may well have given Harris a short statement saying that what was shown to him consisted of a mixture of true characters from Chaldean, Hebrew, Latin (Roman) Assyrian and Arabic. Harris knew that references to known languages would not suffice and asked for a better statement. Anthon then took it back and advised the farmer to beware of being duped.

---

[151]Martin Harris as quoted in Joseph Smith's history, 1838-39, readily found in Jessee, *Papers of Joseph Smith*, I:285; v. Marquardt, *Rise of Mormonism*, 76.
[152] Charles Anthon to Eber D. Howe, in Howe, *Mormonism Unvailed*, 382.

In a second letter, in 1841, to Thomas Winthrop Coit, he mentioned only characters "arranged in columns...Greek, Hebrew and all sorts of letters, more or less distorted..."[153] Egyptian is not mentioned. This assortment of characters indicates that at the time the transcription was created, it had not yet been decided that the plates were written in reformed Egyptian. Smith, at that early stage, would have naively created characters based on characters from these several languages from one or more sources in a reference work. Anthon's description of the paper with the characters cannot be reconciled with Figure 2. He described the characters as being in vertical columns, while those in Figure 2 are in rows.

Michael Hubbard MacKay, Gerrit J. Dirkmaat, and Robin Scott Jensen have published an excellent study of the history of the document in Figure 2 (designated the "charactors" document). David Whitmer was the eventual owner of this document, receiving it either from his older brother John Whitmer, or from Oliver Cowdery. It was bequeathed to his son David J. Whitmer, and then to George Schweich, David Whitmer's grandson. Schweich sold the document to the RLDS. Handwriting analysis shows it to have been copied by John Whitmer. This could only have been done in June of 1829, or later. In 1878 P. Wilhelm Poulsen examined a copy owned by John Whitmer, but his description of it does not match the "Charactors" document. There were many others copies. At some point separate copies were owned by David and John Whitmer. The various known copies suggest "that multiple versions of this same characters document had circulated within the Church, serving to bolster and reaffirm the faith of the Latter-day Saints."[154]"Other documents bearing *Book of Mormon* characters circulated within the early Church as well. In 1828 and 1829, Harris showed a personal document containing characters transcribed from the gold plates to numerous individuals around Palmyra, including the Episcopal preacher John Clark, and others on his travels to New York City. In addition, Harris's document was surreptitiously copied by his future son-in-law Flanders Dyke in 1828 at the behest of Lucy Harris...At least two documents purporting to include *Book of Mormon* characters were created during this period by Oliver Cowdery and Fredrick G. Williams...Smith apparently continued to show the characters to

---

[153] Charles Anthon to Thomas Winthrop Coit, in Vogel, *Early Mormon Documents*, IV:383.
[154] Michael Hubbard MacKay, Gerrit J. Dirkmaat, and Robin Scott Jensen, "The 'Caractors' Document: New Light on an Early Transcription of the *Book of Mormon* Characters," *Mormon Historical Studies*, vol. 14, no. 1.

various visitors later in Nauvoo, such as Reverend George Moore."[155] Smith created more than one document that included copies of the characters on the plates, and one of these was likely copied later in part or in whole to make "Caractors."[156]

Ultimately, Harris' mission was helpful. They had learned that an "expert" statement that the transcript document contained a simple hodgepodge of known characters was not acceptable. At a later date, this would lead to the assertion of Mormon that the plates were written in *reformed* Egyptian characters. Smith would have to devise his own. The original attempt, with characters in columns, was replaced by a text similar to Figure 2; or one of the variations of it.[157]

Harris, scribe and funder, had been satisfied, for the moment. By July of 1828, he and Smith, working in Harmony, Pennsylvania, had produced at least 116 manuscript pages of what Joseph Smith eventually called the *Book of Lehi*. They had every right to feel a profound sense of accomplishment.

The Fate of the Purloined Pages

According to the official LDS account, Martin Harris, a prosperous farmer bankrolling Joseph Smith's *Book of Mormon* project, and his principal scribe at the time, was having difficulties with his wife, who was totally opposed to her husband's relationship with Smith. Quite rightly, she viewed family property to be as much hers as his, and feared that the Smiths would succeed in bilking her husband out of everything. In June of 1828, he requested permission to take 116 pages, all or nearly all of the only copy of the work completed up to that time, to his home in upstate New York, to read them to his wife in hopes of getting her support for his expenses and work as Smith's scribe.[158] Incredibly, according to the official story, Smith allowed Harris to take their only copy of their work into what both knew was enemy territory, even though he himself was planning to make a trip to Manchester, and could have taken them himself.

---

[155] Michael Hubbard MacKay, Gerrit J. Dirkmaat, and Robin Scott Jensen, "The 'Caractors' Document, 136.

[156] Michael Hubbard MacKay, Gerrit J. Dirkmaat, and Robin Scott Jensen, "The 'Caractors' Document, 137-38.

[157] Michael Hubbard MacKay, Gerrit J. Dirkmaat, and Robin Scott Jenson, "The 'Charactors' Document, 131-52.

[158] For a discussion of this episode, see H. Michael Marquardt, *The Rise of Mormonism*, 81-84.

In Smith's 1839 history, Harris had promised to show the manuscript only to his wife, his father, his mother and a sister of his wife.[159]

In late June or early July, Joseph went to visit his parents. The exact date is unknown. His wife had delivered a son that died the day of his birth on June 15 (dated by his tombstone), and Joseph was able to leave his wife in the care of her parents. This was a considerable journey at the time, by stagecoach from Harmony, Pennsylvania to Manchester in upstate New York. On the morning of his arrival Harris was invited to breakfast. According to the account of Joseph's mother, Lucy Mack Smith, Harris arrived over four hours late, and when he arrived, he joined the group at the table but did not eat. She wrote:

> [Harris] cried out in a tone of deep anguish, "Oh, I have lost my soul! I have lost my soul!"
>
> Joseph, who had not expressed his fears till now, sprang from the table, exclaiming, "Martin, have you lost that manuscript? Have you broken your oath, and brought down condemnation upon my head, as well as your own?"
>
> "Yes, it is gone," replied Martin, "and I know not where."
>
> "Oh, my God!" said Joseph, clinching his hands. "All is lost! All is lost! What shall I do? I have sinned—it is I who tempted the wrath of God. I should have been satisfied with the first answer which I received from the Lord; for he told me that it was not safe to let the writing go out of my possession." He wept and groaned, and walked the floor continually.[160]

This is just her recollection, and these words are her composition. Allowing for some embellishment of the language, these histrionics seem extreme, even in a time when apparently women really did swoon.

In the LDS view, this was Satan's plan from the beginning: "Satan hath put it into their hearts to alter the words which you have caused to be written... because they have altered the words, they read contrary from that which you translated and caused to be written..." (D&C 10:10) But God had prepared to foil it (v. the next chapter).

Lucy Mack Smith on the Purloined Pages

Apparently, Lucy Smith, Joseph's mother, and Lucy Harris, Martin Harris' wife, were initially on good terms. We do not know if their

---

[159] Joseph Smith, "History, 1839," in Jessee, *Papers of Joseph Smith*, I:286.
[160] Lucy Smith, in Anderson, *Lucy's Book*, 417-18.

relationship deteriorated due to anything more than the pecuniary interests involved. As it became clear that Mrs. Harris was not going to convert, and was determined to get her husband to withdraw his essential financial support from the *Book of Mormon* project, a great antipathy developed between the two Lucy's. Mother Smith's account reads as follows:

> The manuscript has never been found, and there is no doubt but Mrs. Harris took it from the drawer, with the view of retaining it, until another translation should be given, then, to alter the original translation, for the purpose of showing a discrepancy between them, and thus make the whole appear to be a deception.[161]

Much later (1884), Lorenzo Saunders claimed, in an interview to E. L. Kelley, that he had heard Lucy Harris say that she had burned the papers [the lost 116 pages].[162] Initially Martin Harris was reported as making a statement that seemed to indicate that she had given them to some other person.[163] At a much later date, as he was ill and approaching his death in 1875, he was reported as saying that he believed that Mrs. Harris had burned the pages.[164]

Joseph Smith on the Purloined Pages

Joseph Smith undoubtedly knew Harris' actions in all of this more than anyone else, and must have grilled him regarding the fate of the pages. He wrote of them in the "Preface" to the first edition of the *Book of Mormon*, "which said account [the 116 pages], some person or persons have stolen and kept from me..." In his 1832 History he reiterated essentially the same assertions made in the *Book of Mormon* and his earliest revelations on the subject. Smith says:

> the Lord said unto me let him [Martin Harris] go with them [the 116 pages] only he shall covenant with me that he will not show them to only but four persons and he covenanted with the Lord that he would do according to the word of the Lord therefore he took them and took his journey unto his friend

---

[161] Lucy Smith in Anderson, *Lucy's Book*, 422-23.

[162] E. L. Kelley Papers, "Miscellany," RLDS Church Library-Archives (Independence, MO: 1884).

[163] Claim of John A. Clark, made in a letter addressed to "Dear Brethren" dated August 31, 1840, published in *The Episcopal Recorder* (Philadelphia: 12 September, 1840), 98-99. See Vogel, *Early Mormon Documents*, II:269-71.

[164] Statement of William Pilkington, with his affidavit of 1934; v. Vogel, *Early Mormon Documents*, II:354.

to Palmira Wayne County and State of New York and he brake the covenant which he made before the Lord and the Lord suffered the writings to fall into the hands of wicked men.[165]

We do not know who this friend might be. In his 1838-39 History, Smith wrote:

> Notwithstanding however the great restrictions which he had been laid under, and the solemnity of the covenant which he had made with me, he did shew them to others and by stratagem they got them away from him, and they never have been recovered nor obtained back again until this day.[166]

Harris was strictly told that he could show the pages only to his brother, Preserved Harris, his wife Lucy, his father, his mother, and his wife's sister, Mrs. Cobb.[167] The preface of the 1837 BoM edition made no mention of the issue. This is understandable, as it is not faith-promoting, for either believers or those who might become believers.

This account points the finger at others, not Lucy Harris. If she indeed made the statement that she had burned them, the cause could be nothing more than her fear of what certain persons might do if they thought that she still had them. In effect, such a claim may have been nothing more than, "I burned them. They no longer exist. So leave me alone."

Since Lucy Smith also claimed that Harris had shown the pages to others,[168] one of the things we can take away from the two accounts is that a number of people, not all of them friendly, had had the opportunity to learn what the lost pages contained, especially the first part of them, the part that they were most likely to have read.

Demise of Lehi, Conception of a Bible and Confederates All

The problem that the Smiths faced was detail. If all the material in the *Book of Lehi* that could not be replicated in a new telling were to be eliminated, what would remain would be "slim pickins," surely not enough to constitute a replacement text. The answer to the problem may not have come immediately, and it may not have come from Joseph Jr. He had worked long and hard on a history of the Indians as Jews in America, and

---

[165] Smith, 1832 History, in Jessee, *Papers of Joseph Smith*, I:10. This was most probably written November of 1832.
[166] Smith, 1838-39 History, in Jessee, *Papers of Joseph Smith*, I:286.
[167] *Idem*.
[168] Lucy Smith, in Anderson, *Lucy's Book*, 421-22.

when he arrived back in upstate New York, at his father's home, he was undoubtedly inspired by a keen sense of accomplishment, and pride of authorship. We have no indication that he had any qualms regarding the text he had produced so far. The decision to completely scrap the original conception of what he had done, and start over to produce a very different sort of work, would not likely have come from him, or at least not from him alone. At first he had to return to Harmony and farm to support his family. He would have another opportunity to explore options with his father when his parents visited him in Harmony in August/September 1828. After their visit, he had plenty of time to reflect on the options they had discussed.

When eventually it was decided that the new work should replace the detail with prophecies, preaching and exegesis of Isaiah, out of the ashes of Lehi there arose the phoenix of a new bible, and the birth of a new Christian faith. Book sales would be enhanced by the desire of converts to own a copy of their new bible. And a new church, even one with a lay clergy, might provide the central leadership, the Smiths, with long-term employment and status.

The suggestion that a new bible project began after the loss of the 116 pages encounters an obstacle in the form of articles published in 1840 in the *Episcopal Record*, written by John A. Clark, Pastor of Palmyra's Zion's Episcopal Church. He recounts, apparently from memory, two visits of Martin Harris, who described his activity with Joseph Smith, and mentioned a "gold bible" in the earlier of the two visits, in the autumn of 1827. It is clear that this date cannot be correct since Harris is supposed to have mentioned the characters to be taken to Professor Anthon, which he did not even have until some date in February, 1828[169]. He wrote,

> One thing is here to be noticed, that the statements of the originators of this imposture veried (*sic*), and were modified from time to time according as the plans became more mature. At first it was a gold bible—then gold plates engraved—then metal plates stereotyped or embossed with golden letters. At one time Harris was to be enriched by the solid gold of these plates, and at another they were to be religiously kept to convince the world of the truth of the revelation—and, then these plates could not be seen by any but three witnesses...[170]

It is not clear where this sequence of changes of plan came from. If Harris was at some point supposed to enrich himself from the gold of the plates,

---

[169] Vogel, *Early Mormon Documents*, II:261, note 4.
[170] *Ibid*, II:267.

this would not follow the assertion that the find was a gold bible. A more probable order would be the idea of enrichment from the plates, and then progression to a plan for a gold bible. Harris may have mentioned the gold bible in his second visit, after the loss of the 116 pages. Since this account was written over a decade after the details mentioned, confusing some details would not be surprising. It was a clergyman's effort to discredit Mormonism in an Episcopal publication. In June 26 of 1829 the *Wayne Sentinel* (Palmyra) published a short article announcing the BoM copyright while being scornful of the "Gold Bible." This was followed by *The Palmyra Freeman* (Palmyra, NY) on 11 August with an article titled "Gold Bible;" and by *The Gem* (Rochester, NY) on 5 September, with an article also titled "Gold Bible." The first two of these contained the BoM title page text.

It is not known how many of the Smiths were directly involved in the project to produce a translation of the gold plates prior to the loss of the 116 pages. Joseph's brother Hyrum may have had something to do with it, since he accompanied Martin Harris to Harmony prior to his visit to New York to show the characters to professor Anthon. But in the period immediately following the loss of these pages, it would not have been possible for any Smith to be unaware of the problem, nor to be acutely unaware of two things. First, if ever the stolen pages resurfaced to be compared with any replacement text, they would have to be in the same condition as when they were stolen, or with very obvious changes, and therefore no problem. Second, in any case, Joe Jr. was unable to produce a second copy with the same wording, or even all of the same details. At least at this point, every Smith had to have known that he could not do this, and the correlate as well, that there were no gold plates, nor any translation thereof. Since their involvement henceforth would only grow, it would be in the status of confederates all, united in a family project. According to Irene M. Bates, "Much of Lucy's consciousness during this period was that her *family* was to be the instrument in bringing salvation to the whole human family. It was clearly a Smith family enterprise. As Jan Shipps has pointed out, Lucy employs the pronouns *we, ours,* and *us* rather than simply referring to Joseph's particular role."[171]

After Joseph Jr.'s return to Harmony, Joseph Smith Sr. and Lucy visited their son to meet Emma's parents. The only contemporary

---

[171] Irene M. Bates, "Foreword. Lucy Mack Smith—First Mormon Mother," in Anderson, *Lucy's Book*, 7-8. For her reference, see Jan Shipps, *Mormonism: The Story of a New Religious Tradition* (Urbana: University of Illinois Press, 1985), 107.

document we have for this visit is an entry in doctor Robinson's daybook for medicine for "boy Harrison" [Samuel] dated 11 September. It is difficult to resist associating this date with Lucy Smith's statement that upon their return from Harmony they found Samuel Harrison very sick.[172] Joseph Sr. and Samuel visited Joseph Jr. again in February 1829.[173]

The loss of the *Book of Lehi* had a profound effect on the *Book of Mormon* project:

§ The production of the first text could have been a benefit, as a dry run for the not-so-simple task of creating a new bible.

§ From this point on, no Smith could have had any illusions regarding the nature and objectives of their project.

The BoM canon was not developed by just one person. This is the

BoM Team Issue

―――――――――――――――――――

---

[172] Lucy Smith in Anderson, *Lucy's Book*, 423.
[173] Joseph Smith, *History of the Church*, 1:28.

< Chapter 6 >

Lehi: A History to Bring the Indians to Christ

A now lost text produced as a restored Pre-Columbian history, was drafted by Joseph Smith, assisted by Martin Harris, in the first half of 1828. It came to be known as the *Book of Lehi*.[174] In the summer of that year, a person (or persons) unfriendly to Smith's claims stole the only copy of this work. This has also come to be called the purloined 116 pages. Following this loss came Smith's first recorded revelation, of which at least part is dated July 1828[175] giving us his view of the purpose of the plates at that pivotal moment.

"For This Very Purpose Are the Plates Preserved"

> as the knowledge of a Savior has come into the world, even so shall the knowledge of my people [Nephites, Jacobites, Josephites and Zoramites] come to the knowledge of the Lamanites... and for this very purpose are these plates preserved, which contain these records, that the promises of the Lord might be fulfilled, which he made to his people; and that the Lamanites might come to the knowledge of their fathers, and that they might know the promises of the Lord, and that they may believe the gospel and rely upon the merits of Jesus Christ, and be glorified through faith in his name (BC 2)

Here we find only one set of plates. There is no mention of a new bible, nor of the Jew or the Gentile. At this early date, the objective of the plates was limited to bringing the Native Americans to an awareness of their Israelite origin and to accept Christ. Some seven months later, Smith delivered a revelation for his father on the occasion of his February visit, announcing that "a marvelous work is about to come forth among the children of men..." (BC 3; D&C 4:1) To more fully appreciate the transition from the history to the new bible, one must have a fuller understanding of the contents of the *Book of Lehi*.

God, in His wisdom, had provided some failsafe redundancy in the form of a second set of plates covering the same period of time, i.e. that of the lost pages, in anticipation that the translation of Mormon's abridgment from the Large Plates would be lost. This is made more specific in a

---

[174] Joseph Smith, "Preface" to the 1830 edition of the *Book of Mormon*.
[175] Marquardt, *The Joseph Smith Revelations*, 24.

revelation to Joseph Smith (D&C, 10:10-13, 30-31, & 38-45; compare with D&C 3 & 5):

> 10. And, behold, Satan hath put it into their hearts to alter the words which you have caused to be written...which have gone out of your hands.
> 11. ...because they have altered the words, they read contrary from that which you translated and caused to be written;
> 12. And, on this wise, the devil has sought to lay a cunning plan, that he may destroy this work;
> 30. Behold, I say unto you, that you shall not translate again those words which have gone forth out of your hands;
> 31. For, behold, they shall not accomplish their evil designs in lying against those words. For, behold, if you should bring forth the same words they will say that you have lied and that you have pretended to translate, but that you have contradicted yourself.
> 38. I say unto you, that an account of those things that you have written, which have gone out of your hands, is engraven upon the plates of Nephi;
> 39. Yea, and you remember it was said in those writings that a more particular account was given of these things upon the plates of Nephi.
> 40. And now, because the account which is engraven upon the plates of Nephi is more particular concerning the things which, in my wisdom, I would bring to the knowledge of the people in this account—
> 41. Therefore, you shall translate the engravings which are on the plates of Nephi, down even till you come to the reign of king Benjamin, or until you come to that which you have translated, which you have retained;
> 42. And behold, you shall publish it as the record of Nephi
> 45. Behold, there are many things engraven upon the plates of Nephi which do throw greater views upon my gospel.

The *Book of Lehi*: The More Particular Record

If indeed divine assistance had caused words to appear to Smith in his scryer's hat and he just read them off for Harris to copy down, then surely he could produce a second and virtually identical copy. To duck this challenge, it was decided to replace Lehi with the Book of Nephi. Both books were said to be on the gold plates, covering the same period of the BoM narrative, although the first of these was said to have been engraved on plates called the large plates of Nephi, replete with historical detail. In 1 Nephi 19:2 we read:

> 1. the Lord commanded me, wherefore I did make plates of ore that I might engraven upon them the record of my people....the record of my father...our journeyings in the wilderness, and the prophecies of my father; and also many of mine own prophecies have I engraven upon them.

2. And I knew not at the time when I made them that I should be commanded of the Lord to make these plates; wherefore, the record of my father, and the genealogy of his fathers, and the more part of all our proceedings in the wilderness are engraven upon those first plates of which I have spoken; wherefore, the things which transpired before I made these plates are... more particularly made mention upon the first plates.
3. And after I had made these plates by way of commandment, I, Nephi, received a commandment that the ministry and the prophecies, the more plain and precious parts of them, should be written upon these plates; and that the things which were written should be kept for the instruction of my people, who should possess the land, and also for other wise purposes, which purposes are known unto the Lord.
4. Wherefore, I, Nephi, did make a record upon the other plates, which gives an account, or which gives a greater account of the wars and contentions and destructions of my people. And this have I done, and commanded my people what they should do after I was gone; and that these plates should be handed down from one generation to another, or from one prophet to another, until further commandments of the Lord.
5. this I do that the more sacred things may be kept for the knowledge of my people.

The deliberate contrast is clearly stressed. The phrase "these plates" refers to the plates the reader is currently reading, in this case the small plates of Nephi. The phrase "those first plates" (and "the other plates" or "those first plates") refers to the large plates of Nephi (so called only in Jacob 3:13), which began with the *Book of Lehi*. For the period in the New World, they also contained "an account of the reign of the kings, and the wars and contentions of my people." (1 Nephi 9:4) The details were "more particularly made mention upon the first [large] plates." (1 Nephi 19:2) Of the small plates of Nephi (so called only in Jacob 1:1), he wrote, "I do not write anything upon [these] plates save it be that I think it be sacred." (1 Nephi 19:6) Mormon mentions them again in a brief statement inserted just at the point where the lost pages left off (Words of Mormon): (See Figure 21. Plates Schematic).

3. ... after I had made an abridgment from the plates of Nephi, down to the reign of this king Benjamin, of whom Amaleki spake...I found these plates, which contained this small account of the prophets, from Jacob down to the reign of this king Benjamin, and also many of the words of Nephi.

So for the present discussion, we have 1) the large plates of Nephi, 2) the small plates of Nephi (which translate into the text to replace the lost 116 pages, i.e. the Book of Nephi down to King Benjamin), and 3) Mormon's abridgment of the large plates down to King Benjamin (the lost 116 pages, i.e. the *Book of Lehi*). The small plates were not abridged by Mormon; they are Nephi's own composition. Just to complicate things, at times both the large plates and the small plates are called the Plates of Nephi (1 Nephi 9:2; v. Figure 21. Plates Schematic).

Although the 116-page text is not extant as far as anyone knows, the *Book of Mormon* contrasts this text with the replacement text in sufficient detail for us to reconstruct the basic elements of the *Book of Lehi*. This chapter will also investigate the degree to which the Nephi replacement text struck a radically different course rather than simply replacing Lehi. As Smith moved from the *Book of Lehi* to the gospel-laden Book of Nephi, his history, designed to gather the Pre-Columbian Israelite Americans to Jesus, became a new bible for a far grander mission, to restore Christ's true church for all mankind in preparation for the Second Coming.

Devils in the Details: The First Centuries in the New World

The first of these devils was the persistent fear that once the book was published the purloined 116 pages would somehow resurface and be compared with the text composed to replace them, with disconfirmatory discrepancies. The sort of detail Smith would have included even after their arrival in the New World, according to his mother,[176] is illustrated by the ability of his imagination to invent Indian manners and customs well before he claimed to have the gold plates. If he had decided to merely attempt a reworded version, the events and actors involved in what has been subsequently dubbed the *Book of Lehi* would have proven to be a major challenge to Smith's memory, with numerous opportunities to contradict his original work. The solution to this problem did not require a degree in astrophysics, and probably was rather quickly devised. The new text would eschew detail. As a result, there is a dearth of detail from Nephi to Amaleki (in the book of Omni). Beginning with Mosiah, we suddenly encounter numerous events, and the number of personal names increases, as do the toponyms, including cities and natural features of the BoM setting. This said, it is clear that there should have been no bar on introducing new events that clearly were not in the *Book of Lehi*. A good illustration of this is found in the gospels, with which the BoM authors were quite familiar. The so-called *Slaughter of the Innocents*, when Herod the Great is supposed to have ordered the death of all young male children

---

[176] Lucy Smith, in Anderson, *Lucy's Book*, 345. This would be c. 1824 prior to claiming to have the gold plates.

in the vicinity of Bethlehem, is reported only in Matthew, as well as the flight of the Holy Family with Baby Jesus to take refuge in Egypt. This is a very major event. Yet somehow it escaped the notice of Mark, Luke and John. Similarly, some additional events that had not been reported in the purloined pages would not look out of place in the replacement text.

Devils in the Details: "Our Proceedings in the Wilderness"

The next devil is the very real fear that at least with regard to events and associated detail in Judea and Arabia one might make serious errors. For almost two millennia scholars had studied the Biblical lands and Arabia, including Moab, Edom, Midian, Arabia, Saba (Sheba) and the rest of Arabia Felix (Yemen). Any effort to produce Semitic personal and place names along the way would have been a minefield. But there were so many opportunities to do so. Lehi's group would have had to go across Arabia to the Indian Ocean from oasis to oasis, always finding people there who had limited provisions for their own families, and jealously guarded water sources and family and tribal cisterns. Either they would have had to make a living themselves, or carry with them considerable valuable trade goods, enough for eight years, under threat of nomadic robber-band attacks. Any effort to recount the adventures of this group in the wilderness would encounter many a pitfall. It may be that Joseph Jr. was at least initially naïve respecting the degree to which these areas were known even in his day, but once the project became a Smith family project assisted by Cowdery, this great storyteller must have been reined in and made to understand that it would be better for the eight years to take place mostly in a vacuum, before getting onboard their ship.

  Even so, occasionally some details were included, usually with predictable results. An example is found in Lehi's first two months in the wilderness. It is mentioned that he descended to the shore of the Red Sea, traveled three days and camped in a valley near the mouth of a river that emptied into the Red Sea (1 Nephi 2:5-9):

> 4. And it came to pass that he departed into the wilderness…
> 5. And he came down by the borders *near the shore of the Red Sea*; and he traveled in the wilderness in the borders which are nearer the Red Sea; and he did travel in the wilderness with his family, which consisted of my mother, Sariah, and my elder brothers, who were Laman, Lemuel, and Sam. (emphasis added)
> 6. And it came to pass that when he had traveled three days in the wilderness, he pitched his tent in a valley by the side of a river of water.

7. And it came to pass that he built an altar of stones, and made an offering unto the Lord, and gave thanks unto the Lord our God.

8. And it came to pass that he called the name of the river, Laman, and it emptied into the Red Sea; and the valley was in the borders near the mouth thereof.

9. And when my father saw that the waters of the river emptied into the fountain of the Red Sea, he spake unto Laman, saying: O that thou mightest be like unto this river, continually running into the fountain of all righteousness!

The Arabian peninsula is essentially a wedge that begins near sea level at the Persian Gulf and rises to the Hijaz escarpment overlooking the Red Sea from heights ranging from 3000 feet to over a mile. As the west side of the peninsula was lifted up to form the wedge it exposed the bottom of the Red Sea all along its Arabian shore, forming an arid and highly saline coastal plain, the Tihama.

The absolutely shortest route to a point "near the shore of the Red Sea" is to follow the modern Israeli road to the ancient Israelite port of Eilat on the Gulf of Aqaba. This road passes along the west side of the Dead Sea to Ayn Gedi, then Masada and on down to Eilat. It has a very long stretch in the worst of Wadi Arabah, which as badlands go, is at the top of a scale from one to ten. At Aqaba it is not possible to follow the coast of the gulf due to mountain cliffs that plunge directly into the sea. A winding road follows mountain passes over to Sharma. The total distance is 346 miles according to Google Maps. Since this is a nearly straight route most of the way, there is little room for camels to take shortcuts.

We have solid evidence regarding the distance a caravan travels in a day. Along various trade routes, premodern governments built inns (caravanserai, way stations) where the caravans could sleep overnight, eat and take care of their camels. These are routinely spaced twenty to thirty miles apart. Averaging thirty miles a day, to get to the Red Sea would require about twelve days. From this point they traveled three more days to Lehi's campsite in the Valley of Lemuel. This comes to about fifteen days of rugged travel.

The route followed raises concerns. In 1 Nephi, we find:

we did go forth again in the wilderness, following the same direction, keeping in the most fertile parts of the wilderness, which was in the borders near the Red Sea. (2:5 & 16:14)

Map 1. Jerusalem to the Red Sea

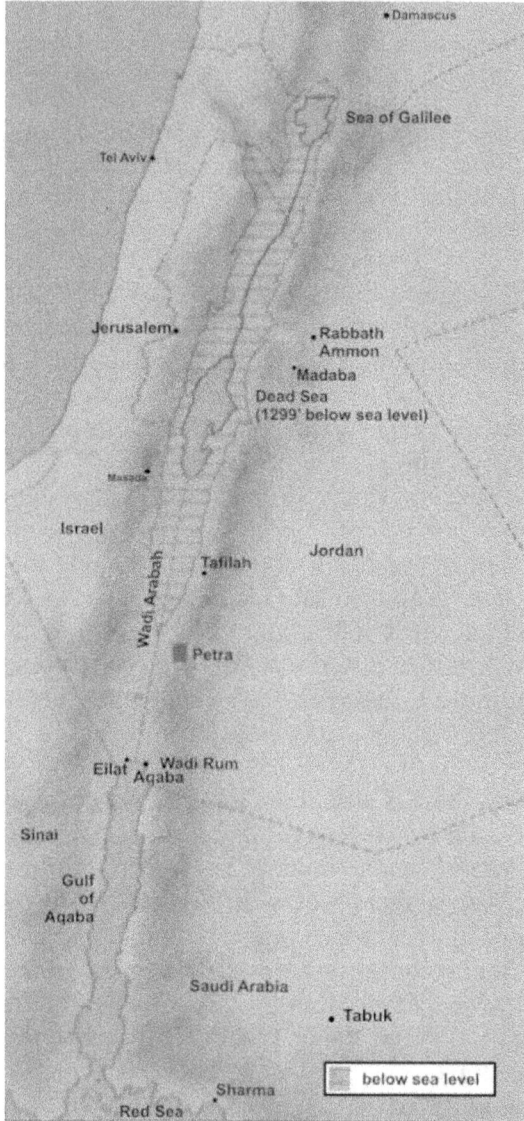

Source: Based on Iain Browning, *Petra*, 12.

Map 2. Arabian Trade Routes

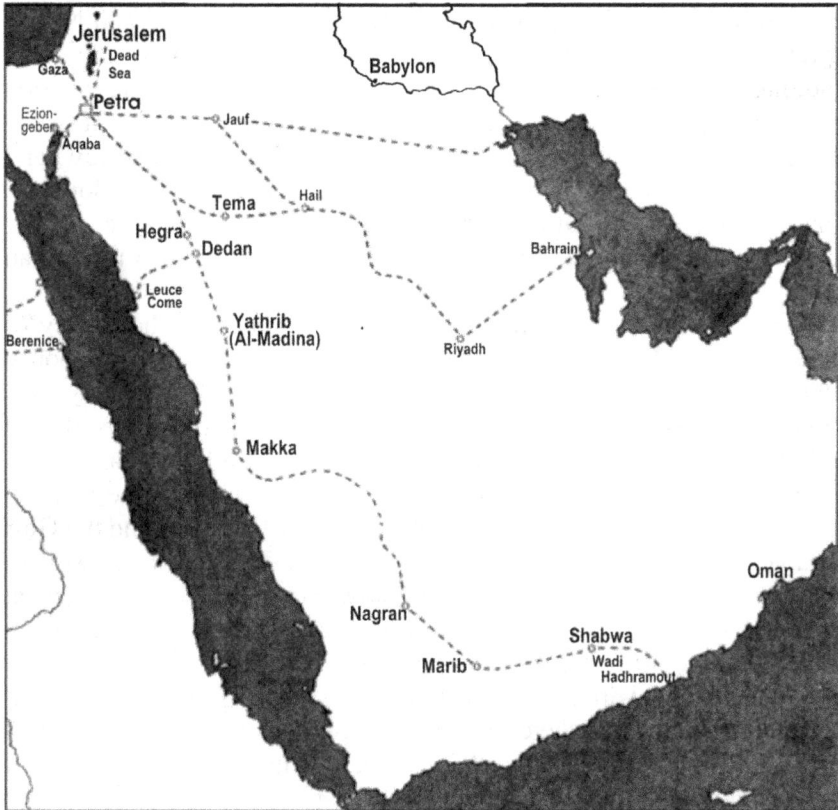

Source: Iain Browning, *Petra*, 14 (slightly edited)

This is the Tihama. It is saline, dry and about as inhospitable as can be to plants other than halophytes, very similar to the wasteland bordering the Great Salt Lake, although much hotter. The "borders near the Red Sea" is absolutely not "the most fertile parts." It is eschewed by the caravans in favor of the very tractable and cooler highland plateau on the east side of the escarpment. (Map 2) The distance from Sharma to Jizan, near the border with modern Yemen, is 1000 miles (Google Maps). I have only driven this route once, just to see it. The normal trade route from Jerusalem to the Indian Ocean crossed Wadi Arabah (part of the Great Rift, 1300 feet below sea level at the Dead Sea) over and up to either Madaba or to Petra at Wadi Musa. The caravan route basically followed the possible, avoiding rugged steep hills while heading for the next oasis, in an unforgiving mountain and desert region. From Petra it made its way south to Hegra (aka Al-Hijr, or Madâ'in Sâlih). Even on the land bordering this escarpment, settlements exist only in scattered oases, such as Tabuk, Al-'Ulâ, Yathrib (Al-Madîna), Makka, At-Tâ'if, Al-Bâha, Abhâ and Najrân (Nagrân in Yemeni Arabic).[177] There it turned southeast to avoid the forbidding mountains of Yemen, where the capital, San'a, perches at 7000 feet. From Najrân it made its way to Ma'rib in ancient Saba (seat of the legendary Queen of Sheba). At Shabwa it entered Wadi Hadhramowt and descended to the Indian Ocean. (Map 2) Proceeding south-east along the Hijaz escarpment, the route either continued on south into what is now Yemen, or to Najrân, and then on to the Hadhramawt and to the Indian Ocean.

Some problems arise. First, from Lehi's campsite at the Valley of Lemuel, Nephi and his brothers had to travel back to Jerusalem twice, once for the Brass Plates of Laban and once for Ishmael and his family, two round trips requiring fifteen days each way, or a total of sixty days of hard travel. All of this could be classified with the Labors of Heracles.

The second is the river Laman. From Petra to Najran, the caravan route stays on the highland plateau overlooking the Dead Sea and the Gulf of Aqaba. I have driven from Amman to Aqaba several times, and always been amazed as the road plunges from the escarpment heights to Aqaba. No river exists in any of this area. Even in wetter times, if one existed in Lehi's time, the formation of a constant river befitting this passage requires a substantial drainage area sloping westward to feed the river. But the plateau slope is from the escarpment eastward, away from Aqaba and the Red Sea, while the drop to the west is precipitous and made up of numerous gorges, hardly a terrain conducive to the formation of such a river. Furthermore, the BoM narrative specifies that Lehi camped near the mouth of the river, pouring into the Red Sea. (1 Nephi 2:5-2:10) What seasonal flows and flash floods exist in the winter mostly disappear into the sand before reaching the sea. At present, no river exists that could qualify, and the terrain militates against such a river in Lehi's time.

---

[177] Apart from considerable literature on the ecology of the area, this passage is buttressed also by the author's personal experience, having lived three years in Jeddah, during which I was the President of the Natural History Society of Western Arabia, and three in San'a, Yemen. I have travelled numerous times along the routes from Tabuk to Najran, and within Yemen, to Hadhramawt and on to Masqat, Oman.

Map 3. Topography of North-West Arabia[178]

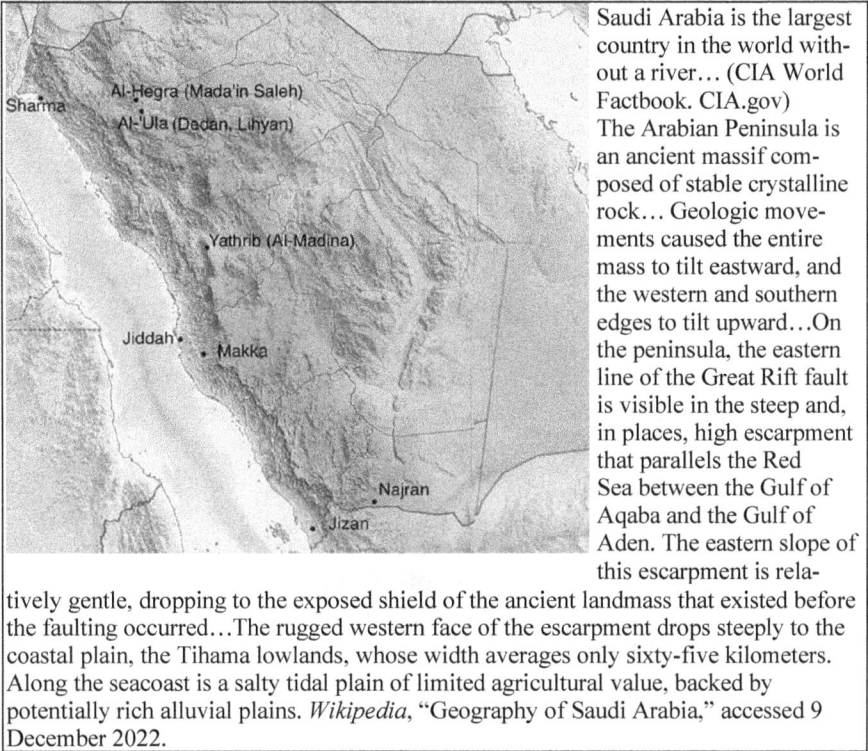

Saudi Arabia is the largest country in the world without a river... (CIA World Factbook. CIA.gov) The Arabian Peninsula is an ancient massif composed of stable crystalline rock... Geologic movements caused the entire mass to tilt eastward, and the western and southern edges to tilt upward...On the peninsula, the eastern line of the Great Rift fault is visible in the steep and, in places, high escarpment that parallels the Red Sea between the Gulf of Aqaba and the Gulf of Aden. The eastern slope of this escarpment is relatively gentle, dropping to the exposed shield of the ancient landmass that existed before the faulting occurred...The rugged western face of the escarpment drops steeply to the coastal plain, the Tihama lowlands, whose width averages only sixty-five kilometers. Along the seacoast is a salty tidal plain of limited agricultural value, backed by potentially rich alluvial plains. *Wikipedia*, "Geography of Saudi Arabia," accessed 9 December 2022.

The historical hydrology of the Arabian Peninsula is not fully known. Certainly in very remote times it was more verdant. In the historical period, ancient sources make it clear that camels had replaced donkeys and mules on the caravan routes by sometime in the second millennium BCE. We also know that the verdant climate in the Sahara dried up one or several thousand years before the predynastic period of ancient Egyptian history, drying up the Nile swamp and forcing North African migration, partly into the Nile valley, resulting in what became the Egyptian people. In Arabia there have long been dry gulches (*wadi, sayl*) that flowed intermittently in the rainy season, often producing raging flash floods. The famous pre-Islamic poet, 'Umru'u l-Qays, commemorated this in an encomium to his horse (a *munjarid*):

---

[178] commons.wikimedia.org/wiki/Category:Topographic_maps_of_Saudi_Arabia#/media/File:Saudi_Arabia_relief_location_map.jpg. The map has been converted to greyscale, and all location labels have been added.

Mikarrin mifarrin muqbilin mudbirin maʿan
Ka-julmūdi ṣaḥrin ḥaṭṭahu s-saylu min ʿāli

Turning, bolting back, charging forth, dashing back, all at once,
Like a stone bolder that the torrent drives down from above.

The period of a wetter Arabia appears to have been up to as late as around 8,000 years ago, an approximate date given to a prehistoric lake in the Great Nefûd Desert.[179] A map of prehistoric rivers in Arabia shows the closest one descending down the escarpment and emptying into the Red Sea at about two hundred miles southeast of the Gulf of Aqaba. Ancient rivers forming on the escarpment further north flowed inland, the closest having been around eighty miles south of Aqaba.[180] Archaeological hydrology studies of the Arabian Desert are under way, including surrounding areas, covering a period from the first arrival of humans to roughly the present time. Hopefully we will know more about when and where real rivers flowed in Arabia.

Apart from warring tribes, one had to face desperate armed robbers. Adult male misfits were cast out (cut off) from their tribe. Like male lions driven from the pride and striving to survive, they banded together. Traveling in Yemen with a caravan, the fearless explorer Ulrich Jasper Seetzen was killed by an armed band that preyed on richly laden caravans.[181] In the area of Makka, a tribe was specialized in attacking caravans, even those taking Muslim pilgrims to Makka. They had to pay *khuwa* (an ironically named "brotherhood tax") for safe passage. Even pilgrims! Perhaps we should think of it as a sort of customs duty. It is unclear how Lehi's party made a living other than hunting. Perhaps with extensive gathering of wild herbs? Lehi left his silver, gold and precious things behind (1 Nephi 2:4). How would they have paid for passage rights, grain, water and fodder or pasturage. As for hunting, the problem of Nephi's steel bow will be addressed in Chapter 11. The party's equipment,

---

[179] Jonathan Gornall, "When Arabia Was Green: Lush Grasslands Helped Early Man Make Leap Out of Africa," *The National* [UAE], 14 May 2015 (http://www.thenational.ae/uae/heritage/when-arabia-was-green-lush-grasslands-helped-early-man-make-leap-out-of-africa, accessed 8 January 2017).
[180] Andrew Lawler, "In Search of Green Arabia." The map was accessed online, 8 January 2017, at http://www.andrewlawler.com/in-search-of-green-arabia/. It is sourced as being adapted from H. Stewart Edgell, *Arabian Deserts, Nature, Origin and Evolution* (New York: Springer Publishing, 2006).
[181] Introduction to *Ulrich Jasper Seetzen's Reisen*, published posthumously by family and friends (Berlin: Verlag bei G. Reimer, 1855).

clothing and beasts of burden would have been attractive goods for desperate robber bands.

The difficulties of making this eight-year trip is further illustrated by the Roman campaign along virtually the same route, a few decades BCE, led by Aelius Gallus by order of Augustus Caesar. Disease significantly reduced his troops, and he encountered armed Arabian resistance. After taking Ma'rib in Arabia Felix (Yemen), and making his way back to the Red Sea, he had lost most of his military. He decided not to attempt a return by the same route, harassed by hostile Arabian warriors, but crossed just north of Bab al-Mandab (The Gate of Wailing) to Abyssinia (now Ethiopia) and marched back to Alexandria, tail between his legs.[182]

Moreover, eight years is excessive. The armed Arab caravans that made the trip successfully traveled from the Indian Ocean to Petra in less than a year. This is a perfect setting for Joseph Smith to fill an eight-year journey from Jerusalem to the Indian Ocean with interesting encounters and adventures. And yet, in Nephi, there is no single mention of any other people, any attempts to announce the gospel of Christ, any conflicts, or any dealings to reprovision themselves with food, water and fodder. This total vacuum is in contrast with the greater detail of the original version, mentioned to in the *Book of Mormon*. Even after the BoM narrative gets the Lehi party to the New World, the need to avoid detail continues all the way up to the Book of Mosiah. This is the period that the purloined 116 pages covered, showing that the threat that they posed was equally responsible for a dearth of detail, even in the land of promise. By having Mosiah relocate the Nephites to lands north of the Isthmus of Panama, the BoM authors provided themselves with a blank tableau, a virgin territory where they could develop a geography replete with many place names, without fear of contradicting toponym detail in the lost pages. (v. 202-03)

A Bible! We have got a Bible!

Initially, the Smith-Harris partnership appears to have been merely to produce a history of the Indians as Israelites in pre-Columbian America, for profit. Smith himself admitted, in his 1832 history, that he had sinned in that he "sought the Plates to obtain riches."[183] It eventually focused on bringing the Native Americans to Jesus. Later the expanded BoM team

---

[182] Strabo, xvi 4:21-25.
[183] Joseph Smith, 1832 history, in Dean C. Jessee, ed., *Papers of Joseph Smith* (Salt Lake City: Deseret Book Company, 1989), I:8.

undertook to produce an Israelite New-World bible to restore the "true" gospel and church.

Here we can make some initial observations. First, Mormon was attracted to the sermons and teachings of the gospel in the small plates of Nephi as opposed to the large plates, the *Book of Lehi*, which was mostly devoid of these (Words of Mormon 1:3-4). Second, the competing claims of Martin Harris and Professor Charles Anthon mentioned only plates bearing curious characters, not a new bible.[184] Third, prior to starting even the Lehi text, Joseph Smith undertook to train as a Methodist exhorter while still in Palmyra, where he was observed exhorting in Methodist camp meetings.[185] He attended a Methodist class after his arrival in Harmony, Pennsylvania, although how long is disputed.[186] It is quite possible that Smith sought training as a Methodist exhorter to acquire the background needed to produce a history of Israelites in America based on the Old Testament, without the audacity of trying to create a new bible per se. The decision to do so required appropriate content in the replacement text.

The Ministry Material

The Nephi replacement text (the Book of Nephi through Words of Moron) focused on "the ministry and the prophecies" (1 Nephi 19:3), the prophecies of the coming of Christ (Words of Mormon vs 4), and other prophesyings and revelation (ibid, 1:6). These materials include chastisements & exhortations (often to Laman and Lemuel), the patriarchal blessings of Lehi to his sons, gospel-related teachings and Isaiah inclusions with commentary. They were absent from the *Book of Lehi*, which contained "the record of my father, and the genealogy of his fathers, and the more part of all our proceedings in the wilderness" (1 Nephi 19:2), and "a greater account of the wars and contentions and destructions of my people." (1 Nephi 19:4) This was probably seen to detract from the desired image of the work as a new bible. Mormon was also pleased by the small plates of Nephi because of "the prophecies of the

---

[184] Charles Anthon, letter to E. D. Howe dated 17 February 1834, in Vogel, *Early Mormon Documents* (Salt Lake City: Signature Books, 2002), IV:377-81. Joseph Smith, Joseph Smith's History of 1838-39, in Jessee, *Papers of Joseph Smith*, I:285.

[185] O[rsamus] Turner, *History of the Pioneer Settlement of Phelps and Gorham's Purchase* (Rochester, NY: William Alling, 1851), 214, 400; quoted here from Marquardt, *Rise of Mormonism*, 30

[186] Marquardt, *Rise of Mormonism*, 30-31.

coming of Christ." (Words of Mormon 4) Presumably this too is in contrast with the content of the *Book of Lehi*, which may have kept closer to the Old Testament with only foreshadowing of Christ, while the Book of Nephi mentions Jesus Christ, baptism and ordination of priests and teachers.

The Isaiah Package

The addition of Isaiah inclusions to the replacement text produced an interrelated chain of changes that constitute a single package.

The Package: the Isaiah Inclusions

The ministry material is bolstered by the lengthy Isaiah inclusions, and the commentary on them: Isaiah 2-14; 48-49; 150-51; 29:3-5; 29:6-24; and 29:13-23; as well as other Biblical passages. Clearly the main purpose of these inclusions was to show that the Old Testament prophets were no strangers to the gospel of Christ, knew of some Israelites going off to distant isles of the sea, the coming forth of the *Book of Mormon*, the New World Israelites' future gathering to Christ and the restoration of the true gospel. Unlike the old approach of the *Book of Lehi*, the Nephi replacement text has a new focus. Up front and center is the *Book of Mormon* arguing the case for the *Book of Mormon*. The text is replete with examples, but a couple will suffice here, such as 1 Nephi 19:21:

> And he surely did show unto the prophets of old all things concerning them; and also he did show unto many concerning us; wherefore, it must needs be that we know concerning them for they are written upon the plates of brass.

Introducing Isaiah 48-49, Nephi says (1 Nephi 19:24):

> Hear ye the words of the prophet, ye who are a remnant of the house of Israel, a branch who have been broken off; hear ye the words of the prophet, which were written unto all the house of Israel, and liken them unto yourselves, that ye may have hope as well as your brethren from whom ye have been broken off; for after this manner has the prophet written. (See also 1 Nephi 19 through 2 Nephi 25 *passim*, and specifically 1 Nephi 19:21-24; 20:21; 22:3-13; 2 Nephi 9:1-7; 11:8; 25:1-4.)

The Isaiah inclusions contain 133 variant readings of the first order, and 326 variants of the first and second orders (Chapter 18).

Note: If these inclusions were in the *Book of Lehi*, Smith would not have been able to replicate the many BoM variants, and would not have put them in Nephi. Since they are in Nephi, they must not have been in Lehi.

Combined with the evidence in Words of Mormon, this is strong presumptive evidence that Lehi did not contain the Isaiah inclusions.

The Package: The Brass Plates

Quoting from Isaiah and the Pentateuch required that the Nephites be in possession of those works. Obtaining a copy of these texts to bring with them was not the only way. Since the Apostle Paul is quoted before he was even born, the reader must surmise that these verses were received by revelation. So too, Isaiah could have been received by revelation, just as Joseph Smith later claimed to have received the *Book of Moses*. Or Providence could have provided a scroll in Hebrew. These options were clearly on the table. Alternatively, the Nephi replacement text of their new Bible could take care of this through the acquisition of the Brass Plates, a sort of pre-exilic Bible, compiled long before the concept of a bible even existed (1 Nephi 5:11-13):

> 11. And he beheld that they [the Brass Plates] did contain the five books of Moses, which gave an account of the creation of the world, and also of Adam and Eve, who were our first parents;
> 12. And also a record of the Jews from the beginning, even down to the commencement of the reign of Zedekiah, king of Judah;
> 13. And also the prophecies of the holy prophets, from the beginning, even down to the commencement of the reign of Zedekiah; and also many prophecies which have been spoken by the mouth of Jeremiah.

They also contained the prophecies of Joseph (1 Nephi 4:2) and Lehi's genealogy (1 Nephi 3:3). For the prospective 19th-century reader, this would seem normal. This band of Israelite immigrants would be analogous to the Europeans who left for the New World, Bible in hand.

In Nephi, this brass bible was in the possession of a wealthy military leader named Laban. Nephi is commanded to get it from him, and when the latter resists and confiscates the precious items brought to exchange for them, Nephi is commanded to kill Laban to take the plates. It is not clear that Lehi lacked some similar episode. This is because in Smith's first revelation, dated July of 1828, in the *Book of Commandments,* the Zoramites, descendants of Zoram, the servant of Laban, are mentioned along with the Nephites, Jacobites and Josephites, in contradistinction to the Lamanites, Lemuelites and Ishmaelites. If the date is correct, and this list is retrospective (to Lehi) rather than prospective (to the intended Book of Nephi), then Zoram would have existed in Lehi. The same list, in the same order, exists in Jacob 1:13. Lehi's sons are listed in order of birth, followed in both cases by a nonrelative (Zoram and Ishmael). In Alma a possibly different group of Zoramites are the enemies of the Nephites. Presumably in 4 Nephi, the Jacobites, Josephites and Zoramites emerge as "true believers" among the Nephites (4 Nephi 1:36) because they had been mentioned as such in the July 1828 revelation. Conspicuously absent from the list is Sam. Moreover, there are no Samites. If there was already a Zoram in Lehi, then conceivably there was also a Laban, and so a conflict between either Nephi or Lehi and Laban, possibly over Lehi's call to repentance, or the genealogy of Lehi, or Lehi's soon-to-be-abandoned property, or a record of the Jews. If this record was part of the story, its contents may not have been mentioned (or possibly just the Law of Moses). None of the foregoing requires a mention of plates of brass. The option of the brass plates was eventually chosen because they had other more intrinsic utilitarian value, as we shall see.

The Package: Egyptian and the Scriptures

It is commonly believed that the text on Smith's gold plates was in "reformed Egyptian." It is not that simple. The portion of the Nephite narrative abridged by Mormon, and the Jaredite narrative abridged by Moroni, is claimed to have been in reformed Egyptian, i.e. the Pre-Columbian Egyptian of their day, in the fourth century CE. But the Egyptian on the Brass Plates must have been that of Lehi's day in Egypt or Judea. This would be the same Egyptian written by Nephi and Jacob, a stage of Egyptian that Egyptologists can read today. So the Book of Lehi, abridged by Mormon, would have been in "reformed Egyptian," and the text of Mosiah on. But the text of Nephi and his brother Jacob would have been in the Egyptian of Lehi (that of 7th century BCE).

One intrinsic value of the Brass Plates lies in the fact that the Nephi replacement text could be crafted to take place in a *linguistic vacuum*, by claiming that their text was in Egyptian, a language they thought would never be deciphered. The gold plates must be in an *epigraphic vacuum* as well; to wit, by making them in "reformed" characters, they hoped to establish a vacuum of script, which made it impossible for anyone to test them by asking Smith Jr. to reproduce known ancient Egyptian characters off the top of his head. By placing the history in pre-Columbian America, a land that no one knew or would ever truly know, or so they thought, they were able to write their history in *a historical and cultural vacuum*, a sort of *tabula rasa*. By contrast, when producing the *Book of Lehi*, Joseph Jr. did not feel constrained by an imperative to avoid detail.

There is no document dated to before 1829 that identifies the characters on the plates as Egyptian. The characters shown to Professor Anthon were a hodgepodge, and there is nothing clearly Egyptian in appearance in the transcription of characters usually associated by the Church with Harris' mission of c. February of 1828 (Figures 2 & 3). Egyptian first clearly emerges in connection with the Brass Plates in the Book of Nephi. This would mean that the addition of these plates provided the opportunity to supply the precedent for the Nephite records to be also in Egyptian, including the gold plates of the *Book of Mormon*. The plates of Laban, Israelite scriptures in Egyptian, thus did double duty. This language was thought to be undeciphered, and never to be deciphered (Mormon 9:34):

> But the Lord knoweth the things which we have written, and also that none other people knoweth our language; and because that none other people knoweth our language, therefore he hath prepared means for the interpretation thereof.

Moreover, making Nephite elites bilingual in Egyptian and Hebrew allowed the authors tremendous linguistic freedom to devise the many Nephite and Lamanite personal and place names.

The Package: Metallic Plates Rather Than Scrolls

Herein lies a second intrinsic value of the Brass Plates. The story of Smith's acquisition of the BoM text imposed on the project the need to assert that indeed a bible could be inscribed on gold plates. This was given a precedent by making the bible brought by Lehi to the New World a text inscribed on brass plates. These two intrinsic values of brass plates gave them the edge over simply having Isaiah be received in Hebrew through revelation, or even penned on a scroll.

The Package: King James English

Initially, Smith Jr. and Harris would have had little inclination to write Lehi's history in anything other than the familiar English of their day, much as Spalding had done in his romance. Knowing their own limitation in the English language, they may have steered away from attempting to write in what they could even have considered a stultified English. When drafting the replacement text, to make the acceptance of the Isaiah passages easier it was necessary to keep them in King James English. But if they were inserted into a larger text written in nineteenth century English, the contrast would make the overall work look like a modern composition quoting KJV Biblical passages. The Biblical inclusions settled this language issue. However, since writing in correct King James English should have lain well within divine capabilities, the work would have to be written in their best approximation to it. Although well versed in the Bible, this BoM A-team made numerous errors, such as confusing "thou," "ye" and "you," as well as verbal conjugation. [187] Fortunately for the project, their prospective readers were not equipped to notice occasional errors of this nature. Indeed, there was an additional compensation for their effort. They could hope that the result would bestow an aura of a sacred text, appropriate to a new Bible.

The Life of Lehi

The BoM begins its list of components of the purloined pages with "the record of my father." This would be the life of Lehi. Since it lists it before the record of the travails in the wilderness, this would include the dealings of Lehi with the Judeans prior to his departure. It is abbreviated in the Nephi replacement text (1 Nephi 1):

> 17. ... I make an abridgment of the record of my father, upon plates which I have made with mine own hands [the large plates]...after I have abridged the record of my father then will I make an account of mine own life.
> 18. Therefore, I would that ye should know, that after the Lord had shown so many marvelous things unto my father, Lehi, yea, concerning the destruction of Jerusalem, behold he went forth among the people, and began to prophesy and to declare unto them concerning the things which he had both seen and heard.
> 19. And it came to pass that the Jews did mock him because of the things which he testified of them; for he truly testified of their wickedness and their abominations; and he testified that the things which he saw and heard, and

---

[187] Royal Skousen, *The History of the Text of the Book of Mormon. Part One, Grammatical Variation* (Provo, UT: The Foundation for Ancient Research and Mormon Studies, 2016), 455-97; & Royal Skousen, *The History of the Text of the Book of Mormon. Part Two, Grammatical Variation* (Provo, UT: The Foundation for Ancient Research and Mormon Studies, 2016), 1144-79.

also the things which he read in the book, manifested plainly of the coming of the Messiah, and also the redemption of the world.

20. And when the Jews heard these things they were angry with him; yea, even as with the prophets of old, whom they had cast out, and stoned, and slain; and they also sought his life, that they might take it away…

In abridging his father's record Nephi says

I, Nephi, do not make a full account of the things which my father hath written, for he hath written many things which he saw in visions and in dreams; and he also hath written many things which he prophesied and spake unto his children, of which I shall not make a full account. (v. 16)

It made only slight mention of the warnings preached to the Judeans, attempts on his life, and possibly miracles of divine protection. One wonders how all of this would have been fleshed out by Lehi, and would have been interfaced with the mission of Jeremiah, as he undertook the same divinely imposed task, and was cast into prison. What details of Jerusalem and the religious and political elites would have been included? Here again is a minefield for an unsuspecting neophyte exhorter, who probably thought he knew more than he actually did.

The Genealogy Quagmire

A major deletion from the *Book of Lehi* in producing the version to replace the purloined 116 pages, is the genealogy of Lehi, said to have been on the Brass Plates of Laban, and then recorded by Lehi (1 Nephi 3:12, 5:14-16, 6:1). The BoM asserts that Lehi was a descendant of Jacob through Joseph. Although there is a lot of genealogy in the Bible, the so-called "begats" are not given for everyone. The focus is on the line of descent from Adam to the patriarchs, from Abraham to Jacob, and then on to David, presumably descended from Judah. Even his genealogy is tricky. The OT text does not provide enough information to trace the genealogy of 7th century BCE nonroyal notables of the northern Kingdom back to Manasseh. It is largely a Judean document, focused on Judean kingship. The New Testament focuses, understandably, on the descent of Jesus from David. Joseph Smith, in attempting to invent Lehi's genealogy, would be rushing in where angels fear to tread. The advice of Paul is clear: "But avoid foolish controversies and genealogies…" (Titus 3:9)

Outlining the Book of Lehi

Based on this description derived from the BoM and Smith's first revelation, it is possible now to get a clear idea of the BoM's view of the lost *Book of Lehi*, albeit minus the details of the text itself. It began with Nephi's abridgment of the record of Lehi (including the genealogy of the fathers of Lehi), his mission to call the Jews to repentance along with their reaction, his calling to lead his family to the New World, an account of eight years in the wilderness replete with details of their travails and dealings and finally a relatively political account of these immigrants once in the New World. It lacked the preaching of the gospel of Jesus, and Lehi's dreams, prophecies, exhortations, calls to repentance and patriarchal blessings, all appropriate for the production of a new bible. Moreover, it lacked the Isaiah package, including the Isaiah inclusions, and commentary on them, to show that Isaiah knew that Israelites would go to the New World, and was himself Christian. Lacking the Isaiah inclusions, it would not have needed their source, the Brass Plates. Without their Egyptian text, the *Book of Mormon* would not have been cast in a linguistic and epigraphic vacuum, and there would be no BoM precedent for recording sacred scripture in Egyptian on metallic plates.

There is enough meat on this skeleton to conclude firmly that the Nephi replacement text was clearly not just a retelling of the Book of Lehi in different words, and perhaps with a few omissions or additions of story details, all justified as being a different composition. Rather, this new version, cast in King James English, was to be a total remake, a totally new concept of what the first fifth of the *Book of Mormon* ought to be, and therefore the *Book of Mormon* itself, and its mission. The wording of Smith's July 1828 revelation, "a marvelous work...about to come forth among the children of men," was incorporated into 1 Nephi 14:7: "For the time cometh, saith the Lamb of God, that I will work a great and a marvelous work among the children of men." This is the

BoM Reconception Issue

< Chapter 7 >

Witnessing Gold Plates thru Spiritual Eyes: *to What End?*

Smith claimed from the beginning that he had been commanded that the gold plates should be shown to no one. Some detractors took the position: "Put up or shut up, Joe." The BoM urtext was no more than half done when it was promised that there would be witnesses, three, or even more. In June of 1829, he led three of his principal collaborators, Oliver Cowdery, David Whitmer and Martin Harris, into a wood near the home of Peter Whitmer Sr. (in Fayette, NY), where they sought a view of the plates.

The Text Attributed to the Three Witnesses

The following text, which the witnesses are said to have signed, asserts a collective experience. It has become the official testimony.

Be it known unto all nations, kindreds, tongues, and people, unto whom this work shall come, that we, through the grace of God the Father, and our Lord Jesus Chris, have seen the plates which contain this record, which is a record of the people of Nephi, and also of the Lamanites, his brethren, and also of the people of Jared, which came from the tower of which hath been spoken; and we also know that they have been translated by the gift and power of God, for his voice hath declared it unto us; wherefore we know of a surety, that the work is true. And we also testify that we have seen the engravings which are upon the plates; and they have been shewn unto us by the power of God, and not of man. And we declare with words of soberness, that an Angel of God came down from heaven, and he brought and laid before our eyes, that we beheld and saw the plates, and the engravings thereon; and we know that it is by the grace of God the Father, and our Lord Jesus Chris, that we beheld and bear record that these things are true; and it is marvelous in our eyes; Nevertheless, the voice of the Lord commanded us that we should bear record of it; wherefore, to be obedient unto the commandments of God, we bear testimony of these things.—And we know that if we are faithful in Christ, we shall rid our garments of the blood of all men, and be found spotless before the judgement (sic) seat of Christ, and shall dwell with him eternally in the heavens. And the honor be to the Father, and to the Son, and to the Holy Ghost, which is one God. Amen.

The Testimony of the Three Witnesses: Smith vs Cowdery

The traditional official account of the testimony simply ascribes some details of what was claimed to have been "seen" and "heard." Harris, and especially Smith, provide important details not even alluded to in this testimony, which most probably was composed by Oliver Cowdery and submitted to the printer with the final gathering of ms𝒫. But according to Smith, initially they failed to get the confirmation they sought:

> Upon this our second failure, Martin Harris proposed that he would withdraw himself from us, believing as he expressed himself that his presence was the cause of our not obtaining what we wished for: He accordingly withdrew from us...I now left David and Oliver, and went in pursuit of Martin Harris, who I found at a considerable distance fervently engaged in prayer; he soon told me however that he had not yet prevailed with the Lord, and earnestly requested me, to join him in prayer, that he also might realize the same blessings which we had just received: we accordingly joined in prayer, and ultimately obtained our desires, for before we had yet finished, the same vision was opened to our view; *at least it was again to me* [emphasis added], and I once more beheld, and seen, and heard the same things; whilst at the same moment, Martin Harris cried out, apparently in an ecstasy of Joy 'Tis enough, tis enough; mine eyes have beheld, mine eyes have beheld'."[188]

Harris has given a similar report:

> The prophet was the spokesman. He prayed with no results twice; then I withdrew from them, telling them that it was on my account that their prayer was not answered. After they had been visited by the angel the Prophet then came over to me so that I might have the privilege also...[189]

In a statement to Anthony Metcalf, he reported:

> They all believed that it was because I (Harris) was not good enough, or, in other words, not sufficiently sanctified. I withdrew. As soon as I had gone away, the three others saw the angel and the plates."[190]

Martin's paranoia had set in. Smith responded to the crisis, and went in pursuit. He found Harris kneeling in fervent prayer, and knelt with him. What was said cannot be known. Harris later claimed that "Jo promised

---

[188] Joseph Smith, "History Drafts, 1838–circa 1841", in JSP, Histories I:320.
[189] John E. Godfrey, in Vogel II, 372.
[190] Reported by Anthony Metcalf, in Vogel II, 347.

him a place next to him in the church,"[191] but we do not know if such a promise was made while kneeling in the wood. But we do know that he was informed that his competition, Oliver and David, had had the promised experience, for Smith reported that he "earnestly requested me, to join him in prayer, that he also might realize the same blessings which we had just received."[192]

The seven most important words in Smith's account are: "at least it was again to me."[193] This comment is important on two levels. First, the nature of the experience: if an angel had appeared with the plates, in a material manifestation such that Smith could see them with his corporeal eyes, Harris would have seen them as well. This comment makes sense only if we are talking about vision in the mind's eye, "spiritual vision" or "second sight." Smith could not know what Harris might have seen with his spiritual eyes. Second, and above all, we find here an admission that Harris might not have seen what Smith claimed to have seen.

The Text Attributed to the Eight Witnesses

The experience of the three was described as being a view given them by the power of God and not of man, presumably referring to the role of the angel and the voice of God. A few days later, Smith led eight others into a wood near the home of his parents in Manchester, near Palmyra, NY: John Whitmer, Christian Whitmer, Peter Whitmer, Jr., Jacob Whitmer, Hiram Page (a Whitmer by marriage), Joseph Smith, Sr., Hyrum Smith and Samuel H. Smith. Since Cowdery was a distant cousin of Joseph Smith, Jr., these twelve were all Smiths and Whitmers, with the exception of Martin Harris, the odd man out. The experience of the eight was described as being a view by the mediation of man, i.e. Joseph Smith:

> Be it known unto all nations, kindreds, tongues, and peoples unto whom this work shall come, that Joseph Smith, Jr. the Author and Proprietor of this work, has shewn unto us the plates of which hath been spoken, which have the appearance of gold; and as many of the leaves as the said Smith has translated, we did handle with our hands; and we also saw the engravings thereon, all of which has the appearance of ancient work, and of curious workmanship. And this we bear record, with words of soberness, that the said Smith has shewn unto us, for we have seen and hefted, and know of a surety, that the said Smith has got the plates of which we have spoken. And we give our names unto the

---

[191] W. Alderman, in Vogel II, 295.
[192] Smith, "History Drafts, 1838–circa 1841" (draft 2), in JSP, Histories I:320.
[193] Idem.

> world, to witness unto the world that which we have seen: and we lie not, God bearing witness of it.

It is possible to marshal a number of points to enable us to understand what sort of event underlay this testimony. Stephen Burnett attributed to Martin Harris a statement that the eight witnesses "never saw them and hesitated to sign the instrument...but were persuaded to do so..."[194] LDS visitors to David Whitmer came largely to hear him testify, but also to see what he claimed to be (or actually thought was) ms$\mathcal{O}$ (although it was ms$\mathcal{P}$). Some thought they would see the original signatures. What they found was the text with signatures apparently in Oliver Cowdery's hand. An editorial comment in *Joseph Smith Papers* says, "It is unknown whether the Eight Witnesses signed the original statement, and it is likewise unknown who wrote the statement."[195] Whitmer suggested that they might be on another copy. No way to know.

We might wonder why we have two sets of witnesses. They result from decisions made by Joseph Smith, and for well-considered reasons. Two sets might have been easier to manage, but additionally, only weeks after the expansion of the project team, he was able to create hierarchy, the vision by the power of God being superior to the vision by the power of man.

One can be readily forgiven for thinking that these testimonies were issued to promote the *Book of Mormon*, and in fact, they have appeared prominently displayed as a forward to the BoM text in every edition from the fourth one (1841) on. But not so in the 1830, 1837 and 1840 editions. Even though the events were supposed to have happened in June of 1829, and the first gathering was taken to the printer in mid August, no mention of these testimonies is found up front. Rather, they were tucked in at the end of the book, where many would not even notice them. Clearly, in the first instance, the testimonies had not been drawn up to promote their new bible. Witnesses were indeed promised in the *Book of Mormon*, but Smith decided the content of the promises and their location in the BoM. These events were initiated and orchestrated by Joseph Smith, but to what end?

❀∽❀❀∽❀❀∽❀❀∽❀

---

[194] Stephen Burnett to Lyman E. Johnson, in Vogel II, 291.
[195] "Historical Introduction," in "Appendix 5: Testimony of Eight Witnesses, Late June 1829," in The Joseph Papers, Documents, Vol. 1: July 1828-June 1831 (Salt Lake City: The Church Historian's Press, 2013), 386

< Chapter 8 >

He Who Pays the Piper Doesn't Always Call the Tune

Much of what happened in Harmony, and then Fayette, is inextricably linked to Martin Harris. The faith-promoting effect of his experience with the Characters transcription was wearing a bit thin.

And yet, his statements are contradictory and sometimes vague. He lived with Joseph and Emma Smith in the three-room log home built by Emma's brother Jesse, while assuming scrivener duties for the composition of what has been dubbed the *Book of Lehi*. How could they have worked together without Harris seeing the plates? Some LDS have imagined that they sat with a veil between them. Various accounts indicate that Harris had been claiming some sort of experience with the plates, prior to the loss of the purloined 116 pages. According to David B. Dille, he reported, "did I not at one time hold the plates on my knee an hour-and-a-half...And as many of the plates as Joseph Smith translated I handled with my hands, plate after plate."[196] Joel Tiffany wrote, "I (Harris) hefted the plates many times and should think that they weighed forty or fifty pounds."[197] Contrasting with this, the *Iowa State Register*, reported that he claimed that the plates weighed forty to sixty pounds. [198] Edward Stevenson stated that Martin and his wife had felt the plates under a cover.[199]

In 1829, not long after the February visit of Joseph Smith Sr., Martin arrived, repentant for having lost the 116 purloined pages, and hoping to get back into the prophet's good graces. Joe Jr. had remained suspicious; having not gotten over his suspicions that Martin might have had more to do with the disappearance of the Lehi pages, perhaps being even himself curious to see if his partner could actually replicate the lost text. Despite the foregoing claimed experiences, Edward Stevenson reported that Martin claimed to have tried to trick Smith before, by switching a river stone for the seerstone. "His countenance betrayed him, and the Prophet asked Martin what he had done."[200] In March of 1829, there seems to have been a standoff. His foregoing claims notwithstanding, Martin insisted on

---

[196] David B. Dille, in Vogel II, 297.
[197] Joel Tiffany (1859), in Vogel II, 306.
[198] Iowa State Register, in Vogel II, 330.
[199] Ibid, 332.
[200] Edward Stevenson, in Vogel II, 321.

having a greater witness for the existence of the plates, emboldened by his awareness that the BoM project was a nonstarter without funds from his farm to publish the new bible. The stakes were high on both sides.

Martin Harris: A Man Convinced of His Own Divine Election

Smith had occasionally worked for Harris. But he was more than just a prosperous and respected farmer. He had had his own religious aspirations. Joel Tiffany reported that Harris claimed that he had been revealed to Joseph by God: "[The angel] told him [Joseph] to go and look in the spectacles, and he would show him the man that would assist him. That he did so, and he saw myself, Martin Harris..." Tiffany reported also that Harris said, "I was not with him at the time, but I had a revelation the summer before, that God had a work for me to do."[201] "He [God] showed this to me ["that it was his work, and that it was designed to bring in the fullness of the gospel"] by the still small voice spoken in the soul."[202] John A. Clark remembered him as having "always been a firm believer in dreams and visions, and supernatural appearances..."[203] He has been called a monomaniac. His deep-seated aspiration to have an exalted position in God's plan made him vulnerable to the flattery of those who wished to play him.

Table 8. Life of Martin Harris.

05/18/1783	Harris was born in Easton, NY, to Nathan Harris & Rhoda Lapham.
1808	Married his first cousin, Lucy Harris.
	Served in the 39th Regiment of Orlando County (NY) militia, war of 1812.
	Inherited 150 acres.
Until 1831	He lived in Palmyra NY on his prosperous farm.
Early 1820s	He employed Joseph Smith to work on his farm.
C. 1824?	Reportedly as early as 1824, Joseph Smith told Harris about the gold plates.
1928	Harris took Smith's gold plate transcript to Charles Anthon.
1828	Harris began scrivener duties for Smith.
1828	Harris took 116 pages of Smith's initial transcript to his farm in Palmyra.

---

[201] Joel Tiffany (1859), in Vogel II,, 302.
[202] Ibid, 309-10.
[203] John A. Clark, interviews (1827-28), in Vogel II, 262.

07/1828	Smith issued a revelation branding Harris a wicked man.
03/1829	Smith issued a revelation with a conditional promise for Harris to view the plates.
June/1829	Smith verbally agreed with Grandin to print the BoM with Harris as guarantor.
08/1829	Harris mortgaged his farm with Grandin to cover the printing.
?	Martin & Lucy split up (Martin is accused of wife abuse & adultery?)
04/06/1830	Harris was baptized.
1830?	Harris prophesied that Jackson would be the last U.S. president.
06/03/1831	Martin was made a high priest in the Church of Christ.
02/12/1834	Sydney Rigdon charged Harris before the Kirtland High Council.
02/17/1834	Harris was ordained a member of the Kirtland High Council.
1834	Harris joined Zion's Camp and marched to Clay County, Missouri.
01/11/1836	Harris married Caroline Young (niece of Brigham Young).
1837	Harris joined with Warren Parrish to form a reorganized church.
1837	Excommunication of Martin Harris.
1847-1860	Harris floated from the Strangites, Whitmerites, Gladdenites and Williamites.
1870	Harris, 87, was rebaptized into the LDS Church & resided in Utah.

Smith had approached this from a more aggressive angle. In the summer of 1828 his God declared "even the man in whom you have trusted has sought to destroy you...for this cause I said that he is a wicked man, for he has sought to take away the things wherewith you have been entrusted; and he has also sought to destroy your gift." (D&C 10:1, 6-7). In the following March, God rebuked him: "because I foresee the lying in wait to destroy thee, yea, I foresee that if my servant Martin Harris humbleth not himself and receives a witness from my hand, that he will fall into a transgression." (5:32) Even so, this is paired with a conditional promise that he might be one of three witnesses. He is ordered to testify, "I have seen them, for they have been shown unto me by the power of God and not of man." This two-pronged approach was risky. Smith here promises that there should be three witnesses. About this time, ms𝒰 should have also reached the promise of three witnesses in 2 Nephi 11:3. Perhaps Harris also sought to be restored to his former scribal position. Smith checked this move when the same revelation ordered, "stop, and stand still, until I command thee, and I will provide means whereby thou mayest accomplish the things which I have commanded thee." (D&C 5:34) There was a bit of hubris in his gamble that he could get three witnesses. But he was pushed. *Smith needed that farm*, and Harris needed a greater witness of the plates.

Then There Were Three, Then Four, and More

In the past, the Smith and Harris duo had been a dichotomous partnership. But that would soon change. On 5 April, Oliver Cowdery arrived, the "means" promised in verse 5:34. This could have found its way into Section 5 if, during his visit in February, Joe Sr. had informed his son regarding these means (Cowdery). Almost two months later, with the addition of David Whitmer to fetch Joseph and Oliver to the Whitmer home in Fayette, NY, the visionary quartette emerged, further complicating the interpersonal relations, and setting the stage for many interpersonal developments during years to come.

Riding the cusp of May/June 1829, three men bound for Fayette rode in a two-horse wagon, Joseph Smith, Oliver Cowdery and David Whitmer—determined, and even religious, in their own way. Scornful of the churches of their day, they were imbued with confidence that they had a better knowledge of the gospel, and could establish a new church, which, having the true gospel, would be the true church. For this they had a strategy. They had very little to recommend themselves as harbingers of the millennial star. This would be better done by prophets of old, in a new bible, revealed and translated by the power of God. Yet a dark cloud hung over their trip. All three knew that if the new bible could not be printed, it would be a dead letter. *They needed that farm.*

Translation recommenced immediately upon their arrival. After all, this was ostensibly their reason for being there. But in fact, producing a cleaned up text (ms𝒪) to show prospective printers was paramount. Cowdery wrote the first three pages, as a model, and soon afterward Fayette scribes wrote two or three more. The typesetter John H. Gilbert later wrote that they showed Grandin only a few pages.[204] They were able to estimate the work's length fairly accurately, undoubtedly based on the length of ms𝒰, which was nearly complete

What Harris needed was a greater witness that the gold plates really existed. He would not give his farm to the Smiths, but he would give it to the Lord. To set the stage, a revelation was issued for Oliver Cowdery, David Whitmer and Martin Harris: "you must rely upon my word, which if you do with full purpose of heart, you shall have a view of the plates, and also of the breastplate, the sword of Laban, the Urim and Thummim...[205].

---

[204] John H. Gilbert, Memorandum, in Vogel II, 543.

[205] These relics are not found in the testimony of the three witnesses, and seem to have been added to the original wording of this revelation. The term Urim and

And it is by your faith that you shall obtain a view of them…And after that you have…seen them with your eyes, you shall testify of them, by the power of God…" (D&C 17:1-3) Clearly Harris aspired to a leadership position in this new church, and he had now been informed that for this he would have to be able to testify. Getting a greater witness was no longer just for his satisfaction; it was a vocational requirement. Having thus been informed what he was to see, with his eyes, Harris then accompanied the other members of the foursome into a wood near the Whitmer home. He had been well groomed and perfectly primed for the experience he had sought, and now all depended on his ability to demonstrate worthiness.

As we saw in the previous chapter, even though the importance of these testimonies to the reader of the BoM ultimately became their value, this was not the original intent. Since the promise was introduced in the March revelation for Harris, the three-witness event served to meet his need for a greater witness that the plates actually exist. It also served to weld the leading group together, they being one Smith, one Whitmer, Oliver Cowdery and Martin Harris. The eight-witness event also bolstered Harris' confidence in this major life decision, which was on the verge of costing him his marriage. Some experience supporting Smith's claims was now shared by twelve, including the prophet. The symbolic value of this number cannot have escaped Martin's notice. Here too the family dimension of the composition of these twelve is worth noting: four Smiths and seven Whitmers. Page had married a Whitmer, and Cowdery was a relative of the Smiths, so the team is not much more than two tight-knit visionary families, Harris being the odd man out. Finally, we might bear in mind that although we have other key 1829 documents (Joseph Smith's contract to buy land from Isaac Hale, his copyright certificate, and some correspondence), the important document with the witnesses' signatures is missing. Even if present, would it stand up to scrutiny?

The timing also indicates that Harris was the target for both sets of witnesses. Again, according to Smith's history, they transpired just before and after the trip to Palmyra to get a printer. It was at this crucial point that Smith needed Harris to pony up with a real commitment to cover the cost of printing the *Book of Mormon*. The Smiths and Whitmers were counting on the witness event to bring Harris to the point of religious commitment

---

Thummim was not yet in use in June of 1829; an earlier version may have read "interpreters". See H. Michael Marquardt, *The Joseph Smith Revelations, Text & Commentary* (Salt Lake City: Signature Books, 1999), 49-51.

sufficiently to make the financial commitment. If he did not, their joint enterprise would be stillborn.

With eleven witnesses in tow, Smith proceeded to organize his church (D&C 18). He began by making Oliver Cowdery and David Whitmer apostles. This is significant inasmuch as even the twelve disciples chosen by Jesus in the BoM were not called apostles. He also appointed these two apostles to the task of choosing twelve disciples. At this point, here too, the twelve are not yet called apostles. Martin was not included in this emerging structure. He would have noticed, and still had a tight grip on the purse strings.

The vocabulary that Smith was coining is quite malleable, facilitating the duty to bear witness. "Seeing" could refer to spiritual eyes and second sight. Even hearing the voice of God was finessed.

> These words are not of men nor of man, but of me; wherefore, you shall testify they are of me and not of man;
> For it is my voice which speaketh them unto you; for they are given by my Spirit unto you and by my power you can read them one to another; and save it were by my power you could not have them.
> Wherefore, you can testify that you have heard my voice, and know my words. (D&C 18:34-36)

So, if you can read "these words" by the Spirit of God, you can testify that you have heard the voice of God. This greatly waters down what you and I might understand by this testimony.

Securing the Copyright in Palmyra

Next came three intertwined tasks, getting a printer, getting Martin Harris to commit to standing surety for Smith to the tune of $3,000 for the printing, and securing the BoM copyright. In his *History*, Smith states in a single sentence:

> We went to Palmyra, Wayne County, N. Y: Secured the Copyright; and agreed with Mr. Egbert Grandon [Grandin] to print five thousand Copies, for the sum of three thousand dollars.[206]

Those who doubt Smith's *History*'s claim to accuracy stress that the copyright issued from the District Court in Utica, and that one could not secure a copyright in Palmyra. Actually, Smith is correct. The copyright

---

[206] Smith, *History* (draft 2), 352.

law in force in 1829 provided that the applicant deposit a *printed* copy of the title page in the office of the county clerk. It further required that the clerk keep a book dedicated to the recording of copyrights, and provided the exact wording that the clerk should enter for each one, with blanks to be filled in for the individual case. The fee for this service was 60 cents. This finished the process, but if the applicant wanted a copy, it would be provided on an official form, with the blanks filled in by the clerk. The fee for this was also 60 cents for each copy.[207] So, all Smith had to do was dispatch a printed copy of the BoM title page with his envoy to Utica (Samuel Smith or John Whitmer come to mind). Since he was going to a printer in Palmyra, i.e. Grandin's Print Shop, he could kill two birds with one stone: get his title page printed for the copyright application, and discuss a rather large print job, that of printing his new bible.

The Quest for a Printer

It was time now to see if Martin Harris would come through. Printers were not falling over each other to get the chance to print this heretical new bible. Penniless, low-repute Smith probably would have had trouble getting the business ear of a printer.

Initially, Grandin turned him down. He and Harris then approached Jonathan A. Hadley, editor and proprietor of the *Palmyra Freeman*. He also turned them down, but recommended that they go to the *Enquirer* in Rochester, founded by Thurlow Weed under whom he had apprenticed. After having already recounted a version of Smith's visit, later Weed, "in his autobiography described a multiday interview." On a first visit, Smith came alone. "That Joseph returned with Martin the next day, suggests that despite Weed's self-serving protestations to the contrary, he had not rejected the work out of hand because of his own moral compass; rather, economics drove his decision." Harris was there this time to offer his farm as surety. Weed again declined, possibly because the proposed job was more than his establishment could handle. Also in Rochester, they then visited Elihu F. Marshall, editor of the *Rochester Album*. According to Pomeroy Tucker, he countered Smith's offer with his own terms for the project.[208]

---

[207] Gordon A. Madsen, Jeffrey N. Walker & John W. Welch, *Sustaining the Law, Joseph Smith's Legal Encounters* (Provo, UT: BYU Studies, 2014). The law, 97-98; photos of the printed title page submission, 101; and Smith's copy of the registration, 102.

[208] Pomeroy Tucker, *Origin, Rise and Progress of Mormonism* (New York: D. Appleton and Co., 1867). This is found in Vogel, *Documents*, III, 114.

Marshall showed enough interest to enable Smith and Harris to return to Grandin and say that the work is going to be printed in any case, that they preferred that Grandin do it, and printing in Palmyra would be logistically easier for them and save money. This time Grandin made a verbal agreement to publish. Gerrit J. Dirkmaat and Michael Hubbard MacKay, in a detailed study of how the *Book of Mormon* got printed, estimated that this quest took about a week.[209] If Smith's copyright envoy to Utica left Palmyra on the ninth, Smith might have left Fayette on the eighth. The witness events could have taken place on either June 6 or 6-7, depending on whether the two events were done on the same day, or not.

Although Smith and Cowdery arrived in Fayette with a nearly complete original draft manuscript (ms$\mathcal{U}$), in order to impress Grandin they probably had attempted to complete several pages of ms$\mathcal{O}$ (originally intended to be the printer's copy, and their back-up, needed in view of the theft of the 116 pages). Typesetter John H. Gilbert stated that they showed Grandin only a few pages of the work, and yet they were able to estimate that the work would be about 500 pages, apparently estimating from the length of the nearly complete ms$\mathcal{U}$.

Chronology

Many of David Whitmer's interviews took place when he was quite old, feeble and even on the cusp of meeting his maker. Perhaps this is why his dates tend to be all over the place. But there is one pair of dates that occur twice: "The translation at my father's occupied about one month, that is from June 1 to July 1, 1829."[210] It is not clear when he, Smith and Cowdery arrived in Fayette. Perhaps June 4.[211] After they arrived at Fayette, Smith recommenced translation, and, in spite of having just met them, he issued revelations for three Whitmers, David, John and Peter Jr. According to David, the visit of the angel was "shortly before the completion of the translation when there were but a few pages left."[212] On another occasion he is reported to have said that he saw the angel "after the translation was

[209] Gerrit J. Dirkmaat & Michael Hubbard MacKay, "Joseph Smith's Negotiations to Publish the *Book of Mormon*," in Dennis Largey, Andrew H. Hedges, John Hilton III & Kerry Hull, eds., *The Coming Forth of the Book of Mormon* (Salt Lake City: Deseret Book, 2015).

[210] David Whitmer, to the *Kansas City Journal*, 5 June 1881. See Vogel V, 76.

[211] See Dan Vogel, "Appendix B: Chronology, 1771-1831," Vogel V:417.

[212] Whitmer in the George Q. Cannon interview, in Cook, ed., *Whitmer Interviews*, 108

completed."[213] In the revelation prior to the "view," it is said, "he has translated the book, even that part which I have commanded him." (v. 2) He also reported that the eight-witness event followed the next day or the day after.[214] The witness events were preceded by D&C 17, and followed by D&C 18. This latter was quoted in a letter from Cowdery to Hyrum Smith dated June 14, making these events June 13 at the latest. The printed title-page submission must have been dispatched from Palmyra no later than early on June 9, so Smith's departure from Fayette can be no later than June 8. It is at this time that the translation was either drawing to a close, or finished, which agrees with Whitmer's timing of the angelic visitation. This means too that Oliver and David were called apostles, and assigned to seek out the Twelve Disciples, no later than June 13. Most of the important events of June 1829 happened in the first two weeks, including the completion of the BoM (ms$\mathcal{U}$). They either have their own firm dates, or are dated in relationship to those that do.

It may seem odd that the Whitmers would be favored to experience a view of the plates so soon after their first encounter with Smith. This, plus the fact that there is no evidence that they were grilled re their worthiness in any way comparable to the treatment of Harris, implies that they had been prequalified, having been recruited to the project by Joseph Smith Sr. and Oliver. Smith clearly timed the witness events as early as possible for the benefit of Martin Harris, to enable him to decide that he had received a greater witness, and would therefore be ready to commit a major part of his farm assets to the printing of the *Book of Mormon*. Smith needed him at his side to give verbal agreement to act as surety to cover Smith's obligation. Smith's history is correct in both detail and sequence. The witness events occurred early on, as prerequisites to the simultaneous occurrence of the quest for a printer, and the performance needed by Joseph Smith to get the copyright, this latter being to get the text professionally printed, most probably at Grandin press, to accompany the application.

Grandin's Circumspect Printing of the BoM Copyright Text

The copyright law further specified that the author should "cause a copy of the said record to be published in one or more of the newspapers printed in the United States for the space of four weeks." The validity of the

---

[213] Whitmer to the *Chicago Tribune*, in Cook, ed., *Whitmer Interviews*, 175.
[214] Whitmer, Interview to Orson Pratt & Joseph F. Smith (Deseret News: 1878), 40.

copyright depended on this being done, although it seems that it was often neglected, partially or wholly.[215] A notice published by Grandin in his *Wayne Sentinel* issue of June 26 has been taken to be a notice that he would be publishing the *Book of Mormon*. Actually, there is no wording in it that states any such intention. Referring to the "gold bible," he states that "Most people entertain an idea that the whole matter is the result of a gross imposition and a grosser superstition. It is pretended that it will be published as soon as the translation is completed." This is followed by the title page text, of which he states "we give it as a curiosity." Its appearance in this notice is probably the result of Smith's effort to comply with the publication requirement. Stuck in Fayette, Smith probably delegated the task of getting this notice into the paper to Martin Harris, a person well known to Grandin. The way this latter crafted the notice, as well as the language used, betrays some concern that his identification with the new bible could negatively influence his readership.

Promulgating the Gospel of the *Book of Mormon*

After the witness events, Smith "continued to translate at intervals, when not necessitated to the numerous enquiries, that now began to visit us; some for the sake of finding the truth, others for the purpose of putting hard questions…whilst at the same time, we were enabled to convince the honest of heart…so that almost daily we administered the ordinance of Baptism…"[216] For his own part, Whitmer said that, "We had preaching during the time that the book was being translated…"[217] With ms$\mathcal{U}$ completed, Whitmer may have thought that ms$\mathcal{O}$ was the original ms (rather than ms$\mathcal{U}$); later he was in possession of ms$\mathcal{P}$ but thought that it was ms$\mathcal{O}$. Without close examination, all of the gatherings looked alike. On the other hand, the Fayette scribes may have known that they were helping to prepare a copy (ms$\mathcal{O}$) for publication. Additionally, although Smith considered the completion of ms$\mathcal{U}$ to be the completion of the BoM, copying it into ms$\mathcal{O}$ was their last opportunity to make changes. In this sense only, the translation continued in the form of making these improvements.

---

[215] Wadsworth, "Securing the *Book of Mormon* Copyright," 105.
[216] Smith, *History*, 325-26.
[217] David Whitmer, Kansas City Journal, in Cook, ed., Whitmer *Interviews*, 65.

The Enforcer on High

God was increasingly available to Smith as whip and salve. His initial revelatory reaction to the loss of the purloined pages had Him not only brand Harris "a wicked man"," but ascribe to him diabolical motives, asserting that he had acted as a willful enemy of the restoration prophet. In March, "my servant Martin Harris has desired a witness at my hand," to which Smith's God replied, "except he...acknowledge unto me the things that he has done which are wrong...he shall have no such views." (D&C 5:1, 28) On some level, Martin knew he could play this game. If he did not get his greater witness, he did indeed have the power to destroy. He could return to his wife and retain his farm. Possibly Smith was suspecting that it was in league with his wife that Harris was throwing down the gauntlet: "If you want my farm to print your bible, now is the time to prove your gift." And yet, the ability to testify to the existence of the plates was a vocational prerequisite to realize his aspirations. His calling (obligation) would be to testify: "Behold, I have seen the things which the Lord hath shown unto Joseph Smith, Jun., and I know of a surety that they are true, for I have seen them, for they have been shown unto me by the power of God and not of man." (D&C 5:25)

When Martin showed up in Harmony in March of 1829, Smith may have had mixed feelings. Still angry and not trusting, he saw that he would have a second chance to get the farm. The fact that Martin had undertaken the long journey to Harmony indicated a psychological vulnerability due to his conviction that he had received a divine calling to play a major roll in preparing the Second Coming. Had he not been led to Smith and the bringing forth of the new bible? If he proved unworthy, would he not suffer a terrible punishment? Not only was he not permitted to resume scrivener duties, but also it was intimated that a competitor was poised to enter upon the stage.

We can picture this scene of August 25, 1829. A very glum, and yet resolute Martin Harris. Joseph Smith Jr., a local scryer, former treasure seeker, but now, in essence, recipient of most of his former employer's farm on behalf of God. And Egbert B. Grandin, a surprisingly young publisher, anxious to get to the business at hand. The legal work was ready, and the papers drawn up for signatures. Smith had contracted with Grandin to print 5,000 copies for a consideration of $3,000 dollars, a debt that was to be secured by Harris mortgaging his farm to Grandin. This arrangement allowed the farm to remain in the possession of Harris, who had the option of paying off the mortgage, if he could.

Harris was loath to lose his family farm. The contract stated that Grandin could auction the property if the debt was not paid by February 25, 1830. At some point Harris tried in vain to get a second mortgage for $1,300 on his property from the New York Life Insurance and Trust Company, presumably to forestall foreclosure. Grandin had still not been paid by March. Harris demanded that Smith give him a commandment.

In previous revelations Harris had been called a wicked man, a person who had already sought to destroy Smith and his work, and who might yet do so. At this time, the Enforcer on High clearly had lost patience with this recalcitrant servant. In D&C 19 (vs. 2, 3, & 5), March of 1830, Smith's revelation was more explicit than ever:

> I command you to repent, repent, lest I smite you by the rod of my mouth, and by my wrath, and by my anger, and your sufferings be sore:
>
> > how sore you know not!
> > How exquisite you know not!
> > Yea, how hard to bear ye know not!
>
> Thou shalt not covet thine own property, but impart it freely to the printing of the *Book of Mormon*,
>
> And misery thou shalt receive, if thou wilt slight these counsels; yea, even destruction of thyself and property. Impart a portion of thy property; yea, even part of thy lands and all save the support of thy family. Pay the debt thou hast contracted with the printer.

Over the course of his life, and after his excommunication, Harris' statements became erratic. According to the *Era*, Seventy, High Priest and Bishop William Waddoups reported that Harris said "I saw the angel of the Lord…saw the plates and the Urim and Thummim and the sword of Laban, and with these ears…I heard the voice of the angel, and with these hands…I handled the plates…"[218] By contrast, Anthony Metcalf attributed a different statement to him: "I never saw the golden plates, only in a visionary or entranced state."[219] And Grandin's printer John H. Gilbert asked, "Martin, did you see those plates with your naked eyes? Martin looked down for an instant, raised his eyes up, and said, 'No, I saw them with a spiritual eye.'"[220]

---

[218] William Waddoups, in Vogel II, 335.

[219] Anthony Metcalf, in Vogel II, 346.

[220] John H. Gilbert, in Vogel II, 548.

In the end, Harris was ruined. In his old age, a collection was taken up to bring him destitute to Utah. When he arrived, he found that his Kirtland wife, Caroline, had remarried without the nicety of a divorce from Martin, this being perhaps the only case of Mormon polyandry. W. Alderman reported, "Martin said that he furnished the means, and Jo promised him a place next to him in the church. 'When they had got all my property, they set me out'."[221]

Joseph Smith was able to use the witness events and promises of leadership positions in his new church to pressure Harris to sacrifice his ancestral farm to pay for the publication of the *Book of Moron*, and to accept the duty to bear testimony to promote missionary work. Already by September 1831, the doctrine linking tithing to exaltation in the hereafter continued the cash flow to build the kingdom. "Behold…verily it is a day of sacrifice, and a day for the tithing of my people; for he that is tithed shall not be burned at his coming." (64:23) The importance of the LDS Law of Sacrifice to the work of the Lord and its link to individual salvation is the

Sacrifice & Testimony Issue

─────────────

[221] W. Alderman, in Vogel II, 295.

< Chapter 9 >

Ms𝒪: The Highly Complex Minimally Edited "Original"

In summer of 1828, after the loss of the purloined 116 pages, Smith issued some verses of a revelation in which Martin was called a wicked man (D&C 10:1). After returning to Harmony, without Harris' funding due to the rupture in their relations, he had no choice but to focus on the seasonal farming. An idea of the agricultural season can be had from the record of Smith's work for his brother-in-law David Hale: threshing buckwheat and plowing in October, husking corn in November; work in December; and chopping wood in January and March. (See p. 392) For the period October 1828 through March 1829, this totaled only eight days of paid labor. Heavy snow was characteristic in Susquehanna County, beginning in December, limiting what farming was possible. Supplemented with occasional loads of basic provisions and money for paper brought by Joseph Knight Sr. by sleigh, once winter set in, Smith would have had the time to start over to produce the text that would become the *Book of Mormon*.

Would the Real Original Manuscript Please Stand Up?

The identification of the original manuscript is clouded by two facts. First, the gatherings (manuscript signatures) looked the same without close inspection and sufficient knowledge. David Whitmer must have known that scribes were writing for Joseph, at least occasionally, for most of June. But although he was later actually in possession of ms𝒫, the printer's copy of ms𝒪, he erroneously believed that it was ms𝒪 itself. Second, during his visit to David Whitmer in Richmond, MO, in 1885, James Henry Moyle sought to see what Whitmer claimed to be the original manuscript of the *Book of Mormon*. He wrote that Joseph Fielding Smith Sr. had advised him that, "it was not the original, but one of the three originals."[222] So there were three?

Evidence presented in chapter ten will show overwhelmingly that ms𝒪 is itself a copy of ms𝒰, the urtext of the *Book of Mormon*. But since there is evidence that some editing was done even in the process of this

---

[222] "James Henry Moyle Interview," 28 June 1885, Richmond, MO, *Conference Reports,* April 1930, in Lyndon W. Cook, ed., *David Whitmer Interviews: A Restoration Witness* (Orem, UT: Grandin Book Co.:1991), 161.

copying, msΟ can still be considered to be the original of the text that appeared in print in the 1830 first edition of the *Book of Mormon*.

The Move to Harmony: Ms𝒰 Is Begun

Having issued some verses of a revelation in which Martin was called a wicked man (D&C 10:1), clearly there had developed a rupture in relations between Joseph Smith and Martin Harris. Without Harris' funding, Smith had no choice but to return to Harmony and work his farm. According to his friend and former employer, Joseph Knight Sr., by the first of winter he had gotten back to work "translating". [223] Before this visit to Knight, Smith had already begun what would become ms𝒰.

Prior to the arrival of Oliver Cowdery on April 5, some writing was done for him by his wife Emma and his brother Samuel Harrison Smith. [224] This rough beginning point agrees with Emma's account that at some point Joseph queried, "Emma, did Jerusalem have walls around it?" When she answered, "Yes," he replied "Oh! I was afraid I had been deceived." [225] This corresponds perfectly with 1 Nephi 4:4. Another view suggests that it might also refer to a presumed similar phrase that could have existed in the nonextant *Book of Lehi*. In view of the fact that the BoM emphasizes that Lehi and Nephi were very different in content, there is no reason to believe that this was the case, while the Nephi passage clearly does exist. Going further into the ms𝒰 timeline, note that the timing works well for 3 Nephi to correspond to Smith and Cowdery's baptism.

The issue of the *terminus ad quem* for ms𝒰 is obfuscated by vagaries in the historical records. David Whitmer's dates for the event of the three witnesses range, from just June, to early June, mid June and late June. In a report in the Richmond Democrat in Richmond, MO, it was stated to have been shortly after his return to Fayette, after getting Smith and Cowdery from Harmony. [226] Moreover, the visit of the angel was "shortly before the completion of the translation when there were but a few pages left." [227]

---

[223] Joseph Knight Sr., "Reminiscence," c. 1835-1847, in Vogel IV: 19.

[224] "Joseph Smith History, 1832," in Vogel I:31.

[225] Emma Smith, as quoted in Edmund C. Briggs, "A Visit to Nauvoo in 1856," *Journal of History* 9 (January 1916): 454, in Vogel, I:530–31

[226] "Richmond Democrat Report," in the Richmond Democrat (26/01/1888), Richmond, MO) in Cook, 229.

[227] Whitmer, George Q. Cannon interview, in Cook, ed., *Whitmer Interviews*, 108.

Furthermore, in his 1838 History, Joseph Smith stated, "Mean time our translation drawing to a close, we went to Palmyra...Secured the Copyright and agreed with Mr Egbert Grandon (sic) to print..." [draft 2]. However, in an alternate text we read, "Having finished the translation we went to Palmyra..." [draft 3].[228] Linking the quest for a publisher to the quest for a copyright has been considered to be a *lapsus memoriae* on Smith's part, quite simply because the registration of copyrights was in the office of the Clerk of the District Court at Utica, *and not Palmyra*.[229] Not so fast. The copyright law at the time required four steps: 1) draft the title page of the book; 2) *get the title page text printed*; 3) deposit the printed copy in the office of the Clerk, and 4) pay the fee. Smith would have drafted the text in Fayette, and in the interest of efficiency, he would have gotten it printed by Grandin during his printing negotiations. At this point Smith's burgeoning staff gave him *l'embarras du choix* of candidates to take the three-day trip to deposit the printed text in Clerk R. R. Lansing's office and pay the fee. So, quite accurately, Smith went to Palmyra to secure his copyright, just as he wrote. The important observation here is the impact on the timeline. Smith's copy of the copyright issuance is dated June 11. Smith must have gotten the title page printed no later than June 8. This is also the latest date for his statement, "Mean time our translation drawing to a close," or "Having finished the translation," depending on which draft one chooses.

The second documented date is June 14, the date of a letter from Oliver Cowdery to Hyrum Smith, which quotes from D&C 18, which follows the witness events, thereby enabling us to fix the limit for their occurrence.

The third date that is oft cited is June 26. The next task was to start getting the title page printed in one or more newspapers, in compliance with the copyright law. Smith was busy in Fayette, and since Harris was on good terms with Grandin, the announcement on this date probably came about after some persistent urging from Smith's former scribe. Some have stated that this is an announcement by Grandin in his *Wayne Sentinel* that he

---

[228] Joseph Smith, JSP, Histories I, "History Drafts, 1838-circa 1841", 352-53.

[229] Smith's registration was signed by R[ichard] R. Lansing, Clerk of the District, Court of the United States for the Northern District of New-York, on June 11. A copy, and detailed study, is in "Securing the *Book of Mormon* Copyright," by Nathaniel Hinckley Wadsworth, in Gordon A. Madsen, Jeffrey N Walker and John W. Welch, *Sustaining the Law. Joseph Smith's Legal Encounters* (Provo, UT: BYU Studies, 2014), 93-112.

would be publishing the new bible. It merely states that *it is claimed* that it will be published as soon as it is finished. Still, this statement is of interest. Typesetter Gilbert, wrote that "A few pages of the manuscript were submitted as a specimen of the whole..."[230] These few pages were probably the cleanest they had, i.e. the first few pages of ms𝒪 (hot off the quill), sporting single-digit page numbers. In order to give convincing reassurance for his estimate of the size of the work, Smith must have made mention of the nearly or recently completed urtext manuscript. We do not know the interval between Smith's visit to Palmyra and Harris's urging, or between that and the date of the publication of this issue of the Wayne Sentinel.

It seems probable that the text of ms𝒰, from Nephi through Mormon, was completed prior to the copyright issuance.

The Mode of Composition

One secular view is that Joseph Smith had amazing mental abilities and was able to dictate the "original" BoM (ms𝒪) text mostly off the top of his head, hour after hour, day after day. This view might not tax one's credulity quite so much if the new bible were a relatively small and straightforward work. But as we can see in the vignette *infra*, it is not only large but also highly complex (at least 22 separate subject matter areas). These items were not done in isolation one from the others, but were woven together into a collage of the Nephite narrative. It is obvious that no one can have dictated ms𝒪 extemporaneously. When Smith made Cowdery a cotranslator (i.e. coauthor), however briefly, he was simply acknowledging the reality of the level of collaboration to research, plan, draft and edit their work.

Vignette | Interwoven *Book of Mormon* Complexity

1. complex storylines, especially the story of getting the Brass Plates, and those found in the missionary and military campaigns;
2. a comprehensive list of recordkeepers, and a complex set of interrelated accounts, records and plates (v. Figure 21 p 447);
3. the development of a complex and extensive onomasticon of proper names, mostly composed by recombining invented pseudo name components;

---

[230] John H. Gilbert, "Memorandum, made by John H. Gilbert Esq., Sep. 8th, 1892, Palmyra, N.Y." This can be found in Vogel, II/543.

4. a complex coinage system;

5. four major KJV inclusions, including one consisting of thirteen highly edited chapters of Isaiah, plus the Sermon on the Mount;

6. Composition of well over a hundred variant readings to rework the texts of these inclusions to comport with the view that they are corrected versions of corrupted Biblical passages.

7. theological commentary on the KJV inclusions;

8. numerous Biblical paraphrases worked into the BoM text

9. a researched and studied roundup of scriptures interpreted to show that some OT prophets knew about the Nephites and that a new bible would come forth;

10. various apologetic arguments in anticipation to opposition to the Book of Mormon (i.e. the BoM in defense of itself);

11. a theory of the Great Apostasy in the Old World, its replication following the nearly two Christian centuries in the New World, and a harsh condemnation of the churches and the Jews of Smith's day;

12. theological disputes with "strawman" anti-Christs to argue against atheism and for a consistent BoM theology;

13. explanation and examination of theological concepts, such as the first and second resurrections; the fall of man; the condescension of Christ; blood atonement; anthropomorphism of God; the infinite sacrifice; the fallacy of infant baptism; OT predictions of the Messiah as shadows or types; and defense of adherence to the law of Moses even while teaching that it has no saving power; plan of redemption, etc.

14. a complex geography, with at least forty cities, that is internally consistent throughout the complexities of the storylines, and a useful and explicit key to BoM geography (in Alma 22);

15. scores of post-Biblical Euro-Christian phrases, drawn from Christian hymns and sermons, and seamlessly integrated into the Nephite narrative;

16. a complex chronology, with regularly reported dates in years after leaving Jerusalem (ALJ dates), years of the judges, years since the sign of the birth of Jesus up to his coming to the Nephites, and years after the birth of Jesus (i.e. CE dates);

17. a continuous diatribe against secret societies;

18. continuously repetitious demonstrations that wickedness is the source of curses and famines:

19. descriptions of military fortification modeled after that used in the revolutionary war (picket walls, berms, ditches, stone walls, watch towers);

20. description of two trips from the eastern hemisphere to the Americas, each with a different type of vessel, including a surface-submarine vessel;

21. scientific explanations to show that ancient prophets knew that the world is round, that it is solid all the way through (to refute hollow earth theories of the followers of John Cleves Symmes) and that the solar system is heliocentric.

22. developing family genealogies, including a list of begats in the Book of Ether, followed by histories corresponding to them.

Ms𝒪 Edits

Regarding the textual criticism that we are about to undertake, there are two basic types of copy errors in terms of how and when they were done. If an error was noticed as soon as it was made, then it was crossed out (with a *linethrough*) and a correction was written immediately after the error, on the same line: *inline edits*. If an error, or a need for improvement, was noticed during proofreading, then there was no alternative to writing the correction above the line: *supralinear edits*. These may be either just an addition, or paired with a deletion (a linethrough) of a word or words in the text already written. The manuscript uses a caret (∧) to indicate where the supralinear text should be inserted. For large insertions, a text on a sheet of notepaper could be pinned to the page where it is to be inserted. This was done in the *Book of Moses* manuscript, but not in ms𝒪.

A *simple linethrough deletion*, with no replacement text, is ambiguous from this perspective. It could have been done immediately after writing the error, as an inline edit, or during proofreading. This is true also of *compound edits* with the correction written over an erasure.

In addition, and by far the largest type numerically, is the myriad *spelling errors*, which are of no import to our current query. All other edits make a substantive, albeit most usually an insignificant change.

These edits in ms𝒪 have been gathered and garnered in Table 9, *infra*.

A look at a few examples of analysis are here used to broach our topic. A simple addition inserted supralinearly is "of the mysteries **of God** wherefore.."[62/3/19/1] Bolding is used to indicate a supralinear addition. Almost certainly it was Oliver Cowdery who added "Of God" during proofreading, above the line, as there was no space on the line of the text. Another example is "blessed art thou **Nephi** because of.." These complete the meaning, without adding much new meaning. But, such an insertion can provide a word that had been dropped in the dictation-writing process, such as "that I may **write** of the things."[81/9/32/1] One of the two longest insertions is "easier to keep the city from falling into the hands of the Lamanites **than to retake it from them**.."[468/354/20/15] This clause is understood without being physically present, but Cowdery rightly judged that it would be better to make it explicit.

Another long supralinear insertion was rethought, and deleted: "not of the ~~Carnal mind but of the spiritual~~ **~~temporal but of the spiritual~~** *temporal but of the spiritual* not of the carnal mind but of God."[320/293'/24/13] An initial six-word deletion was replaced supralinearly by five words. This too was deleted.

> **Note**: the cases discussed in analysis as in the foregoing examples are not repeated in the tables *infra*. The superscript numbers are explained in table 9a.

We usually find a bit more change in meaning when supralinear insertions replace text deleted. Here is a rare case of name confusion: "people of ~~Ameleck~~ **Ammon**"[394/321'/15/14] ["Ameleck" = "Ameleckiah"]. Other cases are somewhat less clear. For example, we find "engraven **upon my** [plates] *upon the plates of Brass*."[159/43/30/2] The italics indicate text added inline. In this case the supralinear text, was intended only to replace "*upon the*," yielding "upon my plates of brass." A similar case is: "take the sword ~~of~~ **or** the simetar to smite"[274/274'/19/13] where "of" may have been dictated under the influence of the very common phrase "sword of Laban." A substantive change can be seen in "those who **fled** ~~were~~ with him,"[388/319'/5/14] where "fled" was added during proofreading, and the linethrough as well.

A case where the error was corrected during dictation is: "which can not ~~to~~ be written."[93/13/40/1] Smith, or Cowdery, or both must have realized instantly that one cannot say "can not to be." In some cases it is not possible to know what was originally intended, as in: "come against the city of Judea ~~of~~ *or* against us to Battle."[443/344/26/15] Perhaps this is just a "typo." A less unclear case is "to be hold ~~to~~ the things which,"[101/16/5/1] where "be hold" was possibly meant to be read "behold," ('behold the things') and "to" was suggested by 'hold to' [the rod of iron?]. An edit made by way of textual improvement is "did ~~give~~ *offer* ~~thank~~ *sacrifice* and offer burnt offerings",[87/11/25/1] where not only is "give" changed to "offer", but presumably an original "thank offering" was changed to "sacrifice." An edit that makes a substantive change is "they called the name of the city ~~Nephi~~ *Moroni*".[408/328/3/15] This *lapsus linguae* would not be the last time for Smith. In his 1838 history, he dictated Angel Nephi instead of Angel Moroni, an error that was corrected by B. H. Roberts. It is clear that Nephi fascinated him; note that there are four books of Nephi, and three recordkeepers. Another name confusion is, "across the River ~~Lemuel~~ *Laman*"[133/30/36/2]

Some corrections were made in ms𝒫 rather than in ms𝒪. A curious blend is observed in "in everl etern glory"[325/295/6/13] ["everlasting" and "eternal" are blended together albeit in two words, whereas ms𝒫 deletes both, yielding "in glory." Occasionally an edit corrects a statement that is impossible in terms of the BoM narrative: "he gave all the land"[381/316`/32/14] was not corrected in ms𝒪, but the BoM reads: "he named all the land."

Others are KJV-BoM Isaiah variants: "~~how should I~~ **I will not** suffer my name to be polluted"[154/21] (Isaiah 48:11). It is interesting to note that one could change one's mind and abort a KJV-BoM variant: "be delivered ~~beca[use]~~ *for* I will..."[159/24] (Isaiah 49:25).

Table 9. The tables below attempt to be exhaustive for MsO Edits by type.

A. Ms𝒪 Proofreading Edits

Bold = supralinear insertion added during proofreading
   A = Skousen's page number   B = msO page number
   C = line number   D = gathering number
	A	B	C	D

running into **the fountain of** all righteousness	62	3	19	1
bring them down **hither** into	65	4	10	1
not required **it** of them	65	4	12	1
the lot **fell** upon Laman	66	4	28	1
after this manner **of language** did My father	78	8	22	1
ware desirous to **return** unto the land	83	10	14	1
that **when** I nephi had spoken	85	10	47	1
most high **God** wherefore	101	16	14	1
the children **of men** wherefore	104	17	12	1
after that he was baptised **of** I beheld	105	17	30	1
pride of the world **& it fell** and the fall thereof	107	18	16	1
apostels of the **lamb** and behold	107	18	21	1
I shall minister **unto** them which shall be plain	121	22	51	1
& its **numbers** were few	122	25	4	2
our father meaneth concerning **the grafting** in of the natural branches	127	27	22	2
the brightness of **a flaming** fire which	130	29	15	2
if their **works** have been filthiness	131	29	29	2
the kingdom **of god** is not filthy	131	29	33	2
that **after** I Nephi had made an end	132	30	5	2
we knew **that** ye could not construct a ship	139	33	37	2
against the true and living **God** & it came to pass that	141	34	32	2
brought with us every **one** according to	146	37	1	2
that they should **do** after that I was gone	150	39	5	2
which were **written** in the Books	153	40	29	2
called by the name of Israel **& are** come forth [Isaiah 48:1]	154	41	1	2
they that swallow**ed** thee up [Isaiah 49:19]	158	43	10	2
shall again in thine ears **say** the place is to strait [Isaiah 49:20]	158	43	12	2
& his burden **depart** from off the shoulders	188	79	36	4
whether they will **that ye shall** come into their land	270	273`	11	13
pure above all **that is pure** & ye shall feast upon	307	287`	19	13
if ye have read these scriptures **if ye have** how can ye disbelieve	309	288`	16	12
will atone for **the sins of** another	312	289`	33	13

I **cried within my heart** O Jesus thou Son of God	323	294`	19	13
I say unto you **my Son** that	323	294`	23	13
& **amon** abominations [among]	330	297`	11	13
the pole which had on the end thereof **his rent coat** & he called it	381	316`	22	14
when Moroni ad proclamed these words **behold** the people came	382	317	8	14
Brethren **in the land** Northward	383	317`	15	14
fearing that he should not gain the point **he** took these of his people	385	318`	5	14
to angar agaist them & **cause them to** come down to Battle	385	318`	10	14
which was composed of the **Lamanites & the** Lemuelites	395	321`	34	14
& now behold **it came to pass** that	403	325`	24	15
by the holy **order** of God	405	326`	34	15
did bring forth unto them **therefore they** did seek to cut	407	327`	35	15
year of the Reign **of the Judges** & it came to pass	409	328`	29	15
year of the Reign **of the Judges** ended in peace	409	328`	29	15
in the **commencement of the** twenty and fourth year	409	328`	31	15
came to pass that there **were** four thousand	415	331`	34	15
Reign of the Judges over the People **of Nephi they** having established	412	330`	13	15
year of the Reign **of the Judges** that Teancum	421	334`	27	15
towards the **land** of Bountiful	421	334`	29	15
your own land **or the lands** of your possessions which is in the land	432	339`	21	15
upon **you** yea even to your utter destructio	432	339`	29	15
with my **two** thousand against the Lamanites	447	346`	30	15
the city **Cumeni** & now	450	348`	4	15
twenty ninth **year** in the latter end	464	353`	14	15
in the **commencement of the** Reign of the Judges	483	364`	10	15
& it bringeth to pass	503	398`	18	15

B. Inline Edits with Deletion Replaced by Supralinear Addition

Strikethrough = deletion Bold = Supralinear Addition	A	B	C	D
we had ~~come~~ **gone** to the land of Jerusalem	66	4	25	1
after that **the angel** ~~he~~ had spoken	69	5	41	1
according to my faith which is in ~~me~~ **thee** wilt thou	86	11	2	1
and it ~~we~~ **was** like	102	16	23	1
the vapor of ~~the earth~~ **darkness** that it	109	18	44	1
& smitten ~~him~~ *them* by the hand of the gentiles	120	22	37	1
the ~~great~~ **plain** and most precious parts of the gospel	120	22	24	1
believing that ye shall ~~believe their~~ **receive with** diligence in keeping	126	27	15	2
wherefore ~~it~~ **there** must needs be a place of filthyness	131	29	34	2
at that time ~~which~~ **when** I made them	149	38	29	2
wherefore ~~we~~ *it* must needs be	153	40	22	2
~~how should I~~ **I will not** suffer my name to be polluted [Isaiah 48:11]	154	41	21	2

in as much as ye will not **keep** ~~his~~ **my commandments** ye shall be	169	48	4	2
at that time ~~will~~ the day **will** com that	190	81	34	4
to him whom the Nation abhoreth ~~for~~ **to** servant of rulers [Isaiah 49:7]	157	42	23	2
according to the time which ~~he~~ **they** laboured	212	225`	13	11
their seed should cause many to ~~suffer~~ **be put to** death	258	268`	19	13
& ~~I then~~ **by then** did establish His Church	280	276`	15	13
I would that ye ~~would~~ **should** remember that God is merciful	302	285`	29	13
when thou liest down at night lie down ~~with~~ **unto** the Lord	333	298`	16	13
did cry out unto the Lord Jesus Christ for mercy ~~& I~~ did **I** I receive	337	299`	35	13
& if ~~his~~ **their** works are evil	349	304`	5	13
be restored to ~~its~~ **their** proper order	349	304`	6	13
if they should ~~go~~ **fall** into the hands of	360	308`	4	14
all things should be restored to ~~its~~ **their** proper order	348	303`	35	13
foundation ~~or~~ *of* liberty	380	316`	14	14
which had **desented** ~~from~~ which were call Ameleckiahites	385	318`	1	14
came down with his men & ~~to~~ surropund the men of Amelickiah	392	32	16	14
peace among the People **of Nephi** ~~were it not for~~ had it not been for	409	328	32	15
of our men ~~of~~ **for** which we have to mourn	442	344`	9	15
a disappointment ~~of~~ **by** being repulsed	417	332`	33	15
orders ~~to have~~ **that** my men	453	349`	16	15
of the ~~forth~~ **fortyeth year of the** Reign of the Judges	487	365`	26	15

C. Simple Deletion Edits

Strikethrough = deletion	A	B	C	D
ye shall prosper ~~in~~ & shall be lead to a land of promise	64	3	47	1
flee ye from the Chaldeans ~~without~~ a voice of singing [Isaiah 48:20]	156	42	1	2
it is by me that ye are lead ~~unto~~ *yea* & the Lord said also	139	33	23	2
promising that he would covenant ~~with~~ & also his people with them	372	313`	16	14
he wrote an epistle & sent it ~~to~~ by the servant of Ammoron	431	339`	13	15
lay down your arms & ~~be~~ subject yourselves	435	340`	20	15

D. Deletion Followed by a Correction or Overwritten

Italics = inline change Strikethrough = deletion	A	B	C	D
one with another ~~I~~ *we* cast lots	66	4	27	1
wisdom ~~of~~ *in* God that we should obtain these records	68	5	2	1
desired ~~his~~ *him* that he would give unto us the records	68	5	18	1
I saw ~~then~~ *that* the blade	71	6	21	1
did ~~give~~ *offer* ~~thank~~ *sacrifice* and offer burnt offerings	87	11	25	1
the space ~~for~~ *of* meny hours	88	11	44	1

many were lost from ~~My view~~/*his view*	92	13	16	1
had ~~to fall in their~~ *fallen away* and	93	13	22	1
and ~~this~~thus it is	95	14	9	1
carried away in the spirit ~~a time~~ *for a space of time*	104	17	4	1
and he ~~said~~ spake unto me	105	17	43	1
shewd ~~it unto them~~himself unto them	109	18	48	1
that the name & apostle of the lamb ["&" is "of the" in ms$\mathcal{P}$ & BoM]	124	26	15	2
the way whither ~~they~~ *we* should go	133	30	31	2
across the River ~~Lemuel~~*Laman*	133	30	36	2
it is the power of the Lord that hath shaken ~~me~~ *us*	145	36	22	2
where ~~had~~ have they been [Isaiah 49:21]	158	43	15	2
be delivered ~~beca~~[use] *for* I will [Isaiah 49:25; BoM variant aborted]	159	43	24	2
for the time speadily shall come ~~which are~~ that all churches	163	45	26	2
the ~~word voice~~ *voice* of Nephi	170	48	34	2
now Amulek ~~saith~~ said	216	227	18	11
let us go down & ~~say~~ *rely* upon the mercies of our Brethren	268	272`	32	13
mercies of ~~the~~ *our* Brethren	268	272`	32	13
land of ~~Nehi~~ *Nephi* [simple spelling error? Or influence from Lehi?]	271	273`	22	13
those which ~~are~~ *were* in favor of the words	317	292`	12	13
may be m ~~anifest~~ ade manifest [be made manifest]	330	287`	9	13
put your trust ~~G~~ in God	336	299`	26	13
the minds of ~~him ch~~ their children	342	301`	23	13
the spirit of the ~~Lord~~ *Devil* did enter into them	344	302`	28	13
upon them ~~so th~~ thus they remain [aborted: "so thus"? or "so that"?]	345	302`	32	13
according to his desires ~~to~~ *of*good	349	304`	11	13
he has desired to do evil all the ~~N~~ *day* long even so ["Night" aborted]	349	304`	12	13
partook of the ~~forbi~~ *forbidden fruit* tree of life	353	305`	15	13
plan of ~~sal~~ *redemption* "plan of salvation" > "plan of redemption"	353	305`	29	13
would he ~~fear~~*be afraid* he should die	355	306`	13	13
& only let ~~thine~~ *your* sins trouble you	356	306`	35	13
& also ~~their~~ *they* were	361	308`	23	14
& his ~~soldiers~~*men* & they were driven	365	310`	12	14
began to fall ~~to~~*upon* them	366	310`	16	14
if ~~Moro~~*they* would spare the remainder of their lives	372	313`	17	14
& came to ~~his~~ *their* houses	372	313`	26	14
would not ~~list~~ *hearken* to the words of Helaman ["list-", "listen"]	378	315`	25	14
~~the many~~ the P~~ow~~*reaching* of Helaman [P|ow from Pow(er)?]	379	315`	35	14
would not ~~forget~~*sake* the Lord [*forsake*]	382	317`	10	14
had supposed ~~by the~~because of the greatness of their numbers	401	324`	24	15
they called the name of the city ~~Nephi~~ *Moroni* [NOTE: Smith, in his 1838 history, called the Angel Moroni Nephi, correct by B. H. Roberts]	408	328`	3	15
there w~~er~~*ould* also have been [were > would]	409	328`	31	15
they were exceding fearful ~~of~~ lest ~~he~~ the army of Moroni	410	329`	8	15
had ~~cov~~ *sworn* or covenanted [original "cov" was to be "covenanted"]	413	330`	29	15
& ~~this us~~ *thus* ended	418	333`	15	15
should maintain ~~these~~*those* Cities	419	333`	26	15
concerning the ~~dead~~ *death* of his Brother	421	334`	17	15
among the ~~Lamaniters~~ *Nephites*	427	337	28	15

there was not a woman ~~or~~ *nor* a child	431	339`	10	15
but he sayeth unto ~~him~~ *them* fear not	437	341`	22	15
now ~~wher~~ *whether* they were over taken ["where" > "whether"]	446	346`	16	15
for many ~~da~~ *nights* ["da" + "days"]	450	348`	8	15
could not come upon us by ~~many~~ *night* & slay us	450	348`	9	15
to the ~~city of Zara~~ *land of Zarahemla*	451	348`	16	15
all those ~~that~~ *who* opposed them	452	349`	6	15
the words ~~th~~ *which* they said unto me ["th" beginning of "that"]	452	349`	10	15
~~w~~ *they* were driven back ["we" changed to "they", or "th" misread?]	452	349`	13	15
they began ~~preparations~~ *to make preparations* to come	459	351	28	15
that ~~remainder of~~ *the remainder* of [insertion of "the"]	467	354`	16	15
head o[f] ~~thei~~ *his* numerous host ["their" changed to "his"]	492	367`	6	15
nor on the East nor on the ~~N~~ *West*	494	368`	9	15
``he feared lest that ~~the~~ *he* should be	496	369`	10	15
your ~~selves~~ *women* shall	505	399`	21	15
the devil which is in him ~~they could~~ *we can* not hit him with our stones	509	401`	19	15
put it unto ~~his~~ *the* heart of Akish	534	462`	22	15
leading ~~him~~ *them* away by fair promises	534	462`	23	15
Akish reigned in ~~the~~ *his* stead	535	463`	17	15

Most of these are one or two words long, and virtually all for clarification or text improvement. There is none that can be said to make a substantive change in the story line or theology. Some were made immediately before moving on, and the scribe made all others during proofreading, which was usually done after the completion of each page (although nothing could prevent Cowdery from making additional edits while copying ms𝒪 into ms𝒫). It was intended to be a cleaned up copy of ms𝒰. This is the

Ms𝒪 Condition Issue

< Chapter 10 >

Evidence for Copying the *BoM* Urtext (Ms*U*) into Ms*O*

Manuscript copying is far from a straightforward process. There are many pitfalls that provide traces of their victims. Errors provide evidence, as do corrections. Both the materials used, and the skills required to use them, tend to engender characteristic errors.

The Mode of Writing

All of the BoM manuscripts were written with a quill pen. Quills are the flight feathers of a bird. They were gathered annually when the birds molt. Initially, they are simply raw material, from which is made a quill pen. Although the quills of specific birds were used for different purposes or effects, goose quills were especially prized and common. Some were an item of commerce. In 1818 the *Kentucky Gazette* advertised "A few Thousand Superior Irish Quills"[231] A writing master in a large school might require thousands. To be used as a pen, a quill must first be cured. Then the writing end must be cut in a correct shape, and slit up the middle, much like the nib of a fountain pen. But the shape and slit must be done properly in order to promote the capillary action for ink flow. From time to time, this tip, or nib, must be reshaped and sharpened. Trimming was needed more frequently if one was using wood pulp paper, which was sufficiently abrasive that its introduction from 1800 to 1850 promoted the early development of steel pens that could hold up to this rough paper. In New England in the 1820s rag paper was probably still the paper in use. A new pen, or a newly sharpened quill, or a newly inked one, had to be tested to be sure it wrote properly. For this purpose, one used a scrap of the same paper one intended to write on. For quill sharpening, it was necessary to have a penknife, and a hone to keep it razor sharp. Special penknives were used to make the curves of the nib. In France a device was invented to guide the cutting of the quill. James Fenimore Cooper used this device.[232] Scribes might cut their own quills, but professionals also offered the service.

---

[231] Joe Nickell, *Pen, Ink & Evidence, A Study of Writing and Writing Materials for the Penman, Collector and Document Detective* (Lexington: The University of Kentucky, 1990), 3. See this work for this section.
[232] Nickel, 7. For pens, see 9-15 & 197. For paper, see 74-79 & 201.

Ink was another issue. It was possible to buy liquid ink in a sealed bottle, which could be used in a pinch as an inkwell. It was cheaper to mix up powdered ink. After all, how many empty ink bottles do you need? The most popular type was iron gall ink. There were various recipes. A scrivener would have an inkwell, or an inkstand with a built-in inkwell and penholder. It would be useful to have one with a stopper; if left unsealed overnight or during a period of inactivity, the ink would thicken due to evaporation. After use, it was essential to clean the quill nib carefully so that ink did not dry on it, especially in its slit.

Inkblots were a perennial problem, whether due to a spill, a poorly made or badly worn nib, excessive pressure, or dragging the nib over the paper, thus making an unwanted stroke. Solutions existed. One literal solution was a bleaching liquid. Several recipes existed. If the ink was dry, there was a special ink eraser knife. Alternatively, there were abrasive compounds, such as pounce, made from powdered cuttlefish bone. If the ink was still wet, one could use a blotter. Large desk blotters were used for a newly written whole page to soak up ink that had not yet dried. Drying took time since the ink was water-based. Rocker blotters were used, often for one's signature. An anecdote has it that FDR refused to use a blotter on his signature because blotting resulted in a less sharp pen stroke. When a large number of documents were ready for his signature, each one was placed on a flat surface to dry, papering his entire office. He jokingly referred to it as his laundry.[233]

Finally, there were a number of styles of cursive letters, which were often formed in ways different from today. New England was peppered with schools of various sizes and formats to teach penmanship. There was a keen competition between these schools, and various instructional methodologies. In some cases, the writing masters were self-taught entrepreneurs. We do not know how much formal training of this sort Smith's scribes had. Moreover, since it seems clear that Smith actually could write, perhaps his need for a scribe stemmed from his inexperience and lack of training with the quill. Or due to myopia?

There are many cases of erasures in Skousen's edition of ms𝒪, and in most cases he was able determine the original character, even when written over by another. It is difficult to make changes that cannot be detected (although Skousen used alternate light sources).

---

[233] Ibid, 59.

Corrections Due to Errors Reading Ms𝒰

Textual criticism has been actively engaged in studying Biblical, Classical and other ancient texts for centuries. Over these many years, a number of standard text copy errors have been observed and studied. They may result in text addition, text loss, or text doubling. They often result from the eye looking aside (*parablepsis*) and then returning to a wrong place in the manuscript being copied. These include 1) word skipping, such as *homeoarchy* (an eye skip forward or back due to words or phrases having the same beginning), and *homeoteleuton* (where the scribe resumed writing but skipped because of the similarity of the endings of two words or lines). If undetected, these result in a loss of text. In the case of ms𝒪, we can only know that it has occurred when the error was detected and corrected. *It is the corrections in ms 𝒪 that provide direct evidence of ms 𝒰* 2) Other errors result in text addition (word, character or phrase doubling; *dittography*). 3) There are various errors that result in text confusion, as in metathesis (reversing the order of two elements, characters or words), confusion of two sounds (usually consonants), and 4) homonym exchange or blends.

Word skipping.

In these cases, Smith, reading from ms𝒰, looked aside from the ms being copied, and when returning to it, he resumed at the wrong place, thereby reading text that he had not yet gotten to. Usually he skipped ahead. *We only know of these errors because Smith, Cowdery or both noticed and corrected them in ms 𝒪.* By contrast, an extemporaneous composer would not be able to skip ahead to a future point that he had not even spoken.

Table 10. Ms𝒪 Word Skipping

with ~~des~~ the bosom of destruction (188:32)
    eye skipped to "destruction", read "des", deleted it, wrote "the..."
yea ~~to d~~ how quick to do iniquity (380:8)
    eye skipped to "to do" & read "to d", delete "to d" & resumed
they became ~~more im~~ more heardened & impenitent (396:3-4)
    eye skipped to "impenitent" & read "im"; "more im" was deleted
fight valiantly ~~fre or~~ for their freedom (416:8)
    eye skipped to "freedom" & read "fre"; corrected & resumed
to the city beyond ~~shore~~ on the boders by the Sea Shore (445:22)
    eye skipped to "Shore" & read "shore": corrected & resumed

to maintain the city ~~Antipar~~ but he did not march until I had gone forth with my little army & came near the City Antiparah (445:25-26)
>   *eye skipped* to "Antiparah", & read "Antipar". The phrase "but he" overwrote "Antipar" and the words, nearly omitted, were written before writing "Antiparah"

Prophets of old ~~concerning~~ all things concerning them (152:21)
>   *eye skipped* to "concerning" & wrote "concerning": word aborted

the vapor of ~~the earth~~ *darkness* that it past from the face of the earth (109:44)
>   *eye skipped* to "of the earth" reading it rather than "darkness"

—In some cases, the eye might skip back.—

the God of Abraham & of Isaac & the God of ~~Isa~~ Jacob (151:26)
>   *eye skipped* back to "of Isaac", read "Isa", deleted it, wrote "Jacob"

your crimes to harrow up your ~~er~~ Soul (340:34)
>   *Eye skipped* back to "crimes"; repeated "cr"; deleted & resumed

like unto them ~~e~~ all save it be a few which shall be called (375:26)
>   *Eye skipped* to "called"; wrote & deleted "c"; & resumed.

Note that in these cases, a temporary dittography happens, but is corrected. Numerous other occurrences are presented in Table 11.

Table 11. Errors from Eye Skipping

Skousen Page #: msⵔ p.	gath- ering no.	Cases in Skousen's Notation / Analysis
63:26 3	1	because of the ~~fl~~ oolish
		eye skipped to "lish" & read "l"; "o" overwrote "l": "fl" > "foolish"
68:22 5	1	that it ~~exeee~~ was exceeding great
		eye skipped ahead to "exceeding" missing "was"
77:19 8	1	A land ~~pr~~ *of* promise
		eye skipped ahead to promise, read "pr"; "of" overwrote "pr"
78:35 8	1	that they ~~re~~ did rejoice
		eye skipped to "rejoice", read "re" & "d" overwrote "re": "re" > "did"
80:5 9	1	also ~~d~~ was a desendant
		eye skipped to "desendant" & read "d"; "w" overwrote "d": "d" > "was"
96:34 14	1	prophet which should come before the masiah ~~whi~~ to prepare
		eye skipped back to "which"; read & deleted "whi": > "to prepare"
116:2 21	1	the gentiles which ~~g~~ had gone out
		eye skipped to "gone"; read "g" & "h" overwrote "g": "g" > "had gone"
130:13 29	2	Justice of God ~~als~~ did also divide
		eye skipped to "also"; read "als"; "did" overwrote "als": > "did also"
137:21	2	thought to make himself a ~~Ru~~ King & a ruler

32		eye skipped to "ruler" & read "Ru"; "K" overwrote "Ru": > "King"
137:23-24	2	came ~~unto~~ & did speak many words unto them
32		eye skipped to & read "unto"; 1st "unto" deleted
141:28	2	they being lead the Lead their God
34		eye skipped back to "lead"; read "Lead": it is "Lord" in BoM
152:21	2	Prophets of old ~~concerning~~ all all things concerning them
40		eye skipped to "concerning" & wrote "com/ncerning": word aborted
157:25	2	thus saith ~~Lo~~ the Lord
42		eye skipped to "Lord"; read "Lo"; & "the" overwrote "Lo"
166:11	2	they shall dwindle in unbelief ~~they~~ after that they hav received
47		eye skipped to "they" [have received]; read & deleted "they"
116:20	1	unto the gentiles & the ~~gen~~ Angel of the Lord
21		eye skipped backto "gentile"; read "gen" & "Angel" overwrote "gen"
120:40	1	the most plain & ~~pre~~ most p{r}ecious parts
22		eye skipped to "precious"; wrote "pre"; "pre" > "most precious"
131:38	2	wherefore the final ~~fi~~ state
29		eye skipped back to "final"& read "fi"; "st" overwrote "fi": > "state"
135:39	2	go ~~u~~ forth up into the top of the mountain
31		eye skipped to up, read "u", deleted it, and proceeded with "forth"
136:1	2	I did slay ~~bea~~ wild beasts
32		eye skipped to "beasts", read "bea", & deleted it
149:37	2	the things wrer **which** were written
38		eye skipped to "written" & read "wr"; & skipped to "were" & read "er"; the word was aborted & "which" was inserted: "wrer" > "which"
164:9	2	to ~~e~~ the commandments
46		eye skipped to "commandments" & read "c"; "t" overwrote "c": > "the"
172:28	3	hedge not up ~~wa~~ my way
		eye skipped ahead to "way", picked up "w", deleted it, picked up "a", replaced it with "m"+"y"
242:5	18	not lay their hands on Ammon or Aaron or Omner or ~~the~~ Himni nor neither of their brethren
		possibly eye skipped to "their" to enounce "their brethren", picked up "the" (to write "their"), overwrote "the" with "Himni..."
261:20	18	that they are ~~w~~ not wasted
		eye skipped to "w" in "wasted", overwrote it with "n", wrote "ot"
277:19	18	& {<%P%>|t}he Power
		eye skipped to "Power"; "P" was written, deleted, overwritten by "t"
279:4	18	all the ends ~~ea of~~ of the earth
		eye skipped to "earth", wrote "ea" of "earth", overwrote it with "of"
288:27	18	~~if A~~ Alma sayeth unto him if ye deny
		eye skipped ahead to "if ye deny"; wrote "if"; skipped back to "Alma"; wrote "A"; deleted "if A"; "Alma sayeth..." was written
297:32	18	which ~~e~~ shall come
		eye skipped to "come" & read "c"; "c" is written & deleted
302:20	18	we shall ~~s~~ know of a surety
		eye skipped to "surety"? "s" was enounced; "k" overwrote "s": "know"
322:12	18	that I could be b ~~ish~~ anished
		eye skipped to "ished" of "banished"; "ani" overwrote "ish": "banished"

323:29	18	& s̶t̶ I stood
		eye skipped to "st" in stood, omitting "I"; "st" deleted: "I stood"
326:30	18	s̶ by small & simple things
		eye skipped to "simple" & enounced "s"; "b" overwrote "s": "by"
326:35	18	it hath b̶e̶ hitherto been
		eye skipped to "been"; enounced "be"; deleted "be"
336:31	18	destruction P̶ among his People
		eye skipped over to see "P" in "People"; "P" was written & deleted
341:9	18	by any f̶o̶o̶l̶ vain or foolish thing
		eye skipped to "foolish"; enounced "fool"; replaced by "vain"
369:5	18	seek not your l̶i̶v̶ blood
		eye skipped to l{e|i}{v}es; wrote "liv"; deleted; & wrote "blood"
369:11	18	delivered up his S̶i̶m̶ sword & his Simetar
		eye skipped to Simetar & enounced "Sim"; "sword" overwrote it
370:18	18	believe that it y̶ is your cunning
		eye skipped to "your" & enounced "y"; "is" overwrote "y": > "is"
370:24	18	that ye will r̶e̶ not return
		eye skipped to "return" and picked up "re" as part of "n"/"r" confusion: "ret" > "not"
372:27	18	year of r̶e̶ the Reign
		eye skipped to "Reign"; read "re"; "th" overwrote "re": > "the"
372:28	18	which w̶r̶o̶ was wrote
		eye skipped to "wrote"; read "wro"; "wa" overwrote "wro": > "was"
372:31	18	which c̶e̶p̶ he} kept
		eye skipped to "kept" & read "cep"; "he" overwrote "cep": "cep" > "he"
375:26	18	like unto them e̶ all save it be a few which shall be called
		eye skipped to "called"; writes & deletes "c": > "all"
380:8	18	yea t̶o̶-d̶ how quick to do iniquity
		eye skipped to "to do" & read "to d", deleted : > "to do"
382:12	18	name of Christ the C̶ Lord
		eye skipped back to "Christ"; read "C"; "L" overwrote "C": "Lord"
383:22	18	as a remnant y̲ of Joseph yea let
		eye skipped to "yea" & read "y"; "y" deleted: > "of"
383:26	18	by the hands g̶ of God
		eye skipped to "God" & read "g"; "o" overwrote "g": > "of"
387:29	18	& o̶r̶d̶ & Helaman & the high Priests did also maintain order
		eye skipped to "order", read it; it was deleted: "o̶r̶d̶"
388:6	18	which we̶n̶t̶ re with him & went up into the land
		eye skipped to "went", read it; "r" overwrote "nt": > **were**
389:25	18	to be a king & a leader over b̶e̶i̶n̶g̶ them being fixed
		DITTOGRAPHY: eye skipped to "being"; read it; "them" overwrote 1st "b̶e̶i̶n̶g̶"
391:12	18	in the t̶ nighttime
		eye skipped to "time"; read "t"; "nighttime" overwrote "t": "nighttime"
392:14	18	would h̶ make him
		eye skipped to "him" & read "h"; "m" overwrote "h": "hake" > "make"
395:26	18	that same s̶e̶ Ameleckiah too that same servant

		eye skipped to "same servant" & read "same se" which was deleted: BoM: "came to pass that Amaleckiyah took the same servant"
396:3-4	18	they became ~~more im~~ more heardened & impenitent
		eye skipped to "impenitent" & read "im"; "more im" was deleted
397:21	18	it came ~~p~~ to pass
		eye skipped to "pass" & read "p"; "to" overwrote "p": "p" > "to"
397:25	18	unto the Lord their ~~L~~ God
		eye skipped back to "Lord" & read "L"; "G" overwrote "L": "God"
402:11	18	towards the ~~N~~ land of Noah
		eye skipped to "Noah" & read "N"; "l" overwrote "N": "Nand" > "land"
410:14	18	& ~~ea~~ it came to pass
		eye skipped to "came" & read "ca"; "it" overwrote "ca": "ca" > "it"
413:31	18	the ~~P~~ voice of the People
		eye skipped to "People" & read "P"; "v" overwrote "P": "P" > "voice"
421:30	18	assist Teancum with his ~~in re~~ men in retaking
		eye skipped to "in retaking" & read "in re"; "men" overwrote "in re"
423:26	18	persueing them ~~ivng~~ in vane
		eye skipped to "in vane", read "i" but missed "n", mistook "e" for "g"; & read "ivng": "ivng" > "in vane"
439:22	18	should fight ~~N~~ with the Nephites
		eye skipped to "Nephites"; read "N" ; "w" overwrote "N": "~~Nᵂ~~ > "with"
443:23	18	which I brought with m ~~y~~ e yea the Sons of mine
		eye skipped to "yea" & read "y" making "my"; "e" overwrote "y": "me"
445:25-26	18	to maintain the city ~~Antipar~~ but he did not march until I had gone forth with my little army & came near the City Antiparah
		eye skipped to "Antiparah", & read "Antipar". "but he" overwrote "Antipar" and the words nearly omitted were written before writing "Antiparah"
450:2	18	we had also ~~als~~ plenty of
		eye skipped back to "also" & read "als"; "p" overwrote "als"
451:32	18	to ~~the~~ go down to the land of
		eye skipped to "to the" [land...]; "to go" overwrote "to the"
455:2	18	behold ~~arm~~ the armies of the) Lamanites
		eye skipped to "armies" & read "arm"; "the" overwrote "arm": "the"
455:11	18	that we might <pre> assist our Brethren in preserving
		eye skipped to "preserve" & read "pre"; > "ass[ist]" overwrote "pre">
480:3	19	he had been a man which ~~v~~ had fought valiantly
		eye skipped to "valiantly"; read "v"; "h" overwrote "v": > "had"
486:14	19	Alma & ~~S~~ Helam}n his Son
		eye skipped to "Son" and read "S"; "H" overwrote "S"
490:25	19	with swords & ~~s~~ with simeters
		eye skipped to "simeters" & read "s"; "w" overwrote "s": "s" > "with"
492:18	19	to go forth a ~~ll~~ gainst all the land
		eye skipped to "all" & read "ll"; "g" overwrote "ll": "against all the"
493:19	19	in the ~~C~~ land of Zarahenla...[ ]...the City of Bountiful
		eye skipped to "City of Bountiful" [line 20] & read "C"; "l" overwrote "C": initially intended "C[ity] of Zarahemla" > "land of Zarahemla"
494:6	19	that it {c|b}ecame

		eye skipped to Coriantumr (line 7) & read "c"; "b" overwrote "c": "cecame" > "became"
496:8	19	this band of ~~see~~ robers & secret murderers
		eye skipped to "secret" & read "sec"; "rob" overwrote "sec": "robers & secret murderers
501:23	20	Son of God ~~re~~ , to [re]edeem
		eye skipped to "redeem", read "re" & deleted "re": "to redeem"
525:2'	22	shall ~~be~~ stand before God to be judged
		eye skipped to "be judged" & read "be"; "be" was deleted: "shall stand"
534:25'	23	is a most abominable ~~ab~~ & wicked above all
		eye skipped to "above" & read "ab"; "ab" deleted; "abominable &
549:20'	23	to avenge himself upon ~~the b~~ Coriantumr of the blood of
		eye skipped th "the blood..." & read "the b[lood]"; "the b" was deleted

Dittography

We know of them because they were detected & corrected in ms$O$.

Table 12. Dittography in MsO.

ishmael and his wife ~~and his Wife~~ and (83:12)
the Nephites greatly ~~feared that~~ feared that (292:32)
if ye keep not his ~~presence~~ commandments ye shall be cut off from his presence (328:18)
was the cov~~eove~~ ennant which they (382:12)
he did place the greater **num ber of men** number of men (397:30)
yea & they ~~& they~~ did obey (452:8)
that we ~~we~~ went (duplication of "we" in "went; 68:13)
came through out of ~~out of~~ captivity (71:1)
and also his **hole** hole. [Possibly it was initially to be "his whole household" so that "whole" & "hold" were written "hole hole", or "house" became "hole" & "hold" became "hole". Note that ms$P$ has "his household insomuch..." (83:6)
the river of water ~~of water~~ ~~of water~~ a great (91:48; *sic*: three times)
the same yester **to** ~~day and~~ to day and for Ever (99:34)
the land the land of promise (*sic*: no deletion; 108:23)
<u>because of the exceeding great length of the war</u> between the Nephites & the Lamanites many had become hardened <u>because of the exceeding great length of the war</u> (480:13; both are retained in the BoM).

Be/To + Infinitive

Throughout our ms$O$ error analyses, the ultimate question is: "Is this something that most probably an extemporaneous text composer would have spoken right off the top of his head, or more probably an error arising from a reader struggling to read a text that was badly written due to being worked over too much, and to an accumulation of deletions and overwriting by persons with inadequate quill competency?" A good example is the "be"/"to" error.

Table 13. Erroneous Use of "Be", Corrected to "To"

he will cause them ~~be~~ *to* **too be** ~~n~~ scattered[167:20-21]
did serve ~~be~~ *to* strengthen (260:2)
things ~~be~~ *to* come (260:4)
according ~~be~~ *to* their prayers (260:7)
suffered themselves ~~be~~-to be slain (268:18)
compeled ~~be~~-*to* be humble (301:15)
cast our garments at they feet ~~be~~ *to* be trodden under (383:16)
as the king came out ~~be~~ to meet him (393:33)
worn them to flee or ~~be~~ *to* prepare for war (398:13)
should have power ~~be~~-*to* harass them (420:6)
marched with the remainder ~~be~~ *to* meet the Lamanites (423:31)
and it came ~~be~~ *to* pass(423:32)
had been left ~~be~~ *to* protect (423:35)
were compeled ~~be~~ *to* behold (429:15)
promises ~~be~~ to do whatsoever (534:23)

Introducing an infinitive with the infinitive of "be" is just not done, and is not something that an extemporaneous speaker (or any speaker) would do. Alternatively, the preposition "to" can be mistaken for "be" in writing. It may have been written over a poor deletion, or with a nib in sore need of being trimmed, or with ink of improper consistency. Furthermore, the "t" may not have been crossed. There is a reason for the expression, "Dot your i's and cross your t's." Skousen has special notation to indicate that a "t" is not crossed: t(-†). If the "t" is not crossed, and its hook at the bottom is too generous, the result will look like a "b". Smith was puzzled and decided to try to sound out the word. When Smith enounced "b", Cowdery heard "be". Smith recognized that the next word was an infinitive, and then enounced "to". Cowdery deleted "be" with a strikethrough, wrote "to", and moved on. As we see from the list above, this was not an altogether rare event.

Compare these with a similar case, where "to" was the added element rather than "be": "which can not <u>to</u> be written."[93/13/40/1]

Consonant Pair Errors

There are many cases where a word requires one consonant but is written with a different one. The following table provides a census with each word pair found, and a nearly exhaustive number of times that it occurs. They can appear in either order (e.g. "d"/"b" or "b"/"d"). An example is "that laban ~~whon~~ *whom* I had slew" (74:13). Alternately, we have "An oath ~~Umto~~ *Unto* us". (76:53) Both of these cases are unlikely from the mouth of an extemporaneous speaker. So did the scribe just hear wrong? Or are "n" and "m" written in such a way, and so badly, that a reader can easily confuse them. Note that the "n"/"m" pair is by far the most common.

Table 14. Ms𝒪 Consonant Pair Errors

"d"/"b":1	"g"/"j":8	"l"/"I":1	"n /"v" :1	"t"/"c/k" :1	"v"/"w":3
"d"/"g":1	"g"/"p":1	"l"/"r":8	"n"/"w" :1	"t"/"d" :42	"v"/ "s":1
"d"/"r":7	"h"/"b":4	"m"/"b":3	"p"/"b" :1	"t"/"f" :5	"w"/ "b":1
"f"/"b":10	"h"/"f"2	"m"/"r"3	"p"/"r" :1	"t"/"h":16	"w"/ "r":1
"f"/"d":1	"j"/"g":3	"m"/"w":2	"p"/"t" :1	"t"/"l":2	"w"/ "t":1
"f"/"p":24	"k"/"f":1	"n"/"d":2	"p"/"y":1	"t"/"r":4	"y"/"g" :2
"f'[ph]/"p":1	"k"/"g":1	"n"/"l":4	"r"/"b":1	"to"/"th":1	"y"/"h" :4
"f"/"r":5	"k"/"h":8	"n"/"m":**148**	"s"/ "d":1	"th"/"w":1	"y"/"j" :4
"f"/"s":1	"l"/"b":3	"n"/"r":**128**	"s"/"h":2	"u"/"w":1	"y"/"r" :1
"f"/"v":2	"l"/"d":5	"n"/"s":5	"s"/"r":10	"u"/"y":1	"&"/"h" :1
"f"/"w":1	"l"/"f":5	"n"/"t":4	"t"/"b":1	"v"/"r":17	"rd"/"nt" :1

Cases where it is improbable that we are dealing with errors from similar sounds include:n/r, k/h, d/b, d/g, f/d, f/r, h/b, k/f, l/b, l/f, l/I, n/s, n/t, n/v, n/w, p/r, p/y, r/b, s/h, t/b, t/f, t/h, t/l, to/th, v/r, v/s, w/r, w/t, y/g, &/h.

The Improbables

Some cases are just too improbable. Note: "to stand before ~~gor~~ *god* to be judged". (131:28) Hopefully we are not going to be judged by "gor". Although not quite in the same category, note too: "a second Prophet of ~~Gold~~ *Old*". (310:21) Capital "O" may have looked like capital "G". These cases are inline, i.e. the error is immediately followed by the correction, and then work resumes immediately after that, all on the main writing line (hence inline). Such immediate resumption is only possible if the error and its correction have already been resolved. Other improbables are:

Table 15. Copying Errors That Produced Improbable Readings

that the ~~bord~~ *lord* t̶ hath commanded (78:28)
My Brethren ~~toof~~ *took* our journey (66:23)
they have ~~regected~~ *rejected* the words(67:51)
& went ~~porth~~ *forth* towards (71:12)
I should ~~hill~~ *kill* Laban (72:23)
he would not ~~kearken~~ *hearken* unto (72:29; cf. 129:33)
and now ~~mephi~~ *nephi* being (83:15)
ye did thrust in the ~~riekle~~ *Sickle* (261:18)
strait and ~~marrogh~~ *narrogh* path (90:27)
is one ~~eternal~~ *etermal* round (99:41)
against the ~~afostels~~ *apostels* of (107:6)
I saw a ~~wist~~ *mist* (108:33)
I know ~~mot~~ *not* (116:9; cf. 350:19, 430:17 , 435:17, 449:28)
will ~~rot~~ *not* this strengthen (304:20; cf. 315:17, 497:29)
the Gospel of the ~~Land~~ *Lord* of whom (117:25; cf. 210:6, 499:1)
to stand before ~~gor~~ *god* to be judged. (131:28)
prophets of ~~oll~~ *old* (152:20)
the prophet ~~Isaiak~~ *Isaiah* (153:31)
& ~~ore~~ *one* shepherd (163:37)
this ~~lard~~ *land* unto me (165:29; 292:29, 441:23)
all the ~~lant~~ *land* (364:22; cf. 386:28, 432:2)
the ~~frophets~~ *prophets* (96:28)
words of the ~~anger~~ *angel* (150:19; cf. 279:4)
belong to the ~~Hingdom~~ *Kingdom* of the devil (163:30)
written ~~ror~~ *nor* (206:1)
their ~~paith~~ *faith* (307:26)
& ~~mone~~ *none* could deliver them (320:18)
one Eternal ~~rount~~ *round* (328:15)
from the ~~fourdation~~ *foundation* of the world (356:28)
of your ~~Chiep~~ *Chief* (371:1)
the day of ~~Mephi~~ Nephi (409:27)
Reign **of the ~~gudges~~ *Judges*** also ended in peace (409:29; cf. 431:2, 449:32)
Reign of the Judges ~~ofer~~ *over* the people
& the ~~freefom~~ *freedom* of the People (412:6)
swoarn to ~~dring~~ *drink* the Blood (414:6, cf. 437:34)
of a ~~numler~~ *number* of their Cities (427:30)
& themselves from ~~bongage~~ *bondage* (430:24)
now ~~dehold~~ *behold* (439:24)
it came to pass that ~~wher~~ *when* he had fortified the city (439:29)
now we were not ~~supficiently~~ *sufficiently* strong (446:5)
that our forces were sufpicient [sufficient; uncorrected] (449:25)
in to our ~~hards~~ *hands* (449:31)
plenty of ~~Prorisiors~~ *Provisions* (450:2)
who did ~~meet~~ ***beat*** the Lamanites (452:13)
which had ~~beer~~ *been* (534:17')
and ~~he~~ *be* kept (326:25)

In all of these, the issue is whether an extemporaneous composer would speak the first, uncorrected word. Unlikely. The errors must be down to Smith's difficulty in attempting to read a manuscript that had been worked over many times and with poor, occasionally messy quill work.

The Unpronounceables

Some copying errors produced sound combinations that depart greatly from the norms in the English language, and some that are nigh unto impossible to be pronounced, at least for denizens of Planet Earth, except perhaps for rare persons capable of remarkable oral-cavity acrobatics. The cases listed in Table 10. Are not vocables that we would expect from someone composing a new bible by way of spontaneous or even extemporaneous dictation to a scribe. We are told that when Smith was narrating an unusual Nephite or Lamanite name, he would spell it.[234] It is probable too that when he was puzzling over a messy word, he would sound it out, letter by letter, a practice of those learning to read. An example is: "thou ~~mi g h~~ *mightest*". (62:18) Cowdery began recording Smith's spelling, treating each letter as a possibility. Suddenly he saw what it was, deleted the spelling, and wrote "mightest." He did not complete the letters he had already written to spell "mightest," probably because they were not written in appropriate cursive. The unpronounceables could have been entered into ms𝒪 in the same manner.

Table 16. Copying Errors That Are Virtually Unpronounceable

I did join my ~~two~~ *two* (442:5)
Akish ~~Reigred~~ *Reigned* (535:17)
we could ~~preserse~~ *preserve* the commandments (80:18)
swallowed ~~uy~~ *up* (298:9)
& they ~~nhall~~ *shall* be brought (161:30)
meaning of the ~~Booh~~ *Book* (116:8)
lost from ~~My   view~~ *his wiew* (92:16)
rod of ~~Iron~~ *iron* (129:3)
according to thr ~~hruth~~ *truth* (132:9)
reckords wpon [*upon*] my plates (174:25; uncorrected)
all these ~~thimgs~~ *things* (273:4)
to ~~gudesgue judesgue~~ (302:35; total phrase was aborted)
led ~~bj~~ *by* a man (364:33, cf. 366:24)
was ~~apfoint~~ *appoint*[ed] (419:23)
Helaman was ~~appoirted~~ *appointed* to fill (495:19)

---

[234] David Whitmer, in the "E. C. Briggs/Rudolph Etzenhouser Interview," 1884, in Cook, 128.

The analysis of a comprehensive list of ms𝒪 edits has shown that there is no edit that introduced substantive change, although some did improve the text, usually in minor ways. It stands in marked contrast with the manuscripts of the *Book of Moses*. A comprehensive list of the many complexities in the BoM reveals a work that could not be composed by extemporaneous dictation to scribes.

There are numerous eye-skips. Composing by extemporaneous narration is unable to skip to a similar word in a text that has not even been composed.

The various types of reading error corrections produce results totally congruent with the eye skip results. Serious whole-word dittographies are unlikely in extemporaneous composition. Introducing an infinitive by preceding it with the infinitive "to be" just does not happen in English, and yet ms𝒪 features fifteen cases, obviously caused by the confusion of "t" wit "b" in ms𝒰. Ms𝒪 has at least sixty-six consonant pairs that give rise to errors. Many of the results are highly unlikely, almost to the point of impossibility. Others are very nearly unpronounceable. These arise from misreading very obscure quillwork, not mistakes on the part of extemporaneous composition, which requires that the words can at least be articulated.

These copy errors and their corrections provide overwhelming evidence that ms𝒪 is a copy of an urtext of the *Book of Mormon*. Many of the errors actually contain bits of text from ms𝒰.

Moreover, these copy errors occur in substantial numbers throughout the extant part of ms𝒪, showing that ms𝒰 had been done for the entire BoM.

So, then there were three: ms𝒰, ms𝒪 and ms𝒫. This is the

Ms𝒪 Redaction Issue.

< Chapter 11 >

Archaeology: New England in Pre-Columbian America

Once the *Book of Mormon* has gotten Israelites into their land of promise in the New World, it proceeds to give an account that includes details of their material culture. These provide ample opportunities for empirical investigation.

Archaeology: Quest for the Nephites

In the nineteenth century, what developed into the school of Higher Criticism undertook to find and apply rational and scientific methods for the study of history, and perhaps especially of the Bible, with seminal works by Julius Wellhousen, Friedrich Schleiermacher, David Friedrich Strauss, Ludwig Feuerbach, Ernest Renan and Rudolf Bultmann. By the end of the twentieth century a number of scholars in Mormon studies had done some similar work, which has laid the foundation for a Higher Criticism of the *Book of Mormon*.

Initially, critics of the *Book of Mormon* were virtually all self-declared foes of this new bible. Their work was built on faded memory, hearsay, rumor and at times deliberate calumny. A century later, pre-Columbian archaeology began providing a scientific basis for a school of Higher Criticism to address BoM issues. Some major civilizations cover only a few centuries. Classical Greece lasted about three. The Mormon bible asserted that for a millennium after 600 BCE, pre-Columbian America had been occupied exclusively by what eventually became millions of Israelites, and gave extensive details of their material culture, geography, cities and villages. We should expect to find scientifically dated remains of items mentioned in the BoM, including fortifications, cities, tools, furnishings, clothing, weapons, and the crops and animals used for food, wool and work.

The Archaeological BoM Item List

To systematize this inquiry in an efficient manner, the following table has been prepared listing items mentioned in the BoM narrative, with indications of what has and has not been found.

Table 17. Archaeological Item List for the *Book of Mormon*

Item in the BoM	Found in Pre-Columbian Archaeological Sites?
Hebrew Texts	none, in either book or inscriptional format
reformed Egyptian Texts	none, in either book or inscriptional format
City walls	yes, but associated with other cultures only
High places, temples	yes, but associated with known Mayan, Olmec, Caral (etc.) cultures
Iron works	no smelted iron has been dated to the BoM time frame (cold hammered meteoric or natural iron objects have been found in the Pacific Northwest)
Steel works	no evidence of steel smelting in the BoM time frame
Brass	no evidence of brass in the New World, but bronze existed in South America
Copper	yes, especially in South America (including smelting)
Gold	yes, but it spread rather late into Mesoamerica
Silver	yes, but it spread rather late into Mesoamerica
Tumbaga	yes, but it spread rather late into Mesoamerica
Ziff	by apologist interpretation: tumbaga (a gold-copper alloy)
Chains	none evidenced, excepting in jewelry
Swords of metal, esp. steel	none
Breastplates of metal	none found in BoM period (Tarascan metallurgy was late)
Bucklers	depends on definition
Cement houses	some use of structural cement is evidenced
Plowshares	none
Wheeled vehicles	none (toys, but no vehicles, there being no draft animals)
Chariots	none
Roads	paved roads for processions and to enable teams of men to carry heave tax/tribute bundles through rainforests and similar terrain
Machinery	see below
Gold & silver coins	no coinage has been found in the New World. (Note: The BoM does not use the word "coin" but "pieces" of silver & gold, each with a different name, which it refers to as "money." The chapter heading used to say "Nephite coins and measures," up to the 1960s, but now says "Nephite coinage")
Torches, candles	possibly torches, but candles are not evidenced
Horses	none found by the Europeans, and no bones have been found of horses dated to within the last 7,000 years
Cattle, bull, calf, ox	no cattle found by the Europeans, nor any bones of cattle
Sheep	no sheep found by the Europeans, nor any bones of sheep
Goats	no goats found by the Europeans, nor any bones of goats (apart from mountain goats)
Ass	not found
Swine	not found
Flocks, herds	none for any of the above animals
Elephants (Jaredites)	mammoths of Siberia went extinct c. 4,000 years ago, and in Pribilof islands c. 6,000 years ago.
Barley	none found, nor barley pollen

Wheat	none found, nor wheat pollen
Corn (maize)	found
Grapes	no *vitis vinifera* (wine grapes), but other species did exist
Winepress	none
Figs	none
Silk	none
Linen	none
Crucifixion cataclysm	see discussion below
Israelite DNA	not found (see discussion below)

There is no way to know what is meant by "machinery" in Jarom 1:8. Noah Webster, in 1828, defined it as:

> A complicated work, or combination of mechanical powers in a work, designed to increase, regulate or apply motion and force as the machinery of a watch or other chronometer.[235]

In this context, one can suggest that minimally it refers to laborsaving and/or task-enabling devices with at least one moving part, based on the principle of the lever, and/or the wheel. Examples of early machinery include the water-driven mill, ox-driven or man-driven mills, weight lifting devices, including the lever (beam on a fulcrum), simple cranes and pulleys, water lifting devices (the simple *shādūf*, in the Middle East by 1500 BCE, and the larger and more complex noria water wheel, developed in Egypt possibly 300 BCE) and simple cog-wheels (using pegs as cogs). The reference is important because it implies an advanced agricultural economy that benefits from devices developed by urban-based artisan specialists, such as one might possibly expect to some degree of the Maya or Olmec civilizations. In any case, if they were in use anywhere, these are items that should have left discoverable remains.

It is clear from this list that nineteenth-century authors replicated their New England farm and town life in the *Book of Mormon*, with an item list that is largely just not found in the pre-Columbian New World.

Pre-Columbian DNA

The result here is quite definitive. It has been best presented in the Mormon context by Simon G. Southerton, an accomplished research scientist, and former Mormon, who served two years as an LDS

---

[235] See Noah Webster, *An American Dictionary of the English Language* (New Haven: S. Converse, 1828).

missionary, and two years as a bishop. His study discusses the scientific findings in detail. His conclusions are succinctly stated as follows:

> The ancestors of Native Americans were Asians who unknowingly became the first Americans as they walked across Beringia over 14,000 years ago. The ancestors of the Polynesians were Asians who honed their considerable nautical skills among the islands of Southeast Asia before sailing out into the Pacific during the last 3,000 years. Regardless of coincidental cultural, linguistic or morphological parallels with the Old World, the peoples of the Pacific Rim who met Columbus and Cook were not Israelites. They were descendants of a far more ancient branch of the human family tree that had existed thousands of years before the Israelite branch sprouted into existence.[236]

It is worth noting here, too, that the languages of the pre-Columbian peoples are in no way similar to the Semitic family or to Egyptian. The Polynesian language group has been identified as being most closely linked to the pre-Chinese people of Taiwan, as well as their DNA.

Grain and Climate

According to the BoM narrative, Lehi's party landed on the west coast of South America. The military and missionary campaigns in and to the Land of Nephi (ultimately occupied mostly by the Lamanites) indicate that it was not far from the Nephites in Central America (see Chapters 14-15). This would place the landing most probably in Columbia or Ecuador, which is as tropical as it gets. Furthermore, the land rises abruptly from

---

[236] Simon G. Southerton, *Losing a Lost Tribe. Native Americans, DNA and the Mormon Church* (Salt Lake City: Signature Books, 2004), 130. See also, Special Issue of *Genes*: "The Peopling of the Americas: A Genetic Perspective": Genes (ISSN 2073-4425)including these four articles: Roca-Rada, X.; Souilmi, Y.; Teixeira, J.; Llamas, B (*Genes* 2020, 11). "Ancient DNA Studies in Pre-Columbian Mesoamerica." Davidson, R.; Fehren-Schmitz, L.; Llamas, B. "A Multidisciplinary Review of the Inka Imperial Resettlement Policy and Implications for Future Investigations" (*Genes* 2021). Lindo, J.; DeGiorgio, M. "Understanding the Adaptive Evolutionary Histories of South American Ancient and Present-Day Populations via Genomics" (*Genes* 2021). Di Corcia, T.; Scano, G.; Martínez-Labarga, C.; Sarno, S.; De Fanti, S.; Luiselli, D.; Rickards, O. "Uniparental Lineages from the Oldest Indigenous Population of Ecuador: The Tsachilas." *Genes* 2021, 12).

the sea to the heights of the Andes mountain chain. The elevation of Quito, capital of Ecuador, is 9,350 feet, the highest capital in the world. Yet it is only about 125 miles from the sea, and lies almost exactly on the equator. Medellin, Columbia, is lower, only 5,000 feet, and also about 125 miles from the sea. Further to the south, Pasto, Columbia, is 8,299 feet above the sea. The rise is so abrupt and rugged that going very far inland would not have been a realistic proposition. These Israelite settlers would have been confined to a relatively narrow equatorial coastal plain (v. Map 4).

Map 4. Topography of Columbia & Neighbors

Based on a copyright-free map from Wikimedia Commons

When strife among them produced a split, Nephi's flight with his followers, a group of families, with their possessions, planting seed and flocks, can only have been up the coastal plain, to the lowlands south or southeast of the Isthmus of Panama. An idea of the totally tropical climate on the west coast can be had by noting that of Buenaventura, Columbia, which has an average high temperature in the nineties, 247 inches of rain annually and average humidity in the mid to high eighties. What a change for a band of Jerusalemites.

Wheat is a temperate climate crop, and prefers moderate rainfall. One wonders if the Middle Eastern grains would have survived at all; certainly their yield and quality would have been miserable.

Grain Detection in Archaeology

This is a hypothetical discussion. There is no evidence that wheat or barley were ever cultivated in pre-Columbian America. Every modern excavation takes systematic soil samples for laboratory examination. A good example is the excavations at Shanidar Cave in northern Iraq, dating 35,000 to 60,000 years ago. There, Ralph and Rose Solecki discovered a burial, next to the Neanderthal cave that they excavated. They took routine soil samples to be analyzed and were informed that the layer of earth associated with the skeletal remains bore a very large concentration of pollen from flowering plants. The conclusion was that these Neanderthals had sufficiently developed feelings for their dearly departed and burial traditions that they had gathered a large number of flowers to throw in on top of the body before covering it with earth. For us, this is a good illustration of the extreme durability of pollen. Wheat and barley culture, during a millennium of Nephite-Lamanite occupation of large parts of the Americas would needs have produced settlement areas with soil saturated with wheat and barley pollen.

Another way of knowing what plants ancient peoples exploited, either as cultivars, or wild plants, comes to us from the excavation at Sandy Hill, Mashantucket, Connecticut. There, archaeologists analyzed stone tools for traces of starchy grains, dated to the ninth millennium BP (before present). They found some, including cyperus esculentus (a sedge) that is suitable as a food source. Indications are that one of the tools was used to process it. Due to the damp ecology, of the 23,000+ bone fragments collected, only white tailed deer could be identified with confidence. [237] Modern archaeology has come to closely resemble CSI forensics. Just as CSI might use sophisticated technology to analyze traces of blood, or explosive residue, archaeology uses similar and equally high-tech methods to analyze trace evidence on ancient tools. This technology would also detect other cultivars in addition to grain.

---

[237] Thomas C. Hart & Timothy H. Ives, "Preliminary Starch Grain Evidence of Ancient Stone Tool Use at the Early Archaic (9,000 B.P.) Site of Sandy Hill, Mashantucket, Connecticut," in *Ethnobiology Letters* (http//:www. ethnobiology.org/ publications/ethnobiology-letters, Vol. 4:87-95, accessed 02 Sept 2013).

Horses, Chariots and Roads

These three are interlinked, although there is no Pre-Columbian skeletal evidence of horses since they had gone extinct in the Americas. When they were reintroduced by the Spanish, they began to spread from tribe to tribe. By collecting the oral history on this subject from the tribes, Francis Haines has traced their dispersion in North America from what emerged as the point of introduction.[238] The modern horse had evolved from the *hyracotherium* (by between 45 to 55 million years ago), to the *mesohippus* (by 32 to 37 million years ago), to the modern horse by c. five million years ago, all in the New World. For reasons poorly understood, the modern horse became extinct in the Americas by 10,000 to 7,000 years ago. Wild horses are of two types, the feral horse, once domesticated but later ranging free, such as the mustang (originally brought by the Spanish), and two species of the true wild horse, Przewalski's horse (or Mongolian horse) in Asia, and the tarpan (European wild horse, found in Europe and much of Asia up to c. 1900). Some LDS scholars have suggested that in a pocket or two in the Americas, the modern horse may have survived extinction at least into the BoM Nephite period. To bring this suggestion from the realm of mere speculation into the realm of empirical reality, one must find and date skeletal remains.

Roads (and Wheeled Vehicles?)

The absence of draft animals in Pre-Columbian America has implications for the probability of chariots. Although a model of a crude wheeled vehicle has been found, this is thought to have been a child's toy, showing that the concept of the wheel existed. So who knows? Even without draft animals, was a king ever moved about with a sort of rickshaw? Not impossible, but more pertinent would be to find remains of a chariot. Such remains have often been found in the Old World. In the Champagne district of France an ancient chariot has been found in a tomb. A 4,000 year-old burial in Georgia (Eastern Europe) has preserved chariot remains. In Bulgaria, a Thracian chariot and two horses were buried, apparently upright. The remains of a beautifully decorated Thracian chariot were also found near a tumulus (burial) in Serbia.[239] In England, a 2,500 year-old

---

[238] Francis Haines, "Where Did the Plains Indians Get their Horses?" *American Anthropologist*, new series, 1938, 40:112-137.

[239] April Holloway, "4,000-year-old Thracian Chariot Unearthed in Serbia," (http//:www.ancient-origins.net, accessed 8/12/2013).

chariot has been found with wheels, their iron rims intact,.[240] Also in England, Iron-Age ornate bronze remains of chariot fittings, and what possibly could be equestrian tools have been found at the fort at Burrough Hill.[241] In China, a Zhou dynasty burial yielded several intact wooden chariots with the complete skeletal remains of four horses, dated as early as 700 BCE, showing how wood can survive if buried.[242] Roman chariots have been found in Greece and Thrace.[243] The archaeological remains of chariots can and do survive.

Finally, it is argued that since the Maya built roads (*sacbeob*, singular *sacbe*), they must have had wheeled vehicles. Indeed, the *sacbe* was a very sophisticated road, often quite narrow, but at times very wide. The majority are intrasite, meaning they were short procession ways connecting buildings inside the city. But others connected cities, and a few were quite long. The Cobá-Yaxuna *sacbe* was 100 kilometers long. In addition to ceremonial functions, these intercity *sacbeob* were used for commerce, bringing in tribute on the backs of slaves and possibly even for moving troops. The *sacbe* was often an elevated road, in places elevated to as much as one, or even up to three meters. They were essential for human foot travel through rugged land, especially land that is overgrown with forest and dense brush. In swampy areas, the elevated *sacbeob* kept the marchers above the flood level. Ancient Roman roads have deep ruts from the passage of wheeled vehicles. No evidence of this nature is associated with the *sacbeob*. Given the great utility of the roads for processions and foot travel, there is no reason to assume that they were used for wheeled vehicles.

Weapons

Relevant to the above are the remains of swords found in Eurasia. Those with blades are found mostly in burials or river beds, since both environments are inimical to oxidation (rusting). Even if fully rusted, a

---

[240] *Deseret News*, 4/12/2003.

[241] "Stunning Discovery of Ancient Chariot Parts, Equestrian Tools", from http//:www. Horsetalk.co.nz, accessed 14 Oct, 2014. "Burrough Hill Archaeologists Find Iron Age Chariot Remains", BBC News, accessed 14/10/2014.

[242] "Trip to the Zhou: Remains of horses and chariots unearthed from tomb dating back to 3,000-year-old Chinese dynasty" (http//:www.dailymail.com, accessed 2/09/2011).

[243] "Roman chariot burial site found [Greece]," with a subtitle "More Roman carts in Thrace" (http//:www.romanhideout.com, 15/02/2003).

sword that for any reason came to be covered with soil, or river or flood silt, would not disappear. Iron oxide is itself a stable compound, retaining every iron atom that went into the formation of the rust. Such a blade would have a bloated form, but would retain a recognizable blade shape. Together with a hilt, the weapon's identity would be certain.

In 2015, hikers in Norway found a Viking sword dated to c. 750 CE. This is a complete steel blade, rusted, but treatable.[244] Of more than a hundred Viking blades found, only around sixteen are swords, apparently because they were very expensive. At least 166 iron swords were found in La Tène at the northern edge of Lake Neuchatel. It is thought that the majority, but not all, of the Celtic swords found in lake beds were votive offerings. Finds have been made in various sites in Britain, such as the Williams and Thames Rivers, Llyn Cerrig Bach, Llyn Fawr, Flag Fen, Blackburn Mill and Carlingwark (Scotland).[245] Two Etrurian swords have been found, one in 7th century BCE Vetulonia and another in 4th century BCE Chiusia. The former was made of five strips of steel of varying carbon content, while the latter was made of a single ferrous bloom. A Roman sword has been found in a drainage system in Jerusalem, possibly dating to c. 66 CE. Another Roman sword has been found in Thrace (Bulgaria). The remains of Roman swords have been found in the excavations of the site of the famous battle of Teutoburg Forest, where the Germans slaughtered three legions led by Publius Quintilius Varus in 9 CE. Several Roman swords have been found in Pompeii. These are just a few of the steel swords that have been found. The reader needs only to visit online dealers specializing in ancient weapons to see images of many others, although the place and details of the find are often not given. Much more common are the sword hilts and scabbards that resist the ravages of time more successfully. Throughout Old World archaeology, one also finds the telltale evidence of sword cuts in the bones of human skeletal remains. Bronze and other copper alloy swords have been found of even earlier date. Given the massive exterminations in the BoM narrative, if they happened, similar finds would be inevitable, professionally dated to the pre-6th-century Americas.

Although our focus is on Pre-Columbian America, it is worth noting that the steel bow of Nephi (1 Nephi 16:18) is highly improbable. Actually, steel bows have existed for perhaps as much as two thousand years. During

---

[244] "1,200-year-old Viking sword discovered by hiker," cnn.com, 22 Oct 2015.
[245] Patrick Hunt, "Celtic Iron Age Sword Deposits and Arthur's Lady of the Lake," (Archaeolog, http//:www.traumwerk.stanford.edu/archaeolog/2008/02/celtic_swords_and_arthurs_lady.html, accessed 10 Feb 2016).

thirty years in the Semitic Middle East, I systematically collected premodern ethnographic artifacts, which eventually came to be my personal very focused museum of same, now on display in my home in Hawaii. I have an antique steel bow, made of spring steel with a silver layer on the front side of the bow and small inlaid gold nuggets. An almost identical one is on display in the museum in Riyadh, Saudi Arabia, dated to the nineteenth century. Although this may have been a ceremonial bow, early steel bows were used in hunting and warfare. The earliest development of steel bows appears to have been in India. There is indirect evidence that Indian metallurgists were experimenting with them perhaps as early as the third century BCE.[246] Such a bow constructed in the seventh century BCE is extremely unlikely. In an intriguing verse (1 Nephi 16:21) Nephi says that his brothers' bows had "lost their springs." This appears to be a double misconception, first of how an ancient bow might have been constructed, and second, the date of the emergence of spring steel. The existence of steel swords in that century, such as the sword of Laban, has to be addressed cautiously. Some sort of sword made of iron is attested perhaps as early as the sixth century BCE. Could a ferrous bow have been made eighty years earlier? We cannot rule this out. Furthermore, since early forms of steel existed, the best might be called "most precious steel" at the time, even if it would be called mediocre at best today. The steel bow found in Wyoming, now in the Jim Gatchell Museum in Buffalo, is in perfect unrusted condition and considered to have been blacksmith-forged in the nineteenth century.[247] King Tut's steel knife is meteoric steel.

Where Did All the Cities Go?

The *Book of Mormon* mentions at least 40 cities by name, including only one Jaredite city. These are clearly distinguished from villages, such as Ani-Anti, and others. (Mosiah 27:6; Alma 8:7 & 23:14 & Mormon 4:22 & 5:5) The fact that this civilization, its cities, inscriptions and artifacts have never been found anywhere in the Americas, has driven some to the assumption that the great Crucifixion Cataclysm at the time of Christ's crucifixion had vaporized everything. Venice Priddis and Arthur J. Kocherhans have made the most extravagant argument, *to wit*, that South America was largely below sea level until the crucifixion. The land that

---

[246] D. Elmy, "Steel Bows in India," in the *Journal of the Society of Archer-Antiquaries*, vol. 12, 1969.

[247] Benjamin Storrow, "Mystery Aiming for Answers. Historic Wyoming Steel Bow's Origins Confound Researchers," *Star-Tribune*, 8 September 2013.

had been above sea level was the land of the *Book of Mormon*. At the time of the crucifixion, South America rose up thousands of feet in about three hours. Still, this leaves the locations prior to that event in the Andes highlands as candidates for exploration, where everything on the item list should be discoverable, in an ideal state of dry highland low-oxygen preservation. To save the day, her cataclysm should not have been just a sudden emergence from the deep, but also a kerplop, a turning over of the whole continent like a pancake, so that BoM remains would wind up at the bottom. A sci-fi kerplop, or vaporization?[248]

Well, this is a lot of fun, but on a more serious note, and to be fair, most *Book of Mormon* cartographers minimize the effect of the cataclysm. After all, only some cities were destroyed, sixteen mentioned by name. (3 Nephi 8:15) Six were burned, five sunk into the earth, one sunk in the sea, three were flooded and one was covered by a mountain. When a city burns, it is still available for archaeology. The fire will just leave a burn level in the stratigraphy. A couple of major cities are said to have been rebuilt, including Zarahemla. This was followed by another four centuries of Nephite-Lamanite urban history, with cities and a material culture. Mormon around 322 CE observed, "The whole face of the land had become covered with buildings, and the people were as numerous almost, as it were the sand of the sea." (Mormon 1:7) Furthermore, the Jaredites also built many cities. (Ether 9:23 & 10:12)

When a city undergoes a major cataclysm, this fact can be observed in the archaeological record. Slipping into the sea leaves a large debris field, and a ready candidate for marine archaeology. Fire leaves a burn level in the stratigraphy. Collapsed buildings not only leave their own debris, but often skeletons and artifacts under it.

It is important to note that north of the Rio Grande cities developed rather late. When they did, these were in the Mississippian region, with the largest city being Cahokia, which existed from about 700 to 1250 CE. Another urban civilization was the Pueblo culture, and particularly Chaco Canyon, where the term Anasazi is often used for the people and culture. Beginning c. 700 CE, it had its golden age from c. 900 CE to 1130 CE, when a 300-year drought brought about its decline. Cities in the BoM Nephite period have not been discovered in North America.

The last battles of both civilizations should have left behind a mass of steel swords, breastplates and helmets. In the Jaredite final conflict, millions of combatants fell to the sword, equipped with these items. In the

---

[248] Priddis, *The Book and the Map*. Arthur J. Kocherhans, *Lehi's Isle of Promise* (Fullerton, CA: Et Cetera Graphics and Printing, 1989).

end-of-days scenario for the Nephites, each of twenty-four commanders commanded 10,000 combatants, similarly equipped, resulting in 240,000 dead, and at least as many Lamanites. Both final confrontations happened in upstate New York. What a field day for weekenders wielding metal detectors.

BOM Cities and Civilian Construction

The *Book of Mormon* mentions at least 40 cities by name, plus only one Jaredite city. These are distinguished from villages, such as Ani-Anti, and others. As people spread out, they built "large cities and villages in all quarters of the land." (Mosiah 27:6; 23:14) The Jaredite ruler Shez "did build up many cities upon the face of the land." (Ether 10:4)

Apologists have argued that all BOM construction was with wood, which rotted away and returned to the earth without a trace. If this were absolutely true, we would be faced with a conundrum. Stone construction was dominant in the parts of the Americas with high civilization, and the construction tradition of Judea was with stone where wood was somewhat scarce. There are a number of references in the BoM of buildings of wood. We also find references to "cities both of wood and cement" in the land northward. This gives rise to the observation that the BoM authors may have confused adobe with cement. (Helaman 3:7-11) Only years, or perhaps a decade after his arrival, Nephi constructed buildings as well as a temple, which he describes in glowing terms (2 Nephi 5):

> 15. And I did teach my people to build buildings, and to work in all manner of wood, and of iron, and of copper, and of brass, and of steel, and of gold, and of silver, and of precious ores, which were in great abundance.
> 16. And I, Nephi, did build a temple; and I did construct it after the manner of the temple of Solomon save it were not built of so many precious things; for they were not to be found upon the land, wherefore, it could not be built like unto Solomon's temple. But the manner of the construction was like unto the temple of Solomon; and the workmanship thereof was exceedingly fine.

There are other mentions of fine spacious buildings, as in Mosiah 11:

> 8. ...king Noah built many elegant and spacious buildings... ornamented ...with fine work of wood, and of all manner of precious things, of gold, and of silver, and of iron, and of brass, and of ziff, and of copper;
> 9. And he also built him a spacious palace, and a throne in the midst thereof, all of which was of fine wood and was ornamented with gold and silver and with precious things.

10. [he] caused that his workmen should work all manner of fine work within the walls of the temple, of fine wood, and of copper, and of brass.

11. And the seats ... he did ornament with pure gold; and he caused a breastwork to be built before them...

12. ...he built a tower near the temple; yea, a very high tower, even so high that he could stand upon the top thereof and overlook the land of Shilom, and also the land of Shemlon...

13. And it came to pass that he caused many buildings to be built in the land Shilom; and he caused a great tower to be built on the hill north of the land Shilom...

In archaeological fact, much has remained of wood-built sites, even without the original wood. These include earthen mounds or walls, and sometimes with stone city walls. Wood Henge in England and a temple in Hierakonpolis in Egypt have been reconstructed (in abstract) from postholes without the posts. In China, earthen walls and other remains have been preserved at Dongzhao, from various ancient periods (Prehistory, Shang and Zhou dynasties). In Yanxu, "excavations have uncovered over 80 rammed-earth foundation sites including palaces, shrines, tombs and workshops." [249] . Rammed-earth foundations often supported wood framing. [250]

> Buildings in China have been supported by wooden framing for as long as seven millennia. The emergence of the characteristic articulated wooden Chinese frame emerged during the Neolithic period. Seven thousand years ago, mortise and tenon joinery was used to build wood-framed houses. (The oldest are at Hemudu site at Zhejiang.) Over a thousand of these sites have been identified, usually with circular, square or oblong shaped buildings. During the Yangshao culture in the Middle Neolithic, circular and rectangular semisubterranean structures are found with wooden beams and columns.

In Spain, a range of remains was found at Los Millares, possibly the largest city in Europe in its day. A mass of information has been collected from the Durrington camp of the builders of Stonehenge. Note too the mound builders in North America.

---

[249] "Yinxu," in Wikipedia, en.wikipedia.org/wiki/Yinxu#Archaeological_ discoveries, accessed 07/03/2020.

[250] "Ancient Chinese Wooden Architecture," Wikipedia, en.wikipedia.org/wiki/ Ancient_Chinese_wooden_architecture#Sructural_features, accessed 07/03/2020.

The ancient cities of Babylonia provide us with a striking example of urban survival. In the plain where the Tigris and Euphrates flow, there is precious little wood and almost no stone. Some use was made of fired brick, and even rarely glazed brick. But most construction was done with sunbaked brick, which over time was covered by the accumulation of a tell and slowly returned to soil. Archaeologists work very carefully to locate the remaining outline of walls, which are almost indistinguishable from the soil that now encases them. After locating a wall, they slowly remove the soil on both sides, sifting every ounce in search of the tiniest object or fragment for analysis. This leaves the wall with just a few inches of soil on each side. One uses a brush to gently remove this soil, and little by little a clear outline of bricks emerges. Unless coated over with plaster before the end of a dig season, or roofed over, these walls become mounds of mud in the winter rains, and only the archaeological photos remain. Even so, with careful painstaking work, the walls and foundations of the city emerge. The objects found are used to identify the use of each structure to the extent possible.

Even if we limit BoM construction to that which the BoM authors knew best in New England, city remains should be found. Many Mormons have generally believed that BoM architecture also involved some stone monumental structures. David A. Palmer flirted with the idea that the Olmecs were the Jaredites.[251] E. L. Peay believed that "the ancient Maya and the Nephites are the same people."[252] A good overview of assertions made regarding connections between the Olmecs, Maya and Aztecs, and the *Book of Mormon* peoples, can be found in the *magnum opus* of John L. Sorenson. [253] As writers become more aware of the wealth of archaeological and written information, this strategy has been losing steam. The sites are decorated with deities that are now well known, and with Mayan inscriptions that we can now read.[254]

---

[251] David A. Palmer, *In Search of Cumorah, New Evidences for the Book of Mormon from Ancient Mexico* (Bountiful, UT: Horizon Publishers, 1981), 125.

[252] E. L. Peay, *Lands of Zarahemla, A Book of Mormon Commentary* (Salt Lake City: Northern Publishing Inc., 1993), vi.

[253] John L. Sorenson, *An Ancient American Setting for the Book of Mormon* (Salt Lake City: Deseret Book Company, 1985), 96-137. Also John L. Sorenson, *Mormon's Codex, an Ancient American Book* (Salt Lake City: Deseret Books, 2013).

[254] Michael Coe, *Breaking the Mayan Code* (London: Thames & Hudson, 1999). See also the DVD documentary *Breaking the Mayan Code*, which shows step by step how Mayan was deciphered.

Crucifixion Cataclysm: A Research Perspective

In the *Book of Mormon*, at the time of the crucifixion of Jesus, the whole land was convulsed and swept with terrible destruction. This great cataclysm was clearly intended to obscure the geography, so as to provide a way to evade the issue of the missing cities, and for many this has been its function in their faith. Such a major cataclysm, on a regional if not a bicontinental level, at a time not so long ago in geological time, would have left very obvious consequences. There are four areas of major investigation, any one of which should have found at least some evidence of this event, over a relatively broad territory and at the same point in time. Such a discovery would have been front-page news.

First, the Panama Canal involved massive earth moving over a long distance, creating a huge geological cross section. A special team of paleogeologists, paleontologists and archaeologists worked feverishly between the creation of the cross-section and the canal construction, to document everything of geological, paleontological and archaeological interest. At present, for the new expansion of the canal, the Smithsonian in collaboration with other institutions is taking advantage of this more recent massive earth excavation, to document geological and paleontological information.

Second, there has been extensive geological research, on land and offshore, in the whole area of the Chicxulub asteroid impact that wiped out the dinosaurs, on the coast of the Yucatan Peninsula. The same area had been extensively investigated by petroleum prospectors who obtained numerous core samples. These were inspected by those studying the asteroid impact. There has also been marine seabed research and investigation into the pattern and formation of the cenotes in relation to this impact. Cenote and other Mesoamerican cave exploration would also reveal the effects of such a cataclysm on these famously fragile structures (stalagmites, stalactites, etc.), datable by the subsequent formation of calcite deposits. Mexico is the site of some of the most outstanding and intricate caverns on the planet.

Third, there have been numerous archaeological excavations covering the first-century timeframe, that have done painstaking stratigraphy research, often with spoons and small brushes, sifting everything, and comparing the strata within and across sites, that would have detected such a disruption. At many sites, continuous occupation straddles the first centuries BCE and CE.

Fourth, there is all the modern development activity in what has become highly populated countries, including geological surveys in search of resources, highway construction and excavations for buildings, all of which have a global history of discovering paleogeological and archaeological elements that were not within the original scope of work.

By the normal standards of secular research, given all of this, it is safe to say that the cataclysm story borders on tales inspired by smoking wacky tabaki.

BoM Fortification

There are many mentions of fortified cities, some with earthen circumvallation, and others with defensive stone walls:

> Yea, he had been strengthening the armies of the Nephites, and erecting small forts, or places of resort; throwing up banks of earth round about to enclose his armies, and also building walls of stone to encircle them about, round about their cities and the borders of their lands; yea, all round about the land. (Alma 48:8)

Here, we have both city walls, and border walls of stone. This is massive. So this being the case, is it conceivable that no stone was used in the construction of monumental buildings, of temples and palaces?

Furthermore, earthen berms or packed earth walls were so high that "the Lamanites could not cast their stones and their arrows at them that they might take effect..." (Alma 49:4) The Nephites "encircled the city of Bountiful round about with a strong wall of timbers and earth, to an exceeding height." (Alma 53:4) Defensive walls were such that one needed "strong cords and ladders, to be let down from the top of the wall into the inner part of the wall." (Alma 62:21) Far from constructions that could have easily disappeared, we read of massive walls of earth and wood, and stone walls, not just around cities, but round about the borders of the land.

The use of berms to enclose an area is ancient. Especially on flat ground the berm is associated with a ditch, not just because of its defensive value, but because the ditch is the source of the soil to raise up a berm. The circumference of a berm is less than that of the ditch, and the soil is less packed than the native soil of the ditch, thereby producing a berm higher than one might expect compared to the depth of the ditch. The use of berm-and-ditch fortification is noted in Alma 49:13, 18.

The first point to note here is that fortified cities of this nature survive extremely well. In England there are from two to three thousand hill forts, built in this manner.[255] Some were constructed in the Bronze Age, but the majority were built in the Iron Age, falling out of favor by the 2nd century BCE. The berm or berm-and-ditch structure is very well preserved in many of them. Originally thought to be nothing more than forts, some are now seen to have been or doubled as fortified towns.

When the early colonists arrived in New England, they noted the existence of raised earthen defense structures, which they attributed to a people prior to the Indians they encountered. Some still survive, but many have been plowed or bulldozed away. In the 1820s, more were in evidence to New England residents than can be visited today. They have been considered by some archaeologists to have been constructed under the influence of the mound builders to the west. Josiah Priest provides us with a description: "They [the fortifications at Marietta, Ohio] consist of walls, and mounds of earth, running in straight lines, from six to ten feet high, and nearly forty broad at their base. There is also, at this place, one fort, of this ancient description, which encloses nearly fifty acres of land."[256]

Although the BoM authors could have known about these earthen fortifications, it might be more probable that they had knowledge of those thrown up by their countrymen in the Revolutionary War and the War of 1812, for this construction persisted into the 19th century. An example is Fort Winchester on the Maumee River in Ohio, but closer to home is Fort George on the Niagara River.[257] A cursory reading of the BoM narrative reveals that its authors had more than a passing interest in military affairs, a trait that manifested itself later in Smith's formation of Zion's Camp and the Nauvoo Legion, which he commanded.

Great Expectations

If the *Book of Mormon* were an authentic history, the first thing that one would expect to find is the massive and extensive defensive stone walls and earthen berms. The latter have been found even in bronze-age forts and towns in England, and both were found at Los Millares, 5,000 years old. The BoM makes it clear that fortified walled cities existed in considerable number among the Nephites and Lamanites. Once found, the

---

[255] About 3,300 are listed in A. H. A. Hogg, "British Hill-forts: An Index" (Oxford: BAR Brit. Ser. 62, 1979). See also "Hillforts in Britain" (Wikipedia, accessed 08/12/16); and D. W. Harding, *Iron Age Hillforts in Britain and Beyond* (Oxford: Oxford University Press, 2012).
[256] Josiah Priest, *American Antiquities*, 40.
[257] Ronald J. Dale, "Fort George National Historic Site" (http://www.eighteentwelve.ca/?q=eng/Topic/37, accessed 9 January 2016).

area enclosed would be investigated for foundations of buildings. Usually one does not find massive ancient temples, apart from Egypt and, of course, Central America. Often there is some sort of a promontory that would have been taken over for the palace or chief temple, an acropolis. The elevation achieved would befit the position and prestige of the ruler or governor, and would enhance its other role as a last redoubt, against invaders, or one's own people. The BoM describes large and impressive buildings. These would have had adequate foundations. At least the thresholds and other recognizable construction elements would have been of stone, and the floors of a sort of burnished clay, lime plaster, stone or bricks. Principal buildings would include a palace, one or more temples or other shrines or places of worship, storage buildings for tribute in kind (crops), etc. In other sites, ancient wood structures are clearly delineated by the large postholes for the large beams. These have been found in many parts of the world. It is the case, for example, of a temple in predynastic Hierakonpolis in Egypt, and at Woodhenge (once paired with Stonehenge) in England.

The site would have no signage. Every little thing found and its location would be photographed, *in situ* when possible, labeled, stored and studied in a dig house, and catalogued. Frequently, buildings are identified by what is found in association with them. Apart from all this, four data sources are potentially very rich. First, the site would typically be littered with pot shards. Some pieces would be distinctive enough to identify the culture, i.e., the people of the site. It is also possible that some otherwise unremarkable shards will bear some writing, a votive text on an offering jar, or graffiti, a curse against the king, a message passed between lovers, or simply, "Jonathan was here," or "made by Jacob". A second source of data would be the findings at a butcher or sacrificial site, where bones of animals would be found. A third, and very rich site would be the midden (rubbish mound), which would be stratified to a degree, with dating possibilities. Finally, a fourth site would be that for the burials. Both Hebrews and Egyptians honored their dead, and took pains to bury them properly. The *Book of Mormon* contains references to a sepulcher (Alma 19:1, 5). There may be humble burials, richer burials of the notables, and more impressive burials of the rulers. Here one would expect to find grave goods appropriate to the culture, possibly bone boxes, and commemorative and blessing inscriptions.

Agricultural activity, food production, preservation, storage and preparation all leave signs, even artifacts. Fields yield valuable information regarding crops. Soil analysis would allow the examination of pollen, which is extremely durable, revealing the crops grown. Wheat is processed at long-term, even ancestral threshing floors, which should be found, and yield pollen and other trace evidence. Then it is taken to winnowing sites. Bread ovens should remain (maize is not suitable for bread). Wheat straw is used for basketry, fodder and dung fuel. Bran is used to fill cushions. One could not just run over to a grocery store like today. Families would have grain storage jars or clay bins, while grain dealers, temples and palaces would have large grain storage buildings sufficient to keep out rain and pests, and to pay their retainers. Wine not only implies the existence of a suitable species of grape, but also wine presses. Wine storage skins or jars would still bear trace evidence.

Every site would have its own history, and ecological/historical vicissitudes. Some may be partially or largely covered over by soil and vegetation. Others may be wind-swept. Lucky sites might have had a mountain (mud slide?) fall on them, or volcanic ash. A site at the bottom of the sea would be in a cold and oxygen-starved environment. Ancient wood ships have been recovered from the sea in good repair, and Viking burials in wood ships fare well under the ground. Pompeii was protected by volcanic ash. They would also vary with respect to pillage. Earthquakes might cause objects to be covered up, including coinage, if it exists. Then there are treasure troves, hidden in response to invaders, or the Gadianton robber threat, at various times, but especially in the last years of the Nephites: "And these Gadianton robbers, which were among the Lamanites, did infest the land, insomuch that the inhabitants thereof began to hide up their treasures in the earth." (Mormon 1:18)

If the Nephite/Lamanite civilization ever existed, all of the items in this study would be found. Most would be collocated in the same find, a whole city.

Lidar & GPR Reveal: Mother, the Emperor Has No Clothes!

Lidar, an aerial-based radar system, does not detect vegetation, but readily penetrates it, reflecting back off of soil and rocks. Time delays allow high resolution 3D maps to be made. Maps vary depending on the resolution: HR (high resolution) and VHR (very high resolution). *The rainforest vanishes.* By contrast, aerial ground penetrating radar (GPR) has now been developed to detect objects beneath the surface of the earth. UAS Vision (Unmanned Aircraft Systems community) has stated that objects have been detected at a depth of 10-16 meters below the ground surface. Once maps are produced, then boots-on-the-ground archaeology takes over, with ground-based GPR, machetes, shovels and trowels. In Guatemala, in a very wide region centered on Tikal, many unknown sites were discovered by aerial Lidar, and initially each was investigated just enough to verify that they were Mayan.[258]

Vignette	**The Quest for Joha's Key**

Joha is searching in the dusty dirt in the lane in front of his humble home.
His neighbor asks: "Joha, have you lost something?"
Joha: "Yes. I have lost the key to my house."
Neighbor: "Did you lose it near here? I will help you find it."
Joha: "No. I lost it in my bedroom."
Neighbor: "In your bedroom? So why are you looking in front of your
home?"
Joha: "Because the light is better here."

The BoM Nephite civilization has been set in the Americas, just as Joha's key is in his bedroom. Focusing one's research on extraneous materials outside the posited locus of the BoM promised land, be they in the Bible or be they in any quarter surrounding Gilead, is like searching in the dusty lane outside Joha's house. Just as Joha must search in his bedroom to find his key, scholars can only evidence the existence of the Nephites by researching in Pre-Colombian America.

Pre-Columbian civilizations define the parameters of the

Relevant-Research Issue

❦❦❦❦❦

---

[258] Press release of UAS Vision (Unmanned Aircraft Systems community) Posted in Electronic Sub-Systems, News on October 18, 2017 by The Editor.

< Chapter 12 >

Reservation for a Promised Land? *Sorry*, No Vacancy!

Apologists focus primarily on Middle Eastern and Biblical topics, rather than the archaeology of pre-Columbian North, Central and South America. Undoubtedly they have found the Americas to be unproductive turf for their objectives. Yet even the average Mormon has heard of problems, such as the consensus among archaeologists, paleontologists and other experts, that horses did not exist in the New World during the past several millennia, in agreement with the eye-witness reports of the first Europeans arriving in the New World, *to wit*, that they found no horses. Indeed, this is just the very tip of the iceberg. Its massive body includes the entire archaeological items list in Chapter 11.

For many, this is enough to conclude that the *Book of Mormon* is a nineteenth-century historical romance. But the faithful for their part base hopes on the view that the remains of Jaredite, Nephite and Lamanite cities lie in some remote valley, yet to be discovered, or have simply vaporized.

The Ultimate Test

And yet, it is what the *Book of Mormon* does not say that provides the ultimate test, and the most ineluctable conclusion. The *Book of Mormon* makes it clear that upon the arrival of the families of Lehi and Ishmael, and the band of Mulek, all leaving Jerusalem in the reign of Zedekiah (c. 597-586 BCE), the new land of their inheritance was empty. It was theirs alone, to preserve a branch of Israel in its purity, to be gathered to Christ in the latter days. Note, in 2 Nephi 1:

> 8. And behold, it is wisdom that this land should be kept as yet from the knowledge of other nations: for behold, many nations would overrun the land, that there would be no place for an inheritance.
> 9. Wherefore, I, Lehi, have obtained a promise that inasmuch as they which the Lord God shall bring out of the land of Jerusalem shall keep his commandments, they shall prosper upon the face of this land; and they shall be kept from all other nations, that they may possess this land unto themselves.

The BoM had to go to atrocious lengths to make this happen, since the non-Israelite Jaredites and their civilization were brought there first, also led there by God, but from the tower of Babel. What to do? Note this statement in Ether 11:

> 20. many prophets... prophesied... and cried repentance unto the people, and except they should repent, the Lord God would execute judgment against them to their utter destruction;
> 21. and that the Lord God would send or bring forth another people to possess the land.

The Jaredites too had divided into two branches. Initially one was more righteous than the decidedly wicked other group, but eventually both became very iniquitous. Warfare between the two ultimately led both leaders to gather their forces to the environs of upstate New York. These were men of might, Coriantumr, leader of the formerly more righteous group, and Shiz, leader of the wicked group. They commanded great masses of people: "the people began to flock together in armies, throughout all the face of the land." (Ether 14:19) In their initial battles, Coriantumr "saw that there had been slain by the sword already nearly two millions of his people ... there had been slain two millions of mighty men, and also their wives and their children." (Ether 15:2 2) So these mighty men, plus wives and children, should total perhaps four million. Just on one side. One can assume that the casualties among the wicked group were no less. So the grand total would possibly reach eight million dead in the initial encounters. This makes every known historical battle a back-alley brawl. At this point, the two leaders realized that this was a fight to the extermination of one group or the other. So they took four years to gather every living human being from Jaredite territories, to have available to them the fighting potential of every man, woman and child. (Ether 15:12-14) While doing this, apparently others fabricated armor and weapons for every man, woman and child: "both men, women and children being armed with weapons of war, having shields, and breastplates, and head-plates, and being clothed after the manner of war." (Ether 15:15) Then, the preparations made, they all fought to the end, to their mutual total extermination. We are left to imagine the horrific scene of child slaughtering child. Only the two leaders were left standing, the classic duel of the chiefs. Coriantumr killed Shiz, and eventually made contact with the successor group, spending the last nine months of his life in Mulekite Zarahemla. Thus the promise was kept, and the Israelite group entered into the land of their inheritance, purged of prior inhabitants, and totally reserved just for them. Ethnic purity in splendid isolation.

The *Book of Mormon* text reinforces this assertion in its historical narrative. There is no single mention of any people or group that is not descended from Lehi, Ishmael, Zoram or Mulek. Realistically, upon their arrival they would have found the land full of occupants. Like the arriving European explorers and settlers (and even the Vikings), they would have found all the best lands taken. In addition to accounts of negotiation and cooperation, there would be accounts of conflict and warfare with these other peoples. The fierce Vikings could not hold out, and the lost colony of Roanoke is famous. Even the Jaredite account makes no mention of other peoples in the New World.

The test based on the omissions in the *Book of Mormon* is more final than that of the commissions, because in the case of the omissions, the data set is fixed. We will not wake up one morning and suddenly find in our BoM copy mentions of numerous other peoples, and wonder, "how did I not notice this before?" Improvements in the table below will only add more peoples that should have been mentioned. In stark contrast with the BoM, the Hebrew Bible is replete with mentions of many other peoples, both near and far.

The Archaeology Cultures List

The many important Pre-Columbian cultures and cities that existed during the time frame of the BoM narrative cannot be fully represented here. Table 18 lists some of the salient ones, and details of interest to the present study.

Table 18. Pre-Columbian Cultures

A. Cultures before or during the BoM Jaredite Period	
Culture	Dates and Details
Clovis	C. 13,000 BCE to 10,000 BCE, a Paleo-Indian population, noted for its arrow heads. They are considered to be the ancestors of most of the indigenous cultures of the Americas. Clovis tips are found in most of North & Central America. A boy preserved in a Clovis culture grave, dubbed Anzick-1, yielded DNA related to the modern Amerindians and the DNA found in eastern Asia.
Folsom	Ca. 9000 BCE, perhaps the principal tradition that replaced the Clovis culture, and appears to have grown out of it. They are more common in the Rocky Mountains and Great Plains, but not as rare east of the Mississippi as once thought.
Las Vegas	8000-4600 BCE (Holocene), 31 sites, primarily hunting, gathering, fish/shell fish, & primitive agriculture, near the Ecuador coast.
Valdivia culture	3500-1800 BCE, impressive ceramic finds (earliest in the Americas), cotton textiles, maize & vegetable cultivation, near the west coast of Ecuador. They used rafts with sails along the coast. Shamanistic religion involving animal figures with fertility objectives.

Norte Chile (Caral)	3,500-1,800 BCE, Peru, largest city of the ancient Americas, with large pyramids (contemporary with ancient Egypt); temple complex, oriented to the worship of various unknown deities.
Chinchuro culture	7,000 to 1,500 BCE, a fishing culture of the Atacama coastal desert. They had complex funerary practices and detailed mummification.
Monagrillo	2500-1200 BCE, Panama, early ceramic site; hearths, post holes, pits, shell, bone, pottery, stone tools, early maize culture.
B. Cultures Overlapping BoM Jaredite & Nephite Periods ⚕ designates some of those with pagan items in the BoM Christian Period	
Casma-Sechin Culture	3600-200 BCE, a complex of multiple ruins in the Andes, including the thirteen towers at Chankillo (solar observatory/calendar?).
Chavín de Huantar	1,500 (up to 400) BCE, Peru, largely a pan-regional ritual center (possibly a religious cult), temples, agricultural economy, gold soldering in jewelry. In addition to others, including feline figures, the three main Chavin deities are the "snarling" god of the Lanzón stele, the caiman of the Tello Obelisk, and the Staff God.
Ancon	10,000 BCE to end of Incan period, a principal center, vast necropolis with thousands of burials.
Montegrande	The civilization in the Peruvian Amazon built a massive earthen burial mound c. 1000 BCE, where a spiral temple was later built. At a second pyramid, the remains of 22 children were found, sick and malnourished victims of human sacrifice. In a lavish burial site the remains of a powerful shaman priest (covered with 180 snail shells) has been discovered, dated to 2,800 years before present.
Acre (Amazon)	In eastern Acre, the westernmost division of the state of Rondônia, and the southern part of the state of Amazonas, ca. 300 geometric earthwork structures have been registered. They represent a regional cultural institution related to ritual and/or sociopolitical institutions, in use from 1200 BCE to the 14th century CE.
Olmecs	1600—400 BCE. Earliest Olmec proto-writing & logograms are accepted by some to have been precursors for the earliest Mayan writing. May have invented the concept of zero and the earliest Mesoamerican calendar. It is considered to be the first major civilization in Mesoamerica.
San Lorenzo	1200—900 BCE, center of early Olmec culture with temples, plazas and royal residences. There are ten colossal stone heads, apparently of rulers. Many also have been found in other Olmec sites.
La Venta	c. 900—c. 400 BCE—followed San Lorenzo as the most important Olmec center. The Great Pyramid was the largest Mesoamerican structure of its time. Even today, after 2500 years of erosion, it rises 34 m (112 ft.) above the naturally flat landscape. Buried deep within La Venta, lay opulent, labor-intensive "offerings" – 1000 tons of smooth serpentine blocks, large mosaic pavements, and at least 48 separate deposits of polished jade celts, pottery, figurines, and hematite mirrors.
Tres Zapotes	Pre-1000 BCE, & flourishing c. 900-800 BCE, the third major Olmec site. It continued after 400 BCE, but gradually transformed into post-Olmec (Epi-Olmec) culture.

Teotihuacan	100 BCE thru 7th century CE, a major site in the Basin of Mexico, with major constructions from 100 BCE to 250 CE, but growing to its apogee at c. 450 CE. Its largest pyramid, Pyramid of the Son, was largely completed by 100 CE and finished by 200 CE. ✝ Its deities include the Storm God, Great Goddess, Feathered Serpent, Old God, War Serpent, Netted Jaguar, Pulque God and Fat God. Many of these are modern names given to them. ✝Hundreds of human sacrifice remains have been found beneath and around the Pyramid of the Feathered Serpent (Quetzalcoatl), which was built from 150 to 200 CE.
Maya	2000 BCE—1697 CE (fall of the last Mayan city). Hieroglyphic writing was in use by the 3rd century BCE. By 500 BCE monumental architecture existed. 400 BCE—250 CE, late preclassic period. 250—900 CE, classical period, with Mayan sites at their height. <u>Deities & other transcendental beings:</u> Acan (wine), Acat, Ah Peku (thunder), Ah-Muzen-Cab, Awilix, Bacab (middle earth & subterranean water), Cabaguil, Camazotz, Chaac (rain), Chin (male-male sex with both deities & humans), Chirakan-Ixmucane (a goddess, one of 13 creator deities), Ek Chuaj, Goddess I (an important goddess of eroticism, human procreation, and marriage), God L (trade; elderly with jaguar traits), Hero Twins (associated with complementary forces), Howler monkey gods (arts & music), Huay Chivo, Hun Hunahpu, Huracan (storm, wind, fire; caused the great flood), Itzamna a sky god & creator deity), Ixchel, Ixpiyacoc, Ixtab, K'awiil, Kinich Ahau (sun god), Kukulkan (feathered serpent; cf. Quetzalcoatl; pre-9th c., never identified as being human, but as presiding over sacrifices), Maize god, Maximón, Moon goddess (sexuality and procreation; fertility not only of human, but also of crops), Nagual (human-jaguar shapeshifter), Tzacol, Q'uq'umatz (cf. Quetzalcoatl), Vision Serpent, Voltan, Vucub Caquix (a bird demon), Wayob, Xbaquiyalo, Xmucane and Xpiacoc, Xmulzencab, Xquic, Xtabay (supernatural femme fatale who preys on men), Yopaat (storm god with a spear thunderbolt), Yum Kaax, Zipacna
Calakmul	Preclassic through late classic; a major site by the late preclassic period, and competitor of Tikal. Check out the Calakmul mask! It is the capital of the snake kings, a major competitor to Tikal.
El Mirador	500 BCE—150 CE, a massive Mayan site and political center with a huge pyramid, other stone architecture, and preclassic glyphs.
Paso del Macho	600-500 BCE, situated in the Yucatan with a find of cocoa used as a condiment.
Tikal	700 BCE-400 CE; the largest Maya dam ever found, 260' long and 33' high. It experienced a cultural florescence in the first century CE. Sometime in the 3rd century CE dynastic kingship was established. ✝ Its Mundo Perdido ceremonial complex, with a pyramid and three temples, was active in the late preclassic and on. Rich burials have been dated to the first century CE.
Kaminaljuy	1500 BCE-1200 CE, a major site with a large population by 700 BCE. ✝A complex pantheon of deities by the middle preclassic period.

u

	✝400 BCE—250 CE, the late preclassic period, with a Principal Bird Deity, maize god and a jaguar deity that was merged with the ruler.
Piedras Negras	7th c. BCE-850 CE, the first population peak being about 200 BCE, and the dynasty list beginning c. 297 CE.
Early Mayan writing	Slowly, a significant corpus of texts is emerging dating within the period from c. the third century BCE to c. 150 CE, i.e., the late preclassic period. See Ch. 6 by J. Kathryn Josserand, and Ch. 7 by Martha J. Macri, in Michael Love & Jonathan Kaplan, eds., *The Southern Maya in the Late Preclassic* (Boulder, CO: University Press of Colorado, 2011).
Lamanai	4th c. BCE thru the classic period, a major site from the 4th century BCE through the 1st century CE, declining but persisting thereafter. It was a major copper center. ✝*Lamanai* is Yucatec Maya meaning "Submerged Crocodile" and a temple features individuals wearing crocodile headdresses.
El Baúl	A center known for obsidian production, with a stele bearing a long count date: 36 CE. Volcanic ash was deposited from a nearby volcano. There are architectural decorations of serpents, and sculptures of gods.
El Zotz (Pa' Chan)	350-400 CE, Temple of the Night Sun, with ornate painted stucco inside and out. It has different phases of Kinich Ahaw (sun god); and *wahob* figures (harmful spirits in animal form).
Xno'ha	400 BCE—600 CE, elite residential complex, with pottery dated to this period, and an early classic tomb.
Tak'alik Ab'aj	700-400 BCE, tomb of a ruler wearing a vulture-headed human figure. ✝ Stele 5 bears two long count dates, the latest being 126 CE. It commemorates a transition of power, and exhibits the serpent.
Chan Chich	770 BCE-850 CE, a midden and neighboring sites being excavated in this much looted Maya site in Belize.
Plan de Ayutla	250-550 CE, a theater, in the palace on top of the acropolis.
Izapa	600 BCE—100 CE, the period within which the site reached its apogee. The site is not clearly Mayan nor Olmec, having elements of both, and purely local elements. ✝ It leads other sites in the number of sculptures, featuring *vucub caquix* (a powerful bird deity), a long-lipped deity (of lightening and rain?), a club-wielding deity with serpents as legs, and a scene of violence among deities with a decapitated god. ✝ A monolithic jaguar was found in 2012 dated to c. 100 CE, the 84th monolith found at the site.
El Tajin	1st century-1200 CE, part of the Classic Veracruz culture. ✝ It was a center of the worship of the god Quetzalcoatl. Monumental architecture began in the 1st century CE. The ball court depicts human sacrifice.
Monte Alban	c. 500 BCE-1000 CE—A major site, considered Zapotec, that reached a population of over 5,000 by 300 BCE and over 17,000 by 100 BCE. During 200-500 CE it was a regional capital with colonies. ✝ Over 300 tortured sacrificed war victims are depicted. The Zapotec language was one of the first written (with a syllabic script, possibly as early as 200 BCE, but in decline by 250 CE).

	✿ The rain god Cocijo was important.
La Mosquitia	A non-Maya culture in Honduras, not yet adequately dated, but notable for a stone head that appears to be a jaguar, or even a were-jaguar (possibly emblematic of a shaman).
Copán	An early Honduran site (across the border from Guatemala), with stone architecture by around 9th century BCE, that grew to importance, but was refounded by a Maya people in the 6th century CE. It is the principal Maya site in a largely non-Maya region.
Los Naranjos	An archaeological region in western Honduras, settled more or less continually from c. 800 BCE and notable for its ceramics, and in particular the highly decorated Yde vessel. The region has two earthen ditches of the BCE period, of unclear use.
Playa de los Muertos	An archaeological zone on the north Honduran coast known from its burials and ceramics, being as ancient as any Mesoamerican region. It has an extensive excavation history.
Talgua Caves	A cave ossuary in northeastern Honduras with numerous burials dated to c. 1000 BCE, possibly indicative of a notable degree of social development.
Yarumela	A major trade center c. 60 kilometers south of Los Naranjos, dating between 1000 BCE to 200 CE, with important mounds. (Honduras)
Sitio Barriles	4600-2300 BCE, the Tropical Forest Archaic period, rock shelter sites in Panama. 300 BCE—400 CE, Conception stage, first pottery 400-900 CE, Aguas Buenas period, featuring large villages & small farmsteads
Sitio Conte	450-900 CE, Panama, primarily a necropolis with ceramic remains. The iconography depicts animals, humans and animal-human beings.
Sitio Sierra	c. 250 CE to the conquest, a significant site in Panama, with periods poorly defined. Sites in the region span 350 BCE to 750 CE.
Chorrera (Ecuador)	1300-300 BCE, noted for its advanced ceramic tradition, particularly hollow figurines.
Moche	100-800 CE, particularly noted for their elaborately painted ceramics, metallurgy, monumental constructions (huacas) and irrigation systems
Muisca	C. 500 BCE-present, an agrarian culture in the Andean highlands of the Columbian Eastern Range. Antecedent cultures go back to 5000 BCE. The Muisca were organized in an extensive confederation. They had large quantities of gold. The chief upon accession covered his body with gold dust. They are famous for the gold Muisca raft, dating between 600-800 CE, & other gold creations.
San Agustín culture	The archeological park (Huila Department in Colombia) contains the largest collection of religious monuments and megalithic sculptures in Latin America and is considered the world's largest necropolis. The statues are believed to have been carved between 5–400 CE. The Mompós Depression is known for its raised fields that work as agricultural drainage systems. High-ranking individuals were buried in earth mounds with pottery and goldwork.
Nazca	100 BCE-800 CE, located in the southern coastal region of Peru, the Nazca were noted for textiles and ceramics. ✿ Their religion focused on powerful nature deities. The shaman cult used hallucinatory drugs. Their so-called trophy heads were either

	trophies from war, or ritual objects. The Nazca are known for their partial burials, of just parts of a body, or of decapitated bodies with a jar painted as a head. The little-understood Nazca lines include zoomorphic and phytomorphic figures, possibly to propitiate some corresponding celestial beings or forces. Cult center: Cahuachi.
Paracas	800-200 BCE, also in the southern coastal region of Peru, the Paracas culture is noted for its knowledge of irrigation and contributions to the textile arts. Their distinctive ceramics use incised polychrome and negative resist decoration. It appears that in some cases the heads of their deceased were used in rituals.
Recuay	200 BCE-600 CE, a Peruvian highland culture with highly elaborate pottery and impressive fabrics. Their iconography featured the so-called 'moon animal,' a fox-like or feline animal.
Tiwanaku	300 BCE-1000 CE, a precursor to the Incan culture, the ritual and administrative capital of a major state power for approximately five-hundred years. The ruins of the ancient city state are near the south-eastern shore of Lake Titicaca in Bolivia.
Pachacamac	A mostly post-420 CE site c. 25 miles SW of Lima, Peru. Named after its creator god Pacha Camaq, its old temple dates to c. 250 CE. They later built a temple of the sun, possibly associated with Inti, the sun god.
Chachapoyas	600 CE, in the Amazonas region of northern Peru. It is possible that they built a settlement called Gran Pajáten where some ceramics have been dated to 200 BC.
Tulor	380 BCE—1200 CE, a village complex in Chile (most surviving structures are post 800 CE). Boreholes were dug for groundwater.
Saladoid period, Venezuela	Hacienda Grande culture (250 BCE–300 CE), Cuevas culture (400–600 CE), Prosperity culture (1–300 CE), Coral Bay-Longford culture (350–550 CE)
Lagoa Santa	The center of Brazilian paleontology, a cave with 15 human skeletons and mega fauna. The oldest human fossil in Brazil, 11,000+ years old.
Pedra Furada	Circa 11,000 BCE Lithic art, possibly prior to the Clovis culture.
Acre	0-700 CE, Brazil Amazonian site, with many massive earthworks, apparently geoglyphs.
North America	Modern information reveals religious details that probably go back to ancient times (much like the case of the Nazca). For example: some concept of a Great Spirit seems to have existed among many others. Some names for the Great Spirit, or its equivalent follow: 1) Sioux: "*Wakan Tanka,*" Great Mystery that organizes the spirits or deities, as every object was spirit, or "*wakan;*" 2) the Shoshone: "*Tam Apo,*" Our Father (although the religion involved various legendary spirits and ghost spirits); 3) Chickasaw: "*Ababinili,*" spirit of fire and manifest in fire and the sun, the giver of life, light, and warmth; 4) Many Algonquian speaking tribes of the Great Plains, such as the Ojibwe: "*Gitchi Manitou,*" Great Spirit (translated as "God" in missionary translations of scripture), along with other spirits pictured above doorways; 5) Blackfoot: "*Apistotoke,*" Our Creator, a formless spirit (translated as "God" in Christian scriptures); Arapaho: "*Chebbeniathan,*" Spider-above, the creator god; 6) Abenaki: "*Gici Niwaskw,*" Great Spirit; 7) Huron: "*Ha-Wen-Neyu,*" the creator god,

	rendered Great Spirit in English, but meaning "Great Voice" or "Great Ruler;" 8) Cheyenne: "*Maheo,*" Great One, creator, but figured in a pantheon including "*Wihio*" (spider trickster), "*Nonoma*" (spirit of thunder), "*Mehne*" & "*Axxea*" (water monsters) and other legendary beings; 9) Seminole: "*Hisagita Misa*" (Creek: "*Hisagita-imisi*"), Breath-maker, associated with the Milky Way. There are others. What they all have in common is that one being is central, although others may exist, and that the religions are shamanistic.
Basket Weaver	1500 BCE-750 CE, a people in the U.S. Southwest, with well-preserved mummies. Antecedent to the Pueblo culture.
Phoenix/Tuscan	From 1,500 BCE on developed irrigation systems were in use in the Phoenix and Tuscan basins. Ancient footprints, c. 1,500 BCE, of what appears to be two adults, two children and a dog, appear to be a family at work opening & closing channel head gates.
Mound Builders	c. 3,400 BCE to the 16th century, a collection of cultures. The Hopewell culture spanned c. 100 to 700 CE. Burial mounds of the Middle Woodland period range from 100 BCE to 400 CE. Kohukia was the first large city in North America, about 1,000 CE. ✝ There are many theories about their religion, but most believe that sun worship was a central element. Evidence of human sacrifice has been found at Kohukia.
Watson Brake	Dated as far back as approx. 3500 BCE, it is in present-day Ouachita Parish, Louisiana, from the Archaic period. It is considered the oldest earthwork mound complex in North America.
Woodlands Culture	c. 1,000 BCE—1,000 CE, in the eastern North America. c. 1,000 BCE—1 BCE, early woodlands period 1 CE—500 CE, middle woodland period, including the Hopewell culture sites, with burial mounds, evidence of hunting and gathering, pottery and some horticulture. Extensive trade system involving exotic items and materials. Sites with Hopewell traits are found in both New York and Ontario (cf. the Saugeen complex). Post-500 CE, introduction of the cultivation of maize, beans and squash. The Adena culture (c. 1000-200 BCE) built many mounds, including Criel mound, a burial site where many skeletons and grave goods (weapons and jewelry) have been found. The effigy mounds (350-1300 CE) were shaped like stylized animals, each having one, two or three people buried but almost totally without grave goods.

In addition to the absence of most of the primary elements of BoM technology and ecology, and a plethora of non-Israelite cultures in all parts of the New World, covering both the Jaredite and Nephite eras, we find a total absence of references to pre-Columbian religion, in the form of texts or representations of known deities or cultic artifacts, in the temples or among the grave goods. By contrast, the Nephite narrative is Christian from the start, even at the beginning of the sixth century BCE.

Although at times many of the Lamanites accept Christianity and are even described as being more righteous than the Nephites, on the whole this is not the case, and the BoM narrative states clearly that it uses the term

Lamanites to refer to those who reject the teachings of God. We find a New England 19th-century stereotype of the Indians, as being dark and loathsome, indolent, savage and bloodthirsty.

In view of the fact that Nephite civilization is placed in an area almost perfectly contiguous with or adjacent to Mayan and Olmec culture, we might expect there to be some mention of the false gods, similar to the OT mention of Baal, Baal-Zebub, Bel, Moloch, Ashtoreth, Amon, Chemosh, Dagon, Tammuz and various other regional deities in competition with Jehovah (Yahweh). Surprisingly, or perhaps not so surprisingly, we find no mention of any other deity in the entire BoM text (although there are occasional condemnations of idolatry). Historically, throughout this region, there were impressive representations of numerous deities, and elaborate rituals, in scores of cities and villages, even throughout the two Nephite Christian centuries.

In New England, English-speakers would mostly have heard of the Great Spirit, including the BoM authors. It is not surprising then to discover that the general religion of the Lamanites, to the extent that the BoM treats it, was based on the existence of the Great Spirit. In Alma 18:2, the Lamanite king Lamoni says, "Behold, is not this the Great Spirit who doth send such great punishments upon this people, because of their murders?" Referring to his belief, "Ammon said: This is God. And Ammon said unto him again: Believest thou that this Great Spirit, who is God, created all things which are in heaven and in the earth?" (Alma 18:28) The king replies in the affirmative.

Conclusions

The claim of the *Book of Mormon* narrative to be a translation of an ancient record of the history and religious affairs of the pre-Columbian peoples of the Americas has been compared with the empirical findings of the archaeological records overlapping the relevant period.

1. The Archaeological BoM Item List was drawn up from the text of the BoM narrative to enable a focused comparison with the archaeological findings. The overwhelming majority of these items have been found to be unevidenced. For all but the most faith-bound, the conclusion is totally disconfirmatory to the BoM authenticity claim.
2. The Archaeological Cultures List was drawn up from a survey of pre-Columbian archaeology to provide an empirical test of the claim that the lands of the proposed Nephite/Lamanite territories had been kept away from the knowledge of all other peoples of the earth, a claim that the BoM

narrative states explicitly and examples clearly by its total lack of any reference to any people other than those descended from the Jaredites, the party of Lehi and the party of Mulek. In fact, we have found that the Americas have been fully populated by numerous cultures. A major civilization, with forty named cities and many unnamed others, covering a period of 1,000 years, must have had important and recurrent contact with the historical cultures of pre-Columbian America.

Highly committed, well-educated and intelligent orthodox LDS scholars laboring at this Gordian knot have produced creative research based on analyses of the BoM text and/or Middle Eastern cultural materials. The unstated premise that all such research is based on is that the *Book of Mormon* is the unquestionably best source for knowledge of pre-Columbian America, and therefore the pre-Columbian archaeological record cannot be totally disconfirmatory. The results from the analysis in chapters 11 and 12 make it clear that this premise is totally untenable, and that no amount of BoM textual or Middle-East cultural or literary analysis can overcome the clear facts on the ground in the New World. This is the

Archaeological Verdict

< Chapter 13 >

The Pre-Columbian Christian Era & Great Apostasy

One God, the Same Yesterday, Today and Forever

As Smith and his partners proceeded to announce the visitation of God the Father, God the Son, the Angel Moroni, and the mission to miraculously translate a new scripture engraved on gold plates, they encountered considerable skepticism, rising to the level of persecution, and condemnation as heretics on theological grounds. The *Book of Mormon* counters (Mormon 9):

> 9. For do we not read that God is the same yesterday, today, and forever, and in him there is no variableness neither shadow of changing?
> 10. And now if ye have imagined up unto yourselves a god who doth vary, and in whom there is shadow of changing, then have ye imagined up unto yourselves a god who is not God of miracles.
> 20. And the reason why he ceaseth to do miracles among the children of men is because that they dwindle in unbelief, and depart from the right way, and know not the God in whom they should trust.

This unchanging god is forever a god of miracles, a god of revelation, who sends angels to his elect, and a god of one true church. As a result, one true Christian gospel fits all, in every time and every clime. In Mormonism, there is little awareness of clear historical evidence that distinctly Christian doctrine and praxis did not exist prior to their establishment by the movements of John the Baptist, Jesus, the Apostles and early church fathers.

Baptism and Christianity in the Nephite Millennium

The Christian issue in the *Book of Mormon* is based on the assertion that the Nephites were Christians already in the 6th century BCE, or at least those who remained faithful to the teachings of Nephi and his prophetic successors. Even more fundamental, a full knowledge of God's plan and its theology was already revealed to Adam. The word "baptism" is found early in the BoM text (1 Nephi 20:1) where it is inserted into the mouth of Isaiah (48:1). Nephi taught basic Pauline theology regarding the coming Savior, and the atonement: "And it came to pass that I, Nephi, did consecrate Jacob and Joseph, that they should be priests and teachers over the land of my people." (2 Nephi 5:26) The name of the Savior, Christ, was revealed to him (2 Nephi 10:3). He states, "…there is none other name given under heaven save it be this Jesus Christ" (2 Nephi 25:20) by which man can be saved; "And we talk of Christ, we rejoice in Christ, we preach of Christ, we prophesy of Christ…" (2 Nephi 25:26) In Mosiah 3:8 (2nd century BCE) we read "And he shall be called Jesus Christ, the Son of God, the Father of heaven and earth, the Creator of all things from the beginning; and his mother shall be called Mary." (See also Alma 7:10)

This is the "Old Testament" as many Christians have always thought it should have been written.

The doctrine of Christ and redemption was accompanied by baptism: "And now, if the Lamb of God, he being holy, should have need to be baptized by water, to fulfill (sic) all righteousness, O then, how much more need have we, being unholy, to be baptized, yea, even by water!" (2 Nephi 31:5). Following that, "… then shall ye receive the Holy Ghost; yea, then cometh the baptism of fire and of the Holy Ghost; and then can ye speak with the tongue of angels." (2 Nephi 31:13; 6th century BCE)

Although in Nephi's time (the first few decades in the New World) a church with ordained clergy existed, the word "church" referring to this church first occurs in Mosiah 18:17 (c. 170 BCE): "And they were called the church of God, or the church of Christ, from that time forward. And it came to pass that whosoever was baptized by the power and authority of God was added to his church." King Benjamin announces that he would give the faithful a new name (Mosiah 1:11), "the children of Christ." (Mosiah 5:7; cf. 5:8-11) The actual name "Christian" first occurs in Alma 46:13-16. In the BoM narrative, the places of worship are variably called churches and synagogues, although Nephi built a temple, and various cities had a temple. The term "holy order of God" is introduced to refer to the divine authority to officiate in the church. Alma stepped down from the judgment seat and "confined himself wholly to the high priesthood of the holy order of God, to the testimony of the word, according to the spirit of revelation and prophecy." (Alma 4:20) After addressing the church established in Zarahemla, Alma "ordained priests and elders, by laying on his hands according to the order of God, to preside and watch over the church." (Alma 6:1; See Alma 13) By the fifteenth year of the reign of judges, "the church had been established throughout all the land…" (Alma 16:21) After some falling away, "... Helaman (son of Alma) and his brethren went forth to establish the church again in all the land, yea, in every city throughout all the land which was possessed by the people of Nephi. And it came to pass that they did appoint priests and teachers throughout all the land, over all the churches." (Alma 45:22; cf. 62:46)

The wavering between belief and unbelief continued, until the wickedness became sufficient that, at the time of the crucifixion of Christ, divine judgment befell the people in the form of the Crucifixion Cataclysm, when many cities were entirely destroyed. Those who were spared were apt to accept Christ when he appeared to them after his resurrection. A new era is ushered in, with Christ personally preaching his gospel and choosing twelve disciples:

> And it came to pass that on the morrow, when the multitude was gathered together, behold, Nephi and his brother whom he had raised from the dead, whose name was Timothy, and also his son, whose name was Jonas, and also Mathoni, and Mathonihah, his brother, and Kumen, and Kumenonhi, and Jeremiah, and Shemnon, and Jonas, and Zedekiah, and Isaiah—now these were the names of the disciples whom Jesus had chosen—and it came to pass that they went forth and stood in the midst of the multitude. (3 Nephi 19:4)

These names are unlikely. Timothy is a well-known Greek name found in the New Testament. In Greek, it means God-fearing. Nephi's brother should not have a Greek name. The BoM authors did not know Greek, and fell into a linguistic trap. Furthermore, unlike the other names of the BoM, there is a concentration of names of the most famous OT figures: Jonas (twice), Jeremiah, Zedekiah and Isaiah. Jonas is especially interesting. It is the New Testament rendering in Greek of Jonah, the *s* being a Greek ending. This too should not appear in a New World disciple list. Furthermore, the governor over the land at the time of the birth of Jesus was Lachoneus, another Greek name (note too Archeantus). Names were chosen for a New Testament atmosphere.

Two Christian Centuries Followed by the Great Apostasy

As noted above, there were earlier periods when the whole land became Christian, although this referred to the Nephite lands. Following the mission of the Twelve to preach to all the surviving people, we are told that the whole land was Christian for about two centuries. This time around, the account refers to truly all the land, presumably North and South America, depicting a Christian era, followed by a post-Christian era, characterized by heresy and apostasy (4 Nephi 1):

1. And it came to pass that the thirty and fourth year passed away, and also the thirty and fifth [after the birth of Jesus], and behold the disciples of Jesus had formed a church of Christ in all the lands round about. ...

2. And it came to pass in the thirty and sixth year, the people were all converted unto the Lord, upon all the face of the land, both Nephites and Lamanites...

23. And now I, Mormon, would that ye should know that the people had multiplied, insomuch that they were spread upon all the face of the land, and that they had become exceedingly rich, because of their prosperity in Christ.

24. And now, in this two hundred and first year there began to be among them those who were lifted up in pride...

26. they began to be divided into classes... they began to build up churches unto themselves to get gain, and began to deny the true church of Christ.

27. when two hundred and ten years had passed away there were many churches in the land; yea, there were many churches which professed to know the Christ, and yet they did deny the more parts of his gospel, insomuch that they did receive all manner of wickedness...

29. And again, there was another church which denied the Christ; and they did persecute the true church of Christ, because of their humility and their belief in Christ; and they did despise them because of the many miracles which were wrought among them.

36. And it came to pass that in this year there arose a people who were called the Nephites, and they were true believers in Christ...

38. And it came to pass that they who rejected the gospel were called Lamanites, and Lemuelites, and Ishmaelites; and they did not dwindle in unbelief, but they did wilfully (sic) rebel against the gospel of Christ...

40-41. And it came to pass that two hundred and forty and four years had passed away...And they did still continue to build up churches unto themselves, and adorn them with all manner of precious things.

The whole land became converted to Christianity, and remained occupied by true Christians for almost the first two centuries, at which point false churches emerged, and eventually one that denied Christ altogether. The BoM authors replicated their own view of what they considered to have been the great apostasy in the early history of Christianity in the Old World, leading to their situation in New England. There is no mention of competition with pagan religions, and the known deities of the New World, nor their worship upon pyramids, or in the caves of cenotes.

This period of the BoM account covers the last two centuries of the late preclassic period of Mayan history. The Mayans and related peoples of Central America are the most relevant pre-Columbian civilizations, due to the specific geographical details in the BoM narrative, situated between the narrow neck of land, which can only be the Isthmus of Panama, and the pass leading northward, which is the erroneous Isthmus of Guatemala, a cartographical error in the 1820s.

It might be expected that at some point specifically Christian remains would be found, churches perhaps, Christian documents, and burials. It is not clear that we would expect cross icons, but it seems that the cross did have some significance in the *Book of Mormon*:

> Now my son, I would that ye should repent and forsake your sins, and go no more after the lusts of your eyes, but cross yourself in all these things; for except ye do this ye can in nowise inherit the kingdom of God. Oh, remember, and take it upon you, and cross yourself in these things. (Alma 39:9)

Jesus says to the Nephites: "For it is better that ye should deny yourselves of these things, wherein ye will take up your cross, than that ye should be cast into hell." (3 Nephi 12:30) The problem is that the cross is one of the common symbols in various civilizations. Its significance depends on the context, and associated inscriptions, especially when found in distinctly non-Christian settings. An explicitly Christian complex should be expected, but none has been found.

From the evidentiary point of view, by far the most important thing is the prevalence of uninterrupted pagan civilization (Mayan, Olmec, Nazca, Moche, etc.). It is now recognized that the essential traits of the classic period (c. 250-800 CE) had already developed in the late preclassic period, including writing, the Mayan calendar, monumental architecture including massive pyramids, statuary and murals, replete with typical Mayan religious iconography.[259]

It is clear that two centuries or more of exclusively Christian civilization just simply did not exist, in this time period, conservatively covering modern Ecuador to northern Mexico. The BoM narrative further describes Christian centers all the way from Nephi to the coming of Christ, indicating that Christian sites should be found even in pre-Christian centuries. This is the

Nephite Christian Issue

Oᵥₑ OO ᵥₑ OO ᵥₑ OO ᵥₑ O

---

[259] See, for example, Michael Love & Jonathan Kaplan, eds., *The Southern Maya in the Late Preclassic: The Rise and Fall of Early Mesoamerican Civilization* (Boulder, CO: University Press of Colorado, 2011).

< Chapter 14 >

The Quest for a *Book of Mormon* Setting

Pre-Columbian archaeological research brings an existential question unavoidably to the fore. Where in the New World is the setting for the sites and events in the BoM narrative? In its pages, readers have found a record of relations between various peoples of Israelite origin that it locates somewhere in the Americas, including wars between well-fortified cities, and descriptions of concrete aspects of the material culture of the Nephites and Lamanites. Once it was established as the founding scripture of a new religion, the believers began to want to see it like the Bible they were familiar with. It should be bound like a Bible, perhaps have gilded pages like a Bible, with a Concordance, and an index. Christians are accustomed to finding in their Bible a map of the Holy Land, and of the travels of the Apostles. So might not the *Book of Mormon* also be similarly equipped, with maps of the lands of the Nephites and Lamanites, showing the cities, rivers and routes of military and missionary campaigns? In 1901 Benjamin Cluff, president of Brigham Young Academy, the forerunner of BYU, conducted an expedition to South and Central America to identify the Land of Zarahemla. In 1921 a General Authority *Book of Mormon* Committee held a hearing of those who had views on the subject of BoM geography. No official conclusions were reached, and since then the LDS establishment has kept aloof from such research. In this absence of enthusiasm, private scholars have taken up

The quest for the Book of Mormon *setting.*

The Abstract Approach

One sort of LDS BoM cartography is both useful and straightforward. It is essentially a reader's guide. The typical map is in the shape of an hourglass, with no features that relate to actual geography. The shape is due to a key passage in Alma 22:32:

> And now, it was only the distance of a day and a half's journey for a Nephite, on the line Bountiful and the land Desolation, from the east to the west sea; and thus the land of Nephi and the land of Zarahemla were nearly surrounded by water, there being a small neck of land between the land northward and the land southward.

A straightforward reading of this passage indicates a land to the north, a land to the south, and a narrow neck of land connecting the two, such that it was a short journey between the east and west seas. These two lands "were nearly surrounded by water… [viz two continents]."

This makes a geographical configuration in the shape of an hourglass. We find an example in *Geography of the Book of Mormon* by Fletcher B. Hammond.[260] The top and bottom lobes are effectively North and South America, as LDS cartographers sometimes map them out. Harold K. Nielsen follows a similar hourglass approach in his *Mapping the Action Found in the Book of Mormon* (1987).[261] These maps are provided as aids to the reader to follow the sometimes confusing travels of persons and armies in the *Book of Mormon*, similar to the ever-popular maps of Middle Earth in Tolkien's *Lord of the Rings*.

The works of J. Nile Washburn are a bit of a composite. The map is drawn to look a lot like one placing the BoM setting in Central America. But he adheres to the principle that "we do not really know" and perhaps "cannot know." While admitting that the narrow neck of land is the key feature, his position waffles as follows: "We must not look too closely for it, however, in terms of modern coastlines. Too much has happened through the centuries." However, "It ought to be noted…that the narrow neck was still a guiding feature of the landscape hundreds of years after the crucifixion of Christ, clear down to the days of Mormon."[262]

So for him, the narrow neck of land endured for possibly two millennia of Jaredite and Nephite history, and even through the Crucifixion Cataclysm, but possibly not through the centuries following 421 CE. Paul R. Cheesman also urges caution regarding associating an abstract (internal) map with current maps of the Americas.[263]

---

[260] Fletcher B. Hammond, *Geography of the Book of Mormon* (Salt Lake City: Utah Printing Company, 1959).

[261] Harold K. Nielsen, *Mapping the Action Found in the Book of Mormon* (Springville, UT: Cedar Fort, 1987).

[262] J. Nile Washburn, *Book of Mormon Lands and Times* (Bountiful, UT: Horizon Publishers, 1974), 207. See also J. A. Washburn and J. N. Washburn, *An Approach to the Study of the Book of Mormon* (Provo, Utah: New Era Publishing Company, 1939), 194-99.

[263] Paul R. Cheesman, *Early America and the Book of Mormon, A photographic Essay of Ancient America* (Salt Lake City: Deseret Book Company, 1972). His view ultimately favors a Central America setting. See also Paul R. Cheesman, *These Early Americans* (Salt Lake City: Deseret Book Company, 1974) and *The World of the Book of Mormon* (Salt Lake City: Deseret Book Co., 1978).

The South America Approach

Finding a BoM setting in South America was given some legitimacy by Orson Pratt as early as 1872.[264] George Reynolds followed his lead in 1888.[265] These deal with the South America that we know.

By contrast, a very different approach is found in *The Book and the Map, New Insights into Book of Mormon Geography* by Venice Priddis (1975),[266] who also attempts to relate BoM cartography to the real world. This map is loosely based on the current elevation contour map of South America. It asserts that the entire continent was thousands of feet lower up to the time of Christ's crucifixion, so that the northern end of the continent, a large swath of the west coast, and nearly all of Brazil and Venezuela were under water. Only the Andean backbone of the continent was above water. It, again, is configured like an elongated hourglass (p. 17). Then came the Crucifixion Cataclysm. Chapter ten is titled "The Land Changed." This is based on 3 Nephi 8:12, which depicts a vengeful God who again destroys cities, men, women and children, in his righteous wrath: "For behold, the whole face of the land was changed because of the tempest and the whirlwinds and the thunderings and the lightnings, and the exceeding great quaking of the whole earth." Priddis finds it possible to write "Geological evidences such as the heaving upward of lower Chile from the ocean's bottom, the rising of Tiahuanaco to about 3,400 feet above its previous level, and the possible rising of the 150-mile 'Darien Gap' at Panama show this to be true. Apparently all the geological changes took place within the space of three hours."[267] (See 3 Nephi 8:19.)

Those who propose a setting in South America have some scenario for expansion into North America, and on to Cumorah, where the gold plates were deposited. A good example of this is the setting proposed by Orson Pratt in 1872. See also the geographical comments in Alvin

---

[264] Orson Pratt, "Nephite America—The Day of God's Power—The Shepherd of Israel" in *Journal of Discourses* (February 11, 1872), 14:324-31.

[265] George Reynolds, *The Story of the Book of Mormon* (Salt Lake City: J. H. Parry, 1888).

[266] Venice Priddis, *The Book and the Map, New Insights into Book of Mormon Geography* (Salt Lake City: Bookcraft, 1975).

[267] Priddis, *The Book and the Map*, 149.

Knisley's dictionary of the *Book of Mormon* (1901), especially under the entry for Zarahemla,[268] as well as the work of Cecil George Le Poidevin.[269]

The assertion that there was a great cataclysm at the time of the crucifixion does not hold up. Archaeologists have excavated numerous sites that straddle this timeframe. Flood layers, lava or volcanic ash deposition, seismic shifts in the strata, leveled structures and burn levels are all indications of some sort of a disaster. If these things are found in the same time period, and at all or at least most of the sites in a region, then one can talk about a major cataclysm. No such thing is evidenced.

Surprisingly, a problem in *Book of Mormon* cartography has arisen from efforts to locate a Hill Cumorah in Mesoamerica, although Joseph Smith claimed to have gotten the Golden Plates at the Hill Cumorah in upstate New York. Riley L. Dixon, in his book *Just One Cumorah*, makes a revealing comment about his methodology: "No external evidence will be used that does not harmonize with the *Book of Mormon*, for that book is the only authentic and divine record that we have of Ancient America."[270] Thus unconstrained by real-world evidence, he locates the land of Nephi in the lands of Bolivia, Peru, Ecuador and the northern half of Chile, with the City of Zarahemla and its environs south of the Isthmus of Panama in the central part of that area, and the land of Desolation stretched out to include the northern reaches of Mexico and the southwestern part of the United States.[271] Thomas Stuart Ferguson's investigation of scriptural references came to the conclusion that Cumorah was exclusively in Central America, as well as the Nephite civilization.[272]

The Central America Approach

From 1900 to the 1980s, most cartography efforts eventually placed the *Book of Mormon* events, towns, cities, bodies of water and other natural features in an area somewhere between the equator and the Rio Grande. Either both the Land of Nephi (Lamanite territory) and the Land of Zarahemla (Nephite territory) were placed in Central America, or the latter

---

[268] Alvin Knisley, *Dictionary of All Proper Names in the Book of Mormon* (Independence, MO: Ensign Publishing House, 1909).

[269] Cecil George Le Poidevin, *Zion, Land of Promise. An Atlas Study of Book of Mormon Geography* (N.P., by author, 1977).

[270] Riley L. Dixon, *Just One Cumorah* (Salt Lake city: Bookcraft, 1958), 12-14. Dixon also locates the principal Lamanite/Nephite territories in South America.

[271] Dixon, *Just One Cumorah*, 46, 65 & 78.

[272] Thomas Stuart Ferguson, *Cumorah—Where?* (Independence, MO: Press of Zion's Printing and Publishing, 1947), 14 & 55.

was there, while the former was placed roughly in the northern part of present-day Columbia. These settings also possibly enjoyed the support of Joseph Smith. In 1842, while he was editor of the *Times and Seasons*, it began publishing selections from a book by non-Mormon John Stephens that reported on his travels in Central America.[273] An editorial comment possibly approved by Smith, says:

> Since our 'Extract' was published from Mr. Stephens' 'Incidents of Travel,' &c., we have found another important fact relating to the truth of the *Book of Mormon*. Central America, or Guatemala, is situated north of the Isthmus of Darien and once embraced several hundred miles of territory from north to south.–The city of Zarahemla, burnt at the crucifixion of the Savior, and rebuilt afterwards, stood upon this land as will be seen from the following words in the Book of Alma: [22:32][274]

It is to be noted that over the course of his career, a variety of comments have been attributed to Smith that many have found to be a bit puzzling in this regard. For Mormons, an LDS prophet has every right to his personal views, which can change over time, and the faithful are not bound by a prophet's opinions, in the absence of a revelation to support it. Still, Smith's connection with this view can be expected to carry some weight.

Benjamin Cluff's expedition report began to redirect the BoM setting to Central America (including Central America plus Columbia).[275] This setting became dominant from 1900 to the 1980s. Two of the earliest works are Holmes (1903)[276] and Palfrey (1903),[277] followed by Shook,[278]

---

[273] John Lloyd Stephens, *Incidents of Travel in Central America, Chiapas and Yucatan* (New York: Harper, 1841).

[274] *Times and Seasons*, 3:23 (1 October 1842).

[275] Benjamin Cluff (1901). . See Joseph Lovell Allen and Blake Joseph Allen, *Exploring the Lands of the Book of Mormon*, 2nd ed. (Orem, UT: *Book of Mormon* Tours and Research Institute, Inc., 2008), 382-83.

[276] Robert Holmes, *Geographical Sketches of the Book of Mormon* (LDS Historian's Office).

[277] Louise Palfrey, *The Divinity of the Book of Mormon Proven by Archaeology* (Lamoni, IA: Zion's Religio-Literary Society, Herald Publishing House, 1903).

[278] Chas. A. Shook, *Cumorah Revisited* (Cincinnati: Standard Publishing Company, 1910).

(1910) Hills (1917),[279], Farnsworth (1947),[280] Ferguson (1947)[281] and many others (v. Table 20 and Bibliography 3).

The Quest for a Fallback Setting

By around 1980, considerable scientific archaeological research had been done in Mesoamerica, and some Maya texts were being confidently translated, including king dynasty lists, the names of the Mayan cities with their imperial vs tributary relationships, and religious beliefs. This heralded a new era in LDS cartography, marked by a growing concern that it might no longer be tenable to superimpose the Nephite/Lamanite territories on top of the Mayan and Olmec regions. An alternative *Book of Mormon* setting was needed.

This turn of events was described in the work of Duane R. Aston (1998 & 2003). He writes that early in 1990

> ...I learned that a Latter-day Saint author had spent nearly 25 years studying and researching *Book of Mormon* archaeology related to Central America, but that he had lost his faith in the authenticity of the *Book of Mormon* [reference must be to Thomas Stuart Ferguson]. It seems that this man had come to the conclusion that there was nothing to be found in the Central American setting that convinced him that the *Book of Mormon* belonged there.... Of course one should not expect to find any external evidence obtained from archaeology that would 'prove' the authenticity of the *Book of Mormon*... Then if *Book of Mormon* lands were not located in Central America, then where might they belong? The only reasonable possible solution that came to my mind was New York.[282]

The Great Lakes setting pays at least some deference to the various mentions of the narrow neck of land, by defining it to be the Erie-Ontario isthmus. To gain access to this area, proponents assert that Nephi sailed from the Arabian coast of the Indian Ocean around the southern tip of Africa, and up to the St. Lawrence River. One has to ask if it would not

---

[279] Louis Edward Hills, *Geography of Mexico and Central America from 2234 BC to 421 AD* (Independence MO: 1917).

[280] Dewey Farnsworth, *The Americas before Columbus* (El Paso, TX: Farnsworth Publishing Co., 1947), and Dewey Farnsworth and Edith Wood Farnsworth, *Book of Mormon Evidences* (Salt Lake City: Deseret Book Company, 1953).

[281] Thomas Stuart Ferguson, *Cumorah—Where?* (Independence, MO: Zion's Printing and Publishing, 1947).

[282] Duane R. Aston, *Return to Cumorah* (Sacramento, CA: American River Publications, 1998/2003).

have been easier to spend eight years getting to Gibraltar to set sail, rather than crossing the wilderness of Arabia.

Beginning in the 1980s, the relocation of the BoM setting to the Great Lakes region has grown and is striving for greater respectability, resulting in the works of Holley (1983),[283] Curtis (1988),[284] Aston (1998),[285] Olive (2000)[286] and Coon (2009)[287].

Map 5. The Great Lakes BoM Setting (without Details)

The place where both Lehi and Mulek disembarked is clearly stated in Helaman 6:10: "Now the land south was called Lehi and the land north was called Mulek, which was after the son of Zedekiah; for the Lord did bring Mulek into the land north, and Lehi into the land south." In the Great Lakes scenario, presumably Mulek must have landed on the north shore of Lake Ontario, and Lehi on the New York shore. Niagara falls would have stopped them from sailing into Lake Erie. As we shall see, Mulek and his descendants remained in the land northward. So Ontario should be the location of Zarahemla, and therefore the land of the Nephites, while the Lamanites should be in New York. Rather than having the Nephites travel to Zarahemla (the Mosiah scenario), the Great Lakes setting usually has the Mulekites traveling south into New York, so that both the Nephites and Lamanites are there.

---

[283] Vernal Holley, *Book of Mormon Authorship. A Closer Look* (Ogden UT: Zenos Publications, 1983).

[284] Delbert W. Curtis, *The Land of the Nephites* (Orem, UT: self-published, 1988).

[285] Aston, *Return to Cumorah.*

[286] Phyllis Carol Olive, *The Lost Lands of the Book of Mormon* (Springville, UT: Bonneville Books, 2000).

[287] W. Vincent Coon, *Choice above All Other Lands. Book of Mormon Covenant Lands According to the Best Sources* (Salt Lake City: Brit Publishing, 2009).

The principal problem with this approach is the location itself. It confuses the sea to the west and the sea to the east with the land with "large bodies of water and many rivers" in Helaman 3:4, speaking of some who had traveled far away from Zarahemla: "And they did travel to an exceedingly great distance, insomuch that they came to large bodies of water and many rivers." This is usually associated with the Great Lakes region. Since the normal term to indicate distance is "many days," this passage stresses the distance much more. The Great Lakes approach, cannot have its cake and eat it too. If the Great Lakes are the east, west, north and south seas, then where are the great bodies of water associated with Cumorah? If they are the lakes in the Cumorah region, then where are these four seas? If the narrow neck of land is the Erie-Ontario Isthmus, then the Nephites should be in the land northward, in Ontario.

A second problem is perhaps equally telling. It arises from the voyages of a shipbuilder named Hagoth (Alma 63:5-7): "... [Hagoth] went forth and built him an exceedingly large ship, on the borders of the land Bountiful, by the land Desolation, and launched it forth into the west sea, by the narrow neck which led into the land northward....and they took their course northward. ...this man built other ships...and set out again to the land northward." The site for embarkation is "on the borders of the land Bountiful, by the land Desolation," where Hagoth launched his ship "into the west sea, by the narrow neck which led into the land northward." In the Great Lakes approach, this site must be at the northeasternmost tip of Lake Erie (called the west sea in this theory), near the Erie-Ontario Isthmus. Launching from this site, the entire "west sea" lies to the south. It is not possible to take one's course to the north, and sail to the land northward.

A third problem is the location of Cumorah, which seems fixed by the Joseph Smith story. The BoM narrative clearly locates Cumorah in the land northward (see below), but this setting places it in the land southward, in upstate New York. Furthermore, the Erie-Ontario isthmus is crossed by the Niagara River, and is dominated by the amazing Niagara Falls. The BoM narrative does not mention it.

Fourth, if Zarahemla is placed in the land northward, Lake Ontario can be to the east, but Lake Erie is to the south. If it is placed in the land southward, Zarahemla can be situated with lake Erie to the west, but Lake Ontario is to the north. As we shall see, in the BoM narrative the sea to the east and the sea to the west are located to the east and west of Zarahemla, respectively.

Finally, this relocation does nothing to facilitate dealing with the archaeological verdict. Where are the Nephite/Lamanite remains?

Even though the Great Lakes proposal patently cannot be reconciled with the BoM narrative, the fact that a number of geographies have been based on it since the 1980s is important. It provides evidence that many LDS scholars are becoming seized of the fact that superimposing the Lamanite/Nephite territories on the Maya and Olmec regions presents serious problems.

Related to the Great Lakes Model are other approaches that locate the BoM setting in the familiar areas of Mormon settlement prior to the move to Utah, particularly Missouri and Illinois, partly associated with the Great Lakes. These are usually only loosely based on BoM geographical references, or proceed by very creative or imaginative interpretations of a few of those passages.[288] An example is the setting of Rod Meldrum. He has proposed the American Heartland Model, which nestles the Nephite setting within the lands of the Ohio, Illinois, Mississippi, and Missouri rivers, largely from the confluence of the Ohio and Mississippi up to Lake Michigan. Even more than the foregoing, his model essentially ignores the narrow neck of land. It makes Lake Michigan the Sea West, Lake Superior the Sea North, Lake Erie the Sea South, and Lake Ontario the Sea East. It is very difficult to imagine a narrow neck of land separating Lake Michigan from Lake Ontario. For these models, selected and liberally reinterpreted quotations attributed to Joseph Smith and early Church leaders clearly trump the BoM text.[289]

A Bible in Search of a Geographical Setting

The BoM setting conundrum is reflected in some book titles: *The Lost Lands of the* Book of Mormon; *Where O Where is the* Book of Mormon? *An Ancient American Setting for the* Book of Mormon; *In Search of Cumorah*; *Cumorah—Where?*

From 1850 through the first half of the twentieth century, Mormon writers clearly felt that there was no real writing in pre-Columbian America, and that their *Book of Mormon* was the best guide to interpreting the

---

[288] One such approach is that to which the website http//:www.bookofmormon geography is dedicated.

[289] Rod L. Meldrum, *Exploring the Book of Mormon Heartland Photobook* (New York: Digital Legend Press, 2011). An online map copyrighted by Meldrum was accessed from "Heartland Model" on 22/01/2016 at http//:www.josephsmith academy.org, Inspira Wiki. See also J. A. Benson, "How Manifest Destiny Destroyed *Book of Mormon* Evidence" (http//:www.millennialstar.org, posted 12/02/2015).

monuments. This has been a natural continuation of the Smith-Cowdery strategy of reserving historical detail for the New World, where certain information regarding such an early period would never be available to test the BoM narrative. The idea that the ruins of the Maya were available for anyone to make a case to support an agenda has been beautifully studied in *Romancing the Maya* by Tripp Evans.[290] Speaking of "a period in the age of the world of which all history is silent," and of "ruins utterly barren of all record of their own history," all the while being sure that the *Book of Mormon* is a true history, John Taylor, yet to become the third LDS prophet, seer and revelator, wrote confidently in 1851 regarding the Mesoamerican glyphs:

> For not only do we find the characters so common to all the ruins of Central America, but tracing them back, without as yet knowing precisely their import, we reach by progressive though receding steps a period when they were identical with and purely the Egyptian hieroglyphs easily deciphered and as easily understood.[291]

The process of deciphering the Mayan glyphs got off to a slow start. The documentation of the many Mayan written materials, and their publication to produce a corpus in a clear scholarly format (photographs plus hand-drawn monographs), was slow, as was the decipherment of the Mayan writing system so that these many texts could be read. From the archaeological, epigraphic and linguistic point of view, LDS insulation from the facts that pre-Columbian civilizations had left behind lasted for over 150 years, from 1830 to at least 1980. The history of Mayan decipherment is summarized in the following table.

Table 19. Decipherment of Mayan Writing

1519	Cortez lands on Cozumel; several screen-fold Mayan books are sent back to Spain.
1561	Diego de Landa has a Mayan friar to help him list the Mayan characters with their Spanish equivalents. He mistakenly thought the Maya used an alphabet, whereas they used a syllabary (as did the Sumerians, and the Japanese today).
1562	Diego de Landa burned all the Mayan books he could find. Only four screen-fold books are known to have survived.
1785	Jose Calderon discovers Palenque.

---

[290] Tripp Evans, *Romancing the Maya, Mexican Antiquity in the American Imagination, 1820-1915* (Austin: University of Texas Press, 2004).

[291] John Taylor, "The Discovery of Ancient Ruins in Northern California" (Salt Lake City: *The Millennial Star of the Latter-day Saints*, vol. XIII, 1851), 93-95.

1810	Five pages of the Dresden codex are published in Paris in a massive volume on the Americas.
18??	Constantine Samuel Rafinesque deciphers some elements of the Mayan numbering system. This is the first decipherment of any Mayan writing.
1862	Brasseur de Bourbourg finds the description of the Maya written by Diego de Landa. He used it to attempt a translation of the Madrid manuscript, but produced a text that bore no similarity to what this manuscript actually says.
1881	Alfred Percival Maudslay begins photographing monuments and inscriptions, producing the first accurate corpus of written Mayan.
1880	Ernst Förstemann, in Dresden, discovered that the Maya invented the concept of zero, and a base-20 counting system. They used rows to record numbers, a ones row (0 to 19), a 20s row, a 400s row, an 8,000s row, etc., much like our system of a one's column, a tens column, etc. They carried over from row to row, just as we carry over from column to column. He also succeeded in working out the Mayan calendar. He used Diego de Landa's notes on the Mayan months, with the Mayan month names written in the Spanish alphabet to be able to read Month glyphs in Mayan. He discovered the Mayan beginning point of the calendar thousands of years ago, the Mayan date of creation. Using Maudslay's photographs, he found that this creation date was used throughout the Mayan world.
1880s	American agricultural scientist Cyrus Thomas discovered that the Maya used a syllabary rather than an alphabet to write, and worked out some characters correctly.
1892	German Mayanist Eduard Seler attacked Thomas' discovery, and Thomas abandoned his efforts. Seler held that the glyphs were pictorial rather than phonological.
1905	A Nevada newspaper man, Joseph Goodman, worked out the correlation between the Mayan dates and the Gregorian calendar. Now Mayan monuments would be dated by their inscriptions.
1900s	In the 1930s through about 1970, Eric Thompson of the Carnegie Foundation catalogued Mayan glyphs, assigning to each a T number. The vast majority could not be read. Unfortunately, Thompson dominated Mayan inscription studies, and held that the Maya did not write, but used symbols in a vague manner to represent priests, gods and their high mysteries. Tatiana Proskouriakoff of the Peabody Museum identified the glyphs for birth dates, ascension to the throne and death. With this she worked out the dynastic succession of Piedras Negras, showing that the Maya wrote their history. The meaning of these glyphs was clear, but she still could not read them in Mayan.
1952	Russian linguist Yuri Knorosov recognized that the characters in the work of Diego de Landa are a partial syllabary, in which, instead of a character for *b*, there are separate characters for *bi, bu, ba, bo, be*, and so on, for all the consonant-vowel combinations of the Mayan language. In addition, the system uses pictorial signs, logograms, where a single sign represents a whole word, as in the Chinese writing system. He knew that some other languages use both phonological characters, and logograms, such as ancient Egyptian. In both Mayan and Egyptian, a word can be represented by a single logogram, or spelled out phonologically.
1953	Anti-Communist Eric Thompson attacked Knorosov's work. This, plus the fact that it had been published in Russian, caused his work to be ignored in the West.

1955	Michael Coe and his Russian-born wife Sophi, discovered a copy of Knorosov's work in Merida, Mexico, and began collaboration with Knorosov. Sophi Coe translated his papers into English. Unfortunately, Eric Thompson's view dominated, and Knorosov remained isolated behind the iron curtain. Heinrich
1959	Berlin identified "city emblem" glyphs that record the names of Mayan cities. Geography could now be identified in the inscriptions, although these glyphs could not be read in Mayan.
1968	Heinrich Berlin identified the glyphs for four rulers at Palenque.
1970s	Merle Greene Robertson founded the Pre-Columbian Art Research Institute.
1973	Merle Robertson organized a *mesa redonda* (round table), the first Mayanist conference. Scholarly collaboration began. During this conference, Peter Mathews, Linda Schele and Floyd Lounsbury picked up where Heinrich Berlin left off, and worked out 200 years of the Palenque dynasty, including six rulers, Lord Hanab Pakal and his five successors.
1974	At a conference at the Dumbarton Oaks research library, using the rubbings from the Hanab Pakal sarcophagus, this ruler's ancestors were added to the Palenque dynasty list, finally covering 400 years, beginning in the late 4th century. Subsequently, similar work was done for other Mayan cities.
1970s	Although a minimum of eighty syllabic signs would be needed to write all of Mayan sounds, by the 1980s fewer than thirty could be read with confidence.
1980	The recognition that the relationship of classical Mayan to modern Mayan is a bit like that of Chaucer to modern English has been extremely useful in achieving a better understanding of the Mayan inscriptional language. This contribution has been much like Champollion's knowledge of Coptic (Egyptian), which he used to decipher ancient Egyptian, once he realized that Coptic was simply the latest development of the former. Since there are some thirty Mayan languages, dictionaries have been written specific to individual languages. An example specific to Yucatec Maya is *Diccionario maya Cordemex*: *maya-español, español-maya*, by Alfredo Barrera Vásquez ((Mérida, Yucatán, México: Ediciones Cordemex, 1980); see other works by Juan Ramón Bastarrachea Manzano and William Brito Sansores.
1985	David Stuart discovered that the Maya used more than one sign for the same sound, much like in English *ch* can be represented by *ch* and by *t* (as in "nature"), and *s* can be represented by *s* and by *c* (as in "cistern"). This opened up a flood gate for the identification of syllabic signs.

Even though there is still much work to be done, by thirty years later, thousands of inscriptions on stone and ceramics have been transcribed, and very adequate translations have been made of many of them.

The pattern we see in LDS apologetics published in the *Improvement Era* and *Ensign* (Figure 34) finds a parallel in the following table, which reflects the penetration of the realities of Mesoamerican archaeology into the circle of LDS scholars wrestling with the issue of locating a plausible setting for the BoM history. The problem arose when ancient Mayan was translated. Until the seventies, Mayan was considered to be untranslatable, or possibly the glyphs were not even a writing system. The Mayan region was fair game for anyone's interpretation. By the mid eighties, much of Mayan could be read with confidence, and progress was being made each year. As this region slipped out of the "fair game" range, orthodox LDS scholars began attempting to relocate the BoM lands elsewhere, always ignoring their violation of clear BoM references. This change in mapping is clear in Table 20 *infra*, as well as its timing with Mayan decipherment. The Mesoamerican setting now has competition. As LDS scholars became increasingly aware of its problems in Central America, they began seeking a new piece of real estate for the BoM narrative. Only time will tell to what extent the new views can prevail among the faithful, being so at odds with the *Book of Mormon* itself.

Table 20. Summary of BoM Cartography Efforts

Abstract	Mesoamerica	South America	North America
	Joseph Smith (1842)		
		O. Pratt, 1872	
		Comer/Maeser, 1880	
		Reynolds, 1888	
	Cluff, 1901		
	Holmes, 1903		
	Palfrey, 1903	Knisley, 1909	
	Shook, 1910		
	Smith, 1911		
	Hills, 1917		
	Young, 1921	Ricks, 1921	
	Ivins, 1921		
	Roberts, c. 1922, c. 1927		
	Driggs, 1928		
Layton, 1938			
Washburn/Washburn, 39			
	Ferguson, 1947		
	Farnsworth, 1947		
	Wilde, 1947		
	Birrell, 1948		
	McGavin/Bean, 1948		
	Stout, 1950		
	Hansen, 1951		
	Hunter, 1956, 1970	Dixon, 1957	
	Ferguson, 1958		
	Reynolds/Sjodahl, 1957		
Hammond, 1959	Hammond, 1959		
	Davila, 1961		
	Jakeman, 1963		
	DeLong-Steede-Simmons	Priddis, 1975	
	1977	Le Poidevin, 1977	
	Cheesman, 1978		
	Ellsworth, 1980		
	Palmer, 1981		Holley, 1983
	Sorenson, 1985		
Nielsen, 1987	Hauck, 1988	Kocherhans, 1989	Curtis, 1988
	Peay, 1993		
	Hansen, 1997		Aston, 1998
	Welch/Welch, 1999		Olive, 2000
	Sutton, 2001		Goble/May 2002

	Calderwood, 2005 Diane Wirth, 2007 Lund, 2007 Allen & Allen, 2008 Johnson, et. Al., 2008	Potter, 2009 Conway, 2012	Coon, 2009 Meldrum, 2011 Neville, 2015

It is interesting that the work of Eric Thompson prolonged the period when it was possible to consider the territory of the Maya to be the Land of Zarahemla, although the Mayan classic period was thought to be the work of the Lamanites in the wake of the war of Nephite extermination. Eric Thompson enjoyed a very high reputation for his knowledge of the Maya, and for his list of Maya characters which even today are referred to by the "T" (Thompson) numbers that he assigned to them. Consequently, his view dominated, that the Maya had no writing, and recorded no history, but used their "glyphs" to represent high mysteries and sacred rites. But at long last evidence accumulated that the Maya used a combination of logograms and phonological characters of a complete syllabic writing system to record historical events and the personal histories of their kings. Since this development, orthodox LDS scholars have been forced to relocate the Nephites to some other place, even when doing so forces them to disrespect the BoM's references to the narrow neck of land. Presumably this results in some degree of cognitive dissonance, since ignoring the references to this key BoM feature is tantamount to editing out a key part of their most sacred scripture.

This is the

Geographic Issue

< Chapter 15 >

BoM Geography Betrayed by a Nonexistent Isthmus

All who undertake BoM cartography have to deal with certain real-world features, including: 1) The Nephite and Jaredite narratives took place in the Americas. 2) There are four seas of note, these being primarily the sea to the east and the sea to the west, and secondarily, the sea to the north and the sea to the south (to all of which eventually Israelites spread). 3) There are two landmasses separated by a "narrow neck of land" that could be traversed at some point by a Nephite in a day and a half. 4) The Nephite Cumorah and the Jaredite Ramah are one and the same and they are where the gold plates with the Nephite record were hidden, which Smith claimed to have found in upstate New York.

Geographic Segmentation

Geographic segmentation is possible when a lengthy text has been composed within a historical framework and has been broken down into sections covering sequential periods of time. In the BoM, it is a process where an earlier section leaves some portion of its territory devoid of geographical detail, with the result that a subsequent section is free to populate its territory with toponyms without fear of contradicting the preceding section. Four segments have been labeled stages one through four.

Table 21. *Book of Mormon* Toponyms

2 Nephi (north)	Omni (land northward)		
	land of Zarahemla	land northward	
2 Nephi (south)	**Omni (land southward)**		
place called Nephi	land of Nephi		
Mosiah (north)	**Alma (land northward)**		
Zarahemla land	Aaron	Lehi city	Riplah hill
	Ammonihah city	Manti	sea east
	Ammonihah land	Melek land	sea west
	Amnihu hill	Minon land	Sidom land
	Antiparah city	Moroni city	Sidon river
	Cumeni city	Moroni land	Sidon head
	Desolation city	Mulek	Sidon land
	Desolation land	Nephihah city	wilderness east
	Desolation of Nehors	Nephihah land	wilder... Hermounts
	Gideon city	Morianton city	wilderness south

	Gideon land	Morianton land	wilderness north
	Gideon valley	narrow pass north	wilderness west
	Judea city	narrow pass south	Zarahemla city
	land northward	Noah city	Zarahemla land
	land southward	Noah land	Zeezrom city
Mosiah (south)	**Alma (land southward)**		
Alma valley	Alma valley	Lemuel city	Siron land
Amulon land	Amulon land	Melek land	
Helam city	Ani-Anti village	Middoni land	
Helam, land	Antionum	Midian land	
Lehi-Nephi city	Antionum land	Mormon fountain	
Lehi-Nephi land	Antipas mount	Mormon forest	
Mormon forest	Bountiful city	Mormon land	
Mormon fountain	Bountiful wilderness	Nephi land	
Mormon waters	Helam city	Onidah hill	
Nephi city	Helam land	Sebus waters	
Nephi land	Ishmael land	Shemlon city	
Shemlon land	Jershon land	Shemlon land	
Shilom city	Jerusalem city	Shilom city	
Shilom land	Jerusalem land	Shilom land	
Mormon (land northward)			
Angola city	Cumorah land/hill	Jashon land	Shem land
Antum land	David land	Jordan city	Shim hill
Boaz city	Desolation land/city	Joshua city	Zarahemla

Stage 1. In the summer of 1828, disaster struck. A thief stole Smith's only copy of nearly all (if not all) of his BoM manuscript completed to that date. It was clear that divine assistance could not be relied upon to replicate this work word for word. His counter was to announce that Providence, ever so prescient, had provided, also engraved on Smith's gold plates, a second and independent account covering the same period of Nephite history. However, there was still a problem. The details in the stolen version might not be correctly remembered for the replacement text (Nephi through Omni replacing Lehi, irretrievably lost). The solution was clear. This new text would have to eschew detail, including geographical place names. The replacement text comprises 23% of the entire BoM narrative, and covers c. 470 years of Nephite history. Yet, it mentions only a place called Nephi (2 Nephi 5:8) and "the land of Nephi" (Omni 1:27), apart from the city and "the land of Zarahemla" (Omni 1:13), and "the land northward" (Omni 1:22), both mentioned at the end, in what was originally chapter one of Mosiah. As for the geographical framework, we are told only that this New World is one of the isles of the sea (2 Nephi 10:20) mentioned in Isaiah (60:9, 24:15).

Stage 2. The Book of Mosiah was thus able to take advantage of the replacement text's lack of detail. In what was originally written to be its chapter one, Mosiah I led the Nephites north, across the Isthmus of Panama, to the Land of Zarahemla. There, the Mulekites incredibly adopted a Nephite identity to the extent that the Mulekites no longer figure in the Nephite narrative. The four sons of Mosiah II travelled throughout the lands of Zarahemla (Mosiah 27:35). People spread north, south, east and west, building large cities (Mosiah 27:6). And yet, all of the stories take place in the territory of the replacement text, i.e. south of the Isthmus of Panama, in the lands of the land of Nephi. Apart from mentioning "the land of Zarahemla," the whole record of Mosiah totally eschews both stories and place names in the region that had become the Nephites adoptive homeland, and even introduces few new toponyms in the south. Only two of the four cardinal points of the compass are used to relate place names. There is a hill north of the land of Shilom (Mosiah 7:5) and Zeniff reigned in the land of Nephi, away south of the land of Shilom (Mosiah 9:14). Alma preached at the waters, fountain and forest of Mormon (Mosiah 18:5, 30). There is no geographical anchor point to situate place names. The Book of Mosiah has left the follow-on book (Alma) a blank slate and total freedom to develop the geography of all the lands north of the narrow neck, including the lands of Zarahemla.

Identifying Features, Cities & Lands in the *Book of Mormon*

Stage 3. The Book of Alma takes full advantage of this *tabla rasa* with a geographical insert, Alma 22:27-34. That it is an insert is indicated in verse 35: "And now I, having said this, return again to the account of Ammon…" His "aside" was obviously intended to provide enough detail with sufficient specificity to give the reader a clear understanding of the geographical framework for the *Book of Mormon*.

Stage 4. Mormon's record of Nephite history in his own lifetime (*infra*).

The Framework

When the BoM project reached Alma, it had become obvious that the envisaged wars, battles and missionary travels would not be even remotely accessible for the readers without populating the Nephite and Lamanite territories with cities, territories, at least one river, and other landmarks.

| Vignette | Alma's Key to Nephite-Lamanite Geography |

The Promised Land that Lehi led his group to is an isle of the sea [i.e. a continent]. (2 Nephi 10:20) In Alma 22, the basics of BoM geography are laid out. The land of the king of the Lamanites in the south stretched from sea to sea. (22:27) After Mosiah had led his people to the Land of Zarahemla, the Nephites and Lamanites were separated by a narrow strip of wilderness stretching from the east sea to the west sea, and along the sea shore as far north as Zarahemla which is situated by the river Sidon, with its headwaters near the city Manti. (22:27) The wilderness stretches along the west seashore from a point west of Zarahemla southward and along the west shore of the Lamanites' Land of Nephi in the south. (22:28) It also extends along the east coast of the lands of Nephi in the south, and of Zarahemla in the north. The Nephites had taken possession of the land north of a land called Bountiful. Lower level Lamanites dwelled in these stretches of wilderness, and so the Lamanites almost had the Nephites surrounded. (22:29) Passing east to west until the Sidon headwaters, one passes by Bountiful, and on the north lay the land they called desolation, filled with bones (of the slaughtered Jaredites). Bountiful is a wilderness that is bountiful with wild animals of every kind, which had come from the land northward to get food. (22:31) This is the place of "their" first landing. Apparently this refers to the landing of the people of Mulek, because Helaman (6:10) states that Mulek landed in the land north, and Lehi in the land south.

> *And now, it was only the distance of a day and a half's journey for a Nephite, on the **line Bountiful and the land Desolation**, from the east to the west sea; and thus the land of Nephi and the land of Zarahemla were nearly surrounded by water [being two "isles of the sea", viz two continents], there being **a small neck of land** between the land northward and the land southward. (22:32)*

The Nephites had hemmed the Lamanites in, in the land southward, while they took exclusive possession of the land north.

At this point Alma ends his geographical key, saying "And now I, after having said this, return again to the account of Ammon and Aaron, Omner and Himni, and their brethren." (22:35)

The most important BoM geographical desideratum is this reference to this "small neck of land." In Ether, it is called a narrow neck of land. (10:20) There is only one location in the Americas that comes even close to his description: the Isthmus of Panama. The distance from Panama City to Colón is 45 miles. The distance from David, Panama, to Chiriquí Grande is 70 miles. At five miles an hour, the crossing at Panama City would take ten hours. At a more believable pace, say 2.5 miles an hour, the crossing could be 28 hours at the David crossing, or very close to a day and a half (allowing for a little sleep). The crossing at Panama City could be done in one day. Actually, a later passage refers to a fortified line taking only one day (Helaman 4:7-8). This crossing point on the narrow neck of land firmly situates the entire BoM geography. After five and one half centuries in the New World, the BoM peoples covered both continents: "...they did multiply and spread... from the land southward to the land northward... they began to cover the face of the whole earth, from the sea south to the sea north, from the sea west to the sea east." (Helaman 3:8)

Moreover, the entire Nephite territory, the land of Zarahemla, is no more than three hundred miles across, from sea to sea, and usually much less. The text is always aware of the presence of these bounding seas.

Map 6. Modern Map of the Americas and the Principal Nephite Territory

Note that the outer (coastal) contour of this map is based on the schoolboys' map.

Our task is not to make BoM geography fit modern maps, but rather the cartographical knowledge of the 1820s. To make a BoM draft map for their work, the 1820s map that the Smiths and Cowdery must have had available is the *School Atlas to Adams' Geography* (Map 7)

Map 7. 1825 Schoolboys' Map of Central America

Cities, lands & Regions

In the *Book of Mormon*, city names are rarely found alone, such as Judea (Alma 57:11). More usually, they are preceded by "the city of" or "the land of." The latter refers to the city plus its hinterland. A few place names can refer additionally to a region. Thus we can have Zarahemla, the city of Zarahemla, the land of Zarahemla (city plus its hinterland), and the land of Zarahemla (the city plus all the cities and their lands in the Zarahemla/Nephite empire). One time only, we find "the lands of Zarahemla" (Mosiah 27:35; i.e. the lands of the empire). Similarly, we have the city of Nephi, the land of Nephi (city plus its hinterland) and the land of Nephi (the region under the sway of the city of Nephi (Alma 50:11). Bountiful is often found alone, referring to a wilderness area: "called Bountiful, it being the wilderness which is filled with all manner of wild animals of every kind." (Alma 22:31) The Jaredite narrative also refers to it: "…they did go into the land southward, to hunt food for the people of the land, for the land was covered with animals of the forest. And Lib also himself became a great hunter. And they built a great city by the narrow neck of land, by the place where the sea divides the land. …they did preserve the land southward for a wilderness, to get game." (Ether 10:19-21) In it we find the city of Bountiful (Alma 53:4), and the land of Bountiful (Alma 52:18), the latter being the hinterland of the city, which is not coterminous with the wilderness Bountiful.

Wilderness vs Desolation

In addition to Bountiful, the BOM has extensive other wilderness. A narrow strip of wilderness has essentially an H form, with the crossbar separating the Lamanites from the land of Zarahemla, and with the legs and arms of the H being narrow strips of wilderness up and down the coastal areas, on both sides of the narrow neck of land, bordering the sea east and the sea west (Alma 22:27). The wilderness areas were occupied by Lamanites living off of hunting and raiding, even on both sides of the land of Zarahemla, such that the Nephites were nearly surrounded (Alma 22:29). Note that at the time of Alma's insert, Bountiful had been occupied by the Nephites (Alma 22:33). So then this crossbar may have passed along the south side of Bountiful, possibly being distinct from it by not being so rich in game (Alma 16:7, 22:27, 31:3, 43:23, 58:13).

There are some regional designations. "Zoram...crossed over the river Sidon...and marched away beyond the borders of Manti into the south wilderness, which was on the east side of the river Sidon." (Alma 16:7) Contrast this with "Antionum, which was east of the land of Zarahemla, which lay nearly bordering upon the seashore, which was south of the land of Jershon, which also bordered upon the wilderness south." (Alma 31:3) Swinging all the way north of Zarahemla and west, we find the wilderness Hermounts (Alma 2:37). The coastline on the east side of the land of Zarahemla is referred to as the east wilderness. There is no corresponding designation on the west side, although captain Helaman has to contend with wilderness used as a Lamanite refuge in his campaign to liberate Manti and other cities there.

Ether (2:5) describes a wilderness as being "that quarter where never had man been." Most usually, the least civilized of the Lamanites make a living by hunting and raiding in the wilderness. Ultimately, it is a land that has not been subjected to human exploitation, under the plow or otherwise. Travel through wilderness occasionally occurs in the BoM, and could represent a considerable challenge. Ammon and his group wander about in the wilderness for forty days before happening upon Shilom (Mosiah 7:4). For the distance from lands that the Lamanites had taken (Shemlon, Shilom and Amulon), just to arrive at the land of Zarahemla (not the city proper), Alma spent a day getting to the valley of Alma, plus twelve days in the wilderness (Mosiah 24:20, 25).

The term "desolation" is just about the opposite of "wilderness." The land Desolation had been extensively occupied by the Jaredites, and had become devoid of their inhabitants, desolate. All of the territory north of the line Bountiful-Desolation was encumbered by the Jaredite ruins found by Mulek upon his arrival. That the first landing of Mulek was in the land north, and that the first landing of Lehi was in the land south, is made clear in Helaman 6:10. Thus the entire land northward came to be called the land of Desolation. The line Bountiful and line Desolation is the point on the isthmus where a Nephite could cross sea to sea in only a day and a half. Bountiful is the northern tip of modern-day Columbia up to this narrow point on the Isthmus of Panama. Although this extensive region went all the way up to the land of large bodies of water, rivers and fountains (the Great Lakes region), over time the land of Zarahemla filled up with cities and was anything but desolate. As a result, a speaker from the vantage point of his home in the Nephite city of Gideon may well refer to the land of desolation as beginning at the northern boundary of the land of Zarahemla.

Similarly we have various directional terms. The southern boundary of "the land northward" was originally the northern side of Bountiful, but over time it could also begin at the northern boundary of the land of Zarahemla. The territory indicated by "the land which was northward" (Alma 50:11; 50:29 & 63:4) is distinct from that indicated by "the land northward." It is the land northward upon leaving the land of Zarahemla: "departed out of the land of Zarahemla into the land which was northward" (Alma 63). "The land southward" may or may not include Bountiful. Even though the narrow neck of land lies on an east-west axis, the city of Nephi lies southeast of the city of Zarahemla, and the continent (South America) lies largely on a north-south axis. But the phrase "on the south" simply refers to the southern side of any place, such as "on the south of the city of Ammonihah" (Alma 8:18); "on the south of the land Bountiful" (Alma 27:22); "on the south of the hill Riplah" (Alma 43:31); "it [the city of Moroni] was on the south by the line of the possessions of the Lamanites" (Alma 50:13); and, the Nephites "had hemmed the Lamanites in on the south" (Alma 22:33).

Water

There is no river mentioned in the Land of Nephi, and but one in the Land of Zarahemla, the river Sidon. Its headwaters are in the southwest of that region, near the city of Manti, which is near the west sea. On the east of the city there is a wilderness and the headwaters. All crossings are from east to west, or vice versa, indicating a northerly flow. Since this river passes on the east side of the capital city, it must be emptying into or near what today is called the Gulf of Honduras.

The explorers sent out by king Limhi in search of Zarahemla got lost and after many days came to a "land among many waters." (Mosiah 8:8) This phrase is used to indicate a large body of water, most notably the Indian Ocean (1 Nephi 17:5; cf. 13:10). There they also found "bones of men, and of beasts, and [it] was also covered with ruins of buildings of every kind." This land, "which had been peopled with a people who were as numerous as the hosts of Israel," most probably corresponds to the great Jaredite city near the narrow neck of land (Ether 10:20). If we were to search for some modern-day referent, it would be the region of the Lake of Nicaragua and Lake of Managua, the former being large enough to be featured on the 1825 schoolboys' map.

No lakes, rivers or springs are indicated for nearly any of the BOM cities. There are however references to the Great Lakes region, said to be at "an exceedingly great distance" (Helaman 3:4), not just "many days." This region has large bodies of water, rivers and fountains (Alma 50:29; Helaman 3:4; & Mormon 6:4, in connection with Cumorah).

The Lamanites and the Land of Nephi

Perhaps two decades after Lehi's landfall in the land southward, Nephi's elder sibling and rival had become irrevocably opposed to his brother's rule, and his Christian message. The Lord warned Nephi to flee. He gathered his followers with their planting seed and flocks, and fled into the wilderness, clearly eastward away from the seashore, and perhaps somewhat northward, into what is now north-central Columbia. This location works for the various subsequent displacements of missionaries and armies. Nephi and his followers established the city Nephi and land of Nephi. The Lamanites continued to grow in numbers, and to move into the region of the land of Nephi. About 450 ALJ the Lord commanded Mosiah to take the Nephites and move to the Mulekite city Zarahemla, north of the narrow neck of land. The Mulekites enthusiastically accepted the Nephite language and the gospel of Christ. Their king, Benjamin, designated Mosiah to be their new ruler. (Omni 1:18, 19; Mosiah 6:2)

A man called Zeniff led a group of Nephites back to the land of Nephi (Mosiah 7:9). The Lamanite king Laman allowed them to occupy the cities of Shilom and Lehi-Nephi in exchange for paying tribute (Mosiah 7:21). Noah, son of Zeniff, built a tower in Shilom, that also overlooked Shemlon. Amulon, viceroy of Helam, was appointed a teacher over the people in the land of Shemlon, the land of Shilom, and the land of Amulon (Mosiah 23:39-24:1). The tower of Shilom overlooked that city and Shemlon (Mosiah 11:12). When the Lamanites sought to destroy the people of Limhi, they went "up to the land of Nephi" (Mosiah 20:7). When

Ammon arrived at Shilom, viceroy Limhi was described as being "the king of the people who were in the land of Nephi, and in the land of Shilom" (Mosiah 7:7). Although viceroy Limhi, son of Noah, reigned in Shilom, two references state that he returned to the city of Nephi (Mosiah 21:1, 12). Clearly these six lands are closely grouped.

Mosiah became concerned about those who had left. A man called Ammon (identified as being a descendant of Zarahemla) succeeded in prevailing upon him to be allowed to take a company of sixteen to learn their fate. When he got to Shilom, he was seized and brought to king (viceroy) Limhi. With the aid of Gideon, and led by Ammon, king Limhi escaped with his people back to Zarahemla (Mosiah 22:5-11). But another hero had yet to get out: Alma, a convert of the prophet Abinadi. When Amulon persecuted Alma and his converts, they began to meet secretly at a place called Mormon (forest called Mormon), where he baptized in the waters of Mormon (Mosiah 18:16). This is geographically important, because it is located "in the borders of the land having been infested, by times or at seasons, by wild beasts." (Mosiah 18:4) This probably describes a location on the east side of Bountiful, and is therefore an anchor point, that helps locate these five lands. Moreover, interaction between king Limhi and the king of the Lamanites indicates at least some degree of propinquity to the city of Nephi (20:12-21:1).

The next Nephite foray into the lands southward was undertaken by another Ammon (a son of Mosiah), and his siblings (Aaron, Omner and Himni). They split up and each headed for a different place with the object of proselytizing. Ammon went to the land of Ishmael. Those who were converted unto the Lord were people of the Lamanites in the land of Ishmael; in the land of Middoni; in the city of Nephi; in the land of Shilom; in the land of Shemlon, in the city of Lemuel, and in the city of Shimnilom. (Alma 23:8-12) There is not enough information to enable us to know specifically where these are located in the land southward. But we can observe that when Ammon and Lamoni are on route to Middoni, they encounter the latter's father apparently coming from the city of Nephi, placing it in some sort of linear relationship with the land of Ishmael and Middoni. Nephi, Shilom and Shemlon overlap the six cities above. All of these are probably within some proximity to each other.

The converts took the name of Anti-Nephi-Lehies and became the target of Lamanite military forces. Ammon and the others met in the land of Midian, and held a council in the land of Ishmael. In view of the Lamanite danger to these converts, Zarahemla decided to give them the land of Jershon. This tells us that Zarahemla still sought to exercise control over at least one land south of Bountiful. Their enemies collected in a neighboring land, Antionum (v. *supra*). Another city has some geographical information. Aaron went to the land of Jerusalem, "away joining the borders of Mormon." (Alma 21:1) And even more clear are the cities of Mulek, Gid and Bountiful (v. *infra*).

The Nephites and the Land of Zarahemla

The group from Jerusalem led by Mulek had made landfall in the land north (Helaman 6:10) and built the great city Zarahemla. "[They] were brought by the hand of the Lord across the great waters, into the land where Mosiah discovered them; and they had dwelt there from that time forth." (Omni 1:16) The place of Mulek's landfall must have been within some reasonable proximity to the land of Nephi. Later, General Moroni fortified "the line between the Nephites and the Lamanites, between the land of Zarahemla and the land of Nephi...the Nephites possessing all the land northward, yea, even all the land which was northward of the land Bountiful." (Alma 50:11)

The city of Zarahemla, the residence of Alma, is on the west side of the Sidon. Alma traveled west to Melek, and then three days north to Ammonihah (Alma 8:3-6; later renamed the Desolation of the Nehors, Alma 16:11). Alma, Amulek and their converts left Ammonihah and went to the land of Sidom (Alma 15:1). In the context of Lamanite forays against the Nephites, the land of Noah is associated with Ammonihah (Alma 16:3; 49:14-15). The land, valley and city of Gideon are across the river Sidon from Zarahemla, i.e. on the east side (Alma 2:26, 6:7). Minon is between Zarahemla and the land of Nephi (Alma 2:24-26). In Alma's war against the Amlicites, the hill Amnihu is on the east of the Sidon, and associated with Gideon, east of Zarahemla (Alma 2:15-20).

Zarahemla was located inland. In Helaman (1:27) we read: "the Lamanites ... had come into the center of the land, and had taken the capital city which was the city of Zarahemla." (cf. Alma 22:28 & 31:3). Furthermore, from Zarahemla one must cross the wilderness to get to the land of Nephi. (Alma 17:8, 22:27, 27:14) The wilderness wraps north and south around to the west of Zarahemla and in the west of the land of Nephi (Alma 22:28). The wilderness also lies east of Zarahemla, having wrapped around and up both the east and west coasts. (Alma 50:9) In 3 Nephi (3:23) we read that a land (unnamed) lay between Zarahemla and the land of Bountiful.

The Lamanite-Nephite wars in Alma began when Lamanites attacked converts called the Anti-Nephi-Lehies. The Lamanites, seeking revenge against the Nephites (Alma 25:1), marched up the west coast of the land of Zarahemla and destroyed the city of Ammonihah (Alma 25:1-2). Finding the Nephites to be too strong for them to continue, they returned to the land of Nephi. When the Anti-Nephi-Lehies (later renamed the people of Ammon) got established in Jershon, the Nephites put military units all about the city to protect them. (Alma 28:1) Zerahemnah collected Lamanites, Amalekites and Zoramites in Antionum, and created an army poised at Jershon. The Nephite chief captain Moroni commanded the army in the borders of Jershon. Rather than confront Moroni, Zerahemnah took his forces through the wilderness, around into Nephite territory at Manti to seize the land. Moroni divides his force, with part just south of the hill Riplah, east of the headwaters of the Sidon, and the other part on the west of the Sidon in the borders of the land of Manti. He and his captain Lehi surrounded the Lamanites on the banks of the Sidon. After some additional fighting, Zerahemnah entered into a peace agreement and was allowed to slip into the wilderness with his remaining forces.

A period of far more serious warfare developed due to the rise of Nephite dissenters under the leadership of Amalickiah. He, after fleeing to the land of Nephi, and considerable maneuvering, incredibly became king of the Lamanites, and sought "to reign over all the land, yea…the Nephites as well as the Lamanites." (Alma 48:2) The Lamanites proceeded again up the west coast of the land of Zarahemla, but when they found Ammonihah rebuilt and very strong, they decide to attack Noah. Lehi commanded its defense and defeated the Lamanites who returned to the land of Nephi.

Enraged by this news, Amalickiah personally commanded a new effort in the 19th year of the judges (19 YOJ), beginning by mobilizing a massive army. Since he decided not to attack the city of Judea (the command center in the west, fortified by Antipus), we assume that it was he who conquered the other cities in that quarter of the Nephite territory, including Zeezrom, Cumeni, Antiparah and even Manti, the prize of the west. (Alma 56:14) Clearly he then left these conquests to be defended by his captains, as Helaman, in his report to Moroni, makes no mention of him. In 28 YOJ Helaman marched into battle with his 2000 stripling soldiers (Alma 53:22). After taking the cities lost, and last of all Manti, he said in his report to Moroni "we have obtained those cities and those lands, which were our own." (Alma 58:33) Geographically, the most we know is that all of these cities are in the course of Amalickiah's campaign to take Manti. None of them figures in Moroni's campaign in the east.

While Helaman was engaged with the liberation of Nephite cities in the west, Moroni became aware that the Lamanites were amassing a huge force to invade the land of Zarahemla, and readied his own land for war. In YOJ 20 he began erecting earthen berms surmounted by picket palisades around all the cities of the land (Alma 50:1-2). He then drove all the Lamanites in the east wilderness "into their own lands, which were south of the land of Zarahemla." (Alma 50:7) In their place, he ordered that Nephites should settle the east wilderness. At this point, "the land of Nephi did run in a straight course from the east sea to the west." (Alma 50:8) He fortified "the line between the Nephites and the Lamanites, between the land of Zarahemla and the land of Nephi, from the west sea, running by the head of the river Sidon—the Nephites possessing all the land northward, yea, even all the land which was northward of the land Bountiful" (Alma 50:11)

Also in 20 YOJ (about 67 BCE), the Nephites began establishing cities in the north (Alma 50:15), including the city of Lehi (Alma 50:15), and the city of Morianton, which "joined upon the borders of Lehi; both of which were on the borders by the seashore." (Alma 50:25) In the same year, the Nephites established the land, city and fortifications of Moroni, "by the east sea; and it was on the south by the line of the possessions of the Lamanites." (Alma 50:13) The "line of the possessions of the Lamanites" corresponds to the northern border of Bountiful. The city of Moroni is therefore in the southeast corner of the land of Zarahemla, to be a counter to Mulek, "which was one of the strongest holds of the Lamanites." (Alma 53:6) In the same year that the city of Moroni was established, the Nephites also establish Nephihah, "joining the borders of Aaron and Moroni." (Alma 50:14)

While captain Moroni was preoccupied with putting down some dissenters in his own land, particularly the king-men, the Lamanites began their invasion of the east. In 25 YOJ, they took the city of Moroni, the people of Moroni fled to the city of Nephihah, and "the people of the city of Lehi gathered themselves together…to receive the Lamanites to battle." (Alma 51:24). Amalickiah proceeded to take possession of a string of cities beginning with the Lamanite stronghold Mulek, and including the city of Gid, the city of Omner, the city of Nephihah, the city of Lehi and the city of Morianton, "all of which were on the east borders by the seashore." (Alma 51:26) So the Nephite cities on this shore, south to north, are Moroni, Nephihah, Aaron, Lehi and Morianton.

At the end of this year, Amalickiah commanded a large force to take the land of Bountiful, but was prevented by Teancum, who slew him (Alma 51:34). He was replaced by his brother Ammoron.

To further preempt the Lamanite attack, in YOJ 27 Moroni ordered Teancum to take the Lamanite fortified city Mulek. He decided that his force was insufficient, and so backed off to the city of Bountiful to wait for Moroni to arrive with his army. In the 28th year, Moroni took possession of Mulek (Alma 52:26). The Lamanites pursued Teancum to the city of Bountiful, which was being defended by captain Lehi. Moroni put Lehi in charge of the city of Mulek. Teancum was commanded by Moroni to fortify the city of Bountiful (Alma 53:3). The Lamanites were keeping their Nephite prisoners in the city of Gid. Moroni took possession of this city, and forced his own captives to fortify it (Alma 55:25), and then to be taken and guarded in the city of Bountiful. The fact that these three cities are near one another, and not far from the northern border of the Lamanite possessions, is seen in the missionary itinerary of the sons of Helaman, who began their entry into the land of Nephi by going first to the city of Bountiful, then on to the city of Gid, and then to the city of Mulek (Helaman 5:14-15).

Again captain Moroni had to put down a rebellion in Zarahemla. Pachus, king of the king men had driven the freemen out of the city, and removed chief governor Pahoran from his judgment seat. He had taken refuge in Gideon, across the Sidon river eastwards, but in the valley of Gideon, i.e. not on the sea. Moroni took a small force to the city of Gideon, and he and Pahoran defeated Pachus, putting him and his recalcitrant followers to death. Then Moroni resolved to end the war with the Lamanites. For some reason, he took Pahoran with him, and they passed up Lehi to march on Nephihah, which they took by stratagem. Moroni doubled back and took Lehi, (Alma 62:30) and the other cities taken by the Lamanites, and set up camp in the land of Moroni. Along the way, they drove the Lamanites from the liberated cities to the land of Moroni, where they "were encircled about in the borders by the wilderness on the south, and in the borders by the wilderness on the east." (Alma 62:34) Commanding his entire force, Moroni "did drive them out of the land; and they did flee, even that they did not return at that time against the Nephites (Alma 62:38).

Vignette   A Tale of Two Cities

The first step in relating this drama is to introduce the principals, the city of Lehi and the city of Morianton, newly established by the sea in the north part of the land of Zarahemla. Before the invasion of the Lamanites, in approximately 63 BCE, Morianton, the founder of the new city of Morianton, attacked his neighbor, the city of Lehi, and undertook to seize territory by force of arms. The people of the city of Lehi took fright and fled to the camp of Moroni, who rendered judgment in their favor. Now Morianton took fright, and convinced the citizens of his city "that they should flee to the land which was northward, which was covered with large bodies of water," (Alma 50:29) i.e. the Great Lakes region. Moroni became concerned, calculating that if Morianton should control the land northward (northward of the land of Zarahemla), it would be to the detriment of the Nephites. He resolved to stop them and sent an army. Teancum at the head of this army headed Morianton at a narrow pass, where a battle ensued and the rebel was killed. The residents of the city of Morianton were escorted back to their homes (Alma 50:36).

Alma described this narrow passage as leading "by the sea into the land northward, yea, by the sea, on the west and on the east." (Alma 50:34) Being flanked by seas on both sides, it is clearly an isthmus. Both the city of Morianton and the city of Lehi are in the land of Zarahemla, and somewhat to the north at that (Alma 50:15, 25; 51:26). So this would-be migratory city (men, women and children) would have to travel to the northern border of the land of Zarahemla, to approach this narrow pass from the south to cross the isthmus heading north, on route to a land covered with large bodies of water. But from modern Honduras to Mexico, inclusively, i.e. on any putative northern border of the land of Zarahemla, there is no such isthmus, nor any narrow area in an appropriate location to serve as an isthmus for this tale. Or is there?

Betrayed by a Faulty 19th Century Map

The solution is provided by the 1825 schoolboys' map that the author of Alma would have used.

The Bay of Honduras separates Honduras and Belize on today's maps, while it ends to the west with a shoreline on Guatemala. It is connected by a very short river to Golfete Dulce, which is connected by a navigable river to Lake Izabal. This body of water is an oval oriented east-west (dimensions, c. 31 miles by 16). The schoolboy's map mistook Golfete Dulce and Lago Izabal for a continuation of the bay of Honduras, and extended the latter even further, slicing across Guatemala east to west, leaving a narrow land bridge to connect the southern slice to the northern one. In his *Geography* (1831), Daniel Adams states, "This country [Guatemala] is divided by the bay of Honduras, into two peninsulas."[292] Jedidiah and Sidney Morse concur in their contemporary geography "for the use of schools": "The bay of Honduras divides this country into two peninsulas."[293] This does violence to geophysical reality, but at least on this 1825 map, there is ostensibly a second isthmus, north of Panama. Crossing it requires a second narrow pass, "by the sea, on the west and on

---

[292] Daniel Adams, *Geography, or a Description of the World*, 13th ed. (Boston: Lincoln and Edwards, 1831), 187.
[293] Jedidiah Morse and Sidney Edwards Morse, *A New System of Geography, Ancient and Modern, for the use of Schools* (Boston: Richardson and Lord, 1822), 153.

the east." The land of Zarahemla is therefore situated between two isthmuses, each with its own narrow pass.

Map 8. The "Isthmus of Guatemala," a Creation of Early Cartography

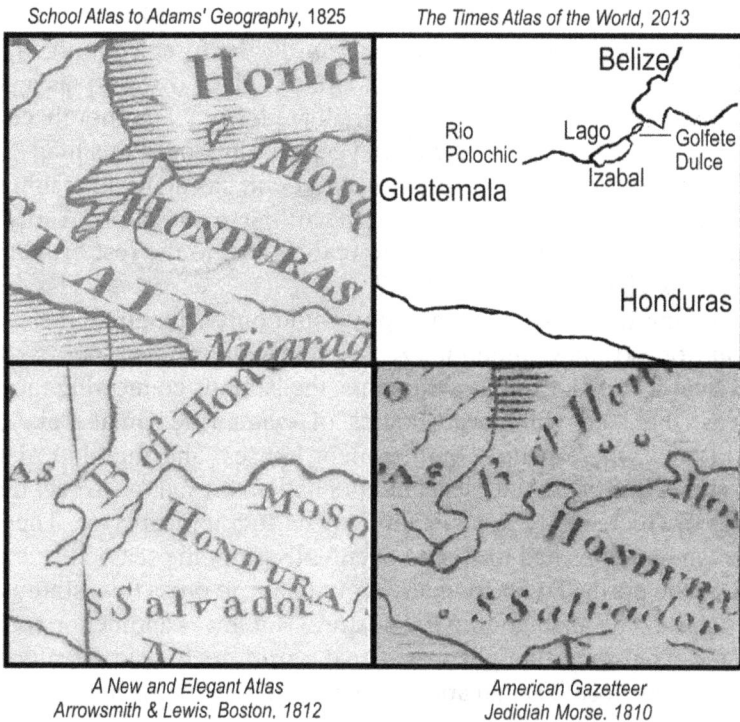

School Atlas to Adams' Geography, 1825   *The Times Atlas of the World, 2013*

A New and Elegant Atlas
Arrowsmith & Lewis. Boston. 1812

American Gazetteer
Jedidiah Morse. 1810

In the 1820s, map engraving was done on a copper plate. Maps were produced for inclusion in large tomes on geography, or as works of art to hang framed on a wall. Perhaps the most illustrious of these artists was Aaron Arrowsmith, hydrographer to the Prince of Wales in 1810, and later to the king of England. He teamed up with Samuel Lewis, a publisher in Philadelphia, for his luxurious *A New and Elegant Atlas*. Although the map of Jedidiah Morse also features this "isthmus of Guatemala," most likely the work of Arrowsmith is the source for both it and Daniel Adams' *School Atlas to Adams' Geography*.[294] Unlike these more high-end productions,

---

[294] Daniel Adams, with H. (Hazen) Morse, engraver, *School Atlas to Adams' Geography* (Boston: Lincoln and Edmonds, 1825). Jedidiah Morse, *The American Gazetteer, Exhibiting a Full Account of the Civil Divisions, Rivers, Harbors, Indian Tribes, &c. of the American Continent* (Boston: Thomas & Andrews, 1810), fold-out map: North America.

this latter work was published as cheaply as possible to fit the budget of the average schoolboy's parents. The entire work is printed on cheap paper, although the cover is a bit heavier than the mere ten sheets inside. Each map is published on one side of a sheet, leaving the verso blank. There is no text at all. Published many times from 1814 to at least 1830, this humble work would certainly be familiar to Joseph Smith Sr., as a member of the Palmyra school board, and to Oliver Cowdery as a school teacher. Moreover, Daniel Adams graduated from Dartmouth college, where Hyrum Smith later studied. He very possibly used this map.

This tale of two cities, Morianton and Lehi, has no relationship to the evangelizing missions in Alma, nor to the military campaigns. Alma 50:25 through 50:36 can be deleted with no real change to the rest of Alma. So why was this vignette inserted at all?

Adhering to real-world geography could only strengthen the *Book of Mormon*, or so they thought. Alma refers to numerous real-world geophysical features: the two continents, the isthmus connecting them, the four seas, the land with large bodies of water (the Great Lakes), the semiarid land where people built cement houses, and the land of many waters (Lago de Nicaragua). The authors had no reason to suspect that the "isthmus of Guatemala" was just an early cartographical error. Their Pre-Columbian Israelites had to spread eventually from the sea on the south to the sea on the north. To do so, many would have to cross this isthmus. The authors could have just ignored this feature. But it was another opportunity to include what they thought was a real-world geophysical feature, and even better, one located at an appropriate point to mark the northern border of the lands of Zarahemla. Since it had nothing to do with their sermons, nor with the evangelical missions to the Lamanites, nor with the wars with the Lamanites, getting this feature into Alma could best be done by means of a stand-alone vignette. The map gave rise to the story, and today the story leads back to the map.

The Land Northward and the Land of Desolation

In Mormon we once again find geographical segmentation. In his two wars with the Lamanites, he traverses the lands of Zarahemla four times, once from his birthplace in the north to the line separating the Nephites and Lamanites, where he begins his military career, a second time retreating into the land northward, a third time driving the Lamanites back into their own territory, and then a fourth time retreating a final time. Yet there are only four places named south of the narrow pass into the north which led into "the land that is northward": the city of Desolation near the southern border of Nephite territory, the land of Zarahemla, the waters of Sidon and the narrow pass to the south. All other toponyms are north of the narrow pass into the north, and are names not encountered elsewhere in the Nephite narrative. The potential for contradiction to arise from name generation in Mormon is thereby obviated.

These two geographical designations evolved over time. The land northward is first found in Omni to identify the direction of the flight of the Nephites under the lead of Mosiah. It became a term for the whole region north of the line Bountiful-Desolation. It is used initially somewhat synonymously with the land of Desolation. Mulek made landfall in the land northward, which had been the territory of the Jaredites. They found it to be full of ruins, still uncorroded weapons, and even skeletons. It was a land desolate of its original inhabitants, "because of the greatness of the destruction of the people who had before inhabited the land." (Helaman 3:6). But the Mulekites began filling the territory between the Isthmus of Panama and the Isthmus of Guatemala with urban and rural settlements, a process that was furthered by the addition of the Nephites. From the perspective of Zarahemla, the land northward lay north of its own lands. And although the original meaning of the land of Desolation persisted, effectively it had become the territory from this northern narrow pass to include the land of many waters, rivers and large bodies of water, i.e. the Great Lakes region.

At age eleven, Mormon's father took him "into the land southward, even to the land of Zarahemla" (Mormon 1:6). So he himself must have originated in "the land which was northward," i.e. in a part of the land of Desolation north of the land of Zarahemla. It is somewhere in this region that Ammaron buried the sacred records, in the hill Shim of the land Antum (Mormon 1:3).

The Lamanites attacked, entering the land by the waters of Sidon. In about 326 CE, the Nephites appointed Mormon to be the leader of their armies. They retreated to the north countries (Mormon 2:3), where they occupied the city of Angola, but were driven out. After also being driven out of the land of David, the Nephites gathered in the city of Joshua on the seashore. After initial success, the Nephites retreated to the land of Jashon near hill Shim. From there the Nephites were driven "northward to the land which was called Shem." (Mormon 2:20) At this point, a Nephite-Lamanite treaty gave the Nephites the land from the narrow pass leading southward, and the Lamanites received all the land southward.

A new war began. Mormon gathered his people to the land of Desolation, to a city by the narrow pass leading to the land southward. In 361 CE the Lamanites attacked the city Desolation. Driven from there, the

Nephites fled to the city Boaz. At this point Mormon took the records from the hill Shim (Mormon 4:23). Next they retreated to the city Jordan. This chief Nephite captain then requested that the Lamanites allow him to gather his people to "the land of Cumorah, by a hill which was called Cumorah." (Mormon 6:2) "and it was in a land of many waters, rivers and fountains" (Mormon 6:4). Although Mormon hid the Nephite records there "save it were these few plates which I gave unto my son Moroni" (Mormon 6:6), Cumorah was later identified as the place where the angel Moroni revealed the gold plates (D&C 128:20).

Apart from the four listed above, no toponym in Mormon is found anywhere else in the Nephite narrative. "The land which was northward" has unique cities founded by the Nephites that had spread into the northern lands. The Book of Helaman has few toponyms. Those that occur are already found in Alma. The principal toponyms found in 3 Nephi are the cities that a wrathful Jesus destroyed just prior to his visit to the new world. The cities of Zarahemla, Moroni, Moronihah and Jerusalem occur in Alma. The remainder do not occur elsewhere in the BoM narratives: Gilgal, Onihah, Mocum, Gadiandi, Gadiomnah, Jacob, Gimgimno, Jacobugath, Laman, Josh, Gad and Kishkumen. There is no information to determine the location of these cities but since we are told that the greater destruction occurred in the north, we may be intended to understand that they too are north of the lands of Zarahemla.

The final Lamanite onslaught begins in 375 CE, and the remainder of the Nephites are gathered at Cumorah by 384 CE. The retreat from the city of Desolation to Cumorah lasted c. nine years.

The Map

The most distinctive feature of the map of the *Book of Mormon* is the extension of the Bay of Honduras, almost to the sea west. The modern Gulf of Honduras is merged with Lake Izabal to form an extension of the gulf that cuts nearly two thirds of the way across modern Guatemala from the sea on the east to the sea on the west, leaving a narrow isthmus between the lands of Zarahemla and the "land which was northward." On maps 6 and 9, the narrow pass at the Isthmus of Panama has been labeled "narrow pass to the south," and the narrow pass at this BoM northern isthmus has been labeled "narrow pass to the north."

Map 9. The Lands of the Nephites and Lamanites

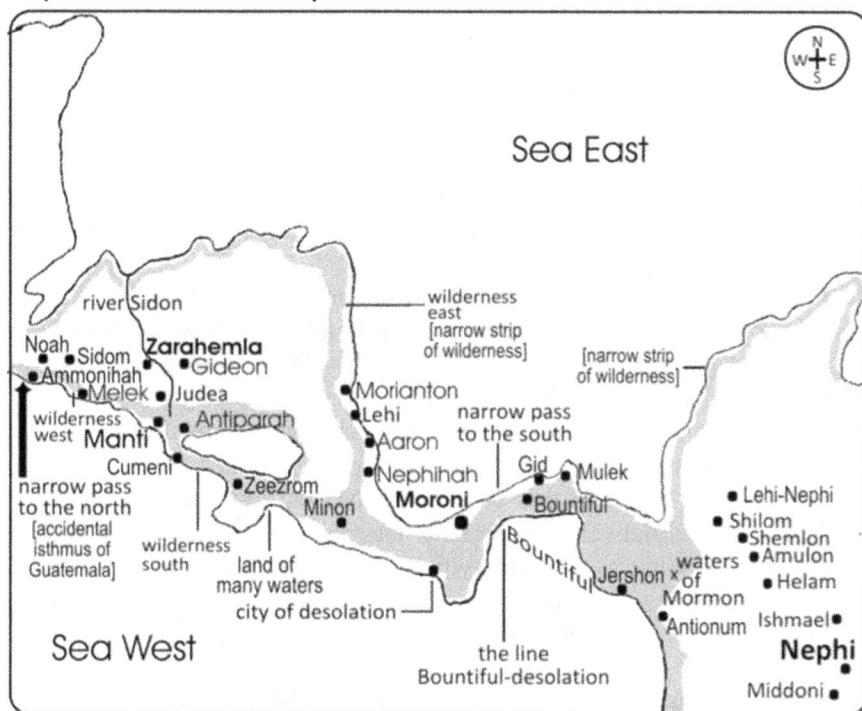

Map 6 was developed using the schoolboys' map that clearly served as the basis for the BoM authors. It was scanned and printed. The coastal outline was then meticulously traced and also scanned to produce an empty map, which has been filled in somewhat sparsely.

The coastal outline for map 9 was taken from that of map 6. The toponyms discussed above were then put into it to the extent that space allowed. Some could be located with considerable accuracy. Others, such as the cities that figure in Helaman's campaign around Manti, were entered into the region to which they belong, but without any pretense that they could be located precisely.

Observations

§ The *Book of Mormon* has a complex history and a correspondingly complex geography. The internal consistency is remarkable. This could not result from extemporaneous narration off the top of one's head.

§ BoM geography proceeds in segmented stages. The replacement text almost totally lacks toponyms to avoid contradiction with the stolen 116 pages, leaving the land southward free for the generation of toponyms in Mosiah. It concentrates its toponyms in the land southward, leaving the land north of the narrow pass for Alma to develop an elaborate geography, while leaving the northerly region for the toponyms of Mormon's flight to Cumorah. Avoiding toponyms in the lands of Zarahemla, Mormon obviates the possibility of contradictions with prior books.

§ The toponyms in Amaleki's record belong to Mosiah, as they occurred in the original Mosiah chapter one before it was moved to Omni and Words of Mormon.

§ This geography was clearly based on the schoolboys' map of 1825. It was the popular text in the 1820s, and undoubtedly known to Smith Sr. and Oliver Cowdery. Its compiler, Daniel Adams, was a graduate of Dartmouth College, where Hyrum Smith studied.

§ Following this map, the Gulf of Honduras was extended westward thereby producing an isthmus along the western coast of present-day Guatemala. As a result of this error, the BoM narrative has the lands of Zarahemla tucked between two narrow passages, one leading southward, and the other leading to "the land which is northward." Incorporated into the *Book of Mormon*, the inaccuracy in this map produced a significant geographical error in the Nephite narrative.

Following the cartography of the era, the BoM incorporated a false geophysical element. This is the

Geographic Issue

< Chapter 16 >

Premature Urbanities & Inadvertent Methuselahs

When the Lehi party arrived in the New World from Jerusalem, they began the process of populating empty continents kept just for them for what they called "the land of our inheritance," to preserve an intact branch of Israel to be gathered to Christ prior to the Second Coming. Initially they numbered no more than 30 individuals, including children born in the wilderness of Arabia (Jacob and Joseph are mentioned). Their population size is important, since population can be viewed both as a limiting factor, and an enabling factor. During the first five decades in their new environment, we find projects that require a population of an adequate size, and events, concerns and comments that only make sense when the population has reached a certain level of urbanization.

Nephites Maximized: Premature Urbanism

The BoM narrative does not provide detailed population data. But for our purpose, this is no obstacle. A population growth model can be constructed with assumptions that yield maximum population growth well beyond what one can reasonably entertain, thereby producing figures that lean very heavily in favor of the BoM narrative.

1) The beginning point is the initial party. We will give Lehi twelve children, a goodly patriarchal number. We will give Ishmael no fewer, twelve children as well. His family was needed so that Lehi's sons might be able to marry. (1 Nephi 7:1-5) The servant of Laban, Zoram, joined this hypothetical twenty-eight. Perhaps there was yet another daughter so that he too could marry. The members who were of eligible age were married up shortly after leaving Jerusalem, in a place that the BoM calls the Valley of Lemuel. The Lehi group did not encounter the group that came over with Mulek until centuries after the period of this study.

2. In order to maximize population growth, we will assume that the generation span was short, i.e. that the average age of marriage was fifteen, with some marrying as early as fourteen, and others at sixteen. Outliers, beyond either side of this range, would have been rare, and would have offset each other. Eventually, all 26 were married.

3. The sex ratio will be 50/50 so that all born will find a mate.

4. The model further assumes that each couple also had twelve children, throughout, at the rate of one every second year without fail.

5. The model also assumes that there was no mortality apart from Lehi, Sariah, Ishmael and his wife, at least for the first six decades; no infant mortality, no death in childbirth, no deaths due to disease. It is assumed that no Nephites were killed in spite of some conflict.

6. Although at first all were charted, after a date estimated for the Nephite-Lamanite division, only the Nephite group was charted. Although eventually Lamanites would outnumber Nephites by a wide margin, in keeping with our intent to maximize Nephites, they were assumed to be the most numerous initially.

There is no population on earth with such an idyllic growth rate.

At journey's end, this project had produced sixty-five pages of charts, one chart every second year from 598 through 546 ALJ, all organized in birth-year groups. As cumbersome as this is, all relationships were kept straight, and each chart was a clear picture of all persons alive in that year, with their marital status, age and descent. Although a hypothetical construct, the assumptions are such that each chart gives the maximum figures that this Nephite-maximized model predicts for each second year.

Using this data, the following summary table was made, including important events at their approximate times.

Table 22. Maximized Nephite Population & Significant Events

Date	Total Population	Elderly	Married	Unmarried (under 14)	Married (no children over 4)	Under Ten Years Old
2 ALJ (c. 595 BCE)	35	4	18	13	18	11
590	67	3	20	44	0	39
New World arrival after eight years in the wilderness, & the oceanic crossing.						
588	77	3	20	54	0	40
578	143	3	48	92	26	55
c. 576-572	Nephi took his people to a new location, which they called the land of Nephi, and they took upon them the name Nephites. Nephi taught his brethren smelting and alloying metals, working in iron, copper, brass, gold and silver. Nephi made many swords to arm Nephites against Lamanites. Construction of the temple. Nephi's brethren sought to make him king, but he refused. The followers of Laman were cursed with a skin of blackness, and made loathsome to the Nephites.					
574 total	198	3	64	131	24	87

From this point, only Nephites were reported, although Lamanites were still being charted.						
574	114	3	34	77	10	50
568	162	1	58	103	26	82
562	244	1	90	153	34	101
c. 572-558	Nephite-Lamanite wars and contentions					
From this point on, only the Nephites were charted.						
558	328	8	114	206	46	144
548	657	14	214	429	80	273
542	824	14	260	550	120	358
c. 55 ALJ (c. 543 BCE)	Nephi dies, most probably c. 80..					

Without the extravagant assumptions to maximize Nephites, and without the three sons of Ishmael and their families included with the Nephites, the figures in the table would be no more than half.

At some point between 578 and 568 BCE, Nephi leads his people to a new land, separate from the Lamanites, and the account focuses largely on the Nephites. At this early date, we are not dealing with individuals, but with a group of nuclear families, possibly living together as extended families. A large proportion was children or very young adults, i.e. no more than twenty years old. The BoM narrative indicates that the families of Nephi, Sam, Jacob, Joseph and even Zoram were among the Nephites. Three of Ishmael's sons were assigned to the Nephites and three to the Lamanites, even though most or all of his sons may have joined the Lamanites. By 400 BCE the Lamanites were more numerous than the Nephites (Jarom 1:6). Later in the BoM, the Ishmaelites are usually numbered among the Lamanites. If this 50/50 division inflates the Nephite count, then it too leans in favor of the BoM narrative. After this separation, the population charts were done only for the Nephites, since it is their events that loom large in this study. And in any case, any assumption that enhances the size of the Nephite population in the first several decades favors the credibility of the *Book of Mormon* narrative within the context of the present inquiry.

The following observations can be made from the charts and this table: 1) Initially, there was considerable inbreeding; 2) the population was very young; 3) the women were either pregnant or recovering from childbirth up to their late thirties, and raising young children up to age fifty; and 4) with so many children, and even with only three elders, the population in the New World had a very high dependency ratio.

When Lehi's party left the Old World, they brought "all manner of seeds of every kind, both of grain of every kind, and also of the seeds of fruit of every kind" (1 Nephi 8:1). Upon their arrival they found "beasts in the forests of every kind, both the cow and the ox, and the ass and the horse, and the goat and the wild goat, and all manner of wild animals, which were for the use of men." (1 Nephi 18:25)

Numbering no more than 67, and with only about a dozen able-bodied men, they set about clearing the land and establishing farmsteads, supplemented by hunting and gathering. Then, only after about 17 years in the "land of their inheritance," the settlers, already warring among themselves, divided into two groups, and Nephi led his group off to a new land, which they named the land of Nephi (2 Nephi 5:8). There they worked hard and "did prosper exceedingly; for we did sow seed, and we did reap again in abundance. And we began to raise flocks, and herds, and animals of every kind." (2 Nephi 5:11) This they did, starting anew, with a population of only about 114, including only seventeen males aged 15 and above (excluding the elderly).

In just a few years, they also established metallurgy, smelting iron, copper, gold and silver, and clearly also tin, to alloy it with copper to produce brass. They made steel adequate for sword blades: "I, Nephi, did take the sword of Laban, and after the manner of it did make many swords." (2 Nephi 5:14) The construction of buildings rounded out their production: "And I did teach my people to build buildings, and to work in all manner of wood, and of iron, and of copper, and of brass, and of steel, and of gold, and of silver, and of precious ores, which were in great abundance." (2 Nephi 5:15) At this time men were laboring to tame the land, putting it under the plow, planting, harvesting and preparing the produce for long-term storage, while women were both pregnant and caring for infants and toddlers. Men also were capturing the animals that they would domesticate. Women would care for some of them, engage in milking and some shearing in order to spin, weave and make clothing. Men also were engaged in the construction of homes and outbuildings. In spite of these overwhelming challenges, men also had to discover iron, copper, gold, silver and tin ores, extract them from the earth, haul them to the settlement, build kilns, make bellows, smelt iron ore to make the tools needed for other metallurgy, make those tools, smelt iron and process it to make steel, smelt and purify copper, gold and silver, smelt tin to alloy it with copper to produce brass, and then manufacture swords and other metallic objects. After the Nephite/Lamanite split, when the Nephites established the city Nephi, they were only 114, i.e. only about 17 men 15 and older. By the time of Nephi's demise, the number of married individuals (i.e. over 15 years old) was only 260, plus 14 elderly.

Even more remarkable, Nephi proceeded to build a temple (2 Nephi 5:16): "And I, Nephi, did build a temple; and I did construct it after the manner of the temple of Solomon save it were not built of so many precious things; for they were not to be found upon the land, wherefore, it could not be built like unto Solomon's temple. But the manner of the construction was like unto the temple of Solomon; and the workmanship thereof was exceedingly fine." To put this into perspective, the Israelites in their thousands were unable to build the temple of Solomon. Hundreds of years after the victories of Joshua, and after the establishment of the Davidic Empire, with the influx of slaves, booty and taxes, the Israelites contracted with the Canaanite Hiram, King of Tyre, to build it, although most grunt labor was probably slaves and Israelite freemen. (1 Kings 5-9, 1 Chronicles 14:1 and 2 Chronicles 2-7)

Yet this tiny band, while establishing their farmsteads, and engaged in warfare with the Lamanites, was able to build a temple like unto that of Solomon, with exceedingly fine workmanship. Incredible.

At the time, one did not go to a lumberyard to buy boards and nails. The construction projects would have required felling trees, splitting logs, cutting wood to required lengths, hewing boards, one after another, probably with an adze, and drilling holes for pegs, or making one's own nails. There is no mention of saw mills, nor rivers to power them. Foundations and floors were possibly made with clay or packed earth. Stone may have been used to make thresholds, cornerstones and even floors of substantial edifices. All this was done while clearing the land, farming, herding, and hunting to put food on the table, as well as engaging in metallurgy to make weapons and tools, all the while fending off the Lamanites.

These events are dated by the comment of Nephi, once his group had become this well established in the new land, "thirty years had passed away from the time we left Jerusalem." (2 Nephi 5:28) Since eight of these were in the wilderness, plus some time at sea, we are dealing with little more than twenty years.

It is not knowable what is meant by the assertion that already the two groups had been engaged in warfare: "it sufficeth me to say that forty years had passed away, and we had already had wars and contentions with our brethren." (2 Nephi 5:34) In the fortieth year ALJ (c. 558 BCE) the Nephite men over fifteen numbered only 57 (half of married Nephites), and the Lamanites about the same. Most must have been at work in the fields. Warfare? "Fighting" would perhaps be a more appropriate term.

The BoM narrative uses the word "people", which implies a larger population than could have existed. When they establish the land of Nephi with a total population of c. 50, we read in 2 Nephi 5:

> 8. And my people would that we should call the name of the place Nephi; wherefore, we did call it Nephi. 9. And all those who were with me did take upon them to call themselves the people of Nephi. 14. And I, Nephi, did take the sword of Laban, and after the manner of it did make many swords, lest by any means the people who were now called Lamanites should come upon us and destroy us; for I knew their hatred towards me and my children and those who were called my people. (Cf. 2 Nephi 5:15, *supra*, and vs. 17-33)

In this context, we read in 2 Nephi 5:

> 17. And it came to pass that I, Nephi, did cause my people to be industrious, and to labor with their hands. 18. And it came to pass that they would that I should be their king. But I, Nephi, was desirous that they should have no king; nevertheless, I did for them according to that which was in my power.

It is totally incongruous that this "people" should ask Nephi to be their king, when they were no more than his brothers, Sam, Jacob and Joseph, their wives, and in-laws (a son or two of Ishmael, married to granddaughters of Lehi), and their children (many still minors), and their children (all quite young). This is a handful of extended families, hardly even a clan. The BoM authors are getting ahead of their story.

Concubines among Kin?

One is also surprised to read Jacob's condemnations of the people of Nephi not so long after the death of Nephi, accusing the rich of neglecting the needs of the poor, and of having concubines and many wives. Nephi died c. 55 ALJ (543 BCE), and in the year 542 BCE the Nephites numbered only 824, with 260 adults, all closely related, cousins, second cousins, etc. At the time of Jacob's condemnation, perhaps a decade later, the demography would not have been seriously different. Socioeconomic stratification, severe divisions between the rich and the poor, excesses of concubinage and polygyny, are all characteristics of societies of considerably larger scale. In the case of plural wives in tribal society, each tribe exists in relationship to many other tribes, and the second wife usually comes from a different tribe, of lower status, a situation that is hard to imagine in Jacob's day. The Nephites then constituted, at best, a small village of blood relatives. Moreover, these population figures have been greatly exaggerated by our maximization model.

This demographic analysis indicates that the BoM authors themselves probably had little awareness of the population they were penning, its size, composition, capabilities and limitations.

Recordkeeper Methuselahs

The *Book of Mormon* records the handing down of the records from which Mormon's abridgment would be made on the gold plates. This information is sufficiently detailed to enable us to study record-keeping periods (how long each recordkeeper recorded on the plates). By simple examination, one notes the difference between two time spans, 600-0 BCE and 0-400 CE. Not counting brothers, who are contemporary with the previous recordkeeper and recorded only a few years, we have 14 recordkeepers in the first period, up to when Nephi son of Helaman passed the plates to his son. There are five in the second period, going up to when Moroni got the records from Mormon. The average recordkeeper time of service in the first period is 42.86 years (600/14), which has been rounded up to 43 in the table (third column from the left). The average record-keeping time of service in the second group is 80 years (400/5). These have been accumulated in the column "Summing Average Time in Service," to see how well the averages track the actual passage of time. Note that in the column "Time Keeping Record," when the date of the passing of the records is not recorded, averages have been used from the previous to the next known date.

Table 23. Plates Transmission & Recordkeeper Recording Time

ALJ: After Leaving Jerusalem YOS: Year Since the Sign (birth of Jesus) YOJ: Year of the Reign of the Judges Note: unknown dates resulted in averaging two or more record-keeping spans.				Summing Averages: accumulation of average recordkeeping times. (*italics*=43-year intervals) (**bold**=80-year intervals) For each recordkeeper, the average is added to the total accumulated to that point.
Record Keeper #	Time Keeping Record	Summing average time in service	date ALJ	Event/Transmission of Plates
1			0	Departure from Jerusalem.
			4	Approximate birth of Jacob, brother of Nephi.
			8 c.	After eight years in the wilderness. (1 Nephi 17:4)
			10	Nephi makes the plates.
	45	*43*	55	**Nephi keeps records.** Approx. death of Nephi.

				Nephi gives plates to **Jacob, his brother**, born in the wilderness. (Jacob 1:-21)
2	c. 62	*86*	?	Plates passed from Jacob to **Enos son of Jacob**.
3	c. 62	*129*	179	Approximate death of Enos **Jarom, son of Enos**, receives plates.
4	59	*172*	238	Approximate death of Jarom. **Omni son of Jarom** receives plates.
5	44	*215*	282	Approximate death of Omni. Passed plates to **Amaron son of Omni**
6	38	*258*	320	**Approximate death of Amaron.** Plates passed to his brother, Chemish. (wrt 1 verse)
No calculation for a brother				Chemish to **his son Abinadom.** (wrote 2 verses)
7	c. 52	*301*	?	Abinadom passes plates to **his son Amaleki.**
8	c. 52	*344*	?	Amaleki passes to **King Benjamin.**
9	c. 52	*387*		Birth of Mosiah I (446)
			476	Mosiah reigns in his father's stead, at age 30. King Benjamin passes plates to his son **Mosiah II.**
			479	King Benjamin dies.
10	c. 33	*430*	509	King Mosiah passes plates to **Alma his son**, Alma the Younger. (Mosiah 28:20) King Mosiah dies, in 33rd year of his reign, age 63. Alma is appointed the first Chief Judge. Alma's father dies, age 82. Years of the Reign of the Judges begin (YOJ).
			518	9th year of the reign of the judges, Alma delivers judgment seat to Nephiha. Moroni at 25 appointed Chief Captain over the Nephites.
11	19	*473*	528	Alma the Younger passes plates to **Helaman** the Elder, and departs (19 YOJ).
12	16	*516*	544	Helaman the Elder dies in 35th year of judges
no calculation for a brother			545	**Shiblon brother of Helaman** takes possession of plates in 36th year of judges (from Helaman).
			548	Shiblon dies in 39th year of judges. Delivers plates to **Helaman the Younger.** Helaman (the younger, son of Helaman) appointed
			551	to the judgment seat, 42nd year of judges.
13	18	*559*	562	Helaman the Younger dies, leaving the plates **to his son Nephi**[1], in 53 YOJ. (Helaman 3:37)
			571	Nephi delivers judgment seat to Cezoram, in the 62nd year of judges.
			575	Cezoram murdered, then his son is murdered, in the 66th year of judges.
14	38	*602*	**600**	Lachoneus is chief judge, in 91st year of judges (date given: 91 YOJ = 600 ALJ; see 3 Nephi 1:1). Nephi[1], son of Helaman, passes plates to **his son, Nephi**[2], son of Nephi (600 ALJ; 3 Nephi 1:2). Years after the Sign (birth of Jesus) begin.
			609	Equals 100th year of the judges (3 Nephi 2:5-6).

17	84	68	630	Equals also 9 years since the sign of the coming of Christ. Lachoneus son of Lachoneus becomes governor (30th year of the sign).
			634	Chief judge is murdered.
			634	A great storm, 34th year, 1st month, 4th day of the sign. (3 Nephi 8:5) "Age of man" defined by Christ as "seventy two years." (3 Nephi 28:2)
17	84	68	684	Nephi[3], son of Nephi the disciple, dies, having kept the record 84 years (4 Nephi 1:19-20). *Some list 1 more Nephi, (without BoM references).*
			710	Plates passed to **his son Amos.** 110 years after the sign equals first generation since Christ (age c. 76, i.e. 110-34)
18	111	762	794	194 years after birth of Christ (after the sign),
			710	Amos dies and passing plates to his son, **Amos son of Amos.**
			801	Dissension begins in 201st year of the sign (or since birth of Christ).
			810	Many churches & schisms 210 years after the sign.
			831	Nephite/Lamanite division reestablished, 231st year after the sign.
19	111	842	905	Amos son of Amos dies and **his brother Ammaron** gets the records, in year 305'
			910	Mormon is born'
			922	Ammaron hides records in 322 AD Mormon (c. 10 years old) receives instructions from Ammaron.
20	40	922	921	Mormon accompanies father to Zarahemla. Nephite/Lamanite warring begins.
			926	Mormon is sixteen in 326 after Christ.
			945	**Mormon** gets the records; begins keeping the record.
21	36	1002	984	Nephites gather at Cumorah.
			c. 985	Mormon hides all records in the Hill Cumorah, except those given to **Moroni.**
			1,000	Mormon is killed. Nephites destroyed; no more Christians (400 CE).
			1,021	**Moroni** seals the plates (c. 421 CE).

The records, written initially in 7th century BCE Egyptian, were passed mostly from father to son, along a line of descent of four families from Nephi through Amaleki, then Benjamin and his son Mosiah, then from Alma through Ammaron, and finally Mormon and Moroni. It was a sequence mostly of prophets, who were spiritual, and sometimes political elites. There were also plates kept by Mormon the disciple of Christ, and the plates of the kings: "Amaleki had delivered up these plates into the hands of king Benjamin. He took them and put them with the other plates, which contained records which had been handed down by the kings, from generation to generation until the days of king Benjamin." (Mormon 1:10)

As we shall see, the period after Christ occupies very few pages in the narrative for a four-hundred-year period. There are few new city and personal names. Everything indicates that once the story had been told of Jesus in the New World, they needed only to record the establishment of the church, the apostasy and the destruction of the Nephites. At this point the BoM authors were anxious just to conclude the *Book of Mormon* and get on with the establishment of their new church.

A consequence of peopling the Nephite narrative with fewer and fewer key figures was to have fewer recordkeepers. During the period from Jerusalem to Jesus, the average number of years covered by each recordkeeper is 43, while from then to the end it was 80 years. This required these individuals to have long life-spans. If on average each recordkeeper received the plates at age 30, his lifespan would be 73 years in the first 600 years, and 110 years in the second.

Nephi is an example at the lower end of the first-period range. He describes himself as being a man large in stature even before leaving Jerusalem, being perhaps about 25. If so, when he handed the plates over to Jacob in 55 ALJ he was approximately eighty. Jacob was on the high end of the range. He was born prior to leaving Jerusalem, when his age was perhaps 15, although possibly as young as 5. We do not have the date for the passage of the plates from Jacob to Enos, but the latter was approaching death in 179 ALJ. The combined time of this service for Jacob and Enos was 124 years. It seems that Jacob would represent at least half of this, given the size of his book. So Jacob's age at death would be approximately 15 + 55 + 62 = 132 years.

Amos son of Nephi received the plates in 684 ALJ, and died in 794. If he was 30 when he got the plates, his age at death was 140. Amos son of Amos died in 905, having kept the record 111 years. If he received the plates at age thirty as well, then he died at age 141. But that would mean that Amos son of Nephi sired him at age 110.

The recordkeepers seem to have enjoyed greater longevity than the general population. For example, Alma the Elder died at age 82 and Mosiah died at age 63. When Jesus asked his disciples what they wished, we read, "We desire that after we have lived unto the age of man, that our ministry, wherein thou hast called us, may have an end, that we may speedily come unto thee," and Jesus replied, "after that ye are seventy and two years old ye shall come unto me in my kingdom." (3 Nephi 28:2-3) So, in this passage, apparently the "age of man" is 72 years. The authors may not have been aware of the much higher ages of the methuselahs that the paucity of recordkeepers was creating.

Jaredite Methuselahs

Although the Jaredite narrative does not say so, one might assume that all Jaredites were quasi Methuselahs. But even if all the progenitors in the begat list in Ether 1:6-32 lived to 900, this is not important for the calculation of the length of their record, from the Tower of Babel and their arrival in the New World to when Coriantumr wandered into Zarahemla.

Table 24. Jaredite Begats (From the Tower of Babel to 600 BCE)
> **Read:** *The date for the tower of Babel is set to precede the earliest documented languages. Jared was born in 3300 BCE & was 30 at the time of the tower of Babel, & 90 in 3210 when he sired Orihah; who was 90 in 3120 when he sired Kib, etc.*

progenitor	year	progenitor	year	progenitor	year	progenitor	year
BABEL	3330	8. Com	2670	16. Kish	1950	24. Shiblon	1230
1. Jared	3300	9. Heth	2580	17. Lib	1860	25. Seth	1140
2. Orihah	3210	10. Shez	2490	18. Hearthom	1770	26. Ahah	1050
3. Kib	3120	11. Riplakish	2400	19. Heth	1680	27. Ethem	960
4. Shule	3030	12. Morianton	2310	20. Aaron	1590	28. Moron	870
5. Omer	2940	13. Kim	2220	21. Amnigaddah	1500	29. Coriantor	780
6. Emer	2850	14. Levi	2130	22. Coriantum	1410	30. Ether	690
7. Coriantum	2760	15. Corom	2040	23. Com	1320	NEPHITES	600

What is really important is the generation span. When a woman lives to 115 or beyond, in our day and age, she still goes into menopause at around age 50. Even when an aging patriarch is matched with a young bride, he rarely procreates beyond the age of seventy. We are not interested in the age of the progenitors listed in Table 24, but the age when each sired the next one in line in the table. The table assumes that on average each one's procreative power expired at age ninety. Average age at death must have been at least 100. Since these are averages, some individuals would have lived longer. One can make different calculations based on other virility expiration dates.

These hypothetical dates begin shortly before languages had begun documenting their existence. The sequence ends with Ether being born 90 some years before Lehi began his career in Jerusalem. As for Coriantumr, the last of the Jaredites, we do not know his birth date, nor the date that he smote off the head of Shiz, nor the period of his wandering before he arrived at Zarahemla. Mulek arrived in the land northward after the Jaredite annihilation. It must have taken some time for these Jerusalemite migrants to establish their new capital in the middle of the land. The Tower of Babel in Genesis has nothing to do with Babylon. Babel is *Bab El*, "Gate to God." Around 3,200 BCE, protowriting was beginning in Mesopotamia and the Nile valley. Around 2,500 BCE the Egyptians were building the great Pyramid, and the Sumerian, Babylonian and Egyptian languages were already being written. Proto-writing was being developed in China. The peoples of the planet had spread to every continent. The arrival of mankind to Australia was more than 40,000 years ago, while evidence of agriculture in South America dates to before 14,000 BCE. Presumably all these people actually did speak, thousands of years before any Babel date, and not all some hypothetical pure Adamic language assumed by some. Sumerian, Babylonian, Egyptian, Mayan and Chinese are all in different language families. We can accommodate the antiquity of language development and global spread by placing the Tower of Babel at an earlier date, but in doing so, the average age that each member of the begat list would have, when he sired his successor, would be greater than 90. Clearly the Tower of Babel story is just that: a story. But in the *Book of Mormon*, it is historical fact.

Millennial Population Growth

One might wonder if demographic realities allow the BoM history to even be possible. In the preindustrial period, global population growth was extremely slow. For the Lehi and Mulek parties, we might assume that their combined initial number was 60. If we further assume that they were all perfectly healthy, carrying no disease, and arrived in a rich but empty land, where no diseases had evolved to prey on humans, and food was plentiful, we might compare the situation with some third-world populations after the introduction of modern medicine and agriculture, resulting in a population explosion. Even though some have achieved a doubling rate of less than twenty years, for a while, let us assume a doubling rate of twenty years. In this case, on average, every generation would leave behind four offspring per couple that survive to produce a new generation of twice the size, and the population would double five times in a century. If this were sustained, then by the time of Christ, the population of the New World would be in the billions, which is totally ridiculous.

Let us make the same initial assumption, but assume that the population growth rate levels off, even with generous help from divine Providence, such that it has five doublings in the first century, four in the next, three in the next, two in the next two, one in the next three, and then is stable. The results are in the following table.

Table 25. A Hypothetical BoM Demography

Date After Leaving Jerusalem	Doublings per Century	Population
100	5	1,920
200	4	30,720
300	3	254,760
400	2	1,019,040
500	2	4,076,160
600	1	8,152,320
700	1	16,304,640
800	1	32,609,280
900	0	32,609,280
1000	0	32,609,280

Admittedly, population-doubling analysis is a rather crude demographic technique, and is in this case, totally hypothetical. A skeptic might argue that this is unrealistic. But we do not know what could have happened if such idyllic circumstances had existed, especially with the operation of divine Providence. For comparison, note that Europe is estimated to have had a population of only fifty-six million in the year 1,000 CE, and only ninety million in 1500 CE. According to the estimate above, by 400 CE, the BoM New World population would have been over 16 million per continent. This does not factor in the decimation of the Crucifixion Cataclysm.

The foregoing analyses allow the role of divine Providence a free hand. John C. Kunich, by contrast, has marshaled data to make a real-world analysis of BoM demographic issues. He argues, among other things, that given the observed growth rates of other preindustrial populations, especially with the limitations on population growth imposed by a hunter-gatherer economy (usually prevalent among the Lamanite majority), and the high level of war casualties, the Jaredite and Nephite-Lamanite societies could not have developed as described in the BoM narrative.[295]

This is the

Demographic Issue

⌀∽◖◗∽◖◗∽◖◗∽⌀

---

[295] John C. Kunich, "Multiply Exceedingly: *Book of Mormon* Population Sizes," in Metcalfe, ed., *New Approaches to the Book of Mormon. Explorations in Critical Methodology* (Salt Lake City: Signature Books, 1993), 231-267.

< Chapter 17 >

The Bible versus the *Book of Mormon*

When the project of composing a New-World bible was undertaken, it was natural to use the existing Bible, the King James Version, as the model, Old Testament and New. A deep awareness must have existed that there would be opposition to any new bible, and deep suspicion regarding its contents. Christian hesitations were to be at least partly overcome by inserting a number of large *Biblical inclusions*.

The Brass Plates of Laban

One of the more astounding claims of the *Book of Mormon* is that a canon of Israelite scriptural texts had already been translated into the Egyptian language and inscribed on brass plates by the close of the seventh century BCE. According to Talmud tradition, the Men of the Great Assembly established the *Tanakh* (Hebrew Bible) in c. 450 BCE. Modern scholars vary, dating it as early as the Hasmonean Dynasty, perhaps as early as 130 BCE, or even later. Among the Dead Sea scrolls, the books attested are found as individual scrolls, not collected into a complete *Tanakh*. The authors of the *Book of Mormon* knew that the Bible had, in their day, been translated into many languages. Bible students are aware also that approximately by the birth of Jesus, books of the Old Testament had been translated into an Aramaic *targum* (pl., *targumim*: *Targum Onkelos*, *Targum Yerushalmi* [Jerusalemite], *Targum Yonathan* [Jonathan], and *Targum Neofiti*); and into Greek (the Septuagint). By only a few hundred years after Jesus, the New Testament had been translated into Latin (Italic first, and then the Vulgate), classical Ethiopic (Geez), Coptic and even Arabic. *All of these OT translations were done at least a century after the Hebrew language was no longer spoken*. The Targumim and Septuagint were translated to meet a very real need, for use in the synagogues, and so that, via an Aramaic or Greek translation, worshippers would have access to the Tanakh. We have no example of Hebrew Scriptures being translated into a Gentile language before the demise of Hebrew.

The claim that Israelite religious leaders had translated their scriptures into Egyptian as early as 600 BCE is surprising. Egypt was seen as a land of the Israelites' bondage, a land of pagan idolatry, a symbol of evil and a land of refuge (cf. Joseph). Moreover, such a translation would have had to have been done by one or more individuals trained as an Egyptian scribe, to write it in the very complex Egyptian writing system.

Furthermore, there is a huge wealth of Egyptian documentary and other artifact evidence, to the extent that Egyptian museums often are forced to double as warehouses. And yet, there is no clear evidence even of an Israelite presence in Egypt. The one clear case of an Israelite settlement in Egypt prior to 600 BCE is that uncovered on Elephantine Island, in Southern (Upper) Egypt. Although this sixth-century BCE community, possibly of mercenaries, had embraced some pagan influences, they had a temple, and left behind a trove of legal documents and letters. Significantly, these were written in Aramaic. Clearly they had not adopted the Egyptian language for their written documents, and there is no trace of their use of written Egyptian for scripture.

When the Rabbinical philosopher and exegete Sa'adiah ben Yosef Gaon (birth in Egypt and death in Baghdad, ninth to tenth century CE) translated the Pentateuch (the five so-called Books of Moses) into Arabic, he not only wrote it using the Hebrew alphabet, but used the Arabic passive participle *ma'bûd* (the one who is worshipped) to translate God (Exodus 20:3),[296] rather than Allah, which is the normal Arabic word for God not only in the Qur'an, but also in the New Testament. This is the extent to which he attempted to cling to at least some Hebrew in his translation, and avoid any hint of non-Israelite religious tainting.

The Age of Scientific Discovery, and the Bible

A list of works considered sacred by the rabbis, may have been drawn up as early as 450 BCE, but probably centuries later, the Hebrew OT (*tanakh*, from *t* for torah, *n* for *nevi'im* [prophets] and *k* for *ketuvim* [writings]). Even as late as the mid-third century CE, there was no Christian scriptural canon, no "bible" in the modern sense. Even when the works included in the earliest canon were selected, and copied into the first manuscript "edition," they were referred to as the sacred *biblia*, which is the plural of *biblion*, meaning little book, booklet. The manuscript was called the sacred books, not the Bible.

Long before the Christian era, the Judeans had begun the process of developing what became Judaism out of earlier Israelite religion or religions. They began the process of identifying various compositions as sacred. Evidence indicates that in many cases, some of these works were

---

[296] Derenbour, J.,ed., *Version Arabe du Pentateuque de R. Saadia ben Iosef Al-Fayyoumi* (Paris: Ernest Leroux, 1893), 109.

edited and augmented over time, arriving at their final form roughly perhaps a century before the time of the Qumran community and the now famous Dead Sea Scrolls.

During these first couple of centuries of Christian history, theology played a major role in determining what works would be selected. Although there are traces of at least some gnostic thinking in the canonic gospels, the gnostic compositions, discovered in Egypt, written in Coptic, were roundly rejected. Early scholars in theology developed their views of the works they accepted, and their authorship.

The nineteenth century witnessed a new age of critical and scientific reevaluation of almost everything. Scholars specializing in ancient literature were not immune to this broader movement. They found themselves confronted by numerous nonidentical manuscript sources for the same composition. The differences between them were called variant readings. They had to produce *critical editions* in an attempt to arrive at the original text, while providing in their footnotes (the *critical apparatus*) the other manuscript readings that they had rejected, so that other scholars could check their work, and choose for themselves. Issues of authorship had to be addressed, and the historical development of a work. This effort focused on the classical works of the Greeks and Romans, Homer, Hesiod, Herodotus, Plato, Aristotle and the dramatists. Over time, the methods they developed were extended, even to include the study of Hammurabi's Code, and the development of the compositions that collectively comprise the so-called Egyptian Book of the Dead. As religious hesitations were overcome, the works of the Bible were also subjected to the same sort of scrutiny, using techniques developed over time.

This work has implications for the *Book of Mormon* with respect to two ancient works, the Book of Isaiah and the Book of Revelations.

Which Isaiah?

Isaiah was especially important to the BoM authors because it was initially the primary OT work that was interpreted to show that the ancient Israelite prophets were aware that a branch of Israel would be taken off by the Lord to distant lands across the sea, and later be reunited with the other branches of Israel in the last days. It provided the basis for the *Book of Mormon* to present its argument for itself. It claims that a seventh-century BCE "bible" inscribed on brass plates in ancient Egyptian contained all of the sacred books of the Hebrews up to King Zedekiah, including Isaiah, and was brought to the New World by Lehi and Nephi. It quotes long passages, including chapters 2-14, 48-49, and 50-51. Nephi makes it clear that he read these passages from the Brass Plates:

> *Isaiah 2-14*:
> 2 Nephi 11:8. And now I write some of the words of Isaiah
> 2 Nephi 25:1. Now I, Nephi, do speak somewhat concerning the words which I have written, which have been spoken by the mouth of Isaiah.
> *Isaiah 48-49*:
> 1 Nephi 19:23. And I did read many things unto them which were written in the books of Moses; but that I might more fully persuade them to believe in the Lord their Redeemer I did read unto them that which was written by the prophet Isaiah
> 1 Nephi 22:1. And now it came to pass that after I, Nephi, had read these things which were engraven upon the plates of brass
> *Isaiah 50-51*:
> 2 Nephi 6:5. And now, the words which I shall read are they which Isaiah spake concerning all the house of Israel
> 2 Nephi 9:1. And now, my beloved brethren, I have read these things that ye might know concerning the covenants of the Lord

The BoM is very clear that Nephi is reading from the Brass Plates, and writing the words of Isaiah onto his plates. His own commentary follows the quotation. This is clear in reading the text, but specified in 2 Nephi 25:1: "Now I, Nephi, do speak somewhat concerning the words which I have written."

Isaiah lived between 750-700 BCE. Even in medieval times, some Jewish scholars already held that the prophet had not authored certain sections of Isaiah, most notably Abraham ibn Ezra in his 1167 commentary.[297] There has been a large amount of excellent research on the received Hebrew text. It analyzes the content, the occurrence of words, terms and syntax, comparison with well-documented historical events and comparison with other books of the OT. The results that enjoy a high degree of consensus among leading scholars are: 1) Isaiah wrote, or dictated to be written, passages of varying length at various times in his life, in response to events and his situation, usually in his capacity as a sort of advisor to each of four different kings. 2) At an early date, these documents were collected by followers of his mission, and edited together. There are passages that were added by these editors, probably sincerely believing that their additions were consistent with and supportive to the materials from Isaiah himself. 3) The initial compilation included chapters

---

[297] George A. Buttrick, *The Interpreter's Bible* (New York: Abingdon Press, 1956), 382.

1-39, which preserve the material done by Isaiah himself, plus some additions to tie them together. It was mostly completed prior to 597 BCE, i.e., the captivity of the leading Judeans during the short reign of Jehoiachin. 4) Chapters 40-55 are a later product, under Isaiah's name, either done during the exile in Babylon, or shortly after. 5) Chapters 56-66 are of even later composition, clearly postexilic. 6) Editing chapters 1-39 continued into or possibly even after the exile, and consequently they contain some later material as well. All of this is contrary to the position of the *Book of Mormon*. Although it is not clear that it asserts that all of chapters 1-66 were contained on the Brass Plates of Laban, minimally, chapters 2-14, 29, 48-51 and 53 are claimed to have been on the plates by 600 BCE, already translated into the Egyptian of that day.

Although these divisions remain the dominant view, the analysis of the Dead Sea material has suggested a different division point. In the Great Isaiah Scroll, the best preserved of the Dead Sea Scrolls, there is no break between Isaiah 39 and 40, but there is a large vacant space between Isaiah 33 and 34. Perhaps more significant, other Isaiah texts included in the find contained portions of Isaiah 1-33, or 33-66, but not both. These pre-Christian manuscripts provide evidence in support of current analysis, differing only on the point of division.[298].

Consequently, having been composed decades after Zedekiah, Isaiah 48-49, 50-51, 53 & 54 could not have been on the Brass Plates of Laban, and were not even written by Isaiah.

The Stick of Judah and the Stick of Joseph

The argument in support of the assertion that the God of Israel had brought part of the tribe of Joseph to the New World and produced a new bible makes use of a naive misinterpretation of several Biblical passages, taken out of context, probably as a result of total ignorance of Biblical history. Few events are more central or more seminal in the OT narrative than the unification of Israel under Saul and David, who used his considerable military assets to bring the tribes under one yoke, as well as many of the neighboring peoples. Like all expansions, the initial take in booty and slaves was considerable. His successor, Solomon, was a major builder.

---

[298] See Marvin A. Sweeney, *Isaiah 1–39: with an introduction to prophetic literature* (Grand Rapids, MI: Eerdmans, 1996); & Marvin A. Sweeney, "The Latter Prophets," in Steven L. McKenzie and M. Patrick Graham, *The Hebrew Bible Today: An Introduction to Critical Issues* (Westminster: John Knox Press, 1998).

Since the Hebrew tribes had neither experience nor expertise in such things, he contracted with the Canaanite king Hiram of Tyre to build first his own palace, then the temple and later his fleet. Having exhausted the initial booty resources, and overstrained the imposed tribute obligations, he resorted to heavy taxation of his own people. After his death, the tribes in desperation inquired regarding taxation, and Rehoboam, the successor in Jerusalem, made his famous reply (1 Kings 12:11): "And now whereas my father did lade you with a heavy yoke, I will add to your yoke: my father hath chastised you with whips, but I will chastise you with scorpions."

This reply fed an already sharp division between Judea and the tribes of the north, led by the tribes of Ephraim and Manasseh (the two sons of Joseph). Rehoboam emerged as the king of the Kingdom of Judah, with Jerusalem as its capital, and Jeroboam became the king of the Kingdom of Israel in the north (composed of ten of the twelve tribes), with its capital in Shechem. This division was a continual irritant to the prophets of Judah, who looked forward to a new David, a Messiah (anointed one, i.e. king) to reunite the twelve tribes. The Kingdom of Israel fell to the Assyrians over about a twenty-year period beginning in 740 BCE, and many were dispersed and/or carried off into captivity, leading to the dissolution of the tribes and the legend of the ten lost tribes.

Around 597 BCE Babylon sacked Jerusalem, carrying many off into captivity in Babylon, and c. nine years later destroyed the temple and walls. Meanwhile many Hebrews, like their Canaanite cousins (called Phoenicians by the Greeks) traveled abroad to seek their fortunes, around the Mediterranean, especially Alexandria, and even Elephantine Island in the far south of Egypt, and as far east as India and Persia

The book of Isaiah began as a collection of some prophetic writings by the prophet himself, gathered together and edited by his followers. It received further editing and considerable augmentation over the next hundred years. In the resulting text, and in the books of Jeremiah and Ezekiel, there are occasional prophecies regarding the hoped-for gathering from captivity and dispersion, even from the isles of the sea (the Mediterranean; cf. Esther 10:1). Ezekiel claimed a revelation that indicated that this reunification would be soon (Ezekiel 37):

> 16. Moreover, thou son of man, take thee one stick, and write upon it, For Judah, and for the children of Israel his companions: then take another stick, and write upon it, For Joseph, the stick of Ephraim, and for all the house of Israel his companions:
> 17. And join them one to another into one stick; and they shall become one in thine hand.

18. And when the children of thy people shall speak unto thee, saying, Wilt thou not shew us what thou meanest by these?

19. Say unto them, Thus saith the Lord GOD; Behold, I will take the stick of Joseph, which is in the hand of Ephraim, and the tribes of Israel his fellows, and will put them with him, even with the stick of Judah, and make them one stick, and they shall be one in mine hand.

20. And the sticks whereon thou writest shall be in thine hand before their eyes.

21. And say unto them, Thus saith the Lord GOD; Behold, I will take the children of Israel from among the heathen, whither they be gone, and will gather them on every side, and bring them into their own land:

22. And I will make them one nation in the land upon the mountains of Israel; and one king shall be king to them all: and they shall be no more two nations, neither shall they be divided into two kingdoms any more at all:

So God shall take the two sticks (the kingdom of Israel and the kingdom of Judah) and make them one people. This all goes back to the division wrought by the dispute between Solomon's sons, Jeroboam and Rehoboam.

LDS scholars interpret the stick of Judah as being the Bible, and the stick of Joseph as being the new bible from the gold plates. LDS exegesis has claimed that the sticks are scroll sticks, each scroll being a book of scripture, which will be united as the twin scriptures of the restored church. The phrase the "isles of the sea" in Isaiah 24:15 is claimed to refer to the Israelites in the New World, those continents being interpreted as "isles." (2 Nephi 8:10 & 29:7) The *Book of Mormon*, it is claimed, is further referred to in Isaiah 29:4, "And thou shalt be brought down, and shalt speak out of the ground, and thy speech shall be low out of the dust, and thy voice shall be, as of one that hath a familiar spirit, out of the ground, and thy speech shall whisper out of the dust." This is said to apply because the gold plates were dug up "out of the ground," speaking, as it were, "low out of the dust." (See also 1 Nephi 22 & 2 Nephi 6:5-18) Actually, "hath a familiar spirit, out of the ground" refers to necromancy calling for a message from a deceased person in Sheol, the great pit underground, as was the case when Saul sought wisdom from the deceased Samuel, with the aid of the Witch of Endor (I Samuel 28:3-25).

The Book of Revelations: Which John?

The *Book of Mormon* relies heavily on the Book of Revelations for the language that condemns all churches existing throughout most of the Christian era, as being the work of Satan. 1 Nephi 14 is explicit:

8. And it came to pass that when the angel had spoken these words, he said unto me: Rememberest thou the covenants of the Father unto the house of Israel? I said unto him, Yea.

9. And it came to pass that he said unto me: Look, and behold that great and abominable church, which is the mother of abominations, whose founder is the devil.

10. And he said unto me: Behold there are save two churches only; the one is the church of the Lamb of God, and the other is the church of the devil; wherefore, whoso belongeth not to the church of the Lamb of God belongeth to that great church, which is the mother of abominations; and she is the whore of all the earth.

11. And it came to pass that I looked and beheld the whore of all the earth, and she sat upon many waters; and she had dominion over all the earth, among all nations, kindreds, tongues, and people.

The attribution that provides the link to the Book of Revelations is in verses 20-22 and 27:

20. And the angel said unto me: Behold one of the twelve apostles of the Lamb.

21. Behold, he shall see and write the remainder of these things; yea, and also many things which have been.

22. And he shall also write concerning the end of the world.

27. And I, Nephi, heard and bear record, that the name of the apostle of the Lamb was John, according to the word of the angel.

Although this is clear enough, it is important to remember that the *Book of Mormon* does not use the title "apostle" loosely. When Jesus visits the New World and chooses a similar body of twelve, he calls them the Twelve Disciples, not apostles.

Traditionally, it was thought that John the apostle authored the so-called Johannine works (the Gospel according to John, the first, second and third epistles of John and Revelations). It is now generally agreed that even the gospel bearing the name of John was written after the apostle's death. Indeed, the majority view is that all four gospels were written by others, possibly by students of the apostles. Note that each is traditionally called the Gospel *according to…* (Mathew, Mark, Luke or John), where "according to" is Greek *kata*, literally meaning "according to" and not implying authorship. The majority view dates the gospels to within the following time frames: Mark: c. 68–73; Matthew: c. 70–100; Luke: c. 80–100; and, John: c. 90–110. Matthew and Luke show clear signs of having been written based largely on Mark, the earliest of the four canonical gospels. These three are called the synoptic gospels because scholars found that if large-format pages were ruled off into three columns, it was possible to print the three texts together, one in each column, collating passages chronologically to facilitate comparison. John does not fit this synoptic scheme. In some cases, the events are not even in the same order. John is unusual also with regard to its beginning verses, referring to the "word" as God (*logos*, in Greek). This follows a Hellenistic philosophical formulation, and argues for an author well-versed in Greek language, literature and philosophy. Some scholars do not accept that the Johannine epistles were written by the same author as the Gospel according to John, although similarities support the view of others that they were. For what it is worth, many now think that the Gospel of Thomas, discovered in a Coptic text, is actually the earliest gospel to have survived. Its focus was the sayings of Jesus, and may have been a source document for Mark.

The odd man out is the Book of Revelations, which is so different in language and style that most agree that it was written by a different author, and most probably around 95 CE. The early second-century author Justin Martyr was the first to write that the author of Revelations was John the Apostle.[299] However, Eusebius in his *History of the Church* (c. 330) argued that one author wrote the Gospel of John and the First Epistle of John, some other author wrote the second and third epistles of John, and there was no agreement on the identity of the author of Revelations.[300] Sophronius of Jerusalem (560-638) held that some other John, John of Patmos (later sometimes called John the Divine) wrote it. John the Presbyter has also been proposed as the author (by Eusebius of Caesarea and Jerome). The subsequent inclination to ascribe it to the apostle was largely due to the theological hesitation to expand the circle of revelators beyond the twelve apostles (accepting Paul as the replacement for Judas), making this revered body the seal of the era of revelation.

John the Apostle, like his brother James the apostle, on the other hand, was a fisherman, the son of Zebedee, possibly also a fisherman. He was undoubtedly a native Aramaic speaker, most probably with little or no classical education in Greek. This background does not support the proposal that he authored a gospel in Greek reflecting Hellenistic learning, much less the Book of Revelations.

---

[299] Justin Martyr, *Dialogue with Trypho*, 81:4.
[300] Eusebius of Caesarea, *The History of the Church*, Book three, point 24.

Recension Histories

It is quite normal, and perhaps universal, for ancient works to have gone through revisions, addition and deletions. Over the course of much of the life of the books of the Bible, their texts have evolved, and for almost as long, scholars have noted evidence for the changes, and have used it to attempt to arrive at their own scholarly evidence-based recensions in an effort to arrive at the original.

This is just the beginning of the BoM issues with the Bible.

< Chapter 18 >

The *Book of Mormon* Version of the KJV Bible

Throughout his career, Joseph Smith claimed to translate by divine power. A BoM prophet sys of Mosiah, "he has wherewith that he can look, and translate all records that are of ancient date…whosoever is commanded to look in them, the same is called seer…" "And the king said that a seer is greater than a prophet." (Mosiah 8:13, 15) "And now he [Mosiah] translated them [the gold plates of Limhi] by the means of those two stones which were fastened into the two rims of a bow." (Mosiah 28:13) Smith's work on the Bible is in two corpus. The first is said to have been on the Brass Plates of Laban, and the second is his undertaking to revise the entire KJV Bible. The latter work was cut short by his untimely death, and has never been canonized. The former, as part of the *Book of Mormon*, is fully canonical.

Biblical Variant Readings in the *Book of Mormon*

The *Book of Mormon* claims that the Nephites brought the Bible with them as it existed by 600 BCE, already assembled as a single sacred book, and translated into Egyptian on brass plates. The BoM text quoted extensively from these Biblical materials on the Brass Plates, especially Isaiah, but also other materials, including the Sermon on the Mount, which Jesus delivered again when he visited the New World after his resurrection, to make the Nephites and Lamanites Christians, at least for two centuries, after which people started falling away from the "truth."

The Biblical materials in the *Book of Mormon* are primarily the King James text. According to the orthodox LDS view, its wording was used in translating the gold plates because people were used to it. According to these reverent scholars, it differs from the King James wording only when the original text required different wording to be a correct translation (cf. 1 Nephi 13:24-29). But according to the critics, the variants were devised to make it look as though the inclusions are not just a rote copy of the King James Version, pure and simple.

These variants, which are supposed to be the correct, divine translation of the original text of Isaiah and other Biblical texts, have been a focus of apologist research. The claim is that some ancient Biblical manuscripts occasionally agree with the *BoM* variants, and since Smith et al. had no access to these manuscripts, and did not know the languages, they could not have come up with variants that enjoy this ancient manuscript support.

The present study has made every effort to be exhaustive. The Biblical passages in the *Book of Mormon* that were gleaned for examination are very close to exhaustive, and certainly include all passages of any significant length.

The insertion of Biblical passages was tricky business. This was supposed to be a divine translation, and so these passages would be expected to be perfect translations of the original text, including much of Isaiah, and the words of Jesus on the Mount. Yet the authors dared not depart too far from the accepted text that their prospective audience knew and cherished. They opted to insert primarily the following (with both Biblical and the BoM references, the latter in parentheses):

Table 26. KJV Inclusions

Longer passages:	
Isaiah 2-14 *(2 Nephi 12-24)*	Isaiah 48-49 *(1 Nephi 20-21)*
Isaiah 50-52:2 *(2 Nephi 7 & 8)*	Isaiah 53 *(Mosiah 14)*
Isaiah 54 *(3 Nephi 22)*	Malachi 3 & 4 *(3 Nephi 24 &25)*
Matthew 5:3–7:27 *(3 Nephi 12:3–14:27)*	
Other passages	
Exodus 20:4-17 *(Mosiah 13:12-24)*	Isaiah 52:11-15 *(3 Nephi 20: 41-45)*
Exodus 20:2-4 *(Mosiah 12:34-36)*	Isaiah 52:8-10 *(3 Nephi 16:18-20)*
Isaiah 29:3-5 *(2 Nephi 26: 14-19)*	Micah 4:12-13 *(3 Nephi 20:18-19)*
Isaiah 29:6-18 *(2 Nephi 27:2-6, 25-29)*	Micah 5:8-14, 15 *(3 Nephi 21:12-18, 21)*
Isaiah 29:13-23 *(2 Nephi 27:25-35)*	Matthew 3:2 *(Helaman 5:32)*
Isaiah 52:1-3 *(3 Nephi 20:36-38; note v. 39)*	Matthew 3:10 *(Alma 5:52)*
Isaiah 52:7-10 *(Mosiah 12:21-24; 13:12-24)*	Acts 3:23 *(1 Nephi 22:20)*

There are other shorter Biblical verses interwoven into the text here and there. These passages are often reworded and blended in to the point that they can be thought of as paraphrases. It is not possible to determine what might be a variant of the KJV text and what might be simply due to the BoM composition into which the paraphrase has been inserted.

The Distribution of the Variants

The process of identifying the *Book of Mormon* variant readings in the longest Biblical inclusions revealed that they vary in importance. Moreover, they did not occur randomly. Although the Isaiah passages on the Brass Plates would be in 7th century BCE Egyptian or early Demotic, this is irrelevant, since Smith's English translation was claimed to be of divine origin, and so would be a revelation of the most accurate English rendition of Isaiah's original Hebrew text.

A *Book of Mormon* variant that simply changes the spelling of an English word does not imply any difference between the King James wording and Isaiah's original Hebrew. A variant that adds a phrase of several or many words does imply that the underlying Hebrew text had this phrase, which is missing in the King James text. These are extreme cases; other variants may or may not imply a discrepancy between the original text and the King James.

To study their distribution, I first divided the variants into the following categories:

I (first order): variants that presuppose at least some sort of difference in the source document (i.e., the wording of Isaiah's own original text required this change).

Ia: first order variants consisting of at least three words.

III (third order): variants that are totally English-language based, and do not raise the presumption of a difference in the underlying text, mostly very minor changes.

II (second order): those that cannot be readily assigned to either order one or three.

The four largest texts listed above were selected for analysis since they are long enough to develop a distribution pattern that can be meaningfully analyzed. The numerical results are found in the following table. I then graphed out the variants according to the categories, as found in Figure 4.

The most obvious observation is that it is always the first quarter of a passage that has the most variants. The probability of this happening, if the distribution should be expected to be random, is a very simple calculation, expressed mathematically as $.25 \times .25 \times .25 \times .25 = .00390625$, or only four chances in a thousand.[301] Minimally, random means that the distribution in each quarter does not affect the distribution in any other quarter. Note that this distribution feature becomes more acute with the more serious variants and that in the case of the Sermon on the Mount, the variants in the first quarter outnumber those in the next three quarters combined.

---

[301] Based on Arthur Chris Eccel, *An Analysis of the Distribution of the BOM-Isaiah Variants* (Chicago: unpublished paper, 1972).

Table 27. Distribution of *Book of Mormon* Variants

Passage	Group	Total	Frequency				Per Cent			
Orders: I, Ia, II & III　　Quarters: 1, 2, 3, 4										
Ia: order I variants that exceed three words in length										
			1	2	3	4	1	2	3	4
Isaiah	Total	374	136	84	70	84	36.4	22.5	18.7	22.5
2:1 to	III	183	54	44	42	43	29.5	24.0	23.0	23.5
14:32	II	124	45	33	20	26	36.3	26.6	16.1	21.0
	I+II	191	82	40	28	41	42.9	20.9	14.7	21.5
	I	67	37	7	8	15	55.2	10.4	11.9	22.4
	Ia	18	12	0	1	5	66.7	0.0	5.6	27.8
Isaiah	Total	141	48	40	29	28	34.0	28.4	20.6	19.9
48:1 to	III	64	18	18	13	15	28.1	28.1	20.3	23.4
49:26	II	38	14	11	6	7	36.8	28.9	15.8	18.4
	I+II	77	30	22	16	9	39.0	28.6	20.8	11.7
	I	39	16	11	10	2	41.0	28.2	25.6	5.1
	Ia	20	9	4	7	0	45.0	20.0	35.0	0.0
Isaiah	Total	113	44	18	29	22	38.9	15.9	25.7	19.5
50:1 to	III	55	22	11	16	6	40.0	20.0	29.1	10.9
52:2	II	31	9	4	7	11	29.0	12.9	22.6	35.5
	I + II	58	22	7	13	16	37.9	12.1	22.4	27.6
	I	27	13	3	6	5	48.1	11.1	22.2	18.5
	Ia	11	8	1	2	0	72.7	9.1	18.2	0.0
Matthew	Total	176	89.	48	23	16	50.6	27.3	13.1	9.1
5:3 to	III	74	29	23	13	9	39.2	31.1	17.6	12.2
7:27	II	36	20	8	1	7	55.6	22.2	2.8	19.4
	I + II	102	60	25	10	7	58.8	24.5	9.8	6.9
	I	66	40	17	9	0	60.6	25.8	13.6	0.0
	Ia	37	21	11	5	0	56.8	29.7	13.5	0.0

The explanation for this distribution is equally obvious. Changes were made for the purpose of calming suspicions regarding the use of the King James Version. Making these changes was both tedious and time-consuming. Once it was thought that the reader had accepted the passage as normal, it was no longer necessary to make as many changes. The process seems to be governed either by a time-efficiency principle, a laziness principle or both. In either case, this pattern is not consistent with the claim that the variants occur because the Bible had been changed (cf. 1 Nephi 13:24-29), and that the *Book of Mormon* is correcting the King James in accordance with the original text divinely revealed in the process of translating the gold plates.

Figure 4. Distribution of *Book of Mormon* Variants[302]
(Percent in Each Quarter)

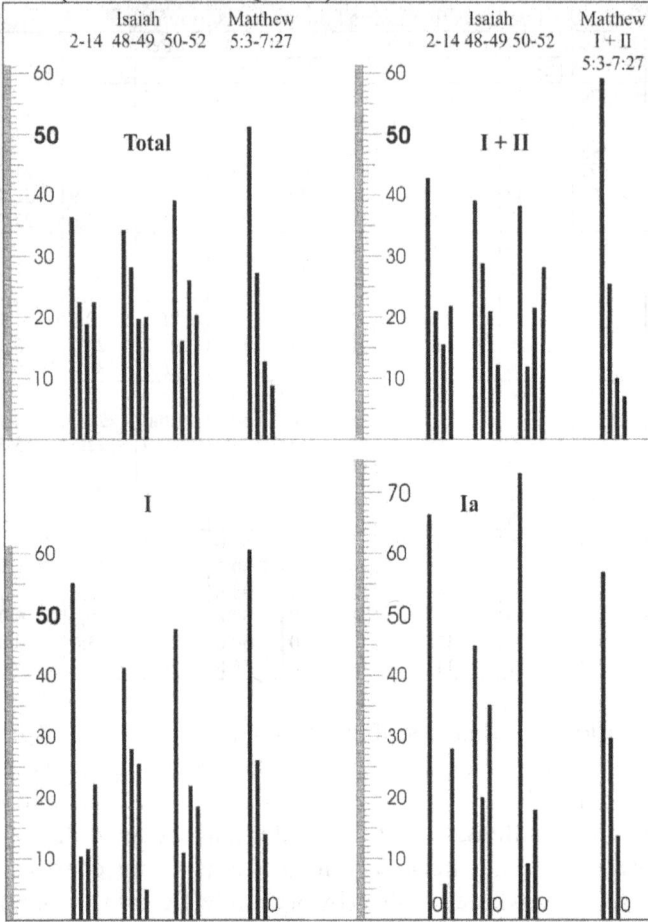

And upon all the ships of the sea

Having a B.A. in Classics (Greek and Latin) and an M.A. in the Semitic languages, I found the study of *Book of Mormon* variants to be especially fascinating, although the research was long and tedious. I not only used the standard critical editions for the Bible (Rudolf Kittel's *Biblia Hebraica*, Alfred Rahlfs' Greek *Septuaginta*, Eberhard Nestle's *Novum Testamentum Graece*, and Alberto Colunga & Laurentio Turrado's *Biblia*

---

[302] Eccel, *An Analysis of the Distribution of the BOM-Isaiah Variants*. Privately distributed (1972).

Sacra iuxta Vulgatam Clementinam), but also the principal editions of the Old and New Testaments in Aramaic, Coptic, Ethiopic, pre-Vulgate Latin (Vetus Latina) and Arabic.[303] Most of these editions are actually rendered unnecessary by the use of the critical editions.

We do not have Isaiah's original manuscript, or a copy of it. What actually exists is a number of ancient Isaiah manuscripts in Hebrew, and these have differences among them, variant readings. An editor, such as Kittel, selects the manuscript that he considers to be the most reliable as his base text. He then compares it with every other source, not only the other Hebrew manuscripts, but Aramaic, Greek, Latin, Coptic and Ethiopic. At times he will decide that a reading in another Hebrew manuscript is more probable than the reading in his base edition, and will make the substitution. When he does, he lists what his base edition originally said as a footnote, as a variant. When he decides in favor of his base edition, the variant from the other manuscript is listed as a footnote as well. In the end, he produces his edition, called a recension, that is thought to be an improvement over the base manuscript, but in the footnotes (critical apparatus) he lists all other readings from all the manuscripts used that could reasonably be important. In this manner, he produces a resource that provides the user all significant evidence from all ancient manuscripts. So no one is required to accept Kittel's decisions. Scholars are able to examine the other possibilities listed in the critical apparatus.

Now, let us consider the Mormon apologists' *pièce de résistance*:[304]

Isaiah 2:16	2 Nephi 12:16	Greek Septuagint
And upon all the ships of Tarshish,	and upon all the ships of Tarshish And upon all the ships of the sea	And upon all the ships of the sea
and upon all pleasant pictures.	And upon all pleasant pictures	And upon every sight of ships of beauty

Defenders of the *Book of Mormon* have been delighted to find that the Greek Septuagint has a phrase that the *Book of Mormon* added: "And upon

---

[303] These are found in Bibliography 1 of Eccel's *Mormon Genesis*.

[304] Sidney B. Sperry, *Our Book of Mormon* (Salt Lake City: Bookcraft, 1950), 172-73. See also in Bibliography 4. John Tvedtnes, "Isaiah Variants in the *Book of Mormon*" (1984; from http//:www.publications.mi.byu.edu/people/john-a-tvedtnes/ (text accessed on 12/04/2015).

all the ships of the sea." Joseph Smith, a farmer's son, knew no Greek, and did not have access to the Greek text. This can only be explained, they say, by the fact that the *Book of Mormon* text is a divine translation of Isaiah's original, which must have had this phrase.

For our analysis, first, note the Biblical context is using a style called *parallelismus membrorum* (parallel members). The larger passage is in Isaiah 2:12-17, a prophesy cursing the proud wicked. Note that the first member is given on the left, and its parallel is to its right:

12	For the day of the Lord of hosts shall be upon	
	every one that is proud and lofty	and upon every one that is lifted up and he shall be made low:
13	And upon all the cedars of Lebanon that are high and lifted up	and upon all the oaks of Bāshan
14	And upon all the high mountains	and upon all the hills that are lifted up
15	And upon every high tower	and upon every fenced wall
16	And upon all the ships of Tarshish	and upon all pleasant pictures
17	And the loftiness of man shall be bowed down	and the haughtiness of men shall be made low
	and the Lord alone shall be exalted in that day.	

The parallelism is partly obscured by the fact that a single word or two words in Hebrew can be best translated by a clause in English. Allowing for that, the parallelism is in the paired items: *ones proud and lofty* parallel with *ones lifted up*; *cedars of Lebanon* parallel with *oaks of Bāshan*; *high mountains* parallel with *lifted up hills*; *high tower* parallel with *fenced wall*; *ships of Tarshish* parallel with *pleasant pictures*; and *loftiness of man* parallel with *haughtiness of men*. The parallelism of verse 16 is also obscured by a KJ mistranslation. Instead of "pleasant pictures," the translation should be "ships of delight (or pleasant ships)." See Table 29.

The addition of a member in the *Book of Mormon* version of verse 16, increasing the members from two to three, violates this parallelism. This alone makes it improbable.

Furthermore, while the *Book of Mormon* adds the phrase, "and upon all the ships of the sea," the Greek does not; rather, it translates Tarshish as meaning "of the sea." So the Greek does not provide support.

The Alexandrian translator, a native speaker of Greek, Hebrew then being already a dead language, knew that Tarshish was a foreign word. He could treat it as a proper name, possibly an unknown toponym as others had done, or he could try to figure out what language it came from, and thereby its meaning. To understand his situation, we must bear in mind these characteristics of Hebrew writing in his day:

1. For the most part, only the consonants were written, although three characters came to do double duty (*matres lectionis*). Initially, *aleph* (א, transliterated as ') was used for the glottal stop (like the pronunciation of *t* in bottle in cockney English [bo'l]), but came also to indicate a long *ā* vowel; *waw* (ו, transliterated as *w*) was used to indicate *w* but came also to indicate a long *ū* vowel; and *yōd* (י, transliterated as *y*) was used to indicate *y* but came to also indicate a long *ī* vowel (pronounced like *e* as in "delete") or a long *ē* vowel (pronounced like *a* as in "snake").

2. Double consonants were not indicated, so *s* could be one *s* or two.

3. The Hebrew alphabet, borrowed from Aramaic, did not have characters for all the Hebrew sounds in use at the time. One example is *t* (ת), which could represent either *t* or *th* (as in "thin").

4. Hebrew has an "extra" sibilant. Sibilants are consonants with a bit of a whistling sound (sibilant being Latin for hissing or whistling). These are:

ש	*sh* (later written with a dot over the right-hand "prong")
ס	*S*
ז	*Z*
ש	a sound that is today unknown, and which came to be pronounced like *s* as a matter of convenience (later written with a dot over the left-hand "prong")

5. Ever since the conquest of Alexander the Great, or even earlier, Greek words had been entering into Hebrew, and when they did, there was often a bit of distortion, much like foreign words adopted by English. One possible source of distortion was the common sound shift, *l/r*. This is because the *r* was pronounced by the end of the tongue, in roughly the same position as *l*. This correspondence is also epigraphically possible since a badly made Hebrew *r* can look like a Hebrew *l*.

The Hebrew word Tarshish is ש י ש ר ת. Here, the characters have been changed to Greek order (the same as English order). When we apply the possibilities listed above, we have:

Hebrew letters:	ת	vowel	ר	vowel	ש	׳	ש
Possible sounds:	*t/th*		*r/l*		*s/sh*	*ī/ē*	*s/sh*

The Greek speaking Jewish translator would know that others had simply transliterated Tarshish as Θαρσις (Tharsis, an unknown place name). He however, spotted a Greek word, which he settled on as the best rendition:

Hebrew letters:	ת		ר		שׁ	׳	שׁ
Greek letters:	Θ	α	λ	α	σ	η	σ/ς
English letters:	*th*	*a*	*l*	*a*	*s*	*ē*	*s*

So, the word is Θαλασσης (*thalassēs*). Θαλασσα (*thalassa*) means sea, and the –ης ending is genitive, like our apostrophe *s*. Just as "Bob's book" means "the book of Bob," so *thalassa* with the ending –*ēs* means "of the sea." For our Hellenistic translator, the presence of what can pass for a Greek genitive ending may have promoted his translation from "highly probable" to "quite certain." A ship "of the sea" may have been a vessel for the open sea, bringing beautiful treasures from afar.

By translating Tarshish as "of the sea" (rather than a totally unknown place name) he got a meaningful phrase, "all the ships of the sea." He did not add this phrase; he just translated "Tarshish," at least to his satisfaction. His version is totally faithful to the Hebrew original, which was transliterated into English letters by the King James translation. The icing on the cake is the fact that it is a nice parallel to "all pleasant ships," the correct translation instead of "all pleasant pictures." The *Book of Mormon* authors, by contrast, added a whole new element, violating the parallelism in the context, and finding no support at all, in any ancient manuscript, neither in the Greek as an additional member, nor in language versions translated from the Greek. In the BoM, "all the ships of the sea" is nothing more than a common English phrase suggested to the BoM authors by the context.

Examples of Variant Analysis

Before proceeding further, a word about Hebrew. The Semitic languages are what I call "Me Tarzan, you Jane" languages. That is to say, Hebrew does not use the verb "to be" unless it is needed. So "He is David" is "He David", (*Hū Dawīd*, where the *w* is pronounced *v* in later Hebrew). The King James translators were determined to be as literal as possible, and when they had to add a word to make good English, such as the verb *is* in this example, they wrote it in italics. It is important to note that *Book of Mormon* variants often occur where one finds italicized words or phrases. It is clear that the authors thought that italics were a sign that there is something a bit odd here, so it is a good place to throw in a variant. This phenomenon will be evidenced here and there throughout the remainder of this presentation, and the portion of the study found in Appendix 2.

The original language of the Old Testament books is Hebrew (except, primarily, for the stories of Daniel, and part of Ezra, which were originally in Aramaic). The original language of the New Testament is Greek. With respect to the biblical passages in the *Book of Mormon*, all other language sources are translations. The Greek Septuagint is translated from the Hebrew, as are the Aramaic targumim. But the Ethiopic, Coptic and Arabic texts are mostly translations of the Septuagint, and so are translations of translations. Therefore, these are not direct evidence for the Hebrew. Scholars use them to evaluate variant readings in the Septuagint. Unless one is faced with two or more variant readings for the same word or phrase in Hebrew for the Old Testament, or in Greek for the New Testament, the Hebrew text trumps all translations of the OT, and the Greek text trumps all translations of the NT. Even so, a perusal of "Bibliography 1" in Eccel, *Mormon Genesis* will show that every language tradition has been extensively examined.

To start off, an interesting variant is Exodus 20:11: "For in six days the Lord made heaven and earth, the sea, and all that in them *is*, and rested the seventh day:" Incredibly, the *Book of Mormon* omits "and rested the seventh day." All versions have this clause, but there is a note in one critical apparatus indicating that only one Arabic manuscript omitted it.[305] So, is there a manuscript that supports this huge omission? Indeed, there is. But effectively, there is absolutely no support for it.

Isaiah 53:9 has a variant: "violence" (KJ) versus "evil" (BoM). The Hebrew uses a noun that means violent treatment, whereas the Greek uses the noun *anomia*, which essentially refers to unlawful behavior, transgression. The *Book of Mormon* receives no support here.

Matthew 5:36 has: "white or black" (KJV) versus "black or white" (BoM). The Greek original agrees with the KJV, while the Syriac translation of the Greek agrees with the BoM. Greek trumps Syriac; furthermore, this is just a simple change in order, with no change in meaning.

Isaiah 10:23 has the phrase "in the midst of all the land" where the *Book of Mormon* omits "midst of." The meaning is the same. The omission occurs also in Greek, Syriac, Latin and Arabic manuscripts. This is an example of a change that better fits a language into which the text is being translated. Hebrew rules.

In Isaiah 9:3 "Thou hast multiplied the nation *and* not increased the joy," "not" was deleted (2 Nephi 19:3). In a number of Hebrew manuscripts, "the nation and not" is absent, producing "Thou hast

---

[305] Robertus Holmes, ed., *Vetus Testamentum Graecum cum Variis Lectionibus*, (Oxford: Clarendon Press, 1798), vol. 1.

multiplied; Thou hast increased the joy." In a sense, one can say that "not" was deleted, but the change is more than that. In Isaiah 29:17 "*Is* it not yet a very little while, and Lebanon shall be turned into a fruitful field," "not" is also deleted here, a change that finds some non-Hebrew manuscript agreement, but the change has only slight difference in meaning, and Isaiah 29 is not quoted word-for-word, but has been rewritten into part of a preachment. These verses are of no significance.

In Isaiah 2:21, "glory of his majesty" is changed to "majesty of his glory" with agreement only in the Arabic text of the *Biblia Sacra Polyglotta Complectentia* (London, 1657), for what it is worth.

An interesting rewording, with no meaning change, occurs in Isaiah 2:20 and 2 Nephi 12:20:

> In that day a man shall cast his idols of silver, and his idols of gold, which they made *each one* for himself to worship... (KJV Isaiah)

> In that day a man shall cast his idols of silver, and his idols of gold, which he hath made for himself to worship,.. (2 Nephi)

In Hebrew, the pronoun is part of the verb (although separate pronouns also exist), and in a couple of Hebrew manuscripts *'āsū* (they made) is changed to *'āsā* (he made), providing agreement for the 2 Nephi version. The BoM change was a result of the deletion of the italicized words *each one* thereby requiring "he hath made" to make the verb agree with "for himself."

A similar case is Isaiah 4:3 where "*that he that is* left in Zion, and *he that* remaineth in Jerusalem" is changed to read "they that are left in Zion and remain in Jerusalem" (2 Nephi 14:3). There is no meaning change, but even so, a couple of Coptic manuscripts translate with wording that involves "they that are" similar to the 2 Nephi version. Again, Hebrew trumps Greek, which trumps Coptic, and the italics prompted the *Book of Mormon* variant.

A less than straightforward variant is found respecting Isaiah 50:2, which reads, "their fish stinketh, because *there is* no water, and dieth for thirst." The BoM reads "I make...their fish to stink because the waters are dried up, and they die of thirst." The Great Isaiah Scroll reads, "their fish dry up for lack of water and die of thirst." The Septuagint has the same. For Tvedtnes,[306] the interesting point is that the latter uses the verb "to dry

---

[306] John Tvedtnes, "Isaiah Variants in the *Book of Mormon*."

up" as does the BoM. But there is a critical difference. In the BoM, the waters dry up, but in the Scroll and Septuagint, the fish dry up. The confusion seems to derive from the similarity in the two verbs: *ybš*, to dry up, and *b'š*, to stink. In any case, the BoM reading does not occur in any manuscript.

A word switch occurs in Isaiah 3:1 ("whole stay of bread") and 2 Nephi 13:1 ("whole staff of bread"). There is no manuscript support for this. The change may have been prompted by the English idea that bread is the staff of life.

A revealing case is the variant in Isaiah 5:30, where "if *one* look" is changed to "if they look." In this case, after the removal of the italicized word, the authors mistakenly thought that 'look' is plural, but in reality it is a subjunctive singular. This grammatical misunderstanding of English prompted the addition of a plural pronoun for the verb. No meaning change is involved.

We should not omit Isaiah 50:2 (2 Nephi 7:2):

Wherefore, when I came, *was there* no man? When I called, *was there* none to answer? (Isaiah)

Wherefore, when I came there was no man; when I called, yea, *there was* none to answer. (2 Nephi)

This change again turns on King James italicization. But in this case, interrogative is changed to assertion. This change plays on the double meaning of the English word 'wherefore.' The Hebrew is unequivocally interrogative (*maddūa'*), and most of the Septuagint manuscripts as well. But a couple change *ti hoti* to *dioti*, an obvious scribal error that produces the change above (since *h* had ceased to be pronounced in Greek). But the Latin Vulgate, following the Septuagint variant, introduces the verse with *quia*, 'because', and so agrees with the BoM variant. Here, meaning is involved, but Hebrew trumps Greek, and the majority Greek reading trumps Latin, especially when the Greek variant has an obvious linguistic explanation.

A variant with some support involves Isaiah 48:14, where the BoM adds 'unto them.' This prepositional phrase is found in the Septuagint and translations based on it (the Latin Vulgate, Targum Jonathan, Arabic mss, the Syriac Hexapla and Coptic). It is not found in any Hebrew ms, which trumps all else, and has little meaning change.

Another interesting case is Matthew 5:22: "whosoever is angry with his brother without a cause shall be in danger of the judgment." 3 Nephi 12:22 says: "whosoever is angry with his brother shall be in danger of his judgment." The phrase "without a cause" is in some Greek manuscripts, but not all; but 'his' in 'his judgment' instead of 'the judgment' has no support.

The *Book of Mormon* also has variants with itself. Isaiah 52:1, as found in 2 Nephi 8:24, begins "Awake, awake, put on thy strength, O Zion; put on thy beautiful garments, O Jerusalem, the holy city..." while in Moroni 10:31 we read, "And awake, and arise from the dust, O Jerusalem; yea, and put on thy beautiful garments, O daughter of Zion;.." This complex rewording enjoys no agreement.

Some *Book of Mormon* passages are so reworked that they are difficult to evaluate. For example, 1 Nephi 10:8 ("he is mightier than I, whose shoe's latchet I am not worthy to unloose") is a composite of Mark 1:7, Matthew 3:11 and Luke 3:16.

Raising the Bar: The Longer Variants

When the *Book of Mormon* variants reach a certain length, and greater significance, there is no longer room for tortuous interpretation:

Table 28. The Longer *Book of Mormon* Variants

Additions
Isaiah 2:5 (2 Nephi 12:5): *yea, come, for ye have all gone astray, every one to his wicked ways*
Isaiah 2:11 (2 Nephi 12:11): *And it shall come to pass that*
Isaiah 2:14 (2 Nephi 12:14): *and upon all the nations*
Isaiah 2:14 (2 Nephi 12:14): *and upon every people*
Isaiah 13:22 (2 Nephi 23:22): *For I will destroy her speedily; yea, for I will be merciful unto my people, but the wicked shall perish.*
Isaiah 14:2 (2 Nephi 24:2): *yea, from far unto the ends of the earth; and they shall return to their lands of promise.*
Isaiah 14:4 (2 Nephi 24:4): *And it shall come to pass in that day*
Isaiah 14:11 (2 Nephi 24:4): *is not heard*
Isaiah 29:6 (2 Nephi 27:2): *And when that day shall come*
Isaiah 29:4 (2 Nephi 26:15): *low in the dust*
Isaiah 29:4 (2 Nephi 26:15): *for the Lord God will give unto him power, that he may whisper concerning them, even as it were*
Isaiah 29:9 (2 Nephi 27:4): *all ye that doeth iniquity*
Isaiah 29:10 (2 Nephi 27:5): *because of your iniquity*
Isaiah 29:16 (2 Nephi 27:27): *But behold, I will show unto them, saith the Lord of Hosts, that I know all their works*
Isaiah 29:17 (2 Nephi 27:28): *But behold, saith the Lord of Hosts: I will show unto the children of men that*
Isaiah 29:20 (2 Nephi 27:31): *assuredly as the Lord liveth they shall see that*

Isaiah 48:1 (1 Nephi 20:1): *or out of the waters of baptism*
Isaiah 48:2 (1 Nephi 20:2): *who is the Lord of Hosts*
Isaiah 48:3 (1 Nephi 20:3): *and they came to pass*
Isaiah 48:5 (1 Nephi 20:5): *and I showed them for fear*
Isaiah 48:7 (1 Nephi 20:7): *they were declared unto thee*
Isaiah 48:11 (1 Nephi 20:11): *I will not suffer*
Isaiah 48:14 (1 Nephi 20:14): *yea, and he will fulfill his word which he hath declared by them*
Isaiah 48:22 (1 Nephi 20:22): *And notwithstanding he hath done all this, and greater also*
Isaiah 49:1 (1 Nephi 21:1): *And again: Hearken, O ye house of Israel, all ye that are broken off and are driven out, because of the wickedness of the pastors of my people; yea, all ye that are broken off, that are scattered abroad, who are of my people, O house of Israel*
Isaiah 49:8 (1 Nephi 21:8): *O isles of the sea*
Isaiah 49:8 (1 Nephi 21:8): *my servant*
Isaiah 49:12 (1 Nephi 21:12): *And then O house of Israel*
Isaiah 49:13 (1 Nephi 21:13): *for the feet of those who are in the east shall be established*
Isaiah 49:13 (1 Nephi 21:13): *for they shall be smitten no more*
Isaiah 49:14 (1 Nephi 21:14): *but he will show that he hath not*
Isaiah 50:1 (2 Nephi 7:1): *Yea, for thus saith the Lord: Have I put thee away, or have I cast thee off forever?*
Isaiah 50:1 (2 Nephi 7:1): *Yea, to whom have I sold you?*
Isaiah 50:8 (2 Nephi 7:8): *and I will smite him with the strength of my mouth*
Isaiah 51:7 (2 Nephi 8:7): *I have written*
Isaiah 51:11 (2 Nephi 8:11): *and holiness*
Isaiah 51:20 (2 Nephi 8:20): *save these two*
Isaiah 52:6 (3 Nephi 20:39): *Verily, verily, I say unto you, that*
Isaiah 52:11 (3 Nephi 20:41): *And then shall a cry go forth*
Isaiah 54:4 (3 Nephi 22:4): *and shalt not remember the reproach of thy youth*
Micah 5:8 (3 Nephi 21:12): *my people who are*
Micah 5:10 (3 Nephi 21:14): *Yea, wo be unto the Gentiles except they repent*
Micah 5:15 (3 Nephi 21:21): *them; even as upon*
Matthew 5:3 (3 Nephi 12:3): *who come unto me*
Matthew 5:6 (3 Nephi 12:6); *with the Holy Ghost*
Matthew 5:12 (3 Nephi 12:12): *ye shall have great joy*
Matthew 12:13 (3 Nephi 12:13): *Verily, verily, I say unto you, I give unto*
Matthew 12:14 (3 Nephi 12:14): *Verily, verily, I say unto you, I give unto*
Matthew 5:19 (3 Nephi 12:19: [total change] *And behold, I have given you the law and the commandments of my Father, that ye shall believe in me, and that ye shall repent of your sins, and come unto me with a broken heart and a contrite spirit. Behold, ye have the commandments before you, and the law is fulfilled.*
Matthew 5:20 (3 Nephi 12:20: *Therefore come unto me and be ye saved.*

Matthew 5:20 (3 Nephi 12:20): *ye shall keep my commandments, which I have commanded you at this time*
Matthew 5:21 (3 Nephi 12:21): *and it is also written before you, that*
Matthew 5:23 (3 Nephi 12:23): *shall come unto me, or shall desire to come unto me*
Matthew 5:24 (3 Nephi 12:24): *unto thy brother, and*
Matthew 5:24 (3 Nephi 12:24): *unto me with full purpose of heart, and I will receive you*
Matthew 5:26 (3 Nephi 12:25): *And while ye are in prison can ye pay even one senine? Verily, verily, I say unto you, Nay.*
Matthew 5:29 (3 Nephi 12:27): *Behold, I give unto you a commandment, that ye suffer none of these things to enter into your heart.*
Matthew 5:30 (3 Nephi 12:30): *ye should deny yourselves of these things, wherein ye will take up your cross, than that ye*
Matthew 5:46 (3 Nephi 12:46): *Therefore those things which were of old time, which were under the law, in me are all fulfilled)*
Matthew 5:47 (3 Nephi 12:47): *Old things are done away, and all things have become new.*
Matthew 6:1 (3 Nephi 13:1): *Verily, verily, I say that I would that ye should do alms unto the poor*
Matthew 6:25 (3 Nephi 13:25): *Remember the words which I have spoken. For behold, he are they whom I have chosen to minister unto this people*
Mark 1:7 (1 Nephi 10:8): *among you whom ye know not; and he is*
Acts 3:24 (3 Nephi 20:24): *Verily, I say unto you*
Acts 3:25 (3 Nephi 20:25): *and ye are of the house of Israel*
Acts 3:26 (3 Nephi 20:26): *and this because ye are the children of the covenant*
1 Corinthians 12:8 (Moroni 10:9): *of God, that he may teach*
1 Corinthians 12:8 (Moroni 10:10): *that he may teach*
1 Corinthians 12:9 (Moroni 10:11): *exceeding great*
1 Corinthians 12:10 (Moroni 10:13): [replacing "prophecy"] *that he may prophesy concerning all things*
1 Corinthians 12:10 (Moroni 10:16): *languages and of divers kinds of*

Omissions

Isaiah 5:8 (2 Nephi 15:8): *that* lay field to field
Isaiah 9:4 (2 Nephi 19:4): as in the day of Midian
Isaiah 13:8 (2 Nephi 23:8): they shall be in pain as a woman that travaileth
Isaiah 29:7 (2 Nephi 27:3): the multitude of
Isaiah 29:7 (2 Nephi 27:3): even all that fight against her and her munition
Isaiah 48:10 (I Nephi 20:10): but not with silver
Isaiah 49:7 (1 Nephi 21:7): *and* the Holy One of Israel, and he shall chose thee
Isaiah 50:10 (2 Nephi 7:10): let him trust in the name of the LORD, and stay upon his God.
Isaiah 51:1 (2 Nephi 8:1): ye that seek the LORD
Isaiah 51:2 (2 Nephi 8:2): and increased him
Isaiah 51:9 (2 Nephi 8:9): in the generations of old

Isaiah 51:15 (2 Nephi 8:15): that divided the sea
Isaiah 54:9 (3 Nephi 22:9): nor rebuke thee
Micah 5:15 (3 Nephi 21:21): in anger
Matthew 3:11 (1 Nephi 10:8): that cometh after me
Matthew 5:18 (3 Nephi 12:18): Till heaven and earth pass away
Matthew 5:20 (3 Nephi 12:20): your righteousness shall exceed *the righteousness* of the scribes and Pharisees
Matthew 5:23 (3 Nephi 12:23): bring thy gift
Matthew 5:24 (3 Nephi 12:24): Leave there thy gift before the altar
Matthew 5:25 (3 Nephi 12:25): the adversary deliver to the judge, and the judge deliver thee to the officer, and thou be cast into prison
Matthew 5:27 (3 Nephi 12:27): Ye have heard that
Matthew 5:29 (3 Nephi 12:27): And if thy right eye offend thee, pluck it out, and cast it from thee: for it is profitable for thee that one of the members should perish, and not that thy whole body should be cast into hell.
Matthew 5:30 (3 Nephi 12:30): And if thy right had offend thee, cut it off, and cast it from thee
Matthew 5:30 (3 Nephi 12:30): one of thy members should perish, and not that thy whole body
Matthew 5:33 (3 Nephi 12:33): ye have heard that
Matthew 5:35 (3 Nephi 12:33): neither by Jerusalem; for it is the city of the great King
Matthew 5:38 (3 Nephi 12:38): Ye have heard that
Matthew 5:43 (3 Nephi 12:43): Ye have heard that
Matthew 5:45 (3 Nephi 12:45): and sendeth rain on the just and on the unjust
Matthew 5:46 (3 Nephi 12:46): For if ye love them which love you, what reward have ye? Do not even the publicans the same?
Matthew 6:10 (3 Nephi 13:10): Thy kingdom come
Matthew 6:11 (3 Nephi 13:11): Give us this day our daily bread
Matthew 6:32 (3 Nephi 13:32): (For after all these things do the Gentiles seek)
1 Corinthians 12:5 (Moroni 10:8): but the same Lord
1 Corinthians 12:6 (Moroni 10:8): And there are diversities of operations
1 Corinthians 13:4 (Moroni 7:45): charity vaunteth not itself
1 Corinthians 13:5 (Moroni 7:45): Doth not behave itself unseemly

Note that the addition to Isaiah 2:5 (2 Nephi 12:5: yea, come, for ye have all gone astray, every one to his wicked ways) was created by inserting wording based on the famous Isaiah verse 53:6, "And we like sheep have gone astray; we have turned every one to his own way; and the LORD hath laid on him the iniquity of us all."

Analyzing Isaiah 13:22, where the BoM adds "For I will destroy her speedily; yea, for I will be merciful unto my people, but the wicked shall perish" (2 Nephi 23:22), Tvedtnes states that the Septuagint adds, "quickly shall it be done, and shall not be delayed" offering some sort of support to the BoM addition. In fact, the Septuagint does not *add* this. It *translates* the KJV clause "and her time is near to come" with "quickly it will come," and the KJV clause "and her days shall not be prolonged" with "and it shall not be delayed." Indeed, a Septuagint variant reading has "and her days shall not be drawn out." The BoM addition finds neither parallel nor support in any version.

Analyzing Isaiah 14:2 where the BoM adds "yea, from far unto the ends of the earth; and they shall return to their lands of promise" (2 Nephi 24:2), Tvedtnes suggests that there is partial support in the Great Isaiah Scroll, which, instead of the KJV phrase "to their place" one finds "to their land and to their place." The BoM variant has "lands of promise," but after "to their place," and after an intervening clause. This is scraping the barrel for lean pickins.

Analyzing Isaiah 48:11 "how should my name be polluted?" where the BoM has "I will not suffer my name to be polluted" (1 Nephi 20:11), Tvedtnes states that there has been a change in the verb, from third person singular to first person singular, with support in the Great Isaiah Scroll, the Septuagint and one Targum. Although this is true of the verb "to pollute," the change in the BoM is in the verb "to suffer" while "to pollute" is an infinitive. No version agrees with the BoM.

An awkward situation exists with respect to the variant involving Isaiah 51:9, where the BoM omits "in the generations of old" (2 Nephi 8:9). Tvedtnes states that some Hebrew mss omit "generations" providing partial support. No Hebrew manuscript omits it according to Kittel's *Biblia Hebraica* or *Biblia Hebraica Stuttgartensia*, or any other source that I have been able to examine. Kennicott does have variant spellings for "generations" (*drt/drwt*, both plural of *dwr*).

These larger, and significantly more substantive variants find no agreement in any ancient manuscript. Sperry and Tvedtnes were of course aware of these much more substantial variants. The rational to ignore them, as well as others, was to assert that these passages are BoM paraphrases, and not taken from the Isaiah of the Brass Plates. On the contrary, they cannot be explained as being simply scribal glosses, (explanatory insertions), since the *Book of Mormon* version is not supposed to be a translation of a text produced by a scribal tradition, but Isaiah's text translated by the power of God. As we have seen in the case of the four long Isaiah inclusions, it is clearly stated that Nephi is simply reading from the Brass Plates. All of the inclusions are commented upon separately, following the reading. The claim that these longer variants are Nephi's glosses is nothing more than a tacit admission that orthodox LDS apologetics can do nothing with them. Furthermore, *the gloss argument cannot apply to the nearly forty omissions.*

BoM Isaiah Failed to Correct King James Mistranslations

The King James translation was begun in 1604 and completed in 1611. Several teams (companies) produced it. The First Oxford Company translated from Isaiah to Malachi. They were John Harding (Professor of Hebrew at Oxford; died in 1610); John Rainolds (Reynolds; 1549-1607; a Greek scholar, educator and Puritan protagonist); Thomas Holland (1539-1612; a Calvinist scholar and theologian); Richard Kilby (1560-1620; Regius Professor of Hebrew, responsible for translating the latter part of the Old Testament); Miles Smith (1554-1624; a Calvinist scholar, accomplished in the Biblical languages); Richard Brett (1567-1637; a clergyman and student of Latin, Greek, Aramaic, Arabic, Hebrew and Ge'ez); Daniel Fairchough (1582-1645; a chaplain and theological disputant, especially in debates against the Jesuits) and William Thorne (1569?-1630; a chaplain and orientalist who had been Regius Professor of Hebrew at Oxford). The translation of the Old Testament was based primarily on the Masoretic text of *The Second Rabbinic Bible*, edited by Jacob Ben Chayyim and printed by Daniel Bloomberg in 1525, but for some passages not present in this edition, recourse was had to *First Rabbinic Bible* edited by Felix Praetensis in 1517-18.

Some lay believers assume that the KJV translation is so good that one can argue from it, word for word, as though it were the Hebrew original. In fact, there are many problems in the translation. The following table presents some of the mistranslations in the book of Isaiah, and compares them with the Jewish Aramaic Targum translation and the Septuagint Greek translation. One must bear in mind that the Hebrew is the original and trumps all else. The translations are important only when they can shed light on Hebrew words or phrases that are still poorly understood, especially the *hapax legomena*, words that occur only once in the whole Hebrew OT. At times, both the Aramaic and Greek indulge in a bit of translator's license, and even some exegesis (theological interpretation). The Aramaic in particular seems to be concerned to tell the reader what one should understand Isaiah to have meant, rather than word for word what he actually wrote. The KJV translators used Masoretic Hebrew manuscripts, and also consulted the Greek and Aramaic when found useful.

The Masoretes were a famous family working in Palestine (Tiberias and Jerusalem) and Iraq (Babylon) that was dedicated to preserving the scriptural tradition (*masorah* means "handing down, transmission, tradition," in Aramaic). Their text did not change the consonantal text, but added marks, a form of diacritics, above or below the consonants to indicate vowels (vocalization) and other marks for liturgical intonation. The timeline is approximately the Great Isaiah Scroll (1Qisaa, carbon-14 dated several times with the following results: 335-324 BCE and 202-107 BCE); the Greek Septuagint (possibly as early as late 2nd century BCE); the Aramaic Targum Jonathan (Yonatan, early 1st century CE) and the Masoretic text of the prophets (c. 900 CE). The antiquity of the Great Isaiah scroll is hugely important, as this text confirms the accuracy of the consonantal text of the Masoretes, and shows the great care that the rabbis have exercised in passing Isaiah's text down to us. Although it is the best preserved of the Dead Sea Scrolls, it does have some small damaged parts, resulting in occasional lacunae in the text.

The *Book of Mormon* Isaiah inclusions are held to be a divine translation, restoring lost or poorly transmitted scriptures. "...they have taken away from the gospel of the Lamb many parts which are plain and most precious" (1 Nephi 13:26). The BoM text is claimed to differ from the King James Version only when such differences were needed to correct errors in the KJV. These BoM emendations are quite numerous. Therefore, the obvious question is: when the King James translation is wrong, or poor, does the BoM "correction" correct or improve upon it?

Scholars who will engage in careful examination of the entries in the following table can check my translations against the published literal translations of the Hebrew Masoretic text, Aramaic Targum Jonathan and Greek Septuagint: Jay P. Green, editor & translator, *The Interlinear Bible, Hebrew-Greek-English*; [307] Lancelot Brenton, *The Septuagint with Apocrypha: Greek and English*[308]; and J. F. Stenning, *The Targum of Isaiah* [Targum Jonathan], *edited with a translation.*[309]

---

[307] Jay P. Green, , editor & translator. *The Interlinear Bible, Hebrew-Greek-English.* (London: Hendrickson Publishers, 2005).

[308] Lancelot Brenton, *The Septuagint with Apocrypha: Greek and English* (Peabody, MA: Hendrickson Publishers, 2015).

[309] J. F. Stenning, *The Targum of Isaiah* [Targum Jonathan], *Edited with a translation.* (Oxford : Clarendon Press, 1949).

Table 29. Mistranslation in the King James Version of Isaiah

HM:	the Hebrew Masoretic text
Q:	the Great Isaiah Scroll found at Qumran
	=Q indicats orthographic differences to HM
T:	the Aramaic Targum Yunathan (Jonathan; Sperber edition)
S:	the Greek Septuagint (edited by Rahlfs)

Editions and dictionaries are listed in the bibliographies.

Transliteration: In keeping with the early (pre-Rabbinacal) date of Isaiah, b, g, d, k, p & t are not aspirated after vowels.

Texts at Issue with Chapter & Verse	Translation & Comments
2:16: pleasant <u>pictures</u>	
HM: *śakîyôt* (=Q)	HM: <u>ships</u> (so in prominent lexica)
T: *kal d-šarān bə-bīrāniyāt šiprā*	T: those dwelling in beautiful palaces
S: πᾶσαν θέαν πλοίων κάλλους	S: every display of beautiful ships
3:2: the <u>prudent (one)</u>	
HM: *qōsēm* (=Q)	HM: <u>soothsayer</u>, diviner
T: *mištə'ēᵞl*	T: diviner
S: στοχαστὴν	S: diviner
3:18: <u>bravery</u>	
HM: *tip'eret* (=Q)	HM: <u>beauty, glory</u>, ornament
T: *tūšbəḥat*	T: praise, glory
S: δόξαν	S: glory
4:1: <u>to take away</u> (infinitive)	
HM: *'ᵉsōp* (=Q)	HM: <u>take away!</u> (the form is <u>imperative</u>)
T: *kənōš*	T: sweep away! (imperative)
S: ἄφελε	S: take away! (imperative)
4:5: every <u>dwelling place</u> of mount	
HM: *kol məkôn har-ṣîyôn* (=Q)	HM: *məkôn*: "<u>place</u>": "every place of ..."
T: *kōl miqdaš ṭūrā də-ṣiyōn*	T: every sanctuary of Mount Zion
S: ῥᾶς τόπος τοῦ ὄρους Ζιων	S: every place of Mount Zion
5:25: their carcases <u>were torn</u> in the midst of the streets	
HM: *wat-təhî niblātām kas-sûḥâ bə-qereb ḥûṣôt* (Q reads: *w-thyh*; no meaning difference)	HM: "their carcases <u>are like rubbish</u> (or dung) in the midst of the streets" *sûḥâ* is a noun meaning rubbish, sweepings, or alternatively faeces.
T: *wa-hwa'ā nəbīlathōn məšuggərā kə-siḥūtā bə-gō šūqayā*	T: "their corpses were cast out like offal in the midst of the streets"
S: ἐγενήθη τὰ θνησιμαῖα αὐτῶν ὡς κοπρία ἐν μέσω ὁδοῦ	S: "their corpses were like dung in the midst of the street"

5:15: the <u>mean</u> man shall be brought down, and the <u>mighty</u> man shall be humbled	
HM: *way-yiššaḥ ʾādām way-yišpal ʾîš* (=Q, except Q lacks *way-*)	HM: both "a man shall be bowed low, and a man shall be abased". *ʾādam* & *ʾîš* mean "man" or "a man". There is no word in the text to be translated "mean" or "mighty" (words introduced by the KJ translators).
T: *yimʾak ʾanāšā wə-yiḥlaš təqōp gūbrīn*	T: "man shall be debased and the might of men shall grow weak"
S: *καὶ ταπεινωθήσεται ἄνθρωπος καὶ ἀτιμασθήσεται ἀνήρ*	S: "man shall be brought low and man shall be dishonored"
5:30: in <u>the heavens</u> thereof	
HM: *ba-ʿarîpeʸhā* (=Q)	HM: "by its [the land's] clouds" unless emended: *ʿarîpīyā* (in cloud). There is nothing that can mean "heavens".
T: *min qədām bištā*	T: "from before the shame [or evil]"
S: *ἐν τῇ ἀπορίᾳ αὐτῶν*	S: "in their distress (perplexity)"
6:13: shall be <u>eaten</u>	
HM: *wə-hāyətâ lə-bāʿēr* (Q: *w-hyyth l-bʿr*; no meaning difference)	HM: *bāʿēr* means "to kindle" and thus ([the tenth that returns] "shall be <u>to kindle</u>", and like the mighty trees shall sow the holy seed (certainly, this tenth will not be eaten!)
T: *w-îhōn lə-ṣārābā*	T: "it will be for burning" (the remnant)
S: *ἔσται εἰς προνομὴν*	S: "it wll be for plunder"
9:5: for every <u>battle of the warrior</u> is with confused noise	
HM: *kî kol səʾôn sōʾēn bə-raʿaš* (=Q)	HM: "for every <u>shoe (boot) of the wearer</u> (marcher) is with noise (tumult, din)". *səʾôn* occurs only here in the whole OT but is common in Aramaic (Syriac: *səʾūnā*,where the verbal root means "to wear a shoe") and Jewish Babylonian Aramaic (*sēʸnā*); while *raʿaš* means a din or noise (not necessarily "confused").
T: *kol miʸsabbəhōn we-mittanhōn bi-ršaʿ*	T: "all their taking and giving is with wickedness" (v. Jastrow, p. 777)
S: *ὅτι πᾶσαν στολὴν ἐπισυνηγμένην δόλ ω*	S: "for every garment gathered by treachery"
10:4: <u>without me</u>	
HM: *biltî* (=Q)	HM: "<u>except</u>" This is a negative or privative particle, often meaning "not" and "lest"; note 48:9 , "that ... not"
T: *bar min*	T: "except for"
S: *τοῦ μὴ*	S: "to not (lest)..." End of v. 10:3.

10:26: <u>slaughter</u> HM: *makkat* (=Q)	HM: "<u>blow</u> (or defeat)". The root means to strike. Slaughter is a totally different root.
T: *maḥḥat* S: *πληγὴν*	T: "smiting (blow)" S: "blow"
10:18: a <u>standardbearer</u> fainteth HM: *məsôs nōsēs* (=Q)	HM: "an <u>invalid</u> pines away(despairs)." *nōsēs*, a *hapax legomenon*, was interpreted by the KJ based on *nēs* (flag) and *hitnôsēs* (to rally about the flag). Taking *nōsēs* to mean "standardbearer" is pure KJ guesswork, over against T, S & the lexica. The root *nss* (*nōsēs* is the active participle) is found in post-Biblical Hebrew & Jewish Aramaic (*nəsîs*, grieved), Syriac (*nassīs*, frail, sick) and Akkadian *nasāsu* (to lament, bewail). T takes *nōsēs* from *nws*, "to flee." *məsôs* is a better attested root, meaning "to melt, disolve," and hence "to pine away, despair, become faint."
T: *təbīr wə-ᶜārīq*	T: "a lame [broken] person and a fugitive"; as if putting "and" between *məsôs* and *nōsēs*. T & S derive from Hebrew *nās* (nws), to flee.
S: *ὁ φεύγων ὡς ὁ φεύγων ἀπὸ φλογὸςκαιομένης*	S: "the fugitive like one fleeing from burning flame"
13:14: <u>roe</u> HM: *ṣəbī* (=Q) T: *ṭəbēʸ* S: *δορκάδιον*	HM: "gazelle" T: "gazelle"; possibly also deer S: "fawn" of the gazelle in the Mid East,
11:8: <u>cockatrice</u> HM: *ṣipᶜônî* (=Q)	HM: "<u>a poisonous snake</u>"; not specifically identified, while the cockatrice is a mythological serpent or dragon born of a cock's egg.
T: *ḥiwēʸ ḥurmān* S: *ἀσπίδων*	T: "poisonous snake" (for *ḥurmān* [poisonous] v. Dalman, p. 161) S: "asps "
13:12: <u>golden wedge</u> of Ophir HM: *ketem ʾôpîr* (=Q)	HM: "<u>gold</u> of Ophir". There is no word for wedge here.
T: *məsannənā də-ʾōpīr* S: *ὁ λίθος ὁ ἐκ Σουφιρ*	T: "refined [gold] of Ophir" S: "the stone from Souphir

10:28: <u>carriages</u>
HM: *kēlāᵞw* (=Q)

HM: "his weapons (equipment? vessels?)". The word primarily means "vessels", used often of the vessels of the temple, altar, sanctuary or tabernacle, but can mean vessels (ships), equipment, and weapons

T: *yəmannēᵞ rabbānēᵞ mašrəyātēᵞh*

T: "he appoints the heads of his camps, troops"

S: *σκεύη*

S: "equipment"

11:1: a Branch shall <u>grow</u> out of his roots
HM: *nēṣer miš-šorāšāᵞw yipre* (=Q)

HM: "a shoot from his roots shall <u>bear fruit</u> (be fruitful)"; *yipre* comes from the common word for fruit, *pərî*; while the phrase "shall grow" would come from "*yipraḥ*"

T: *məšîḥā mib-bnēᵞ bənōhî yitrabbē*

T: "the Messaiah shall be reared from the sons of his sons"

S: *ἄνθος ἐκ τῆς ῥίζης ἀναβήσεται*

S: "a flower shall come up from the root"

13:21: <u>owls</u>
HM: *bənôt yaᶜᵃnâ* (=Q)
T: *bənāt naᶜāmyāᵞn*
S: *σειρῆνεσ*

HM: "<u>ostriches</u>"; an unclean animal.
T: "ostriches"
S: "sirens" or rather, demon ghosts of the desert

14:22: son, and <u>nephew</u>
HM: *nîn wā-neker* (=Q)
T: *bar wə-bar bar*
S: *κατάλειμμα καὶ σπέρμα*

HM: "offspring and <u>progeny</u>"
T: "son and son's son"
S: "offspring and seed (progeny)"

13:2: <u>high</u> mountain
HM: *har nišpe* (=Q)

HM: "<u>wind-swept</u> (bare) mountain". Other words from this root mean to clean off, polish off, while a form in later Hebrew means to make smooth. Roots from cognate languages have similar meaning, and never mean "high"

T: *ᶜal karkā yātēᵞb šēlēᵞwā zəqūpū ᵓātā*

T: "on the fortified place standing at ease, set up the sign"

S: *ὄρους πεδινοῦ*

S: "a mountain of a plain"

13:22: the wild beasts <u>of the islands</u>
HM: *ᵓîyîm* (=Q)
T: *ḥātōlīn*
S: *ὀνοκένταυροι*

HM: "jackals" (possibly hyenas)
T: "cats"
S: "donkey-centaurs"

13:22: desolate <u>houses</u>
HM: -*ᵓalmənôtāᵞw* (=Q)
T: *bīrānyāthōn*
S: *ἐκεῖ*

HM: "<u>palaces</u>"
T: "palaces"
S: " there"

14:4: golden city HM: *madhēbâ* (Q reads: *marhēbâ*)	HM: Mss. differ. Some have *madhēbâ* while Q has *marhēbâ*. *madhēba* does not mean "golden" in Hebrew (much less golden city), the word for gold being *zāhāb*, and no "m" preformative from this root exists to read "golden"; while *marhēbâ* comes from a root meaning "to assault, storm, act insolently"; so that one can read with Q: "the insolence (insolent one) has ceased"
T: *sāp təqōp ḥayyābā* S: *ἐπισπουδαστής*	T: "the strength of the guilty has ceased" S: "taskmaster" ceased
14:23: bittern HM: *qippōd* (=Q)	HM: "hedgehog" (earlier *qinpoḏ = Arabic *qunfuḏ*, hedgehog)
T: *qūppədīn* S: *ἐχίνους*	T: "hedgehogs" (Dalman, Levy) S: "hedgehogs"
48:3: from the beginning (also 48:7) HM: *mē ʾāz* (=Q)	HM: "from then , in advance"; note *me-ʾāz* is rendered "from that time" in 48:8
T: *mib-bə-kēʸn* S: *ἔτι*	T: "from there on"; with the sense of prior time (v. Dalman, p. 201) S: "already"
51:6: abolished HM: *tēḥāt* (=Q)	HM: "to be broken". This is the passive of a common verb meaning "to break".
T: *u-zkūtī lā titʿakkab* S: *δικαιοσύνη μου οὐ μὴ ἐκλίπῃ*	T: "and my judgment will not be delayed [variant: broken] " S: "fail"
51:9: Art thou not it HM: *hᵃlô ʾat hî* (=Q)	HM: "Art thou not she". *ʾat* ("thou"), *hî* ("she") and the verb are feminine (also in 51:10; all referring to Jerusalem).
T: pronouns not used S: *οὐ σὺ εἶ*	T: The circumlocution does however have a feminine verb: *šēʸṣītī* S: "Is [it] not thou?" Greek does not have gender in verbs or in these pronouns.
51:15: divided HM: *rōgaʿ* (=Q)	HM: "stirred up". A number of passages involving the sea and requiring a meaning such as this have brought some lexicographers to separate the verb in these instances from the more common root having to do with calm and quiet.
T: *nāzēʸp* S: *ταράσσων*	T: "rebuke" S: "one who stirs up (troubles)"

51:20: wild bull HM: *tô'* (Q: tô) T: *mizrəqēʸ* S: σευτλίον ἡμίεφθρον	HM: "antelope"; possibly the oryx, or the ibex (a species of wild goat). T: "vessels" (to sprinkle blood on the altar; followed by "of the snare, net". Hmm. So, what does thhis mean?) S: "beet"; both words together "half-boiled beet".
3:22: crisping pins HM: *hā-hᵃrîṭîm* (=Q) T: *maḥakayā* (variant: *maḥaṭṭayā*) S: *διαφανῆ Λακωνικὰ*	HM: "purses" T: *maḥakayā*: girdles or breast holders. A variant is: pins, needles (for sewing, or decoration). S: a type of Laconian shear (transparent) garment
3:3: the cunning artificer HM: *hᵃkam hiʳāšîm* (=Q) T: *sīb* S: σοφὸν ἀρχιτέκτονα	HM: "magician", one skilled in magic. This may be a gloss to explain the following phrase. T: scholar, senior scholar S: skilled master-builder
3:3: the eloquent orator HM: *nəbôn lāḥaš* (=Q) T: *sōklatān bə-ʿēʸṣā* S: *συνετὸν ἀκροατήν*	HM: "skilled in incantation". The verb means to utter, & to whisper incantations (against snakes, etc.). T: one intelligent in counsel S: intelligent listener
3:8: to provoke the eyes of his glory HM: *l-amrôt ʿênê kəbôdô* (=Q) T: *margəzīn qədām yəqārēʸh* S: ἐταπειψώθη ἡ δόξα αὐτῶν	HM: "to rebel against the eyes of his glory". The verbal root means "to be rebellious". T: who provoke anger before his dignity S: their glory has been brought low
3:19: muflers HM: *raʿālôt* (=Q) T: *hᵃnisnəsayā* S: τὸν κόσμον τοῦ προσώπου αὐτῶν	HM: veils (possibly with an eye slit) T: veils S: their face ornamentation

The passages in the above table are part of a larger study of KJV translation deficiencies in the relevant Isaiah passages. The total included in this study is 103. Table 29 has 35. The remaining 68 can be found in Appendix 2. By far the majority are clear mistranslations, but there are some included that are most probably mistranslations, and a few that are simply very weak. Linguists will find numerous lexical resources in Bibliography 2 of *Mormon Genesis* (2018). There too, Bibliography 1 has an annotated list of the published texts used in this study. Even though the

Greek and Aramaic texts are interesting in their own right, since the original was in Hebrew, the bottom line is: Hebrew rules.

Of the 103, the BoM has the KJV wording 100% intact in 100. They underwent no change at all. Each of the remaining three has a variant, which however does not involve the mistranslation. *The BoM fails to correct or in any way improve even one KJV mistranslation.*

In spite of the fact that the rational for the changes made in the KJV Isaiah text was to correct it, the BoM text retains all of the KJV mistranslations verbatim, except three, where its version is equally incorrect. In Isaiah 51:9, the KJV says "Art thou not it," while the BoM says "Art thou not he," and the Hebrew says "Art thou not she." In Isaiah 51:15, the KJV says "that divided the sea," while the Hebrew says "that stirs up the sea" and the BoM omits the clause. In Isaiah 51:17 the KJV says "wrung *them* out," while the BoM says "wrung out," and the Hebrew says, "drained [it]." Apart from the fact that "wrung out" is a mistranslation of the Hebrew, the BoM does tangentially delete "them," not present in the Hebrew text, while the KJV has it in italics, which the BoM frequently deletes.

Isaiah 8:3 is a serious mistranslation defect. Most Hebrew names have meaning, and they are not usually translated. But the carnal intercourse of Isaiah and the prophetess was to produce an oracle. Yahweh himself speaks, telling Isaiah to name the boy "*maher-shalal-hash-bazz*" [*Hurry, take booty; hasten, take plunder.*] A bilingual Tanakh online translates it "*hasten loot, speed the spoils*" This is the text of the divine oracle itself, and the whole purpose of the story. It was a revelation that the enemies of Israel were soon to be defeated, and is usually taken to refer to the expected Messiah, the long-awaited new David. Yahweh only rarely speaks to his prophet, and when he does, his oracle must be translated. Note that it was translated in both the Aramaic Targum Jonathan and the Greek Septuagint.

This study has arrived at the following observations:

1. The King James translation is seriously defective.
2. Table 29 contains numerous opportunities for correction or improvement by a totally or nearly perfect, divine translation of Isaiah.
3. In 100 of 103 cases, the version of Isaiah in the *Book of Mormon* retains the KJV wording *verbatim*. The BoM version introduced some change in only three cases (above), which neither correct a KJV mistranslation, nor improve upon an improbable translation..

4. The BoM Isaiah text has numerous variant readings. These do not find support in the ancient manuscripts. Above all, as many as they are, they do not correct KJ mistranslations or dubious translations. Not even once.

The division of the Isaiah text into chapters evolved over time. We do not know what this division might have been prior to the Great Isaiah Scroll (Q). The beginning and end points of the three long Book of Isaiah inclusions correspond to the chapter divisions in the King James. These divisions were determined by content, so it is not surprising to find that the divisions in Q largely correspond to those in the KJV, but not altogether. The KJV break between 51:23 and 52:1 does not exist in Q. Having all chapter breaks in agreement with KJV breaks is consistent with a nineteenth century origin for the BoM.

BCE New Testament Inclusions

Old Testament material in the Nephite record is explained by the Brass Plates of Laban, presumably essentially most of the Bible through 1 Kings, along with Isaiah. Passages dating after Lehi's departure from Jerusalem are thought to have been given to the Nephites by revelation. Remarkably, these even include New Testament material that appears hundreds of years before Christ, by *Book of Mormon* chronology. Phrases familiar to New England Christians occur throughout. The following table gives some of the passages.[310]

Table 30. Some Pre-Christian NT Passages in the *Book of Mormon*

ye must pray always, and not faint (2 Nephi 32:9)	men ought always to pray, and not to faint (Luke 18:1)
they shall depart "into everlasting fire prepared for the devil and his angels." (Mosiah 26:27)	Depart from me, ye cursed, into everlasting fire, prepared for the devil and his angels (Matthew 25:41)
And then shall the righteous shine forth in the kingdom of God. (Alma 40:25)	Then shall the righteous shine forth as the sun in the Kingdom of their Father. (Matthew 13:43
ye should be steadfast and immovable, always abounding in good works (Mosiah 5:15)	be ye stedfast, unmovable, always abounding in the good work of the Lord (1 Corinthians 15:58)
when my mortal shall put on immortality Enos 1:27)	this mortal must put on immortality (1 Corinthians 15:53)
in the nurture and admonition of the Lord (Enos 1:1)	in the nurture and admonition of the Lord (Ephesians 6:4)

---

[310] Marquardt, *The Rise of Mormonism*, 104-05.

he that fighteth against Zion, both Jew and Gentile, both bond and free, both male and female, shall perish (2 Nephi 10:16)	There is neither Jew nor Greek, there is neither bond nor free, there is neither male nor female (Galatians 3:28)
the Spirit is the same yesterday, today and forever (2 Nephi 2:4)	Jesus Christ the same yesterday, and to day, and for ever (Hebrews 13:8)
the righteous...who have endured the crosses of the world, and despised the shame of it (2 Nephi 9:18)	Jesus...endured the cross, despising the shame (Hebrews 12: 2)

New Testament influence can be found in other ways. For example, when Jesus comes to the Nephites, he chooses twelve disciples. One of them is Timothy, a good New Testament name, which, however, happens to be a Greek name. It was only after the conquests of Alexander and the spread of Hellenism in the Middle East that Greek names occurred among the Jews, as can be readily observed in the Old Testament. Timothy should have had a good Nephite or Hebrew name.

These passages were worked over in private, with pen and ink, and display many types of variants. Still, the basic phenomenon is the same: some changes are clearly suggested by similarity between the KJV word and the BoM word. The *Book of Mormon* throughout reflects the linguistic and religious environment of its authors.

New Testament themes are also used. The story of Salome, with the dance of the seven veils, and the head of John the Baptist on a platter, is given new life in the Jaredite *Book of Ether*. The daughter of the king's son in exile, who is "exceeding fair," says "And now, therefore, let my father send for Akish, the son of Kimnor; and behold, I am fair and I will dance before him, and I will please him, that he will desire me to wife; wherefore if he shall desire of thee that ye shall give unto him me to wife, then shall ye say: I will give her if ye will bring unto me the head of my father, the king." (Ether 8:10)

Observations.

§ Several aspects of the BoM narrative conflict with the Bible, such as the existence of a Bible at 600 BCE, especially in Egyptian.

§ Portions of Isaiah are quoted from the Brass Plates that were not written by Isaiah, and that date to decades after Lehi's departure.

§ The Book of Revelations is erroneously attributed to John the apostle.

§ The distribution of the variant readings in the Biblical inclusions are concentrated in the first quarter, being seemingly governed either by a time-efficiency principle, a laziness principle, or both.

§ The variant readings in the Biblical inclusions lack support in ancient manuscripts.

§ The KJV has may mistranslations, and the BoM variant readings fail to correct even one.

§ The preparation of the KJV inclusions in the BoM text required considerable effort, as well as the commentary on them, and the paraphrases worked into the Nephite narrative. This was not something that was done by casual composition, and most especially not by extemporaneous dictation.

§ If these Biblical inclusions existed in the lost 116 pages, Smith could not replicate their variants, and they would not exist in Nephi. Since they were inserted into Nephi, they clearly did not exist in Lehi.

This is the

Biblical Issue

< Chapter 19 >

Linguistic Pitfalls in BoM Name Creation

A major task faced by the BoM authors was the creation of a name list for all the personal and geographic names in their narrative. Research into a somewhat similar phenomenon has been done on speaking in tongues. In 1972, a linguist, William J. Samarin, published his now classical study of speaking in tongues, using recordings made in religious meetings in Italy, the Netherlands, Jamaica, Canada and the USA. He included Puerto Ricans of the Bronx, the snake handlers of the Appalachians and others. One of his main findings was that those presumably speaking in tongues never used sounds alien to their own language. Their discourse was made up of syllables, combined in various ways, with language-like intonation and rhythm, but lacking internal organization.[311] In another study, Felicitas Goodman found similar results.[312]

The generation of names for the Nephite narrative shares some of these traits. But it differs in that not all of the names had to be unique to the BoM. The repertoire could include names from the Bible. On the other hand, since many names need not have any referent outside the fertile minds of the authors, their analysis is fraught with hazards.

The Brass Plates of Laban: Establishing the Language Base

For our analysis, the Brass Plates of Laban raise the question: To what extent does one expect to find Hebrew in the *Book of Mormon*, and to what extent Egyptian? Nephi states that his father had lived all his days in Jerusalem, while at the same time referring to Egyptian as the language of his (Nephi's) father. It is hard to imagine that these two statements are not at odds. He claimed to be descended from Joseph. This implies that he would have hailed from the tribe of Joseph. When the tribe of Levi was made into a priestly cast and scattered among the other tribes, their territory was reallocated, along with that of Joseph, making tribes of each of Joseph's sons, Manasseh and Ephraim. These tribes were located in the north, in what had become the northern kingdom, after the conflict

---

[311] William J. Samarin, *Tongues of Men and Angels: the Religious Language of Pentecostalism* (New York: Macmillan, 1972).
[312] Felicitas D. Goodman, *Speaking in Tongues: a Cross-cultural Study of Glossolalia* (Chicago: University of Chicago Press, 1972).

between Solomon's sons, Jeroboam and Rehoboam, which had divided the tribes into two Kingdoms, Judah in the south, and Israel in the North. When Nephi says that he went to the land of his inheritance to get the silver, gold and other precious things (left there by his father) to buy the Brass Plates, he might have gone to the north, to the land of Israel. Lehi was of the tribe of Manasseh (Alma 10:3), perhaps with relatives in the Hebrew-speaking capital city Shechem. It would appear that one or some of Lehi's forebears had moved from this land of their inheritance to Jerusalem, possibly during the time of the Assyrian conquest of the Kingdom of Israel in the north, but certainly before his birth. Nephi and his siblings too must have been reared in Jerusalem, with their father. Surely their first language must have been Hebrew.

Even so, Nephi made plates with his own hands (1 Nephi 1:17) and wrote his history in Egyptian. (1 Nephi 1:2) This must have been the Egyptian of the period of the plates, 7th century BCE Egyptian or early Demotic, rather than reformed Egyptian. Nephi states (1 Nephi 3:19 "And behold, it is wisdom in God that we should obtain these records, that we may preserve unto our children the language of our fathers." That Egyptian was an acquired language even for Lehi is clear.

> For it were not possible that our father, Lehi, could have remembered all these things, to have taught them to his children, except it were for the help of these plates; for he having been taught in the language of the Egyptians therefore he could read these engravings, and teach them to his children, that thereby they could teach them to their children, and so fulfilling the commandments of God, even down to this present time. (Mosiah 1:4)

So he spoke Hebrew, but was taught Egyptian. Even though the first language of the people must have been Hebrew, and in spite of the sacred stamp of the Hebrew language, and its symbolic value for ethnic and religious pride, inexplicably he chose to write in Egyptian. (1 Nephi 1:2) When Alma passed the records to his son Helaman, he said (Alma 37):

> 2. And I also command you that ye keep a record of this people, according as I have done, upon the plates of Nephi, and keep all these things sacred which I have kept, even as I have kept them...
> 3. And these plates of brass, which contain these engravings, which have the records of the holy scriptures upon them, which have the genealogy of our forefathers, even from the beginning

Each member in this line of succession taught the Egyptian language to his sons, to pass on the ability to read and continue the record. The fact that this instruction was necessary shows that Egyptian was not their spoken language, but rather a scriptural, literary, liturgical but otherwise dead language. The *Book of Mormon* claim is, therefore, that an elite among the people were bilingual, speaking Hebrew, but using Egyptian largely as a scriptural and possibly a liturgical language, a bit like Latin in Italy, confined to the Vatican.

This is reflected in the statement of Mormon, when speaking of his production of the text on the gold plates, saying that he wrote in reformed Egyptian which had been "handed down and altered by us, according to our manner of speech," due to a shortage of gold, apparently implying Egyptian was a more compact language. Notably he added, "if we could have written in Hebrew, behold, ye would have had no imperfection in our record." This indicates that he was able to write in Hebrew better than in Egyptian. Clearly, the first language of the Nephites was Hebrew, although among them there was an elite who handed down sufficient knowledge of the Egyptian needed to read the Brass Plates in 7th century BCE Egyptian or early Demotic (Mosiah 1:4; Mormon read Nephi.).

The assertion that both Egyptian and Hebrew had been altered over the course of a millennium in the New World is not unusual. Language always changes. Even so, the Semitic languages display remarkable resistance to change, largely due to their triconsonantal structure and the forms used to generate vocabulary. Even Coptic resembles ancient Egyptian to such an extent that Champollion, who knew Coptic, was able to use it to decipher the Rosetta Stone text, once he had identified enough of the phonological characters. Two of the principal factors that promote language change are the adoption of a language by a substrate population that speaks some other language, and influences from neighboring languages, especially languages with considerable cultural dominance. Egyptian and Hebrew among the Nephites would have suffered neither of these influences, since the land is claimed to have been devoid of human beings prior to Lehi's arrival. Especially Egyptian, existing in splendid isolation, and used mostly as a written scriptural language, should have remained largely intact. For example, the transformation from classical Latin to church Latin did not produce a major change in the language, and almost no change in script. Modern Hebrew is written in virtually the same script as the Great Isaiah Scroll, although this "square" script developed from an earlier, but similar, Aramaic script.

Even the nature of change that had befallen Egyptian among the Nephites seems to have affected mostly the system of writing. In Mormon 9:32, Moroni says, "we have written this record according to our knowledge, in the characters which are called among us the reformed

Egyptian..." Even so, there would also have been some change in the language itself, similar to the shift from classical to church Latin.

Many other records existed. In Helaman 3:15 we read "But behold, there are many books and many records of every kind, and they have been kept chiefly by the Nephites." By the time of Mosiah, there is a Lamanite language and Nephite languages (Mosiah 9:1: "all the language of the Nephites"). The latter may have included the 7th century BCE Egyptian or early Demotic of the Brass Plates, and already a modified Egyptian in their record-keeping, as well as some regional dialects of Hebrew. Apparently early (classical) Nephite was preferred, the "language of Nephi." Steps are taken to make Nephite the linguistic coin of the realm (Mosiah 24):

> 4. he appointed teachers of the brethren of Amulon, in every land which was possessed by his people: and thus the language of Nephi began to be taught among all the people of the Lamanites.
> 6. they taught them that they should keep their record, and that they might write one to another.

Perhaps what are termed languages are more properly dialects, since Alma says "I attempt to address you in my language." (Alma 7:1)

At this point, the Lamanites "began to increase in riches, and began to trade one with another, and wax great, and began to be a cunning and a wise people, as to the wisdom of the world" (Mosiah 24:7). This trade would require written documents.

Communications by sending epistles was very common (Moroni 8:1; Alma 54:14-15; 56:1; 57:1-3; 59:3-4; 60:1; 60:25; 61:1 & 9; 61:19; 3 Nephi 3:1; 3:10; Mormon 3:4; 6:2; Ether 15:4-5; 15:18; and Moroni 8:6). Messages were often sent, and though some may have been delivered orally, others may have been written (Alma 15:4; 43:24; 47:12; & 47:33). Decrees were issued (Alma 23:2). Proclamations were "published throughout all the land" (Alma 22:27; 23:1; 30:57; 47:1; 61:6; Helaman 9:9; 3 Nephi 3:22 Mosiah 2:1; 7:17; & 27:2). The scriptures were sent out to teach the people: "Now behold, all those engravings which were in the possession of Helaman were written and sent forth among the children of men throughout all the land, save it were those parts which had been commanded by Alma should not go forth." (Alma 63:12) A case of book burning (burning of the scriptures) shows that a burnable material was used for copies of sacred writings: "they also brought forth their records which contained the Holy Scriptures, and cast them into the fire also, that they might be burned and destroyed by fire." (Alma 14:8)

The Nephite/Lamanite civilization is described as being very advanced, with numerous cities, many of them fortified, kingship, coinage, advanced metallurgy, wheeled vehicles, large armies and a written tradition in two languages. Writing must have been essential to keep inventories, write contracts and conduct business. Indeed, in parts of the ancient Middle East, these mundane applications were the earliest and most common use of writing. Since the account of the Nephites and Lamanites spans a period of over 1,000 years, certainly they would have left written material, in both languages, monumental inscriptions, commemorative inscriptions, signet rings, seal stamps and bullae, texts on jars used in votive offerings, royal and business correspondence, documents (contracts, inventories, marriage and divorce writs, and scriptures), tomb inscriptions and inscribed bone boxes. Some principal cities would have had a royal archive. Apparently, metal plates were a common medium for records in the *Book of Mormon*.

Even if the Hebrew writing system was altered, the alphabet has only twenty-two characters. Its form at the end of the seventh century BCE is known to scholars from inscriptions. If a text in altered Hebrew were to be found, a specialist would readily identify the alphabet, and basic translation would be possible in probably no more than a year. Subtle shifts in the meaning of some words, and neologisms, would provide grist for the scholars' publication mills for many years. It is even now so with Biblical Hebrew, as well as the Qumran corpus and extra-Biblical classical Hebrew inscriptions.

The unsealed plates were at least 30% in 7th century BCE Egyptian (Nephi, Jacob and part of Lehi). Today's Egyptologists are quite familiar with it. Even if reformed Egyptian were dug up, in time these texts would be readily recognized as a later form of Egyptian, although its decipherment would be more complex and take longer than reformed Hebrew. Possibly the character set would be larger, and logograms would exist alongside phonological characters. Even so, there is no reason to assume that this challenge would be greater than that faced by Champollion. Above all, minimally, archaeologists should be digging up textual material that is unidentified, i.e. neither Mayan nor any part of the Zapotec/Oaxacan/Aztec systems. In spite of massive archaeological exploration and excavation in the New World, no unidentified writing has been found that could be a candidate for a Nephite or Lamanite text.

Some Conclusions

§ The claim is extremely unlikely that the Hebrew scriptures had been collected as a sort of Bible, and translated into Egyptian, by the end of the seventh century BCE.

§ The *Book of Mormon* shows that Hebrew was the first language of the Nephites, and Egyptian was a written scriptural language.

§ The *Book of Mormon* states that there were many records of every kind, and correspondence.

§ If the Nephite/Lamanite civilization existed in the Americas without a substrate population and language, or neighbors using other languages, then their Hebrew and Egyptian would have persisted in ideal circumstances to resist change.

§ Such a large and advanced civilization, existing for over 1,000 years in the Americas should have left written artifacts that can be deciphered, or at the very least, there should be unidentified texts that are candidates for ancient Nephite texts. No Nephite or Lamanite written material has ever been found, or any unidentified text that could be a candidate for it.

Approaches to the Study of BoM Language Issues

Distribution of BoM Personal Names

The fact that BoM names consist of some taken from the Bible, and others that are decidedly non-Biblical, provides us with our first approach, without even dealing with the analysis of any individual non-Biblical name. The first part of the gold-plates translation (Lehi) was initially written with considerable detail, and the rewrite of that important section omitted much of the detail. Thus the events that took place in the portion that dealt with the Middle East are written in a social, cultural and political vacuum, thereby reducing the chance of errors that could be checked. The authors were much more comfortable giving their imaginations greater reign once they had gotten their little band established in the New World, and more so after King Benjamin. The history and cultures in the Pre-Columbian Americas, so long ago, could never be known well enough to prove them wrong, or so they thought. This is reflected in the roster of personal names that populated their narrative.

The band of Israelites arriving from Jerusalem obviously had to have Hebrew names. This was best done by drawing heavily from the Bible. As soon as the founding generation had died, they switched to made-up names, to give an exotic expression to a world that is uncharted and unknowable, apart from what one learns in their new bible. Even so, they felt that using such names exclusively for the disciples of Jesus would be just too strange for devout readers. To give a sacred cachet to the story of Jesus in the New World, they used some of the most illustrious names in the Bible associated with their period: Isaiah, Jeremiah, Jonas, Timothy and Zedekiah. These are joined by the name of their founding hero and prophet, Nephi. The two Christian centuries were followed by apostasy, a reemergence of the Nephite/Lamanite division, and the annihilation of the Nephites. This period is once again dominated by made-up names.

Table 31. Distribution of Nephite and Lamanite Names

Biblical Names Are in Bold Type.			
Israel	Enos to the Birth of Christ	The Christian Centuries (34-231 CE)	Apostasy & Annihilation (231-421)
Lehi, **Laman**, **Lemuel**, Nephi, **Jacob**, **Sam**, **Joseph**, **Sariah**, **Ishmael**, Zoram **Laban**	Enos, **Shem**, Jarom, Omni, Amaron, Chemish, Abinadom, **Amaleki**, Mosiah, **Benjamin**, Mosiah, Mormon, **Aaron**, Abinadi, Amulon, Helorum, Helamon, Himni, Antipus, **Antipas**, Ammon, Helam, Helem, **Hem**, Limhi, **Amaleki**, Ammon, **Noah**, Zeniff, Laman, Laman, Alma, Alma, Aminadi, Amulon, Helaman, Mulek, Omner, **Gideon**, Amlici, Ammonihah, Zeram, Amnor, Manti, Limher, Antinephilehi, Isabel, Nephihah, Amulek, Giddonah, Ishmael, Zeezrom, Seantum, Zoram, Zoram, Lehi, Aha, Zoram, Antionah, **Lehi**, Lamoni, Abish, Muloki, Antiomno, **Ammah**, Korihor, Helaman, Nephi, Shiblon, Corianton, Gazelem, Zerahemnah, Moroni, Nehor, Amalickiah, Laman, Lehonti, Teancum, **Lehi**, Pahoran, Ammoron, **Jacob**, Paanchi, Pacumeni, Pahoran, Gid, Morianton, Cumeni, Teomner, Pachus, Moronihah, Hagoth, Coriantumr, Tubaloth, Gadianton, Kishkumen, Cezoram, **Aminadab**, Nephi, **Lehi**, **Samuel**, Lachoneus, Lachoneus, Giddianhi, Gidgiddoni, Zemnariha, **Jacob**	**Jesus Christ**, Nephi, **Timothy**, **Jonas**, Mathoni, Mathonihah, Kumen, Kumenonhi, **Jeremiah**, Shemnon, **Jonas**, **Zedekiah**, **Isaiah**, Nephi, **Amos**, **Amos**	Ammaron, **Aaron**, Mormon, Mormon, Moroni, Gidgiddonah, Lamah, Limhah, Joneam, Camenihah, Moronihah, Antionum, Amoron, Shiblom, **Gilgal**, **Shem**, Josh, Archeantus, Luram, Emron, Zenephi
11 8 Biblical (70%)	106 17 Biblical (15%)	16 9 Biblical (56%)	21 3 Biblical (17%)

Note: A few Biblical entries are not identical with Biblical names, but very close (e.g. Sariah; cf. Sarah, Sarai, Saraiah). Excluding them would not change the results. Sources:

Alvin Knisley, *Book of Mormon Dictionary*, and "An Alphabetical Table of the Proper Names in the Old and New Testaments", in *The Holy Bible* (Philadelphia: M. Carey & Son, 1821).

Book of Mormon Phonology

The distribution of words by the first letter in the Nephite narrative is equally interesting. We cannot analyze Jaredite phonology in any meaningful way, since, according to that narrative, their language escaped the Tower of Babel confusion of languages, and so we are left to assume that they spoke the language of Noah, which theological creativity can assume to have existed, and to have been Adamic, the language of Adam, or some approximation to it. The linguistic heritage of Nephite/Lamanite inhabitants is said clearly to have been Hebrew, as a spoken language, and Egyptian as a scriptural/liturgical language. BoM names should reflect their phonology.

Using Knisley's *Dictionary of All Proper Names in the Book of Mormon*, we can make the following observations regarding non-Biblical personal names in the Nephite narrative:

1. There are no personal names beginning with *b* or *d*, although these are common in both Hebrew and Egyptian.
2. The exception to this is "deseret," which the BoM defines as "honey bee." Note that there is no phonologically similar word in Middle Eastern languages with this meaning.
3. The letter *c* is used as in English, for both *s* (Cezoram) and *k* (Corianton).
4. The sound *ch* is found pronounced as in "choice" (Chemish) although there is no such sound in Hebrew; while the closest in Egyptian is pronounced differently (more like *ts*).
5. The letter *j* pronounced as in "justice" does not exist in Hebrew. The letter usually written as *j* is *y* in Hebrew. So Jerusalem in Hebrew is *Yerushalayim* (*yərūšālayim*) and Joseph is *Yoseph* (*yōsēp*). When words from Latin passed into French, this sound shifted to the French *j* and so Latin "*justitia*" (i.e. *iustitia*) became *justice* in French, and was so borrowed into English. Many Biblical names that should be pronounced with initial *y* came into English with initial *j*. Some north-European languages have retained the original *y* pronunciation for *j*.
6. This said, many Hebrew words beginning with *y* came into English with initial *I*, such as Israel and Ishmael. In Hebrew, these are *Yiśrā'ēl* and *Yišmā''ēl* respectively. These are often names that are actually third person singular imperfect verbs ("May he [El, God] strive" and

"May he [El, God] hear", respectively). These names are common in Hebrew. But in the BoM, there are no names beginning with *y* at all, and none beginning with *I* that were not taken from the Bible.

7. The absence of initial *f* and *ph* personal names is consistent with Hebrew, since it has no letter *f*. Even in late Hebrew this is true in the initial position. In Egyptian, initial *f* is used in names.

8. The sound *w* existed in Egyptian, and in early Hebrew (although in late Hebrew it shifted to *v*). No BoM personal name begins with either sound.

Given the number of personal names in the Nephite narrative, it is obvious that there are inexplicable gaps in its phonological lineup, which is consistent with the artificial nature of BoM name creation.

BoM Name Generation

We will never know as much as we would like to know about the generation of the names found in the *Book of Mormon*. It is not possible to learn of all of the source elements that were used in this process, and, above all, one cannot get into the minds of the BoM authors. This said, once again, it is hoped that a real-world comparison might throw some light on the subject. Since it is the Bible that the authors took as their model, at least to a significant extent, one beginning point is to examine its names, and in particular, the degree of multiple occurrence of the same name, but borne by different individuals. The following list has been culled from a dictionary of Biblical names.[313] It is a collection of names that are not borne by more than one person in the Old Testament (and almost always in the New Testament as well), and are sufficiently prominent as OT heroes or eponymous ancestors that one might think that they would have been among the first choices of parents seeking a name for their child.

Table 32. 118 Personal Names Borne by Only One Individual in the OT

Abel (also in five compounds), Abigail, Abinadab, Abram/Abraham, Absalom, Adam, Ahab, Ahaz, Ahaziah, Ahijah, Asher, Baruch, Benjamin, Dan, Daniel, David, Deborah, Delilah, Dinah, Elijah/Elias, Elkanah, Ephraim, Er, Esau, Esther, Eve, Ezekiel, Ezra, Gad, Gideon, Gog, Goliath, Habakkuk, Hagar, Haggai, Ham, Hannah, Hosea, Jacob, Japhet, Jeconiah, Jehoash,

---

[313] "An Alphabetical Table of the Proper Names in the Old and New Testaments," in *The Holy Bible Containing the Old and New Testaments, together with the Apocrypha* (Philadelphia: M. Carey & Son, 1824), 1067-73.

Jehoiachin/Jeconiah, Jehoiakim/Eliakim, Jephthah, Jeroboam, Jerusha, Jesse, Jethro, Jezebel, Jonah, Joram/Jehoram, Josiah, Isaac, Isaiah, Israel, Issachar, Ithamar, Jubal, Judah, Judith, Kish, Laban, Lamech, Leah, Lemuel, Levi, Lot, Magog, Malachi, Manoah, Medan, Melchisedek, Menahem, Merab, Methuselah, Michal, Miriam, Moab, Mordecai, Moses, Na'am, Na'ashon/Nashon, Nahum, Naomi, Naphtali, Nehemiah, Ner, Nimrod, Noah, Nun, Onan, Ozem, Rachel, Rahab, Rebekah/Rebeccah, Remaliah, Rephael, Reuben, Ruth, Salmon, Samson, Samuel, Sarah/Sarai, Saraiah, Saul, Seth, Shem/Sem, Simeon, Solomon, Terah, Tubal, Uriel, Zebulun, Zeruiah, Zillah, Zilpah, Zipporah

It is surprising that so many prominent names do not recur in the OT books, especially given the large number of names and the near notoriety of some books for their "begats" and genealogical references. This is in spite of the fact that our reference, "The Scripture Dictionary," contains over 3,000 entries.

Our source for BoM names is the work of Knisley,[314] which contains only 506 entries. Both contain entries for locations, and some important words, in addition to personal names. "The Scripture Dictionary" contains some entries that derive from outside the Biblical lands (foreign place names, deities, etc.), while Knisley's work contains names from Biblical inclusions. All in all, they are comparable name lists.

First we note significant BoM name underpopulation. Although the BoM covers over 1,000 years of history, its name list is under 20% of the number in the OT.

Second, a large proportion of the BoM names are applied to two or more individuals. Unlike the OT, prominent names are especially given to this trend.

Table 33. BoM Name Recurrence

The number of persons bearing the name is in parentheses
Exact Personal Names:
Aaron (3), Alma (2), Amaleki (2), Ammon (2), Amos (2), Cohor (3), Com (2), Coriantum (2), Coriantumr (3), Corihor (2), Helaman (3), Heth (2), Ishmael (2), Jacob (3), Jared (2), Jonas (2), Lachoneus (2), Laman (4), Lamoni (2), Lehi (4), Lib (2), Mormon (3), Moroni (2), Moronihah (2), Mosiah (2), Nephi (4), Noah (2), Pahoran (2), Shez (2), Shiblom/n (3), Zoram
Similar Personal Names:
Abinadi/Abinadom/Aminadab, Aminadi, Aha/Ahah, Amaleki/Amalickiah/Amlici, Amaron/Ammaron/Ammoron/Amoron/Moron/Moroni/Moronihah, Ammon/Ammonihah, Amos/Amoz Amulek/Amulon, Anti-Christ/Anti-Nephi-Lehi, Antiomno/Antionah/Antionum/Antum, Antipas/Antipus, Cezoram/Seezoram/Zeezrom, Com/Comnor, Corianton/Coriantor/Coriantum/Coriantumr, Corihor/Korihor, Cumen/Kumen/Kumenonhi/Kish/Kishkumen/Pacumeni, Emer/Emron, Esrom/Ezrom,

[314] Knisley, *Dictionary of all Proper Names in the Book of Mormon.*

Ethem/Ether, Gadiandi/Gadianton/Gadiaomnah,
Gideon/Giddianhi/Giddonah/Gidgiddonah/Gidgiddoni, Gilgah/Gilgal,
Helam/Helaman/Helem/Helorum, Jashon/Jershon, Jonas/Joneam, Kib/Kim/Kimnor,
Lamah/Laman/Lamoni, Limah/Limher/Limhi/Limnah, Morianton/Moriantum,
Mulek/Amulek/Mulok/Muloki, Nephi/Nephihah, Nimrah/Nimrod, Omer/Omner/Omni/Teomner,
Riplah/Kish/Riplakish/Ripliancum, Seantum/Teancum,
Shemlon/Shemnon/Shiblon/Shiblom/Shiblum, Zonock/Zenos, Zeram/Zerin,
Zarahemla/Zerahemnah

City Names (Often from Personal Names)

Nephi, Zarahemla, Helam, Lehi-Nephi, Shemlon, Shilom, Aaron, Ammonihah, Bountiful, Gideon, Jerusalem (Lamanite), Lemuel, Shimnilom, Zarahemla, Antiparah, Judeah, Lehi, Moroni, Mulek, Nephihah, Onmer, Zeezrom, Gid, Gad, Gadiandi, Gadiomnah, Gilgal, Gimgimno, Jacob, Josh, Kishkumen, Laman, Moronihah, Onihah, Angola, Desolation, Jashon, Jordan, Shem, Teancum

The first group in this table reflects the need for efficiency, since duplication is the easiest way to generate names. The second group is name generation by free association, where a slight modification or recombination of elements already used can readily produce additional names.

Syllable Generation

The production of speech-like utterances in the practice of speaking in tongues differs from the BoM generation of names, in that the former is an extemporaneous phenomenon. Although the BoM authors still did need to develop a number of syllables that they could recombine, they could do so in a more studied and deliberate manner. An example is the ending *antum* and its permutations. These include: Antum, Irreantum, Coriantum (twice), Coriantumr (thrice), Corianton, Coriantor, Gadianton, Gadianti, Morianton, Ripliancum, Seantum and Teancum. Although we cannot be certain as to the source of this element, we may not have to look further than to the first settlement of Indian converts to Christianity in New England, Nonantum, founded by John Elliot, the Apostle to the Indians, whose work was used as an example and goal in the Second Great Awakening, which exercised the minds and aspirations of so many in the first four decades of the nineteenth century.

Some other examples of syllable components are worth mentioning:

Table 34. Names Ending in *hor*

Cohor (1)	the first rebel in the Jaredite narrative
Cohor (2)	a rebel who killed his own father to gain power
Cohor (3)	one of a group who refused repentance
Corihor (1)	rebelled against his father, raised an army in the Land of Nehor, imprisoned his father
Corihor (2)	mentioned with other impenitents

Korihor	an anti-Christ who opposed Alma
Nehor	a false teacher who murdered Gideon
Nehors	Order of the Nehors, a false religious system
Nehor	the refuge, land and apparently city of Corihor

Free association also appears manifest in the *-hor* (whore) names. All such occurrences are names of bad men, impenitents, patricides, and an anti-Christ. In this context, we remember that Nephite theology holds that there is only one true church, and all others are collectively the work of Satan, and are the *Whore of All the Earth*, a key BoM *cri de guerre*.

Table 35. Evil vs Good: Gad and Gid Names

Gad Names	
Gad	a wicked city that was burned as divine punishment
Gadiandi	a wicked city that was sunk in the earth as divine punishment
Gadianton	the founder of the Gadianton Robbers, based on oaths and secrets inspired by Satan
Gadiomna	a wicked city that was sunk in the earth as divine punishment
Gid Names	
Gid	a victorious Nephite military officer
Gid	a Nephite city, captured by Lamanite Amalickiah, but retaken by Nephite Moroni
Giddianhi	a leader of the Gadianton Robbers
Giddonah	presiding High Priest over the Nephite church
Gideon	a Nephite military leader & teacher, who delivered Limhi's people of from bondage
Gideon	
Gidgiddonah	a Nephite city, threatened by woe by Samuel; not listed among the cites destroyed
Gidgiddoni	a Nephite commander slain in the battle of Cumorah
	Commander in Chief of all Nephite armies in the Gadianton-Nephite war

All Gad names are of bad men or cities, while nearly all Gid names are good, including four Nephite heroes and one High Priest. The exception is Giddianhi. In this case, we may have a deliberate dissimulating alteration of the name Gadianton. The association of Gad with evil may have come simply from its rhyming with "bad," or from the fact that the tribe of Gad had joined the rebellion of the Israelite tribes of the north against the Davidic kingdom, and the prophets of Judah, including Isaiah and Jeremiah. Or it may have been drawn from the city name Baal-gad, the northernmost city smitten by Joshua (Joshua 11:17). On a more popular level, it may have derived this connotation from the expression "Egad!"/"Ye Gad!" (By God!), a euphemism for taking the name of God in vain. Even worse was the original more heathen expression, "Egads!"/"Ye Gads". In the still puritanical New England, especially in religious circles, such profanity was not taken lightly.

Another element used in name generation is the Greek prefix *-anti,* as in: Anianti, Anti-Nephi-Lehi, Antiomno, Antionah, Antionum, Antiparah, Antipas, Antipus and Archeantus. These have a double derivation. The first is *anti,* a Greek element that has become an English word. The second is Antipus, a variation of Antipas, a martyr in the Book of Revelations, and Herod Antipas. Antipas is a nickname for Antipatros, a Greek name that should not appear in the *Book of Mormon.*

Where Are the Expected Hebrew Elements?

There are recurrent elements in language. We would expect personal and location names given by a people speaking Hebrew to have at least some such elements from Hebrew.

Table 36. Name Elements in Biblical Hebrew

Personal Names			
adon-	'dn אדנ	lord, as in Adonijah (Adoniya), Adonizedek	None
ab-/abi-	'b/'by אב/אבי	father of	Abinadi, Abinadom—compare both with Biblical Abinadab
aḥi-	'ḥi אחי	brother of, as in Aḥijah (Aḥiya), brother of Jehovah	None (Note that the sound *j* does not exist in Hebrew; but *y* became *j* in French and English got it through French.)
ben-/beni-	bn/bny בנ/בני	son of, as in Benaiah Son of Yahweh (Jehovah), Bənēbəraq, Sons (clan) of Bəraq	None, except Biblical Benjamin
bat-/bit-	bn+t בנ+ת	daughter of (the n combines with the t, a feminine ending	None
yo-/-yah-/yahu	y+hwy י+הוי	Short versions of Yahweh (Jehovah), extremely common	Mosiah is possible, pronounced Mosyah, but it is hard to make it have meaning in Hebrew; Elijah (Eliyah) is Biblical
el-/-el	'l אל	God (El)-as in Samuel and Elhanan	Only Elijah (Eliyah), which is Biblical
ebed-/abd-	'bd עבד	servant of	None
ezer-ezr-azar-	'zr עזר	help, as in Azarel, Ezra, Azar, Azariah (Azar-ya)	None
uzz-azaz-aziz-	'zz עזז	strength, refuge, as in Uzziah (Uzzi-ya/Uzzi-yahu)	Uzziah (Biblical)

malk-/melk-/milk-	mlk מלכ	king, usually as in "my king is (God)": cf. Malkiyah, Malkiel	Melek (Biblical), Malachi (Biblical) Mulek, Muloki—no Hebrew names with God
mika-	my-k-'l מיכאל	Mikah is short for Michael; mi-who (is)+ka-like+el (God): Who is like God	None
Place Names			
bet-	byt בית	house of, clan of-, as in Bethlehem	Bethabara (Biblical)
en-	'yn עין	spring of, as in Engedi, Endor	Enosh, but making this work in Hebrew requires gymnastics
migdal	gdl גדל	tower of, as in Migdal-El, Migdal-Gad	None
qirya-qiryat-	qry קרי	town of, as in Qiryatsefer (book city)	None
rama-/ram-	rwm רום	an elevated town, hence defensible, as in Ramah	Ramath (cf. Biblical Ramoth-Gilead); Ramah (Biblical); Rameumpton (needs to be broken up for interpretation)

These pairs are inseparable. *Aḥijah* (*Aḥiya*) is "Brother of Yahweh" (Jehovah). His name would never be just *Aḥi* (brother), nor could you call him Jehovah. Brother of Jehovah would have had the sense of Godly, as well as one favored by Jehovah. Aḥimelek, brother of the King (God) has similar connotations. Abiel is (my) Father is God, where the close relationship of father has a function similar to *Aḥi*. When I had a beard in Egypt, some Arabs called me *Ibn liḥya*, son of a beard, i.e., bearded one. 'Obadiah (*'Obadya*) is Servant of Jehovah. In some cases, there may have been hypocorism (short forms, or nicknames). How this might have been done can be seen in Arabic, were *'Abdallah* (servant of God) can be shortened to 'Abduh, His (God's) Servant. The second element is removed only by adding -*uh*, the suffixed possessive pronoun.

The same is true of place names. Engedi, "Gedi Spring," is never just Spring, nor just Gedi. Just as my hometown, Green River is never just Green, nor just River. Bethlehem was never just *bēṯ*, nor just *leḥem*. Both *bēṯ* (house, place of, clan of) names and *'ēn* (spring) names are common in Hebrew.

It is inconceivable that a Hebrew people, speaking Hebrew at least as their first language, would not have a good share of these elements, which are not just standard in Hebrew, but in the Semitic languages generally. The *Book of Mormon* names are mostly made up, and the common types of names expected in Hebrew are virtually nonexistent. But given the lack of relevant background of the prospective readership, this defect was not an obstacle to successful proselytism.

Investigation into Specific Names

The easiest names to analyze are those that should not be in the *Book of Mormon*, such as Timothy, Jonas, Antipas, Lachoneus, Archeantus and the Greek prefix *anti-* (all analyzed above).Obviously key names in the Nephite narrative are of greater intrinsic interest.

Vignette	Walker's Name Bazaar—Best Selection in Town

One could readily find key Book of Nephi names in the ever popular classic A Critical Pronouncing Dictionary *by John Walker (1732-1807) published in Boston in 1823,[315] which lists La'ban, Lah'man, Lehi, and Lem'u-el in close proximity to each other on page 361, and Ne'phi on page 363. This very popular and nearly ubiquitous classic was first published in London in 1791. The first American edition was published in1803, and republished by various publishers: in Philadelphia (1803, 1808, 1810, 1811, 1815, 1818, 1819, 1822, 1830, 1832, 1847, 1863); New York (1807, 808,1814, 1815, 1818, 1819, 1823, 1825, 1826, 1827, 1828, 1831, 1836, 1840, 1846); Hartford (1823 & 1828, 1830, 1832, 1851); Boston in 1823 and 1829; Bellows Fall, VT (1822); Middletown, CT (1807); and Cooperstown (1839). These are by no means an exhaustive publication roundup. Note that Nephi is also found in the Catholic Douay-Reims Bible, where it is a toponym in 2 Maccabees 1:36. These are names that were available. But there are many others that did not make their way in to the BoM narratives. Why were these chosen and not others?*

Other factors made some names more appealing than others. For example, Lehi is the place where Samson slew a thousand Philistines with a new jawbone of an ass (Judges 15:14). Given the emphasis on slaughter in the *Book of Mormon*, it is easy to think that this passage would have appealed to Joseph Smith. The name could have been further recommended by the phonology and meaning of Le High: the Le High River, Valley and Pass. In 1822, Le High was made a county of Pennsylvania. Was not Lehi a "high" leader in the eyes of the Lord? To the extent that young Smith identified with Nephi, he may have associated

---

[315] John Walker, *Walker's Critical Pronouncing Dictionary, and Expositor of the English Language* [including Scripture Proper Names] (Boston: Lincoln & Edmands, Samuel T. Armstrong, and Charles Ewer, 1823). It has 468 pages with thousands of entries, and was frequently reprinted by publishers in New England.

Lehi with his own father, whom he made the new church's first Patriarch, a position comparable to Lehi.

The BoM project was conceived, framed and carried out during part of the Second Great Awakening with one of its emphases being the conversion of the Indians. During this period, Indians who converted to Christianity and were taking their first steps in their new faith were at times called "neophytes". This is an old theological term, meaning a new growth, a term not only applied to converts, but to those entering into a religious calling, such as a person in training to become a monk. Although used for Indian converts commonly in the Catholic missions in the Southwest, the first Methodist mission to western Canada (Alberta) used the term for Indian converts (e.g., Rev. Robert Rundle, 1840).[316] In Smith's fertile imagination, "neophytes" as a term for the Christianized Indians could have readily become "Nephites" for the BoM Christians.

This could have been reinforced by Smith Jr.'s own experience, when he entered into training to be a Methodist exhorter. Like the believer in training to join a monastic order, the exhorter trainee was also a neophyte. In an 1885 source we find a reference to a Methodist "neophyte ministry,"[317] which probably was not a neologism at that time. All of this gelled: Christianized Indians were neophytes, Christian Pre-Columbians are Nephites, the Nephites descend from Nephi, akin to Joseph Smith's own Methodist moniker, neophyte.

The neophyte exhorters were in the first stage of possibly becoming a minister, and so were already set apart from the lay members of the church, the laymen. Similarly, Nephi found himself at odds with his older brother, Laman.

As reasonable as this can be made to sound, we must remember that we cannot really put ourselves into the minds of the BoM authors.

The Generation of Aliases

Joseph Smith apparently came to delight in name generation, to the point that he devised various aliases for himself and some of his associates. One, Gazelem (cf. crystal gazer), is found in the *Book of Mormon* (Alma 37:23)

---

[316] John Blue, *Alberta, Past and Present, Historical and Biographical*, Vol 1, Chapter XIV, "Church History in Alberta" (Chicago: Pioneer Historical Publishing Co., 1924).

[317] Bishop H. M. Turner, *The Genius and Theory of Methodist Polity, or the Machinery of Methodism* (Philadelphia: Publication Department, A. M. E. Church, 1885), v.

in connection with a "stone, which shall shine forth in darkness unto light, that I may discover unto my people who serve me, that I may discover unto them the works of their brethren…" This name is used for Joseph Smith in D&C 78:9, where he is called Gazelem (also Enoch). Twenty-four aliases were used in five sections of the 1835 D&C, 78, 82, 92, 96 and 103. These aliases were not found in the original language of the revelations, which used only the real names. Their substitution seems to have been in order to instruct members how to refer to people and places in any situation that could involve persecutors or creditors. It is no accident that all of these refer to the United Firm (United Order) that Smith had established in Kirtland, which was having difficulties with its creditors, and eventually defaulted. In addition, aliases were also used in two sections of the 1844 edition of the D&C, 104 and 105.[318]

Table 37. Names & Aliases after *Book of Mormon* Publication

Name	Meaning & Section References to the 1835, 1864 and Current D&C
Gazelem	the seerstone gazer, foretold in the BoM, & used later by Joseph Smith Jr.
Ahashdah	Newel K. Whitney (1835, 75; D&C 78)
Enoch	Joseph Smith, Jr. (1835, 75; D&C 78)
Pelagoram	Sidney Rigdon (1835, 75; D&C 78)
Alam	Edward Partridge (1835, 86; D&C 82)
Mahalaleel	Sidney Gilbert (1935, 86; D&C 82)
Horah	John Whitmer (1835, 86; D&C 82)
Olihah	Oliver Cowdery (1835, 86; D&C 82)
Shalemanasseh	William W. Phelps (1835, 86; D&C 82)
Mahemson	? Jesse Gause, or Martin Harris? (1835, 86; D&C 82)
Shederlaomach	Frederick G. Williams (1835, 93; D&C 92)
Zombre	John Johnson 1835, 96; D&C 96)
Seth	Joseph Smith (1835, 96; D&C 96)
Tahhanes	Tan<n>ery (1835, 98; D&C 104)
Shinehah	revealed name for Kirtland, Ohio (1835, 86; D&C 82)
Lane-shine-house	printing office (1835, 86; D&C 82)
Shinelah	print ("to shinelah my words;" 1835, 86; D&C 82)
Shine-lane	printing (1835, 86; D&C 82)
Ozondah	revealed name for the LDS store in Kirtland, Ohio (1835, 86; D&C 82)
Mahemson	Martin Harris (1835, 86; D&C 82)

[318] Orson Pratt, "Explanation of Substituted Names in the Covenants," *Millennial Star,* 16 (March 18, 1854): 171–73; & Steven C. Harper, "Selected Teachings on Why Code Names Were Used in the D&C," published online on http//:www.scottwoodward.org (accessed 21/01/2017).

Shule	Ashery (converts hardwood to lye, potash and pearl ash; 1835, 86; D&C 82)
Talents	dollars (1835, 86; D&C 82)
Cainhannoch	New York (1835, 86; D&C 82)
Baurak ale	Joseph Smith (1864, 102; D&C 103)
Baneemy	Sidney Rigdon according to Orson Pratt, but currently "my elders;" (1864, 102; D&C 103)
Ahman	Possibly: the LDS deity, the Son & Redeemer (Jesus), presumably a name from the pure Adamic language
Adam-ondi-Ahman	Generally held to be the place of Adam and Ahman, i.e. Eden
Master Mahan	Cain "master of the great secret, that I may murder and get gain", who "gloried in his wickedness" (also Lamech)
Nauvoo	name chosen for the LDS capital in Illinois

Names with Middle Eastern Referents

Since they assumed that the knowledge of Egyptian would never be known, and some other languages of the Middle East were at least not known by their prospective audience, it would be safe to be more adventurous in the realm of linguistics. Not so. Efforts, in the *Book of Mormon* and *The Book of Abraham*, to show off a knowledge of these languages backfired royally.

Table 38. Names with Invented Semitic or Egyptian Content

Word	Translation	Found in Middle Eastern Languages?
Mormon	more good (source: a statement attributed to Joseph Smith)	Neither component (mor & mon) means 'more' or 'good' in any Middle Eastern language. (As a powerful military man, 'more man' makes more sense, but who knows the authors' thinking?)
Liahona	compass (to guide Lehi in the wilderness south of Canaan/Negev)	There was no compass, much less a word for one; no word with appropriate meaning can be found in any Middle Eastern language
Irreantum	many waters	No
Ripliancum	large, to exceed all	No
Rameumpton	the holy stand	No
Deseret	honey bee	No
Ziff	an unknown metal	No
Elkenah	an Egyptian god	No
Libnah	an Egyptian god	No
Mahmackrah	an Egyptian god	No
Korash	an Egyptian god	No
Rahleenos	hieroglyphics	No
Kolob	the first creation, nearest to the residence of God,	No

Enish-go-on-dosh	first government, a measurement of time one of the governing planets, the sun	No
Kae-e-vanrash	the grand Key, the governing power, governing 15 other fixed planets or stars	nothing in Egyptian to answer to this range of meanings (nor in astronomy)
Floese	the Moon, the Earth and the Sun in their annual revolutions	No
Kli-flos-is-es or Hah-ko-kau-beam	the star represented by the numbers 22 & 23	no for the Egyptian (#'s 22 & 23 in Facsimile 2 are not stars); as for the Hebrew, the second is Smith's rendition of hak-kōkābīm (stars); Smith was studying Hebrew, but was not faring well.

Not one of these made-up words corresponds phonologically to a word in any Semitic language.[319] However, note rabbanah (powerful, great king) is not actually a made-up name (cf. NT rabbi and rabboni).

Ziff is a BoM word that has interesting phonological problems. First, even though Early (3rd-millennium) Egyptian shows evidence of the sound *z*, as a legacy from an Afro-Asiatic past, it was mostly merged with *s*, to the extent that Egyptian dictionaries do not list words under the letter *z*. This sound was lost in Middle Egyptian, and absent in the Egyptian, of the 1st-millennium BCE, or the time of the destruction of Jerusalem. Second, the letter *f* does not exist in Hebrew. To be sure, the letter *p* shifts to *f* after a vowel in Post-Biblical Hebrew, a phenomenon that developed under Aramaic influence, i.e. during and after the captivity in Babylon, or, more probably later, after Hebrew ceased to be a spoken language. Under the influence of the Aramaic speaking rabbis of Babylon, centuries after Christ, this pronunciation was preferred even for reciting Old Testament passages, probably initially for recitation in the synagogues, but made "official" for the OT in the Masoretic text. Even so, a double *p* never shifted to *f*, so there has never been a double *f* in Hebrew. Finally, even allowing for all reasonable phonological alternatives (*zff, zwf, zyf, sff, swf* & *syf* for Egyptian, and *zpp* for Hebrew, *zff* for Arabic, and *zpp* for Aramaic and Akkadian), there is no word even roughly corresponding to *ziff*, with the meaning "metal" or any specific metal. Nor is there any pre-

---

[319] See Arthur Chris Eccel, *Sembase, a Database for the Semitic Languages* (http//:www.sembase.org), prepared for a comparative dictionary of the Semitic languages; work in progress).

Columbian metal that did not have a common English name in the 1820s, thereby requiring the use of a Nephite word (with the possible exception of the tumbaga alloy of gold). Ziff is phonologically improbable, is unattested in Middle Eastern languages, and lacks a real-world referent.

The *Book of Mormon* also falls into linguistic pitfalls in some of its expressions. A good example is the use of the phrase "straight and narrow". Compare Matthew with 2 Nephi:

> Enter ye in at the strait gate: ... Because strait is the gate, and narrow is the way, which leadeth unto life... (Matthew 7:13-14)

> ..enter into the narrow gate, and walk in the straight path which leads to life... (2 Nephi 33:9)

> straight is the gate, and narrow is the way (3 Nephi 14:14)

> And again, it showeth unto the children of men the straightness of the path, and the narrowness of the gate, by which they should enter... (2 Nephi 31:9)

That *straight* is not just a misspelling, but is intended to mean *not crooked*, is seen in 2 Nephi 9:41:

> Behold, the way for man is narrow, but it lieth in a straight course...

Popular preachers confused *strait* with *straight*, which seems to be a confusion arising from the English language, the two words being homophones, and a confusion between "straight" in Matthew 3:3 ("make his paths straight") and Matthew 7:13-14, above. Actually, the phrase in the New Testament uses a common Semitic form of emphasis through repetition, by using two words with the same meaning: "strait and narrow" means "truly narrow."

The BoM has a tendency to produce words suggested by a word in English. Here are some examples:

> my hand hath found the kingdoms of the idols (KJ Isaiah 10:10)
> my hand hath founded the kingdoms of the idols (2 Nephi 20:10)

> everyone that is found shall be thrust through (Isaiah 13:15)
> everyone that is proud shall be thrust through (2 Nephi 23:15)

> the raiment of those who are slain (Isaiah 14:19)
> the remnant of those who are slain (2 Nephi 24)

I will break the Assyrians in my land (Isaiah 14:25)
I will bring the Assyrians in my land (2 Nephi 24:25)

As we have seen, producing language-like made-up words from words in one's own language has been found to be a common phenomenon in the speech of persons claiming to be speaking in tongues.

One Nephite name appears to be a modification of a famous Hebrew OT name: Cumorah from Gomorrah? Today, Cumorah is almost a Mormon pilgrimage site, the Hill Cumorah being where Moroni buried the plates and then revealed them to Joseph Smith. But in the *Book of Mormon*, it is the place where the Jaredites totally annihilated each other. (Jaredite Ramah being Nephite Cumorah). Under the name Cumorah, it is the place of the last battle where the Lamanites totally annihilated the Nephites. In both cases, it is the place where a people are visited by God with total extinction due to their sins, not unlike Gomorrah. This association could well have been the basis for producing the name Cumorah. Note as well Hermounts, apparently a modification of Mount Hermon.

Another interesting possibility occurs in a passage of the *Book of Moses* (5:31 & 49), which was undertaken only months after the BoM: "And Cain said: Truly I am Mahan, the master of this great secret, that I may murder and get gain Wherefore Cain was called Master Mahan, and he gloried in his wickedness." In the 1820s, there was a campaign against the Freemasons. Given this context, it is impossible to ignore the possibility that Master Mahan is adapted from Master Mason.

Local Sources for Names?

Vernal Holley has made a gallant effort to find names in the New York region that could have been the source or inspiration for some *Book of Mormon* names[320]

Table 39. Name Generation from Toponyms in the Wider Local Area

Name in the BoM	NY Region Place Name	Comment
Ogath	St. Agathe des Monts, Québec	No. Founded in 1849.
Alma, Valley of	Alma, NY	No. Founded in 1854.
	Alma, WV	? When was it founded?
Antum	Antrim (Hamlet in Ramapo, NY?)	? Difficult phonology.
Ani-Anti	Antioch, IL	No. Named in 1843.
Boaz	Boaz	No. Named in 1878.

---

[320] Vernon Holley, *Book of Mormon Authorship*.

Comnor	Conner	Where?
Ephraim, Hill	St. Ephrem de Beauce, Quebec	No. Founded in 1866.
Helam	Hellam, PA	Possible.
Hill Onidah	Oneida County, Oneida Castle, Oneida Indian Nation[321]	Very possible. The Oneida Indian Nation is headquartered in Verona, Oneida County, NY, east of Oneidah Lake. An Oneida band came to Great Bend, Susquehanna County, during a land dispute in New York, and left (1790).
Jacobugath	Jacobsburg	Difficult phonology.
Jordan	Jordan, NY	No. Settlement began in 1825, incorporated in 1835. Why not Biblical Jordan?
Lehi	Lehigh (river, valley, pass, etc.)	Possible.
Manti	Mantu? (Mantua, OH?)	Possible.
Moroni	Monroe, NY	Difficult phonology.
Morianton	Moraviantown	Difficult phonology.
Moron	Morin, Ontario	No. Founded in 1855.
Noah, Land of	Noah Lakes (Noah Lake, MI?)	Why not Biblical Noah?
Omner	Omer, MI	No. Founded in 1866.
Ramah	Rama	Why not Biblical Ramath?
Shilom	Shiloh, NJ	Difficult phonology. Why not Biblical Shiloh?
Sidom	Sodom, NY	Possible; date unknown.
Land of Minon	Minonian Indians	Possible.
Waters of Ripliancum	On the banks of Lake Superior: Ripple Bay, Ripple Creek, Ripple Reef, Ripple Lake	Possible, as well as a name suggested by *ripple*.
Hill Ramah	Rama Indian Reservation & Rama Township, Ontario, Canada	Rama Township, Ontario is possible, but the Chippewa moved there in 1836. Why not Biblical Ramah?
Angola (fortified city)	Angola, New York (Or Angola, Indiana?)	No. Evans Station was renamed Angola in 1855 due to Quakers who were giving aid to Angola, Africa. Angola, Indiana, dates to even later. Perhaps, Angola

---

[321] Patricia Bell Scott, *The History of Agriculture in Susquehanna County from 1787* (by author? Lebanon Valley College, History 44: 1957-1958), p. 3.

		Plantation (infamous for enslaving Indians)?
Teancum (city)	Tecumseh (Tenecum), Canada	Possible.
King Gideon	Chief Tadeuskund, baptized in 1750 and christened "Gideon"	Possible, but note Biblical Gideon (place & angel).
Kishkumen (city)	Delaware Indian village Kishkiminetas, near Pittsburgh	Possible. It is about 30 miles northeast of Pittsburgh. Or BoM Kish + Kumen?

Holley's list was made to support the Spalding or Spalding/Rigdon theory of BoM authorship. His names are said to be some that these men would have been familiar with. Many turn out to be names that the Smiths and Cowdery might have been familiar with. Another is Irreantum, the name given to the point in Arabia, on the coast of the Indian Ocean, where Lehi and his band constructed a boat and set sail. The narrative says it means "many waters." The BoM authors were quite familiar with both Erie the lake and the canal. The name would simply be Erie with the syllabic element -antum (treated above), or the lakes Erie- Ont(ario)> Irreantum.

One drawback is that many of these names are small, little known and remote locations. It is unclear that the BoM authors would have known them. At the time, such places did not figure on the maps of the day. Moreover, for the BoM authors, the important thing was probably to have names with a good ring to them. They may even have tended to avoid local names.

Observations.

§ The generation of names shows considerable thought, and even some strategy. It is improbable that they were produced in casual composition or extemporaneous dictation.

§ The names lack the most expected Hebrew elements, while prominent names in Nephi are found in Walker's nearly ubiquitous *Dictionary*. The name list includes Greek names. Many were produced by repeating the same name for several individuals, and recombining name elements in a manner commonly found in the utterances of persons exhibiting the gift of tongues. The ending occurring in various forms, "antum", is found in "Nonantum", a Christian tribe in Eliot's town, Natick, for converts. This is the

Onomastic Issue

< Chapter 20 >

The Post-Biblical Euro-Christian Text

When Christianity became rooted in Europe, a process began of developing a new culture, to replace the pre-Christian cultures. This process occurred in widely different European regions, and drew upon pre-Christian elements (especially Greek philosophy) and the creativity of numerous theologians, church clerics, poets and hymnists. In England, and its New World offshoots, many common cultural elements merged with Biblical elements, to the extent that it was not easy to avoid confusing the two. This was clearly true in the case of the BoM authors, and as a result the BoM text includes Euro-Christian elements that are incompatible with the premise that it was written by pre-Columbian authors, or even pre-Columbian Christian authors.

Post-Biblical Euro-Christian phrases in the BoM text pose a significantly different issue as compared to the Biblical phrases. They cannot be said to be identical elements of divine revelation received by prophets on both sides of the world. In some cases, they are clearly a product of later Christian thought, and in the most serious cases, they are instances of incorrect Biblical interpretation, or even pseudoscientific apologetics.

The assertion that the BoM text quotes Shakespeare helps bring the current study into better focus. The phrase is from lines 79 and 80 in Hamlet, Act 3, Scene 1:

> The undiscovered country from whose bourn
> No traveller returns.

The BoM verse states (2 Nephi 1:14):

> the cold and silent grave, from whence no traveler can return

A tough-minded assessment must not only ask whether these three or four words, in substantially different contexts, are sufficient to warrant the assertion, but also must face the serious question of transmission. Can we really assume that any of the BoM authors had such familiarity with Hamlet that this phrase would have come to mind? Alternatively, was it part of the common parlance of clerics in rural New England, to the point that they might have heard and acquired it, perhaps not even knowing where it came from? Perhaps. Perhaps not. This example illustrates the

298

problems of asserting the existence of post-Biblical Euro-Christian phrases and/or concepts in the BoM text.

Unsustainable Biblical Interpretation

In some cases, the inclusion is a Euro-Christian notion that is an unsustainable interpretation of a Biblical passage. In other cases, it is scientifically wrong. But in most cases, it is a phrase coined in English Euro-Christian devotional or theological literature.

Lucifer

17. an angel of God...had fallen from heaven; wherefore, he became a devil, having sought that which was evil before God. (2 Nephi 2)

2 Nephi 24:12 (quoting Isaiah 14:12)

How art thou fallen from heaven, O Lucifer, son of the morning! How art thou cut down to the ground, which didst weaken the nations!

The issue here is not the story itself. The doctrine of a war in heaven is found in the New Testament as well: (Revelation 12:7-9; See also Luke 10:18; 2 Corinthians 11:14; & Jude 1:6) The issue is the interpretation of Isaiah 14:12, as being Old Testament support for this story. The BoM text makes this identification by using *lucifer* as the proper name Lucifer. Actually, this passage does not refer to Satan, but is part of a proverb (similitude, tantamount to a curse) that Isaiah was commanded by God to declare against the king of Babylon. The curse follows (Isaiah 14, KJV), with the Lord saying:

4. That thou shalt take up this proverb against the king of Babylon, and say, How hath the oppressor ceased! The golden city ceased!

9. Hell from beneath is moved for thee to meet thee at thy coming: it stirreth up the dead for thee, even all the chief ones of the earth; it hath raised up from their thrones all the kings of the nations.

10. All they shall speak and say unto thee, Art thou also become weak as we? Art thou become like unto us?

12. How art thou fallen from heaven, O Lucifer, son of the morning! How art thou cut down to the ground, which didst weaken the nations!

13 For thou hast said in thine heart, I will ascend into heaven...

14. I will ascend above the heights of the clouds; I will be like the most High.

15. Yet thou shalt be brought down to hell, to the sides of the pit.

18. All the kings of the nations, even all of them, lie in glory, every one in his own house.

19. But thou art cast out of thy grave like an abominable branch, and as the raiment of those that are slain, thrust through with a sword...

20. Thou shalt not be joined with them in burial, because thou hast destroyed thy land, and slain thy people: the seed of evildoers shall never be renowned.

21. Prepare slaughter for his children...

22. For I will rise up against them, saith the LORD of hosts, and cut off from Babylon the name, and remnant, and son, and nephew…

This proper name, Lucifer, occurs in the King James Version only once; nowhere else is it used to refer to the Great Serpent. It renders the Hebrew word הֵילֵל (*hēlēl*) in Isaiah 14:12. This word also occurs only once in the Hebrew Bible, and means "shining one, morning star." The Latin Vulgate translated הֵילֵל as *lucifer*, meaning "the morning star, the planet Venus," or, as an adjective, "light-bringing." The Septuagint renders הֵילֵל in Greek as ἑωσφόρος (*heōsphoros*; literally "bringer of dawn"), a name for the morning star.

In this passage Isaiah applies to a king of Babylon the image of the morning star fallen from the sky.

Later Christian tradition came to use the Latin word for "morning star," lucifer, as a proper name ("Lucifer") for Satan as he was before his fall. As a result, Lucifer has become a byword for Satan in much of Euro-Christianity, and in popular literature, as in Dante Alighieri's *Inferno* and John Milton's *Paradise Lost*. However, unlike in English, the Latin word never came to be used almost exclusively in this way, and was applied to others also, including Christ. This star is Venus, which was a pagan deity in the Roman pantheon. This may have influenced the evolution of the Roman church's interpretation of Isaiah, and of the Euro-Christian name.

It is incongruous for a divine translation of Isaiah to use this proper name. It should rather have been "O morning star!"

Father of Lies

that old serpent, who is the devil, who is the father of all lies (2 Nephi 2:18; 9:9)	Ye are of your father the devil…When he speaketh a lie, he speaketh of his own: for he is a liar, and the father of it. (John 8: 44)

The Greek (καὶ ὁ πατὴρ αὐτοῦ.) can say, literally, "the father of it" or "the father of him" or "its/his father." Some modern translations take the interpretive liberty to render the last clauses: "for he is a liar and the father of lies." "Father of Lies" is the title of a "topic page" of "gospel.com." Similarly, "openbible.info" has a page titled "100 Bible Verses about Father Of All Lies." It appears to have become a normal Christian phrase.

Author of All Sin

Helaman 6:30. And behold, it is he [Satan] who is the author of all sin

The designation "author" is used in the KJ Bible in reference to God ("God is not the author of confusion," 1 Corinthians 14:33) and Jesus ("he became the author of eternal salvation," Hebrews 5:9). By contrast, in English Euro-Christianity, Satan has been called the "author of sin." Ironically, originally it was applied to God. This assertion first appeared in the affirmative by the Gnostic Florinus (c. 180), which was immediately attacked by Ireneaus (130-200), who published a discourse entitled: "God, not the Author of Sin." Florinus' doctrine reappeared in another form later in Manichaeism, of which Augustine was initially a member for nearly a decade before converting to Catholicism. A similar rejection of the charge is found in the work of the American theologian Jonathan Edwards. The assertion that Satan is the author of all sin is found in English Euro-Christianity, but has rarely been stated as boldly and unequivocally as in the BoM passage, since sin is normally treated as being a complex problem involving three actors, God, Satan and man. We find in a sermon of John Wesley ("The End of Christ's Coming"), "'For the devil,' saith the Apostle, 'sinneth from the beginning;' that is, was the first sinner in the universe, the author of sin..."

Son of Righteousness
3 Nephi 25:2. But unto you that fear my name, shall the Son of Righteousness arise with healing in his wings.

This is the BoM version of Malachi 4:2, where the text reads "shall the Sun of righteousness arise with healing in his wings." This phrase is possibly inspired by the ancient Egyptian image of the winged sun. In Hebrew, sun is *shemesh*, while son is *ben*. The phonological basis for this sun/son confusion is found only in English. In the BoM text, the passage is spoken by none other than Jesus Christ to the Nephites.

It occurs prominently in "Hark! The Harold Angels Sing" by Charles Wesley (1707-1788), and other hymns. In many printings, the word "Sun" is changed to "Son," deliberately or inadvertently. Given this variation found in printed versions, it is clear that members of congregations, while hearing and/or singing the hymn, would tend to understand "Son of Righteousness."

Red Sea (dubious identification, in a dubious Biblical account)

The Red Sea is mentioned in the BoM narrative in two contexts, the geography of Nephi's travel in Arabia (1 Nephi 2:5; 1 Nephi 2:8; 1 Nephi 16:14), and the story of Moses leading the Israelites out of Egypt:

1 Nephi 4:2. Therefore let us go up; let us be strong like unto Moses; for he truly spake unto the waters of the Red Sea and they divided hither... (See also 1 Nephi 17:26-27; 2 Nephi 19:1; Mosiah 7:19; Alma 36:28 & Helaman 8:11)

Red Sea is a direct translation of the Greek *Erythra Thalassa* (Ερυθρὰ Θάλασσα) and Latin *Mare Rubrum*. The OT has the Sea of Reeds (Hebrew יָם סוּף). The BoM usage can be simply an affirmation that its identification with the Red Sea is correct, or, if it is not, then it is a post-Biblical identification that was incorporated into the BoM.

Convincing of the Jews
2 Nephi 26:12. And as I spake concerning the convincing of the Jews, that Jesus is the very Christ, it must needs be that the Gentiles be convinced also that Jesus is the Christ, the Eternal God (see also 2 Nephi 25:18).

This phrase originally meant to refute the claims of the Jews, or to condemn them and their rejection of Christ. In English, the meaning of "to convince" changed. The obsolete meaning is "to refute or prove wrong," but eventually this gave way to the current meaning, "to show to the satisfaction of someone else that one's own claims are true." The BoM usage is based on an understanding of the Bible based on this later meaning, while the King James translators were intending the now obsolete meaning. It is this meaning that we find in the original languages:

Greek: (ἐλέγχει [*elengchei*): to expose wrongdoing, charge, show fault, prove wrongdoing, convict.
(διακατηλεγχετο) to confute.
Hebrew: (מוֹכִיחַ; argue, dispute)
Job 32:12
there was none of you that convinced Job, or that answered his words (מוֹכִיחַ; dispute, refute)
John 8:46
46. Which of you convinceth me of sin? And if I say the truth, why do ye not believe me? ([ἐλέγχει; accuses, charges with, convicts)
Acts 18
28. For he mightily convinced the Jews, and that publickly, shewing by the scriptures that Jesus was Christ. (διακατηλεγχετο; to confute)
1 Corinthians 14:24-25
24. But if all prophesy, and there come in one that believeth not, or one unlearned, he is convinced of all, he is judged of all:
25. And thus are the secrets of his heart made manifest; and so falling down on his face he will worship God, and report that God is in you of a truth. (ἐλέγχεται; he is convicted)
Titus 1:9
Holding fast the faithful word as he hath been taught, that he may be able by sound doctrine both to exhort and to convince the gainsayers. (ἐλέγχειν; to convict, charge)
James 2:9

But if ye have respect to persons, ye commit sin, and are convinced of the law as transgressors. (ἐλέγχομενοι; convicted [by the law])
Jude 1:15
15 To execute judgment upon all, and to convince all that are ungodly among them of all their ungodly deeds which they have ungodly committed... (ἐξελέγχαι; to convict)

Freemasonry

It is not surprising to find influences from Freemasonry in the *Book of Mormon*. In 1827 Hyrum Smith received Masonic degrees in Palmyra's Mount Moriah Lodge #112. Joseph Smith became a Freemason after the publication of his new bible, a Masonic lodge was organized in Nauvoo, and the rituals of the LDS temple were strongly influenced by Masonic rites. (v. p. 558) In a draft of Lucy Smith's biography, regarding the early 1820s, she mentioned "trying to win the faculty of Abrac..."[322] Abrac "derives from Abracadabra and Abraxas." Masons claimed to know the way of obtaining the faculty of Abrac.[323] An encyclopedia of Freemasonry states, "In the so-called Leland Manuscript [sometimes called the Locke Manuscript], it is said that Freemasons 'conceal the way of wynninge the facultye of Abrac.' That is, that they conceal the method of acquiring the powers bestowed by a knowledge of the magical talisman that is called Abracadabra (see Abracadabra and Leland Manuscript).[324]

Secret Combinations
2 Nephi 9:9. Secret combinations of murder and all manner of secret works of darkness. (See also: 2 Nephi 26:22; Alma 37:30-31)

The *Book of Mormon* has numerous passages that warn against "secret combinations," with their oaths and secret signs. It seems that this phrase is used in lieu of "secret societies." The historical context is the Freemasonry controversies that were raging, exacerbated by the anti-Freemason accusations made by Captain William Morgan, stirred up by his persecution, kidnapping and mysterious disappearance, and present in

---

[322] Lucy Mack Smith, in Lavina Fielding Anderson, ed., *Lucy's Book, A Critical Edition of Lucy Mack Smith's Family Memoir* (Salt Lake City: Signature Books, 2001), 323.
[323] Marquardt, *Rise of Mormonism*, 67 n. 22.
[324] Albert C. Mackey, *Encyclopaedia of Freemasonry and Its Kindred Sciences* (http://www.phoenixmasonry.org/mackeys_encyclopedia/f.htm, accessed 29/03. 2017).

the Presbyterianism of the Second Great Revival in New York, due to the disaffection of revivalist Rev. Charles Finney and others.

The Wayne Sentinel (March 23, 1827) quotes the *Rochester Daily Advertiser*:

The Freemason, too—not only those who took off Morgan, but every one who bears the masonic name—are proscribed, as unworthy of 'any office in town, county, state, or United States!' and the institution of masonry, . . . is held up as DANGEROUS and detrimental to the interests of the country!

Regarding the 1827 elections, *The Wayne Sentinel* printed the following (November 16, 1827):

The election in this county (says the Ontario Messenger) has resulted in the choice of the entire ANTI-MASONIC ticket.

Ironically, the BoM authors were not consistent in their attitude towards Freemasonry, reflected in their use of the following phrases, and the subsequent adoption of Masonic rites and symbols in the Mormon temples.

One Eternal Round
1 Nephi 10:19. The course of the Lord is one eternal round (Also Alma 7:20; 37:12)

The circle had long been a symbol for eternity, although not in the Bible. This is because the line that circumscribes it has neither beginning nor end. However, referring to it as an eternal round is distinctly Masonic. It has been found as early as 1731, in "The Generous Freemason" (well before Mozart's *Magic Flute*, 1791) by William Rufus Chetwood, the first Freemason to write the libretto of an opera. It contains the passage:

Let Love and Friendship then our cares confound,
And halcyon days be one eternal round.[325]

---

[325] W R Chetwood, *The generous Free-Mason, or, The constant lady: with the humours of Squire Noodle, and his man Doodle: a tragi-comi-farcical ballad opera in three acts: with the musick prefix'd to each song* (London: J. Roberts, 1731). Richard Northcott, "The Generous Freemason, A short History of the First Masonic Opera," published on the website of the Grand Lodge of British Columbia and Yukon (http://www.freemasonry.bcy.ca/fiction/generous_free mason/generous.html, accessed March 2016).

Tabernacle of Clay
Moroni 9:6. We have a labor to perform whilst in this tabernacle of clay

Biblically, this phrase is related to 2 Corinthians 5:1 "For we know that if our earthly house of this tabernacle were dissolved, we have a building of God, an house not made with hands, eternal in the heavens."

The BoM phrase is found in a Freemason funeral ceremony text:

Master: This evergreen is an emblem of our faith in the immortality of the soul. By it, we are reminded of our high and glorious destiny beyond the 'world of shadows' and that there dwells within our tabernacle of clay, an imperishable, immortal spirit, over which the grave has no dominion, and death not power.[326]

Since the phrase is found in other Euro-Christian sources, it cannot be said to be exclusively a Freemason expression. More recently, we find in a poem, "Tabernacle of Clay," on the web under the name of LateefahFreeWOMAN (2014), the line: "In this temple, this tabernacle of clay."

All-searching Eye
Mosiah 27:31. The glance of his all-searching eye
Jacob 2:10. The glance of the piercing eye of the Almighty God

This post-Biblical phrase has been thought to have its source in the eye iconography of ancient Egypt, and Freemasonry. The all-seeing eye of God (or Eye of Providence) is often represented as an eye surrounded by rays of light, usually within a triangle. Today, the Eye of Providence is usually associated with Freemasonry, although many associate it primarily with the reverse of the Great Seal of the United States, which appears on the one-dollar bill. It is found in various early hymns:

Charles Wesley: (339) Thou to Whose All-Searching Sight...; and (279) they searching eye...
Isaac Watts (1775), "Almighty God, they piercing eye."
Christopher Wordsworth (Canon of Westminster Abbey. Born, 1807) in *Holy Year; or, Hymns for Sundays, Holidays, and other Occasions*: "God, in Whose all-searching eye Thy servants stand..."

---

[326] Most Worshipful Grand Lodge of Ancient Freemasons of South Carolina, "Funeral Service" (Abbeville, SC: Hugh Wilson, Printer, 1899).

Influences from Hymns

Popular hymns of the day not only influenced those who heard them, but provided expressions in use in common parlance. In many cases, worshippers tended to confuse these expressions with those in the Bible itself. As a result, a writer intending to use Biblical expressions might include post-Biblical expressions by mistake. Or one might draw freely and knowingly from both sources, all the while aware that the reader would not be able to distinguish them. These phrases enabled the creation of a text that would have a familiar sound.

Redeeming Love (sing redeeming love, or song of redeeming love)
Alma 5:9. They did sing redeeming love
Alma 5:26. If ye have felt to sing the song of redeeming love
(Also Alma 26:13)

This English post-Biblical Euro-Christian phrase is found in a number of hymns, most notably "Redeeming Love," often published as "Now begins the heavenly theme," erroneously attributed to John Langford, who, in 1765, began to preach in a chapel in London, and in 1776, published a collection of *Hymns & Spiritual Songs*. This hymn has been published in 326 hymnals. However, the earliest form in which it is found differs widely from that followed in modern hymnals. In 1763 it appeared in the Appendix to M. Madan's *Psalms and Hymns*, as No. clxxii, thus:—

"Redeeming Love"
Now begin the Heav'nly Theme,
Sing aloud in Jesu's Name,
Ye, who Jesus' Kindness prove
Triumph in Redeeming Love.

This is followed by seven additional stanzas, each ending with a "Redeeming Love" phrase.[327] The phrase occurs twice in the sermons of John Wesley, such as "You cannot taste his redeeming love," in sermon #29, "Upon Our Lord's Sermon on the Mount, Discourse Nine." It is found four times in the sermons of George Whitefield, and once in *The Works of Jonathan Edwards*, Chapter XI. It is also found in hymns of Charles Wesley, (129) "the covenant of redeeming love," (147) "the greatness of

---

[327] John Julian (ed.), *A Dictionary of Hymnology : Setting Forth the Origin and History of Christian Hymns of All Ages and Nations* (London: John Murray, 1907).

redeeming love," (162) "thy all-redeeming love" (119, 133, 202, 216, 278, 300, 319, 436, 507, 542, 549, 605, 691 & 798)

Glad Tidings of Great Joy/Glad Tidings of Salvation

Mosiah 3:3. For behold, I am come to declare unto you the glad tidings of great joy (See also Alma 13:22)
Alma 39:15 he cometh to declare glad tidings of salvation

This is an English variation of "I bring you good tidings of great joy" in Luke 2:10. It is not known when the popular variation developed, with "glad" instead of "good," but already we have it in a hymn by Charles Wesley (121):

mighty dread had seized their troubled mind;
'Glad tidings of great joy I bring to you and all mankind'.

It is also in Leonard Marshall (1809—1890), as the first line: "Glad tidings of great joy I bring." "Glad tidings of salvation" is likewise extra-Biblical. It developed in English Euro-Christianity, and is evidenced in the famous declaration of John Wesley (*Journal*, June 11, 1739.), "I look upon all the world as my parish: thus far I mean, that, in whatever part of it I am, I judge it meet, right, and my bounden duty to declare unto all that are willing to hear the glad tidings of salvation." This phrase is the title and first line of a hymn by Donald S. Lundin, and is the title of a hymn by Robert O. Smith.

Condescension of God

1 Nephi 11:16. Knowest thou the condescension of God? (Cf. 2 Nephi 4:26)

This post-Biblical Euro-Christian phrase is a standard Christian theological term. We find it prominently in a Hymn by the famous and prolific hymnist Isaac Watts (1674-1748), "God's Condescension to Human Affairs."[328] Considered the "Father of English Hymnody," he is credited with some 750 hymns. Many of his hymns remain in use today and have been translated into numerous languages.

2. He that can shake the worlds he made,
Or with his word, or with his rod,
His goodness how amazing great!
And what a condescending God!

---

[328] Isaac Watts, *Hymns and spiritual songs, in three books* (Coventry: M. Luckman, 1793).

References to the condescension of God or Christ abound in the hymns of Charles Wesley. The phrase is common in English-language sermons as well. Note "The Condescension of Christ, A Sermon (No. 151), Delivered on Sabbath Morning, September 13, 1857, by the REV. C. H. Spurgeon at the Music Hall, Royal Surrey Gardens."

Rejoice My Heart
2 Nephi 4:28. Awake, my soul! No longer droop in sin. Rejoice, O my heart, and give place no more for the enemy of my soul.

"Rejoice my heart" is a phrase found in 18th-19th century Christian devotion. See for example "Rejoice my heart, be glad and sing" by Paul Gerhardt (1607-1676, Lutheran), which was translated into English and became cross-denominational:

Rejoice, my heart, by glad and sing,
A cheerful trust maintain;

Note too that hymn 388 in the *Complete Collected Hymns of Charles Wesley* has the line "Come, Lord! The drooping sinner cheer..."

Judgment Bar
2 Nephi 33:15. For what I seal on earth, shall be brought against you at the judgment bar...
2 Nephi 33:11. I shall stand face to face before his bar
Alma 5:22. The bar of God (See also 11:44 & Moroni 10:27)

This English phrase is not Biblical; compare with "barrister" and "bar-at-law." "Bar" is defined as the whole body of lawyers, the legal profession (1550s), a sense that derives ultimately from the railing that separated benchers from the hall in the Inns of Court. It is found in a hymn, "God's Judgment bar! Justice complete" (music composed in the late 19th century, for words by Emily Leader). "How wilt thou stand at the judgment bar?" is found as a refrain of a hymn written and composed in 1917 by Harry D. Loes. The early adaptation of the term to religious discourse is documented in a sermon of John Wesley, "...wherein to Stand at the bar of God in the day of judgment." His brother Charles made reference to the bar in his hymns (55):

Thou judge of quick and dead, Before whose bar severe,
With holy joy, or guilty dread, We all shall soon appear

God of Nature

1 Nephi 19:12. "The God of nature suffers"

This phrase is not Biblical, and developed in Euro-Christianity. Note, in particular, a poem/hymn by James Montgomery (1771-1854, son of John Montgomery, a Moravian minister). He wrote many poems, some of which were made into hymns, such as the stanza:

The God of nature and of grace
In all His works appears;
His goodness through the earth we trace,
His grandeur in the spheres.

Compare with the hymn of Jeremiah Eames Rankin (Pseudonym: R. E. Jeremy), born at Thornton, New Haven, Jan. 2, 1828: "O God of nature, come and grace our harvest;" as well as a sermon by Charles Kingsley, "The God of Nature (Preached During a Wet Harvest)". A hymn of Charles Wesley states (33): "On each leaf is written, Nature's God is there." "Nature" is not an OT concept, and was developed in Greek literature, where *physis* (nature) and *nomos* (convention, law) were at times in opposition. From Greek thought, it went into the epistles of Paul, but not regarding the deity.

The Veil of Unbelief

Ether 4:15. Behold, when ye shall rend that veil of unbelief (See also Alma 19:6)

This is a common extra-Biblical English Euro-Christian phrase, found as early as in a hymn by Charles Wesley (1707-1788 ; 113, also 122):

4. The veil of unbelief remove,

The phrase occurs as a theme in Christian sermons and devotional articles.

Valley of Sorrow

2 Nephi 4:26. ...why should my heart weep and my soul linger in the valley of sorrow

Compare with "Vale of tears," Psalm 84:6.

This phrase does not occur in the Bible. We do find it in "Resurrection of Christ" by M.H. Ware, Jr. (1794-1843):

But Jesus hath cleared the dark valley of sorrow,

In the hymn "I have been through the valley of sorrow and weeping" of Clement Cotterill Scholefield (1839-1904) we have:

I have been through the valley of weeping,
The valley of sorrow and pain

Note too "Rays Of Light In The Valley Of Sorrow" by Henry Wheeler.

Blood from Every Pore
Mosiah 3:7. Blood cometh from every pore, so great shall be his anguish

As part of the cult of Christ's Blood, this is a post-Biblical Euro-Christian interpretation of Luke 22:44:

his sweat was *as it were* great drops of blood falling down to the ground [Emphasis added]

This description is found only in Luke, and even he qualifies it with "as it were." Contrast it with the couplet in the hymn "O Love Incomprehensible" by Anne Steele (1717 –1778), an English Baptist hymn writer:

16. What pain, what soul-oppressing pain, The great Redeemer bore;
While bloody sweat, like drops of rain, Distilled from every pore!

In "Agony in the Garden" one sings, "His sweat like drops of blood ran down; In agony he prayed," attributed to (Thomas?) Haweis (1734-1820). [329] Reverend Spurgeon (1834-1892), in an oft-quoted sermon, exclaims, "every pore is open, and it sweats!" In "Feast of the Sacred Heart," a devotional by Fr. Francis Xavier Weninger, 1877, we find: "His precious blood burst forth from every pore.".

Apply the Atoning Blood of Christ
Mosiah 4:2. O have mercy, and apply the atoning blood of Christ
Charles Wesley (346): The atonement of thy blood apply (also 28, 35, 85, 96, 128, 125, 150, 180, 184, & others). (307): Through the atoning blood (also 84, 101, 351, 530 & others).

Note here the phrases to "apply" and the "atoning blood," as though it were a medicinal ointment.

---

[329] Found in J.G. (John Greenleaf) Adams and E.H. (Edwin Hubbell) Chapin (compilers), *Hymns for Christian devotion; especially adapted to the Universalist denomination* (Boston: B. Bradley & Co., 1853).

The phrase "atoning blood" is also found in hymns of Isaac Watt. Note Hymn 1:97, "Christ our wisdom, righteousness, &c."

Our guilty souls are drown'd in tears
Till his atoning blood appears

The phrase also occurs in hymns 1:98 and 2:36.

Gulf of Death
Alma 26:20 Behold, he did not exercise his justice upon us, but in his great mercy hath brought us over that everlasting gulf of death and misery

An example in English Euro-Christianity is found in the works of Felicia Hemans (1793-1835). In "Communings with Thought" she wrote:

Go, visit cell and shrine!
Where woman hath endured!—through wrong, through scorn,
Uncheer'd by fame, yet silently upborne
By promptings more divine!

Go, shoot the gulf of death!

In Charles Wesley's hymn #288, similar wording occurs:

Thy love shall burst the shades of death,
And bear me from the gulf beneath
To everlasting day.

In "Encouragements to Walk with God" in the *Sermons of George Whitefield*, we read, "Death may seize thee, judgment find thee, and then the great gulf will be fixed between thee and endless glory forever and ever."

Bounty of His Love
Alma 26:15 "they are encircled about with the matchless bounty of his love"

This is an English Euro-Christian phrase, found as early as a hymn published in 1756 by Thomas Cradock, and containing the lines:

All by the bounty of his love are fed;

Word of Truth and Righteousness
Alma 38:9. Behold, he is the word of truth and righteousness.

This extra-Biblical phrase is found among various denominations, such as in "A Hymn" by James M. Whitfield (1822–1871):

And grant that many souls may hear
The words of truth and righteousness

It is found in a newspaper, *The Gospel Trumpet*, of 1899 (o4/06), and in a meditation by Don Swagger (online) we find: "Do you trust in God's grace and mercy and do you submit to his life-giving word of truth and righteousness (moral goodness)?"

Mankind Fallen
Alma 42:14. And thus we see that all mankind were fallen
(See also 1 Nephi 10:6; Alma 12:22

Phrases characterizing mankind as "fallen" is post-Biblical. One finds it in the English language as early as John Wesley, in his sermon "God's Love to Fallen Man." Hymns of Charles Wesley use the phrase "fallen race" (1, 4, 34 & 39). Compare this with his brother's hymn #33. It is also found in a hymn by Isaac Watts (1674–1748), beginning:

Ah, how shall fallen man
Be just before his God!

Redemption of the World
Mormon 7:7. He hath brought to pass the redemption of the world

This post-Biblical phrase is found as early as St. John of Damascus (hymn writer, c. 760),

We bless you for our creation, preservation,
and all the blessings of this life;
but above all for your immeasurable love
in the redemption of the world by our Lord Jesus Christ

It comes into English usage at least as early as "A Rationale upon the Book of Common Prayer" by Anthony Sparrow, D.D. (London, 1672): "For the Te Deum, Benedictus, Magnificat, and Nunc Dimittis being the most expressive Jubilations and rejoycings for the redemption of the world, may be said more often than the rest." The phrase became common in English. We find it in *"The Worship of the Church (28; v. 632); A Witness for the*

Redemption of the World, a Sermon" by F. D. Maurice (1805-1872). It is also in "Plenteous Redemption," (Sermon No. 351, delivered by Rev. C. H. Spurgeon: "and in that day he purchased the redemption of the world from its curse."

Eye of Faith
Alma 5:15. Do you look forward with an eye of faith...? (Alma 32:40; Ether 12:19)

This is a common English Euro-Christian phrase, as in the hymn "The Eye of Faith" by J. J. Maxfield (19th –century, dates unknown). Another hymn is "Through the Eyes of Faith" by Stephen Hurd. We find it in sermon 4, "Of Contentment" by Isaac Barrow (1630-1677):

Will it not much please us with an eye of faith to behold our Redeemer sitting in glorious exaltation at GOD's right hand...?

In a hymn of Charles Wesley we find (272): "To him mine eye of faith I turn..." See also hymns 75, 122, 128, 133, 493, 876 and 920.

The Life and Light of the World
Making Jesus not only the light, but also the life of the world, is extra-Biblical. Since this phrase occurs among various denominations, it is not unique to the *Book of Mormon*, even though nineteenth-century occurrences have not been found. It appears to be a combination of two titles, as indicated in the hymn of Isaac Watts, "The Names and Titles of Christ."

What winning titles he assumes!
Light of the World, and Life of Men

The hymn "All Things Are of God"[330] states:

Thou art, O God, the life and light of all this wondrous world

Clasped in the Arms of Jesus
Mormon 5:11. ...they might have been clasped in the arms of Jesus.

---

[330] So titled in *Hymns for Christian Devotion Especially Adapted to the Universalist Denomination*, 1846, with attribution to "61 moore" [dates?]; but alternatively, "God's Presence in Nature", the title in Samuel Johnson & Samuel Longfellow, *Book of Hymns for Public and Private Devotion*, 10th ed. (Boston: Ticknor & Fields, 1857/1846).

This phrase is similar to several hymns, including a hymn of Charles Wesley written after his daughter Sarah died, with the line, "clasped in the arms of His love."[331] We also find, "Safe in the arms of Jesus" (343). In the *Free Methodist Hymnal*,[332] "The Savior's melting mercies yearn to clasp thee to his breast." We also find "He leadeth me, for I can feel the clasping of that pierced hand so." (Helen S. Arnold, Charles H. Gabriel, "He Leadeth Me") We note that another hymn reflecting the same idea was written in 1868 by Fanny Crosby: "Safe in the Arms of Jesus."

Theological Euro-Christian Phrases

In addition to hymnodists, Euro-Christian theologians developed their own phraseology.

Typifying of Him (a Shadow, or Similitude)
Early Christianity was essentially an offshoot of the Judaism of Jesus' day. One accusation that the first believers had to face was that Jesus just is not in the pre-Christian scriptures, and certainly not the essential claims regarding the mission of their Christ. There was no way that they could challenge the sacred texts, and certainly they would never have thought to argue that important parts had been deleted. Rather, they argued that certain verses, and the sacred law itself, were typifications or foreshadowings of Jesus, the crucifixion and redemption. The Israelites, they held, were not ready for the literal truth. Instead, the law was given as a schoolmistress for Israel, to prepare them for the Advent of the Messiah. Paul taught that the law had been fulfilled in the crucifixion, the passion of Christ.

2 Nephi 11:4. For this end hath the law of Moses been given; and all things which have been given of God from the beginning of the world, unto man, are the typifying of him
Alma 33:19. Behold, he [Christ] was spoken of by Moses; yea, and behold a type was raised up in the wilderness, that whosoever would look upon it might live (See also: Alma 13:16; 25:15; 37:43-45)
Mosiah 3:15. And many signs, and wonders, and types, and shadows showed he unto them, concerning his coming
Jacob 4:5 offering up his son Isaac, which is a similitude of God and his Only Begotten Son. (See also Helaman 8:14)

The inspiration for this is in the commentaries on the Epistle of Paul to the Hebrews, 11:17-19:

---

[331] Sir Thomas Moore, *The English Hymnal*, no. 298.
[332] *Free Methodist Hymnal* (Chicago: Free Methodist Publishing House, 1910).

17 By faith Abraham, when he was tried, offered up Isaac: and he that had received the promises offered up his only begotten son,
18 Of whom it was said, That in Isaac shall thy seed be called:
19 Accounting that God was able to raise him up, even from the dead; from whence also he received him in a figure.

In his *Interpretation of Hebrews 11*, Theodoret, Bishop of Cry (Cyrrhus; 393-466 AD), wrote (commenting on Hebrews 11:19):

Figuratively speaking, he did receive him back, that is, by way of a symbol and type of the resurrection. Put to death by his father's zeal, he came back to life at the word of the one who prevented the slaughter. In him the type of the saving passion was also prefigured. Hence the Lord also said to the Jews, "Your father Abraham rejoiced at the prospect of seeing my day; he saw it and was glad."

This rationale is present in English Euro-Christianity, at least as early as John Wesley ("The End of Christ's Coming", Sermon 62), who wrote:

3. May we not reasonably believe it was by similar appearances that He was manifested in succeeding ages to Enoch, while he "Walked with God;" to Noah, before and after the deluge; to Abraham, Isaac, and Jacob, on various occasions; and, to mention no more, to Moses? This seems to be the natural meaning of the word: "My servant Moses is faithful in all my house. – With him will I speak mouth to mouth, even apparently, and not in dark speeches; and the similitude of Jehovah shall he behold;" namely, the Son of God.
4. But all these were only types of his grand manifestation.

His commentary on the Bible has at least 170 instances of asserting that an OT personage or event was a "type" of Christ, or of the Savior. His brother Charles put the doctrine into a hymn (706):

The types and figures are fulfilled; Exacted is the legal pain;
The precious promises are sealed; the spotless Lamb of God is slain.

Closer to home we have the work of Jonathan Edwards, "Types of the Messiah." Of OT sacrifices, he wrote:

Gideon was not only the captain of the host of Israel, but was immediately appointed of God to be a priest to build the altar of God, and to offer sacrifice to God, to make atonement for that iniquity of Israel that had brought them sore judgment upon them, that he came to deliver them from. Jdg. 6:20-28. And he offered a sacrifice acceptable unto God, and of which God gave special testimony of his acceptance, by consuming his sacrifice by fire immediately enkindled from heaven. Verse 21. And his sacrifice procured reconciliation and peace for Israel, Jdg. 6:24. These things are exactly agreeable to the prophecies of the Messiah.

And in his "Dissertation Concerning the End for Which God Made the World," Edwards wrote:

those two great temporal salvations of God's people, the redemption from Egypt, and that from Babylon, often represented as figures and similitudes of the redemption of Christ

The word similitude does occur in the Bible, but only to indicate the form of God, or a graven image, or allegories made by Jesus. It does not occur to indicate that an OT event or precept was a similitude of Christ.

As for "shadow" we read in Hebrews 10:1:

For the law having a shadow of good things to come, and not the very image of the things, can never with those sacrifices which they offered year by year continually make the comers thereunto perfect.

The verse says that the law "has" a shadow, not that it "is" a shadow. It asserts that this shadow is impotent, unable to "make the comers thereunto perfect." This did not prevent later interpretation to mean that the law was a shadow of Christ and redemption, a sort of revelation of them. The use of the word "shadow" in English Euro-Christianity is illustrated in John Wesley's Commentary on the Bible, Notes on Joel," 3:18:

Of the flowing waters in this verse, he wrote, "This no doubt is a shadow of the purifying blood of Christ, and his sanctifying spirit and word."

Of the words "type," "similitude" and "shadow," only the last was used in the Bible with a meaning that can be easily confused with the meaning it acquired in English Euro-Christianity, the meaning that found its way into the BoM narrative.

Plan of Salvation or Plan of Redemption

Jarom 1:2. For have not they revealed the plan of salvation? (See also: Alma 24:14; 34:9; 42:5)

Alma 12:30. ...the plan of redemption, which had been prepared from the foundation of the world (See also Alma 12:25; 18:39; 22:13; 29:2; 34:16; 39:18; 42:13)

Although Christians have always perceived that the Bible teaches God's provisions for salvation, the phrases "plan of salvation" and "plan of redemption" are not Biblical. At least in English Euro-Christianity, the phrases have become common to Catholics and various Protestant denominations. A sermon on the topic was delivered by John Wesley, "The Way of Salvation," in which he states, "Here I design to take a brief view of the gospel plan of salvation, and exhibit it especially in contrast with the original plan on which it was proposed to save mankind." His brother Charles refers to "the saving plan" (444).

Ends of the Law
2 Nephi 2:10. Wherefore, the ends of the law which the Holy One hath given, unto the inflicting of the punishment which is affixed...

This post-Biblical Euro-Christian phrase is common in English, both in theology and in legal studies. We have an example in the sermon "The Law Established Through Faith, Discourse 1" by John Wesley:

Their grand plea is this: That preaching the gospel...answers all the ends of the law. But this we utterly deny.

Forbidden Fruit
2 Nephi 2:15. The forbidden fruit in opposition to the tree of life

All Judeo-Christians have heard that there was a fruit forbidden to Adam and Eve in the Bible. But this phrase "forbidden fruit," although a common Christian phrase, is not in the Bible. Surprisingly, the word "forbidden" is found only three times. Its incidence in English Euro-Christianity is exampled in the sermon "On the Fall of Man" by John Wesley:

"That Adam sinned in his heart before he sinned outwardly; before he ate of the forbidden fruit;" ... by loving the creature more than the Creator.

In the Sermons of George Whitefield, this phrase occurs nineteen times, and twenty times in *The Works of Jonathan Edwards*. Although I have not found it in hymns, it is common in modern music and film.

Eternal Head
Helaman 13:38. That righteousness which is in our great and Eternal Head

This non-Biblical phrase may have been introduced by James (Jacob) Arminius (1560-1609) who wrote: "that Christ may be the eternal head of the predestinate." His work and theology became especially dominant in the United States, through John Wesley and Methodism.

Eat, Drink and Be Merry, for Tomorrow We Die
2 Nephi 28:7. Yea, and there shall be many which shall say: Eat, drink, and be merry, for tomorrow we die; and it shall be well with us
1 Corinthians 15:32. Let us eat and drink; for to morrow we die

Ecclesiastes 8: 15. Then I commended mirth, because a man hath no better thing under the sun than to eat, and to drink, and to be merry
Isaiah 22:13. Let us eat and drink; for to morrow we shall die

The English phrase has four elements: 1) eat, 2) drink, 3) be merry and 4) tomorrow we die. All four are found in the BoM verse, but no single Biblical verse has all four elements of the later Euro-Christian phrase.

Upon the Wings of His Spirit
2 Nephi 4:25. Upon the wings of his Spirit hath my body been carried

This phrase occurs in devotional material of various denominations. For example,

the sound of God's voice is being borne upon the wings of His Spirit...[333]

In the Presbycan (Presbyterian) Daily Devotional we find:

let us rise on the wings of His Spirit to praise and glorify His name

Clearly this is an English Euro-Christian phrase, not limited to the BoM.

Join the Choirs Above in Singing the Praises of a Just God
Mosiah 2:28. That … my immortal spirit may join the choirs above in singing the praises of a just God (cf. 1 Nephi 1:8; Mormon 7:7)
Psalms 148:1 Praise ye the LORD. Praise ye the LORD from the heavens: praise him in the heights. 2. Praise ye him, all his angels: praise ye him, all his hosts. 3. Praise ye him, sun and moon: praise him, all ye stars of light. 4. Praise him, ye heavens of heavens, and ye waters that be above the heavens.
Luke 2:13. And suddenly there was with the angel a multitude of the heavenly host praising God, and saying, 14. Glory to God in the highest, and on earth peace, good will toward men.

In the Bible, an angel (less commonly angels) is sent for specific purposes: to deliver a message, to protect, to destroy, to reap men for judgment, to gather the elect, etc. In Psalms 148, they are commanded to praise God, but apparently figuratively, since they are included with inanimate objects, such as stars and waters. This is reflected in the Hebrew word for angel, *mal'akh*, envoy, from a Semitic root "to send." In the New Testament, the word *angelos*, envoy, is a translation of the Semitic.

---

[333] Stephen T. Kia, "Christ, the Synthesis of Independent Fellowship" (online at http//:www.2liveischrist.net/articles/synthesis.htm, accessed March 2016).

"Choir" does not occur in the Bible, and there is no mention of a group of angels singing, in a "choir" (from Greek χορός [*choros*], a group of dancers or singers). At some point in the development of Euro-Christianity, the image of a "choir" of angels developed. Eventually, the angels were divided into orders called choirs (9 choirs according to some), each with its own function. No choir has singing, or singing praises, as its function. Even so, in popular religion, this terminology (choir) gave rise to the image of angels floating on clouds playing the harp, or singing praises. Whatever the meaning in this passage in Mosiah, this phrase obviously comes from post-Biblical Euro-Christianity. The phrase is found in a hymn of Charles Wesley (357):

Thy will by me on earth be done, As by the choirs above,
Who always see thee on thy throne, And glory in thy love.

In Spurgeon's sermon "Royal Homage" (no. 1102, 1873): "Nor can we expect that untrained voices should be admitted into the choirs above."

Chains of Hell

Alma 26:14. Has loosed our brethren from the chains of hell.
2 Peter 2:4. For if God spared not the angels that sinned, but cast them down to hell, and delivered them into chains of darkness

A common extra-Biblical English Euro-Christian phrase, found in *A Gospel Glass*, Part IV, Chapter 21: "Their Pride" by John Wesley:

Knock off the chains of hell from your children while you may.

It is found in later devotional material, such as a sermon of Dieter Reinstorf, Cape Town, "Sermon for the Sunday Cantate." We find the phrase in an 1827 sermon of Rev. John Chambers, Presbyterian Church:

for it will entail upon your souls the everlasting chains of hell, where there will be nought but weeping, wailing, and gnashing of teeth.[334]
We also find the passage "let monarchs now in the chains of hell bear witness to their own utter confusion" in the sermon delivered in 1854 by

---

[334] Rev. Mr. John Chambers, "Sermon delivered by the Rev M. John Chambers delivered at the Presbyterian Church in Thirteenth Street, Philadelphia, on the evening of December 2, 1827, from these words, 'Ye shall not surely die.'" (Philadelphia: 1828), 15.

C. H. Spurgeon. The image found its way into literature, such as the chains of Jacob Marley in Dickens, *A Christmas Carol*, first published in 1843.

Weeping and Wailing and Gnashing of Teeth

Alma 40:13 there shall be weeping, and wailing, and gnashing of teeth,

This is a case of combining wording from various Biblical sources to produce the Euro-Christian version. "Weeping and gnashing of teeth" is found in Luke 13:28 and Matthew 8:12, 22:13, 24:51 and 25:30. "Wailing and gnashing" is found in Matthew 13:42 and 13:50. The phrase "weeping and wailing" is found in Jeremiah 9:10, Esther 4:3, and Revelation 18:15 and 18:19. None of these has the phrase "gnashing of teeth." The common Euro-Christian composite is found at least as early as the 1827 sermon of Rev. Chambers *supra*.

The Damned Soul

Alma 36:16. Racked, even with the pains of a damned soul

This is a post-Biblical English Euro-Christian phrase, made popular if not introduced by none other than John Bunyan (author of *The Pilgrim's Progress*) in *A Few Sights From Hell, or the Groans of The Damned Soul or An exposition of those words in the Sixteenth of Luke* (1658). Closer to home, it is found in "Surprised by God's Judgment" by Jonathan Edwards (1703-1758):

Even those proud and sturdy spirits, the devils, tremble at the thoughts of that greater torment which they are to suffer at the Day of Judgment. So will the poor damned souls of men.

It is probable that the phrase developed in early Christianity.

Cup of Wrath

Mosiah 3:26: Therefore, they have drunk out of the cup of the wrath of God
Revelation 14:10: he also will drink of the wine of the wrath of God, which is mixed in full strength in the cup of His anger

This has long been a common Christian phrase, although not found in the Bible in this form. It is found in "The Life of Christ, the Pith and Kernel of All Religion," by R. Cudworth, B.D., preached before the Honorable House of Commons, 1647: "will prepare flaming ingredients for the cup of wrath…" It is found in Hymn 1:56 of Isaac Watts, "The Song of Moses and the Lamb; or Babylon Falling":

The cup of wrath is ready mix'd
And she must drink the dregs

Note too, its usage in a hymn penned by Witness Lee, "Thou didst drink the cup of wrath." In a sermon, "Jesus Sweats Blood," preached by Pastor Mark Driscoll out of Luke 22:39–46, we read:

the cup he [Jesus] is so grieved about? It is the cup of the wrath of God.

Sword of Justice

Helaman 13:5: the sword of justice hangeth over this people (See also 3 Nephi 20:20; 29:4 & Alma 60:29)
3 Nephi 2:19: the sword of destruction did hang over them

This non-Biblical expression derives from other Biblical material about God's judgment and the common expression of the sword of Damocles, hanging over the head of his guests. Perhaps it was popularized among preachers by Thomas Watson (c. 1620-1686), who still has many works in print, including *The Ten Commandments*, "The Wrath of God":

but the sword of God's justice hangs over a sinner, and when the slender thread of life is cut asunder it falls upon him.

Reap the East Wind

Mosiah 7:31: they shall reap the east wind, which bringeth immediate destruction. (Cf. Mosiah 7:30)
Hosea 8:7: For they have sown the wind, and they shall reap the whirlwind.
Ezekiel 17:10: shall it not utterly wither, when the east wind toucheth it?

This phrase is not Biblical, but is a blend of "reap the whirlwind" and "the east wind" (the latter being found in the OT as a wind of destruction). Since Hosea was not on the Brass Plates, there is no OT basis for the blend in the BoM. The phrase has been found in "Truth — Pyrrhonism — Dogmatism — Christianity," in *The Bible Treasury*, 04-1863.

Isabel in Siron

Alma 39:3: into the land of Siron...after the harlot Isabel

The sirens were legendary alluring women appearing to sailors at sea who (mis)led them onto rocky shoals and to a watery grave. In English, a siren became a woman of low morality who uses her charms to seduce a man into danger or sin. Isabel seems suggested by the name Jezebel (Hebrew אִיזֶבֶל, Izabel), a Canaanite princess who married Ahab, king of the northern kingdom Israel, and caused him to worship Baal and Asherah. (See 1 Kings 16, 18 & 21) The co-occurrence of the possible Isabel/Jezebel association, and the possible Siron/Siren association, seems like more than a coincidence.

Cross Yourself

Alma 39:9: Oh...take it upon you, and cross yourself in these things

The sign of the cross, or blessing oneself or crossing oneself, is post-Biblical, but became a ritual act done by members of many branches of Christianity. The use of the cross as a symbol of Christianity was rare in early Christianity, but apparently established by 200 CE. Signing the cross on one's forehead was common by the time Tertullian wrote "We Christians wear out our foreheads with the sign of the cross." The LDS Church later rejected the use of the cross, regarding it to be a symbol of torture unworthy of their faith in Jesus.

A Bitter Cup

Alma 40:26. ...they drink the dregs of a bitter cup

"A bitter cup" is not a Biblical expression, but became common in English Euro-Christian culture. We find it in a popular eighteenth-century hymn, "Jesus drinks the bitter cup" by Charles Wesley (1707-1788). In the sermon "On Eternity" by his brother John Wesley we read:

I know not if it would not seem as a thousand years. But (astonishing thought!) after thousands of thousands, he [the damned] has but just tasted of his bitter cup! After millions, it will be no nearer the end than it was the moment it began!

The *Book of Hymns for Public and Private Devotion* has a hymn by Jane Roscoe, "The Bitter Cup." The same collection has two other hymns containing this phrase. In the hymn "Agony in the Garden" (referenced above), we find "Father, remove this bitter cup."

Kingdom of the Devil

1 Nephi 22:23: all those who belong to the kingdom of the devil (See also v. 22 & 2 Nephi 28:19; Alma 5:25; 41:4)

This is a common post-Biblical English Euro-Christian expression, most usually referring to this world, before the coming of the kingdom of Christ. For a reference in the work of Martin Luther, see *Devotional Writings I.*[335]

---

[335] Jaroslav Jan Pelikan, Hilton C. Oswald and Helmut T. Lehmann, eds., *Devotional Writings I* (Philadelphia: Fortress Press, 1999), 38-39.

In "The Happy Ascetic," a sermon of Anthony Horneck (1641-1697), we find:

how men, under a show of strictness, would prohibit what GOD had…permitted to his creatures; under pretence (sic) of doing more than GOD has commanded, would set up the kingdom of the Devil.

We find it in John Wesley's notes on Genesis 3:

A perpetual quarrel is here commenced between the kingdom of God, and the kingdom of the devil among men

State of Nature
Alma 41:11. And now, my son, all men that are in a state of nature.

A non-Biblical Euro-Christian concept, it was developed as early as Thomas Aquinas, for the concept of natural law in political philosophy. Alternatively, it has been used to refer to man's natural sinfulness. In the sermon by John Wesley, "Awake, Thou That Sleepest," we read:

The state of nature is a state of utter darkness; a state wherein "darkness covers the earth, and gross darkness the people."

Nature of God
Alma 41:11. They have gone contrary to the nature of God

This is a post-Biblical Euro-Christian concept/phrase that became common in Christian devotional material and speculative theology. We find it in Disputation #15 of James (Jacob) Arminius, "On the Nature of God". In his sermon (# 15) on the "Nature of God," John Wesley wrote:

Now God saw that all this, the whole thereof, was evil; -- contrary to moral rectitude; contrary to the nature of God, which necessarily includes all good.

Days of Probation
1 Nephi 15:32. The works which were done…in their days of probation
Mormon 9:28. Be wise in the days of your probation (See also: 1 Nephi 10:21; 2 Nephi 2:30; 2 Nephi 33:9; Alma 12:24; Alma 42:4, 10, 13; and Helaman 13:38)
This is an English Euro-Christian concept and expression, not found in the Bible. In the commentary on the Bible of Daniel Whedon (1808-1885), we find:

Acts 3:22-26. Those prophecies—which are being fulfilled during the Saviour's residence in heaven, namely, during these days of probation under the Christian dispensation—of a predicted, and once present, but now absent Christ.

Example of the Son
2 Nephi 31:16: in following the example of the Son of the living God.

The path to perfection of the soul developed to a high point in Euro-Christianity. Although implied in 1 Corinthians 13:1, this phrase is not in the KJV (although it has been used in more loosely translated modern versions). The classical Catholic work to assist the believer is *Imitatio Christi*. In English-language Protestant worship, following the example of Jesus has long been a theme for sermons, usually adding words to focus on a particular behavior, such as example of Jesus in charity, in praying, etc. Methodism also stresses the example of Jesus in its path to perfecting the soul. In an introduction to John Wesley's sermons, we find: "Wesleyans to this present day still believe that holiness of heart and life is essential to the Christian sojourn. Love perfected in the individual, mirrored after the example of Jesus, will always be a mainstay of a Wesleyan understanding."[336]

Strangers to God
Alma 26:9. They would also have been strangers to God

This phrase is an extra-Biblical English Euro-Christian phrase, found in devotional material and hymns, such as "The Strangers to God," by Charles Austin Miles (1868-1946). In John Wesley's Commentary on the Bible, his note for Genesis 6:4 states: "The sons of God—those who were called by the name of the Lord, and called upon that name, married the daughters of men—those that were profane, strangers to God." In the same spirit, we find it in sermon #104 "On Attending the Church Service" by John Wesley: "Can we imagine that they who are themselves strangers to the grace of God will manifest that grace to others? ...Were not the priests, and public teachers, equally strangers to God, from this time to that of the Babylonish captivity?" Note as well its usage in later sermons: "I once was a stranger to God and his grace" by Adrian V. Miller; and "Stop Being a Stranger to God," preached in the Bethany Bible Church.

---

[336] Ryan N. Danker, "The Sermons of John Wesley [1872 Edition] - An Introduction," in *The Sermons of John Wesley* - 1872 Edition (Thomas Jackson, editor; online version at Wesley.nnu.edu, accessed 03/05/2017).

Wanderers in a Strange Land
Alma 13:23 because of our being wanderers in a strange land
Acts 7:6 That his seed should sojourn in a strange land

In the Bible, this phrase refers to alien residents in a city or land, not wanderers. But the wording with 'wandering' has become common, to the extent that it occurs in some so-called modern-English translations. The earliest occurrence I have found is dated 1832:

Friends, my attachment to my native land was strong—that cord is now broken; and we must go forth as wanderers in a strange land. ("George W. Harkins [Chief of the Choctaw Tribe] to the American People, February 25, 1832," posted on ushistory.org, accessed 09/18/2016)

Give thanks to his holy name
Alma 26:8. Let us give thanks to his holy name (see also 2 Nephi 9:52)

This verse poses an interesting problem. The closest in the Bible is Psalms 30:4, "give thanks at the remembrance of his holiness" (KJV). Strangely, various modern translations render it "give thanks to his holy name" (Jewish Publication Society Tanakh of 1917, English Standard Version, New American Standard Bible, NET Bible, English Revised Version). However, the Hebrew text is clear: *və-hōdū lə-zēker kodšō*, "praise (or give thanks to) the remembrance (or at the mention) of his holiness." The word for name, *šem*, is not even present. Other modern translations remain faithful to the Hebrew text. Since it is found in Christian sermons as well as translations of Isaiah, this too qualifies as a Euro-Christian phrase.

Although not identical, similar phrases occur in the hymns of Charles Wesley: "Give glory to his holy name" (559), "We bless thy holy name" (573 & 945) and "Praises, then, with one accord, to his holy name be given" (1).

Enlightened (Lamanites, i.e. Savages)
Helaman 15:10. And now, because of their steadfastness when they do believe in that thing which they do believe, for because of their firmness when they are once enlightened, behold, the Lord shall bless them and prolong their days, notwithstanding their iniquity

Enlightening people, and especially the "savages," is not Biblical. The term emerged to describe the transformation from an earlier benighted state to the scientific age, the age of enlightenment. It developed in the missionary work, as an English equivalent of *"la nation civilisatrice"* (France). Samuel Purchase justified colonialism: "[God] enriched the Savage Countries, that these riches might be attractives for Christian suters, which there may sowe spirituals and reape temporals."[337] It is evidenced in a journal entry of Rev. Cyrus Byington on his 1820 mission:

> The Missionary Boat has arrived from Marietta on her way to the Choctaw Nation. The plan of enlightening the Savages is certainly philanthropic, to say nothing of the importance of giving them the gospel.

Similarly, as we have seen, Thorowgood held that "If we meane the Indians shall be Gospellized, they must first be civilized..."

Addressing Modern Issues

The advent of the scientific age and a more liberal culture had its own effect. The BoM authors wanted to show that God knows science. They also felt a need to address what some thought was a scourge of atheism.

No God and No Hell

The *Book of Mormon* has a number of passages attacking atheism. These BoM passages reflect a preoccupation of later Euro-Christian writers and preachers.

> 2 Nephi 2:13. And if ye shall say there is no law, ye shall also say there is no sin. If ye shall say there is no sin, ye shall also say there is no righteousness. And if there be no righteousness there be no happiness. And if there be no righteousness nor happiness there be no punishment nor misery. And if these things are not there is no God. And if there is no God we are not, neither the earth; for there could have been no creation of things, neither to act nor to be acted upon; wherefore, all things must have vanished away.
> 2 Nephi 28:22. ...there is no hell; and he saith unto them: I am no devil, for there is none.

Disputation regarding the deity in the Bible was mostly a contest between the deity of Israel and its competition among the divinities of Israel's neighbors. The word "atheism" does not occur in the Bible. A reference to the lack of belief in God is extremely rare. When it occurs at all, it is in the form of a condemnation of evildoers (Psalms 10:4; 14:1; 53:1).

Our interest here is not just the concept of atheism, but disputation over the issue using the classical arguments against it. It developed as a philosophical concept, in the West in pre-Socratic Greek philosophy. By the eighteenth century, in the face of the emergence of modern science,

---

[337] Samuel Purchas, *Hakluytus Posthumus, or, Purchas his Pilgrimes (a Discourse on Virginia)* (Glasgow: James MacLehose & Sons, 1905), XIX, 232-233).

atheism had become a matter of concern for Christian preachers. In the sermons of John Wesley, "atheist" occurs sixteen times. In "Without God in the World" he maintains "I do not mean that they are Atheists, in the common sense of the word. I do not believe that these are so numerous as many have imagined...who seriously disbelieved the being of God...nay, I have found only two of these (to the best of my judgment) in the British Islands." Even though the majority of Americans believe at least in a "higher being," it is clear that the concern among preachers remains considerable.

What we might translate as "hell" in the OT is *šə'ōl*, sometimes rendered as the "pit" (i.e. the grave). It comes from a common Semitic root meaning "to ask" and possibly derives from necromancy. The witch of Endor brings Samuel up from *šə'ōl*. The curse uttered against the king of Babylon (Isaiah 14) says, "All they shall speak and say unto thee, Art thou also become weak as we?" This has been taken to imply that the original Hebrew view of Hell was the great leveler, much like Hades among the Greeks, wherein both the exalted and the lowly are weak shades (ghostly beings). Closer to home, Joseph Smith Sr. was at one point a member of the Universalists, who held that all mankind will be saved. Regarding disbelief in the existence of hell, not evidenced in the Bible, in a sermon of George Whitefield, "The Lord Our Righteousness," when the Earl of Rochester remains unconvinced of the "invisible realities of another world," he is told "Well, my lord, if there be no hell, I am safe. But if there should be such a thing as hell, what will become of you?" Hell has often been used as a sort of theological terrorism.

Your Nothingness, & Unworthy Creatures

Mosiah 4:5. For behold, if the knowledge of the goodness of God at this time has awakened you to a sense of your nothingness. (See Mosiah 4:11. "your own nothingness, and his goodness and long-suffering towards you, unworthy creatures.")

Reducing man to nothingness, or abject unworthy creatures, is not Biblical. Likewise, it has now gone out of fashion. But it was emphasized in certain Euro-Christian doctrines. This negative view of humanity is especially famous in the theology of some New England Puritanism. (v. p. 382) In BoM sermonology, it is most extreme in Mosiah.

This self-denying view of the worth of man developed in Euro-Christianity. An explanation of the Greek Orthodox way of life states: Saint Theophan says that the ancient Church Fathers tell us, "The feeling of one's nothingness and dedication to God unfolds best under constant sorrows and especially through extreme, providential crosses..." A Roman Catholic comments on the view of St. Therese of Lisieux: "When asked what she meant by 'remaining a little child before God', Therese responded: 'It is to recognize our nothingness, to expect everything from God.'" The views of New Englander Jonathan Edwards are well known. He wrote: "whereby there has been wanting a sense of the awful and holy majesty of God as present with them, and their nothingness and vileness before him."[338] A hymn by Greg Metcalf has a line "Your blessings are to us as creatures unworthy." In hymn 135, Charles Wesley wrote, "Loathsome, and vile, and self-abhored I sink beneath my sin."

The Earth

Helaman 14:21. The rocks which are upon the face of this earth, which are both above the earth and beneath, which ye know at this time are solid, or the more part of it is one solid mass, shall be broken up

The BoM authors inserted comments to show that scripture is not unaware of scientific truth. In Helaman 12:15 we find a description of a solar-centric system. Even so, they explain God's stopping the sun in its path by asserting that actually, it is the earth that stops its rotation. In 14:21, they address the structure of the earth, and reveal a view of the earth that is unaware of the earth's complex structure, with a solid crust, a mantle that is largely ductile, and a core that behaves like a liquid. At the time, a lively debate was ongoing between the emerging science of the origin, history and structure of the earth, and various scripture-based arguments to counter what was perceived to be a challenge to the validity of scripture. The BoM authors thought that they had a sufficient understanding of the issues that they could include a scientifically valid statement to show that BoM prophets had a sound understanding of the truth on this topic.

God and Country

Alma 56:11. Died in the cause of their country and of their God (See also Alma 58:8; 59:13; 60:29, 36; 61:6, 21; 62:1-2; 62:4, 9; 62:37; Helaman 6:23-24; & 3 Nephi 3:2)

Prior to the era of the nation state, one did not think in terms of "our country," but rather, our city, people, tribe, or land (of Judea, etc.). Country, as an abstract political or nationalist idea, did not exist. "Country" and "God and country" fit perfectly into nineteenth-century

---

[338] Jonathan Edwards, *Some Thoughts Concerning the Present Revival of Religion in New England*, Part IV. Sect. III, 2. *The Works of Jonathan Edwards*, Peabody, MA: Hendriksen Publishers, 1993).

American discourse. For the emergence of the idea of the nation state, see the classic *Idea of Nationalism* by Hans Kohn.[339]

To assess these passages, keep the following in mind:

§ It is not easy to retrieve the religious discourse of the early nineteenth century. There is a huge amount of material that no longer exists, and what does exist is not easily searched. Nor has it been possible to resurrect a random sample of Upstate New York inhabitants of the 1820s. These examples only scratch the surface of what must still be extant, waiting to be discovered.

§ One's analysis should not hinge on any particular example. Taken altogether, one can readily see that the BoM text is replete with English post-Biblical Euro-Christian phrases and concepts.

§ There is no intention here to imply that any BoM author consulted the sermons of John Wesley, or any other source cited above. Even Wesley most probably did not invent the phrases in his sermons, but drew from language that had already become the common coin of the Christian realm in England. English is a language of idioms and expressions. For the religiously inclined, growing up Christian meant acquiring fluency in this heritage.

What is not clear is whether the BoM authors wrote in this manner totally unaware that certain phrases are post-Biblical and therefore inappropriate, being the creations of later times and religious culture; or if they deliberately used these phrases to make their text more familiar and easily accepted; or, perhaps more probably, as a combination of the two. In any case, BoM text is replete with inappropriate Euro-Christian phrase. This is the

BoM Euro-Christian Anachronism Issue

ᕀᱤᱤᕀᱤᱤᕀᱤᱤᕀ

---

[339] Hans Kohn, *The Idea of Nationalism, a Study in its Origins and Background* (New York: Macmillan, 1944).

< Chapter 21 >

Fabricating Egyptian Documents, Language & History

Even before the *Book of Mormon* was completed, Joseph Smith's calling to restore lost scripture was envisaged as extending beyond it.

The Book of Abraham

Reformed Egyptian Exists

Egyptian writing has had a very long and continuous history of change. Characters resembling hieroglyphs have been found on Gerzean pottery, dating to c. 4,000 BCE. Günter Dreyer found about 300 clay labels in tomb U-j bearing protohieroglyphs dated to the 33rd century BCE. The first full sentence discovered so far is from the tomb of Seth-Peribsen of the 28th century BCE, at Umm el-Qa'ab. By the 25th century BCE an extensive sign list had developed (note the pyramid text at the pyramid of Unas). These included logograms, i.e. signs representing a complete word, independent of phonological content. Other signs were phonological, including signs for one consonant, for two consonants, and even for three. For the most part, vowels were not indicated (unlike ancient Sumerian and Akkadian).

But also very early, those who needed to write in their daily activities, primarily merchants and administrators, needed something less time-consuming than having to draw a picture of a particular species of bird, just to represent the letter *m* (for example). The same logogram was used, but simplified, requiring fewer strokes. This process resulted in hieratic. It is mostly possible to recognize the original hieroglyph in the hieratic character. Much later, a further development occurred, demotic. This was now so different that it is generally not possible to see the hieroglyph in the character, but the connection with the hieratic antecedent is clearer. Finally, the latest form of Egyptian, before it went extinct as a spoken language, is Coptic (*copt* related to *-gypt* in Egypt). To write this, the Greek alphabet was used, supplemented by Egyptian-origin characters for sounds not in Greek. Now, finally, the language was rewritten to reflect much of the linguistic change that had happened in the spoken language over two millennia. But Coptic remains, at base, still Egyptian. For example, the word for god is *n-tch-r* (vowels not written) in hieroglyphic, but *noute* in Coptic (dialects varying slightly). The freestanding pronouns are as follows:

Table 40. Middle Egyptian and Coptic Pronouns Compared

Person	Singular		Person	Plural	
	Egyptian	Coptic		Egyptian	Coptic
1. c. (I)	ínk	Anok	1. c. (we)	ínn	anon
2. m. (you)	nt.k	Ntok	2. c. (you)	nt.tn	ntôten
2. f. (you)	ntt	Nto			
3. m. (he)	nt.f	Ntof	3. c. (they)	nt.sn	ntôou
3. f. (she)	nt.s	Ntos			

Champollion had studied Coptic, and when he succeeded in deciphering some of the Egyptian characters on the Rosetta Stone, he suddenly had a breakthrough realization: "Hey, I already know this language, sort of. It is the antecedent of Coptic." Coptic had never gone fully extinct, and is still used as the liturgical language for Coptic Christian services in Egypt today. It was a great aid in deciphering earlier stages of Egyptian.

But note, some sort of "reformed" Egyptian as a code has never been found, where one character can represent a sentence, a paragraph or even a high mystery of the initiate.

Joseph Smith's Notion of, and Rational for Reformed Egyptian

The mention in the *Book of Mormon* that the Brass Plates of Laban were written in Egyptian is remarkable, being the record of Lehi's Hebrew fathers (the Old Testament up to his departure). It is not impossible, of course, that that family had returned to Egypt, possibly to carry on commerce, and had become bilingual. Even if they were bilingual, certainly Hebrew would have been their choice, the sacred language. A more remarkable mention of this language is found in connection with the gold plates, in Mormon 9:32-34:

> 32. And now, behold, we have written this record according to our knowledge, in the characters which are called among us the reformed Egyptian, being handed down and altered by us, according to our manner of speech.
> 33. And if our plates had been sufficiently large we should have written in Hebrew; but the Hebrew hath been altered by us also; and if we could have written in Hebrew, behold, ye would have had no imperfection in our record.

34. But the Lord knoweth the things which we have written, and also that none other people knoweth our language; therefore he hath prepared means for the interpretation thereof.

We find here some interesting points. First, apparently their first language was Hebrew, although it also had undergone change. They could write in it more correctly. Second, the use of reformed Egyptian was dictated by a shortage of gold, indicating a belief that writing in reformed Egyptian is more compact than in reformed Hebrew. That this most probably is not the case, or not to any great degree, can be seen in Figure 5. Even with this description we are not able to know what "reformed" means, since it states that the characters had been reformed. Were only the characters reformed, or the vocabulary, morphology and syntax as well? The same holds true regarding the reference to Hebrew. In what sense had it been altered?

Figure 5. Does Egyptian Have a More Compact Script?

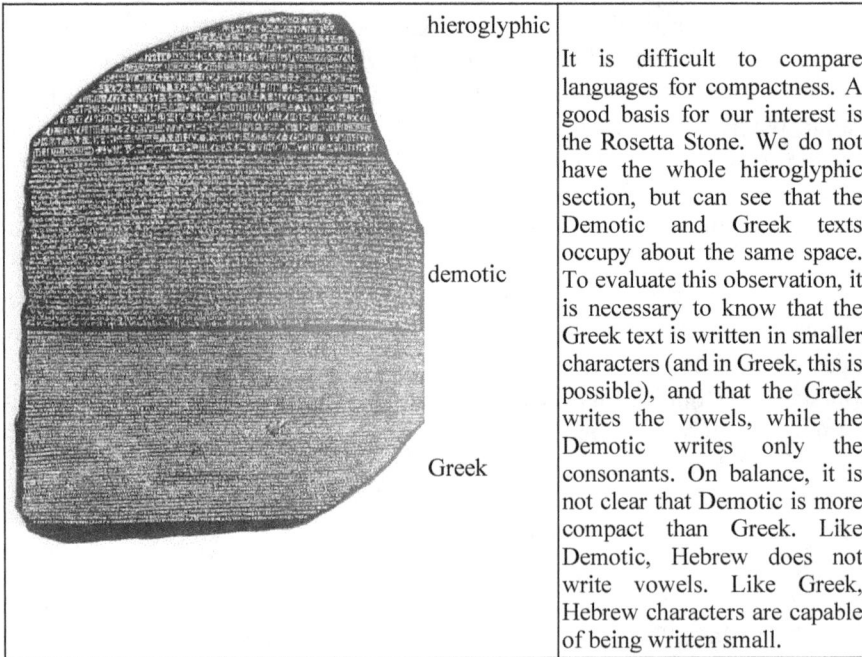

hieroglyphic

demotic

Greek

It is difficult to compare languages for compactness. A good basis for our interest is the Rosetta Stone. We do not have the whole hieroglyphic section, but can see that the Demotic and Greek texts occupy about the same space. To evaluate this observation, it is necessary to know that the Greek text is written in smaller characters (and in Greek, this is possible), and that the Greek writes the vowels, while the Demotic writes only the consonants. On balance, it is not clear that Demotic is more compact than Greek. Like Demotic, Hebrew does not write vowels. Like Greek, Hebrew characters are capable of being written small.

The text seems to also make clear the real reason for the Brass Plates to be in Egyptian, and the gold plates in reformed Egyptian. It is said in the statement, "none other people knoweth our language." The introduction of the Brass Plates in Egyptian is intended as an explanation for their ability to write the gold plates in Egyptian, albeit in reformed

Egyptian. And the gold plates are in Egyptian in order for Joseph Smith to have plates in a language that he believed, at that time, to be unknown. Indeed, in the statements of his contemporaries, both believers and detractors, I have never seen a mention of Champollion. The authors of the *Book of Mormon* could not be called to task in regard to the language of the plates.

Before the discovery of the Rosetta Stone, and the subsequent decipherment of ancient Egyptian, a common view was that in Egyptian writing, a single character could represent a whole sentence, or more. Thus even small texts were being "translated" into long documents. The most famous and influential of these was the work of Athanasius Kircher (c. 1601-1680). He, for example, translated two characters, dd Wsr ("Osiris says") to mean: "The treachery of Typhon ends at the throne of Isis; the moisture of nature is guarded by the vigilance of Anubis."[340]

The famous Egyptologist, Sir E. A. Budge wrote of him:[341]

> Many writers pretended to have found the key to the hieroglyphics, and many more professed, with a shameless impudence, which is hard to understand in these days, to translate the contents of the texts into a modern tongue. Foremost among such pretenders must be mentioned Athanasius Kircher, who, in the 17th century, declared that he had found the key to the hieroglyphic inscriptions; the translations which he prints in his *Oedipus Aegyptiacus* are utter nonsense, but as they were put forth in a learned tongue many people at the time believed they were correct.

On several occasions Joseph Smith said that he was working on the composition of his *Egyptian Alphabet, and Grammar*. The text of this work has been preserved in the Church historian's office and has been published. Included in his papers is a work that one can call the translation document, which lists characters from one of the papyri in a column, and opposite each, a phrase or sentence found in *The Book of Abraham*.

In America, the reigning concept of the Egyptian language seems to have been untouched by Champollion's work, and so it is not surprising to find, in Joseph Smith's *Egyptian Alphabet and Grammar* a similar pre-19th century approach, reproduced below (for Whitmer on this, v. 396).

---

[340] Examples of his translations may be found in his *Sphinx mystagoga: sive Diatribe hieroglyphica, qua Mumiae, ex Memphiticis Pyramidum Adytis Erutae...* (1676 edition).
[341] E. A. Wallis Budge, *Egyptian Language: Easy Lessons in Egyptian Hieroglyphics* (Mineola, NY: Dover, 1983 [1910]),15.

Table 41. Examples from Smith's Egyptian Alphabet and Grammar[342]

Character	Some of Smith's Rules
1.	This is called Za Ki-oan hiash, or chaslidon hiash. This character is in the fifth degree, independent and arbitrary. It may be present in the fifth degree while it stands independent and arbitrary. That is, without a straight mark inserted above or below it.
2.	By inserting a straight mark over it thus, (2) it increases its significance five degrees;
3.	by inserting two straight lines thus, (3) its signification is increased five more.
4.	By inserting three straight lines thus, (4) its signification is again increased five more degrees than the last. By counting the number of straight lines, or considering them as qualifying adjectives, we have the degrees of comparison. There are five connecting parts of speech in the above character, called Za Ki-on hish. These five connecting parts of speech [are] for verbs, participles, prepositions, conjunctions, and adverbs. In translating this character, the subject must be continued until there are as many of these connecting parts of speech used as there are connections, or connecting points, found in the character. But whenever the character is found with one horizontal line, as at (2), the subject must be continued until five times the number of connecting parts of speech are used, or the full sense of the writer is not conveyed. When two horizontal lines occur, the number of connecting parts of speech are continued five times further—or five degrees. And when three horizontal lines occur, the number of connecting parts of speech are continued five times further. The character alone has 5 parts of speech increased by one straight line thus: 5 x 5 is 25; by two horizontal lines thus: 25 x 5 = 125; and by three horizontal lines thus: 125 x 5 = 625.
5.	When this character has a horizontal line under it reduces it to the fourth degree, consequently it has but four connecting parts of speech.
6.	When it has two horizontal lines, it is reduced into the third degree and has but three connecting parts of speech,
7.	And when it has three horizontal lines it is reduced into the second degree and has but two connecting parts of speech.

Among comparative linguists, there are those who specialize in language universals. Enough universals have been found to seriously suggest that the human brain has evolved to be "hard-wired" for language. All languages (even the so-called ergative languages) have subjects, verbs and objects. Writing systems all have a way to unambiguously represent each of these, whether through logograms (Chinese), phonological signs (English) or a combination of logograms and phonological signs (Egyptian, Akkadian and modern Japanese). It is inconceivable that a

---

[342] The best analysis, is Dan Vogel, *Book of Abraham Apologetics. A Review and Critique* (Salt Lake City: Signature Books, 2021).

system such as that attempted by Smith could work. Still wedded to the approach destroyed by Champollion, he is trying to answer the question, "OK, so how can one know how much meaning a single sign can represent." For Smith, it can be huge. It is hard to understand how he planned to use such a method, since the Egyptian characters in the papyrus don't have these lines above and below. The Egyptians, on one line, could place one character above another. What Smith may have thought was a line is possibly the letter *n* (a horizontal zigzag line like saw teeth: ∾). In a late text, this can look like a horizontal line.

What Should Be Found, and Actually Has Been Found

The written materials, in books (metallic plates, vellum, etc.) or stone inscriptions, of the Nephite/Lamanite civilization, from the later period, can be expected to look like the writing that Smith claimed to have transcribed from his gold plates. Earlier texts should more closely resemble 7th century BCE Egyptian. He claimed that he made this transcription from the engraving he found on the plates, for his first scribe, Martin Harris, to take to some "learned men." (See Figure 3) This was in the RLDS church archives when I was sent off as a Mormon missionary armed with a plastic-laminated copy to show my contacts. Although it may be our best clue to what archaeologists should dig up, note that Anthon's two descriptions stated that the characters were arranged in columns, casting doubt on this copy. Perhaps Smith made two versions.

The assertion that this transcript was in reformed Egyptian poses an interesting issue. Joseph Smith transcribed it just after arriving in Harmony when he first began his translation with Martin Harris as scribe. When Mormon had completed his abridgment of the large plates of Nephi, he came upon the small plates of Nephi. When translated, these latter became Nephi through Omni in the BoM. Mormon did not abridge these, but says of them, "But behold, I shall take these plates, which contain these prophesyings and revelations, and put them with the remainder of my record" (Words of Mormon 1:6) The bulk of these were written by Nephi and his brother Jacob. As for the large plates, Nephi states: "I make an abridgment of the record of my father, upon plates which I have made with mine own hands" (1 Nephi 1:17). "I did make plates of ore that I might engraven upon them the record of my people. And upon the plates which I made I did engraven the record of my father" (1 Nephi 19:1). "And I knew not at the time…that I should be commanded of the Lord to make these plates [with] the record of my father, and the genealogy of his fathers" (1 Nephi 19:2). "I, Nephi, do not give the genealogy of my fathers in this part of my record; neither at any time shall I give it after upon these plates which I am writing; for it is given in the record which has been kept by my father" (1 Nephi 6:1; also 1 Nephi 10:15) As a result, we have two works, the first called the Book of Lehi (as abridged by Mormon from the large plates), which was stolen from Harris, and the replacement text, the Book of Nephi (written by Nephi). Of the 520 pages of the current printed English BoM text, about 133 represent the material on the small plates of Nephi. The text of the Book of Lehi may have been about the same size, and if included in the printed text, the BoM would be more than 600 pages. For the Book of Nephi, the language used must certainly have been the same 8th century BCE Egyptian as that found on the Brass Plates, which is distinctive and well known to Egyptologists. Although the large plates at least up to Enos would also have been in Late Egyptian, we do not know what form of Egyptian Mormon used to abridge it (i.e. the Book of Lehi lost by Harris). As a result, Smith could have originally copied characters from either character set, reformed Egyptian, or the well-known script used for 7th-century BCE Egyptian (early demotic or hieroglyphic). And if Nephite texts were to be found in Pre-Columbian America, they could date from from the period of Nephi and Jacob, or as late as 400 CE.

What we have actually found is totally different. As it turns out, the only fully literate civilization in Pre-Columbian America was that of the Mayans. Aztec writing was much later and never well developed. Only one Olmec seal may represent early Mayan writing. The Incas did not write, nor any other pre-Columbian group that we have studied.

An amazing documentary, *Breaking the Mayan Code*, shows blow by blow how Mayan was deciphered. One can also consult the book, *Breaking the Mayan Code*, by Michael Coe. The bottom line is that, like Egyptian, there is a mixture of logograms and phonological characters. But unlike Egyptian, Mayan phonological signs are syllabic (like Sumerian, Akkadian, Japanese, and ancient Ethiopic). That is to say, there is a character for *bi*, another for *bo*, another for *ba*, another for *bu*, and so on, for all the consonants. Here again, one cannot get a sentence or a whole paragraph out of a single character. One of the great breakthroughs was the realization that Mayan, and indeed Aztec, are still spoken languages in Mexico. As a student at Harvard, I met a native Aztec speaker. At some point in the decipherment process, it was realized that spoken Mayan had not changed hugely from the Mayan of the stelae and the few books that survived the book-burning priest, Diego de Landa. Grammar books and a dictionary already written for a modern Mayan language were a great help. Certainly there are issues remaining to be solved, including words yet to be figured out. But this is always the case in ancient languages.

Mayan is a very distinctive language, and is absolutely in no way related to Hebrew, or any other Semitic language, or to Egyptian, or any other Hamito-Semitic language. There is no way around the bottom line: the assertions of the *Book of Mormon* require that we find some sort of Hebrew or Egyptian, and if ever it were found, it will not be hard to recognize.

Abraham Found?

An American in Philadelphia, Michael Chandler, somehow came into possession of eleven mummies around 1833. Apparently he collected them from the customs house in New York, possibly under contract with representatives of the estate of the late Antonio Lebolo of Castellamonte, a rich Italian merchant, who had acted as superintendent of the archaeological digs in Egypt for Bernardino Drovetti, the Italian-origin French Consul-General in Cairo. In this capacity, he had acquired eleven mummies. The identification of Lebolo's mummies with those Chandler took possession of is not completely proven, but a very likely case has been made for it by H. Donl Peterson and H. Michael Marquardt.[343] Chandler was not only touring to exhibit them for profit, but was occasionally selling a mummy, and was to pay a share of the profits to Lebolo's estate. Unwrapping them, Chandler found some Egyptian papyri. Presumably while on tour with his mummy exhibit he heard of Joseph Smith, who claimed to have translated a gold bible from Egyptian, but his angel had taken the plates back. Certainly he would like to have something of this nature, to show his followers and prospective converts.

One can imagine the buzz in the Mormon community when, in June of 1835, Chandler arrived with his mummies and papyri in the Mormon center at that time, Kirtland, Ohio. Joseph Smith purchased four mummies and a collection of papyri. Reportedly he was only interested in the papyri, but Chandler insisted on a package deal. When later he had had an opportunity to study the papyri a bit, he announced that one of them was *The Book of Abraham*. In the eyes of his followers, the mission of their prophet to bring forth lost scriptures was ongoing, but now, even better, as the Egyptian documents were there for all to see.

---

[343] H. Donl Peterson, *The Story of The Book of Abraham, Mummies, Manuscripts and Mormonism* (Salt Lake City: Deseret Book Company, 1995). H. Michael Marquardt, "Joseph Smith's Egyptian Papers: A History," in Robert K. Ritner, *The Joseph Smith Egyptian Papyri, A Complete Edition* (Salt Lake City: Signature Books, 2013), 11-68.

Smith said that the project of translation required preliminary work. He wrote, "The remainder of this month (July, 1835) I was continually engaged in translating an alphabet to '*The Book of Abraham*,' and arranging a grammar of the Egyptian language as practiced by the ancients."[344] After some tumultuous years, and when the Mormons had moved to Nauvoo, Illinois, in March of 1842 he published what he called *The Book of Abraham*, claimed to be a translation from one of the papyri. Eventually, the LDS Church accepted this work as divine scripture. It has been a source of some uniquely LDS theology, making it indispensable. In the turmoil accompanying and following the murder of Joseph Smith, the mummies and papyri disappeared. Many were certain, and perhaps wished to believe, that they had found their way to a museum in Chicago that was destroyed in the Chicago fire.

In 1967, the founder of the Middle East Center at the University of Utah, Dr. Aziz Suryal Atiya, a renowned expert on the Crusades and on the history of the Coptic Christians in Egypt, being himself a Copt, was searching the storage area at the Metropolitan Museum of Art for Coptic materials, where he found the Joseph Smith papyri, with a bill of sale signed by Joseph Smith's first wife, Emma. This included some, but clearly not all, of the papyri (at least, a hypocephalus, or solar disk, published in the *Pearl of Great Price*, had gone astray and has not been recovered). On 27 November 1967, the Museum presented them to the LDS Church. Later they were locked up in the university's vaults, and many feared that they would become inaccessible. Rumor had it at the time that the staff of *Dialogue, a Journal of Mormon Thought*, put pressure on the Church to make them available. Apparently fearing nothing, the Church published them in very beautiful images in *The Improvement Era*, its official organ. Subsequently, Egyptologists translated them. The papyrus that had been identified conclusively as being the one that Smith said he translated into *The Book of Abraham* turned out to be an ancient Egyptian funerary text called the *Sensen* (breathing) document, or Breathing Permit of Hor, for the reanimation of the mummy. This, of course, created a great stir, and some intellectual exodus from the Church. How could the Mormon establishment respond to this challenge?

---

[344] Joseph Smith, *History of the Church of Jesus Christ of Latter-day Saints* (Salt Lake City: Deseret News, 1902), 2:238.

Facsimile No. 1: The Lion Couch Scene

The identification of the *Sensen* papyrus with the papyrus that Joseph Smith claimed to have translated into *The Book of Abraham* has been made decisively by "*Facsimile No. 1*," a detailed reproduction in the BoA of a distinctive vignette found in the papyrus.

Figure 6. Facsimile No. 1 (*The Book of Abraham*)

Fig. 1. The Angel of the Lord. 2. Abraham fastened upon an altar. 3. The idolatrous priest of Elkenah attempting to offer up Abraham as a sacrifice. 4. The altar for sacrifice by the idolatrous priest, standing before the gods of Elkenah, Libnah, Mahmackrah, Korash, and Pharaoh. 5. The idolatrous god of Elkenah. 6. The idolatrous god of Libnah. 7. The idolatrous god of Mahmackrah. 8. The idolatrous god of Korash. 9. The idolatrous god of Pharaoh. 10. Abraham in Egypt. 11. Designed to represent the pillars of heaven, as understood by the Egyptians. 12. Raukeeyang, signifying expanse, or the firmament over our heads; but in this case, in relation to this subject, the Egyptians meant it to signify Shaumau, to be high, or the heavens, answering to the Hebrew word, Shaumahyeem.

Source: *The Book of Abraham* (including the "Explanation").

Figure 7. Egyptologist Bell's Proposed Reconstruction

Source: Lanny Bell (v. Bibliography 4)

This "vignette of the corpse in the process of reanimation is common in Books of Breathings..."[345] with the deceased lying on the lion couch, the jackal-headed mummification god Anubis standing behind, and the *ba* spirit of the deceased in the form of a bird with a human head. Beneath the couch are the four standard canopic jars, holding the key organs of the deceased that were extracted during mummification. Each jar is identified by its head (lid). To communicate reanimation, the ancient artist depicts the posture of the deceased with arms uplifted and legs apart, with one leg uplifted.[346]

In an early criticism of *The Book of Abraham*, it was claimed that Facsimile No. 1 had been modified, that the head of the figure behind the lion couch must originally have been Anubis, the mummification god, with the head of a jackal. Now that the original papyrus has resurfaced and has been studied, it turns out that a large area is missing, including the head of Anubis, the hand of Anubis' outstretched arm including what he is grasping, the arms of the deceased, and part of the head of the *ba* spirit. In the gap, in pencil, the head of Anubis is drawn as a human head. His outstretched hand holding a sacrificial knife, the two arms of the deceased and the head of the ba spirit were drawn in to befit *The Book of Abraham* story. This was drawn on the paper upon which the papyrus had been mounted.

Figure 8. The Papyri used for a part of *The Book of Abraham* (JS 1.1 & 1.2

---

[345] Ritner, *The Joseph Smith Egyptian Papyri*, 115.

[346] The reconstruction of Figure 7. is from Lanny Bell, "The Ancient Egyptian 'Books of Breathings,' the Mormon 'Book of Abraham,' and the Development of Egyptology in America," in Stephen E. Thompson & Peter Der Manuelian, eds., *Egypt and Beyond, Essays Presented to Leonard H. Lesko upon his Retirement* (Providence, RI: Brown University, 2008), 30.

Figure 8 shows the text found to the left of the lion couch scene. Parts of the Abraham translation document and hypocephalus (v. *infra*) draw from the first four of these lines. These are shown more clearly in Figures 10, and 11 where the lines have been numbered to facilitate discussion.

Figure 9. Smith's Modified Papyrus for Facsimile No. 1

Note that the edges of the papyrus are frayed, except those of this missing section, which are cleanly removed, indicating that we have here, not a misguided reconstruction, but a removal of unwanted material to be replaced in the guise of restoration. This fabrication runs counter to the claim of some that Smith somehow sincerely thought that he was actually translating.

Several leading Egyptologists have worked on these papyri. The first to do so was John A. Wilson, Andrew MacLeish Distinguished Service Professor of Egyptology at the Oriental Institute of the University of Chicago,[347] and Richard A. Parker, Wilbour Professor of Egyptology and Department Chairman at Brown University. They were followed by Klaus Baer, Associate Professor at Chicago's Oriental Institute,[348] and more

---

[347] *Dialogue, a Journal of Mormon Thought*, Vol. III, No. 2, 67-85.
[348] *Dialogue, a Journal of Mormon Thought*, Vol. III, No. 3, 109-134.

recently, Robert K. Ritner, Professor of Egyptology also at the Oriental Institute, who has published a complete definitive edition.[349]

Figure 10. The Passage to the Left of the Lion Couch Scene (from JS 1.2)

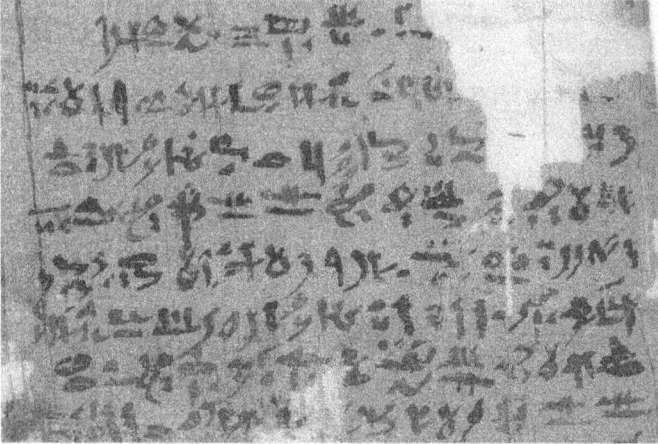

Figure 11. The Texts Used to Produce Abraham and the Hypocephalus

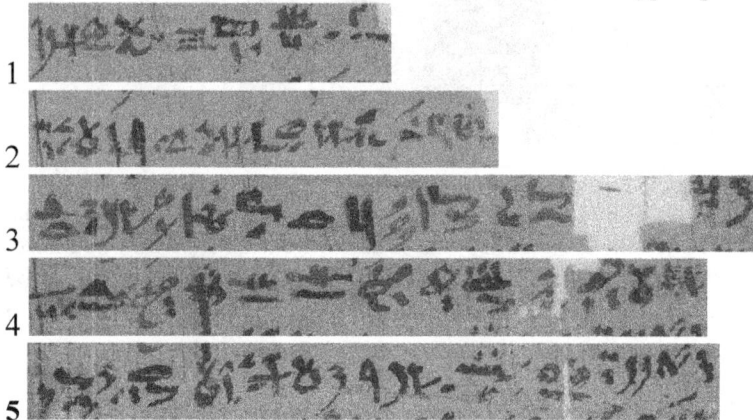

Some have claimed that although Smith's BoA papyrus has been correctly identified, he mistakenly thought he was translating it, while at the time he was actually receiving the text of *The Book of Abraham* by revelation. He was killed before he could realize or correct his error. This argument is also impossible, because in *The Book of Abraham*, Abraham himself makes a first-person reference to Facsimile No. 1:

[349] Ritner, *The Joseph Smith Egyptian Papyri*.

the priests laid violence upon me, that they might slay me also, as they did those virgins upon the altar; and that you may have a knowledge of this altar, I will refer you to the representation at the commencement of this record. (12) It was made after the form of a bedstead, such as was had among the Chaldeans, and it stood before the gods of Elkenah, Libnah, Mahmackrah, Korash, and also a god like unto that of Pharaoh. (13)

Table 42 is based on a Joseph Smith translation document. In the column on the left, it lists characters from Figure 11. There we see the photographed character on the left, Smith's rendition next to it, the Egyptologist's translation of the character below these, and Smith's translation opposite each character in the column on the right.

Table 42. Smith's BoA Translation of Characters from the Abraham Papyrus

Egyptologist Translation (photo from the papyrus, with Smith's rendition, and below these, the Egyptologist's translation.)	Joseph's Attempted Translation of the Character.
Egyptologist: The, this (Figure 11, line 1)	*Book of Abraham* text 11. Now, this priest had offered upon this altar three virgins at one time, who were the daughters of Onitah, one of the royal descent directly from the loins of Ham. These virgins were offered up because of their virtue; they would not bow down to worship gods of wood or of stone, therefore they were killed upon this altar,
Egyptologist: pool, lake (Figure 11, line 1)	*Book of Abraham* text: and it was done after the manner of the Egyptians. 12. And it came to pass that the priests laid violence upon me, that they might slay me also, as they did those virgins upon this altar; and that you may have a knowledge of this altar, I will refer you to the representation at the commencement of this record.
Egyptologist: Water determinative (for clarification, not for translation) (Figure 11, line 1)	*Book of Abraham* text: 13. It was made after the form of a bedstead, such as was had among the Chaldeans, and it stood before the gods of Elkenah, Libnah, Mahmackrah, Korash, and also a god like unto that of Pharaoh, king of Egypt. 14. That you may have an understanding of the figures at the beginning, which manner of the figures is called by the Chaldeans Rahleenos, which signifies hieroglyphics.
	Book of Abraham text: 15. And as they lifted up their hands upon me, that they might offer me up and take away my life,

Egyptologist: great (Figure 11, line 1)	behold, I lifted up my voice unto my God, and the Lord hearkened and heard, and he filled me with the vision of the Almighty, and the angel of his presence stood by me, and immediately unloosed my bands;
  Egyptologist: Khonsu (the moon god of Thebes) (Figure 11, line 1)	*Book of Abraham* text: 16. And his voice was unto me: Abraham, Abraham, behold, my name is Jehovah, and I have heard thee, and have come down to deliver thee, and to take thee away from thy father's house, and from all thy kinsfolk, into a strange land which thou knowest not of; 17. And this because they have turned their hearts away from me, to worship the god of Elkenah, and the god of Libnah, and the god of Mahmackrah, and the god of Korash, and the god of Pharaoh, king of Egypt; therefore I have come down to destroy him who hath lifted up his hand against thee, Abraham, my son, to take away thy life. 18. Behold, I will lead thee by my hand, and I will take thee, to put upon thee my name, even the Priesthood of the father, and my power shall be over thee. 19. As it was with Noah so shall it be with thee; but through thy ministry my name shall be known in the earth forever, for I am thy God.
  Egyptologist: Born of (Figure 11, line 2)	*Book of Abraham* text: 29. Now, after the priest of Elkenah was smitten that he died, there came a fulfilment (sic) of those things which were said unto me concerning the land of Chaldea, that there should be a famine in the land. 30. Accordingly a famine prevailed throughout all the land of Chaldea, and my father was sorely tormented because of the famine, and he repented of the evil which he had determined against me, to take away my life. 31. But the records of the father, even the patriarchs, concerning the right of Priesthood, the Lord my God preserved in mine own hands; therefore a knowledge of the beginning of the creation, and also of the planets, and of the stars, as they were made known unto the fathers, have I kept even unto this day,
  Egyptologist: Tai (first part of a name) (Figure 11, line 2)	*Book of Abraham* text: And I shall endeavor to write some of these things upon this record, for the benefit of my posterity that shall come after me.

Egyptologist: Khibit (second half of the name) (Figure 11, line 2)	*Book of Abraham* text: 1. Now the Lord God caused the famine to wax sore in the land of Ur, insomuch that Haran, my brother, died; but Terah, my father, yet lived in the land of Ur, of the Chaldees. 2. And it came to pass that, Abraham, took Sarai to wife and Nehor, my brother, took Milcah to wife.
Egyptologist: determinative for a woman's name (not to be translated) (Figure 11, line 2)	*Book of Abraham* text: Who was the daughter of Haran.
Egyptologist: Justified (&) likewise (Figure 11, line 2)	*Book of Abraham* text: 3. Now the Lord had said unto me: Abraham, get thee out of thy country, and from thy kindred, and from thy father's house, unto a land that I will show thee. 4. Therefore I left the land of Ur, of the Chaldees, to go into the land of Canaan; and I took Lot, my brother's son and his wife, and Sarah my wife; and also my father followed after me, unto the land which was denominated Haran. 5. And the famine abated; and my father tarried in Haran and dwelt there, as there were many flocks in Haran; and my father turned again unto his idolatry, therefore he continued in Haran.
Egyptologist: After (Figure 11, line 3)	*Book of Abraham* text: 6. But I, Abraham, and Lot, my brother's son, prayed unto the Lord, and the Lord appeared unto me, and said unto me: Arise, and take Lot with thee; for I have purposed to take thee away out of Haran, and to make of thee a minister to bear my name in a strange land which I shall give thee for an everlasting possession, when they harken to my voice. 7. For I am the Lord thy God; I dwell in heaven; the earth is
Egyptologist: grasped (placed) (Figure 11, line 3)	*Book of Abraham* text: my footstool; I stretch my hand over the sea, and it obeys my voice; I cause the wind and the fire to be my chariot; I way to the mountains … Depart hence …and behold, they are taken away by a whirlwind, in an instant suddenly. 8. My name is Jehovah, and I know the end from the beginning; therefore my hand shall be over thee. 9. And I will make thee a great nation, and I will bless thee above measure, and make thy name great among all nations,

This comes from a collection of translation material.[350] Much of it is unclear. Ritner has selected the passages where Smith's Egyptian characters are clear enough to be recognized in the papyrus text in Figure 10. His translation of the characters in the column on the left, put together as they originally were to form a continuous text, albeit out of context, reads: "the great lake of Khonsu, and likewise born of Taikhibit, the justified, after his two arms have been [placed/grasped] at his heart,.."[351]

To emphasize how wrong Smith's translation is, note the character on row three that was transcribed to look like a backwards E (Ǝ, but should be three horizontal lines). This is a determinative. Far from writing in a way that allowed a single sign to be interpreted as having lengthy meaning, the ancient scribes were concerned to reduce ambiguity. They developed a set of semantic category signs to help clarify the word associated with it, by indicating what semantic category it belonged to. An example is the word for sun, written with a circle and a tiny circle inside it, a logogram, representing the sun. It could also be written phonologically, with the two consonants—*r*'—(no vowel indicated, but English writes it *re, ra* or *ra*'). When it meant simply the sun itself, the object we see in the sky, it could be accompanied by the circle sign. But if it meant the sun god Re, it could be accompanied by a deity determinative, a picture of a seated god. The determinative only clarified the word it accompanies, without adding meaning, and is neither pronounced nor translated. The scribe is simply indicating that the word "lake" is in the water category, and should not be mistaken for any homonym. A rough example in English is our use of quotation marks, signs to eliminate ambiguity, distinguishing what is quoted from the rest of the text. Quotation marks are not translated into sentences, or verses. To render quotation marks separately, and make them into two verses of *The Book of Abraham*, would be as silly as doing just that with the Egyptian water determinative. Smith also translated the determinative for a woman's name. A name sign is useful. I was born in Green River, located on the Green River. In Egyptian, the first might have a city determinative just so no one would mistakenly think that I was born in a river.

Apparently Smith continued to think that no one would ever be able to read Egyptian, or come to know the many gods of the Egyptians, and their names. The sacrifice of virgins on an altar is not Egyptian practice. The four gods mentioned are the four canopic jars for the deceased's key

---

[350] H. Michael Marquardt, *The Joseph Smith Egyptian Papers* (Cullman, AL: Printing Service, 1981).
[351] Ritner, *The Joseph Smith Egyptian Papyri*, 127.

organs, typical of a funerary papyrus illustration. By the time of this papyrus, they also represented the four points of the compass: Hapi (the baboon-headed god—north; jar for the lungs), Duamutef (jackal-headed god—east; jar for the stomach), Imseti (human-headed god—south; jar for the liver), and Qebehsenuef (falcon-headed god—west; jar for the intestines).

The Egyptians Never Occupied Ur of Chaldea

Between the 10th and 11th centuries BCE, tribes of West Semitic origin migrated into southern Iraq. These are identified as the Suteans and Arameans, followed perhaps a century later by a tribe called the Kaldu, usually referred to as the Chaldeans or Chaldees. After the Chaldeans had become masters of Babylon (9th century BCE), the term Chaldea became synonymous with Babylonia. The Assyrian empire prevented them from expanding into northern Iraq, and in 689 BCE the Assyrians cemented their control by completely razing the city. To put this in historical perspective, David ruled Israel in the 10th century, long after the time ascribed by the Bible to its great patriarch, Abraham.

Ur, located in the deep south-east of Mesopotamia (Iraq, ten miles from the modern city of Nasiriyah), became a significant settlement in the 4th millennium BCE, and the capital of an empire in the 21st century BCE. It fell into serious decline in the 1st millennium BCE.

Due to its considerable distance from the Fertile Crescent, it has been felt by some devout scholars that the city referred to in the OT in connection with Abraham must have been some other city. This has led to a search for place names sounding like Ur. The only plausible identification is Urha, in present-day southern Turkey. Since the Chaldeans were clearly far too late to be associated with Abraham, even some LDS scholars have joined the quest for an alternate Ur.

Although Canaanites had established a realm in the eastern Egyptian delta in the 18th century BCE, the principal contact that ancient Egypt had with the Semites was the invasion of the Hyksos, who invaded the delta in c. 1650 BCE, and ruled there until expelled by the campaigns of Seqenenre Tao, Kamose and Ahmose, around a century later. The Egyptians used a term for peoples east and northeast of the delta that Egyptologists have usually translated as "Asiatics," which includes the Semites and peoples of Anatolia and Persia. Apart from the initiatives of Senusret I in the land of Canaan, the beginning of Egyptian expansion into Canaan and Syria was the military campaigns of Thutmose I. After quelling a Nubian revolt, he led a military campaign across Canaan and to the northern reaches of

Syria. After crossing the Euphrates, he set up a stele to commemorate his presence (although this has never been found), and returned to Egypt. As long as his military force was present in Syria, cities there conveniently capitulated and paid tribute, but as soon as he returned home they stopped their payments and began preparations to repel a possible recurrence of this invasion. His son and successor, Thutmose II, only made raids into Nubia to the south and to a limited extent north into Syria,. The most penetrating of the Egyptian campaigns was conducted by Thutmose III, after acceding to the throne in the wake of the regnant queen Pharaoh (usurper) Hatshepsut. Of most importance is the fact that he kept a personal record (daybook) of his exploits.

We cannot expect that the Pharaoh's own account would be an understatement of his campaign. In it we learn that he traveled across the full extent of modern Syria, and, in his eighth campaign, as far north as Carchemish, on the west bank of the Euphrates, in what is now southern Turkey (mid-15th century, BCE). The only real kingdom opposing him was Mittani, in what is now eastern Turkey. Its king had not expected that the Egyptian campaign would be anything more than brief incursions, and certainly not that Thutmose III would cross the river. When they arrived on the east bank of the Euphrates, the Mittani king was not prepared for war, and withdrew most of his forces. The Pharaoh erected a stele, destroyed some Mittani towns, and withdrew. He did not go as far as Orhay (Syriac; Urha, Urfa, Edessa and Turkish Şanlıurfa). His time on the east side of the Euphrates was limited, and purely military.[352]

Donald B. Redford, the preeminent authority on the campaigns of Thutmose III, wrote:

> While Thutmose lived, the administration of the Levant (if we can even use this formal term) was rudimentary in the extreme. The Egyptian army marched forth at such regular intervals that "resident governors" were unnecessary, and specific tasks in the north were assigned on an ad hoc basis to civil administrators. Only later in the reign (year 47) is mention made of permanent troops in the Akkar plain (Ullaza [north of Biblos, now north Lebanon]), and they have been stationed there for three purposes: to guard the stores in the "harbors," to supervise the cutting and transport of timber and to keep Eluetheros valley under surveillance.[353]

---

[352] George Steindorff & Keith C. Seele, *When Egypt Ruled the East* (Chicago: The University of Chicago Press, 1957), 58-59; and Donald B. Redford, *The Wars in Syria and Palestine of Thutmose III* (Leiden: Brill, 2003), 220-228.
[353] Redford, *Wars in Syria and Palestine of Thutmose III*, 256-7.

The Mittani became more prepared for Egyptian incursions into their territory, and a new power moved south into north Syria, the Hittites. This formidable kingdom effectively kept the Egyptians out of lands north of Kadesh, famous as the site of the great battle where the Hittite Muwatalli II and Ramses the Great fought to a stalemate, ending with the Hittites remaining in control of this city.

The bottom line is that the Egyptians never had a presence in southern Turkey, certainly not anywhere near Urha, nor even in Syria, that would involve a religious establishment overseen by the priest of Pharaoh. The account in *The Book of Abraham* is historically impossible. The Egyptians were not in Ur, and the Chaldeans were in southern Iraq, and even there only from about the time of King David. No other city has been found that could be a plausible Ur to meet the needs of *The Book of Abraham*.

Map 10. The 8th Campaign of Thutmose III

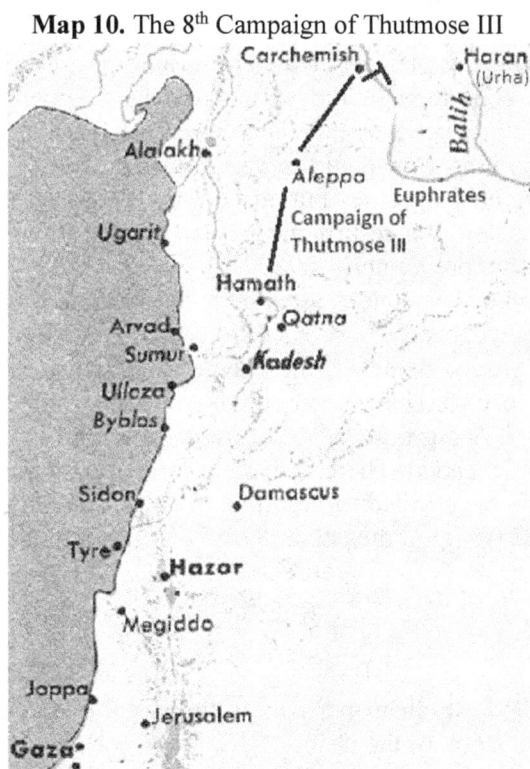

Human Sacrifice and the Egyptians

Human sacrifice in its most normal form is the ritual killing of an individual to propitiate a god or the gods. It can be a relatively routine practice, such as among the Aztecs, or a special-circumstance practice, such as when a people face conquest by am enemy, or prior to launching a military campaign (cf. Euripides' tragedy *Iphigenia at Aulis*), or to seek divine help in a time of plague or famine. This form of human sacrifice is not evidenced in Egypt. This is notable, in that Egypt has been documented by many thousands of structures, statues, stelae, inscriptions, bas relief scenes and documents. All of this has a strong focus on religious matters, and some sort of evidence of human sacrifice should have been discovered, if the institution existed.

Another form of human sacrifice is retainer sacrifice. During the first dynasty (c. 3080-c. 2886 BCE) pharaonic burials contained burials of retainers of the pharaoh as well as his own burial. Since these tombs were covered over by a continuous roof, it is believed that the retainers must have been killed to be buried with their master, to serve him in the afterlife. This was discontinued in the second dynasty, apparently because the retainers no longer believed that their demise was needed for the Pharaoh's well-being, and that they could serve him better alive to maintain his cult. Also, the *ushabtis*, figurines buried with the deceased to come alive and serve their master after resurrection, were viewed to be just as good, and could be much more numerous.

Those who desperately attempt to have human sacrifice in Egypt make reference to representations of executed prisoners of war. There are usually two groups depicted, those who will be prisoners and probably slaves, and those who have been killed. An iconographic device is used to distinguish the two groups. The captives are bound by a cord, while the executed are beheaded. There is never a reference to the latter to indicate that they have been killed to propitiate a deity. Rather, the message is to emphasize the power of the pharaoh, and the fate of those who dare to fight him.

Summary

§ The so-called Abraham papyrus is the Book of Breathing (Breathing Permit) of the Book of the Dead.

§ This papyrus was seriously and deliberately modified to make it fit the story in *The Book of Abraham*.

§ Because in Smith's text, Abraham himself refers to Facsimile 1, speaking in the first person, it is not possible to divorce this papyrus from *The Book of Abraham*.

Facsimile No. 2—the Deliberate Forgery of the Hypocephalus

Figure 12. BoA Facsimile No. 2: Smith's Hypocephalus Fabrication

Source: The *Book of Abraham*, first printing in *The Times and Seasons*.

Figure 13. BoA Facsimile No. 2: Scribe's Copy Showing the Missing Sections

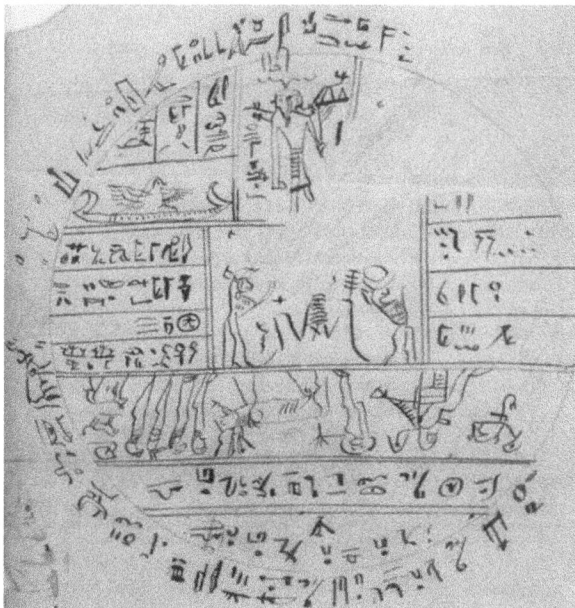

Vignette   Cobbling up Papyri to Forge a Hypocephalus

The focus of this chapter is not Smith's translation, or his effort to create an Egyptian language, but the fact of deliberate falsification of the facsimiles. We have already seen this in the remake of the lion couch scene. It is equally severe in the assembly of unassociated text materials to fabricate the hypocephalus. For example, the original text around the circumference is in cursive hieroglyphs, whereas the text copied in is in hieratic script. This is like suddenly shifting a text, say on the front of a Washington government building, from block printing to handwriting. Furthermore, the meaning of the hieratic text does not fit that of the cursive hieroglyphic text. It is interesting that this hieratic text was copied in upside-down,[354] apparently on purpose.

That it was no accident can be seen by examining the text on the horizontal lines 12-15. Not only is it also upside down, but note that the numbers are also upside down in the 1842 Times and Seasons *first printing (Figure 12). This means the scribe was holding the hypocephalus upside down when copying the text. It was easy to get the source text (Figures 8, 10 & 11) right side up since it was from the section of the papyrus to the left of the lion couch scene, an image clearly indicating the correct orientation. The scribe deliberately rotated the papyrus 180° before copying. He copied upside down to obscure the source of his borrowed texts, a clear sign of deliberate albeit clever deception. Presumably, Smith expected that the printer would not print the numbers upside down as well; their orientation was corrected in subsequent editions.*

Figure 14 shows another source papyrus used to obtain authentic material to occupy part of the missing section. The boat scene at the bottom right was copied into the empty space of what was originally a damaged hypocephalus (right-hand side of the 1st register). There was no rational for doing this, other than to produce an impressive and "complete" graphic to accompany his Book of Abraham. *It is not part of the Abraham story. Smith seemingly hoped to use it to demonstrate his Egyptian language credentials, much as he had attempted to do with his* Egyptian Alphabet and Grammar. *The text to the left of the lion couch scene (Figure 8, 10 & 11) was used to fill in some of the remaining damaged parts, which were labeled 12 through 15 (upside down in Figure 12). Note that on these lines the scribes had made an effort to copy some indistinct text still remaining on the hypocephalus, leaving the far right of each line empty. This can be seen in the scribe's copy (Figure 13), where the missing parts are blank. The fabricated lines were achieved by combining the indistinct effort of the scribe with the bits of text taken from the lines of Figure 11. Figure 15 shows the steps in the production of the final graphic. There, the result of combining the existing indistinct text and the inserted text can be seen in the image at the top right, and in the last four lines at the bottom, labeled 12-15. Clearly, this project required considerable time, planning and determination.*

---

[354] Ritner, *The Joseph Smith Egyptian Papyri*, 263-66.

Figure 14. Papyrus JS IV: Smith's Source for the Boat Insert

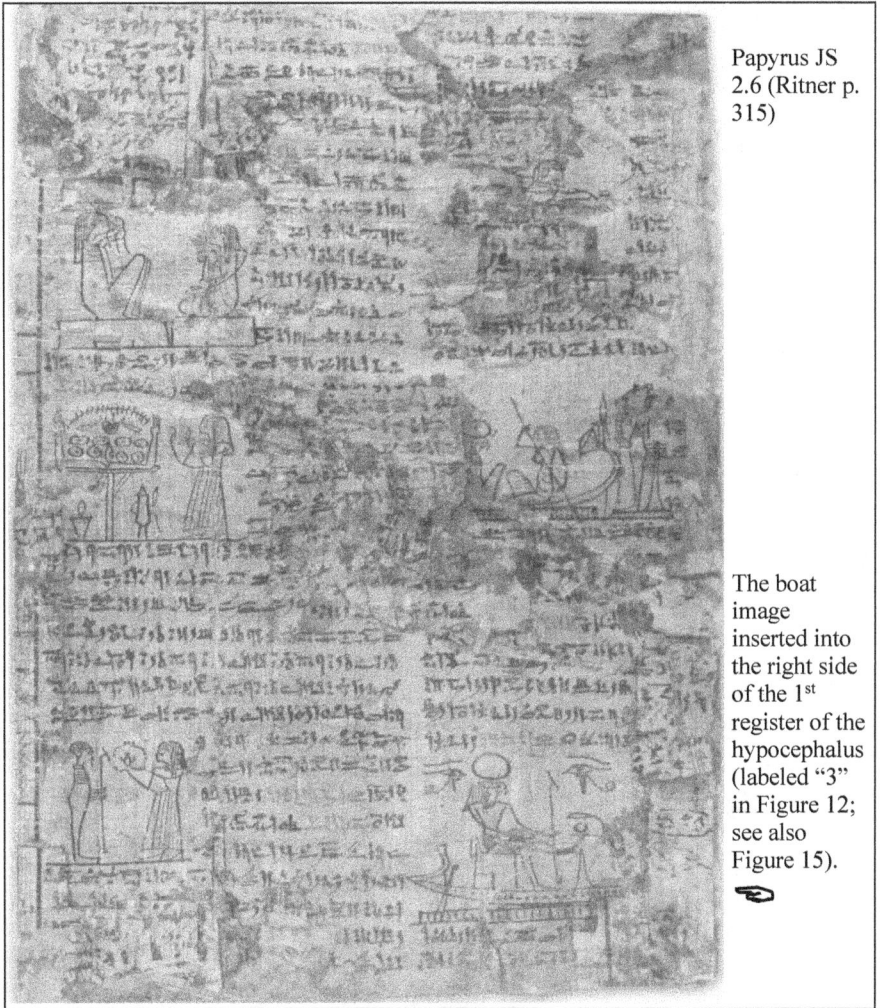

Papyrus JS 2.6 (Ritner p. 315)

The boat image inserted into the right side of the 1st register of the hypocephalus (labeled "3" in Figure 12; see also Figure 15).

The discovery and translation of these papyri are important largely because they show how the facsimiles were created, which shows conscious deception. Logically, it is not possible to conclude that Smith sincerely thought he was translating. The original hypocephalus has gone astray. Fortunately the copy in Figure 13 was made by one of Joseph Smith's scribes.

Figure 15. How to Customize a Hypocephalus
Combination of the scribe's copy of the hypocephalus, plus texts in JS 1.2 & JS 2.6.

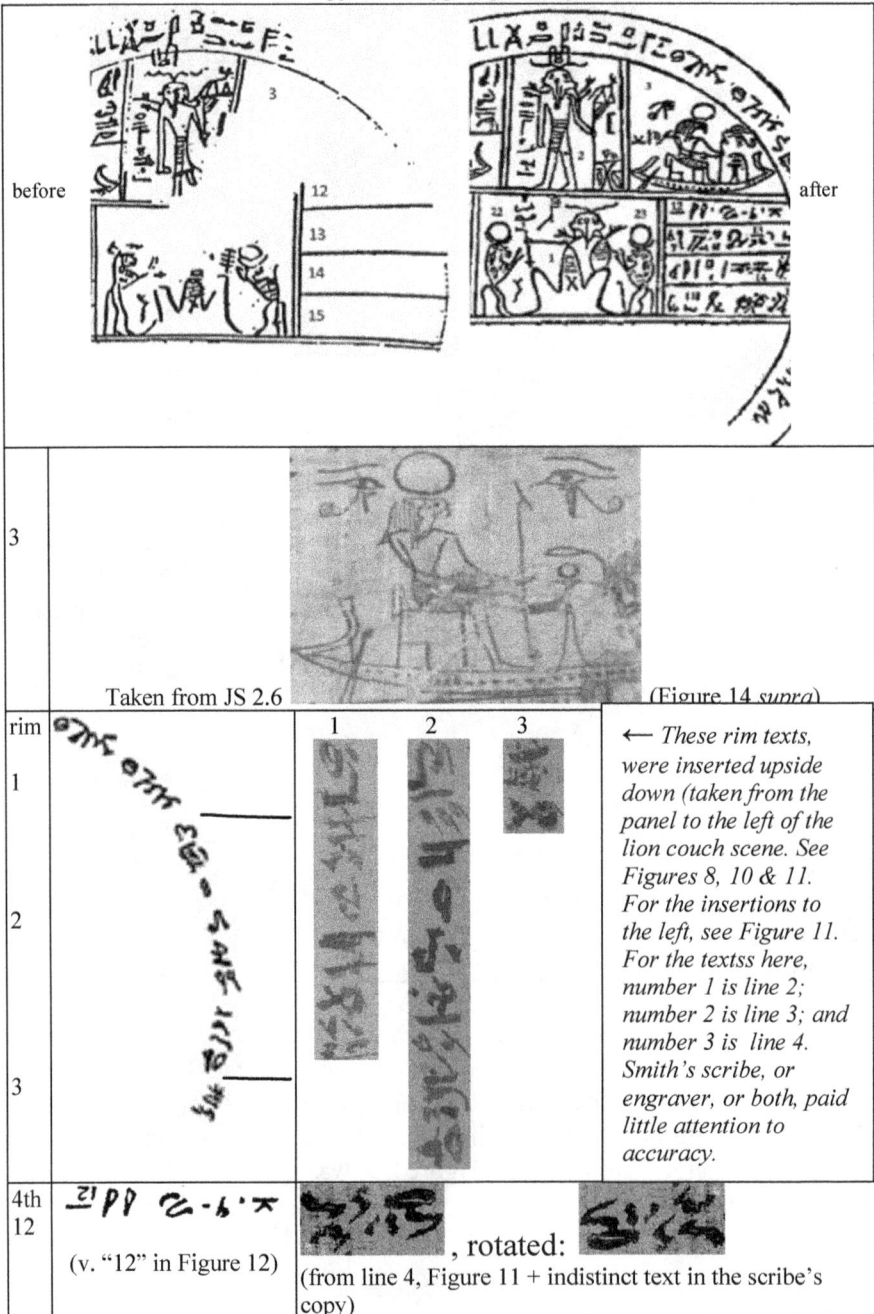

before					after

3		Taken from JS 2.6			(Figure 14 *supra*)

rim 1 2 3		1 2 3			← *These rim texts, were inserted upside down (taken from the panel to the left of the lion couch scene. See Figures 8, 10 & 11. For the insertions to the left, see Figure 11. For the textss here, number 1 is line 2; number 2 is line 3; and number 3 is line 4. Smith's scribe, or engraver, or both, paid little attention to accuracy.*
4th 12	(v. "12" in Figure 12)	, rotated: (from line 4, Figure 11 + indistinct text in the scribe's copy)			

5th 13	 (characters) (v. "13" in Figure 12)	 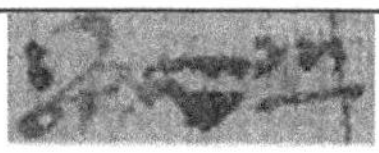 (characters) , rotated: (characters) (from line 4, Figure 11 + indistinct text in the scribe's copy)
6th 14	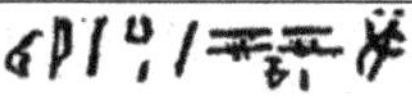 (characters) (v. "14" in Figure 12)	  (characters) , rotated: (characters) (from line 4, Figure 11 + indistinct text in the scribe's copy)
7th 15	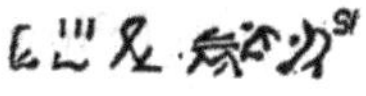 (characters) (v. "15" in Figure 12)	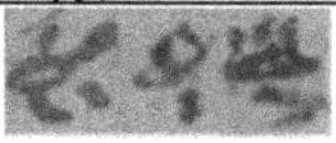 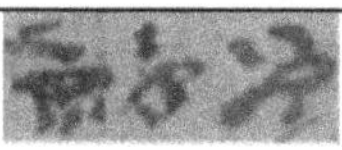 (characters) , rotated: (characters) (from line 4, Figure 11 + indistinct text in the scribe's copy)

Facsimile No. 3

Joseph Smith attributed a third illustration to Abraham (Figure 16). Unfortunately, the original was not among the papyri recovered by Dr. Atiya. Smith's "Explanation of the Above Cut," again, has nothing to do with the vignette.

Figure 16. *Book of Abraham* facsimile No. 3

EXPLANATION OF THE ABOVE CUT

1. Abraham sitting upon Pharaoh's throne, by the politeness of the king, with a crown upon his head, representing the Priesthood as emblematic of the grand Presidency in Heaven; with the scepter of justice and judgment in his hand.
2. King Pharaoh, whose name is given in the characters above his head.
3. Signifies Abraham in Egypt—referring to Abraham, as given in the ninth number of the Times and Seasons. (Also as given in the first facsimile of this book.)
4. Prince of Pharaoh, King of Egypt, as written above the hand.
5. Shulem one of the kin's principal waiters, as represented by the characters above his hand.
6. Olimlah, a slave belonging to the prince.
Abraham is reasoning upon the principles of Astronomy, in the king's court.

Source: The *Book of Abraham* (including the "Explanation").

The Book of Ether

Although the *Book of Ether* was published as a companion work along
with the *Book of Mormon*, it is a separate history, included possibly as a
relatively late decision, just in case there should turn out to be Pre-
Columbian ruins dating prior to the Nephites. It also helps explain how it
is that Lehi et al. found animals in the Americas that should have been
exterminated in Noah's flood. This record of the Jaredites is sufficiently
interesting to warrant inclusion here. The basic points are as follows:

1. A prophet Jared sought an exception from the Lord from divine wrath
at the Tower of Babel, so his group would not suffer the confusion of
tongues.
2. Wroth as he was, the Lord obliged him, and, guided Jared's group
through a wilderness to the sea for the voyage to the New World, kept
empty, just for them for an inheritance.
3. The Lord instructed them so they could build eight barges, totally sealed
"like a dish" with only a small pluggable hole in the top, so when plunged
to the depth of the sea they would not drown. Water pressure is not taken
into consideration; these submarines are made of wood.
4. The brother of Jared "did molten out of the rock sixteen small stones"
and the Lord touched each to emit light, providing light in the vessels when
submerged.
5. They gathered "flocks of every kind; and also of the seed of the earth of
every kind," the "fowls of the air," "a vessel in which they did carry with
them the fish of the waters" and honey bees. Thus each barge was a scaled-
down submarine Noah's ark. (Ether 1:41 & 2:1-3) Apparently the authors
wrote on the assumption that most or all animal life might not have existed
on isolated distant lands after Noah's flood (even fish?).
7. The Lord gave him two special stones, interpreters (seerstones).
8. They included food for themselves and all of these animals, sufficient
for their voyage of 344 days at sea.
9. They arrived in the New World and quickly populated much of the same
area where the Nephites and Lamanites would later be (but only as far
south as the "narrow neck of land"). Imitating the book of Genesis, the
Book of Ether begins with "begats." One individual has 31 children.
10. Shortly after their arrival, a leader named Shule smelted ore from a
mountain, and made steel swords, before the Iron Age elsewhere (not
bronze, or just iron, but steel).
11. They filled the land with many cities.

12. At the end, shortly before the arrival of Lehi, their internecine wars totally exterminated every last soul. In one sequence of battles, about two million warriors were killed on just one side. Then, during a truce of four years, each side rounded up every last soul of the Americas to what is now upstate New York, near the Hill Cumorah, for the last major confrontation: on each side, "when they were all gathered together, every one to the army which he would, with their wives and their children—both men, women and children being armed with weapons of war, having shields, and breastplates, and head-plates, and being clothed after the manner of war..." Eventually all were dead, except the two enemy commanders: Coriantumr and Shiz. The former killed the latter. Then Coriantumr wandered until eventually he arrived in Zarahemla, where he spent the last months of his life. In this manner, the *Book of Mormon* authors manage to provide for the possibility of pre-Nephite ruins, while retaining a central theme of the gold plates, to wit, that Lehi was guided to an empty land for his people's exclusive inheritance.

The Book of Moses

Even though the *Book of Mormon* is the founding scripture of the Mormon community, it contains little of what would become their distinctive theology. In June of 1830, shortly after the publication of the *Book of Mormon* and the founding of the new church, Joseph Smith turned his attention to more theological matters. From June of 1830 through February of 1831, he produced for his followers another book of scripture, in keeping with his role as having been called by God to restore important and precious truths in lost scripture. The work went through a redaction process (see also pp. 400-402):

> Examination of the original manuscripts of the JST shows that soon after the initial writing, Joseph further modified and revised these early chapters in a number of ways. This included a complete rewriting of the early chapters of Genesis, which was then followed in the editorial process by a number of interlinear inserts and deletions. In some instances, additional material was written on small pieces of paper and pinned to the manuscript at places needing still further correction.
>
> Thus, there were two drafts of the manuscript for the first twenty-four chapters of Genesis, with the second copy being more complete and presenting a more extensive text than the first draft...

> The portions of the JST that were published in the *Evening and Morning Star* and later incorporated into the *Book of Moses* are as follows: August 1832—Moses 7:1-69; March 1833—Moses 6:43-68; April 1833—Moses 5:1-16; Moses 6:52, 58-61; Moses 7:5-11; Moses 8:13-30.[355]

This redaction process, to produce not just one but two versions, is a good indication how ms$\mathcal{U}$ was done to produce the BoM ms$\mathcal{O}$ (the partially extant manuscript of the entire work dubbed "Original"). There were initial drafts edited to become completed drafts. Work on the BoM drafts was also done with the assistance of scribes. For the *Book of Moses*, these were (with the portion he assisted in): Oliver Cowdery (1:1-5:43), John Whitmer (5:43-6:18), Emma Smith (6:19-52), John Whitmer (6:52-7:1) and Sidney Rigdon (7:2-8:30). This list does not track specifically with the production of two versions. We are left to wonder who did what of each version. It is also not clear how the scribal work interfaced with the edits and insertion of additional material.

The mss were in the possession of the Reorganized Church of Jesus Christ of Latter Day Saints (currently the Community of Christ), and the material published above, and a partial copy in the possession of the LDS Church served as the basis for an inadequate version published in the 1851 edition of the *Pearl of Great Price*. Orson Pratt prepared the current version for the 1878 edition. It was officially canonized in 1880.

This text has been called a revision of Genesis. Although similar to parts of Genesis, it is inaccurate to call it a simple revision. Although it more or less revises Genesis in some chapters, it contains major totally extraneous expansions. In Moses 1, God is speaking to Moses regarding a mission for him, partially to show the close relationship between the deity and his prophet. Even in the chapters shadowing the Genesis text, there are theologically major insertions, such as: all things having been created spiritually in heaven before their material creation on the face of earth (3:5, 7); freewill (3:17); trees, beasts of the field and fowls of the air having souls (3:9, 19); God working with his Beloved Son from the beginning (4:1-4, 28, 5:6-15, 5:57-59; animal sacrifice as a similitude of the sacrifice of the Son of God (5:7); evil arising even in Adam's day in the form of secret combinations (5:51, 6:15); the institution of priesthood (6:7, 8:19); Cainan called the promised land (6:17); the atonement of the Son of God for original guilt (6:53) and the baptism of Adam and his receiving the gift of the Holy Ghost (6:65). The passages Joseph Smith chose for publication

---

[355] Robert J. Matthews, "How We Got the *Book of Moses*," *Ensign*, January 1986. (JST is the Joseph Smith Translation of the Bible.)

are an almost total miss with respect to these passages. Those published in his lifetime dealt exclusively with the stories of Enoch and Noah, comprising material not found in Genesis. It may be that he was hesitant to publish at that time yet more direct modifications of the KJV that his followers had grown up with. Perhaps too the passages he did not publish were those he wished to modify further.

One important point of its difference from Genesis is that the creation story purports to be the word of God himself, not the inspired writing of Moses or of some other ancient author or redactor. The creation in six days, the seventh day of rest, the creation of Adam from the dust, and of Eve from his rib, are all literally the word of the Lord, a point that is specifically emphasized in Moses 4:32. This does not mean that all or even most Mormons have been unable to reason their way around the details, to embrace the modern geological and biological sciences, but for some this text rendered the process more complicated, if not more difficult, and certainly more sensitive.

The Enoch story in the *Book of Moses* is not in itself notable, although it has been expanded beyond the original in Genesis. There, we find two Enochs. The first is a son of Cain, in Genesis 4:17: "and [the wife of Cain] bare Enoch: and he [Cain] builded a city, and called the name of the city, after the name of his son, Enoch." This Enoch sired Irad. The second Enoch is in the line of Adam in Genesis 5:18, 21-24 (cf. Moses 6:21). The main Enoch story in KJV Genesis follows:

21. And Enoch lived sixty and five years, and begat Methuselah:
22. And Enoch walked with God after he begat Methuselah three hundred years, and begat sons and daughters:
23. And all the days of Enoch were three hundred sixty and five years:
24. And Enoch walked with God: and he was not; for God took him.

The statement "and he was not; for God took him" has been interpreted to mean that he was not made to suffer death. We find in Hebrews 11:5, "By faith Enoch was translated [i.e. carried across] that he should not see death; and was not found, because God had translated him: for before his translation he had this testimony, that he pleased God."

The *Book of Moses* elaborates on this passage, detailing the calling God gave to Enoch and the message of his testimony. Enoch teaches the word and name of Jesus Christ, baptism and the gift of the Holy Ghost. This Enoch also builds a city, which is named Zion. Enoch saw the seed of Adam "save it was the seed of Cain, for the seed of Cain were black, and had not place among them."

This Enoch story is not remarkable in itself, apart from the fact that it has become a focus of LDS apologetics, beginning with a work of Hugh Winder Nibley, to be treated in Appendix 1.

The Doctrine and Covenants

Smith began by translating the words of an ancient prophet, but ultimately decided that he could cut out the middle man. Even before completing the *Book of Mormon*, Joseph Smith had discovered that he could simply receive a revelation from God, without the aid of gold plates, or even a seerstone. By the violent end of his career, he bequeathed to his church a large number of revelatory texts. These included instructions to the prophet himself, the will of God regarding the role of the cofounders of the church and other later principal persons, and details regarding the organization of the Church and the affairs of the community. But they also contain elements of an inchoate theology.

Revelations received and published were not final. Some of them have a history of revision, even from printing to printing. The early revelations exist in a few original copies, but mostly in copies and early publications. In 1831 a series of conferences were held in Hiram, Ohio, and on 1 November it was decided that 10,000 copies should be printed of what was to be called the *Book of Commandments*. Cowdery and John Whitmer arrived in Independence, Missouri, on 5 January 1832, where William W. Phelps was to establish his press and printing company. Although Smith Jr., Harris, Cowdery, Whitmer, Rigdon and Phelps were made stewards over the revelations and commandments, it appears that the person actually in editorial charge of the project was Cowdery. On 30 April, in a meeting of the council of the Literary Firm, the project was scaled down to an initial printing of 3,000 copies. Apparently as a stop gap, between June 1832 and July 1833, the earliest to appear were published in the *Evening and Morning Star*. Meanwhile, work was progressing on the publication of the *Book of Commandments*. But, on 20 July, citizens of Independence demolished the printing office throwing the press from the upper story window and scattering the type. Sheets of what had been done up to then on the *Book of Commandments* were gathered up, from which it was possible to assemble around 100 copies comprising 160 pages of the unfinished work. Between January and June 1835 the *Evening and Morning Star* again published commandments. After extensive research, H. Michael Marquardt[356] found that "if any original manuscripts (previous to 1835) were used, their exact wording was not adhered to... [the Star] altered texts, deleted previously published material and inserted editorial comments by Cowdery." Cowdery wrote, "On the revelations we merely say, that we were not a little surprised to find the previous print so different from the original."[357]   As an explanation, RLDS Church historian Richard P. Howard wrote:

> It may be that Cowdery's surprise at the remarkable differences between the "original" and that which he had previously published arose from the fact that in late 1834 or early 1835, as he was beginning to republish the revelations, he was working from a *different* "original"—different, that is, from the one he and John Whitmer had copied from in 1831 in preparing the *Book of Commandments* manuscript for the Independence printer.[358]

These changes do not include those done in the process of arriving at the text of the earlier "original" drafts. This skeletal review indicates the degree to which the revelations were subject to editing and modification. The revisions of those involved can be found in Marquardt's work.[359]

Other doctrines, now popularly associated with the Mormon community, were given in the *Doctrine and Covenants*. These include the text that counsels against tobacco, wine or strong drink, and hot drinks, given as a word of wisdom, and not a commandment, but the will of God (Section 89). It also includes the institution of polygamy, or plural wives, and a justification for concubinage at least for some (D&C 132). Another doctrine of interest came in Section 19, addressing relations with non-Mormons:

> 21. And I command you that you preach naught but repentance, and show not these things unto the world until it is wisdom in me.

---

[356] H. Michael Marquardt, *The Joseph Smith Revelations, Text and Commentary* (Salt Lake City: Signature Books, 1990), 10-11. See Marquardt, ibid, 3-19).

[357] Oliver Cowdery in the *Evening and Morning Star* (Kirtland reprint) 1 (June 1832), 16; reprinted Jan. 1835; see Marquardt, ibid, 11.

[358] Richard P. Howard, *Restoration Scriptures* (Independence, MO: Herald House, 1969), 202; Marquardt, *Joseph Smith Revelations*, 11.

[359] Marquardt, Joseph Smith Revelations. See also, *The Joseph Smith Papers, Vol. 2: Revelations and Translations, Published Revelations (Joseph Smith Papers: Revelations and Translations* by Robin Scott Jensen, Richard E. Turly, Jr., Riley M. Lorimer (Salt Lake City: Church Historian's Press, 2011).

22. For they cannot bear meat now, but milk they must receive; wherefore, they must not know these things, lest they perish.

In the BoM Book of Alma (12:9) we find the earliest articulation of this policy:

> And now Alma began to expound these things unto him, saying, It is given unto many to know the mysteries of God; nevertheless they are laid under a strict command, that they shall not impart only according to the portion of his word, which he doth grant unto the children of men, according to the heed and diligence which they give unto him.

This is essentially a doctrine of collective dissimulation when replying to prying questions about doctrines or practices outsiders might consider disturbing and/or unorthodox. It does not encourage telling untruths, but simply says that it is not always wise to tell the whole truth.

The *Book of Abraham* purports to be the writing of the patriarch by his own hand. At least chapters two through four of the *Book of Moses* clearly claim to be the word of God himself spoken to Moses. Likewise the D&C is mostly the word of the Lord spoken in the first person to Joseph Smith. When we see how they were produced, edited and partially rewritten as needed, we gain an understanding regarding their purely human character. But beyond this, we are given considerable insight into the process of producing the initial drafts of the books of the *Book of Mormon*, and of their Smith-Cowdery collaborative redaction to produce ms$\mathcal{U}$, prior to being copied to produce ms$\mathcal{O}$.

Orthodox LDS scholars have generally not attempted to defend Smith's efforts to translate the Abraham papyri, or to create an Egyptian language, but have primarily attempted to distance their prophet from these efforts. Dan Vogel has published the most comprehensive and competent critique of their efforts in *Book of Abraham Apologetics. A Review and Critique*, referred to *supra*.

The present study focuses on Smith's combination of unrelated elements from his Egyptian papyri to forge new papyri that comport with the text that he ascribed to Abraham, as evidence of the probity of his canonical output. This is the

Egyptology Issue

< Chapter 22 >

Heresy, Complicity and Self-Justification

Joseph Smith Sr. and Jr. were fully alienated from the religions that they knew. Although many have found the religious teaching of the BoM to be disorganized, in fact Smith and his colleagues had a clear vision of what they wanted, and even had to champion, not only to defend against condemnation as heretics, but to feel that they personally would stand in good stead before the bar of God.

Heresy: Charging All Christian Churches with Apostasy

Although John of Patmos, most probably the author of the *Book of Revelations*, directed his bitterness and the indignation of God against Rome, Christian writing by the time of the fall of that empire had already extended it to apply to religious movements that were deemed to be antichrist. The *Book of Mormon* continues this tradition, calling other churches the church of the devil, that great and abominable church, the *Whore of All the Earth* (1 Nephi 14:10). An angel tells Nephi (13:5):

> Behold the formation of a church which is most abominable above all other churches, which slayeth the saints of God, yea, and tortureth them and bindeth them down, and yoketh them with a yoke of iron, and bringeth them down into captivity.

This sounds born of Protestant antipapist fervor, but its terrible judgment is extended to all churches (1 Nephi 14:10): "Behold there are save two churches only; the one is the church of the Lamb of God, and the other is the church of the devil."

Similarly, we note the statement of Jesus to Joseph Smith in his First Vision account of c. 1832,

> behold the world lieth in sin and at this time and none doeth good no not one they have turned aside from the gospel and keep not <my> commandments they draw near to me with their lips while their hearts are far from me and mine anger is kindling against the inhabitants of the earth to visit them according to their ungodliness.

Needless to say, the LDS Church is not a likely candidate to sit at any ecumenical conference table. In opposition to the church(es) of the devil, its mission is to build the kingdom of Christ, and call all mankind to its true restored church, destined to become Christ's world government after his victory over Satan, when he comes again to reign on earth.

The Jews were not overlooked. They are treated as being Christ-killers, a stiff-necked people that also killed the prophets of God. 2 Nephi 10:3 declares:

> it must needs be expedient that Christ...should come among the Jews, among those who are the more wicked part of the world; and they shall crucify him..., and there is none other nation on earth that would crucify their God.

In Alma, notwithstanding some differences, one cannot help but feel that the Jews are caricatured in the form of the Zoramites. They worship in synagogues rather than churches, and deny the Christ. They believe that they were separated from others by God, and are His chosen children:

> Holy God, we believe that thou hast separated us from our brethren; and ...we believe that thou hast elected us to be thy holy children; and also thou hast made it known unto us that there shall be no Christ. (31:16)

Christian anti-Semitism is well represented in the BoM text.

The faithful in BCE pre-Columbian America were eventually organized into churches, were baptized and took upon themselves the name of Jesus Christ, i.e. they were called Christians (2 Nephi 31:5-17, Mosiah 18:13-18, Alma 19:35 & Helaman 3:24-26). They were taught the doctrine of repentance and redemption from their sins by the power of the sacrifice of Jesus on the cross. They even were urged to cross themselves (Alma 39:9). But, even when the Nephites were Christians, and baptized into the faith, the believers in the New World were commanded to obey the Law of Moses and keep all of its performances, from the seventh-century BCE to the crucifixion of Christ. Although left somewhat vague, it appears that the law was given to the Israelites to keep them sufficiently in line that their society would be suitable for Christ's mission. This anomaly is accentuated by the fact that the law's performances cannot save.

Heresy: Gazelem, a Prophet like Moses, a Patriarch like Joseph

Joseph Smith not only claimed to be a prophet, but virtually the greatest prophet of all. In the BoM he is referred to as Gazelem. "And the Lord said: I will prepare unto my servant Gazelem, a stone, which shall shine forth in darkness unto light, that I may discover unto my people who serve me, that I may discover unto them the works of their brethren..." (Alma 37:23-24) The stone is called an "interpreter." When his new church moved to Kirtland, the chief leaders were assigned aliases. An alias Smith assigned to himself was Gazelem. Moreover,

> Joseph [who was sold into Egypt] truly said: ... A choice seer will I raise up (2 Nephi 3:7)...And he shall be great like unto Moses... (2 Nephi 3:9) and unto him will I give power to bring forth my word unto the seed of thy loins. (2 Nephi 3:11) And his name [Joseph Smith] shall be called after me [Joseph, patriarch, son of Jacob]; and it shall be after the name of his father [Joseph Smith Sr.]. And he shall be like unto me. (2 Nephi 3:15)

To complete Smith's claim, we are informed, "And the king said that a seer is greater than a prophet." (Mosiah 8:15) So this seer is a latter-day prophet like unto Moses, and a patriarch like unto Joseph.

The condemnation of false prophets goes back millennia:

> Deuteronomy 18:20: But the prophet, which shall presume to speak a word in my name, which I have not commanded him to speak, or that shall speak in the name of other gods, even that prophet shall die.
> Jeremiah 23:16: Thus says the Lord of hosts: "Do not listen to the words of the prophets who prophesy to you, filling you with vain hopes. They speak visions of their own minds, not from the mouth of the Lord."
> Matthew 7:15: Beware of false prophets, who come to you in sheep's clothing but inwardly are ravenous wolves. (cf. 2 Peter)
> Revelation 20:10: And the Devil who had deceived them was thrown into the lake of fire and sulphur, where the Beast and the false prophet were, and shall be tormented day and night forever and ever.

In the early Christian era, after the decrees of the various ecumenical councils began to accumulate, and when religious and secular authority began to merge, conditions became favorable for judgments of heresy to be issued and implemented. The first Christian heretic, Priscillan, was executed in 385. After the edict of Theodosius (435) some were put to death just for possessing writings of Arius. Determination to extinguish the Albigensian heresy resulted in the Albigensian Crusade in 1208 and the Albigensian massacre in 1209. In 1239, 183 men, women and children were burned at the stake on the orders of the Dominican inquisitor. In 1826, the last person executed by the Spanish Inquisition was the Spanish schoolteacher Cayetano Ripoll after a two-year trial. Although John Wycliff, founder of the Lollard English translation (of the Bible) heresy, was protected by the queen, others of the Lollards were not. Sir John Oldcastle's revolt failed, and he was burned at the stake in 1417, while others were also executed. Heresy often has a political dimension. The most famous case is that of Joan d'Arc, who claimed to have had a vision of Saint Michael, as well as Saint Catherine and Saint Margaret, telling her to support the French against England, and support Charles VII for the French throne. When she was captured by the British, she was tried as an ally of Satan, and burned at the stake (30 May 1431).[360]

The LDS missionaries in England occasioned charges of heresy.[361] The *Book of Mormon* came under attack.[362] But the primary concern was Joseph Smith, whom they called a false prophet. Again in England, when the missionaries encountered mob violence, it was often instigated by religious leaders:

> 1839: Preston, religious leaders stirred up a mob ... stoned missionaries; 1840: Rector of the Church in Dymock (Gloucestershire) stirring up mobs; 1841: West Bromwich, much opposition from Methodist preachers; religious leaders in Preston stirred up the local citizenry with cries of 'false teacher' and 'false prophet'; 1841: West Bromwich, much opposition from Methodist preachers; village of Swan, a Primitive Methodist leader organized citizens; 1841 Tirley (Gloucestershire) a member was beaten & shortly later he died; 1840s at Tenby, Pembroke & Fishguard Methodist preachers harassed missionaries; 1856 Luton, a Wesleyan preacher urged an audience to drive the Mormons out of town; Southwold, Smith caricatured as having four horns.[363] (Zechariah 1:18; Revelations 9:13)

Track Record: Smith's Score Card as a Prophet

Although Smith succeeded in establishing his church, he disappointed on some important occasions. In early 1830, he received a revelation for four trusted brethren to travel to Kingston, Ontario, stating: "I grant unto my servent (sic) a privelige (sic) that he may sell <a copyright> through you speaking after the manner of men for the four Provinces (of Canada)." They understood that a buyer would be there. One assumes that this was

---

[360] *A History of Heresy in Ancient and Medieval Christianity*, downloaded on 23/07/2022, from www.Brewminate.com /a-history-of-heresy-in-ancient-and-medieval-christianity/

[361] Anonymous, *The New Heresy!! An Exposure of Mormonism* (Dunstable: Harper Twelvetrees, 1850)

[362] John Brindley, "A Short and Easy Method with the Mormonites," in *The Antisocialist Gazette* 8, 1 May 1842, 142.

[363] Wilford Woodruff, journals, quoted in Malcolm R. Thorp, *Sectarian Violence in Early Victorian Britain: The Mormon Experience, 1837-1860*, downloaded on 23/07/2022 from www.escholar.manchestwer.ac.uk.

when Smith was growing increasingly concerned as to whether Harris would pay the printer in Palmyra. They returned empty-handed and a bit confused. This revelation has not been included in the LDS canon.[364]

In 1833, disgruntled Missourians attacked Mormon settlers in Missouri. Some fled to Clay County. On February 24, Smith received a revelation to assemble a force and march to relieve his brethren there. About 200 arrived led by Smith. Zion's Camp, as it was called, withdrew without engagement. On June 22, a second revelation attributed the untoward consequences to transgressions. Zion's Camp's combatants suffered a cholera attack, with c. 70 sick and 14 dead.

Heresy: A New Bible to Correct the Corrupted Christian Bible

> The Gentiles do stumble exceedingly, because of the most plain and precious parts of the gospel of the Lamb which have been kept back by that abominable church, which is the mother of harlots, saith the Lamb... I will bring forth unto them...much of my gospel, which shall be plain and precious, saith the Lamb [i.e. the *Book of Mormon*]. (1 Nephi 13:34)

The historical heretical movements have been based on unorthodox interpretations of scriptures in the Bible. They do not introduce an entirely new bible. A partial exception is certain extra-Biblical Gnostic books; for example, the *Gospel of Thomas*, or the *Gospel of Mary*. Some of these were written before the canonical era. They were declared heretical primarily in that they were not selected for inclusion in the Christian canon due to contents rejected at Nicaea. A more striking exception is the (late) *Gospel of Barnabas*, written to promote Islam. Considered to be pseudepigraphic (i.e. falsely ascribed) it is in two manuscripts, one in Italian, and the other in Spanish. The introduction of a whole new bible is unprecedented and not evidenced.

The *Book of Mormon* is well aware that its introduction will draw fire from the Christians. It anticipates that they will say, "A *Bible! We Have Got a Bible!*" (2 Nephi 29:3).

Before the establishment of organized Christian churches, even though sacred books were revered, some were translated when the people no longer understood the language of the original text. Respecting what eventually became the books of the Hebrew Bible (*tanakh*), translation into Aramaic was done in Babylon and Palestine. Translation into Greek was done in Alexandria. For the early Christian churches, the NT and OT

---

[364] *Manuscript Book 1*, in *Joseph Smith Papers*.

were initially translated into Vetus Latina, which preceded the Vulgate, the translation achieved by Jerome in the fourth century CE. This text was elevated to some sort of inviolable status, and it became forbidden to translate it.

In translating, some leeway is allowed in rendering the meaning: viz, translator's license. But how much change can one permit? A somewhat draconian measure is zero translation. The popes of Rome have a long history of exacting penalties for translating the Vulgate Bible. In 1215 Pope Innocent III issued a law commanding "that they shall be seized for trial and penalties, who engage in the translation of the sacred volumes."[365] Many popes have maintained this legacy. In England, John Wycliffe sparked and led a movement to translate the Bible from the Vulgate. First, he and hi colleagues completed most or all of the English NT, and then the OT (c. 1382-1395). Rome attempted to imprison him, but he was protected by the Queen. He was declared a heretic posthumously, and in 1428, 43 years after his death, the Roman Catholic Church exhumed his bones and burned them. On October 6, 1535, in England, William Tyndale was first strangled and then burned at the stake for translating both the OT, from Hebrew, and the NT, from Greek. It seems possible to assume that introducing a totally new bible, while asserting that the Christian Bible had been corrupted, having undergone changes and deletions, would have been deemed an even greater heresy.

Joseph Smith, and possibly also his colleagues, had reason to be concerned for their security. He had to face legal procedures in 1826 and 1830. These were possibly mere harassment. Smith had to be tried as a disorderly fellow, apparently due to the lack of a more specific law, and possibly the judge was uncomfortable with this, being cognizant of the old established legal principle: *nullum crimen sine lege*. On March 24, 1832, Joseph and Sydney Rigdon were tarred and feathered, possibly in connection with Church financial issues. While yet in Kirtland, Ohio, Smith engaged Orrin Porter Rockwell to be his personal bodyguard. In Missouri, the Mormon press was attacked and destroyed (1833). Smith was arrested (1838) and charged with treason. In Nauvoo, the city charter allowed a militia and Smith made himself its commander. In spite of all

---

[365] Author unknown, *Illustrations of popery. The "mystery of iniquity" unveiled: in its "Damnable heresies, lying wonders, and strong delusion* (New York: J.P. Callender [?], 1838), 387. Callender appears on the title page where one usually finds the notice of the publisher, although it is he who registered the work in "the clerk's office of the district court of the southern district of New York." We also find: "stereotyped by Francis F. Ripley." Apparently he was the printer.

his precautions, he was murdered by an anti-Mormon mob on June 27, 1844. Although the issues for the Missouri anti-Mormons were various, the issues that brought the initial charges against him that landed him in Carthage Jail arose from the destruction of the press of the *Nauvoo Expositor*, which had charged him with teaching principles contrary to long-held Christian beliefs: polygamy, polytheism and exaltation (the doctrine that worthy Latter-day Saints can become gods and goddesses).

Heresy: A Polytheistic Godhead, & Deification by Exaltation

Most early converts would have assumed that their new religion asserts monotheism, a fundamental defining doctrine of Christianity. They could not have anticipated that the LDS godhead would be polytheist, nor also that worthy members can be exalted, by which they too can become gods and goddesses. This is a case where more is less.

> If a man marry a wife by my word, which is my law, and by the new and everlasting covenant, and it is sealed unto them by the Holy Spirit of promise, by him who is anointed, unto whom I have appointed this power and the keys of this priesthood; and it shall be said unto them– Ye shall inherit thrones, kingdoms, principalities, and powers, dominions, all heights and depths...it shall be done unto them in all things whatsoever my servant hath put upon them, in time, and through all eternity; and shall be of full force when they are out of the world; and they shall pass by the angels, and the gods, which are set there, to their exaltation and glory in all things, as hath been sealed upon their heads, which glory shall be a fulness and a continuation of the seeds forever and ever.
> Then shall they be gods, because they have no end; therefore shall they be from everlasting to everlasting, because they continue; then shall they be above all, because all things are subject unto them. Then shall they be gods, because they have all power, and the angels are subject unto them. (D&C 132:19-20)

The companion doctrines of polytheism and exaltation continue to be a major obstacle to accepting LDS theology as Christian, since these concepts are seen to be the antithesis of what Christianity is. Today, Most LDS are unaware that their B*ook of Mormo*n strongly asserts the doctrine of the trinity, a three-in-one godhead: "behold, this is the doctrine of Christ, and the only and true doctrine of the Father, and of the Son, and of the Holy Ghost, which is one God, without end." (2 Nephi 31:21; also Alma 11:38; Alma 11:39; Mosiah 15:16) This may have scored points for the LDS if Joseph Smith had not subsequently replaced this key doctrine with polytheism. Moreover, LDS deities are anthropomorphic and corporeal: "The Father has a body of flesh and bones as tangible as man's; the Son also; but the Holy Ghost has not a body of flesh and bones, but is a personage of Spirit. Were it not so, the Holy Ghost could not dwell in us." (D&C 130:22)

Heresy: Polygamy, Practiced by Worthy LDS

The issue of polygamy fanned the existing flames of sectarian opposition and fueled violence against Mormons. It was seen as being contrary to Christian law, unjust to women and detrimental to the family. Its role in radical splinter groups has continued this negativity to the present day. The law that made polygamy illegal was challenged twice all the way to the Supreme Court, once in a Utah case and once in an Idaho case. For a long time it undercut efforts on the part of the Church to lay claim to the moral high ground.

Complicity: Testimony in Support of Heresy

Some critics of the founders of the Mormon movement focus mainly on Joseph Smith, for whom they have little good to say. Some are less harsh on Oliver Cowdery. Here, our focus is on how these key individuals might have seen themselves, and how in their own mind they might have justified their project and what they were willing to do to implement it. Here we are narrowing our focus on testimony. How substantial were the events that they testified to, events that cannot have been true (Table 43), and how often might they have been called upon by converts and others regarding their testimonies? (Table 44)

Orthodox LDS scholars have been desirous to identify as many pre-1830 kin and friends of Joseph Smith who presumably claimed to have had first-hand experience with the gold plates or associated relics. Testimonies may attest to visual and/or tactile experience. The latter usually refers to hefting them. These testimonies are of two different provenances. Assertions may have come down to us either from the individuals themselves, or from statements in writings of others. An example of the first of these is statements by Lucy Smith about her own experience, published in her book. A trickier example is the statements of the eleven witnesses, presumably signed by them, although we lack the documents with the signatures. A clearer example of the second type is the statement attributed to Alvah Beeman (Beman/ Beaman), that when he helped to modify a box originally for glass window panes and helped to put the plates into the box, "he heard them jink."[366] Joseph B. Noble, his son-in-law, wrote that Beeman "was permited (sic) to handle the plates with a thin cloth hovering over them."[367]

In addition to handling the plates through a tow frock, Mother Lucy Smith stated that, after returning from the hill, he [Joseph] placed [the Urim and Thummim]

> into my hands, and upon examination, [I] found that it consisted of two smooth three-cornered diamonds set in glass, and the glasses were set in silver bows, which were connected with each other in much the same way as old fashioned spectacles...
>
> Soon after this, he came in from work, one afternoon, and... handed me the breastplate spoken of in his history.
>
> It was wrapped in a thin muslin handkerchief, so thin that I could see the glistening metal, and ascertain its proportions without any difficulty.
>
> It was concave on one side, and convex on the other, and extended from the neck downwards, as far as the centre of the stomach of a man of extraordinary size. It had four straps of the same material, for the purposes of fastening it to the breast, two of which ran back to go over the shoulders, and the other two were designed to fasten to the hips. They were just the width of two of my fingers, (for I measured them,) and they had holes in the end of them, to be convenient for fastening.
>
> The whole plate was worth at least five hundred dollars: after I had examined it, Joseph placed it in the chest with the Urim and Thummim.[368]

In a similar vein, Emma Smith stated that during the translation,

> ...the plates often lay on the [table in our home], without any attempt at concealment, wrapped in a small linen tablecloth, which I had given him [Joseph Smith] to fold them in. I once felt... the plates, as they thus lay on the table, tracing their outline and shape. They seemed to be pliable like thick paper, and would rustle with a metallic sound when the edges were moved

---

[366] Martin Harris, *Tiffany's Monthly* 5 (Aug. 1859), 167.

[367] Joseph B. Noble, Journal, LDS archives, in Marquardt, *Rise of Mormonism*, 58n45.

[368] Lucy Smith, *Biographical Sketch of Joseph Smith the Prophet and His Progenitors for Many Generations* (Liverpool: published for Orson Pratt and S. Richards, 1853) 101, 106-7; also Milton Backman, *Eyewitness Accounts of the Restoration* (Salt Lake City: Deseret Book Company, 1986).

by the thumb, as one does sometimes thumb the edges of the book... I did not attempt to handle the plates, other than [through the linen cloth][369]

Here follows a review of testimonies:

Table 43. Claimed Experiences of Persons Purported to Be Witnesses

Name	What They Claimed to Have Seen or Heard	provenance
Joseph Smith, Jr.	saw gold plates, Urim & Thummim, breastplate, sword, God the Father, the Son, angel Moroni, John the Baptist, Peter, James & John. Heard the voice of all of the above. Laying on of hands of John for the Aaronic priesthood. Same by Peter, James & John for the Melchizedek priesthood.	Self
Oliver Cowdery	saw gold plates, Urim & Thummim, breastplate, sword, angel Moroni, John the Baptist, Peter, James & John. Saw the plates & Urim & Thummim. Heard the voice of all of the above. Laying on of hands of John for the Aaronic priesthood.	Self
Martin Harris	saw gold plates, Urim & Thummim, breastplate, sword, angel Moroni. Hefted the plates in Smith's home under a cloth. Held the plates on his knee an hour and a half. May have seen the Urim and Thummim in the chest; handled the plates one by one. Heard the angel's voice.	Self
David Whitmer	saw gold plates, Urim & Thummim, breastplate, sword, director, Brass Plates, angel Moroni. Heard the angel's voice.	Self
Joseph Smith Sr.	handled and hefted the plates at the Smith home in a frock. Saw, handled and hefted the plates in the woods.	Self
Samuel Smith	handled and hefted the plates at the Smith home in a frock. Saw, handled and hefted the plates in the woods.	Self
Hyrum Smith	handled and hefted the plates at the Smith home. Saw, handled and hefted the plates in the woods.	Self
Peter Whitmer Sr.	saw, handled and hefted the plates in the woods.	Self

[369]Emma Smith, statement to her son, Joseph Smith III, February 4-10, 1879, cited in *The Saints' Herald* 26 (October 1, 1879), 289-90; in Backman, *Eye Witness Accounts*, 107.

John Whitmer	saw, handled and hefted the plates in the woods.	Self
Christian Whitmer	saw, handled and hefted the plates in the woods.	Self
Jacob Whitmer	saw, handled and hefted the plates in the woods	Self
Hiram Page	saw, handled and hefted the plates in the woods.	Self
William Smith	handled and hefted the plates at the Smith home in a frock.	Lucy Smith
Lucy Mack Smith	handled and hefted the plates, examined the breastplate, all under a thin cloth, allowing her to see them. Handled and examined the Urim & Thummim.	Self
Emma Smith	handled the plates under a cloth & moved them from place to place to do her work.	Self
Alvah Beeman	helped put the covered plates in the glass-box.	Martin Harris
Lucy Harris	handled & hefted the plates under a cloth according to her husband.	Martin Harris
Harris' daughter	handled & hefted the plates under a cloth.	Martin Harris
Mary Musselman Whitmer	reportedly saw the gold plates	David Whitmer
Katherine Smith Salisbury	hefted the plates & found them to be very heavy	self

What are we to understand from these claims? When Smith and Harris had the visitation event in the grove, Smith described it as follows: " the same vision was opened to our view; at least it was again to me...whilst at the same moment, Martin Harris cried out...'Tis enough, 'tis enough; mine eyes have beheld, mine eyes have beheld.'"[370] It seems that for Smith it was possible for him to once again apprehend the angel, the plates, and the relics, but possibly not Harris. One can readily conclude from this that the vision was with "spiritual eyes." Otherwise, both should have beheld the same thing.

Spiritual sight is mentioned in the testimony of Newel Knight. He affirmed that Smith had cast a devil out of him and that he had seen the devil. When asked what the devil looked like, he first got this questioner, Mr. Seymour, to admit that he personally did not understand "the things of the spirit." Knight then replied, "it will be of no use to tell you what the

---

[370] *Joseph Smith History*, 1839, in Vogel I, 85.

devil looks like, for it was a Spiritual Sight, and Spiritually discerned; and of course you would not understand it."[371]

The early accounts refer to material, tactile experiences, including handling directly, hefting, feeling through a flimsy sheer cloth cover, and hearing the metallic sounds of the plates. Since the gold plates and associated relics never really existed, one is tempted to conclude that these bearers of testimony were either easily deluded or quite minimally had a facile commitment to notions of truth. Moreover, when they express their experiences that they themselves consider to be instances of spiritual sight, or spiritual discernment, they use language that they know will be understood by many if not most people as being conventional material experiences. In this practice, there is a degree of dissimulation.

The frequency that one might be called upon to bear this sort of testimonial depends in part on activity in the new Church. In these offices, it is impossible that there would be any dearth of situations where bearing one's testimony would be expected, even when accosted at Church functions. The accounts of Smith and Cowdery regarding their ordination by John the Baptist and Peter, James and John, clearly indicate that Cowdery was already a total confederate. Martin Harris' claim regarding the visitation, plus his claim to have held the plates on his knee, shows that at some point he too had become confederate.

Table 44. Activities of Key Founders

Oliver Cowdery	apostle, Assistant President of the Church, Presiding High Council Member and editor or editorial board member of several Church publications,
Martin Harris	a high priest, served a mission to the Midwest, Pennsylvania & New York, member of the Kirtland High Council and marched from Kirtland to Missouri with Zion's Camp.
David Whitmer	apostle, a High Priest, President of the High Council of Zion (in Missouri) and President of the Church Zion
Joseph Smith Sr.	missionary, first Presiding Patriarch of the Church.
Hyrum Smith	presiding officer of the Colesville branch, proselyting missions to Missouri & Ohio, marched with Zion's Camp, Second Counselor in the First Presidency of the Church, Presiding Patriarch
Samuel Smith	served a number of missions, one of 12 members of the new High Council

---

[371] *Newel Knight Journal*, circa 1846, in Vogel, IV, 33.

William Smith	an inaugural member of the Quorum of the Twelve, ordained an apostle, editor of the pro-Mormon *The Wasp* in Nauvoo and Presiding Patriarch
Peter Whitmer Sr.	—
John Whitmer	First Church Historian, a High Priest, Second Counselor to the President of the Church Zion, Editor of the *Latter Day Saints' Messenger and Advocate*, a cofounder of Far West (with Phelps)
Christian Whitmer	a leading elder in Jackson County, MO, and a member of the High Council in Far West, MO.
Jacob Whitmer	—
Hiram Page	moved to Kirtland, then Missouri, helped found Far West
Lucy Smith	Active in supporting her family in their Church duties, author of her book (a history of her family, and material for Church history)
Emma Smith	compiled the first Church hymnal (with W.W. Phelps), first Relief Society general president

NOTA BENE: We are not investigating the nature of the witnesses' experience, such as asking "Was it material/corporeal?" Or, "Was it spiritual?" "Did they see with their bodily eyes, or with their mind's eyes?" What we are addressing is what they testified to, regardless of the actual nature of their experience.

Complicity: Baseless Fears, a Lame Cover-up and Confederates All

The issue of collusion is clarified by matters associated with the loss of the 116 pages. When the *Book of Lehi* was stolen, the unlikelihood of Smith's cover-up must have been quite obvious to his colleagues. They may well have thought, "The prophet doth protest too much, methinks." He issued a revelation to explain his reaction. All LDS accounts are based on an assertion claimed to be from God, i.e. that "Satan hath put it into their hearts to alter the words which you have caused to be written... because they have altered the words, they read contrary from that which you translated and caused to be written... that by lying they may say they have caught you in the words which you have pretended to translate." (D&C 10-13)

Was this really a possibility, or even conceivable? Clearly one could not erase passages in the lost pages, written in ink, and then write in new wording. A note by Skousen regarding ms𝒪 is pertinent:

Normally, a deletion is a crossout (or lining out of the text)...Sometimes deletions were effected by erasure or blotting of ink...Of course, erasures and blotting typically lead to ink smearing. A further indicator of erasure is paper abrasion, so that if the erased text is overwritten, the overwriting is uneven and may show ink feathering...In addition, there are cases where the scribe first tried to erase the text, then lined it out [apparently seeing that overwriting would not turn out well].[372]

If Smith did redo the text word-for-word, and the original did surface largely modified, but with substantial unmodified sections word-for-word the same as Smith's original text, the improbability of even this achievement would already be proof of his divine assistance in producing the two texts. To be truly convincing, such an imposture would have required redoing the entire text or nearly all sections of it, with important differences. This would require writing a very long text in the handwriting of Martin Harris, and two other scribes known to have taken dictation on occasion. Surely this was likewise impossible.

In other words, the threat alleged in Smith's revelation patently did not exist. Most of the witnesses had enough practice with the quill to know this. The first thing a beginner would learn, the hard way, was if one makes a mistake, attempting to correct it risks making a bigger mess. Cowdery, the entire Smith family, and indeed the Whitmers as well, must have known this, and must also have detected his ruse, and realized that Joe Jr. could not reproduce the same text. Moreover, its corollary was equally patently obvious, that there were no gold plates. This being the case, his revelation was based on an impossible claim, devised partly to sidestep the thief's challenge, *but principally to justify replacing Lehi with the Book of Nephi, which was necessary to make a new start on a new Bible*. Tough-minded scholarly analysis of this episode has to comport with the clear fact that the claimed threat was impossible, and all key members of the BoM team were fully aware of the imposture, although, as long as they drew breath, they continued to pursue their own self-interest in testifying to the plates (i.e. the BoM heresy).

The decision to replace all of Lehi with a replacement text enabled Smith to get on with the BoM project without delay and with a clean slate. Even so, the fact that he chose to address this issue in his preface to the *Book of Mormon*, shows the enduring degree of his concern.

---

[372] Royal Skousen, *The Original Manuscript of the Book of Mormon: Typographical Facsimile of the Extant Text* (Provo, UT: Foundation for Ancient Research and Mormon Studies, 2001), 21.

Clearly the twelve witnesses (including Joseph Jr.) had all become confederate to a significant extent. Their claims, plus the level of their involvement in the early history of the church and its scriptures, all indicate this. In the case of others, some sort of plates or heavy object wrapped up in linen or a tow cloth pillowcase could have given rise to their experience, such as that of Alvah Beeman, Mrs. Harris and her daughter, whose "testimonies" are ascribed, and not directly quoted.

However, all involved could have agreed with the general historical outline of the BoM as being something close to what they thought must have actually happened, and they may have agreed that the doctrinal teachings in the BoM narrative were in some measure inspired.

Hell & Salvation: Then Ye May Know with a Perfect Knowledge

The Christian hell has generally been eternal fiery torment. The BoM reaffirms the existence of the most terrible traditional Christian hell:

> And assuredly, as the Lord liveth, for the Lord God hath spoken it, and it is his eternal word, which cannot pass away, that they who are righteous shall be righteous still, and they who are filthy shall be filthy still; wherefore, they who are filthy are the devil and his angels; and they shall go away into everlasting fire; prepared for them; and their torment is as a lake of fire and brimstone, whose flame ascendeth up forever and ever and has no end. (2 Nephi 9:16; cf. 2 Nephi 9:19 & 2 Nephi 9:19)

From as early as the composition of Alma, the foundation was being laid to escape the charge of offending God, impersonating God and exploiting, distorting, adding to, deleting from and rewriting His word. The founders were sufficiently well-grounded in religion to be grievously cognizant of the accusations that they would face. It seems probable that Mormon founders testifying to experiences that cannot have happened, thereby creating and promoting the Mormon heresies, might fear that doing so would put the testifiers' souls in eternal jeopardy. Very early on, they needed a rational for exculpation and justification, as well as signs that the new bible and their church were from God. We find these in the *Book of Moroni*:

> I show unto you the way to judge; for every thing which inviteth to do good, and to persuade to believe in Christ, is sent forth by the power and gift of Christ; wherefore ye may know with a perfect knowledge it is of God. (7:16)

But whatsoever thing persuadeth men to do evil, and believe not in Christ, and deny him, and serve not God, then ye may know with a perfect knowledge it is of the devil; for after this manner doth the devil work, for he persuadeth no man to do good, no, not one; neither do his angels... (7:17)

a bitter fountain cannot bring forth good water; neither can a good fountain bring forth bitter water; wherefore, a man being a servant of the devil cannot follow Christ; and if he follow Christ he cannot be a servant of the devil. (7:11)

Their works being good must be of God. They will guide persons of faith away from that church of the Devil, and its corrupt teachings into the true gospel. Their new bible will enable the Indians to know that they descend from Israel, and will bring them to Christ in preparation for His imminent Advent. It will likewise urge both Jew and Gentile to embrace the true teachings of the Lord, and a life of good works. Such praiseworthy works can only come from God.

How Ye May Know: Active Cultivation of Subjective Confirmation

A bible without believers is an empty vessel. From the beginning, the *Book of Mormon* narrative has sought to present evidence for itself, as an authentic collection of writings of Israelite prophets in the New World. Early in this effort, the BoM adduces Biblical evidence: the mention of isles of the sea (Isaiah 24:15/2 Nephi), of a stick of Joseph that would be joined to the stick of Judah (Ezekiel 37:15-17/2 Nephi), of speech low out of the dust (Isaiah 29:4/2 Nephi) and of a sealed book that the wise could not read (Isaiah 29:11-12/2 Nephi). This initial approach, found in Nephi, was calculated to appeal to those who rely on the rational analysis of scripture.

Perhaps due to increased experience on the part of Smith in teaching others, or perhaps due to the wisdom of colleagues, further into the BoM narrative, more weight is given to feeling rather than scriptural reasoning. The metaphor is of a seed (the word of God) growing in one's bosom, if it is properly nurtured (by faith, etc.). The word "seed" refers exclusively to progeny in all passages up to Alma 32: 28-29, 36-37 & 41, where it is used to school the reader re how to recognize mildly euphoric feelings to "know" that the "word" (minimally, the BoM) is true:

28. Now, we will compare the word unto a seed. Now, if ye give place, that a seed may be planted in your heart, behold, if it be a true seed, or a good seed, if ye do not cast it out by your unbelief, that ye will resist the

Spirit of the Lord, behold, it will begin to swell within your breasts; and when you feel these swelling motions, ye will begin to say within yourselves—It must needs be that this is a good seed, or that the word is good, for it beginneth to enlarge my soul; yea, it beginneth to enlighten my understanding, yea, it beginneth to be delicious to me.
29. Now behold, would not this increase your faith? ...
36. Behold I say unto you, Nay; neither must ye lay aside your faith, for ye have only exercised your faith to plant the seed that ye might try the experiment to know if the seed was good.
37. And behold, as the tree beginneth to grow, ye will say:
Let us nourish it with great care, that it may get root, that it may grow up, and bring forth fruit unto us. And now behold, if ye nourish it with much care it will get root, and grow up, and bring forth fruit.
41. But if ye will nourish the word, yea, nourish the tree as it beginneth to grow, by your faith with great diligence, and with patience, looking forward to the fruit thereof, it shall take root; and behold it shall be a tree springing up unto everlasting life.

This is all about feeling: "when you feel these swelling motions."

The seed, faithfully planted and nurtured, must be kept safe from the buffeting winds of contrary information. Smith delivered a revelation to assist members with their interlocutors:

And I command you that you preach naught but repentance, and show not these things unto the world until it is wisdom in me.
For they cannot bear meat now, but milk they must receive; wherefore, they must not know these things, lest they perish. (D&C 19:21)

This is a strategy of information nondisclosure to the point of collective dissimulation. However, by circumscribing the recommended range of missionary discussion, it also reduced the probability that an elder would be led into difficult discussions that could undermine his own faith. As we were counseled in the French East Mission in the 1960s, "Remember, you have been sent to teach, not to be taught."

Fruits Good Fruits vs Evil Fruits

for there is nothing which is good save it comes from the Lord;
and that which is evil cometh from the devil. (Omni 1:25, cf. Alma 5:40)

Ye shall know them by their fruits. (Matthew 7:16)

Fruits: Mission to the Cursed Israelites of America

The *Book of Mormon* overall strives to give Native Americans an Israelite identity, and a role in ushering in the new millennium, by accepting Jesus as their Savior, and eventually rejoining the other tribes of Israel. Some Eurocentric-Americans might consider this to be an ethnic upgrade.

> As the knowledge of a Savior has come into the world, even so shall the knowledge of my people [Nephites, Jacobites, Josephites and Zoramites] come to the knowledge of the Lamanites... and for this very purpose are these plates preserved...and that they may believe the gospel and rely upon the merits of Jesus Christ, and be glorified through faith in his name (BC 2)

Euro-Americans might have thought that the Lamanites would jump at the chance to be Israelites, albeit fallen, cursed with a dark and loathsome skin, and a wild and indolent character. In fact, if successful, this would rob them of their own history and culture in which they can legitimately take great pride.

The religion of the Lamanites has next to nothing to do with the Pre-Columbian Americas. In religious debates with non-Christians, these antagonists of the Nephite narrative are depicted as being godless. The closest thing to a Pre-Columbian non-Christian deity mentioned in the BoM text is what is sometimes called the Great Spirit. Settlers had derived this from beings such as *Wakan Tanka* of the Lakota, which is more accurately translated Great Mystery, a force possibly beyond human understanding, which is the power of the sacredness that resides in all things. It may be that before European contact, it referred to a group of sacred beings. Another religious entity with similar import is Manitou (of the Algonquian peoples), the spiritual and fundamental life force. Christian missionaries found that creating the English term "Great Spirit" drawn from these concepts was the most effective way to explain their own concept of "God." This practice would have been familiar to Joseph Smith and his colleagues.

None of the indigenous North American religious beings occur in the BoM, nor any of the many deities of Central and South America. Ultimately, the bottom line is that all of Lamanite and Nephite religion derives from the religious culture of nineteenth-century New England. This includes the condemnation of idolatry, found in the Bible and sermons. There is no trace of the religions of the territories where Nephite missionaries should have been in competition for the hearts and minds of the indigenous populations such as the Lakota, Maya and Olmecs.

Potential converts in an age imbued with millennial expectations would view this BoM teaching in a very positive light.

Fruits: Smith's Early Missions to Convert the Indians

Only months after the establishment of the Church, Smith sent a mission to the borders of the Lamanites. During 1830-31 they met with and taught Indians along the way. After being ordered out of the [Delaware] "Indian Territory", they returned to Independence, Missouri. In 1843, Smith sent a mission to the Society Islands. This was inspired by the BoM story of Hagoth, a shipbuilder who took Nephites into the sea west. This gave rise to th notion that some Pacific Island peoples might be descended from these Nephites. During the 1830-31 period, the missionaries in Missouri failed to baptize any Indians, at least as far as can be documented. But their labors in the Polynesian Islands achieved a greater harvest, such that today Tonga is largely LDS. Overall, results have been slow and uneven.

Fruits: The Rejection of Infant Baptism

The doctrine of infant baptism derives from the doctrine of the *total depravity of man*. Many readers will have encountered the teachings of Edwards in this regard:

> Seeing you thus disregard so great a God, is it a heinous thing for God to slight you, a little, wretched, despicable creature; a worm, a mere nothing, and less than nothing; a vile insect, that has risen up in contempt against the Majesty of heaven and earth?[373]

> Faith abases men and exalts God, it gives all the glory of redemption to God alone. It is necessary in order to saving faith, that man should be emptied of himself, that he should be sensible that he is "wretched, and miserable, and poor, and blind, and naked."[374]

Compare this with the BoM text:

> if the knowledge of the goodness of God at this time has awakened you to a sense of your nothingness, and your worthless and fallen state (Mosiah 4:5)

---

[373] Jonathan Edwards, *The Works of Jonathan Edwards*, vol. 1 (Edinburgh: The Banner of Truth Trust, 1990), 673.

[374] Jonathan Edwards, *Selected Sermons of Jonathan Edwards*, edited with introduction and notes by H. Norman Gardiner (New York: MacMillan, 1904).

I would that ye should remember, and always retain in remembrance, the greatness of God, and your own nothingness, and his goodness and long-suffering towards you, unworthy creatures (Mosiah 4:11)

O how great is the nothingness of the children of men; yea, even they are less than the dust of the earth. (Helaman 12:7)

The three protestant traditions that strongly influenced the early religious formation of the Mormon movement founders are the Congregational Church (Oliver Cowdery was raised Congregational), the Presbyterian Church (Lucy Mack Smith, Hyrum, Samuel and Sophronia all became members of the Presbyterian Church)[375] and the Methodist Church (Joseph Smith Jr. studied to become a Methodist Exhorter). The first two of these were essentially Calvinist, and adhered to the doctrine of the *total depravity of man*, whether directly or through Arminianism. These two would be comfortable with the verses quoted *supra*.

The rational for this precept, the *total depravity of mankind*, has its roots in the garden of Eden. Adam and Eve, while yet in the Garden, disobeyed a direct order from God. This says something about their naturally depraved inclination. And all of mankind is in their bloodline, and have inherited the same depravity.

Even an infant, drawing its first breath, has inherited the same depravity, is therefore in some sense not sinless, and so needs baptism as soon as possible. In this context, the BoM is eclectic. Even though it seems to echo aspects of Calvinist doctrine, it declares that the doctrine of infant baptism is evil and detestable. This is at least partially due to Joseph Smith Jr.'s deep feelings regarding the fate of his eldest brother Alvin, who died before the restored Aaronic Priesthood and valid baptism. These feelings were reinforced when he had to bury his first-born son shortly after his first taste of the air at Harmony, PA. He could not accept the idea that his brother and his infant son would be barred from heaven for dying unbaptized, and condemned to the torments of eternal damnation.

For the Christians of the day, the doctrine of the total depravity of mankind helped explain Jesus' statement, "unless one is born of water and the Spirit he cannot enter into the kingdom of God." (John 3:5) All of mankind before Jesus' crucifixion, and most of the population of the earth

---

[375] Milton V. Backman and James B. Allen, "Membership of Certain of Joseph Smith's Family in the Western Presbyterian Church of Palmyra," *BYU Studies* 10 no. 4 (1970): 482-484.

ever since who have never heard of Jesus, presumably must go to Hell, or some possibly less painful appendage to Hell (in Roman Catholicism, this used to be Limbo). Smith Jr. was probably also influenced by his father's involvement with Universalism. The LDS solution came in the form of baptism for the dead by proxy, based on 1 Corinthians 15:29.

Fruits: The Iron Rod of the Word of God

One strategy to confront the charge of heresy was to seek the moral high ground so as to disarm the reader's natural skepticism, by challenging his own religiosity and morality, and calling him too to repentance. While condemning the pursuit of the riches of this world, BoM morality roundly condemns *whoredoms, adultery, concubines and plural wives.* (Jacob 1:15, 2:24-27, Mosiah 11:2, Ether 10:5) Already in the first pages of the BoM text a major rift develops between the protagonist, Lehi's younger son, Nephi, and the antagonists, his two elder siblings, Laman and Lemuel. Nephi was chosen before his conception, to be the founder of the true Christian gospel in the Promised Land early in the seventh century BCE. As he asserts his spiritual and temporal leadership in the family, his two older brothers are affronted, feel threatened, and revolt. This scenario gives father Lehi and Nephi opportunities for speeches calling them to repent, to hold to the word of God, to seek the spiritual life in preference to the material, and to withstand the mockery of the great many who despise the truth under the influence of Satan. They serve also as Nephi's foil to rebut anticipated objections to the BoM claim that a Hebrew party had settled in the New World, where they produced their own scriptures.

Fruits: The Millennium of Christ Draweth Nigh

Those implementing the BoM project were able to associate it with the enthusiastic Adventist expectation that the millennium of Christ's reign on earth was drawing nigh, to divert the skepticism of their interlocutors.

Hippolytus of Rome likened the history of the world to the six days of creation plus the Sabbath, and argued that six millennia must precede the millennium of Christ's rule on earth. Some have suggested an apostasy-restoration cycle, although not sticking literally to a 1,000-year period for each cycle. Mormonism has generally accepted a version of this view. For what concerns us here, it is important to note that the *Book of Mormon* holds that each of the main prophets, including Adam, Abraham and Moses, was a Christian and had the full gospel. God's true church has been the same over the millennia, with the exception of the major change occasioned by Jesus' accomplishment of his mission upon the cross. In later LDS theological development, this led some to adopt some version of dispensationalism.[376] It is no accident that general Mormon, author of the new bible whose name it bears, is killed in 400 CE, exactly one thousand years ALJ. This is the Nephite millennium.

It seems that in every generation for many centuries, some portion of various Christian populations have become convinced that Jesus' return was imminent. The proximity of this event is at times pegged to some notion that the divine calendar is based on intervals of 1,000 years, i.e. millennia. It has been argued that some of the fervor of the crusades was inspired by their proximity to the year 1,000, or thereabouts (since it is not easy to know when a millennium began, or if a millennium is an exact or a proximate unit). In the 1820s, a substantial degree of Adventism was underway in New England.

Fruits: Refutation of Atheism

Rather than condemning belief in false gods by name, or other supernatural beings in Pre-Columbian America, the *Book of Mormon* has passages attacking atheism, a prevalent concern in 18th and 19th-century New England, in the context of the perceived conflict between science and religion. Ammoron writes in reply to an epistle received from Moroni, "And as concerning that God whom ye say we have rejected, behold, we know not such a being; neither do ye; but if it so be that there is such a thing, we know not but that he hath made us as well as you." (Alma 54:21) There are several debates over the existence of God:

> 2 Nephi 2:13. And if ye shall say there is no law, ye shall also say there is no sin. If ye shall say there is no sin, ye shall also say there is no righteousness. And if there be no righteousness there be no happiness. And if there be no righteousness nor happiness there be no punishment nor misery. And if these things are not there is no God. And if there is no God we are not, neither the earth; for there could have been no creation of things, neither to act nor to be acted upon; wherefore, all things must have vanished away. (cf. 2 Nephi 28:22 & Mormon 9:2)
> Alma 30:43-44. The scriptures are laid before thee, yea, and all things denote there is a God; yea, even the earth, and all things that are upon the face of it,

---

[376] See William C. Watson, *Dispensationalism before Darby. Seventeenth-Century and Eighteenth-Century English Apocalypticism* (Silverton, OR: Lampion Press, 2015).

yea, and its motion, yea, and also all the planets which move in their regular form do witness that there is a Supreme Creator. (cf. Alma 11:22)

Our interest here is not just the concept of atheism, but the nature of the disputation over the issue, and the classical arguments against it. Alma's argument here is anachronistic. Verses in the Bible used in Christian theology to adduce the wonders of nature as evidence of the existence of God were composed by the Biblical authors to praise God, rather than as part of a reasoned argument against atheism (i.e. the *vestigia dei* argument). Alma uses the marvels of nature in his disputation just as they have been used in Euro-Christian theology. By the eighteenth century, in the face of the emergence of modern science, atheism had become a matter of concern for Christian preachers. Even though the majority of Americans believe at least in a "higher being," it is clear that the concern among preachers remains considerable.

The Witnesses: Demise and Apostasy

Within fifteen years of the publication of the *Book of Mormon*, all twelve witnesses to the gold plates had been murdered, had died of natural causes or had left the Church. The only remaining ties to the period prior to 1830 were Lucy Mack Smith, Emma Hale Smith and William Smith (albeit in the RLDS Church). Martin Harris did return at the end of his life, destitute and frail, having no other viable option. In desperation, sick and frail, after having accepted baptism into the Methodist Church, Oliver Cowdery was willing to return to the LDS fold in Utah, but succumbed to his illness and died on March 3 1850 in David Whitmer's home in Richmond, Missouri. The entire Smith family had been almost eradicated from the main LDS Mormon movement.

Table 45. Death and Apostasy among the Witnesses

Natural Deaths
1835 Christian Whitmer died.
1836 Peter Whitmer Jr. died.
1840 Joseph Smith Sr. died.
1844 Samuel Smith died (cause of death then called a "bilious fever").
Excommunication
1837 Martin Harris was excommunicated (died 1875)
1838 Oliver Cowdery was excommunicated (died 1850).
1838 David Whitmer was excommunicated (died 1888)
1838 Jacob Whitmer was excommunicated (died 1856)
1838 Hiram Page was excommunicated (died 1852)

1845 William Smith was excommunicated after disputes with Brigham Young.
Murder Victims
1844 Joseph Smith murdered.
1844 Hyrum Smith murdered.
The Last Ones Standing
1856 Lucy Mack Smith, wavered between moving to Utah and joining the Strang group, but stayed in Nauvoo with her daughters and Emma Smith (died 1856).
1875 Martin Harris, died after returning to the Church in Utah
1878 William B. Smith joined the Reorganized Church of Jesus Christ of Latter Day Saints
1879 Emma Smith died, a member of the Reorganized Church of Jesus Christ of Latter Day Saints.
1893 William B. Smith died in Osterdock, Iowa (brother of Joseph Smith Jr.)

Any Confessions?

Due to the central importance of the statements of those claiming to have seen, hefted or handled the plates and the associated BoM relics, the LDS establishment has controlled the spin on this issue. It is framed in terms of whether or not they ever *denied their testimonies*. In any normal investigatory situation, one would frame the issue in terms of whether or not any ever *confessed*. This is of great importance, because it is axiomatic in criminology that "there are no guilty men in prison;" many found guilty with the most clear forensic evidence continue to insist on their innocence. Confession is the last thing we would expect.

A theological backdrop exists to the issue of confession: Mormons do not shrive. They have no concept of dying unshriven.

There were several reasons for the witnesses to remain loyal. First, people are concerned about what their family, wife, children and grandchildren would say. They do not want to cast themselves in a light that would impair the family's standing in the community. Far better to be remembered *as a man of God than a fraud*.

Second, there had come into existence a vigilante group, self-styled the Danites, who roughed up dissidents who took actions to undermine the church, roughed them up, or worse. The greater one's prominence, the more apostasy is tantamount to persecuting the Church. To know that the LDS establishment could pose a threat, we need only recollect the passage in Smith's polygamy revelation, where presumably God speaks, saying: "But if she [Emma Smith] will not abide this commandment [polygamy] she shall be destroyed, saith the Lord" (D&C 132:54, 64). Emma waited until Joseph was dead, and Brigham Young and his followers were at a safe distance in Utah, before she began to proclaim that, to her knowledge, her husband had never taken any wife but her. This has been shown to be patently untrue, and itself shows how people say what they must to survive. In her case, she and her son, Joseph Smith III, were being welcomed by the dissident saints who stayed behind, and never had adopted polygamy. Still, the revelation itself, and her later claim, show she was not in agreement with polygamy, but was made to keep mum.

Third, there was another motivation to maintain one's testimony: the BoM-based agendas that many of these men nurtured. Shortly after the *Book of Mormon* was published, Hiram Page made his move. He set his seerstone to work and received some revelations. Joseph clearly detected the rivalry, and instructed Oliver Cowdery to inform brother Hiram that his revelation had come from Satan. Oliver succeeded in this, and Page withdrew his claim. In the conference of the new church, the assembly voted unanimously that only Joseph could receive revelation for the Church. Others, such as David Whitmer, attempted to become the new prophet, seer and revelator, at the head of the presidency of the Church, in the aftermath of Smith's murder, and when that failed he established his own congregation, also based on the *Book of Mormon*. Martin Harris and Warren Parrish in Kirtland attempted the formation of a new church, the Church of Christ, to take over from Smith. Even Sydney Rigdon engaged in intrigue, declaring that the keys had been taken from the Church; when confronted by Smith, he recanted. Others, who never did attempt to take over the new church, had been given positions in the LDS establishment and were thereby coopted.

The Saints have gone to great effort to track the lives of the witnesses, take subsequent testimonies and claim that they can show that not one of them ever denied his testimony, even on his deathbed. Although it seems that there were no documentable denials, there were apostasies.

The Predestinates: Smith's Prebirth Election

The interrelated doctrines of *predestination, election,* and the *total sovereignty of God* are Calvinist keystones. They may have come to influence the *Book of Mormon*, and Smith's evolving post-1830 thought, from preachers of the Second Great Awakening, strongly influenced by Jonathan Edwards. The doctrine of election has the potential to strengthen one's resolve no matter what the means might be to establish the true church: namely, the conviction that one has been elected for this mission by God from the most ancient times. As for his own case, Smith was clear: "Every man who has a calling to minister to the inhabitants of the world was ordained to that very purpose in the Grand Council of heaven before this world was. I suppose I was ordained to this very office in that Grand Council."[377] God says to Smith, "Behold, thou art Joseph, and thou wast chosen to do the work of the Lord..." (D&C 3:9)

In addition to one' self-assurance that the fruits of one's works are good, and so of God, the conviction of one's election can calm whatever qualms one might have regarding the means necessary for the mission. Another Calvinist doctrine would strengthen this resolve: the *total sovereignty of God*. This holds that any attempt to impose human notions of morality on God would reduce Him by impinging upon His sovereignty. Such human impudence would also be very sinful.

> Being merely the instrument in the hand of God,
> then whatever is expedient for God
> can be permitted to, or even incumbent upon
>
> His Prophet.

[377] Joseph Smith, in *Teachings of the Prophet Joseph Smith, sel. Joseph Fielding Smith* (Salt Lake City: Deseret Book, 1938), 365.

< Chapter 23 >

Fayette: Where Ms$\mathcal{U}$ Was Completed & Ms$\mathcal{O}$ Born

After the loss of the 116 pages, Smith returned to Harmony. He had issued a revelation branding Harris "that wicked man," who had assisted Satan in an attempt to destroy the work of the Lord. At that time, he could hardly expect a continuation of financial support from his former partner and scribe. His only way forward as head of household, whose wife had recently lost her first child, was to "man up" and get to work farming. True, he did announce that he was himself punished by the temporary loss of his gift. But the solution was easily formulated. Having a good knowledge of the scriptures, he knew well that in the OT, the books of 1 and 2 Chronicles mirrored Genesis through 1 & 2 Kings, producing two accounts by different authors but covering largely the same period, from different perspectives. Even more obvious, there are four gospels, four accounts of the mission of Jesus, by different apostles, in different words, and from different perspectives. Certainly, his gold plates must also contain a second version of the stolen material. Shortly after his arrival back home, his parents visited. They must have discussed how the new bible could explain to its readers why the Lord would have allowed the theft to happen in the first place, and His plan to thwart the plotting of the Father of all Lies. So then, when did he recommence?

On two occasions David Whitmer estimated that the time required to translate the *Book of Mormon* portion of the gold plates was eight months.[378] This would begin c. December 1, 1828. Lucy Smith quotes her son: "I continued my supplications to God, without cessation, and on the twenty-second of September, I had the joy and satisfaction of again receiving the Urim and Thummim with which I have again commenced translation, and Emma writes for me."[379] Since he makes no mention of Samuel, presumably this is prior to February. Additional information regarding this undefined period is provided by a statement of Joseph

---

[378] David Whitmer Interview on 15/12/1885, published in the *Chicago Tribune*, 17/12/1885. See Vogel 5, 153. Also, an interview on 10/10/1886, published in the *Omaha (NE) Herald* 22, 17/10/1886. See Vogel 5, 178. David Whitmer's confusion over what was done in the summer of 1829 probably stems from his confusion between the various mss. Later on, when he was in possession of ms$\mathcal{P}$, he claimed that it was the original manuscript.

[379] Lucy Smith, *Lucy's Book*, 428.

Knight. Joseph and Emma approached him seeking material assistance "the first of winter 1828."[380]

Two of those actually involved in events of June, 1829, Joseph Smith Jr. and his mother Lucy Smith, gave virtually the same timeline. Immediately after arriving at the Whitmer home, Joseph and Oliver got to work to finish up the translation. This must have taken only a few days. Joseph wrote, that the three witnesses had their experience in Fayette, and then, "Having finished the translation we went to Palmyra"[a] (or "the translation drawing to a close"[b]), secured the copyright (v. p. 129) and engaged Grandin for publishing.[381] Exactly the same timeline is given by Lucy. First Joseph sent a messenger to Manchester to summon his parents to come to celebrate the completion of the *Book of Mormon* translation. They brought Martin Harris with them. The next day, the three witnesses and Joseph repaired to a grove where they saw an angel and the plates. The following day, the Manchester party returned home, followed later by Joseph, Oliver and the Whitmers. After their arrival, there was the experience of the eight witnesses. She writes, this was Thursday and the following Monday they went to Grandin for the printing of the book. After the Whitmers' returned to Fayette, Joseph undertook to get the copyright [while yet in Manchester].[382] It is important that these two relatively independent accounts agree so closely, especially on the events of interest here: the translation text was completed (or nearly so), then the three witness event, and then the copyright, which issued on June 11.

David Whitmer's estimate of eight months for the completion of the translation could place the beginning of the work perhaps as early as late November, since the work had already been under way prior to the Smiths' visit to Knight. Emma wrote for her husband as much as possible through January, and into February, until the arrival of Joseph Smith Sr. and Joe Jr.'s brother Samuel. He then began to serve as a scribe, according to Smith Jr.[383] Among the important observations made by Skousen is the fact that, most notably, the handwriting of these two does not occur in the extant parts of ms$O$ (including Nephi). Actually, there is no mystery here. Emma and Samuel were writing into gatherings of the *translation manuscript*, ms$U$, not in ms$O$. In an interview with Edmund C. Briggs, speaking of a time when she was writing for her husband translating the

---

[380] Joseph Knight, Sr., "Manuscript of the History of Joseph Smith" (c. 1836-47), in Vogel 4, 18-19.

[381] Joseph Smith, 1835-c. 41 *History*, in JSP, 353 (draft 3[a], or draft 1 &2[b]).

[382] Lucy Smith, Lucy's Book, 457, 459.

[383] Joseph Smith, 1834-36 History, in JSP, 16.

Book of Mormon, Emma attributed to her husband a query: "Emma, did Jerusalem have walls around it?" She affirmed that it did, and he replied, "Oh! I was afraid I had been deceived."[384] This is important because there is only one reference to the walls of Jerusalem in the entire *Book of Mormon*, in 1 Nephi 4:4. This verse should be in Emma's hand, but occurs in ms O on manuscript page six, which was written by John Whitmer. It is not in ms O because she was writing ms U.

It was during Joe Sr.'s visit in February that his prophet son issued a revelation for his father announcing that a marvelous work and a wonder was soon to come forth. Samuel began writing for him then, and was available to assist until March 20. On that date, an entry in the store ledger of David Hale records that Samuel Harrison was paid 81 cents for working a day and a half.[385] He could have written for Smith until the Lord commanded the prophet to stop and wait, presumably for the arrival of Oliver Cowdery on April 5, 1829. (D&C 5:30) Then Samuel must have returned to Manchester, since it was he who escorted Oliver to Harmony. A documented date for the beginning of Oliver's presence in Harmony is found in the contract for Smith's purchase of a small piece of land from his father-in-law, drafted and signed as a witness by Cowdery (April 6, 1829).[386]

Although relations were being repaired with their funder, Martin Harris, Joseph, Emma and Oliver were going through lean times. Smith found occasional work for his brother-in-law David Hale, recorded in his store ledger: 1828 (Oct 18th) half a Day threshing Buckwheat; (Oct 24) one day plowing by oxen; (Nov) two Days and a half husking corn; (Dec. 1-4) four Days work; 1829 (Jan 3) half a Days work- chopping &c; (March 20th) one Day chopping.[387] This was certainly welcome, but was ultimately slim pickins. He recorded how thankful he was for a "quantity of provisions" that Joseph Knight Sr. brought him. (History, 1839) Things got worse when "my wifes (sic) father was about to turn me out of doors & I had not where to go." (History, 1832) He, Oliver

---

[384] Emma Smith, "A visit to Nauvoo in 1856," *Journal of Mormon History* 9, 10/1916, 454. See Vogel I, 530-31.

[385] David Hale's entry in his store ledger in Mark Lyman Staker and Robin Scott Jensen, "David Hale's Store Ledger. New Details about Joseph and Emma Smith, the Hale Family, and the Book of Mormon," *BYU Studies Quarterly* 53:3, 2014, 105, 111.

[386] "Joseph Smith Harmony (PA) Land Records," in Vogel 4, 427-28.

[387] David Hale's store ledger, 110-11.

and the BoM project were rescued by the arrival of David Whitmer at the end of May to take them to the home of David's father, Peter Whitmer Sr. in Fayette, NY (approximately 30 miles east by southeast of Manchester). There they were to be assisted and provided for during the completion of the *Book of Mormon.*

The Origin and Nature of MsO and MsP

The orthodox LDS view is that over a period of approximately three months (April, May and June) in 1829, a manuscript was produced that LDS scholars call manuscript O, dubbed the *original* manuscript because it is the first manuscript of the entire *Book of Mormon*, as it was published in 1830, written by scribes as Smith read the words revealed by the power of God. Joseph Smith placed it in the cornerstone of Nauvoo House, which was to serve as his boarding house. Some forty years later, when the second husband of Emma Smith, Lewis Bidamon, removed it, he found it had been seriously damaged by water and mold. Fortunately, the scribes of Joseph Smith, primarily Oliver Cowdery, had produced for the printer a highly faithful copy of it (apart from the correction of some scribal errors and English mistakes), which has been called manuscript P, the printer's manuscript. Royal Skousen of BYU has produced an excellent professional edition of both manuscripts.[388] He has estimated that the surviving parts of O constitute about twenty-eight percent of the original.

A number of sheets of foolscap paper, often around six, but in one case twenty-eight sheets (96 pages, most of Alma), were folded and sewn together, each group into a "gathering." For most of the extant work, the fold was "widthwise," made by bringing the top of the sheets in portrait orientation to the bottom, and folding across their width. A few were folded "lengthwise," by bringing the left edge of the sheets in portrait orientation over to the right edge (or vice versa), and folding. The text was written in ink on both sides of each page, thereby producing four pages per sheet. The pages were numbered much like the signature of a book. For a six-sheet *gathering*, there were thus twenty-four pages. The outer side of the gathering had page one (of the first gathering) on the right side of the fold, and page twenty-four on the left side. This work was done prior to writing, to enable the scribe to avoid the gutter.

---

[388] Skousen, *The Original Manuscript*, and Royal Skousen, *The Printer's Manuscript of the Book of Mormon: Typographical Facsimile of the Entire Text in Two Parts,* (Provo, UT: Foundation for Ancient Research and Mormon Studies, 2001).

The extant pages of ms𝒪 were written mostly in the hand of Oliver Cowdery, but with two Fayette scribes doing parts of 1 Nephi. The hand of Joseph Smith occurs, but oddly, for only about two lines in part of Alma 45:22. The extant pages and the scribe for each can be found in Appendix 4, which gives line numbers to allow the reader to have some idea of the degree of preservation. One caveat: since many deteriorated pages have large lacunae, including sometimes the absence of the whole left or right half or top of a page, for scholarly use one must consult Skousen's edition and the JSP *Facsimile Edition*.[389]

From Ms𝒰 to Ms𝒪: What Documents Are Extant?

By comparison, the most famous nonextant source for serious scriptural scholarship is the *Gospel according to Q*. Q is an acronym for German *Qwelle*, which means "source." Mark has long been accepted as a source document for Matthew and Luke. Q is considered to be a source for elements found in both Luke and Matthew, but not found in Mark. It has been considered to have been oral material, or nonextant mss, or both. The initial reaction to the Q hypothesis was, "Q? What is that?" Now, it is one of the foundational concepts for modern NT scholarship.

Ms𝒰

Similarly, in BoM scholarship, no part of the original composition manuscript (ms𝒰) is physically extant. Even so, many bits of it are witnessed in the scribal errors made when it was copied into ms𝒪 (v. Chapter 10). Apart from this, it is a conclusion drawn principally from one salient observation. Ms𝒪, which orthodox LDS scholars have come to accept as the original manuscript, is virtually clean, largely free of significant edits (words crossed out or added, insertions of larger texts, or deletions of text composed of one or several lines, etc.; v. Chapter 9). It is ideal for the orthodox believer, being just what one might expect: Smith read off the divinely revealed text while his scribe copied it down.

But the secular scholar does not base his understanding on visions of the divine. So what is his alternative? Many find it implausible that Joseph

---

[389] Skousen, Royal, & Robin Scott Jensen, , *Original Manuscript of the Book of Mormon, Facsimile Edition*, in *The Joseph Smith Papers*, volume 5 (Salt Lake City: The Church Historian's Press, 2021).

Smith could compose a text extemporaneously as complex as the *Book of Mormon*, even assisted by notes and outlines. An alternative is more probable. Smith and his collaborator(s) must have produced one or more original texts, the earliest manuscript(s), which, after considerable editing, collectively became the source text, or urtext, ms$\mathcal{U}$ (*ur* in German = *ear* in "early"). The observable complexity in ms$\mathcal{O}$, the earliest extant text (i.e. as supplemented by Cowdery's copy of it made for the printer, ms$\mathcal{P}$) provides the clear evidence for ms$\mathcal{U}$.

Table 46. The BoM Complexities Include:

1. complex storylines, especially the story of getting the Brass Plates, and those found in the missionary and military campaigns;
2. a comprehensive list of recordkeepers, and a complex set of interrelated accounts, records and plates (v. Figure 21 p 449);
3. the development of a complex and extensive onomasticon of proper names, mostly composed by recombining invented pseudo name components;
4. a complex coinage system;
5. four major KJV inclusions, including one consisting of thirteen highly edited chapters of Isaiah, plus the Sermon on the Mount;
6. Composition of well over a hundred variant readings to rework the texts of these inclusions to comport with the view that they are corrected versions of corrupted Biblical passages;
7. theological commentary on the KJV inclusions;
8. numerous Biblical paraphrases worked into the BoM text;
9. a researched and studied roundup of scriptures interpreted to show that some OT prophets knew about the Nephites and that a new bible would come forth;
10. various apologetic arguments in anticipation to opposition to the Book of Mormon (i.e. the BoM in defense of itself);
11. a theory of the Great Apostasy in the Old World, its replication following the nearly two Christian centuries in the New World, and a harsh condemnation of the churches and the Jews of Smith's day;
12. theological disputes with "strawman" anti-Christs to argue against atheism and for a consistent BoM theology;
13. explanation and examination of theological concepts, such as the first and second resurrections; the fall of man; the condescension of Christ; blood atonement; anthropomorphism of God; the infinite sacrifice; the fallacy of infant baptism; OT predictions of the Messiah as shadows or types; and defense of adherence to the law of Moses even while teaching that it has no saving power; plan of redemption, etc.;
14. a complex geography, with at least forty cities, that is internally consistent throughout the complexities of the storylines, and a useful and explicit key to BoM geography (in Alma 22);

> *15. scores of post-Biblical Euro-Christian phrases, drawn from Christian hymns and sermons, and seamlessly integrated into the Nephite narrative;*
> *16. a complex chronology, with regularly reported dates in years after leaving Jerusalem (ALJ dates), years of the judges, years since the sign of the birth of Jesus up to his coming to the Nephites, and years after the birth of Jesus (i.e. CE dates);*
> *17. a continuous diatribe against secret societies;*
> *18. continuously repetitious demonstrations that wickedness is the source of curses and famines;*
> *19. descriptions of military fortification modeled after that used in the revolutionary war (picket walls, berms, ditches, stone walls, watch towers);*
> *20. description of two trips from the eastern hemisphere to the Americas, each with a different type of vessel, including a surface-submarine vessel;*
> *21. scientific explanations to show that ancient prophets knew that the world is round, that it is solid all the way through (to refute hollow earth theories of the followers of John Cleves Symmes) and that the solar system is heliocentric;*
> *22. developing family genealogies, including a list of begats in the Book of Ether, followed by histories corresponding to them.*

Each of these items would be challenging enough, taken alone. But these items were not done each in isolation of the others; they were woven together into the fabric of the Nephite narrative. A text of this complexity requires collaboration on a working document and considerable editing and development. At times, it may have been necessary to scrap a whole page, or to add one. This is not ms 𝒪.

The Orthodox Understanding of How the Translation Was Done

The contemporary orthodox LDS understanding of Ms 𝒪 is that it is a divinely executed primordial translation into English. That is, its text was revealed by divine instrumentality, and is not the product of any 1829 human activity from any earlier draft, notes or other written or memorized material. Words were presented to Joseph Smith by the power of God. He read out what he saw, and his scribe wrote them down. The correctness of the work extended even to spelling, as Emma Smith wrote,

> I wrote a part of it, as he dictated each sentence, word for word, and when he came to proper names he could not pronounce, or long words, he spelled

them out, and while I was writing them, if I made any mistake in spelling, he would stop me and correct my spelling…[390]

David Whitmer stated,

> A piece of something resembling parchment would appear, and on that appeared the writing. One character at a time would appear, and under it was the interpretation in English. Brother Joseph would read off the English to Oliver Cowdery, who was his principal scribe, and when it was written down and repeated to Brother Joseph to see if it was correct, then it would disappear, and another character with the interpretation would appear.[391]

These reports are given here solely to illustrate the understanding of Smith's contemporary associates: O was exclusively the scribe's writing of the words that were presented to Smith by divine instrumentality.

The Quest for Emma and Samuel's Handwriting

Joseph Smith reported in his 1832 History that both Emma and Samuel Smith had written for him prior to the arrival of Oliver Cowdery. Because the handwriting of Emma and of Samuel is not found in the extant part of ms$O$, Nephi through Enos, the orthodox position is that it must be in Mosiah, although no part of it is extant. Much of the defense of the LDS position focuses on the segment of translation done by these two scribes, and therefore the period of the work done.

Vignette **Estimating Emma & Samuel's Translation Time**
Prior to Cowdery's arrival Emma and Samuel Harrison Smith wrote for Smith. Their handwriting was not found in the extant parts of msO. In 1970, Dean C. Jessee published a study concluding that Smith must have recommenced his work with Mosiah, and that their handwriting must be found in this totally nonextant book. This assertion assumes further that Emma and Samuel, having begun at Mosiah 1:1, did not get far enough in their scrivener service for Joseph to write all the way through Mosiah, and certainly not far enough into Alma to have broached the first undisputed extant fragment, beginning at 10:31. If they had, their handwriting would be found there.

---

[390] Emma Smith, as reported by Edmund C. Briggs, "A Visit to Nauvoo in 1856," *Journal of History,* Jan. 1916, 454.
[391] David Whitmer, *An Address to All Believers in Christ* (Richmond, MO: Snell's Printshop, 1887), 12.

Samuel accompanied his father to visit Joseph in Harmony in February 1829, although we do not know when in February. We do know that his name occurs in the ledger of Smith's brother-in-law David Hale, dated March 20.

Prior to Samuel's arriving, Emma wrote for her husband. Regarding an event in which he was a principal participant, Joseph Knight Sr., a long-time friend of Joseph Smith, wrote that the Smiths came to him for help at the first of winter of 1828/29. At that time, they told him that Joseph had already been translating, with Emma writing for him, but due to their other work, translation was slow.[392] He also provided some money to buy paper. The world was at the end of the little ice age (c. 1600 to 1850). The farmer's "first of winter" must have been earlier than our meteorological definition of 21 December. Perhaps it would be closer to Whitmer's estimate, i.e. early December. Furthermore, this is just the date of the Smiths' visit to Knight; Smith had already been translating by that time, and we have no way to know how long before.

Lucy Smith quotes her son: "…on the twenty-second of September, I had the joy and satisfaction of again receiving the Urim and Thummim with which I have again commenced translation, and Emma writes for me."[393]

On two occasions, David Whitmer estimated that the time taken for the whole BoM was eight months.[394] He also made statements re the completion of the translation at his father's home. The one most usually accepted is, "The translation at my father's occupied about one month, that is from June 1 to July 1, 1829."[395] So his eight months would be c. December 1 to July 1.

These three individuals were very close to the translation process, and provide our best evidence. Although we do not know the date of father Smith and Samuel's visit to Harmony, Emma's writing for Joseph might have been from December 10 to February 10, i.e. for 62 days. Samuel is mentioned in David Hale's ledger on 20 March. If he wrote for his brother from February 11 through March 21, that would be 38 days of scrivener service.

Although disputed, there may be another extant Alma fragment located much earlier, beginning at 3:5. Clearly, it is in the interest of the orthodox case to minimize the amount of progress that Emma and Samuel could have made, thereby minimizing how far into Mosiah their work could have reached, into Mosiah and even beyond into Alma. It is also in the interest of the orthodox

---

[392] Joseph Knight, Sr., "Manuscript of the History of Joseph Smith" (c. 1836-47), in Vogel 4, 18-19.

[393] Lucy Smith, *Lucy's Book*, 428.

[394] Interview on 15/12/1885, published in the *Chicago Tribune*, 17/12/1885. See Vogel V/153. Also, an interview on 10/10/1886, published in the *Omaha (NE) Herald* 22, 17/10/1886. See Vogel 5, 178. David Whitmer's confusion over what was done in the summer of 1829 probably stems from his confusion between the various mss. Later on, when he was in possession of ms𝒫, he claimed that it was the original manuscript.

[395] David Whitmer, to the *Kansas City Journal*, 5 June 1881; see Vogel V/76.

case to fend off any encroachment of Alma fragments prior to 10:31. The two Chicago leaves have been included in the JSP *Facsimile Edition* of ms$O$, albeit in Appendix 1, with a forward in which Robert Scott Jensen makes the case for their authenticity, and Royal Skousen makes the case for their inauthenticity. In the first case, we note that the leaves appear to be in the hand of Oliver Cowdery; that the archival records of the University of Chicago special collections indicate that the leaves were acquired in the 1920s; and that using sophisticated Scanning Auger Microscopy (SAM) a determination was made that the ink of the leaves dates to 1830 plus or minus five years. Their acquisition by the Church was in the wake of the infamous Mormon bomber (document forger extraordinaire). Skousen promptly undertook to alert Church authorities that he considered these leaves to be most probably yet another forgery. His initial alert has been expanded for inclusion in the *Facsimile Edition*. Having examined evidence from both sides, the Church rendered no judgment of its own, but notably, after getting the views of experts, it did decide in favor of their inclusion in this landmark JSP edition.

For our approach to estimating the likelihood that Emma and Samuel should have reached either Alma 3:5 or 10:31, we need a unit of measurement. The best available is manuscript pages. Fortunately we have a sample of one ms$O$ gathering (24 pages in length), extant in both ms$O$ and ms$P$, that was done by the same scribe (Oliver Cowdery): 1 Nephi 14:11, page 25 through 2 Nephi 1:30, page 48, in ms$O$; and 1 Nephi 14:21, page 25 through 2 Nephi 1:24, page 48, in ms$P$. A few pages in the ms$O$ sample are a bit damaged, but their condition does not compromise our ability to know the number of lines per page. We not only can know the number of pages in each gathering, but we can also observe that Cowdery did this part of ms$P$ virtually in lockstep with ms$O$. This provides a means to estimate the number of pages to various points along ms$O$, which us missing the long section from Enos 1:14 to Alma 10:31. We need to estimate the number of pages from 2 Nephi 1:24 to Mosiah 1:1. Then we need to know the number of pages from there to Alma 3:5 and to 10:31. Our only basis for these estimates is ms$P$.

1) The first of these interstices extends from 2 Nephi 1:24 to Mosiah 1:1, viz. page 48 to page 117 in msP, which is 70 pages.
2) The manuscript page number for Enos 1:14 is 114 in both ms$O$ (an extant page) and ms$P$. Cowdery is still copying ms$O$ in lockstep.
3) Mosiah begins in ms$P$ on page 117, only three pages from Enos 1:14. Both manuscripts clearly must have begun Mosiah on this same page.

4) In msP, Mosiah ends on page 169. So it has 52 pages. Alma 3:5 begins on page 176, 60 pages from Mosiah 1:1, or there abouts.
5) Alma 10:31 begins on page 195 in msP, 79 pages from Mosiah 1:1 in msP. Curiously, Skousen's estimated page number for Alma 10:31 in ms O is 225.
5) How can Alma 10:31 begin 30 pages later in m O than in msP (225-195)? This is not possible.

This massive discrepancy has nothing to do with Lehi, which was lost prior to msO. It cannot arise from any estimate of the assumed lost first chapter of Mosiah, since Mosiah chapters were no where near this long. After all, in msP, all of Mosiah is only 52 pages.

In view of this, the present study will use the following numbers for the manuscript interstices (each being pages from Mosiah 1:1): to Alma 3:5, 60 pages; and to Alma 10:31, 79 pages.

For Emma' service, December 10 to February 10 equals 48 days. If Emma was only able to average 2/3 of a page per day in view of her chores, this would still add up to 32 pages done before Samuel's arrival. If we count Samuel's scrivener duty from February 11 to March 21, this comes to 38 days. If he averaged only 1.33 pages per day, he could have written 50.5 pages. Both together equal 82.5 pages. These modest rates of page copying should take them well into the 10:31 fragment. Even much more modest rates of writing would take them to and beyond the first page of the Chicago leaves. It seems that even without additional fragments being found, we should minimally see Samuel's hand in these leaves.

This prompts us to ask, how much could they do between December 10 (or earlier) and March 21. This is winter time, a period when essential farmwork is not pressing. Northern Susquehanna is known for heavy snow. We know that Joseph Knight Sr. had loaned his sleigh to Joseph to court Emma, and in winter of 1828-29 he used his sleigh to bring Joseph and Emma provisions. We get an idea of the winter chores from the store ledger of David Hale where we observe that essential work was limited to tasks like chopping wood. It could be a time for projects, such as repairs to fences or a chicken coop. On this occasion, Smith probably gave priority to translating, especially being partially supported by provisions from Joseph Knight Sr.

The Mosiah priority argument requires that the translation before Cowdery be so short that it cannot have extended from Mosiah 1:1 to any point within the first generally accepted extant Alma segment, which begins with 10:31. The twin prongs of this argument holds that Smith did not begin early, and was too busy farming to do much.

The problem now is the segment after Cowdery. As the orthodox shorten the before-Cowdery segment, the segment after Cowdery grows by the same amount. It is claimed that this segment could have been done in a three-month period. Yet work did not start with Cowdery until April 7. Furthermore as we shall see (Table 61), over half of June was not available for translation due to other activity. At best, only twelve weeks were available for translation, i.e. 84 days. To be generous, let us say that the number of days from 7 April to late June is 100. Estimating from ms$P$, the total number of pages in the whole BoM is 462 manuscript pages. Since 82 pages would get Samuel from Mosiah 1:1 into the fragment beginning with Alma 10:31, allocating 380 pages (462 minus 82) for the period after Cowdery would get Samuel's handwriting into that Alma fragment. To avoid this, Cowdery and Smith would have to exceed c. 3.8 pages per day, every day.

We do not know how fast the work could have gone with assistance from divine Providence, but the secular approach must bear in mind that under its hypothesis, one also had to compose the text, not just write it. Note too that should just one small fragment from Moroni surface, it would be enough to determine paper type, to see if it is the same as that in Ether, or that in Nephi, or neither.

Contrasting Manuscripts: MsO and the *Book of Moses*

At some point, as a young adult, Smith claimed to have a calling to restore lost, hidden or corrupted scripture. During about one year after the publication of the *Book of Mormon*, Smith labored on a new corpus of restored scripture: The *Book of Moses*. He had already become enamored with improving the Bible when he prepared lengthy Isaiah inclusions for his "Book of Nephi." Although retaining the King James Version as his base text, he introduced numerous variants, ranging from the most insignificant to others that are rather large.

By 1830 Smith realized that he had no need for gold plates. The *Book of Moses* was his first effort outside of the BoM. Moses was to be an expanded version largely of Genesis, newly divinely revealed to Joseph Smith. Its seriously reworked and edited mss are an example of what the ms$O$ urtext would have looked like (v. pp. 357-58, *supra*).

Figure 17. A) An Edited Page from the *Book of Moses*, Ms 2.

A) Moses 6:53-63. The highlighted passage was to be replaced by the chit *infra*)

by <in> water And the Lord said unto Adam Behold I have
forgiven thee thy transgression in the garden of Eden Hence
came the saying abroad among the people that Christ **the son of God** hath
atoned for original guilt. Wherein the sins of the parents
cannot be answered upon the heads of the Children, for they
are whole from the foundation of the world. /21 And the
Lord spake unto Adam, Saying, inasmuch as thy children
are conceived in sin, even so, when they begin to grow
up ÷ Sin conceiveth in their hearts, & they taste the bitter,
that they may know to prize the good. & it is given
unto them to know good from evil; Wherefore, they are agents
unto **unto** themselves. /22 And I have given unto you another law
& & commandment; Wherefore, teach it unto your Children,
that all men evry where, must repent, or they can in
no wise inheret the kingdom of God. For no unclean thing
can dwell there or dwell in his presence; for, in the
language of Adam, Man of Holiness is his name; & the
name of his only begotten, is the son of a man even Jesus
Christ a righteous Judge which **who** shall come **in the meridean of time**. /^23^ Therefore I give
unto you a commandment to teach these things freely unto
your Children Saying that in as much as they were born
into the World by **reason of** the fall which bringeth death by
water & blood & the Spirit which I have made & so became
of dust a living soul even so ye must be born again
of water & the spirit & cleansed by blood even the blood
of mine only begotten into the mysteries of the kingdo
m of Heaven that ye <they> ye may be sanctified from all Sin; &
enjoy the words of eternal life in this world; & eternal life
in the world to come; even immortal glory. /24 for, by the
water ye keep the commandment; by the spirit ye are
Justified & by the blood ye are Sanctified. / that **Therefore** in you **it** is
given **to abide in you** the record of Heaven, the comforter, the peacible
things of immortal glory **keys of the kingdom of heaven** the truth of all things that
which quickeneth all things, which maketh alive all
things, that which knoweth all things, & hath all power,
according **to** wisdom, mercy, truth, Justice, & Judgement. /25 & now,
Behold, I say unto you, this is the plan of salvation
unto all men, **through** the blood of mine only begotten, which
shall come in the maridian of time. </> And, Behold, all

B) Moses 6:58-59. This is the chit marked to replace the deletion from verse 23, *supra*.

<23/> Therefore, I give unto you a commandment, to teach
these things unto freely unto your children, saying,
that by reason of the trangression cometh the fall,
which fall bringeth death, And in as much as they
were born into the world by watter, and blood, and
the spirit which I have made, and so became of
death <dust> a living soul; even so ye <they> <ye>must be born
again, into the kingdom of heaven, of watter, and of
the spirit, and be cleansed by the blood, of even the
blood of mine only begotten.

Source: "Old Testament Revision 2," p. 18 & 0, accessed Jan 14, 2002.
https://josephsmithpapers.org/papersummary/old-testament-revision-2/22

Figure 18. A Page of MsO
(1 Nephi 4:20-33, copied from MsU for the Printer)

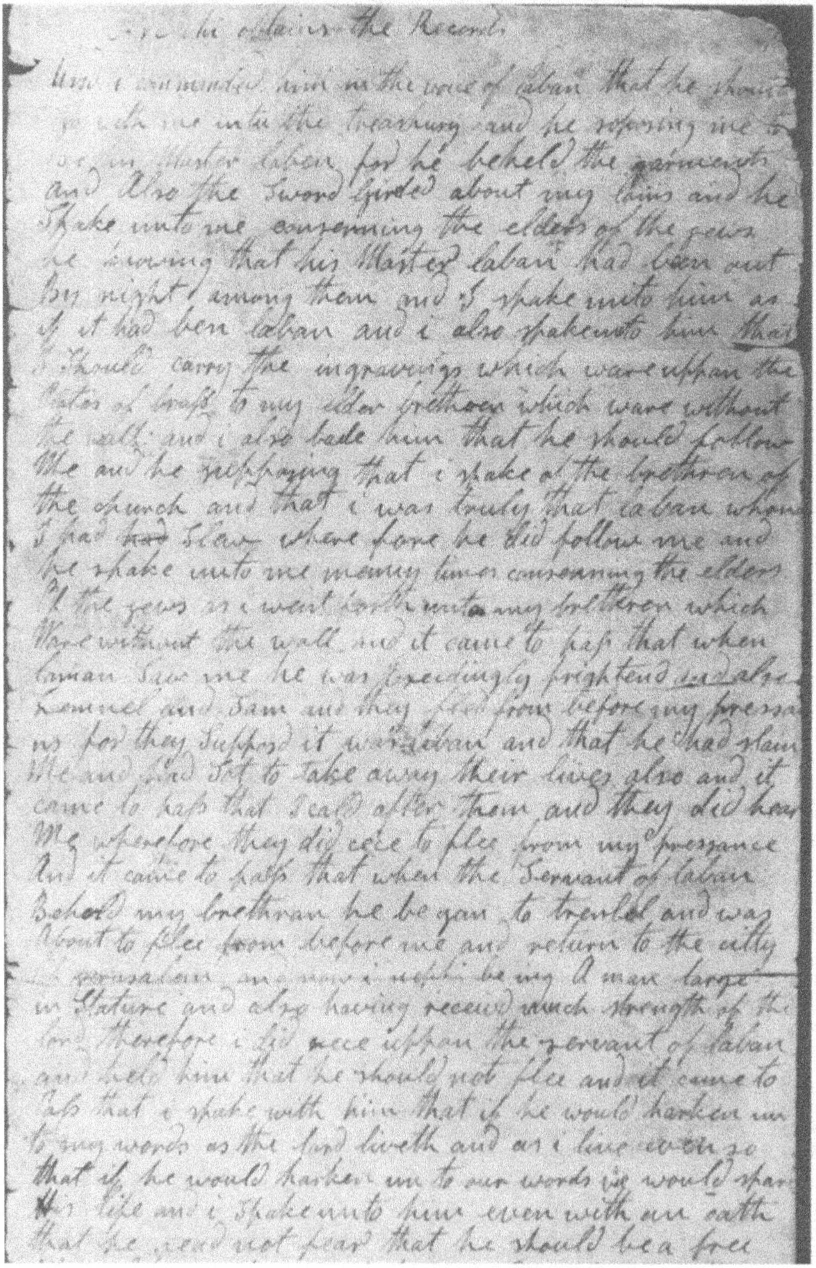

Skousen, *Original Manuscript*, plate 7, p. 45.

There is evidence that ms$U$ drafts were eventually also written on gatherings similar to those of O and P. Robert J. Espinosa, conservator at the Harold B. Lee Library at BYU, found that the first gathering of O used a paper type not found elsewhere in the extant materials.[396] This paper was very possibly left over from a quire used for the final gathering of ms$U$. Its pages too would have been stitched together in gatherings. Initially Smith and Cowdery would have considered it their original translation manuscript.

In Chapter 10 we found that O contains substantial empirical evidence for U, in the form of numerous copy errors throughout the extant portion of O. These frequently contain bits of U fossilized in the text. There is also testimony of a contemporary. Joseph Fielding Smith Sr. stated regarding the copy in the possession of David Whitmer, that "it was not the original, but one of the three originals"[397] (viz mss U, O and P).

The Walls of Jerusalem and the Composition Date of Nephi

As mentioned, Emma recounted that once, while translating the *Book of Mormon*, Joseph queried, "Emma, did Jerusalem have walls around it?" There is only one reference to the walls of Jerusalem in the entire *Book of Mormon*, in 1 Nephi 4:4. This text occurs in ms$O$, but there it was penned by Fayette scribe John Whitmer, not Emma. The timing works perfectly for this to be the ms$U$ text being written in the winter of 1828/29, when Emma was writing for Joseph.

Alternatively, it has been suggested that it refers to when she was writing part of the *Book of Lehi* (the purloined 116 pages) for Joseph at the beginning of 1828. The problem with this is that the content of the *Book of Nephi* is not at all the same as the *Book of Lehi*, retold in slightly different words. It is radically different in subject matter. The small plates were reserved for "the things of God" (1 Nephi 6:3); a "small account of the prophets, from Jacob down to the reign of this king Benjamin" (Mormon 1:3); "the prophecies of the coming of Christ" (WoM 1:4) and other "prophesyings and revelations" (WoM 1:6). By contrast, the larger plates (from which Mormon abridged the *Book of Lehi*) contain "an abridgment of the record of [Nephi's] father [Lehi]"; the "genealogy of his fathers"; "an account of [Nephi's] own life"; "the more part of all [their] proceedings in the wilderness"; "the proceedings of this people, their wars,

---

[396] Skousen, *Original Manuscript*, 37-38.
[397] Whitmer, in Cook, ed., *Whitmer Interviews*, 161. See supra, p. 126.

and their contentions"; and the records "of the reigns of their kings," "*handed down by the kings*, from generation to generation" (Nephi 1:17; 9:4; 19:2; Jacob 3:13; WoM 1:10). The content of the small plates (the things of God, the prophecies of the coming of Christ, and other prophesyings and revelations) is what Mormon found lacking in the larger plates, the *Book of Lehi*. The prophets and prophecies mentioned as being the subject matter of the small plates are largely a reference to the Isaiah inclusions taken from the Brass Plates, with Nephi's commentary. To have these inclusions it was necessary to obtain the Brass Plates. No parallel content ascribed to the *Book of Lehi* serves as a requirement for the story of getting those plates from Laban, the story that makes reference to the walls of Jerusalem. It is not even known that the Brass Plates were part of the Lehi story. *If these inclusions were in the Book of Lehi, Smith would not have been able to replicate them, and would not have put them in Nephi. Since they are in Nephi, they must not have been in Lehi.*

So there is a substantial probability that the walls of Jerusalem were not even mentioned in Lehi. We at least do know that they are mentioned in Nephi. The only documented mention is in Ms𝒪. Emma's account refers to her work writing its antecedent, ms𝒰.

Moreover, Emma said that Joseph's query was while translating the *Book of Mormon*. It is unclear that she would include the *Book of Lehi* under that rubric. For her, by the time of this interview, this title referred primarily if not exclusively to the published Mormon scripture.

As seen in Figure 18, the nearly edit-free condition of 𝒪 contrasts sharply with the manuscripts of the *Book of Moses*, which is what we should expect to see in an original composition manuscript.

No Part of Ms𝒪 Can Be Dated to Prior to June 1, 1829

We know that ms𝒪 existed in Fayette due to the work of the Fayette scribes. We have no part of ms𝒪 that can be shown to have ever existed in Harmony. This is because it was not even begun in Harmony. Ms𝒪 has page numbers; pages 1 & 2 are not extant, page 3 was done by Cowdery; and page 4 was done by a Fayette scribe, but edited by Cowdery. The BoM urtext (ms𝒰) was all but complete when David Whitmer took Smith and Cowdery to his father's home. It seems probable that Cowdery did pages 1-3 of ms𝒪 shortly after his arrival, partly because the two Fayette scribes had barely been converted, partly to produce three pages as a model for these new scribes, and partly to have some more finished sample pages to show a prospective printer as soon as possible. The finding that ms𝒰 was completed shortly after the move to Fayette is consistent with Smith's statement that the BoM (ms𝒰) was completed, or nearly so, prior to his trip to Palmyra to make arrangements with a printer.

Table 47. Pages in Ms𝒪 with Visible Page Numbers[398]

Scribe	ms pages	Corresponding BoM Text
Cowdery	6, 44, 111-114	1 Nephi 4:2-20, 22 4-14; Jacob 6:11-7:6 thru Enos 1:9-14
John Whitmer	20, 22	I Nephi 13:1-18; 13:29-35
Scribe 3	5, 7, 11-18	1 Nephi 3:18-4:2; 4:2-37; 7:17-12:8
Note: Page 30, with no extant page number, done by John Whitmer, is the last page done by a Fayette scribe. It contains 1 Nephi 15:36-16:14. From here on, Cowdery is the sole scribe for the extant pages of ms𝒪.		

The abrupt cessation of scribal service done by the Fayette scribes may be explained as marking the rough date when Smith and Cowdery left the Whitmer home, having achieved their purpose there, i.e. to complete the BoM, which for them was still ms𝒰. After leaving the Whitmer home, the Fayette scribes were no longer available. Alternatively, at least for a while, Smith and Cowdery may not yet have left Fayette, but were entirely engaged in teaching their new gospel. In any case, the page numbers provide *prima facie* evidence that ms𝒪 was barely begun in Fayette. As far as can be empirically determined, there is no extant part of ms𝒪 that can be dated to any time prior to June 1, 1829.

Fayette: Preparation for the End Game

Without doubt, on that long trip from Harmony to Fayette, Smith's first concern was his meeting with the Whitmers. This family was to join his own for the completion of the BoM project, and ultimately to get the new church established. One Whitmer would be one of the three witnesses to the gold plates, and others would be five of the eight witnesses (including in-law Hiram Page). He had not yet met them, and they had heard so much about him. He must not disappoint. Beyond that, he must establish his prophet persona. He succeeded in baptizing two, received revelations for David, John and Peter Jr., and recruited a couple to work as scribes.

Second, he had to get a contract and a funder for the publication of

---

[398] Skousen, *Original Manuscript*, 33.

the *Book of Mormon* (in Palmyra) and his copyright (in Utica, NY).

The hurry to get the work into print as soon as possible was partly due to the urgency they felt to establish their church and get on with recruiting members. But for Smith, it was also governed by his need to get back to Harmony fall farmwork to support his family.

A trip was made to Palmyra to arrange for the printing of the *Book of Mormon*. The distance from Fayette to Palmyra is c. 30 miles. Initially, a friend of Harris, and Smith's preferred publisher, Egbert B. Grandin, declined.[399] After approaching two other printers, they visited Elihu F. Marshall in Rochester, editor of the *Rochester Album*. According to Pomeroy Tucker, he countered Smith's offer with his terms for the project[400] (v. pp. 120-21). The tentative positive outcome with Marshall enabled Smith and Harris, back in Palmyra, to assure Grandin that since the work was going to be published anyway, it would be better for them to publish in Palmyra due to the expense of maintaining someone in Rochester, and Grandin might as well get the job. This time, Grandin accepted. Dirkmaat and Mackay estimate that the entire quest just for a printer took a week.[401]

What Text to Show Prospective Publishers?

To secure the agreement with Grandin, Smith needed a manuscript better than ms$\mathcal{U}$, with all of its edits. This would be $\mathcal{O}$, the original printer's copy. Since one of the Fayette scribes began work in 1 Nephi 2, it is clear that it was begun in Fayette for this purpose. At this point, only a few manuscript pages had been copied into the first gathering. This comports with the statement of Grandin's typesetter, John H. Gilbert, that "A few pages of the manuscript were submitted as a specimen of the whole, and it was said there would be about 500 pages."[402] That was enough for Grandin to have Gilbert calculate the cost. When Martin Harris indicated that he would

---

[399] Gerrit J. Dirkmaat & Michael Hubbard MacKay, "Joseph Smith's Negotiations to Publish the *Book of Mormon*," in Dennis L. Largey, Andrew H. Hedges, John Hilton III, and Kerry Hull, Editors, *The Coming Forth of the Book of Mormon. A Marvelous Work and a Wonder* (Salt Lake City: Deseret Book Co., 2015), 157. See this source for most of this paragraph.

[400] Pomeroy Tucker, *Origin, Rise and Progress of Mormonism* (New York: D. Appleton and Co., 1867 This is found in Vogel, Documents, III, 114.

[401] Gerrit J. Dirkmaat & Michael Hubbard MacKay, "Joseph Smith's Negotiations

[402] John H. Gilbert, "Memorandum, made by John H. Gilbert Esq., Sep. 8th, 1892, Palmyra, N.Y." This can be found in Vogel, II, 543.

mortgage his farm and serve as guarantor, Grandin was ready to begin what was for him a very large project. The relatively accurate estimate of the total pages was possible, estimating from ms U.

The Fayette scribes did not write for Smith after 1 Nephi 16:14. Their work is limited to the first 26 extant pages of ms O. Four pages are missing from the first gathering, which originally had 24 pages. Six pages from the second gathering gives us 20+6=26. The tally is: pages 3 (the first extant page of gathering one), most of 4 and the last fourth of page 6 done by Cowdery (S^1); twelve pages done by the first unidentified scribe (S^2, John Whitmer), and twelve by the second (S^3). So, nearly all of the scribal work was done by these two, S^2 and S^3, up to when quite suddenly they no longer appear in ms O. (See Appendix 4.) These two men were among Smith's most faithful supporters, who would go on to make important contributions for the rise of the early church. Certainly they would not walk off the job. And it is equally certain that it was important to free up Cowdery's time to enable him to further polish the translation document, perhaps also to get a start on ms P, and possibly even to copy Ether into ms O (a separate history, which occupies a separate gathering in ms P).

David Whitmer later wrote that the *Book of Mormon* was completed in his father's home, "from about June 1 to July 1."[403] Smith wrote, "Having finished our translation [or "translation drawing to a close," c. June 7], we went to Palmyra, Wayne County, NY, and Secured the Copyright" (dated June 11; History, 1839). This is an important note because the date of the copyright (June 11) obtained in Utica, NY, after agreeing on details with Grandin, is several days later than when the translation was "finished."[404] This statement indicates that nearly all of ms U had already been done in Harmony, and was completed before June 11. It is consistent with a revealed statement, prior to the three witnesses event, that "he has translated the book, even that part which I have commanded him." (D&C 17:6) Grandin published the copyright text in the *Wayne Sentinel* of June 26, and stated that "It is pretended that it will be published as soon as the translation is complete." Since this statement does not comport with the foregoing texts, it was probably based on assurances made by Smith referring to the preparation of gatherings of the printer's copy, at that time ms O, which was just getting under way.

---

[403] David Whitmer, to the *Kansas City Journal*, 5 June 1881; see Backman, *Eyewitness Accounts*, 124.

[404] Third draft of Smith's 1838-c. 1841 history. The first and second drafts say, "our translation drawing to a close..." JSP, *Histories*, vol. 1, 352-53.

Although Lucy Smith stated that "as soon as the *Book of Mormon* was translated," there was a celebration, for which she, Joseph Sr. and Martin Harris traveled to Fayette,[405] even so, the completion of the *Book of Mormon* does not refer to the entire book of New World scripture that the LDS cherish. The copyright document has two parts. The first is for the *Book of Mormon*, the record of the Nephites, and the second is for the record of Ether, the account of the Jaredites. So the completion of the *Book of Mormon* does not necessarily include Ether, which Mormon had nothing to do with, and as we shall see, the Book of Moroni was not yet even envisioned, being an add-on book done c. February of 1830.

We get our best idea of the early view of the relationship between these two books, the *Book of Mormon* and the *Book of Ether,* from the text division in the printed copyright text submitted by Joseph Smith in Utica. This text makes it clear that the *Book of Mormon* is Mormon's abridgment. The words "Also, which is a record of the people of Jared" begins a new paragraph (v. Figure 19), making it the second of two companion works. In ms𝒫, Ether begins a fresh gathering as is appropriate for an independent work. Unfortunately, this part of Ether is not extant in ms𝒪.

Based on word counts, the portion of the replacement text (1 Nephi 1:1 through Words of Mormon) that was copied into ms𝒪 in Fayette (i.e., by the Fayette scribes, 1 Nephi 1:1 through 1 Nephi 16:14) is only 28%, which is only 5% of the Nephite narrative. Since this completion of the *Book of Mormon* cannot be in reference even to the extant portion of ms𝒪, it can only refer to ms𝒰, the translation text.

According to Lucy Smith, it was after the completion celebration that her son received a commandment that a second copy should be prepared for the printer (ms𝒫). This enabled Smith to present ms𝒪 to the world as his original, a nearly perfect manuscript (a clean copy of ms𝒰), claimed to have been made by Cowdery as the revealed text was read out by Smith, viz. just what the believer would expect. Thus after the demise of ms𝒰, there would still be two copies to avoid another tragedy should one be purloined. Fortunately, Grandin did not have enough type for much work to get done even after it began in mid August, and his order for additional type did not arrive until around the end of November. It is very possible that the ms𝒪 copy was also completed before Smith returned to Harmony to farm his small patch of land in early October.

---

[405] Lucy Smith, Lucy's Book, 451.

Figure 19. *Book of Mormon* Copyright Text
The printed copy submitted in Utica to apply for the copyright.

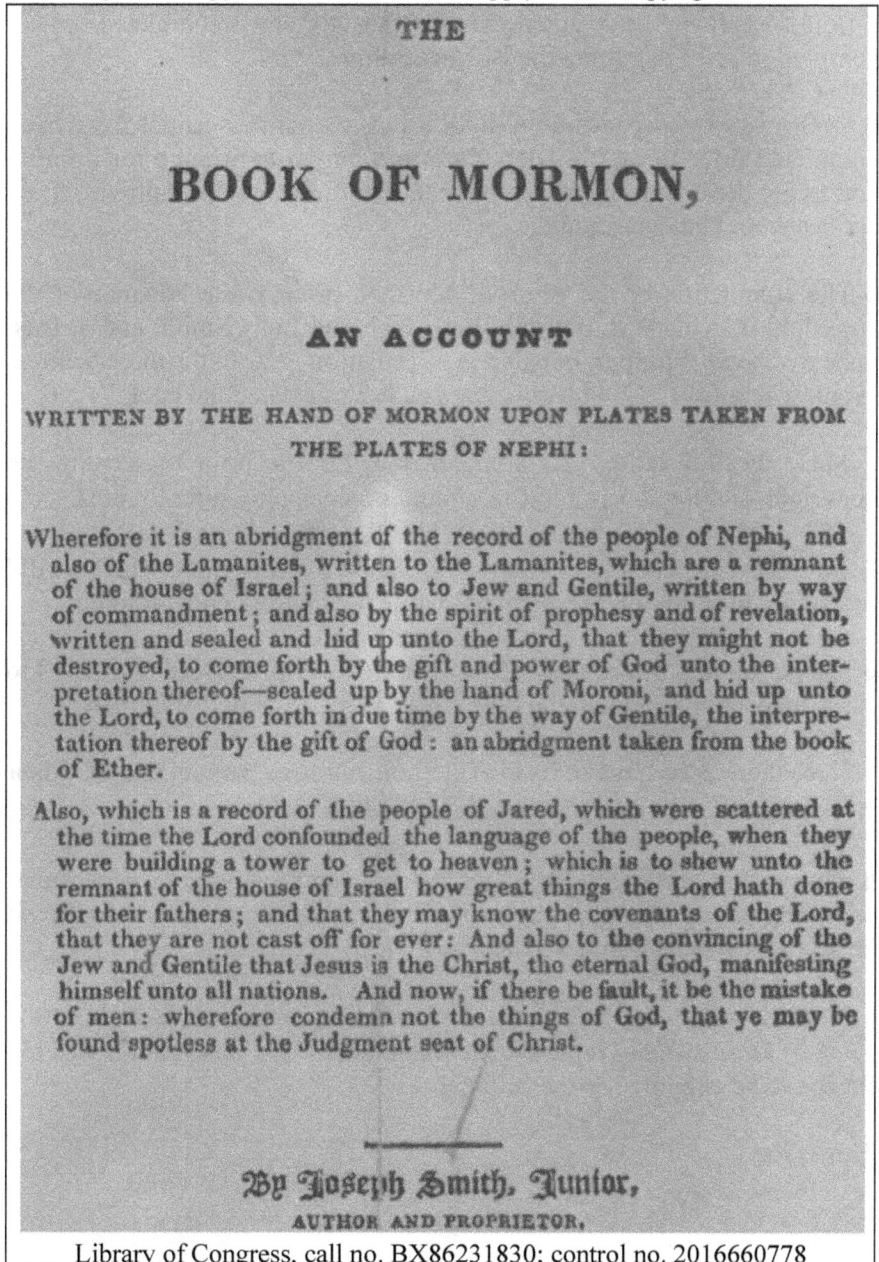

THE

BOOK OF MORMON,

AN ACCOUNT

WRITTEN BY THE HAND OF MORMON UPON PLATES TAKEN FROM THE PLATES OF NEPHI:

Wherefore it is an abridgment of the record of the people of Nephi, and also of the Lamanites, written to the Lamanites, which are a remnant of the house of Israel; and also to Jew and Gentile, written by way of commandment; and also by the spirit of prophesy and of revelation, written and sealed and hid up unto the Lord, that they might not be destroyed, to come forth by the gift and power of God unto the interpretation thereof—sealed up by the hand of Moroni, and hid up unto the Lord, to come forth in due time by the way of Gentile, the interpretation thereof by the gift of God: an abridgment taken from the book of Ether.

Also, which is a record of the people of Jared, which were scattered at the time the Lord confounded the language of the people, when they were building a tower to get to heaven; which is to shew unto the remnant of the house of Israel how great things the Lord hath done for their fathers; and that they may know the covenants of the Lord, that they are not cast off for ever: And also to the convincing of the Jew and Gentile that Jesus is the Christ, the eternal God, manifesting himself unto all nations. And now, if there be fault, it be the mistake of men: wherefore condemn not the things of God, that ye may be found spotless at the Judgment seat of Christ.

By Joseph Smith, Junior,
AUTHOR AND PROPRIETOR,

Observations

§ Both Joseph and Lucy assert that the translation was completed or near completion prior to getting the BoM copyright.

§ Even just the 26 pages done by the Fayette scribes cannot have been completed prior to Smith's departure to Palmyra to arrange for printing and to get the copyright text printed. While Smith was in Palmyra, these scribes would have been idle.

§ The completion of the Book of Mormon prior to the issuance of the copyright is evidenced, not only by Joseph and Lucy Smith, and at least once by David Whitmer, but also in a revelation prior to the three-witness event, where D&C 17:6 affirms that "he has translated the book."

§ Since the translation was completed in Fayette prior to seeking the copyright, and ms$\mathcal{O}$ was not, this completion can only refer to ms$\mathcal{U}$.

§ Smith also took action in Palmyra to secure his copyright, which he did by getting his copyright text printed while negotiating with Grandin.

§ The period to produce the BoM was from November/December 1828 to early June, approximately the time stated twice by David Whitmer.

§ Since there is no trace of handwriting of Emma or Samuel in ms$\mathcal{O}$, their work of writing for Joseph would have been in ms$\mathcal{U}$.

§ The scribal work done by Emma and Samuel was almost certainly enough to have gotten well into Alma 10:31, which is extant, and so should be at least partly in Samuel's hand.

§ Our best example of what ms$\mathcal{U}$ looked like is the manuscripts of the *Book of Moses*. Being replete with emendations, its presentation was too flawed to be exhibited as the original.

This is the

ms$\mathcal{U}$ completion issue

< Chapter 24 >

Ms𝒰 to Ms𝒪, and the Creation of Second Nephi

Apart from examining occasional editorial changes in ms𝒪, scholars have been seized of some formatting issues, such as pagination, page headings, summaries at the head of certain books and the division of Nephi into two books.

The Page Headings: A Nonissue?

Ms𝒪 provides additional evidence of a preexisting text, ms𝒰. First, there is evidence that a <u>book synopsis</u> was placed at the beginning of principal books. Unfortunately, book beginnings survived only for two traditional BoM books: 2 Nephi and Helaman (Helaman the Younger). It also has a book synopsis for Helaman the Elder (located between Alma 44 and 45) and for a presumptive 3 Nephi B (see below). Furthermore, the first line of each page contained a page content heading. Unfortunately, this part of the pages tended to fall victim to water and mold damage. Some wording of extant page content headings, and book content synopses, are provided in Table 48. Those found in the printer's copy (ms𝒫) were most probably also in ms𝒪.

Table 48. Page Content Headings and Book Synopses in Mss 𝒪 & 𝒫

Book Synopsis (𝒫)

   First   Chapter 1 st
The ^ Book of Nephi ^ his reign and ministry. An account
of Lehi, & his wife Sariah, & his Sons, being called, beginning at
the eldest‹,› Laman, Lemuel, Sam & Nephi —the Lord warns Lehi to dep
art out of the land of Jerusalem because he prophesieth unto the people co
ncerning their iniquity—and they seek to destroy his life—he taketh three days jou
-rney ‹un› into the wilderness with his family—Nephi taketh his brethren & retur
-ns to the land of Jerusalem after the record of the Jews—the account of their
sufferings—they take the daughters of Ishmael to wife—they take their
families & depart into the wilderness—their sufferings & afflictions in
the wilderness—the course of their travels—they come to the large waters
—Nephis Brethren rebelleth against him he confoundeth them & bu|i|
-ldeth a ship—they call the place Bountiful—they cross the large waters
Into the promised land &C. this is according to the account of Nephi

---

or in other words I Nephi wrote this record.

Relatively intact wording from the longer passages of page content headings:

1 Nephi 2:2: "Nephi crieth unto the Lord for his Brethren" (Facsimile Edition, 741)
1 Nephi 2:23: "(N)ephi goeth up to Jerusalem to bring the Records of the jews"
1 Nephi 3:18: "The brethren of Nephi Smite him with a Rod"
1 Nephi 4:2: "Nephi slayeth Laban &C"
1 Nephi 4:20: "Nephi obtains the Records"
1 Nephi 4:38: "Lehi searcheth the Records"
1 Nephi 5:14: "Lehi Prophesyeth conserning his seed"
1 Nephi 7:3: "Laman and lemuel rebelleth Against Nephi"
1 Nephi 7:17: "laman and lemuel Repent g[ ] with Nephi"
1 Nephi 8:11: "Lehies dream of the Pressious fruit"
1 Nephi 8: 27: "Lehies p/fears for laman and lemuel and he exorts (th)e(m)"
1 Nephi 9:4: "Lehi Prophesies of the messiah and so forth"
1 Nephi 10:11: "(N)ephi Desireth the Spirit of (P)rophesy"
1 Nephi 11:1: "Nephi caught Away in the Spirit an(d so fo   )"
1 Nephi 11:18: "Nephi beholdeth the Lam of God &{C}"
1 Nephi 11:32: "The Masiah Crusafied &C"

Book Synopsis (𝒪 & 𝒫)

2 Nephi:

~~+~~

~~Chapter V VIII~~

    Second   Chapte[r] I
The ^ Book of Nephi ^ An account of the death of Lehi ~~the Lord~~ Nephis Brethren
rebelleth against him—the Lord warns Nephi to depart into the wilderness — &C
his journeyings in the wilderness—&C

Book Synopsis (𝒫)

The Book of Jacob (‹Chapter I.)›
          Chapter I
The Brother of Nephi ^ the words of his preaching unto his Brethren—He
confoundeth
a man who seeketh to overthrow the doctrine of Christ—A few words concerning the
histo
-ry of the People of Nephi

Book Synopses (in either 𝒪 or 𝒫)

No synopsis for Enos, Jarom, Omni, the Words of Mormon or Mosiah.

Book Synopsis (𝒫)

Alma (Alma the Younger)

the Book of Alma Chapter 1/st
_____the son of Alma
   The account of Alma who was the Son of Alma the First and
Chief {g|J-}udge over the people of Nephi & also the high Priest over the
Church. An account of the Reign of the Judges and the wars & contentions
Among the people, And also an account of a war between the Nep
-hites & the Lamanites According to the Record of Alma the first and Chief Judge

Section Synopsis: Alma 17-26 (𝒫)

Alma the Younger (drawing from the account of Ammon)

An ac{c}ount of the Sons of Mosiah, w[h]o reje{c}ted the{i}r rights to the {K}ing
-{d}om for the word of God, & went up {ro} the land of Nephi, to prea{c}h to the
Lamanites. [T]heir sufferings & deliverance{e}, according to the record of Alma.

Relatively intact wording from the longer passages of page content headings:

Alma 23:7: "(AntiNe)phiLehi Ie(ig)ns in (h)is s(te[ad])"
Alma 25:16: "Alma & his (   )"
Alma 26:24: "Ammo{n}s discours(   )"
Alma 26:35: "(h)is Brethren {of th}e People of
AntiNephi[L]ehi"
Alma 27:12: "[th]e Peo{[}le of Anti{N}eph{i}Lehi   )"
Alma 27:24: "(th)e People [o]f Ammon &C."
Alma 28:6: "exertation of Al(ma   )"
Alma 30:2: "Korihor who is called (A)n(ti   )"
Alma 30:28 "Korihor before A(lm   )"
Alma 30:53: "[K]orihor is trodden to (D)e(a   )"
Alma 35:1: "([the people of Am]mon) [go to] the land of Melek [&]C"
Alma 35:14: "Amas [C]harge to (   )"
Alma 36:10: "(   ) his Son Helaman &C"
Alma 37:30: "(n)dments to his Son Helaman &C"
Alma 38:8: "(e)nts to his Son Corianto{n}"
Alma 43:47: "the La{m}anites ensercl{e}d"

Book Synopsis (𝒪 & 𝒫)

Helaman the Elder (text inserted between Alma 44 & 45)

T{he} account{n}t of the {P}eople of Nephi and the{i}r wars & d{e}se{n}sions in
the days of Hela{m}an accord{i}ng to the Reckor{d} of H{e}lam{a}n which {he}
{k}ept in his days

Relatively intact wording from the longer passages of page content headings:

Alma 47:23: "[A]melecki{a}h Caus{e}s the King to (d   )"
Alma 49:9: "the La{m}anites go to the C(ity   )"
Alma 50:1 "Moroni drive[s] the (L)ama(nite   )"
Alma 50:26: "Morionton slain [&]C the Ch(ief   )"
Alma 51:8: "A[m]eleck{i}ah comes up to a({tta[k]   )"
Alma 52:17: "Moron{i} {u}ses stratagem to (   )"
Alma 53:22: "Moroni sends a{n} Epistle"
Alma 54:24: "Moroni sends Laman to (de   )"
Alma 55:28: "Helama{n} sends an Ipistle   )"

Book Synopsis (𝒪 & 𝒫)

Helaman the Younger

    The Book of Helaman
        Chapter I
  An account of the Nephites t(h)eir W(a)rs & Conten(TIONS & THEIR DISSENSIONS & ALSO) the Prop(h)es{i}es of many Holy Prophets before the coming (Of CHRIST ACCORDING TO THE REC)k[o]rd of Helaman which was the Son of Helaman & also a(cCORDING TO THE RECKORDS OF HIS SONS) even down to (t)he comeing of Chr{i}st & also many of the Lam(aNITES ARE CONVERTED AN ACCO)ount of their conve[r]sion an account of the r{i}ghteousness o(f tHE LAMANITES & THE WICK)e{d}ne{s}s & abominat{i}ons of the Nephites accord{i}ng to the Reckord of (H)el{a}m(an (& HIS SONS EV)en do{wn} to the come{i}ng of Chr{i}st wh{i}ch is c{a}lled the Book of Helaman &C.

Relatively intact wording from the longer passages of page content headings:

Helaman 1:17: "the [Lam]a[n]it[es] take [City [of] [Za]r[a](hem   )"

Book Synopsis (in either 𝒪 or 𝒫)

No synopsis for 3 Nephi (just preceded by his genealogy). However, there is a synopsis between chapters 10 and 11:

    Jesus Christ shweth himself unto the people of Nephi, as the multitude were gathered together in the land of Bountiful, and did minister unto them; an [and] on this wise did he shew himself unto them.

On this basis, 3 Nephi is divided presumptively into 3 Nephi A and 3 Nephi B.

No synopsis exists for 4 Nephi, Mormon, Ether or Moroni.

Some LDS scholars are concerned to show that the heading line was left blank when beginning a page, and after finishing it, the heading was written in the blank space. This appears to be because the content of the page should not have been known, even to Joseph Smith, before receiving the translation. Royal Skousen refers to ms*O* page 6, where the heading is in the hand of Cowdery, but the page was done by unknown scribe two down through line 40, and Cowdery took over at line 41, to the end. If the heading line was left blank, then Cowdery, being the last scribe standing, pen in hand, would naturally fill in the heading to finish the page.

At least for some time, scribe three did headings. On pages 7-18 the heading and the text body were both done by scribe three.

Scribe two does not do page content headings. In two cases, two was the last scribe standing, but scribe three did the heading. The text of page four was done mostly by Cowdery, following his work on page three, but on line 49 he inserts a supralinear edit, after which scribe two continues to the end. The heading is done by scribe three. On page 5, scribe two did the text and scribe three did the heading. In other cases, the heading was left blank. Page nineteen was begun by scribe three, who did just three words, and then scribe two took over to the end. Although the area for the heading is intact, no heading was written. On pages 20 and 22, scribe two wrote the page number and the text, but no heading, although the space is intact. On the extant pages 21 & 25-29, scribe two wrote the text, but put in no heading.

Skousen explains the absence of headings, where clearly a line was left blank (mostly pages where scribe two did the text), as follows: "It appears that unknown scribe 2 did not like to do these headings..."[406] On the other hand, when beginning a page, scribe two always left a space for a heading.

Most of the pages 31-233 have damage in the heading area, but there is evidence that Cowdery had also ceased to put in headings. He did the text for all of these pages. Pages 111-114 (Jacob 6:11 through Enos 1:14) are sufficiently intact to see that Cowdery did not put in their headings. Later he resumed putting in page content headings. The next extant undisputed page (after 1 Nephi 2:2-Enos 1:14) is page 225' (Alma 10:31). Skousen uses the prime ['] to indicate his extrapolated page numbers.). From this point on, Cowdery did all of the remaining extant pages, up to 472' (ending with Ether 15:17). All of these pages have headings, and both

---

[406] Skousen, *Original Manuscript*, 25.

they and the texts are in the hand of Cowdery. He also did both the heading and text of the first extant page, page 3.

I say undisputed due to the disputed Chicago Leaves (two sheets from the University of Chicago special collections, containing Alma 3:5–17, 3:17–4:2, 4:20–5:10 and 5:10–23. These have 42 or 43 lines.

A more important issue than whether the heading line was left blank or not is why the headings were done in the first place. It seems to be a bit of work, and must have had a function. Perhaps they were first done simply to emulate the appearance of the Bible and its headings. Then, both Cowdery and Smith must have realized that the pages of ms$\mathcal{O}$ would not track with the pages of the printed edition. At this point they were abandoned. But when they accumulated more and more pages, and got into the more complex books, with many city and personal names, articulations of theological positions, and geographical locations, the need became apparent to be able to go back, efficiently, to crosscheck with what had been written 30, 50 or 200 pages earlier. The headings were recommenced to serve as a sort of index to facilitate finding the key locations relevant to this crosschecking process. In addition, they would have enabled the work to resume without confusion or duplication after a hiatus, due to a lunch or coffee break or an unexpected visitor. They were not inserted into the copy made for the printer, and ms$\mathcal{O}$ was thought to be safe from prying inspection, at first in Smith's possession, and then in the foundation stone.

Actually, the heading issue is not as threatening to the LDS position as one might think. If divine power could translate reformed Egyptian, surely it could supply page headings prior to translating the page. Similarly, BoM critics can be perfectly at ease with the view that the page headings were done after the pages. The nature of the drafts for the *Book of Moses* is known to us, with supralinear edits and additions, and slips of paper pinned to pages with additional text to be inserted. If Smith was reciting from such a complex draft, it may not have been clear how much draft material would fill a page. Putting in page headings after the fact would accommodate this uncertainty. In any case, Wisdom counsels that we not presume to know more than we do.

Furthermore, this issue is irrelevant to the Mosiah priority issue since that question goes to the order of the production of the chapters in ms$\mathcal{U}$. As we shall see in chapters 27-28, there is evidence of multiple authorship. Different drafters may have done Nephi, Alma and possibly even Mosiah simultaneously. Furthermore, ms$\mathcal{O}$ has page numbers showing that when the drafts were copied into it, the work began with Nephi. Unfortunately, neither Mosiah nor Moroni is found in the extant ms$\mathcal{O}$ materials.

Book Summaries and the Division of the Book of Nephi Draft

In any case, the introductions present in the body of the text, introducing 2 Nephi, Helaman the Elder (between Alma 44 &45) and Helaman (the Younger), cannot be explained away in this manner. These three book-content introductions were retained in Cowdery's printer's copy. There, we find a similar book content introduction for the Book of Jacob, but none for the very small works, from Enos through the Words of Mormon. It is also lacking at the beginning of Mosiah, which has an unusual beginning, having been at first treated as a continuation of Words of Mormon, to the extent that the title, "the Book of Mosiah," was omitted, and had to be added in as a correction. An introduction is found for 3 Nephi B (between 3 Nephi 10 and 11). Given the extreme care to copy ms$O$ exactly, and the presence of two book introductions, it is highly likely that the other introductions in ms$P$ were retained from ms$O$. Even so, some books lack this introduction, at least in the printer's manuscript. The book-content summaries constitute additional evidence for the use of a prior draft, ms$U$.

When Cowdery arrived in Harmony, the duo's first task was to study and revise work drafted so far. They would have integrated books already in draft into an initial overall work, the emergent urtext, ms$U$. Texts already done could be edited as needed, not only with text edits, but with text additions or deletions. In addition to his scrivener duty, Cowdery was able to serve as a sort of (imperfect) grammar and spell check for Smith, and the two would discuss the next day's work. His typically neat work indicates that Cowdery did not hurry. At any time, they could pause and consult each other. The issue of multiple drafters will be investigated through analyses of the distribution of style.

While we are on this topic, note that there is evidence from the earliest extant manuscript that Nephi was originally intended to be just one book. The replacement text was ordered to be called the record of Nephi, a single work. We see this in D&C 10:42: "...you shall publish it as the record of Nephi..." Even when this work was divided into two books, the title, the Book of Nephi, persisted for each book. Even in the printer's ms, both First Nephi and Second Nephi were originally titled the Book of Nephi. Editing his work, Cowdery inserted "First" between *the* and *Book* for First Nephi, and "Second" between *the* and *Book* for Second Nephi [the *second* Book of...]. Thus the first of these begins "The ^first Book of Nephi, Chapter 1," followed by a book summary. (NOTE: The chapters are the longer ones found in the 1830 BoM first printed edition, shortened later for LDS printings.)

The persistence of "The Book of Nephi" even after dividing it probably came from D&C 10:42. Note that Nephi in its original form was not as long as Alma. If Smith and Cowdery had already accepted Alma, a double book (AlmaY and HelamanE) to be a single book, they probably would not have felt a need to divide Nephi, especially when doing so meant countermanding a direct order from God to publish it as the Book of Nephi.

> ... the last day and thus it is Amen ~~Chapter {V|I} VIII~~
> **Second**   Chapter 1
> The⌃Book of Nephi⌃An account of the death of Lehi...
>
> Brethren rebelleth against him...

This is an attempt to represent the manuscript just using a word processor. The source is a grey-scale image in the Facsimile Edition of ms$\mathcal{O}$. All three lines in grey represent the dim quill work, in its current aged condition. The spaces seen here between lines are a bit exaggerated. The first observation to be made is that the last words of 1 Nephi ("thus it is Amen") end just before the half-way point of the line, and "The Book of Nephi..." begins the next line. "T" of "The" and the "B" of "Book" seem to have been written with a bit of a flourish. The book summary follows immediately.

These three lines, are spaced very much the same as the line spacing on the rest of the page. Skousen's introduction of line 13 does not exist in the ms. I assume that it was thought useful for editorial purposes. For the complex supralinear chapter additions, Cowdery took advantage of the space at the end of the last line of chapter 7, after the word "Amen."

The entire page has roughly equal ink weight. The exception is the supralinear addition "second," which is substantially heavier. It may be that the chapter corrections were done while proofing the page, and that the addition of "second" was later.

A workable scenario for the process of entering ms$\mathcal{U}$ into ms$\mathcal{O}$ is as follows. First, Nephi was written in ms$\mathcal{U}$ as a single book, with chapters numbered continuously, including chapter 8 (etc.) following chapter 7. Then it was decided to divide the book in two, and a new book summary was composed. This was written on a small chit that was pinned in at the point where the division was to occur. Adhering to the commandment for the title, at the point of division "The Book of Nephi" was written, followed immediately by the book summary, and the beginning of 2 Nephi to the end of the page. The issue of the chapter divisions arose, and Cowdery took advantage of the space at the end of 1 Nephi. Smith followed the chapter numbers in ms U, and read out chapter eight. But just when Cowdery wrote the V of VIII, Smith said "Wait, let's make it chapter one." So Cowdery overwrote the V (of an intended VIII) with I. Then Smith changed his mind, and said, "No, let's go with chapter eight." So Cowdery drew a line through his V (overwritten with I), and followed it with VIII. Then Smith changed his mind again and went back to "Chapter 1." Cowdery decided that the line he had been using was now irretrievable, so he struck out the whole line, and wrote "Chapter 1". Finally, at some later time, "second" was placed supralinearly above "The Book of Nephi". In ms O, ∧ was written to locate the points where these edits were to be inserted.

The new book summary begins: "An account of the death of Lehi ~~the Lord~~ Nepis [Nephi's] Brethren rebel against him—the Lord warns Nephi to depart into the wilderness..." The phrase "~~the Lord~~" was accidentally written because Smith's eye had skipped to "Nephi's Brethren rebel..." and he started with "The Lord [warns]". Realizing what he had done, he deleted "The Lord" and continued with "Nephi's Brethren rebel..." followed by "The Lord warns..."[407]

Based on the evidence regarding the original drafts, I will use the following seventeen-book divisions for the analysis of BoM style:

Traditional BoM Books	*Books Based on Chapter Synopses*	
1 Nephi	1 Nephi	[Nephi, is used for Nephi 1 &
2 Nephi	2 Nephi	2 together, as a single book.]
Jacob	Jacob	
Enos	Enos	
Jarom	Jarom	
Omni	Omni	
Words of Mormon	Words of Mormon	
Mosiah	Mosiah	
Alma	Alma the Younger (Alma 1:1-44:24)	
	Helaman the Elder (Alma 45:1-60:17)	
Helaman	Helaman the Younger	
3 Nephi	3 Nephi A (1:1-10:19)	

---

[407] Skousen, *Original Manuscript*, 164; and in the facsimile edition, Royal Skousen, Robin Scott Jensen, , *Original Manuscript of the Book of Mormon, Facsimile Edition*, in *The Joseph Smith Papers*, volume 5 (Salt Lake City: The Church Historian's Press, 2021), 134-35.

	3 Nephi B (11:1-30:2)
4 Nephi	4 Nephi
Mormon	Mormon
Ether	Ether
Moroni	Moroni

Although Nephi was originally one book, the traditional division (1 Nephi and 2 Nephi) has been retained for citations. It is taken as a single book in studies of style distribution. The importance of the draft divisions will become clear as we get into the study of stylistic distribution among the books.

The Book of Mormon (i.e. the published work) is always italicized, even when it is found in the title of a cited work that does not italicize it. This is to distinguish it from Mormon's record, also called The "Book of Mormon", which is never italicized.

Careful analysis of ms$\mathcal{O}$ repays with interesting observations. Of these, one of the most important is the fact that its largely unedited condition requires the conclusion, at least for the secular scholar, that it is the result of dictation from a highly developed draft. The analysis of Mosiah in Chapter 26 will provide additional evidence. At least as important is the phenomenon of ms$\mathcal{U}$ empirically revealed in the numerous ms$\mathcal{O}$ copy errors (Chapter 10).

< Chapter 25 >

Origin of Ms𝒰: The Spalding-Rigdon Theory

The fundamental argument that led to the Spalding-Rigdon theory is a syllogism. When the *Book of Mormon* was published, those who took the trouble to read it were somewhat impressed. Although judging it to be a hoax, they were nonetheless surprised to find it more complex and theologically substantial than they had expected. This was occurring in an environment of efforts to undermine the credibility of the Smith family, to brand them a people of bad character, semiliterate and uneducated. So the three-point argument emerged. 1) The book required some sophistication and background (major premise); 2) the Smiths and Cowdery lacked these characteristics (minor premise); 3) so *therefore* someone else must have written it (conclusion). But who?

Shortly after the *Book of Mormon* was published, a new church was established, then called the Church of Christ. Some felt strongly that they were witnessing a dangerous heresy, a new church, based on a new bible authored by a person claiming to be a latter-day prophet, who challenged the authority of the Bible. Without doubt some of these considered it to be the work of Satan to undermine the true Christian faith at a time when they expected the events of the Apocalypse and the Second Coming of Christ. The more activist among them felt that the best offensive against this heresy was to prove that the new bible was false. At that time the means for conclusive archaeological investigation did not exist. The best vehicle to challenge the book was to brand it a plagiarism of a work done around two decades earlier, penned by Solomon Spalding. The accusation of plagiarism was first leveled at Sidney Rigdon, whose work was recast into the BoM narrative by Smith and Cowdery.

The Spalding/Rigdon Theory

One of the principal early arguments to ascribe authorship is based on statements alleging that a one-time minister, Solomon Spalding, wrote a historical romance based on the premise that the Indians descend from a lost tribe of Israel. Although he died in 1816, it is argued that he took his manuscript to a publisher in Pittsburgh. Years later, a Baptist minister, Sidney Rigdon, came to possess it and plagiarized it, in particular adding some religious material, to become at least a precursor draft of the BoM text. Smith and Cowdery published it, having made modifications of their own to adapt it to their needs. Consequently, whether the text published in 1830 was the work mostly of Spalding, or Rigdon or Smith and Cowdery, the new bible is nothing more than a plagiarized version of Spalding's work. Table 50 presents key points in Spalding's life.

Table 49. Solomon Spalding (also Spaulding)

Date	Event
1761	Born in Ashford, Connecticut.
1782	Entered Dartmouth College in Hanover, New Hampshire.
1785	Graduated with the class of 1785.
1787	Ordained a Congregationalist preacher.
1795	Married Matilda Sabin (Sabine].
	Opened a store with his brother in Cherry Valley, New York.
1799	Moved the store to Richfield, New York.
18??	Bought land and lived in Conneaut, Ohio.
18??	Wrote "Manuscript Found," the Oberlin ms, or both (1809-1812?).
1812	Moved to Pittsburgh, Pennsylvania.
	Reportedly took his manuscript to printers Patterson & Lambdin.
1814	Moved to Amity, Pennsylvania.
1816	Died in Amity.

In 1812 Spalding moved to Pittsburgh, Pennsylvania, and in 1814 to Amity, Pennsylvania, where he died in 1816. The argument usually made is that an alleged Israelite-origin manuscript had been taken to a publisher in Pittsburgh but was never published. It is also claimed that at a later date Sidney Rigdon, then working as a tanner, periodically visited the publisher and acquired or stole the manuscript. The Spalding-Rigdon argument got its start when individuals who claimed some knowledge of a Spalding manuscript alleged similarity to the *Book of Mormon*.

Hurlbut & the Syllogism's Minor Premise & Conclusion

Originally a Methodist lay minister, Doctor Philastus Hurlbut (1809-1883), "Doctor" being his first name, was converted to the Mormon faith and ordained an elder.[408] He was excommunicated in June of 1833. Sidney Rigdon, who had ordained him, wrote that this was due to his "using obscene language to a young lady, a member of the church," a charge that Hurlbut denied. Although there certainly is a difference between anti-Mormons and Mormonism critics, Hurlbut was the epitome of the former.

---

[408] Dan Vogel, "Preface" in Howe, *Mormonism Unvailed*, i-xxvii, and "Addenda" to the same, & 408-12.

Initially he began simply lecturing against Mormonism, but soon he obtained funds from a group of anti-Mormons to collect statements from individuals in both Palmyra and Harmony expressly to expose Joseph Smith, the entire Smith family and the *Book of Mormon*. These supplied material to support the minor premise that the BoM could never have been written by Smith whose bad character would certainly not qualify him to be a prophet of God. Believing that he had secured the minor premise and the syllogism conclusion, he then needed to address the question it posed, to wit, so "who did it?" To this end, he also collected statements regarding the historical romance of Solomon Spalding from Spalding's brother and sister in Conneaut, Ohio, from his widow Matilda Spalding Davidson in Massachusetts, and others who claimed an association with Spalding. With these he claimed he had identified the ultimate source of the precursor to Smith's new bible. Both sets of statements were published in Eber D. Howe's book *Mormonism Unvailed* (sic) in 1834. Later, Hurlbut had an association with Oberlin College, becoming a member of the board of trustees in 1847.

Table 50. Doctor Philastus Hurlbut ("Doctor" Being His First Name)

Date	Event
1809	born in Chittenden County, Vermont.
Late 1820s	became a Methodist class leader, exhorter & lay minister in Jamestown, New York.
Late 1832	converted to Mormonism.
March, 1833	ordained an elder by Sidney Rigdon; sent on a mission to Pennsylvania.
1833	told by a Methodist, Lyman Jackson, in Albion, that the BoM resembled a manuscript of Solomon Spalding.
1833	left his mission to interview John and Martha Spalding, Solomon Spalding's brother and sister, in Conneaut.
June 3, 1833	while interviewing the Spaldings he was excommunicated.
June 21, 1833	reinstated because of his "liberal confession".
1833	excommunicated again for attempting to discredit Joseph Smith.
1833	Collected funds from anti-Mormons Orrin Clapp, Nathan Corning, Grandison Newell and others "to obtain affidavits showing the bad character of the Mormon Smith family".
c. 9/1833-?	Collected statements, first from the Spaldings, regarding the "Manuscript Found" connection.
12/21/1833	on complaint of Joseph Smith, a writ against Hurlbut was issued by John C. Dowen, Justice of the Peace.

1/13-15/1834	in preliminary hearings, Hurlbut said he would kill Joseph Smith, by which Dowen said he meant he would kill Mormonism.
2/1834	Eber D. Howe agrees to publish Hurlbut's collected statements in a book authored by Howe, paying Hurlbut in books.
2/9/1834	Hurlbut's letter to Charles Anthon for his statement.
4/9/1834	the decision of the Geauga County Court issued deciding that "the said complainant had ground to fear that the said Doctor Ph Hurlbut would wound, beat or kill him, or destroy his property" setting bail at $200, & charging Hurlbut to keep the peace.
11/1834	publication of his collected statements in *Mormonism Unvailed*.
1846	ordained an elder in the United Brethren Church.
1847	member of the Board of Trustees of Oberlin College.

Hurlbut's Spalding-Related Statements

Howe's exposé of Mormonism included statements of persons claiming that Solomon Spalding had written a fictional history of persons from the Old World coming to America, which was very similar to the text of the *Book of Mormon*. Even after two decades, some of them claimed to remember that it was titled "Manuscript Found." In 1885, a former Ohio antislavery editor Lewis L. Rice went through antislavery manuscripts in his possession, and happened to find a Spalding manuscript. His search was on the occasion of the visit to his home then in Honolulu of James H. Fairchild, President of Oberlin College. Rice gave his friend some mss, including the Spalding manuscript, to be donated to the Oberlin Library. The document was not titled, but was accompanied by a wrapper on which Rice had written in ink "Solomon Spalding's Writings." Earlier writing in pencil identifies the contents in the wrapper. When computer-analyzed, it clearly reads "Manuscript Story Conneaght Creek". Proponents of the Spalding-Rigdon theory have taken this to correspond to Conneaught River, the site that the manuscript identifies as the location where marooned Romans had deposited twenty-eight sheets of parchment over fifteen hundred years earlier. They have used this wrapper to ascribe the title "Manuscript Story Conneaught (Conneaut) Creek," or simply "Manuscript Story" to this historical romance of Solomon Spalding. Two camps of researchers developed, one claiming that both this designation and "Manuscript Found" apply to the same manuscript, and the other claiming that these are titles identifying two different Spalding compositions, one donated to the Archive of Oberlin College, and the other lost. I will follow the lead of many others, and call the only existing one "the Oberlin Manuscript." Spalding would be surprised to know that it was eventually published (in 1885 by the Reorganized Church of Jesus Christ of Latter Day Saints, and in 1886 and 1910 by the Church of Jesus Christ of Latter-day Saints).

About October of 1833, Spalding's widow Matilda informed Hurlbut that she knew her husband had produced some manuscripts but that she did not know anything of their contents. She also stated that her husband's papers were stored at a cousin's home in Otsego County, New York. When he located them, and the manuscript thought to be the one in question, he found very little similarity to the *Book of Mormon*. He described its contents as follows:

> This is a romance purporting to have been translated from the Latin, found on 24 rolls of parchment in a cave, on the banks of Conneaut Creek, but written in modern style, and giving a fabulous account of a ship's being driven upon the American coast, while proceeding from Rome to Britain, a short time previous to the Christian era, this country then being inhabited by the Indians.[409]

This description is more than sufficient to identify the Otsego manuscript as being the Oberlin manuscript. Undaunted by this untoward discovery, and being convinced already that Smith had plagiarized Spalding, he saved his argument by concluding that in fact Spalding must have had two manuscripts regarding old-world visitors to the Americas, the one later found among the mss of Lewis L. Rice in Honolulu, wherein the visitors are Romans, and a lost manuscript wherein a tribe of Israel comes to the Americas and eventually becomes the American Indians. For Hurlbut, Howe and those arguing the Spalding-Rigdon origin of the *Book of Mormon*, the manuscript hypothesized by Hurlbut is referred to as "Manuscript Found."

Table 51. Hurlbut's Statements Collected in 1833 re Spalding's Manuscript

John Spalding, brother of Solomon, Crawford County, PA	• About 1812, he visited Solomon, who was working on a book titled "Manuscript Found" which he hoped would pay off his debts. • Solomon read "many passages" to his brother John. • It was a historical romance to show that the Indians are the descendants of Jews who had come to America.

---

[409] Howe, *ibid*, 404.

	• The protagonists were Lehi and Nephi, and the group divided into Nephites and Lamanites. • He wrote it in the old style. • He had recently read the BoM.
Martha Spalding, Wife of John, Crawford County, PA	• Visited Solomon a short while before he left Conneaut. • He was writing a historical novel. • In it the Indians are some of the lost tribes of Israel. • The protagonists were Lehi and Nephi. They divided into Lamanites and Nephites. • It was written in the older style. • She had read the BoM, which brought these details fresh to her recollection.
Henry Lake, Conneaut, Ashtabula County, OH	• Partnered with Spalding to build a forge in Conneaut. • For many hours, Spalding read passages from a manuscript he said had been found in Conneaut called "Manuscript Found." • It represented the Indians as being descendants of the lost tribes. • He remembered the tragic account of Laban. • Later he had examined the BoM and said it is the source of the historical part of the BoM.
John N. Miller, Springfield, PA	• He had lodged with Spalding for several months. • Spalding often read to them from "Manuscript Found." • It tells how the Indians came from Jerusalem. • He remembers the protagonists were Nephi, Lehi and Moroni, and that the group landed at the Straits of Darien which he called Zarahemla. • He had recently read the BoM and found it contains religious material the he did not see in Manuscript Found.
Aaron Wright, Conneaut, Ashtabula County, OH	• He became acquainted with Spalding in 1809 or 1810. • On day in Spalding's home, he read to him from a history he was writing. • Apart from the religious material, it was the same as the BoM. It traced a lost tribe of Israel from Jerusalem to America. It had the same names as the *Book of Mormon* with no alteration.
Oliver Smith, Conneaut, Ashtabula County, OH	•Spalding boarded at his home for about six months. •Oliver read and Spalding read to him at least one hundred pages from his manuscript.•It told how Lehi and Nephi brought Israelites to America. •He had read the BoM which had added religious text.

Nahum Howard, Conneaut, Ashtabula County, OH	• He frequently saw Spalding at his house and his own. • Spalding frequently showed him his writings. • "When I later read the BoM, I found it to be the same as what Spalding wrote, apart from the religious material." • He said he planned to get it published in Pittsburgh.
Artemas Cunningham, Perry, Geauga County	• Spalding showed him a manuscript that he hoped would raise the money to pay his debt to Artemas. • It was an account of Israelites being the first Americans. • It was found buried in the earth, or in a cave. • He had partially examined the BoM and found it to be the same as Spalding's work, except for the religious part. • He remembered the name of Nephi. • He intended to publish it in Pittsburgh.

Source: Eber D. Howe, *Mormonism Unvailed*, 392-402.

Although she did not make a signed statement, Howe ascribes to Solomon Spalding's wife Matilda Sabin Spalding Davison the following: she remembered Solomon had many manuscripts, of which one was called "Manuscript Found." She could not remember any of its contents, but thought it was the one he took to Patterson & Lambdin in Pittsburgh to be published. She did not know if he had brought the manuscript back home or not.[410]

There are two sets of statements collected by Hurlbut, and printed in Howe's *Mormonism Unvailed*, those presented to demean the Smith's and their associates, and those that assert that the BoM text closely resembles that of Solomon Spalding. As for the first set, Dan Vogel quote Cornelius R. Stafford, who "remembered that Hurlbut arrived at 'our school house and took statements about the bad character of the Mormon Smith family, and saw them swear before him.'"[411] He balances this with a statement with the statement of Benjamin Saunders, who said Hurlbut "came to me but he could not get out of me what he wanted; so [he] went to others."[412] These are introduced as depositions, and the testimonies of eight of these are followed by the form and signature of a justice of the peace.[413] Many

---

[410] Howe, *Mormonism Unvailed*, 403.
[411] Vogel, *ibid*, xvi.
[412] Vogel, *idem*.
[413] Howe, Mormonism Unvailed, 325-378

others are named concurring with the general tenor of their testimonies, but without certification by a justice of the peace.

Howe introduces the second set as witnesses, listed in Table 51, supra. The most we can assume is that they were signed.

Given the circumstances of his exit from Mormonism, and the preliminary judgments against him in the Joseph Smith v. Hurlbut case, it is clear that he was about as anti-Mormon as one can get. Furthermore anti-Mormons were funding him specifically to expose Joseph Smith, the *Book of Mormon* and Mormonism in general. He had to get results. He was a man on a mission, aided by the anti-Mormon atmosphere of the day. Still, he did not invent the Spalding issue. Persons unfriendly to Joseph Smith, the *Book of Mormon* and Mormonism were discussing a Spalding romance before Hurlbut began his mission.

Rumor Dynamics and Memory Reconstruction

The publication of an American bible, and establishment of a new church headed by a latter-day prophet caused no little stir at a time when many were expecting some sort of end-of-times scenario leading up to the Second Coming. In Ohio, the conversion of a well-known and influential clergyman named Sidney Rigdon became a topic of concern. Since he had been a prominent Campbellite figure, Alexander Campbell himself made a trip to Ohio to determine how much damage had been caused to his own movement. On 24 March 1832, both Joseph Smith and Sidney Rigdon were tarred and feathered. Hurlbut's mission was conducted in special circumstances, marked by intense anti-Mormon feelings and rumor dynamics. His informants were not randomly selected, but at least partially self-selected. What percent of the persons he contacted actually came to be numbered among his informants? We cannot know. As he went about, news of his coming probably preceded him. Whatever one's belief might have been regarding life after death, people are also interested in how they are remembered among the living. In normal circumstances, after the passage of three or four generations, our entire existence is summarized by a name on a tombstone, at best. Hurlbut offered the opportunity to have one's name and statement published in a book, and to be numbered among a chosen group who had helped to end a heresy mounted by Satan leading up to the coming of Jesus. This is heady stuff.

Rumor dynamics have been studied for many decades. The seminal study is the 1947 *Psychology of Rumor*, by Gordon Allport and Joseph

Postman.[414] They identified three processes: *leveling, sharpening,* and *assimilation.* In the first, there is a loss of detail as a result of the process of transmission facilitating the spread of the rumor. Sharpening involves the selection of the key elements to be included in its transmission. The process of assimilation refers to distortion as a result of subconscious motivations and the intrusion of extraneous information. There can be considerable competition or one-upmanship. A stereotypical example is a housewife saying to her neighbor over the clothesline, "Very interesting. But wait till I tell you what *I've* heard she did." Those who had known Spalding were ideally situated to participate. "I've been thinking a lot about this lately, and suddenly I remembered…"

The importance of rumor in this discussion is that it provided an important backdrop for the process of memory reconstruction. Suggesting this process is not an accusation directed at any individual. It is the way memory works for us all. In this context, it means that the process of memory reconstruction was already underway even before Hurlbut came along. To complete their qualifications for participation in the rumor mill, even those who had a claim to having had an association with Spalding should have some knowledge also of the *Book of Mormon* in order to say that they had noticed a similarity. At least they should have read the first ten or twenty pages. This provided the occasion for the more salient details of the BoM narrative to be subconsciously incorporated into and to shape their old and faint memories. This is not simply speculation; a statement collected from John N. Miller refers to the phenomenon: "The names of Nephi, Lehi, Moroni, and in fact all the principal names, are bro't fresh to my recollection, by the Gold Bible."[415] In the *International Encyclopedia of the Social & Behavioral Sciences* we read:

> Cognitive processes are active. When we perceive and encode events in the world, we construct (rather than copy) the outside world as we comprehend the events. If perceiving is a construction, then remembering the original experience involves a reconstruction. Reconstructive memory refers to the idea that remembering the past reflects our attempts to reconstruct the events experienced previously. These efforts are based partly on traces of past events, but also on our general knowledge, our expectations, and our assumptions about what must have happened. As such, recollections may be filled with errors, when our assumptions and inferences, rather than traces of the original events, determine our recollections. Errors—false

---

[414] Gordon Allport and Joseph Postman, *Psychology of Rumor* (New York: Henry Holt and Company, 1947).
[415] Howe, *Mormonism Unvailed,* 398.

memories—constitute the prime evidence for reconstructive processes in remembering. Several different sources of error (inferences during encoding, information we receive about an event after its occurrence, our perspective during retrieval) exist. Contrary to popular belief, memory does not work like a video-recorder, faithfully capturing the past to be played back unerringly at a later time. Rather, even when we are accurate, we are reconstructing events from the past when we remember. (H. L. Roediger)[416]

Simply accessing one's memory many years later is one thing. Doing so at the behest and under the influence of an interviewer is another. At this point memory reconstruction is influenced by the questions. This introduces the issue of the leading question. Having myself taught survey methods at the university level, I can assure that one of the most common mistakes of untrained interviewers or questionnaire designers is to ask leading questions. It is not only possible, but even probable that Hurlbut committed this fallacy, with or without conscious intent of coaching the informant. For example, instead of asking "Do you remember any of the names in the manuscript Spalding read from?" he might very well have asked, "Now try hard. Did the name 'Nephi' occur, or Lehi? How about 'Laban?'" In this manner, an informant's statement can be influenced, even coached. Usually a long discussion ensues, and then the interviewer draws up a draft statement and asks, "Is this a fair summary of what you have just told me?" We have all seen this in CSI documentaries.

Furthermore, even though John and Martha Spalding knew Solomon very well, it is his widow Matilda who actually lived with him throughout the period that he worked on his romance, and she could not remember anything about the contents.

Spalding died in 1816. He moved from Conneaut to Pittsburgh in 1812. By 1833, the statements listed *supra* would have been made *circa* twenty years later. The now considerable psychological evidence regarding memory, especially over time, informs us that normally it is impossible to access a memory without altering it. The act of trying to remember an old and faint memory is itself a process of memory *creation*. Reading the *Book of Mormon* feeds details into the mind, to supplement memories.

---

[416] H.L. Roediger III, "Psychology of Reconstructive Memory," *International Encyclopedia of the Social & Behavioral Sciences* (Amsterdam: Elsevier B.V., 2001), 12844–12849; accessed online, 04/02/2017.

Depriving Informants of Relevant Key Information

A statement by Howe regarding the Otsego (i.e. Oberlin) manuscript reveals the nature of Hurlbut's method in obtaining statements from his informants. He stated as follows:

> This old [Oberlin] M.S. has been shown to several of the foregoing witnesses, who recognize it as Spalding's, he having told them that he had altered his first plan of writing, by going farther back with dates, and writing in the old scripture style, in order that it might appear more ancient. They say that it bears no resemblance to the "Manuscript Found."

This is located on the third page from the end of his book, after Hurlbut's Spalding-related statements summarized above. The title "Manuscript Found" occurs in the statements of Solomon's brother John, Henry Lake and John N. Miller. The claim made regarding "several of the foregoing witnesses" is strange since in their statements there is absolutely no mention of having been shown a second manuscript bearing no resemblance to "Manuscript Found." If Hurlbut had indeed shown the Otsego manuscript to his informants, and gotten the reply indicated by Howe, this would have been the purest gold for his campaign, and he would certainly have included it in the statement of each informant making this denial. The fact that it is absent from the statements shows that he did not share this document with them even though it was in his possession. We have one telling example. After the interviews, he returned to Aaron Wright to get a statement that the Otsego ms was not the one he had described in his original statement, which described Spalding's ms as being the account of a tribe of Israel that became the first settlers in America, with BoM names. Already on record, Wright had no choice. He could only say, in his follow-on statement, that the Otsego ms was not the one mentioned in his statement.[417] The letter is not in Wright's handwriting, but closely resembles Hurlbut's,[418] indicating that the latter may have composed a summary of their conversation that the former agreed to.

---

[417] Aaron Wright draft letter dated 31 December 1833 in the New York Public Library. Photos of the letter and a transcription can be fount at "Ashtabula county, Ohio: Spalding Source Part Three" on Dale Broadhurst's Solomon Spalding website (http//:www.solomonspalding. Com, accessed 25/03/2017).

[418] Dale Broadhurst, "Ashtabula county, Ohio: Spalding Source Part Three," on his website (http//:www.solomonspalding. Com, accessed 25/03/2017).

Since he was in possession of the Oberlin ms and did not reveal it when obtaining the initial statements, clearly Hurlbut had decided that if he had a cooperating informant merging a faint memory with *Book of Mormon* details, it was not advisable to share with him a document that would only confuse his memory. Howe, or Hurlbut's backers, or both decided rather belatedly that the authors of these statements certainly should have been shown the manuscript Hurlbut had acquired, and should have been asked if it was the one that they remembered. Hurlbut's visit to Wright may well have been at Howe's prompting, to get from Wright an addition to his original statement to provide a basis for him to supplement their original statements with the foregoing quote.

When Names Are a Double-edged Sword

The most damning aspect of the statements is their feature that Howe thought to be one of their strongest points: "most of the names" of the *Book of Mormon* were found in the Spalding manuscript.[419] In fact, we find only Lehi, Nephi, Laban, Nephites, Lamanites, Moroni and Zarahemla in the foregoing statements. Aaron Wright stated, "the names more especially are the same without any alteration."[420] The specificity here, after two decades, is indicative of reconstructive memory. We are asked to believe that the Smiths and Cowdery were so stupid that in plagiarizing Spalding's work, they did not even think to change the names of the most important protagonists. Since the Spalding-origin claim is usually argued in the form of the Spalding-Rigdon origin, we are actually asked to believe that the Smith, Cowdery and Sidney Rigdon combo were all so stupid as to retain the most obvious evidence of their plagiarism

The Origin of the Title for a Second (also) Missing Manuscript

As we have seen, in their original statements, the informants make no mention of two Spalding historical romances. Hurlbut had already become convinced that a Spalding manuscript would look very much like the BoM narrative at least in broad outline. When he acquired the Otsego (i.e. Oberlin) manuscript and found that it dealt with Romans, he must have been greatly disappointed. The idea that there had to have been a second manuscript probably came to him rather quickly. As we have seen, his initial strategy was to fail to reveal the manuscript that he had acquired.

---

[419] Howe, *ibid*, 405.
[420] Howe, *ibid*, 399.

Later writers would supplement Hurlbut's second-manuscript claim by giving it a title.

Using the wrapper found with the Oberlin manuscript as their evidence, they called it "Manuscript Story Conneaught (Conneaut) Creek" or with more effect, simply "Manuscript Story." If Hurlbut had seen the wrapper, or Howe, he could have construed it as evidence for a title for this manuscript to differentiate it from the "Manuscript Found" mentioned by the informants. This too would have been the purest gold, and Howe would not have failed to mention it. In fact, the "Manuscript Story" title occurs neither in Hurlbut's statements nor in *Mormonism Unvailed*. This establishes a time frame for the wrapper: sometime after Howe's book and before Rice found it.

Figure 20. Computer Enhanced Oberlin Ms Wrapper

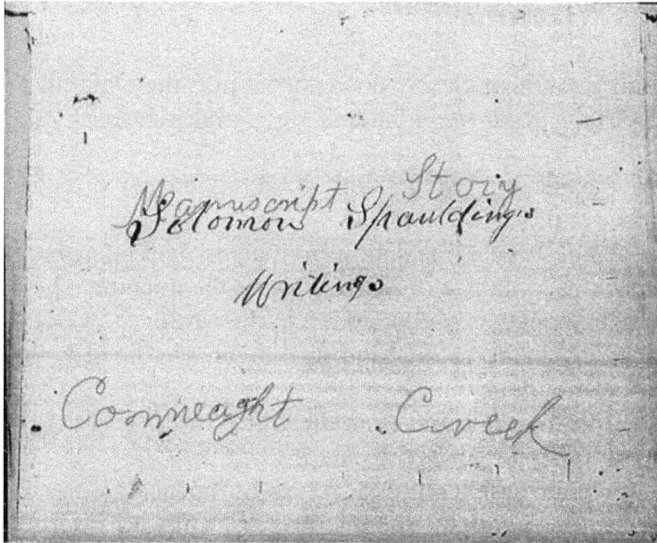

Furthermore, this title appears to read "Conneaght Creek."[421] Connaught is the name of a very large and celebrated region in Ireland. Both the Irish and the English would know about it. It was at one time almost a separate kingdom, and was under the Duke of Connaught. An equally celebrated Irish regiment in the English Army was the Connaught Rangers, established in 1793. There is a Connaught Road on Hong Kong Island, and a Connaught Man's Rambles (a jig), as well as a hotel, the Connaught, in

---

[421] Dale R. Broadhurst, "The Oberlin Spalding Manuscript, An Overview" solomonspalding.com, accessed 2 February 2017.

London. This said, the creek or river in question has been variously spelled. According to the Geographic Names Information System, Conneaut Creek has been known historically as: Conneaut Creek, Caneaught Creek, Conneaut River, Coneaught Creek, Conneaut River, Conneought Creek, Conyeayout Creek and even Counite Riviere.[422] It does not list Conneaght.

The first line of Spalding's "Introduction" refers to Conneaught River as the place the ancient document was found. Whoever penciled this title on the wrapper would have read at least this line and when writing on the wrapper he erroneously wrote Conneaght Creek instead of Conneaught River, an error that Spalding would never have made. This evidence also indicates that the title attributed to the extant Spalding romance only came into existence decades after 1816. The actual manuscript is untitled.

The Oberlin Manuscript

Although this document clearly does not support the claim that it was the origin of the *Book of Mormon*, interesting similarities exist:

1. It is the account of an Old World (Roman) discovery of and settlement in the New World.
2. It professes to be a translation from an ancient language.
3. The supposed translator himself found the document he translated.
4. The document was found hidden in the earth.
5. The cavity made to hide the document was lined with stone and covered with a flat stone.
6. The "author" originated from the Old World.
7. He and his group arrived by ship.
8. He anticipated the coming of future Europeans.
9. The "author" hid the document specifically to inform the future Europeans about his people.
10. Some Indians are described as having been a great, relatively enlightened people who later declined.
11. Just as the *Book of Mormon* begins in the first person, this document begins "My name is Fabius..."

---

[422] "Conneaut Creek". Geographic Names Information System (https://geonames. usgs.gov/apex/f?p=gnispq:3:::NO::P3_FID:1067126, retrieved 25/03/2017).

12. A storm arises at sea and the people onboard become very frightened. They turn to their god for help, a prophet communes with the divinity, and calm is restored.

13. Those who arrived at the New World are Christians, so there were Christians in the New World prior to Columbus.

14. The history has a "Reign of Judges."

15. They hold their property in common.

16. Some Indians are described as "savages."

17. The color distinction is made between the white Christians and dark Indians.

18. Churches were built.

19. The Indians worship the Great Spirit.

20. The heliocentric solar system is mentioned.

21. New World fauna includes mammoths.

22. The natives produced a sort of iron.[423]

There is plenty here to feed the memories of any who might have read it, or part of it, or heard Spalding read from it. Some informants stated that they remembered after a hiatus of two decades that "Manuscript Found" was similar or identical to the historical part of the *Book of Mormon*, without the religious material. The similarities here are sufficient to become the manuscript the informants strove to remember. The process of memory leveling eliminated some details, sharpening focused on others, and assimilation merged the memory with details from personal prejudice, anti-Mormon rumor and the *Book of Mormon* itself, under a bit of coaching from Hurlbut. For Hurlbut, this similarity, unenhanced by reconstructive memory, was not sufficient to make his more specific and extravagant claims, and after his disappointment in Otsego County, he proposed the existence of a second document.

Note too that we have no reason to believe that each informant signed a summary of the discussion with him. Those who could not agree to a statement that Hurlbut could use were never mentioned. He may have deemed their memories inadequate. In the case of the others, he probably

---

[423] Solomon Spaulding [Spalding], *The "Manuscript Found" or "Manuscript Story," of the Late Rev. Solomon Spaulding; from a Verbatim Copy of the Original Now in the Care of Pres. James H. Fairchild, of Oberlin College*, Ohio, *Including Correspondence Touching the Manuscript, Its Preservation and Transmission until It Came into the Hand of the Publisher* (Lamoni, Iowa: The Reorganized Church of Jesus Christ of Latter Day Saints, 1885); *Manuscript Found: The Complete Original* (Provo, UT: BYU Religious Studies Center, 1997).

wrote a discussion summary that they agreed to. This accounts for the considerable uniformity in their comments.

Sidney Rigdon

The argument that Rigdon contributed to the text of the *Book of Mormon* was made possible primarily by the fact that the image of Joseph Jr. as an uneducated farm boy, with the rest of the family in the shadows, was successful then, and still impresses the minds of some BoM critics even today. Some knowledge of Rigdon's life leaves little doubt that he could not have been involved. Instead he was totally absorbed in Campbellism and the Reformed Baptist movement, in which he was competing for a leading role. Failing to rise to prominence in that movement, he undertook to achieve his aspirations with the Mormons.

Table 52. Sidney Rigdon

1793	Rigdon was born in St. Claire Township, Allegheny County, PA.
	He remained on the family farm until his mother sold it in 1818. Rigdon completed basic education (elementary school?).
1817	He was baptized Baptist at Peter's Creek, a tributary of the Monongahela River.
1818	He moved to North Sewickley to apprentice to Baptist minister Rev. Andrew Clark.
1819	He received his license to preach for the Regular Baptists.
1819	He moved to Trumbull, Ohio, and preached there until 1822.
1820	Rigdon moved to Warren (Western Reserve).
01/04/1820	He delivered his first sermon to the small Warren congregation.
12/06/1820	He supplemented this monthly service as a circuit preacher. Rigdon and Phebe [Phoebe] Brooks were married.
1820	Rigdon, his cousin Charles Rigdon and his brother-in-law Adamson Bentley were asked to draft the "Corresponding Letter," used for various Baptist associations to keep in touch.
1821	Rigdon's daughter Athalia was born.
07/1821	Rigdon and Bentley meet with Alexander Campbell, noted for his beliefs in dispensationalism, New Testament supremacy over the Old Testament and baptism by immersion. Both joined the Disciples of Christ movement.
1822	Rigdon's daughter Nancy was born.
28/01/1822	Rigdon reported as minister of the First Baptist Church of Pittsburgh.
1823	Rigdon's daughter Elizabeth (or Eliza) was born.

1823	Rigdon worked to advocate Campbell's reforms, and argued against infant damnation (should they die unbaptized) in a debate with Rev. John Winter. The latter formed an opposition group within Rigdon's congregation. Each claimed that its group was the First Baptist Church of Pittsburgh. Each, Rigdon and Winter, expelled the other. A commission was set up to investigate the heresy charges brought by Winter against Rigdon.
11/10/1823	Rigdon is excluded (cut off, a form of excommunication) from the Baptist denomination, valid only within the Redstone Association of Baptist churches.
Fall, 1823	Rigdon's group lost its meeting house and informally joined with Walter Scott's Independent Church, holding joint meetings. Even so, at this point, Rigdon had no income.
1824	Rigdon's daughter Phebe Jr. was born.
1824-26	Rigdon first worked as a journeyman tanner, then as a tanner, possibly acquiring part ownership of the tannery. It had dealings with publishers, possibly supplying material for leather book binding. Apparently he took occasional preaching engagements to keep in touch with his chosen clerical occupation.
12/1825	A new tannery opened up in Bainbridge, Geauga County, Ohio, and Rigdon moved there. Reportedly he was called there by a small Baptist congregation. This group embraced a Calvinistic creed, but Rigdon was not required to endorse it. At Bainbridge, he was forced to resort to circuit preaching
1826	A new tannery opened up in Mentor, Ohio, and Rigdon moved to work there. Rigdon appears to have become the minister of this congregation, but served the area as a circuit preacher, which required him to travel about.
c. 11/1826	Rigdon became the new minister, or preaching elder, at Mentor, Ohio.
1826-1830	Rigdon's circuit preaching continued. He preached in the Kirtland area: Bainbridge, Mentor, Kirtland, Warren, etc.
1827	The first eight months of Rigdon's ministry in Mentor are described as being "turbulent."
Early 09/1830	Rigdon's associate, Parley P. Pratt, was baptized into Smith's Church of Christ.
08 /11/1830	Sidney and Phebe Rigdon were baptized into the Mormon faith.
30/08/1831	Smith rebuked Rigdon for exalting himself (D&C 63:55).
05/ 07/1832	Rigdon declared the Keys of the Kingdom have been taken away. (Quinn, *Mormon Hierarchy*, 42)
06/07/1832	Rigdon was disfellowshipped. (Quinn, *Mormon Hierarchy*, 42)
07/07/1832	Smith rebuked him again and took the high priesthood from him.

28/07/1832	Smith re-ordained Rigdon to the high priesthood. (Quinn, *Mormon Hierarchy*, 42)
1844	Joseph Smith was murdered.
03/08/1845	Rigdon claimed a revelation for him to be the "Guardian of the Church."
08/09/1845	Sidney Rigdon was excommunicated.
1845	He established The Church of Jesus Christ of the Children of Zion.

Sidney Rigdon's pre-Mormon life was a struggle. In his youth, according to his son John W. Rigdon, "He was never known to play with the boys; reading books was the greatest pleasure he could get. He studied English Grammar alone and became a very fine grammarian. He was very precise in his language."[424] Like many men of the cloth, he may have sought a career in the ministry to escape from the drudge of farm labor. He was ordained a Regular Baptist minister in 1819, preached in Trumbull, Ohio, until 1822, when he reported to be the minister of the First Baptist Church in Pittsburgh, PA. This was the peak of his Baptist career. His upward trajectory ended as a result of a fateful meeting with Alexander Campbell, the prominent leader of a theological reform movement that sought a return to his version of early Christianity, teaching New Testament primacy over the Old Testament, and dispensationalism. Rigdon became a major proponent of Campbellism, in the face of growing opposition from the Regular Baptists. In 1823, he was opposed in his own congregation by Rev. John Winter, who argued more orthodox doctrine. Rigdon was investigated for possible heresy and was cut off from the Redstone Baptist Association to which he belonged. He took those loyal to him to found an independent Baptist congregation, but was unable to raise enough money to pay the rent at his new location, and found himself without a parish, without employment, and without an income. This devastating blow came when he was struggling to support his wife and three daughters Athalia, Nancy and Elizabeth (or Eliza), with a fourth daughter on the way, Phebe. Since his father-in-law was an established tanner, it was possible for him to hire on as a journeyman tanner. At this juncture, he could have been swallowed up in the tannery business.

But Sidney persisted. He made use of his contacts and began networking at a time when that meant personal visits, going to and from on foot in muddy or dusty streets. He sought every opportunity to preach, at a church service, or for a funeral. This consumed much of his time when

---

[424] John Wycliffe Rigdon, "The Life and Testimony of Sidney Rigdon," *Dialogue: A Journal of Mormon Thought*, 1:4, 1966, 20.

he was not working as a tanner, but it paid off. At the end of 1825, a tannery had opened up in Bainbridge, Geauga County, Ohio, which may be the reason he moved there. But he was also reportedly called to serve as the preacher for its congregation. Due to its small size, his clerical position could not have supported him and his growing family. In the next year, a tannery opened up in Mentor, Ohio, and he moved there, where he may have served as the preacher of its congregation. This, however, marked a return to his earlier more junior status working as a circuit preacher, traveling about to various congregations in the area. A circuit preacher was a bit like a circuit judge. He did not travel with the speed of the pony express. A distance of thirty miles took a day on horseback or horse-drawn conveyance. The next day he would preach, attending to other pastoral duties, baptisms, marriages, counseling and funerals. The following day would be another travel day. The life was hard, and far from his glory days in Pittsburgh. From 1826 to 1830, he continued his circuit preaching operating out of Mentor, preaching at Mentor, Kirtland, Bainbridge, Warren, etc. Fawn Brodie has given us a list of official acts of Sidney Rigdon as a preacher in Ohio from November 1826 through November 14, 1830, from which she concluded, "It is clear from the following chronology that he was a busy and successful preacher..."[425]

According to Eber D. Howe, in 1823 Rigdon abandoned his preaching and employment to study the Bible for a year. Actually, it was not until 11/10/1823 that his release from his position at the First Baptist Church of Pittsburgh issued. After attempting to form an independent congregation and losing their meeting house due to inability to pay rent, he and his flock informally joined with Walter Scott's Independent Church, holding joint meetings. In May of 1824, Rigdon wrote the Preface to Campbell's report on his debate with Reverend W. L. McCalla, *A Debate on Christian Baptism*, published that summer. Rigdon worked as a journeyman tanner in Pittsburgh from sometime in 1824 up to his move to Bainbridge in December of 1825. There is no place in this period for Howe's claim to be correct.

The author/s of the *Book of Mormon* must have had some serious involvement with the plight of the American Indians, the efforts to convert them to Christianity and the claim that they descended from Israelites. Rigdon's total involvement was with congregations of settlers, and the doctrines of the theological reforms of Campbellism. There is no

---

[425] Fawn Brodie, *No Man Knows My History. The Life of Joseph Smith*. Second edition, revised and enlarged (New York: Alfred A Knopf, 1986 [1945/1971]), 453-55.

indication that he was concerned regarding the Indians, either in his proselyting or his theology. By contrast, Lucy Smith reported that her son Joseph had been fascinated by the Indians as a youth. His brother, Hyrum, attended Dartmouth, a school established to educate and convert the Indians. Ethan Smith, author of *View of the Hebrews* (1823), graduated from Dartmouth in 1790 and was installed pastor at Poultney, Vermont on 21 November 1821 where he preached until December of 1826. The family of William Cowdery Jr. was listed in the Federal Census as living in Poultney as late as 1820, and it was about 1825 that Oliver Cowdery left Vermont. His exposure to the ideas of Ethan Smith is highly probable.

After Sidney Rigdon's encounter with Alexander Campbell in July of 1821, his efforts to promote Campbellism with all his characteristic fervor not only included its rejection of infant baptism, a growing position in his day, but also the belief in the primacy of the New Testament over the Old Testament, and opposition to speculative theology, with his *cri de guerre* "The Bible Alone." As Campbell's father had put it, "Where the Bible speaks, we speak, and where the Bible is silent, we are silent." The latter of these positions is inconsistent with a major effort to produce a new bible, and reminds us of Nephi's anticipated opposition to the *Book of Mormon* saying, "A Bible! We have got a Bible" (2 Nephi 29:3-6). Downgrading the Old Testament is in contrast with the extensive Isaiah inclusions in the BoM, its adoption of the interpretation of some OT texts as prefiguring the coming of Christ and other OT texts to show a knowledge that some Israelites would go to the isles of the sea and produce a new bible. Campbell opposed Mormonism, referring to it as "delusions and religious imposition." After his conversion, Rigdon met his former friend in Kirtland and found him unreceptive to efforts to convert him.[426] It is hard to imagine that in former days a dyed-in-the-wool Campbellite such as Rigdon would be the originator of a new bible inconsistent with the positions for which he was risking his career in the Baptist ministry.

Furthermore, manuscript $\mathcal{O}$ is full of grammatical errors. Subject and verb often do not agree in number. The past form of the verb is used as a past participle, such as "When I had came..." Its deplorable English rules Rigdon out as an author (as well as God), due to his reputation for good grammar, and experience as a writer. Judging from the published "Manuscript Found," even Spalding's English was much better.

[426] Richard S. Van Wagoner, *Sidney Rigdon, A Portrait of Religious Excess* (Salt Lake City: Signature Books, 1994), 96.

A Multiple-Contingency Hypothesis: Beware the Weakest Link

The Spalding-Rigdon argument is a multiple-contingency hypothesis, dependent on the following contingencies:

1. Did Solomon Spalding write not just one but two historical romances on pre-Columbian migration to America, the Oberlin manuscript featuring a party of Romans, and a second history featuring Israelites? (This might be inferred from the follow-up interviews done by Hurlbut.)
2. Did Spalding take a manuscript to a publisher in Pittsburgh, possibly Patterson &Lambdin, hoping to get it published? (Hurlbut's statements.)
3. If so, was the manuscript taken to Pittsburgh the Israelite one, not the Roman one? (Totally unevidenced.)
4. Although the publisher did not undertake to publish it, did Spalding simply leave it there, rather than reclaiming it for submission elsewhere, or to keep it with his prized manuscripts out of pride of authorship? Did this manuscript languish with the publisher after Spalding's death, even for years? If so, did it stay there until Rigdon showed up in 1822? (Totally unevidenced.)
5. Did Sidney Rigdon gain sufficient access to the publisher's office to rummage through accumulated papers and discover this manuscript? The time window is very narrow, since his release from the Pittsburgh congregation was near the end of 1823, he became a journeyman tanner in 1824, and moved to Bainbridge at the end of 1825. (A late statement suggests a possibility, but his having done so is totally unevidenced. This would be nearly a decade after Spalding might have left it there.)
6. Did Rigdon, who had never shown any interest in the claim that pre-Columbian populations are of Israelite origin, or interest to gospelize them, nevertheless take interest in this manuscript? (Totally unevidenced.)
7. Did Rigdon get possession of the manuscript, either by theft, purchasing it or receiving it for free? (Totally unevidenced.)
8. In spite of his difficult circumstances, dedication to Campbellism and work as a tanner to support his growing family, did Rigdon get the many months free that would be required to plagiarize Spalding's work to produce what would become the precursor to the *Book of Mormon*? (Totally unevidenced, and seemingly impossible.)
9. Did Rigdon, living in Ohio, have some sort of encounter with either the Smiths or Olive Cowdery, or both? (There is a vague report of contact with some stranger, but actual contact with Smith or Cowdery is totally unevidenced.)

10. Overcoming his own pride of authorship or personal agenda, did Rigdon provide this manuscript to the Smiths, with whom he could only have had the slightest acquaintanceship, but probably none at all? Was Rigdon the sort of man to just give his work away? (Totally unevidenced.)
11. Did Smith decide to plagiarize this work? If so, in the process, were he, Cowdery and even Rigdon not even clever enough to change the names of the principal protagonists? (Totally unevidenced.)
12. Did Rigdon provide a replacement text for the 116 lost pages? (Totally unevidenced. This suggests a scenario where Smith or Cowdery approach Rigdon to say, "Sidney my friend. It seems I have lost the first quarter of my work, and need a replacement text with less history and more religion. Can you help me out?")
13. Would Rigdon keep this secret all his life, even after leaving the LDS Church, and in his lowest and bitterest moments.

One might be tempted to treat this as a simple multiple probability problem. Just for illustration however, let us reduce the first eleven contingencies to only six, each with an independent probability of fifty-fifty (p=.5). Then the probability is $.5^6$ (i.e. .5X.5X.5X.5X.5X.5), which yields .015625, or less than two chances in 100. In fact, the Spalding-Rigdon hypothesis is more complex. It hangs from a chain of contingencies, and if even just one fails, out of at least the first eleven, the hypothesis falls entirely.

Sophisticated content analysis has been done in an attempt to provide independent evidence for the conclusion of the Spalding-Rigdon hypothesis. The results are far from proof, and are refuted by other equally good statisticians. For a researcher who feels he has very strong stylistic evidence for his hypothesis, there can be the temptation to feel so sure that the hypothesis is true that it can be used to prove the contingencies. This line of reasoning proceeds as follows. Since Smith plagiarized a Spalding-Rigdon BoM-precursor text (or so this research is said to show), therefor "Rigdon must have provided it." Since he did, therefore "Rigdon must have known Smith or Cowdery." Since he did, he must have had a manuscript to provide. Since he did, "Rigdon must have found the time to dedicate himself to produce such a text." Since he did, "he had so much interest in the native American issues that he was motivated to do so." This mode of argument continues all the way down the chain to therefore, "Spalding wrote a history featuring Israelites." In this approach, the hypothesis proves the chain of contingent premises upon which it rests. This is as fallacious as it gets.

Vignette　　Rise and Fall of a Hypothesis?

The opponents to Mormonism felt that it was a false church founded by a false prophet. On the other hand, Mormonism burst on the scene with a firm belief that all the churches of the day were false, and branded them churches of the devil. At the time, the plagiarism charge seemed like the best avenue to destroy this brash new kid on the block, perhaps even a godsend. This charge attracted followers, supporters and researchers determined to show its merit. For many, it seemed like the most viable approach.

Today, in the realm of modern Mormon studies, we see very few prominent secular researches drawn to it. This is probably because it is not the only critique out there, and certainly not the best. For some, the Mormon claims are simply countered with a superior smile and snide retort, "An angel with gold plates? Really?" With the advent of Pre-Columbian archaeology, and the fiasco of the Abraham papyri, most secular scholars treat the issue of Book of Mormon *authenticity as long-since decided in the negative, and yesterday's news. The Spalding-Rigdon theory is just no longer needed by anyone.*

< Chapter 26 >

Producing Ms𝒰: Where to Recommence?

Joseph Smith stated that prior to the arrival of Oliver Cowdery in Harmony, PA, his wife Emma Mack Smith and brother Samuel Harrison Smith had written for him (v. Smith, 1832 History). The role of Emma is independently corroborated by Joseph Knight Sr. Later, when scholars examined ms𝒪, they found that 1 Nephi had been penned by three scriveners, including Oliver. They naturally assumed that the other two were Emma and Samuel. When handwriting analysis discovered that these two hands did not belong to either, those in the Church apprised of the potential implications of this untoward development had to face up to a handwriting crisis. This was most probably coming to a head in the 1960s.

The orthodox LDS solution was found in finessing the order of composition of the BoM books, which resulted in the division of scholars into two camps: those who argue that after the loss of the *Book of Lehi*, Smith began from the beginning with Nephi (Nephi priority), and those who argue that Smith began where he left off *in the storyline* at the beginning of Mosiah, and later returned to Nephi and worked back up to Mosiah (Mosiah priority).

Dean C. Jessee and the Orthodox LDS View of Translation Order

In 1970, Dean C. Jessee wrote,

> The location of the Cowdery writing at the beginning of the text of 1 Nephi [in ms𝒪] followed by the apparent hand of John Whitmer, may indicate that Oliver began writing at a point in the manuscript beyond the loss of the 116 pages [i.e. at Mosiah], and that the "plates of Nephi" [Nephi through Words of Mormon] were written after the completion of the rest of the Book.[427]

This handwriting crisis in Ms𝒪 became the launchpad for the Mosiah Priority hypothesis. Kent Metcalfe collected nineteen studies supportive of this theory, nearly all by orthodox LDS scholars. The earliest was the

---

[427] Dean C. Jessee, "The Original *Book of Mormon* Manuscript," in *BYU Studies* 10 (Spring, 1970), 278.

highly specific 1970 Dean C. Jessee study, "The Original *Book of Mormon* Manuscript."[428]

The problem encountered by orthodox LDS scholarship arises from the question, "What part of the Nephite narrative were Emma and Samuel writing?" The extant part of Ms𝒪 begins with chapter two of Nephi (1 Nephi 2:2) and is not in the hand of Emma or of Samuel. The explanation that Jessee suggested is that Joseph must have decided to take up his work where he left off in the storyline, i.e. at Mosiah. So the work, first of Emma and then of Samuel, would be found in Mosiah. This is not at all evidenced. Unfortunately, no part of Mosiah is found in the extant ms𝒪 material.

Some secular scholars also adopted the LDS view, but with additional speculation. Brent Metcalfe argued that, "The misplacement, theft, or destruction of the *Book of Lehi*, eventually [led] the despondent prophet to dictate 1 Nephi–Words of Mormon last... Smith resumed dictation in Mosiah... perhaps hoping that chapter one and the rest of the *Book of Lehi* would be recovered." (For the issue of Mosiah Chapter 1, see page 453.

The Secular Approach: Drafting the BoM

By definition, secular approaches do not begin their analysis with the aprioristic premise that the text of the gold plates was translated by divine instrumentality, with Smith just dictating the revealed words for Cowdery to write down into ms𝒪. The secularist's primary premise is evidence-based, i.e. that Smith could not have produced a 500-page nearly edit-free manuscript, as complex as the *Book of Mormon*, by composing it extemporaneously off the top of his head. Moreover, copy-correction errors in ms𝒪 retain fossilized fragments of the draft being copied. The necessary conclusion is that the true original manuscript must be a draft, initially in rough form, but edited and improved to become ms𝒰. The use of drafts answers a variety of questions, including what text Emma was writing regarding the walls of Jerusalem, what document would have borne her and Samuel's handwriting, and the timing of a few BoM passages with events during the production of ms𝒰, such as Smith's and Cowdery's baptism. Furthermore, the Nephi priority vs Mosiah priority issue is not the order of the books in ms𝒪, but rather their order in ms𝒰.

---

[428] Dean C. Jessee, "The Original *Book of Mromon* Manuscript," 259-78.

The Gorilla in the Room: Ms𝒪 Page Numbers

The pages of ms𝒪 were numbered, beginning at the beginning, Nephi. Due to the fact that the space for page numbers is missing for all extant pages after the Book of Enos, they have no page numbers. Skousen assumes that originally all pages were numbered, and he extrapolates to assign provisional numbers to these pages, distinguishing them with a prime (`). This said, he further clarifies,

> It appears that scribe 3 neglected to put page numbers for pages 8–10 since the complete top of the page is extant for these pages (that is, the corners are not missing), yet no numbers are apparent for these pages.

> In two cases, it is possible to determine that the scribe wrote the page number at the same time he wrote the summarizing head at the top of the page— namely, page 5 (by scribe 3) and page 6 (by Oliver Cowdery). As previously noted, these headings were added after the text for the page had been written down.[429]

The impact of these page numbers depends on timeline assumptions:

An orthodox LDS Nephi prioritist who treats ms𝒪 as the original with no prior draft can hold that the numbering started with 1 Nephi 1:1 to the end. In this approach, the handwriting issue cannot be resolved by Jessee's Mosiah priority solution.

Any Mosiah prioritist who treats ms𝒪 as original, without positing a prior draft, has to explain how Emma knew what page number to assign to Mosiah 1:1. An orthodox scholar might argue that ever prescient Providence revealed the correct page number. Alternatively, the scribes might have left the space blank for the page numbers to be entered after ms𝒪 was otherwise complete. The problem here is the three pages that never were numbered. Perhaps they were somehow missed, or perhaps no final page numbering happened at all. At least in the pages of the replacement text, there is evidence that the page numbers were entered at the same time as the page summaries. As for producing Nephi priority from a Mosiah priority text, one needed only to rearrange the gatherings.

Any Mosiah prioritist who treats ms𝒪 as original, but being the result of entering the text from a prior draft that was done in Mosiah priority order, and subsequently copied into ms𝒪 in Nephi priority order, can hold

---

[429] Skousen, The Original Manuscript, 33.

that the numbering was then done from 1 Nephi to the end. Since either Mosiah or Alma would have been done in January, 1829, this requires the position that Emma's comment regarding the walls of Jerusalem refers to her work on the Book of Lehi.

A secular Nephi prioritist scholar that treats ms𝒪 as having been produced by copying the text from a Nephi priority draft can hold that Emma and Samuel were writing into the draft, and that the page numbers were entered page by page as they were being written from the draft.

Since the first gathering had six sheets, originally its pages were numbered from 1 through 24. Since the outer sheet is not extant, pages 1, 2, 23 and 24 are not extant. Skousen lists the readable page numbers as follows:[430]

> Cowdery: 6, 44, & 111-114.
> S²: 20 & 22.
> S³: 5, 7, & 11-18.

Another observation complicating the thesis that Nephi followed Moroni is the probability that the latter was not even thought of until long after Nephi had been printed. Moroni is an add-on book (*infra*, 543).

The Plethora of Plates and BoM Complexity

First, we need to bear in mind Joseph Smith's statement that only part of the gold plates were permitted to him for translation. The remainder were sealed.

The most important references to the various narratives in the *Book of Mormon* are to metallic plates, especially the Brass Plates and the Plates of Nephi. The former is the Bible in an earlier originally longer version (1 Nephi 13:23), written in Egyptian and brought with the Lehi group from Jerusalem. The latter are two sets of plates bearing the same name, a deliberate obfuscation: "the plates upon which I make a full account of my people I have given the name of Nephi; wherefore, they are called the plates of Nephi, after mine own name; and these plates ["of the ministry"] also are called the plates of Nephi." (1 Nephi 92-3) Nephi refers to the former as being the "first" or the "other" plates. (1 Nephi 19:2, 4; 2 Nephi 4:14) The first plates are mostly secular, a highly detailed account of the affairs of the people, "engraven, according to the writings of the kings, or those which they caused to be written (Jarom 1:14)" and were "had by the

---

[430] Skousen, *Original Manuscript*, 33.

kings, according to the generations." (Omni 1:11) The LDS refer to them as the large plates of Nephi, although this designation occurs only once in the BoM, in Jacob, where he calls them the "larger plates" (but possibly "larger" only in number of plates) and characterizes them as containing "their wars, and their contentions, and the reigns of their kings." (Jacob 3:13) The religious plates of the ministry are usually referred to as the small plates of Nephi by the LDS. This name is also referred to only once in the BoM, also in Jacob (1:1). Nomenclature flexibility is illustrated by the fact that Jacob records his record on the plates made by Nephi, obviously the small plates, which he also calls the Plates of Jacob, a term that occurs only once. (Jacob 3:14) Apart from these two sets, we find "the record of my [Nephi's] father," which Nephi abridged. Since such records are usually inscribed on plates, we may have here another set, the Plates of Lehi (?). (1 Nephi 1:17; 5:16; 6:1; 19:2) The record of the Jaredites were inscribed by Ether on gold plates. (Mosiah 8:9; 28:11)

When the term "the Plates of Nephi" occurs, which set is intended can only be known by context, bearing in mind the remarkably different content of each set. On the other hand, the authors were very consistent in their use of the demonstrative pronouns. It seems that the religious (small) plates are always near at hand, and so are called "these plates." The plates with the highly detailed secular content are called "those plates," as well as the "first" and the "other" plates."[431]

The larger Plates of Nephi, kept by the royal administration, begin with Lehi and continue up to King Benjamin (who is also found in the record of Amaleki, in the Book of Omni).

It is commonly the case that recordkeepers specify that they are recording their record on the Plates of Nephi, these being a continuation of the affairs of the ministry, religious teachings and prophecies, i.e. the small plates. Since Amaleki had filled up the original plates made by Nephi, these plates would be a separate set intended to be a continuation of Nephi's small plates. Even so, Mormon abridged them. The LDS Church has adopted a novel term: the Plates of Mormon. No such designation exists in the BoM. At least in one Church source, this includes all of the unsealed plates in the set delivered to Joseph Smith.[432] For others, it includes just those of Mormon's abridgment, presumably not including the original small plates of Nephi.

---

[431] This dichotomy is found in 1 Nephi 6:1, 3; 9:4; 19:2-4, 2 Nephi 5:29-33; Jacob 7:27; Jarom 1:4; WoM 1:3-6, 10

[432] https://www.churchofjesuschrist.org/study/ensign/2020/01/which-plates-did-the-book-of-mormon-come-from?lang=eng

Figure 21. Plates Schematic

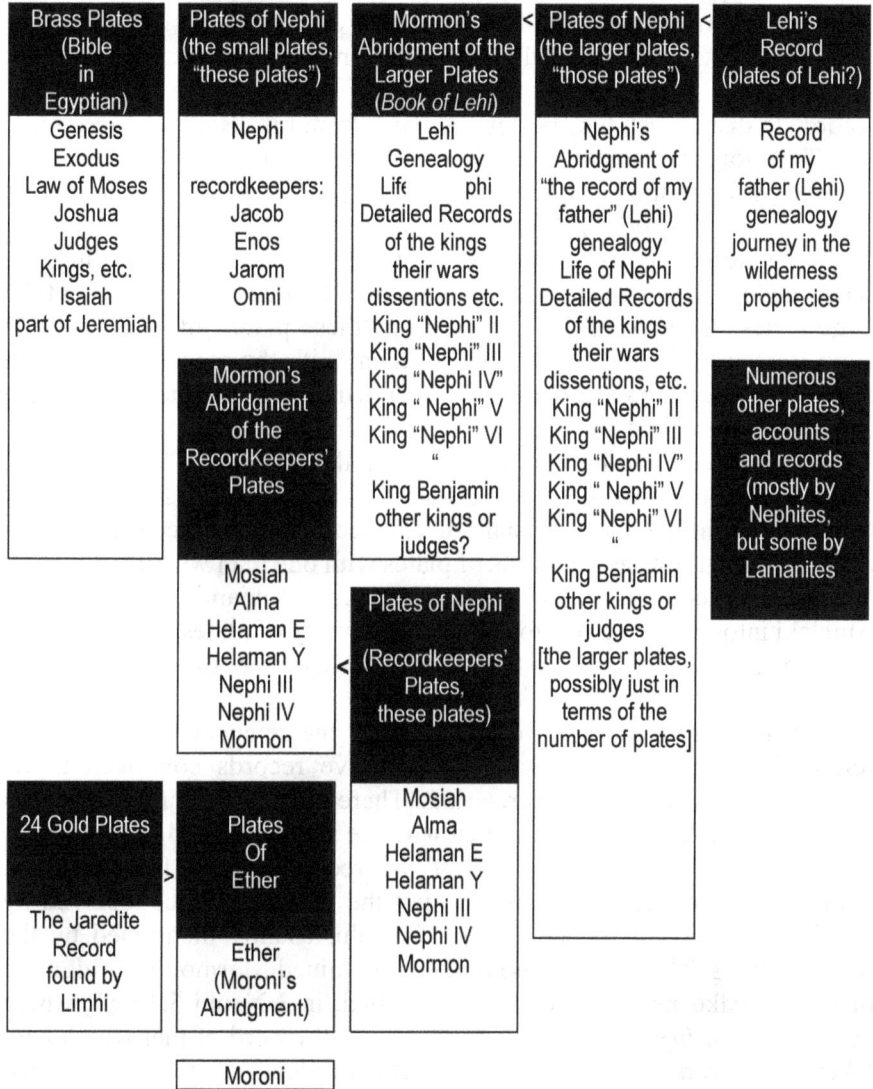

Brass Plates (Bible in Egyptian)	Plates of Nephi (the small plates, "these plates")	Mormon's Abridgment of the Larger Plates (*Book of Lehi*)	<	Plates of Nephi (the larger plates, "those plates")	<	Lehi's Record (plates of Lehi?)
Genesis Exodus Law of Moses Joshua Judges Kings, etc. Isaiah part of Jeremiah	Nephi recordkeepers: Jacob Enos Jarom Omni	Lehi Genealogy Life phi Detailed Records of the kings their wars dissentions etc. King "Nephi" II King "Nephi" III King "Nephi" IV King " Nephi" V King "Nephi" VI " King Benjamin other kings or judges?		Nephi's Abridgment of "the record of my father" (Lehi) genealogy Life of Nephi Detailed Records of the kings their wars dissentions, etc. King "Nephi" II King "Nephi" III King "Nephi" IV King " Nephi" V King "Nephi" VI " King Benjamin other kings or judges		Record of my father (Lehi) genealogy journey in the wilderness prophecies Numerous other plates, accounts and records (mostly by Nephites, but some by Lamanites
	Mormon's Abridgment of the RecordKeepers' Plates					
	Mosiah Alma Helaman E Helaman Y Nephi III Nephi IV Mormon	Plates of Nephi (Recordkeepers' Plates, these plates)	<	[the larger plates, possibly just in terms of the number of plates]		
24 Gold Plates The Jaredite Record found by Limhi	Plates Of Ether Ether (Moroni's Abridgment)	Mosiah Alma Helaman E Helaman Y Nephi III Nephi IV Mormon	>			
	Moroni					

After having abridged the large plates up to King Benjamin, Mormon had three sets: the large plates, the Plates of Nephi (the recordkeepers' plates, from Mosiah and including the beginning of his own record), and the plates of his abridgment (the *Book of Lehi*). He then found another set, the small Plates of Nephi, from Nephi through Omni, which Amaleki had completely filled up. He was delighted with the religious content of these. From this we know that he could read 7th-century BCE Egyptian.

"Wherefore, I chose these things, to finish my record upon them, which remainder of my record I shall take from the plates of Nephi...I shall take these plates, which contain these prophesyings and revelations, and put them with the remainder of my record" (WoM 1:5-6, 10) He uses "my record" to distinguish his abridgment work from his "Book of Mormon."

The story of Mosiah I and King Benjamin, begun in the record of Amaleki, is continued by Mormon in WoM 1:9-18, and further continued in the current chapter 1 of Mosiah.

Although Nephi's supporters insisted that he be their king, he succeeded in setting up a separate royal line. Their administration kept the large plates. After Amaleki delivered up "these plates into the hands of King Benjamin, he took them and put them with the other plates, which contained records which had been handed down by the kings from generation to generation until the days of King Benjamin." (WoM 1:10). They are passed on to his son Mosiah II, so that the large Plates of Nephi are given into the possession of Mosiah II, as king, and the small plates of Nephi are continued by Mosiah II, as recordkeeper (succeeding from Amaleki). We now have two sets of plates with one man wearing two hats. We also have continuity: continuity of the King Benjamin storyline from Amaleki into the record of Mosiah, and continuity of plates, with the small plates of Nephi followed by the record of Mosiah, both in the hands of Mosiah.

Meanwhile, although Mosiah replaced the reign of kings with the reign of the judges, historical/administrative records continued to be created in the government secretariats. There are at least three references to a larger secular record in contrast with the smaller record.[433]

However, the compositions of the recordkeepers, from Mosiah, Alma, Helaman and so on, are also not the unsealed plates received by Smith. These constitute the Plates of Nephi, usually mentioned by the recordkeepers. The unsealed gold plates contained Mormon's abridgment of the recordkeepers plates. This is clarified, in 3 Nephi 5:15-17, where Mormon says, *first*, that he will make a "small record of that which hath taken place from the time that Lehi left Jerusalem, even down until the present time..." [beginning with the Book of Lehi] to be made "from the accounts which have been given by those who were before me, until the commencement of my day [i.e. the previous recordkeepers]." *Second*, he also makes his own recordkeeper account: "And then I do make a record of the things which I have seen with my own eyes." And *third*, he was also

---

[433] Helaman 3:13 ("particular and very large"); 3 Nephi 5:9 (records with "all the proceedings of this people"); & Mormon 2:18.

writing the last bit of the large plates before the extinction of the Nephites: "upon the [large] Plates of Nephi I did make a full account...but upon these plates [small Plates of Nephi] I did forbear to make a full account."[434] Of these, it was Mormon's "small record" (Mosiah through Mormon) that was included in the unsealed plates provided to Joseph Smith, along with his abridgment of the Book of Lehi from the large plates, and Nephi through Omni (the small plates made by Nephi's hand and filled up by Amaleki). Mormon states, I "hid up in the hill Cumorah all the records which had been entrusted to me by the hand of the Lord, save it were these few plates which I gave my son Moroni."[435] This is conceivably not the same cache where Moroni hid up the gold plates that Smith received. Mormon inserts: (3 Nephi 5:8-16, 19):

> 9 But behold there are records which do contain all the proceedings of this people; and a shorter but true account was given by Nephi.
> 10 Therefore I have made my record of these things according to the record of Nephi, which was engraven on the plates which were called the plates of Nephi.
> 11 And behold, I do make the record on plates which I have made with mine own hands.
> 12 And behold, I am called Mormon...after the land of Mormon,
> 15 Yea, a small record of that which hath taken place from the time that Lehi left Jerusalem, even down until the present time.
> 16 Therefore I do make my record from the accounts which have been given by those who were before me, until the commencement of my day;
> 19 now I...proceed to give my account of the things which have been before me.

Mormon's account is his abridgment of "the things which have been before me" (i.e. prior to his calling to abridge the records, and to command the Nephite forces). He made his own plates, as did Nephi, which explains how it would be that the plates delivered to Smith could all be of the same size.

Mormon at the Hill Shim

In the year 320 CE, Ammaron, the record keeper before Mormon, hid up the sacred records of the Nephites in the Hill Shim (4 Nephi 1:48; Mormon

---

[434] Mormon 2:18.
[435] Mormon 6:6.

1:3). He instructed Mormon to go there at about age 24, and "take the plates of Nephi unto yourself, and the remainder shall ye leave in the place where they are, and ye shall engrave on the plates of Nephi all the things that ye have observed concerning this people." (Mormon 1:4). This record will be Mormon's own record of his day, the "Book of Mormon." He also uses "the plates of Nephi" (the large plates), saying "…upon the plates of Nephi I did make a full account of all the wickedness and abominations; but upon these plates I did forbear to make a full account of their wickedness." (Mormon 2:18)

In 375 CE, the Lamanites attacked again. At some point after this year, Mormon relented, and once again took up the burden of leading the Nephite forces. The first BoM date after this is 379. It appears that for thirteen or fourteen years, Mormon was free to pursue his abridgment duty. During this time we find references to writing. (Mormon 3:17, 19) In the year 364, fearing that the Lamanites would get to and destroy the records in the Hill Shim, he removed all of the records. It is most probably during this time that he was able to abridge the larger Plates of Nephi, from the first of the history of Nephi's father up to King Benjamin. Perhaps in the process of removing the records from Hill Shim and finding a new repository for them, he happened upon the record that Nephi made on the small plates, covering the same period. He is clear on this: "…after I had made an abridgment from the plates of Nephi, down to the reign of this king Benjamin…I searched among the records which had been delivered into my hands, and found these plates, which contained this small account of the prophets, from Jacob down to the reign of this king Benjamin, and also many of the words of Nephi." (WoM 1:3)

The Plates and the Order of Translation

As far as we know, Nephi's first plates, or the larger plates, were not among those delivered to Joseph Smith (although we know nothing regarding the sealed plates). This record began with Nephi's abridgment of the record of Lehi, followed by a genealogy of his fathers, then the life of Nephi, and finally the records of the kings over the centuries all the way down to Mosiah I. This text, on the larger plates, was abridged by Mormon down to King Benjamin to become the *Book of Lehi*, lost in the purloined 116 pages.

The small Plates of Nephi had been handed down from Nephi to Amaleki, a discreet set of plates made by Nephi, but now filled up. When they were entrusted to Mosiah, the recordkeeper who followed Amaleki, obviously he had to make additional plates for his own account, since

Amaleki had finished the plates made by Nephi. (Omni 1:30) He continued to call them the plates of Nephi. These were passed on to the other recordkeepers, generation after generation, all the way down to and including Mormon. Periodically additional plates needed to be made, all the while being called the Plates of Nephi. Mormon found the original set, the small Plates of Nephi that had been conformed to Nephi's command to fill them with the teachings that would be most precious to his people.

After completing his abridgment of the larger plates as far as King Benjamin, thereby producing the *Book of Lehi*, Mormon discovered the small plates of Nephi. He read them enough to be deeply impressed by the exclusively religious character of the plates, and wrote, "I chose these things [the ministry, gospel, prophecies, etc.] to finish my record upon them [i.e. to continue the remainder of his abridgment emulating them], which remainder of my record I shall take from the Plates of Nephi...." So he will continue his work, at Mosiah, by abridging the recordkeepers' plates of Nephi. (WoM 1:5) He then added, "I shall take these plates, which contain these prophesyings and revelations, and put them with the remainder of my record..." (WoM 1:6). That is to say that he will not abridge them, but include them directly as he found them, being the compositions of Nephi, Jacob, etc. down to Amaleki. It seems fair to presume that he added them to his work thus far done (Lehi), and then continued with the remainder of his work (Mosiah on down to his own recordkeeper account). In this regard, note that the history of Mosiah I and King Benjamin is begun in Omni, continued in WoM, and further continued in Mosiah. This sequence bridges the small Plates of Nephi to Mormon's abridgment of the Plates of Nephi, strongly implying that the former was placed after the *Book of Lehi*, and before Mosiah.

Unfortunately, none of Mosiah has survived in the extant portions of ms𝒪. But in the printer's manuscript (ms𝒫), usually almost a rote copy of ms𝒪, it initially had neither title nor synopsis.

The Great Mosiah Mystery

In ms𝒪 (evidenced in ms𝒫), Mosiah originally began with "Chapter II" after the removal of chapter one. There was neither a book title, nor a book synopsis. The title, "book of Mosiah" was added in above the line, and "Chapter II" was changed to "Chapter III, when Omni became chapter I and Words of Mormon became chapter 2 d (second)." Then it was decided to make these three separate books, and a linethrough changed III to I̶I̶I̶.

Table 53. Chapter Numbering in msP (Omni, Words of Mormon, Mosiah)
(Bold italics indicate supralinear emendations)

Omni Beginning
`[line 10]` ~~The Book of Omni~~
`[line 11] The Book of Omni Chapter first^^^^^^^Behold it`
Note: The Book of Omni was repeated to start the book on a new line.

Words of Mormon Beginning
`end of my speaking.~~~~~~~~~~~~~~~~~~~~~~~~~~~~~~~~~~~~` `~~~~~~~~~~~~~~~~~~~~~~~~~~~~~~~~~~~~~~~~~~~~~~~~~~~~~~~~~`
Chapter .2.d I
`The words of Mormon ^ And      [ Mormon being about to...`

Mosiah Beginning
`  ...the prophets, wherefore they did once again establish`
the Book of Mosiah
`peace in the land~~~^~~~~Chapter I‡‡~~~~And now there...`
NOTE: read this as: first `II`, was changed to `III`, & changed again to `I‡‡`.

Mosiah chapter mix-up

chapter numbers in msP	1830 chapter numbers	chapter numbers in msP	1830 chapter numbers
		8th	
`I‡‡ [II→III→I‡‡]`	1	~~IX,~~ `|I|X`	8
`II`	2	`I|X`	9
`III {~|X}~~~`	3	`X‡`	10
`IIII`	4	`XI‡`	11
`V ~~{~|{X}}~~~`	5	`1{3}`	12
`VI`	6	*3* `14\th`	13
`VII. —`	7		

The next six chapters follow this corrected numbering sequentially (i.e. 1 through 7), but from chapter eight to the end (chapter thirteen, these being the long chapter divisions seen in the 1830 edition of the BoM) the chapters are all numbered one ahead. Chapters 8-11 and 13 are corrected, although Cowdery neglected to correct 12. This erroneous sequence is based on the first chapter originally being II in the draft, after the original Mosiah 1:1 was removed, the first chapter became chapter III. It became I (I‑‑) when Omni and WoM were made separate books.

Omni, Words of Mormon and Mosiah 1-13 (1830 chapter numbers) are all in the hand of Cowdery, so the initial error, and then the return to that error for Chapter 8 were not due to a shift in scribes. All evidence indicates that Smith's dictation to Cowdery was making a rote copy of ms $\mathcal{U}$ to the extent possible. Therefore, this is a reversion to numbering that must have been present in ms $\mathcal{U}$, viz ms $\mathcal{O}$ errors arising from a failure to fully update chapter numbers in the draft. It is improbable that either Cowdery or Smith would suddenly revert to out-of-sequence numbering at chapter eight without a trigger indicating what alternate number to use. Smith was clearly reading from a text that had been finished to such an extent that it already had numbered chapters that had become out of date when chapter one was moved to Omni and WoM. At chapter eight he began to read out the unupdated chapter number in ms $\mathcal{U}$ (chapter nine). Initially, Cowdery did not catch the error, but corrected it while proofing his work. The ultimate cause for this numbering error in both mss can only be that the original draft of Mosiah had a first chapter.

A curious unknown: "Whence Omni?" When Omni, WoM and Mosiah were all one book, what was the name of that book? The word "omni" occurs in many English words, already listed in the dictionaries of Samuel Johnson and Noah Webster. These would be familiar to students of religion by 1829, through words such as omnipresent, omniscient and omnipotent. It may have been intended to embrace the many persons of Omni through the Book of Mosiah. Clearly a book name of this (Latin) nature cries out for an explanation.

Stylistic evidence will indicate that Nephi through Jacob had been done by Smith, while Mosiah was being done by another author. When Joseph Jr. and Oliver began work together, and began interfacing the small plates of Nephi (the replacement text) with Mosiah, they faced important issues. The first was chronology. Nephi died around 540 BCE. Mosiah begins the lead-up to the coming of Christ, and so begins around 130 BCE, followed by Alma & Helaman. Their *terminus ad quem* is fixed by the birth of Jesus. The gap of 400 years is major. Even after Jacob, Enos and Jarom, there remained a major gap. The Book of Omni, only the equivalent of one chapter in length, is attributed to recordkeepers Omni, Amaron, Chemish (his brother), Abinadom and Amaleki. This fast-forward book filled a major chronological gap in only a few pages. The BoM authors were clearly not prepared to come up with enough additional large books to fill this gap.

Second, there was a need to reduce the feeling of disjuncture in the storyline from Nephi to Mosiah. This was addressed by inserting part of the first chapter of Mosiah into the Nephi material (the small plates of Nephi). The assertion that these plates had to be translated all the way to King Benjamin (D&C 10:41, which curiously lacks any mention of

Mosiah) is a reference to the initial part of the Mosiah saga, a part that that was not lost with the purloined pages.

Third, an explanation was needed for how it came to be that there were two sets of plates. This was done in Words of Mormon. Taking only eight verses, as a stand-alone it looked suspicious. To disguise its real purpose, it was amplified with a second part of the first chapter of Mosiah.

Mosiah Chapter One Restored

Here I give my restoration of the beginning of Mosiah. The verses are renumbered, with the verse numbers of Omni and Words of Mormon in parentheses.

Table 54. The Restoration of Mosiah, Chapter One

[The portion from Omni.]
Chapter I **1** (12). Behold, I [Mormon, proceed from the record of Amaleki, the son of Abinadom, regarding] Mosiah, who was made king over the land of Zarahemla; for behold, he being warned of the Lord that he should flee out of the land of Nephi, and as many as would hearken unto the voice of the Lord should also depart out of the land with him, into the wilderness— **2** (13). And it came to pass that he did according as the Lord had commanded him. And they departed out of the land into the wilderness, as many as would hearken unto the voice of the Lord; and they were led by many preachings and prophesyings. And they were admonished continually by the word of God; and they were led by the power of his arm, through the wilderness, until they came down into the land which is called the land of Zarahemla. **3** (14). And they discovered a people, who were called the people of Zarahemla. Now, there was great rejoicing among the people of Zarahemla; and also Zarahemla did rejoice exceedingly, because the Lord had sent the people of Mosiah with the plates of brass which contained the record of the Jews. **4** (15). Behold, it came to pass that Mosiah discovered that the people of Zarahemla came out from Jerusalem at the time that Zedekiah, king of Judah, was carried away captive into Babylon. **5** (16). And they journeyed in the wilderness, and were brought by the hand of the Lord across the great waters, into the land where Mosiah discovered them; and they had dwelt there from that time forth. **6** (17). And at the time that Mosiah discovered them, they had become exceedingly numerous. Nevertheless, they had had many wars and serious contentions, and had fallen by the sword from time to time; and their language had become corrupted; and they had brought no records with them; and they denied the being of their Creator; and Mosiah, nor the people of Mosiah, could understand them.

7 (18). But it came to pass that Mosiah caused that they should be taught in his language. And it came to pass that after they were taught in the language of Mosiah, Zarahemla gave a genealogy of his fathers, according to his memory; and they are written, but not in these plates.

8 (19). And it came to pass that the people of Zarahemla, and of Mosiah, did unite together; and Mosiah was appointed to be their king.

9 (20). And it came to pass in the days of Mosiah, there was a large stone brought unto him with engravings on it; and he did interpret the engravings by the gift and power of God.

10 (21). And they gave an account of one Coriantumr, and the slain of his people. And Coriantumr was discovered by the people of Zarahemla; and he dwelt with them for the space of nine moons.

11 (22). It also spake a few words concerning his fathers. And his first parents came out from the tower, at the time the Lord confounded the language of the people; and the severity of the Lord fell upon them according to his judgments, which are just; and their bones lay scattered in the land northward.

12 (23). Behold, [I,] Amaleki, was born in the days of Mosiah; and [I have] lived to see his death; and Benjamin, his son, reigneth in his stead.

13 (24). And behold, [I have seen there arose] in the days of king Benjamin, a serious war and much bloodshed between the Nephites and the Lamanites. But behold, the Nephites did obtain much advantage over them; yea, insomuch that king Benjamin did drive them out of the land of Zarahemla.

14 (25). And it came to pass that [I Amaleki] began to be old; and, having no seed, and knowing king Benjamin to be a just man before the Lord, wherefore, [I shall he did] deliver up these plates unto him, exhorting all men to come unto God, the Holy One of Israel, and believe in prophesying, and in revelations, and in the ministering of angels, and in the gift of speaking with tongues, and in the gift of interpreting languages, and in all things which are good; for there is nothing which is good save it comes from the Lord; and that which is evil cometh from the devil.

15 (26). And now, my beloved brethren, I would that ye should come unto Christ, who is the Holy One of Israel, and partake of his salvation, and the power of his redemption. Yea, come unto him, and offer your whole souls as an offering unto him, and continue in fasting and praying, and endure to the end; and as the Lord liveth ye will be saved.

16 (27). And now I would speak somewhat concerning a certain number who went up into the wilderness to return to the land of Nephi; for there was a large number who were desirous to possess the land of their inheritance.

17 (28). Wherefore, they went up into the wilderness. And their leader being a strong and mighty man, and a stiffnecked man, wherefore he caused a contention among them; and they were all slain, save fifty, in the wilderness, and they returned again to the land of Zarahemla.

18 (29). And it came to pass that they also took others to a considerable number, and took their journey again into the wilderness.

[Here the portion put into Words of Mormon begins.]

19 (12). And now, concerning this king Benjamin—he had somewhat of contentions among his own people.

20 (13). And it came to pass also that the armies of the Lamanites came down out of the land of Nephi, to battle against his people. But behold, king Benjamin gathered together his armies, and he did stand against them; and he did fight with the strength of his own arm, with the sword of Laban.

21 (14). And in the strength of the Lord they did contend against their enemies, until they had slain many thousands of the Lamanites. And it came to pass that they did contend against the Lamanites until they had driven them out of all the lands of their inheritance.

22 (15). And it came to pass that after there had been false Christs, and their mouths had been shut, and they punished according to their crimes;

23 (16). And after there had been false prophets, and false preachers and teachers among the people, and all these having been punished according to their crimes; and after there having been much contention and many dissensions away unto the Lamanites, behold, it came to pass that king Benjamin, with the assistance of the holy prophets who were among his people—

24 (17). For behold, king Benjamin was a holy man, and he did reign over his people in righteousness; and there were many holy men in the land, and they did speak the word of God with power and with authority; and they did use much sharpness because of the stiff-neckedness of the people—

25 (18). Wherefore, with the help of these, king Benjamin, by laboring with all the might of his body and the faculty of his whole soul, and also the prophets, did once more establish peace in the land.

[Chapter II begins here, as it originally appeared in the draft.]

Chapter II

1 (1). And now there was no more contention in all the land of Zarahemla, among all the people who belonged to king Benjamin, so that king Benjamin had continual peace all the remainder of his days.

[Chapter II continues (first renumbered Chapter III, and then Chapter I).]

The flow of topics and even wording, ending at Omni 29 to resume at Words of Mormon 12, and ending at Words of Mormon 18 to resume at Mosiah 2:1 (renumbered 1:1), indicates the unity of these passages. The chapter numbers in ms$P$ underlying the Great Mosiah Mystery are explained by the chapter numbers in O, which goes back to the numbering in the pre-O Mosiah, in ms$U$.

Note too that some books of the BoM narrative begin with the author speaking in the first person. This is true of Nephi through Omni (as well as the accounts within Omni), as well as Mormon, and Moroni (including his abridgment of Ether, and the Book of Moroni). The portion written by Mormon stretches from Words of Mormon through 4 Nephi. This pattern ("I Mormon") had to be deleted from Mosiah Chapter I when it was inserted into Omni, but is followed at the beginning of the explanation of the two sets of plates (Words of Mormon 1:1), and, once again, when Mormon begins his account of Mosiah, "And now I Mormon..." (WoM 1:9) In addition, if the Mosiah draft originally began with a book summary, it had to be sacrificed when Chapter 1 was split between Amaleki and Words of Mormon.

Another observation is important to this analysis. Mosiah, as it stands in the 1830 edition of the BoM, uses *therefore* (122 occurrences) to the total exclusion of *wherefore*. By contrast, the much smaller Mosiah texts in Omni and Words of Mormon use *wherefore* (five occurrences) to the total exclusion of *therefore*. If Smith began again with Mosiah, he would not have used his characteristic *wherefore*-dominant style for chapter one, to then switch over to an exclusively *therefore* style for the rest of Mosiah. The original chapter two, which is chapter one in the 1830 BoM edition, already has five occurrences of *therefore*, and not one of *wherefore*.

After losing the 116 pages, Smith was commanded to translate Nephi "even till you come to the reign of king Benjamin, or until you come to that which you have translated, which you have retained." (D&C 10:41) If a collaborator would do Mosiah, using the retained pages as a starter, he would ignore Smith's deliberate archaizing using *wherefore*. The pages retained provided some initial storyline and Smith's idea of what an ancient New World prophet would sound like. Moreover, Mosiah immediately begins with King Benjamin's teachings to his sons, and then his lengthy speech. This speech could be done by another ancillary drafter. This transition enables a collaborating BoM author to compose Mosiah without seeing Omni and WoM. As we shall see, *wherefore* was rarely used in the 1820s, so the rest of Mosiah would use *therefore*. In addition to this first chapter, someone (Emma? Samuel?) could have prepared a basic one-page outline of Nephi. Moreover, if the 116 pages consisted of completed gatherings, then the retained pages may have been retained because they began a new gathering not entrusted to Harris, beginning with Mosiah chapter one deliberately archaized with a sprinkling of *wherefores*. Note too that no story lines of missionary travels, of Nephite settlers or military engagements occur in Mosiah in pages one through six (current LDS page numbering). At that point, a collaborating author could develop Mosiah as he wished, and possibly all the while being in communication with the author of Alma.

By the way, additional confusion arose regarding King Mosiah and

King Benjamin. Ether 4:1 states in the first edition, "for this cause did king Benjamin keep them [the records of the Jaredites]." In later editions, Benjamin was changed to Mosiah.

Vignette | **D&C 10: The Nephi Revelation's Unlikely Prefatory Date**

At issue is the date in the prefatory comment: May 1829, and the total disconnect between it and the content of the revelation. Notably, it informs Smith that, although his gift had been taken away, "Nevertheless, it is now restored unto you again." If it was only at this time that his gift was restored, then he could not have been translating before Cowdery's arrival, when Emma and Samuel were writing for him. If the text is correct, then the prefatory comment is in error.

A related issue is found in the Manuscript History of the Church, *which inserts revelations into the historical narrative, but failed to do so in the case of D&C 10. So it was included after the fact, in four numbered pages, with instructions written supralinearly in the top margin of page one: "N.B. This Revelation will read, after the interlined words in page 11 & line 17ᵗʰ." At this point the narrative reads, "After I had obtained the above revelation, both the plates, and the Urim and Thummin were taken from me again, but in a few days they were returned to me, when I enquired of the Lord, and the Lord said thus unto me. ˄ [This carat indicates the place for D&C 10 to be inserted.]*

After the D&C 10 insertion, the narrative resumes: "I did not however go immediately to translating, but went to laboring with my hands upon a small farm which I had purchased of my wife's father, in order to provide for my family. In the month of February, Eighteen hundred and twenty nine my father came to visit us at which time I received the following revelation for him." [D&C 4, dated in the prefatory comment February, 1829.]

The Reorganized Church of Jesus Christ of Latter Day Saints (now the Community of Christ) dated this revelation July 1828 in their 1897 edition of the Doctrine and Covenants. *Possibly as a result of B. H. Roberts' research, the LDS Church changed the date to "summer of 1828" in the 1921 edition of the D&C. The present introduction reads, "likely around April 1829, though portions may have been received as early as the summer of 1828."*

In the fall of 1829, Smith returned to Harmony to work his farm in the first week of October. Minimally, this would be plowing, possibly harrowing, and getting seed in the ground. He may also have been doing some clearing of his land. Laboring the land in 1828 would have had a similar seasonal schedule. The little ice age lasted from 1600 to 1850, so we can expect that winter came earlier, and was colder. It may still have been aggravated by the effects of the Mount Tambora eruption of 1815. That wicked man (Harris) was not funding him at that point, and his in-laws expected him to man up. He had to get seed in the ground during a foreshortened season.

This fits well with his changing relations with Martin Harris. Comments in D&C 10 reflect his lingering swells of anger (that "wicked man") and perhaps the darkly smoldering embers of suspicion (who "has sought to take away the

> *things wherewith you have been entrusted; and he has also sought to destroy your gift."). In March, Harris was in Harmony and Smith received a revelation for him, in which God calls him "my servant Martin Harris," and cautiously gives a conditional promise that he might get the view of the plates that he so desires.(D&C 5) However much the harsh language directed at Harris in D&C 10 can be expected in the fall of 1828, it hardly comports with events from March through June of 1829.*

D&C 10 has been broken into pieces based on content, and how it comports with a hypothetical sequence of events, usually dictated by theories espoused by some orthodox researchers.[436] Smith is admonished, "see that you are faithful and continue on unto the finishing of the remainder of the work of translation as you have begun." (D&C 10:2-3) This may be a double instruction. He began "faithful" and he began with Lehi in Jerusalem ("as you have begun").

D&C 10 progresses in ordered segments. Verses 6-29 describe how Satan has planned to thwart this work of the Lord. In verse 29 we read, "Now, behold, they have altered these words." In verse 30, he is instructed how he must resume his work: "you shall not translate again those words which have gone forth out of your hands..." (i.e. the words of the record of Lehi); "...if you should bring forth the same words they will say that you have lied and that you have pretended to translate but that you have contradicted yourself." (10:31) Verses 31-40 describe how the Lord will defeat Satan's plan. Instead of going back to retranslate the *Book of Lehi*, in verse 41-42, we read:

> Therefore, you shall translate the engravings which are on the [small] plates of Nephi, down even till you come to the reign of king Benjamin, or until you come to that which you have translated, which you have retained;
> And behold, you shall publish it as the record of Nephi; and thus I will confound those who have altered my words.

This verse sounds like an instruction to proceed with the small plates of Nephi, and produce the Book of Nephi. I see nothing in D&C 10:2-3 that can serve to override this.

---

[436] See Max H. Parkin, "A Preliminary Analysis of the Dating of Section 10," *The Seventh Annual Sidney B. Sperry Symposium: The Doctrine and Covenants* (Provo, UT: Brigham Young University, 1979), 68-84; and Tim Barker, "The Dating of Doctrine and Covenants 10-Part 1" (updated April 11, 2010), downloaded from lds-studies.blogspot.com on 23/9/2019.

Mosiah-thru-Mormon Dependence on a Prior Nephi Text

Just as Biblical books refer to signal events and outstanding persons in earlier books, one can expect that later books in the BOM narrative will refer to the important events and persons for the establishment of the Nephites in their promised land.

Textual elements. For the most part, the BOM books do not quote each other verbatim. There are exceptions with significant continuous text. The later books can quote or paraphrase earlier books. When a quote is identified, the obvious first issue is "Which text came first?" In the case of 1 Nephi 1:8, below, the answer to this question is clear. The Nephi passage refers specifically to Lehi, and his vision. The Alma passage paired with it makes reference to this passage, which is an integral part of the Nephi narrative. The second Nephi passage, also quoted in Alma, makes specific reference to a declaration spoken by God to Lehi. This is also an integral element of the Nephi narrative.

> [even as our father Lehi] "saw God sitting upon his throne surrounded with numberless concourses of angels in the attitude of singing and praising their God." (Alma 36:22 quoting Nephi 1:8, **verbatim**)

> [the words which he (God) spake unto Lehi, saying that] "Inasmuch as ye shall keep my commandments, ye shall prosper in the land." [And again it is said that:] "Inasmuch as ye will not keep my commandments ye shall be cut off from the presence of the Lord." (Alma 9:13 & 37:13 quoting 2 Nephi 4:4, **verbatim**; cf. Alma 36:1; 36:22; 36:30; 38:1 & 50:20; 3 Nephi 5:22)

Since both of these refer specifically to passages in Nephi, quoting verbatim, it is hard to imagine that an outline of Nephi was not available to the drafters of Alma [or failing that, these quotes were edited in later].

A passage in Revelation, below, is often paraphrased. Two distinctly different versions are quoted, one in 2 Nephi (quoted in Alma) and the other in Jacob (quoted in Mosiah).

> NT Revelation 14:10-11. "he shall be tormented with fire and brimstone in the presence of the holy angels, and in the presence of the lamb: And the smoke of their torment ascendeth up for ever and ever" (cf. 20:10 & 21:8)
> "And the devil that deceived them was cast into the lake of fire and brimstone" (20:10)
> 2 Nephi 9:16: "their torment is as a lake of fire and brimstone, whose flame ascendeth up forever and ever" (cf. Jacob 3:11)

Alma 12:17: "their torments shall be as a lake of fire and brimstone, whose flame ascendeth up forever and ever"
Jacob 6:10. "ye must go away into that lake of fire and brimstone whose flames are unquenchable, and whose smoke ascendeth up forever and ever"
Mosiah 3:27. "their torment is as a lake of fire and brimstone, whose flames are unquenchable, and whose smoke ascendeth up forever and ever" (cf. 2:38)

Other passages quoted are one in Ether, Mosiah, 3 Nephi and Mormon:

"a land which is choice above all other lands" (Ether 2:10 quoting 1 Nephi 2:20 and 2 Nephi 1:5, **verbatim**)

"unto every nation, kindred, tongue and people" (Alma 45:16 & Mosiah 3:20 quoting 2 Nephi 26:13)

3 Nephi 21:21: "his people may be gathered home to the land of their inheritance"
2 Nephi 9:2: "they shall be gathered home to the land of their inheritance"

Mormon 9:14: "he that is filthy shall be filthy still; and he that is righteous shall be righteous still"
2 Nephi 9:16: "They who are righteous shall be righteous still; and they who are filthy shall be filthy still"

In the following verse, two BOM variants in Smith's edited version of a verse from the New Testament is retained in a quote in 3 Nephi.

Acts (KJV) 3:23: "every soul, **which** will not hear that prophet, shall be **destroyed** from among the people."
1 Nephi 22:20: "all those **who** will not hear that prophet shall be **cut off** from among the people."
3 Nephi 20:24: "every soul **who** will not hear that prophet shall be **cut off** from among the people."

We find an obvious paraphrase in 3 Nephi:

"all the proud, yea, and all that do wickedly, shall be stubble; and the day that cometh shall burn them up" (3 Nephi 25:1)
"all the proud and they who do wickedly shall be as stubble and the day cometh that they must be burned" (1 Nephi 22:15)
"all those who are proud, and that do wickedly, the day that cometh shall burn them up...for they shall be as stubble" (2 Nephi 26:4)

References to the plates of Nephi. In some passages, there is a degree of ambiguity regarding Nephi's two sets of plates. Mosiah, Alma and Helaman all state that they were writing on the plates of Nephi. In 3 Nephi, Mormon states that "there are records which do contain all the proceedings of this people [records on the plates of Nephi]; and a shorter but true account was given by Nephi. Therefore I have made my record of these things according to the record of Nephi, which was engraven on the plates, which were called the plates of Nephi. And behold, I do make the record on plates, which I have made with mine own hands." (3 Nephi 5:9-11) Mormon calls this a "small record." (3 Nephi 5:15) Mormon also writes that he wrote the "more part" of Jesus' teaching on the plates of Nephi, but a lesser part in his own account. (3 Nephi 26:7-8) Further, Mormon, in his own record, states that he wrote a full account on the plates of Nephi, but says "upon these plates I did forbear to make a full account" (Mormon 2:18). In 4 Nephi, Mormon clarifies the difference between these two records. He wrote, "he [the record keeper Nephi] that kept this last record (and he kept it upon the plates of Nephi) died, and his son Amos kept it in his stead; and he kept it upon the plates of Nephi also." (4 Nephi 1:19) Then Amos died, "and his son Amos kept the record in his stead; and he also kept it upon the plates of Nephi; and it was also written [by Mormon] in the book of Nephi, which is this book [Mormon's abridgment]." (4N1:21). So the account was written twice, first on the plates of Nephi, and the a second time in Mormon's account, which Mormon terms "the book of Nephi." The BoM "Book of 4 Nephi" was written on both sets of plates, so we are apparently intended to understand this book of Nephi to mean that he was considering his record to be a continuation of Nephi's record on the small plates.

Overall, Mormon's comments show that the drafters of these books were aware of both sets of plates, the large plates and small plates of Nephi.

The distribution of Nephi elements. The table below is an exhaustive list of Nephi elements found in the BOM books from Mosiah through Moroni, with references showing which books contain each element.

Table 55. Nephi Elements in Mosiah, Alma, Helaman, et al.

Key: N=Nephi, J=Jacob, M=Mosiah, A=Alma, H=Helaman 3N=3 Nephi, 4N=4 Nephi, MR=Mormon, E=Ether, MN=Moroni	
Nephi element	Reference
Nephi	M10:13; A3:17; H1:1; 3N10:18; 4N1:39; MR1:5; E8:21
Nephites	M7:15[+]; A2:11; H1:15; 3N1:28; 4N1:2; MR1:8; E3:17; 9:3, 31; MN1:2
Lehi	M1:4; A9:9; H6:10; 3N1:1; MR4:12; E13:5
Laman	A3:7; A24:29; 43:13; MR1:9
Lamanites	M1:5[+]; A2:24[+]; H1:14; 3N1:5; 4N1:2; MR1:8; E4:3; MN1:1
Lemuel	A3:7; A24:29; 43:13; MR1:9
Plates of Nephi	M1:6[+] A37:2; H2:14; 3N5:9 & 26:7; 4N1:19; MR1:4
Plates of Nephi are a more particular record	3N26:7; MR1:4
Recordkeepers write on the plates of Nephi	M1:6; A37:2 & 44:24; 3N26:7 & 26:11; 4N1:19 & 4N1:21; MR1:4, 2:18 & 6:6
Plates of brass	M1:3[+] 3N10:17; A3:11; A37:3; 3N1:2
Plates of brass contain the genealogy of our fathers	A37:3
Lehi taught in the language of the Egyptians	M1:4
Records which contain the prophecies which have been spoken by the holy prophets, even down to the time of our father, Lehi, left Jerusalem...also, all that has been spoken by our fathers until now	M2:34
If this ...people should fall into transgression...they become weak like unto their brethren	M1:13
the sword of Laban	M1:16
the ball or director...that thereby they might be led...according to the heed and diligence which they gave	M1:16; A37:38

the Nephite-Lamanite division	M1:5[+]
city of Nephi	M9:15[+]; A23:11
land of Nephi	M7:6[+]
the land of Nephi, land of our father's first inheritance	M9:1; A54:12
faithfulness of Nephi when crossing the sea	M10:13
Alma being a descendant of Nephi	M17:2
Brass Plates were written in the language of the Egyptians	M1:4
Brass Plates contain the mysteries of God	M1:3
Lehi (or Nephi) was brought out of Jerusalem	M10:17; H7:7; 3N1:2; 3N2:6; E13:5
Promised land	M10:15; A37:44; H7:7; E2:7-8, 12
Lehi was promised a land for his people's inheritance	M28:20; cf. 3N15:13 & 20:14
Lehi was a descendant of Manasseh (i.e. of Joseph)	M10:3; A10:3; cf. 46:23
Sons of Ishmael & Ishmaelites	A3:7[+]; MR1:9
Mark put upon Laman and Lemuel, and on the sons of Ishmael and the Ishmaelitish women	A3:7
The sons of Ishmael, and the Ishmaelitish women, are joined with Laman and Lemuel	A3:7; 17:19; 18:38
Those who mingle their seed with Lamanites get the same curse	A3:9
Rebellions of Laman and Lemuel	A18:38
Laman was the eldest son of Lehi	A56:3
Righteous siblings: "Nephi, Jacob, and Joseph, and Sam."	A3:6
Zoram, "whom your fathers pressed and brought out of Jerusalem."	A54:23
Zedekiah	H6:10; H8:21
Mulek, son of Zedekiah. Lehi was brought to the land south, and Mulek to the land north	M25:2; H6:10; 8:21
Lehi was cast out of Jerusalem	A10:3; cf. H5:5-6
"Our father Lehi was driven out of Jerusalem because he testified of these things." Also Nephi.	H8:22
If the Nephites fall into transgression, they shall be destroyed from of the face of the earth	A9:24
Judeans attempted to kill Lehi. ???	
"Jerusalem was destroyed according to the words of Jeremiah."	H8:20
Extra-Biblical prophets in Nephi: Zenock (Alma) and Zenos (Alma)	A33:15; 33:3; H8:19-20; 3N10:16
the land of Nephi and the land of Zarahemla were nearly surrounded by water (i.e. isles of the sea)	A22:32
Faithful Nephi took the lead in the wilderness (in Arabia)	M10:13
Lamanites were made to believe that they were driven out of Jerusalem because of the iniquities of their fathers.	M10:12
Laman & Lemuel were wronged in the wilderness by their brethren	M10:12
Laman & Lemuel were wronged while crossing the sea	M10:12
Laman & Lemuel were wroth with Nephi because he took the rule over them in the promised land	M10:15; A54:17

Nephi departed in the wilderness by God's command leaving the initial settlement in the Promised Land	M10:16
Nephi took with him the records which were engraven on the plates of brass when he fled	M10:16
records and scriptures from the time that Lehi left Jerusalem down to the present time	A18:38
Tree of life	A5:34
True vine; grafted into the true vine (N15:15; J5:60)	A16:17
T=55 M=32 M$^{1-10}$=28 M^{1}=12 M^{10}=12 A=31 H=13 3N=11 4N=6 MR=10 E=5 MN=2	

Of these 55 Nephi elements, Mosiah alone has 32, nearly enough coverage to draw up a skeletal outline of Nephi. They are front-loaded, with twelve in the first chapter, and twenty-eight in the first ten chapters. Twelve are in chapter ten. Alma has a bit less, with thirty-one elements. With this evidence added to that in the foregoing sections, there can be little doubt that an outline of Nephi was available to the drafters of Mosiah and Alma. The elements are front-loaded in Mosiah to make the transition from the replacement text seem more normal. Surely the most straightforward explanation is some version of the Nephi priority or a multiple drafter theory of composition order.

On the other hand, if Nephi was done by Smith in Harmony prior to Cowdery's arrival, he and Cowdery could have worked there on separate drafts. Cultivating an optic of Oliver being merely a scribe, and Joseph solely a translator, may have been purely to enhance Joseph's persona. A multiple-authorship theory can be equally consistent with the presence of numerous Nephi elements in Mosiah.

If a Mosiah prioritist were to adopt the draft approach, then it could be argued that Mosiah was the first draft done, and that the Nephi elements were later edited into Mosiah et al. As for the sequence after Mosiah, note that the Abinadi story (Mosiah 11:20) continues in Alma 5:11; and the Gideon story (Mosiah 19:4) continues in Alma 1:8. This is no problem for any sequential theory. If one were to posit that Mosiah and Alma had different drafters, it would be necessary to assume that they worked in reasonable proximity to each other, and collaborated.

Clearing the chronology hurdle. As for the possibility of simultaneous drafting of two or more books, by drafters in different locations, note that beginning Mosiah faces no chronology problem. Nephi establishes a dating system in terms of years after leaving Jerusalem (ALJ dates). Since the birth of Jesus is fixed in time, the main problem for the drafter of Mosiah was to date its beginning sufficiently early to allow enough time for the anticipated books covering that interval. The drafter could expand or squeeze the account of Helaman to fit. Note that its first half covers thirty years, and the second half only twenty-one. This allows 3 Nephi to begin in 600 ALJ. The dating in the fast-forward books (Enos through Omni) could be set to enable Amaleki's dates to accommodate the date of the beginning of Mosiah.

The real date issue arises with Alma. If this book was also drafted in Manchester, how could one know the date for the end of Mosiah? This seems to have been solved by timing the establishment of the regime of the judges so that Alma could begin exactly in the first year of the judges. Suspicious? Readers could always use the date in Mosiah to calculate the ALJ dates for Alma's years of the judges. Beginning this new dating system (i.e. the first year of the judges) in Alma 1:1 is convenient for a multiple-drafter approach.

The Nephi quotes in Alma virtually require the availability of a prior Nephi outline. The numerous Nephi elements in Mosiah give additional weight to this view. Additionally, Mormon at times is clearly referring to the small plates of Nephi. The links between Mosiah and Alma indicate that if these two had separate drafters, they must have done at least a first draft in Manchester, and collaborated. If they had only an outline of Nephi in Manchester, additional Nephi elements could have been inserted in Harmony. The same is true of the Mosiah prioritist approach.

The Issue of Mosiah Priority: The Folds of the Gatherings

Some have used the gathering folds as evidence for the sequence of producing the books. All of Alma, and up to 3 Nephi 4:2 are folded *widthwise* (and also 1 Nephi 14:11 through Enos 1:14). Skousen records that the gathering containing 3 Nephi 19:26 to 27:7 was folded *lengthwise*, as well as the gathering containing the extant part of Ether, 3:9-15:17. From this, some have speculated that lengthwise folding continued to the end of Moroni, and then into the first gathering of 1 Nephi, with 2:2-13:35 extant. If true, this might serve as evidence for the orthodox Mosiah prioritist scholars, *viz* that the text composed to replace the purloined 116 pages (the *Book of Lehi*) were added by Moroni at the end of his own record. Secularist Mosiah prioritists could take this gathering folding observation as evidence that somehow it took a long time for Smith to arrive at the Nephi solution to his dilemma, and to not lose time, he began again where he had left off in the storyline. It is not at all clear that either was the case.

First, this evidence is only relevant to the copying of the text into ms$\mathcal{O}$. It says nothing about the initial composition in ms$\mathcal{U}$; whatever the order of initial composition, the books of ms$\mathcal{U}$ could have been copied into ms𝒪 in any order. *Second*, the ms𝒪 texts of Mosiah, 4 Nephi, Mormon and Moroni are not extant. We have no evidence for how they were folded. *Third*, we need to know *why* some gatherings are folded widthwise and others lengthwise. Note that Cowdery was the sole scribe for all extant portions of 2 Nephi and on to 3 Nephi 4:2. These were folded widthwise. Cowdery, who was very consistent in his procedures, was also the scribe for the text of 3 Nephi 19:26-27:7 (extant), and the text of Ether 3:9-15:17 (extant). Even though the first gathering of 1 Nephi has lengthwise folds, its second gathering has widthwise folds. Cowdery was the chief scribe for both of these. Why does the same scribe, and a somewhat fussy one at that, change the fold orientation? This may be a simple matter of paper grain (grain long = lengthwise, and grain short = widthwise). It may be easier quilling going with the grain, and harder on one's quill going cross-grain. So it may depend on which paper grain was acquired.

Table 56. Gathering Information
(Skousen's gathering numbers are in parentheses)

gathering	extant gathering content (LDS chapters)	paper type	fold	paper size width	paper size length
1 (B1)	1 Nephi 2:2–13:35	F	lengthwise	13"	16.45"
2 (B2)	1 Nephi 14:11–2 Nephi 1:30	A	widthwise	13"	16.45"
3 (B3)	2 Nephi 4:32–9:42	A	widthwise		
4 (B4)	2 Nephi 23.0–25:28	A	widthwise		
5 (B5)	2 Nephi 33:4–Jacob 4:14	A	widthwise		
6 (B6)	Jacob 5:46–Enos 1:14	C	widthwise		
10 (?)	Alma 3:5–17, 3:17–4:2, 4:20–5:10 5:10–23 [CHICAGO LEAVES]	?	widthwise	7.25" (just 1 leaf)	matches other Alma leaves
11 (A10)	Alma 10:31–13:16	D^B	widthwise		
12 (A11)	Alma 19:3–20:22	D^B	widthwise		
13 (A12)	Alma 22:22–60:22	D^B	widthwise	12.7"	16.2"
14 (A13)	Alma 61;11–Helaman 3:21	D^B	widthwise		
15 (A14)	Helaman 13:36–3 Nephi 4:2	D^B	widthwise		
17(A16)	3 Nephi 19:26–27:7	D^B	lengthwise		
18(A17)	Ether 3:9–15:17	E	lengthwise		

NOTES: **D^B**. Some of this paper type was originally typed as B, and the rest as D, but it was later determined that both are the same type, which Skousen labels B/D.
Gathering 16. No part of this gathering is extant. Even so, Skousen assigns five sheets, folded lengthwise, and apparently blank, to this gathering, without explanation.

Paper was probably acquired by the quire, i.e. 24 sheets. This explains why six sheets (24 pages) was a common size for a gathering, with four pages per sheet, and four gatherings per quire. So, was the paper for Ether, 3:9-15:17 (extant) and 1 Nephi 2:2-13:35 (extant) from the same quire?

This is not the case. The evidence is in the paper type. Robert J. Espinosa, conservator at BYU, identified five different paper types in ms$\mathcal{O}$, and these two gatherings are of different paper types.[437] So 1 Nephi 2:2-13:35 may not follow from the last extant books of the BoM. Actually, the next four gatherings (1 Nephi 14:11 through Jacob 4:14) are of yet another type, clearly coming from the same quire. The first gathering of ms$\mathcal{O}$ used a paper type not found elsewhere in the extant materials, likely left over from another quire and possibly one used in producing ms$\mathcal{U}$ in Harmony.

The first gathering of Ms$\mathcal{O}$ appears to have been composed of 6 sheets, equaling 24 pages. Under the Mosiah prioritist hypothesis, when Moroni was completed, Smith circled all the way back to Nephi and began it with a new gathering. But we note that Ether was done on a paper type also otherwise not found in the extant part of ms$\mathcal{O}$, which Skousen labels type E. Since the six previous gatherings were type B/D, Ether was done on paper taken from a new quire, a quire that could have finished Moroni with just one (or maximum two) six-sheet gatherings. If Nephi followed Moroni, then one might expect that it would use a new gathering from this quire. Why not? The required sheets were at hand. Instead, the first gathering of Nephi is also a unique paper type, labeled F. If paper type trumps gathering folds, then even if Moroni turns out to have had lengthwise folds (like the first gathering in Nephi), this fact does not lead us to conclude necessarily that Nephi followed Moroni in the writing of ms$\mathcal{O}$.

The identification of paper types was done by conservator Espinosa.[438] Paper was made on a wire mesh similar to today's window screens, but with very fine wire weaving producing squares. The principal feature looked for is the number of wires per centimeter. Skousen has provided Espinosa's data used to determine paper types in ms$\mathcal{P}$.[439] The wire marks were not sufficiently visible for this determination in one ms$\mathcal{P}$ gathering. The others exhibit considerable variation. Six gatherings used 31 wires per cm, and four used 28 wires per cm. But three used only 17 wires per cm. Even if just one substantial fragment of ms$\mathcal{O}$ Moroni surfaces, the wires per cm used for it could provide strong evidence for whether or not Nephi followed Moroni, independent of its folding orientation, if the fragment is sufficient to show its folding orientation.

---

[437] Skousen, Original Manuscript, 37.

[438] Ibid, 37-38.

[439] Skousen, *The Printer's Manuscript*, I:33-34.

The Issue of Mosiah Priority: The Role of the Retained Pages

We read, in D&C 10:41, the phrase: "or until you come to that which you have translated, which you have retained." Ostensibly the purpose of this phrase is to indicate how far to translate the plates of the replacement text.

One gathering has six x four = 24 pages. Four gatherings are 96 pages. 116 pages = four six-page gatherings, and one five page gathering. This could be how Smith knew how many pages had gone missing. Beyond this, an additional gathering, only partially done, and not entrusted to Harris, might have been the pages retained.

The inclusion of the first part of the Mosiah story in the record of Amaleki, along with D&C 10:41, indicates that this part of the account had already been begun on a gathering following the purloined pages and had to be covered on the small plates of Nephi. It is interesting to note that D&C 10:41 makes no mention of Mosiah. The continuation of the account, found in Words of Mormon, is recorded by Mormon on plates of his own making, emulating the small plates that he admired so much, emulating in both size and content. Consequently, they continue from the small plates of Nephi, and are the beginning of the remainder of his work to be included among Smith's gold plates. These Omni and WoM texts, together, were originally the first chapter of Mosiah. As we have seen, it is *wherefore*-dominant, while the remainder of Mosiah is *therefore*-dominant. Presumably the 116 pages were *wherefore*-dominant.

It was not necessary to publicize that some Lehi pages were retained. There are a couple of possible reasons for doing so. First, if the Mosiah draft was being composed by someone in Manchester, perhaps it was feared that this had been suspected. This assertion would give assurance that Mosiah had been begun in Harmony before any pages even went missing. Second, and perhaps more probable, this may have been extra insurance against an attack from whomever might have the stolen pages. Even with Smith's new strategy, the worst case scenario would be for the pages to be produced totally intact after the new bible had been printed, with a carefully forged 117th page with content incompatible with the published text. If these subversives thought that pages had been retained, they might not attempt it. If they did, this verse laid the groundwork for the BoM authors to produce "retained" pages to refute the attack.

The Issue of Mosiah Priority: References outside the BoM

Another argument adduced in support of the Mosiah priority position is found in a comment once attributed to Joseph Smith in his 1839 history, that in the process of translation they had come across a reference to the promise that there would be three witnesses to the gold plates, and that upon seeing this, Oliver Cowdery, David Whitmer and Martin Harris begged Smith to seek of the Lord on their behalf that they could be the three. Shortly after doing so, they were shown the plates. There is a reference in this passage to 2 Nephi 11 (see 2 Nephi 27:12 in the current LDS chapter divisions), seemingly linking the translation (or composition) of Nephi to this late event. However, in his edition of this history, Jessee points out in a note that this reference is an insertion in pencil in a different hand.[440] It is not Joseph Smith. Unfortunately for the Mosiah priority case, the calling of three witnesses is also mentioned in Ether 5:4, near the end of the *Book of Mormon*. To the extent that this story has any historicity, it could be the translation or composition of the passage in Ether that gave rise to this trio's desire to be the three witnesses.[441] Also, references of this sort could have been added in the process of editing the drafts, after some discussion: "Should we say it here, or perhaps there? Better yet, let's say it in both places." Neither passage has anything new. The promise that there would be three witnesses was already in D&C 5:11, dated in March 1829.

Yet another argument in support of the Mosiah priority position has to do with child baptism. In a letter from Oliver to Hyrum Smith, dated 14 June 1829, he wrote, "he commandeth all men every where to repent and ~~not only~~ [be] baptized *and not only men but women [and] children which have arrived to the years of accountability* (sic; emphasis added)."[442] This has been argued to have been drawn from Moroni 8:20: "he that saith that little children need baptism denieth the mercies of Christ," and therefore evidence that Moroni was written prior to that date. However, a similar view is already expressed in Mosiah 3:18: "the infant perisheth not that dieth in his infancy." More to the point, in June 1829 a revelation with identical wording stated, "For all men must repent and be baptized, *and not only men, but women, and children who have arrived at the years of*

---

[440] Jessee, *Papers of Joseph Smith*, I:295.

[441] For a major analysis of this issue, made in support of Mosiah priority, see Brent Lee Metcalfe, "The Priority of Mosiah: A Prelude to *Book of Mormon* Exegesis," in Brent Lee Metcalfe, ed., *New Approaches to the Book of Mormon*, 395-444.

[442] Oliver Cowdery letter to Hyrum Smith dated 14/06/1829, in Vogel, *Early Mormon Documents*, II:403.

accountability." (D&C 18:42; emphasis added) This was probably the personal view of both Cowdery and Smith, shared by many others at the time. Infant mortality was high, many dying unbaptized. In 1810, Ephraim Smith, a sibling of Joseph Smith Jr., lived only eleven days, and in 1823, another brother, Alvin Smith died without the benefit of baptism by the restored priesthood authority.[443]

Metcalfe further bolsters his argument by adducing the language found in the copyright, dated 11 June 1829, which refers to Mormon's abridgment and to the Book of Ether: "sealed by the hand of Moroni, and hid up unto the Lord." Because the Book of Moroni 10:3 states, "I seal up these records;" he argues that it must have been composed before the date of the copyright. But Moroni makes no mention of hiding up the records. This is found only in Ether 4:3, "I am commanded that I should hide them up again in the earth," and 4:5, "And he commanded me that I should seal them up." Consequently there is no need for Moroni to have been composed prior to the copyright. Moroni can only be a partial referent for the copyright text, while Ether is a complete referent.

Moreover, it is probable that he had already used the name of Moroni for this messenger by the time he was working with Martin Harris on the *Book of Lehi*, and in any case no later than early 1829. Even so, Smith's own oral comments regarding the visitation of the messenger, his receipt of the plates, and the role of Moroni are probably the referent for both the copyright text and the Ether passage.

Nephi and the Nephites are well known from Mosiah on. This is especially true of Mosiah, being the follow-on text to the replacement text. We find therein: the plates of Nephi, the brass plates, the sword of Laban, the ball or director, the Nephite-Lamanite division, the land of Lehi-Nephi, land of Nephi, city of Nephi, faithfulness of Nephi when crossing the sea and Alma being a descendant of Nephi. Alma knows that Lehi was brought out of Jerusalem, had received a promise for a land for his people's inheritance and was a descendant of Manasseh (i.e. of Joseph). Alma also knows that Laman was the eldest son of Lehi. The Book of Helaman knows that Lehi was brought to the land south, and Mulek to the land north. A detailed knowledge of the contents of Nephi was known before Mosiah was commenced.

Note that front-loading the Nephi references in Mosiah is another

---

[443] Metcalfe rejects the argument based on Cowdery's reference to child baptism in a letter to Hyrum, as well as the argument based on 2 Nephi 27:12 regarding the three witnesses, and Joseph's query asking Emma if Jerusalem had walls, in "The Priority of Mosiah," 399, 400 & 401, respectively.

effort to bridge the Nephi-Mosiah gap seamlessly.

Nephi Priority vs Mosiah Priority: Heuristic Timelines

In Table 58, Smith's work recommences in early December, but he might have gotten his new start earlier. David Whitmer said that the translation took eight months (i.e. December 1 to July 1). This comports well with Joseph Knight Sr., who wrote that the Smiths came to him at the first of winter of 1828, at which point they were already translating.

Table 57. *Therefore* (t) and *Wherefore* (w) in the BoM & BoC

Light grey marks *therefore* dominant texts, & dark grey *wherefore* dominant texts.											
Nephi priority					date	Revelations & Docs				Mosiah priority	
book	%/% t/w	t	w	multiple drafters		BoC	t	w	%/% t/w	%/% t/w	book
					28-07	2	2	0	100/0		
1 Nephi	12/88	14	99	1 Nephi[1]	28-12					100/0	Mosiah
1-2 Nephi	4/96	6	135	2 Nephi[1]	29-01					99/1	Alma
2Nephi Jacob	2/98	1	53	2 Nephi[1] Jacob[1]	29-02	3	2	0	100/0	100/0 100/0	Alma Helaman
Jacob Enos Jarom Omni WoM	 0/100 0/100 0/100 0/100	 0 0 0 0	 6 3 6 4	Jacob[1] Enos[1] Jarom[1] Omni[1] WoM[1]	29-03	4	0	0	0	99/1 100/0	3 Nephi 4 Nephi
Mosiah Alma	100/0 99/1	122 288	0 3	Mosiah[2] Alma[3]	29-04	5 6 7 8	8 0 2 2	0 0 0 0	100/0 0 100/0 100/0	100/0 28/72	Mormon Ether
Helaman 3 Nephi 4 Nephi	100/0 99/1 100/0	63 82 5	0 1 0	Helaman[1] 3 Nephi[1] 4 Nephi[1]	29-05 (15-05?)	9 10 11 baptism	10 4 4	0 0 0	100/0 100/0 100/0	0/100	Moroni
Mormon Ether	100/0 28/72	22 24	0 61	Mormon[1] Ether[1]	29-06 **June** (1-14) (11) (14-30)	12 13 14 copy- right 15	3 0 0	1 2 1	75/25 0 0 0/100 0/100	12/88 1/53 0/100 0/100 0/100 0/100	1 Nephi 2 Nephi Jacob Enos Jarom Omni WoM

Moroni	0/100	0	38	Moroni		**D&C** **(1835)** **42**			0/100	
					29-06	Cowdery revelation	2	0	100/0	
					29-07	preface	1	1	50/50	
					1830 **30-03**	16	0	8	0/100	
					30-04	22	0	2	0/100	
					30-06	24	2	3	40/60	

BoC|D&C key: 2|3; 3|4; 4|5; 5|6; 6|7; 7|8; 8|9; 9|10; 10|11; 11|12; 12|14; 13|15; 14|16; 15|18; 16|19; 22|21; 24|20. For the BoC, see the *Joseph Smith Papers*. ¹drafter 1 ²drafter 2 &³drafter 3.

The observation that Joseph Smith had made a style shift was most thoroughly argued by Brent Metcalfe.[444] The column on the far left is done with a single author assumption, i.e. Joseph Smith. Note that in this table BoM books Mosiah through Mormon use *therefore* to the total exclusion of *wherefore*, except for the minor exceptions seen in Alma and 3 Nephi. From the recommencement and well into March, the entire replacement text was done, and only two revelations. These were done for Smith Sr. and Harris, and the latter may have been done at the time that Smith put his work on hold waiting for Cowdery's arrival. Even with the multiple drafter assumption, the entire replacement text was done by Joseph Smith. With the Mosiah priority assumption, on the far right, for this same period (December through March), Mosiah through 4 Nephi is done. It is totally *therefore*-dominant, as is the revelation for Harris. All three assumptions totally avoid a comparison with Smith's revelations.

Although Ether is strongly *wherefore*-dominant, Moroni is the first book to show a total reversal, with *wherefore* being used to the total exclusion of *therefore*. For the chronological assumptions used here, this is just the opposite of the revelations that it might correspond to (v. BoC 9). Note that this Mosiah priority presentation assumes that the work was being done directly into ms𝒪 (begun with Fayette scribes), thereby compressing 1 Nephi through WoM into part of a single month, June.

1 Nephi partially reverses, with only **88%** *wherefore*. In 2 Nephi and Jacob, *wherefore* dominates, until we finally see the Moroni pattern of *wherefore* exclusivity again in Enos through Words of Mormon, all very tiny books. What we totally lack here is what Metcalfe termed a "gradual

---

[444] Using data from John L. Hilton and Kenneth D. Jenkins, "Vocabulary and Numerical Count of all Words from the King James Old Testament, New Testament and the 1830 *Book of Mormon*," *Preliminary Report*. (Provo, UT: FARMS, n.d.)

transition from '*therefore*' to '*wherefore*'."

Table 58. *Therefore-Wherefore* in Ether & 1 Nephi

Chapters	*therefore*	*wherefore*	total	*% therefore*	*% wherefore*
Ether 1-5	14	8	22	64	36
Ether 6-10	8	23	31	26	74
Ether 11-15	2	30	32	6	94
Moroni (all)	0	38	38	0	100
1 Nephi 1-7	10	23	33	30	70
1 Nephi 8-14	3	26	29	10	90
1 Nephi 15-21	1	51	52	2	98

Metcalfe then dissected Ether into thirds and found an impressive progression from *therefore* to *wherefore* (Table 59). He concluded that Smith's style shift took place while doing this book.

Although Moroni accordingly uses *wherefore* to the total exclusion of *therefore* (an impressive 38 occurrences), we find that 1 Nephi, which is supposed to have followed Moroni, has a more complex distribution. In fact, although not as extreme, it mirrors the distribution found in Ether, in that it shifts from *therefore* to *wherefore*. But, in the first third, *therefore* still represents almost one third.

In addition to the BoM and BoC evidence, note that the copyright text (Smith's composition?), composed no later than June 10, has two occurrences of *wherefore* and none of *therefore*. Smith declared that this text was on the gold plates and is a part of the divine translation. It should thus be expected that it would follow the pattern of the replacement text, also done most probably by Smith. The preface to the 1830 edition has one *therefore* and one *wherefore*. There is no way to date this text. In ms*P*, these two documents are on a piece of paper folded in half, separate from the first gathering that began Nephi. The preface could have been composed anytime from mid June to some time in August when the printing began. It exhibits no clear distribution pattern, possibly due to its short length.

It is interesting to note that the Articles of the Church of Christ, composed by Oliver Cowdery in June, is 100% *therefore* (Ryder copy).

The dating of preferences in the 1829 revelations is a different story. *Therefore* is used three times roughly in the first third of BoC 12, and *wherefore* but once, in the last third. Smith wrote in his 1839 history that BoC 12, 13 and 14 were given in succession to three Whitmers (David, John and Peter Jr.). According to Vogel, this would have been most probably before seeking the BoM copyright, and therefore also prior to the trip to Palmyra to arrange for the printing of the *Book of Mormon*. June 7 would be the latest date for these revelations. The second important revelation is BoC 15 (D&C 18), which uses *wherefore* exclusively (as well as all subsequent revelations through March 1830 (BoC 16 & 22). It is only at this point that we have documentary evidence that Smith had begun to use primarily *wherefore*. Vogel dates it after the issuance of the copyright, i.e. from 11-14, since the copyright issued on June 11. According to D&C 17:6, the Nephite narrative was already completed prior to the three-witness event. It may be that after completing this text, Smith decided that *wherefore* could be appropriate for his revelations, at least for a while.

If we assign this revelatory preference a putative date of June 14, then the Mosiah prioritist can logically expect a book with a totally *wherefore* distribution, such as Moroni, within some proximity to this date. Since BoC 12 (D&C 14) is still 75% *therefore*, and Moroni is 100% *wherefore*, it seems improbable that Moroni would have been completed using exclusively *wherefore* directly on the heels of BoC 12.

Another key date in the pre-June timeframe is May 15, commonly accepted as the date of Joseph and Oliver's baptism. The argument has been made that this date would correspond to the baptism passage in 3 Nephi 11:21-26. Both Nephi priority and Mosiah priority can be timed to correspond nicely to this BoM passage.

Wherefore: Just Another Archaism for BoM KJV English

The information displayed in table 60 casts a very different light on the *therefore-wherefore* issue by revealing to what extent *wherefore* was even used in the late eighteenth and early nineteenth centuries in New England.

Table 59. Usage of *therefore, wherefore & save* in Early 1800s and the Bible

Author/Preacher	Works (The number of pages are in parentheses.)	therefore/ wherefore	percent wherefore	save/ except	% save
Jonathan Edwards	*Complete Works* (5,964)	3159/99	3%	2/325	0.6%
George Whitfield	*Selected Sermons* (1,172)	629/18	3%	1/23	4%
Charles Finney	*Works of C. Finney* (1,188)	1599/59	4%	20/413	5%
Bellamy, Joseph	*Works of J. Bellamy* (1,048)	706/45	6%	0/31	0%
John Wesley	*Complete Sermons*	1233/51	4%	7/112	6%
Ethan Smith	*View of the Hebrews* (235)	21/0	0%	0/17	0%
Isaac Worsley (1829)	*View, American Indians* (149)	17/0	0%	0/17	0%
Thomas Thorowgood	*Jews in America* (28)	22/0	0%	1/0	100%
Elias Boudinot	*The Second Advent...* (607)	140/14	10%	0/19	0
James Adair	*History, America Indians* (604)	52/2	4%	1/99	1%
Josiah Priest	*American Antiquities* (499)	98/1	1%	0/47	0%

Charles H. Spurgeon	*Sermons, vol. 1-6* (5,755)	1149/31	3%		
KJV	*Genesis*	48/20	29%		
KJV	*Isaiah*	73/13	13%		
KJV	*Jeremiah*	162/24	13%		
KJV	*Ezekiel*	88/14	14%		
KJV	*Matthew*	49/13	21%		
Joseph Smith	*1832 history*	16/0	0%		
Joseph Smit (et al.?)	*Book of Abraham*	11/1	8%		

Searches of these thousands of pages reveal that *wherefore* was rarely used in the 1820s. It is quite improbable that Smith's own idiolect used it any more, at any time. But it was used noticeably more in the Bible. Joseph Smith was quite familiar with it and its King James English, so much so that he decided that his own bible should be written in that same archaic language. In order to create a BoM English, he also added various words and phrases: "*Behold!*" ("*I beheld.*"), "*unto,*" "*save*" (for *except*), "*thereof,*" "*and it came to pass...*" and the overuse of "*and.*" He observed that *wherefore* was used quite a bit in the Bible, so he added it to this list. A person just learning to cook sometimes decides that if a little salt is good, even more would be better. Similarly, he went to extremes in adding his linguistic spices and aromatics. *Wherefore* was just another word thrown in deliberately and purposefully. The texts of his own revelations did not meet the minimal criteria for this treatment. They were not ancient, and were not the product of Nephite prophets writing two millennia ago.

Another factor may have been at play. The writers of Mosiah thru 3 Nephi were not fond of *wherefore*. Perhaps he or they just did not get the memo. We note that Cowdery's revelation (Ryder copy) has two instances of *therefore*.

The frequency of these words is all about Smith creating an archaic BoM English, and has nothing to do with personal style shifting over time.

The Smith (June 1829) Timeline

The June timeframe is defined roughly by a statement of David Whitmer: "The translation at my father's occupied about a month, that is from June 1 to July 1, 1829."[445] After the vision of the eight witnesses, Smith wrote, "Mean time we continued to translate at intervals,"[446] and later, "Mean time our translation drawing to a close, we went to Palmyra...Secured the

---

[445] David Whitmer, to the *Kansas City Journal*, 5 June 1881; also see Backman, *Eyewitness Accounts*, 124.
[446] Ibid, 324.

Copyright [v. p. 129] and agreed with Mr Egbert Grandon (sic) to print..."
[draft 2], or "Having finished the translation we went to Palmyra..." [draft
3].[447] This leaves so little time after their arrival that, if we take Smith at
his word, progress in composing ms𝒰 must have been very advanced
while in Harmony. His mother Lucy wrote that "As soon as the *Book of
Mormon* was translated, Joseph dispatched a messenger to Mr. Smith [Sr.],
bearing intelligence of the completion of the work, and requesting that Mr.
Smith and myself should come immediately to Waterloo. The same
evening, we conveyed this intelligence to Martin Harris...the next
morning we all set off...and before sunset [arrived at Fayette]...The
evening was spent in reading the manuscript... The next morning...
Joseph, Martin, Oliver and David repaired to a grove" [for the experience
of the three witnesses].[448]

The following table has been developed to put June into sharper
focus, respecting what happened, but also how much time was actually
available for work on the *Book of Mormon* text.

Table 60. Estimated Days Not Available (☒) in June for Translation

☒	date	Event and comment [NOTE: SMTWTFS represent days of the week]
		In his 1839 history, Smith states that David Whitmer arrived to take them to Fayette, "in the beginning of the month of June."[449] He also wrote that he came to have us "accompany him to his father's place, and there remain until we should finish the work."[450]
3	1-3 MTW	We do not know what day Whitmer arrived. Smith stated that it was "in the beginning of the month of June." In Harmony, after a long trip, his horse would require rest and feed. Smith & Cowdery would have to pack personal effects, the completed BoM texts, any prepared but blank gatherings, materials and equipment for the work, all covered securely against the possibility of rain. Whitmer stated that the trip alone took 2½ days. Vogel states that the earliest arrival date would be June 4.[451] We will use Wed. June 3.
1	4-6 TFS	Getting settled in, socializing with and getting to know the Whitmers, and preparing revelations for David, John and Peter Jr. Whitmer. Preparation of ms𝒪 pages to show to a prospective publisher.

---

[447] Ibid, 352-53.
[448] Lucy Harris, Lucy's Book, 451-52. She attended this celebration.
[449] Joseph Smith, JSP, *Histories I*, "History Drafts, 1838–circa 1841" draft 2, 306.
[450] Idem.
[451] Vogel, 5 (2003), 417.

1		Rites: Smith baptizes Hyrum Smith & David Whitmer. Cowdery baptizes Peter Whitmer Jr. (in Seneca Lake or River) The distance from the Whitmer log home is 4 miles, or eight miles round trip. It is not known in what manner those at the Whitmer home celebrated the Sabbath, but it seems that they must have done so. The total time that would otherwise have been available for dictation/composition, but was needed for baptisms and Sabbath observance, must collectively account for the equivalent of no less than one day.
1		Prior to the 3-witnesses event, D&C 17 says "he has translated the book, even that part which I have commanded him…" The 3 witnesses event in Fayette, c. Monday June 6
		Lucy's party arrive back in Manchester, June 6 (1 day travel; Lucy Smith says it took them one day to get to Waterloo. *Lucy's Book*, 451))
2 1	7-14 SMT WTF SS	NO TRANSLATION DURING THIS PERIOD Joseph Jr. & Whitmers travel to Manchester (June 7). According to Lucy, Joe Sr., she and Martin Harris were summoned to Fayette for a translation completion celebration. They returned the next day; Joseph Jr.and five members of the Whitmer family went to Manchester after that for the event of the eight witnesses, which agrees with her son's timeline. The next day, the eight-witnesses event in Manchester (c. June 8. One day for the event of the eight witnesses). Grandin Press prints the BoM title page text to be sent to Utica for the copyright. Smith wrote, "we went to Palmyra… Secured the Copyright and agreed with Mr Egbert Grandon (sic) to print…" The copyright was issued on June 11 (Thursday) in Utica (signed by Clerk Lansing), not in Palmyra. Yet, unless Smith was spiking his sassafras, we have to take his statement seriously. The copyright law of the day required that a printed copy of the description of the work be submitted with the application. Smith could have taken care of this on Grandin's press along with his efforts to arrange for printing. The copyright application could have been submitted by an assistant. John Whitmer and Samuel Smith come to mind.
5		At least five days in Palmyra and Rochester to arrange for printing of the BoM, culminating in a verbal agreement with Grandin. (minimum estimate of Dirkmaat & MacKay; c. June 9-13)
		Introductory comment re the trip to Palmyra: draft 2 of his *History* says, "mean time our translation drawing to a close," while draft 3 says, "having finished the translation." The BoM (i.e. ms𝒰) is completed or all but completed by c. June 7.
1		Smith's travel to return to Fayette: one day.

1		TRANSLATION ONLY AT INTERVALS After the Palmyra trip: "Mean time we continued to translate at intervals, when not necessitated to attend to the numerous enquirers, that now began to visit us; some for the sake of finding the truth, others for the purpose of putting hard questions, and trying to confound us..." Even though this seems to be a distraction from translating that could add up considerably, only one day is accounted here.
1	c. mid to late June	TRANSLATION WHEN POSSIBLE Missionary work: This seems to have taken up some time. "Many [of the people of Seneca County] opened their houses to us in order that we might have an opportunity of meeting with our friends for the purpose of instruction and explanation. We met with many from time to time...from this time forth [i.e. after Hyrum, David and Peter Jr. were baptized], many became believers and were baptized."[452] These activities must account for at least a day.
1		The composition of D&C Section 18 relating to the calling of the twelve apostles and instructions for church organization.
		June 26, Grandin publishes the BoM copyright text, probably after urging from Harris. Since Gilbert reports that they showed Grandin a few pages, this probably was the first few pages of ms𝒪, chosen for this purpose due to its very clean appearance. Grandin and Gilbert would have noticed that ms𝒪 was not done. As a basis for estimating the length of the work, Smith must have given assurance that it was nearly complete (referring to the completed ms𝒰 text), which in turn gave rise to Grandin's comment "as soon as it is complete." His June 26 notice does not indicate that his press will be the publisher.
1		Smith & Cowdery prepared to leave Fayette. The Fayette scribes were no longer available to them & Cowdery assumed all scrivener duties.

❖ As for time spent preaching and baptizing, the Whitmer farm is on Aunkst Rd., a location that is alternatively associated with Waterloo and Fayette. Smith is often said to be baptizing in Seneca Lake at the home of Peter Whitmer Sr. Specific contemporary documentation is generally lacking. B. H. Roberts wrote that Smith baptized Edward Partridge in Seneca River.[453]

---

[452] Ibid, 313-14.

[453] *History of the Church of Jesus Christ of Latter-day Saints*, ed. B. H. Roberts, 1st ed. (Salt Lake City: Deseret News, 1902), 129n. See Larry C. Porter, note 46, in *The*

Geography favors this site. Baptismal parties probably rode to either location by wagon, and there is no direct road from the Whitmer farm to Seneca Lake. But this property fronts on Aunkst Road. Taking it to the east one quickly gets to what is now highway 96, which goes due north to Waterloo, and Seneca River. From 1829 through 1831, it was still pristine, prior to being built up by Waterloo expansion. Travelling as the crow flies, but without passable roads, the distance to Seneca lake is c. 4 miles, and about the same to Seneca river near Waterloo, but with passable roads. A round trip would be eight miles. Each baptism event would take at least half a day, officiated by Smith, Cowdery or both.

1829

	S	M	T	W	T	F	S		S	M	T	W	T	F	S
Jan	...	...	...	...	1	2	3	July	...	...	...	1	2	3	4
	4	5	6	7	8	9	10		5	6	7	8	9	10	11
	11	12	13	14	15	16	17		12	13	14	15	16	17	18
	18	19	20	21	22	23	24		19	20	21	22	23	24	25
	25	26	27	28	29	30	31		26	27	28	29	30	31	...
Feb	1	2	3	4	5	6	7	Aug	...	...	...	...	...	...	1
	8	9	10	11	12	13	14		2	3	4	5	6	7	8
	15	16	17	18	19	20	21		9	10	11	12	13	14	15
	22	23	24	25	26	27	28		16	17	18	19	20	21	22
									23	24	25	26	27	28	29
									30	31					
Mar	1	2	3	4	5	6	7	Sept	...	...	1	2	3	4	5
	8	9	10	11	12	13	14		6	7	8	9	10	11	12
	15	16	17	18	19	20	21		13	14	15	16	17	18	19
	22	23	24	25	26	27	28		20	21	22	23	24	25	26
	29	30	31						27	28	29	30			
April	...	...	...	1	2	3	4	Oct	...	...	...	...	1	2	3
	5	6	7	8	9	10	11		4	5	6	7	8	9	10
	12	13	14	15	16	17	18		11	12	13	14	15	16	17
	19	20	21	22	23	24	25		18	19	20	21	22	23	24
	26	27	28	29	30	...	...		25	26	27	28	29	30	31
May	...	...	...	...	...	1	2	Nov	1	2	3	4	5	6	7
	3	4	5	6	7	8	9		8	9	10	11	12	13	14
	10	11	12	13	14	15	16		15	16	17	18	19	20	21
	17	18	19	20	21	22	23		22	23	24	25	26	27	28
	24	25	26	27	28	29	30		29	30					
	31														
June	...	1	2	3	4	5	6	Dec	...	...	1	2	3	4	5
	7	8	9	10	11	12	13		6	7	8	9	10	11	12
	14	15	16	17	18	19	20		13	14	15	16	17	18	19
	21	22	23	24	25	26	27		20	21	22	23	24	25	26
	28	29	30						27	28	29	30	31	...	...

19th century almanac : a complete calendar from 1800 to 1900
Philadelphia : Allen, Lane & Scott, 1886

The days in June taken up by other business total at least eighteen.[454] This leaves far too little for those who argue that the replacement text was done in June. Even during some of these available days, translation was done only at intervals. We must bear in mind the complexity of the texts to be composed in less than two weeks. This timeline might work a bit

---

Peter Whitmer Log Home: Cradle of Mormonism, in Religious Educator, vol. 12 no. 3, 2011. P. 201.

[454] For some details regarding this timeline, see Vogel 5 (2003), 417-21.

better for the LDS scholars, since Smith needed only to dictate to Cowdery what was revealed by his seerstone. But if Smith and Cowdery had to compose these texts from scratch, getting it all done in two weeks places a major strain on one's credulity.

Map 11. TheVicinity of the Whitmer Farm, from Seneca Lake & Seneca River

Source: adapted from Wikipedia: "The Cayuga-Seneca Canal"

Time Calculations

There are three dates commonly referred to in the context of the progress towards completing the BoM: June 1, 11, and 26. The first is for the beginning of the Fayette period. Although David Whitmer gives June 1 for this, Smith says that David arrived to fetch them "In the beginning of June." Whitmer said the trip took 2 ½ days. Vogel suggests that the arrival was probably on June 4. Initially they had to settle in and meet their new project team. This, plus the revelations for three Whitmers, probably took up most of June 5. It is reasonable to assume that the real start of translation was on June 6, although one cannot exclude June 5.

When Smith first approached Grandin to get the BoM printed (v. p. 406) he refused. Smith had to approach others, in Palmyra and Rochester, before Grandin relented and accepted. This process took at least five days.

The copyright application was received in Clerk Lansing's office on June 11. It is assumed that he signed readily, since this is also the date of copyright issuance. The application was itself the copyright certificate that was returned to the applicant, while the court copied an original into a copyright book; in a sense, the application was made in duplicate. However, in addition to the application (on a formally printed form of the court), it was required that it be accompanied by a printed copy of the book title page. Both survive. Smith could have Grandin press print a copy at the same time that he approached Grandin to print the BoM. This makes sense of Smith's statement that he went to Palmyra to arrange for printing, and to secure the copyright. June 11 translates into June 8 for the application to be carried by an envoy.

The next issue is Grandin's notice regarding the prospective printing of the *Book of Mormon*, published in his June 26 edition of the *Wayne Sentinel*. For the copyright to be validated, it was required by law that its text be published in one or more newspapers. This notice does not say that he intended to print the BoM. He makes the notice appear to be a rather disparaging article about the Gold Bible, and adds, "It is pretended that it will be published as soon as the translation is complete." He then introduces the BoM title page text, saying "we give it as a curiosity." Grandin must have surmised from the few ms$\mathcal{O}$ pages shown him that the manuscript was not yet done, but must have been assured that what he saw was the printer's copy they were preparing for Gilbert. This accounts for Grandin's comment "as soon as the translation is complete." Grandin needed some assurance of a firm basis to estimate how many pages they were negotiating for. Their assurance that an original draft (ms$\mathcal{U}$) was all but complete may have been sufficient for him. Moreover, we do not know at what point it was in his paper's print cycle when he agreed to publish the copyright text. The bottom line is that his comment re the completion of the manuscript most probably relates to the date of their initial verbal agreement. If the copyright arrived at the Smith log home on the 1th, one of the Smith's could have notified Harris to take action to get the title page into Grandin's *Wayne Sentinel*.

Smith's comment regarding his printer and copyright objectives in going to Palmyra makes sense when we consider the requirement to get the title page printed for his application. To accommodate the June 11 issuance date, he must have left Fayette no later than June 7. This is the latest date for his comment that translation was drawing to a close, or was finished. Similarly, since June 26 is the date that the title page notice was printed, undoubtedly after some prodding by Harris, Grandin's memory that the work still needed to be completed would go back to when he and Smith first made their agreement, i.e. c. June 10. Once Smith got back to Fayette, and he and Cowdery finished their translation document (ms$\mathcal{U}$), they could then focus on ms$\mathcal{O}$, the original printer's copy. In early July, they decided to make a second copy, ms$\mathcal{P}$, since they did not want to keep ms$\mathcal{U}$ around for scrutiny; its editing betrayed the human hand, and in any case, it may not have been identical to ms$\mathcal{O}$. Two clean manuscripts, ms$\mathcal{O}$ and ms$\mathcal{P}$, were just what converts would expect to see.

The completion of the translation of the *Book of Mormon* might have referred to the completion of Mormon's abridgment, leaving Ether yet to be done. The completion of both the BoM and Ether, possibly by July 1, may be the basis for David Whitmer's completion date for the *Book of Mormon*.

The orthodox LDS scholars have wanted to push the completion date as far back as possible. Now we go full circle, back to the untoward discovery that the handwriting of Emma and Samuel is not found in any extant text of ms$\mathcal{O}$. This was initially the handwriting crisis that seems to have surfaced in the 1960s. Whose handwritings are these in ms$\mathcal{O}$? How can we accommodate an $\mathcal{O}$ commencement date in June? Dean C. Jessee came up with the orthodox LDS solution: Smith must have recommenced his work with Mosiah, in the winter of 1828-29, resulting in Nephi through WoM being left to last, namely in June.[455] Mosiah priority was born. The problem is that there is just not enough time available in June to complete this portion of ms$\mathcal{O}$. By ignoring the comments of their founding prophet they buy more time to complete the translation in their timeline. Since the time, from Smith's recommencement of his work in the winter or fall of 1829 to Samuel's departure in late March, was sufficient for Emma and/or Samuel to write from Mosiah 1:1 to Alma 10:31, and more, once again, we ask, "Where is their handwriting, if not in ms$\mathcal{U}$?"

This is part of the

Timeline Issue

---

[455] Jessee, "The Original *Book of Mormon* Manuscript," 259-78.

< Chapter 27 >

BoM Books in Ms𝒰: One Drafter or More?

The arguments that Joseph Smith authored the entire *Book of Mormon* have prompted a concern among LDS scholars to show that just one person could not have authored the *Book of Mormon*. In fact the BoM narrative itself asserts multiple authorship. For example, Mormon did not abridge the small plates of Nephi. He simply put them with his own abridgment of Lehi. These plates are said to have separate compositions by Nephi, Jacob, Enos, Jarom, Omni, Chemish, Abinadom, and Amaleki. In addition to the abridgment of Mormon, and Words of Mormon, the BoM, when it was published, also included the works ascribed to Moroni. Fortunately, multiple authorship can be consistent with some BoM-critic perspectives as well. This has led to content analysis, which unfortunately is fraught with more potential issues than Medusa has snakes.

Multiple Authorship as Evidence for BoM Authenticity

In 1978, three BYU scholars, Wayne A. Larsen, Alvin C. Rencher and Tim Layton, began by identifying the sections of the *Book of Mormon* that they believed to have been written by different authors.[456] They reasoned that these pre-Columbian Nephites would have had different writing styles. Showing that this is the case, even in an English translation of their works, would constitute evidence in favor of the BoM, and against the view that a single author had written it in the person of Joseph Smith.

The interpretation of differences between the texts attributed to these authors is complicated by the fact that they may be due to the differential subject matter treated by the texts, rather than multiple authors. The method they adopted holds that authors have distinct styles that they cannot mask, and that authors can be stylistically identified through their "wordprints," a term taken from CSI "fingerprints." To control for the effects of differential subject matter, they established a list of

---

[456]Wayne A. Larsen, Alvin C. Rencher and Tim Layton, "Who Wrote the *Book of Mormon*? An Analysis of Wordprints," in Noel B. Reynolds, ed., *Book of Mormon Authorship* (Salt Lake City: Bookcraft, 1982), 157-188. They identified twenty-one authors, including speeches of some, and even the Lord. See also Glade L. Burgon, *An Analysis of Style Variations in the* Book of Mormon (Provo UT: BYU MA thesis, 1958).

noncontextual words, such as *and*, *with*, *the*, etc., and analyzed the rate of usage of these in each sample text. One might think that if this is done for two texts by the same author, the rates would be the same. However, the rates of usage in two texts by the same author will never be identical. So how different can they be, and still be by the same author? Statistical procedures were used in an effort to determine the probability that just one author could produce each observed difference. If the probability is sufficiently low the conclusion is that most probably the texts were authored by different individuals.

Responding to challenges to the 1978 BYU study,[457] John Hilton, an adjunct professor in the Department of Statistics at BYU, decided to narrow the quest, by comparing just two presumptive authors, Nephi and Mormon. He developed a more refined approach, adapting the analysis of word-pattern ratios developed by Rev. A. Q. Morton in Scotland.[458] This technique uses an analysis of *patterns* of noncontextual words, rather than just occurrences of those words. One must not be overly impressed by the word "pattern." For example, one pattern is the article *a* as the first word of a sentence; another is *a* as the next to last word. A third is *a* followed by a space, a word, another space and *and* (as in "a Nephite and..."). Hilton adopted Morton's method, which used sixty-five such patterns.

His study analyzed the occurrences of these patterns in three 5000-word texts from Nephi and three from Alma. These texts were sampled from the longest "didactic" passages in each book. Selection from "didactic" (e.g. preachment) material was done to further reduce the effect that differing subject matter might have on the results. Without going into statistical detail, the conclusion reached was that it is statistically improbable that the same person authored the English texts of both Alma and Nephi.[459] A study by Utah State University professors Todd K. Moon, Peg Howland and Jacob H. Gunther extended Hilton's study by analyzing BoM texts from Nephi and Mormon. They found evidence consistent with

---

[457] In 1981 *Sunstone* published a challenge to the work of Larsen, Rencher and Layton, by D. James Croft, titled "*Book of Mormon* 'Wordprints' Reexamined," which was published with a rejoinder by Larsen and Rencher (Salt Lake City: Sunstone 6/2, March-April, 1981), 15-21 & 22-26. Vernal Holley published a critique in *Book of Mormon Authorship*, 2nd ed. e-text version (UT, self-published: 1989).

[458] A. Q. Morton, *Literary Detection: How to Prove Authorship and Fraud in Literature and Documents* (New York: Charles Scribner's Sons, 1978). For his later work used by Hilton, v. John L. Hilton, "On Verifying Wordprint Studies: *Book of Mormon* Authorship," Appendix 1, in *BYU Studies* 30, no. 3 (1990).

[459]Hilton, "On Verifying Wordprint Studies."

the Hilton study, and claimed that their results distinguished the underlying actual compositions of these personages.[460] Remember that for these researchers, Nephi was written by Nephi in the BoM, and Mormon was written by Mormon, as was Alma; all writing reformed Egyptian.

John C. Fortier criticized the wordprint method, having found the method deficient when attributing three anonymous works to Hobbes.[461]

Identifying 19th-Century BoM Authors: A Bridge too Far?

D. I. Holmes, Senior Lecturer in Statistics at Bristol Polytech in the UK, attempted to take stylistic research to the next level. He used stylometry to identify BoM authors. To this end, he included in his sampling three text blocks from Joseph Smith's personal writings, either in his own hand, or that of scribes who stated that they had taken the dictation from Smith. BoM samples include: one from 1 Nephi, one from 2 Nephi, one from 3 Nephi, one from Jacob, one from Lehi (in 2 Nephi), two from Moroni, five from Mormon (found in various books) and two from Alma. His work also has less bias *prima facie* than the work of the BYU scholars, in that he felt no inhibition deterring him from including samples from non-BoM LDS scriptures for comparison. Accordingly, he included three independent samples from the D&C, three from the BoM Isaiah (KJV) inclusions, and one from the *Book of Abraham*.

The study analyzed the occurrence of nouns in the passages (a richness of vocabulary approach), using methods established by others before him. The conclusion was that most of the BoM authors, two of his three D&C samples and his *Book of Abraham* sample clustered together, indicating common authorship. He did not find evidence for separate authorship of individual record engravers (or prophets) in the BoM, although 1 Nephi was somewhat of an outlier (as Hilton might have predicted). His three Isaiah samples, each from a different large Isaiah BoM inclusion, grouped together but apart from the others, indicating that the BoM authors may have imitated King James English, but could not

---

[460] Todd K. Moon, Peg Howland and Jacob H. Gunther, "Document author classification using Generalized Discriminant Analysis," Proc. Workshop on Text Mining, SIAM, 2006.

[461] John C. Fortier, "Hobbes and a 'Discourse on Laws': The Perils of Wordprint Analysis," in *The Review of Politics*, vol. 59, no. 04, fall 1997, 861-88.

replicate King James style.[462] Unfortunately, his samples were quite small: text blocks of approximately 1000 words, of similar subject matter.

G. Schaalje, John L. Hilton and John B. Archer took this work to task in a follow-up to Hilton's study.[463] Their work does not attack the mathematical validity of Holmes' approach, but rather claims that a richness of vocabulary method inherently lacks the comparative power to adequately differentiate authors.[464]

In another effort to identify 19th-century authors of the BoM, yet a different mode of analysis was adopted by researchers at the time at Stanford University, Matthew L. Jockers (Dept. of English), Daniela M. Witten (Dept. of Statistics) and Craig S. Criddle (Dept. of Civil and Environmental Engineering).[465] Their work examines the entire BoM text, with each chapter being a text for comparison with samples from the following authors: Oliver Cowdery, Parley P. Pratt, Sidney Rigdon, Solomon Spalding, Isaiah-Malachi, and inexplicably Henry Wadsworth Longfellow and Joel Barlow. The basic unit of analysis is words, which can be either contextual or noncontextual. They have a complex procedure to select the set of words to be included. The first hurdle to qualify is that a word must have occurred at least once in the works of each author listed above, and once in the entire BoM text. This yielded a set of 521 words. Across their 456 samples, those that did not have at least a mean relative frequency of 0.1% were eliminated, yielding a subset of 114 words. Finally, the following words were eliminated as being too religious: *god, ye, thy* and *behold*. The effect of this is that many words that are typical of BoM English or subject matter can be excluded simply because they do not occur in any one of the other author's material. Arguably it is just this type of material that one might focus on to consider authorship. Its elimination assures a greater similarity between BoM passages and at least

---

[462] D. I. Holmes, "A Stylometric Analysis of Mormon Scripture and Related Texts," in the *Journal of the Royal Statistical Society. Series A (Statistics in Society),* vol. 155, no. 1 (1992).

[463] G. Bruce Schaalje, John L. Hilton and John B. Archer, "Comparative Power of Three Author-Attribution Techniques for Differentiating Authors," *Journal of Book of Mormon Studies,* 6/1 (1997).

[464] In this critique, their list of noncontextual words is: *a, an, and, any, all, of, the, as, but, by, in, it, no, not, that, to, up, upon, with, without* (deleting *you* from Morton's list, and adding *up* without explanation).

[465] Matthew L. Jockers, Daniela M. Witten and Craig S. Criddle, "Reassessing authorship of the *Book of Mormon* using delta and nearest shrunken centroid classification," *Literary and Linguistic Computing* Advance Access (17 February 2009).

some of the comparison authors, enhancing the possibility of getting results that can be interpreted to be influence from them. Note too that they did not include the primary authorship candidate, Joseph Smith, in their study. These criteria open the door for an accusation of indirect methodological manipulation.[466]

They concluded that their NSC (Nearest Shrunken Centroid) results were consistent with the Spalding-Rigdon theory of authorship. G. Bruce Schaalje, Matthew Roper and Gregory L. Snow did a sophisticated analysis of this work, showing that an *open-set NSC* method produced dramatically different results compared to the *closed-set NSC* method of Jockers, et al. They found that less than 9% of texts were attributed by their methodology to Rigdon or Spalding, and these were randomly distributed in the BoM text, presumably refuting the closed-set results supporting the Spalding-Rigdon thesis.[467] They conclude, "The writing styles throughout the book do not credibly match Rigdon, Spalding or any of the other candidates, as claimed by Jockers et al. (2008)."[468]

One unsettling observation is obvious: statisticians have not been able to produce the same or even similar results across the board. In some cases, an important claim is largely asserted, without sufficient research to back it up. An example is the claim that an author cannot alter or disguise his wordprint (or any other patterns). This claim is partially at odds with the work of two researchers at the Department of Computer Science, Drexel University, Michael Brennan and Rachel Greenstadt, showing that persons can engage in obfuscation attacks and imitation attacks sufficiently to defeat at least some authorship recognition techniques.[469] Even Hilton acknowledges that "deliberately writing to an externally imposed pattern which restricts the normal noncontextual word choices of the writer or repetitively using normally contextual words in textually important ways

---

[466] Additional potential issues arise from not only using such small samples, but samples of radically different size.

[467] G. Bruce Schaalje, Matthew Roper and Gregory L. Snow, "Extended nearest shrunken centroid classification: A new method for open-set authorship attribution of texts of varying sizes," *Literary and Linguistic Computing*, vol. 26, no. 1, 2011.

[468] Schaalje, Roper & Snow, "Extended nearest shrunken centroid classification," 84.

[469] Michael Brennan and Rachel Greenstadt, "Practical attacks against authorship recognition techniques," Association for the Advancement of Artificial Intelligence, 2009.

can also change the wordprint patterns."[470] The use of KJ English might function as just such an externally imposed pattern.

In the style research in the next chapter, the term is used a bit loosely. I rather expect that Hemingway had a style of his own, as did Melville. In the BoM, the true style of the authors is not just masked by using an approximation to KJV English, but by other deliberate archaization. Just as we found that the BoM variant readings in the Isaiah inclusions were concentrated in the first quarter of each one, we note that Moroni lacks some typical archaizations. This extra effort was deemed to be no longer needed.

The primary validation for Hilton's adaptation of Morton's word pattern method was the use of control texts to test it. Works of eleven authors were used, and tests were done within and between authors. When the method was tweaked sufficiently to differentiate authors, without differentiating works by the same author, it was deemed ready to apply to BoM tests. Minimally, Hilton's conclusion that Nephi and Alma were not authored by the same person is sufficiently probable to be used as a hypothesis for further testing.

Wordprinting Egyptian?

For those hoping that the results of wordprinting would differentiate between presumed Nephite authors, the selection of words used by Morton and Hilton is problematic. Egyptian grammar, syntax and even some vocabulary are radically different from English. Egyptian lacked the word *and* altogether. "Middle Egyptian had no word for 'and.' Conjunction is normally expressed just by one noun following the other."[471] "Egyptian has no special word for 'and'."[472] Although Egyptian had a definite article, it was usually unexpressed. Originally, there was no indefinite article, although later *w'* (one) was occasionally used: "One [a] man once told me…"[473] The genitive is expressed, as in Hebrew, using the construct state: "wife the priest" means "the wife of the priest." No word for 'of' is used in this case. *Any* and *all* are also a problem: *nb* (*neb*) means *all, any* and *every*, depending on context.[474] These words are particularly a

---

[470] Hilton, "Verifying wordprint studies," 107, note 4.

[471] James P. Allen, *Middle Egyptian. An Introduction to the Language and Culture of the Hieroglyphs* (Cambridge: Cambridge University Press, 2000), 40.

[472] Alan Gardiner, *Egyptian Grammar, Being an Introduction to the Study of Hieroglyphs* (London: Oxford University Press, 1973), 68.

[473] Gardiner, *Egyptian Grammar*, 29, 194.

[474] Gardiner, *Egyptian Grammar*, 47.

problem for the wordprint method because each occurs in more than one word pattern, magnifying the distortion. The bottom line is that a wordprint analysis of an English translation of an Egyptian document cannot differentiate the authorship of underlying Egyptian texts. If it does show multiple authors, these must be English-language writers in the 1820s.

BoM Segmentation: A Facilitator for Division of Labor

The BoM narrative is highly segmented. It is composed of longer major segments, each with a distinct function, and shorter fast-forward segments, intended to jump to a significantly later date. These segments are ideally suited to collaboration by multiple authors.

Israelites in the New World. The first two segments (originally one) are major: 1 and 2 Nephi. They have perhaps the most important functions, which are to describe and explain the migration of the Lehi band to what will become the land of their inheritance in the New World (1 Nephi), and to use extensive OT material to provide Biblical support for this radical innovation in Israelite history (primarily 2 Nephi). This is done with the large Isaiah inclusions and extensive commentary interwoven with Isaiah and other OT paraphrases. Laman and Lemuel, depicted as somewhat irksome naysayers, serve as foils for Lehi's arguments against various objections. Nephi is the earliest work in BoM apologetics.

This is the Book of Mormon arguing in defense of the Book of Mormon.

Filling the Time Gap. The first fast-forward material consists of the books of Enos through Omni, collectively, which occupy only 7 pages, but a huge amount of time, from c. BCE 500 to c. BCE 130.

Material to Recover from the loss of the Book of Lehi. Words of Mormon has the essential function of explaining the two sets of plates of Nephi, thereby providing the material for the replacement of the lost *Book of Lehi*, and enabling a total redesign and reorientation of the BoM project. Since this sensitive text required only eight verses, the book was given a more normal appearance by including the second part of the relocated Mosiah 1:1 text.

Why Zarahemla and the Mulekites? The pivotal Book of Mosiah relocates the Nephites to continue the BoM narrative beyond the lost *Book of Lehi*.

Unable to replicate its geography with certainty, the best strategy for the replacement text was to totally avoid place names apart from Nephi. But the Old Testament simulation found from Mosiah on would require geographical context for the wars and missionary expeditions. The solution was for Mosiah to lead his people out of Lamanite territory, north, across the narrow neck of land (the Isthmus of Panama), to a territory not found in the purloined pages. On the other hand, it was not acceptable at this point for the Nephites to be led with their flocks and seed to start over as simple settlers in a new land. Their narrative now needed a major population, with established cities. Enter the Mulekites, a second group led to the New World by God, by Mulek, said to be a son of Zedekiah. They adopt Nephite speech and become themselves Nephites. This expanded Nephite population centered in Zarahemla, the Mulekite capital. This solves another problem. Christianity had always held that the lost tribes resulted from the diaspora, resulting from the Assyrian dispersal of the tribes in the north and the captivity of Judeans by Babylon, not from a flight of Jerusalemites prior to that catastrophe. Having performed these functions, *the Mulekites disappear as a people and never figure in the events of the BoM narrative.* The history can now be developed once again in a new land, with no danger of contradicting the geographical detail of the purloined pages, with a ready-made sizable population, large cities, and a migration presented as part of the traditional diaspora. It links to Nephi by quoting or paraphrasing Isaiah, and contains the BoM version of the Decalogue. The earlier references to Christianity are followed up by the establishment of the Christian Church in BCE America.

The Core: Geography, and the Theological Arguments. Alma is a major segment. It contains a fuller presentation of BoM Pauline theology, nearly all of the BoM geographical detail and many of the proper names. It builds extensively on the Lamanite-Nephite conflicts, and missionary activity to Christianize the Lamanites. This book alone occupies over 30% of the *Book of Mormon.* By comparison, First and Second Nephi together occupy only 20%. Its size resulted from joining the records of Alma the Younger and Helaman the Elder to form a single book.

Alma begins in the first year of the judges (1 YOJ), giving it its own chronology, allowing composition independent of earlier books.

Preparation for the Advent of Christ in the New World. The Book of Helaman (the Younger) prepares the reader for the coming of Christ, details the hardening of the hearts of many to justify the divine wrath that will result in the Crucifixion Cataclysm, and foretells the signs of the birth and death of Jesus.

The Crucifixion Cataclysm and Christ in America. The Third Book of Nephi is a central segment, detailing events in the New World leading up to the Crucifixion and the events of the Crucifixion Cataclysm (3 Nephi A). It covers the time of Jesus' ministry among the Nephites and the establishment of the Christian Church (3 Nephi B). Here we find some Church establishment material currently in use in LDS chapels today.

The Great American Apostasy. Although Fourth Nephi covers the two-century period of Christianity in all the land, and the apostasy, it is also another fast-forward segment. Being recorded by several people, in only four pages it covers 286 years.

The Annihilation of the Nephites. The BoM book titled the "Book of Mormon" is largely the history of the destruction of the Nephites at the hands of the Lamanites. Its other essential contribution is the account of Mormon engraving the BoM text onto the gold plates. It was originally written to conclude the *Book of Mormon*.

Postscript: Adding Church Establishment Material. The Book of Moroni is very short, and was added essentially to supplement the church establishment material in 3 Nephi, drawing from a revelation received by Oliver Cowdery months earlier. Its addition was essentially a late pragmatic decision. With this material, they would be ready to establish their new church immediately following the printing of their new bible.

Pre-Nephite America: Earlier Ruins and Fauna. Incongruously tucked in just before the Book of Moroni is the Book of Ether, which is the history of the pre-Nephite Jaredite civilization. Since its themes are largely the same as the story of the Nephites, its principal *raison d'être* is to cover the possibility that pre-Columbian remains might be discovered dating to a period prior to 600 BCE, and to account for the presence of various animals found by the Nephites in postdiluvian America. The placement of the discovery of the twenty-four gold plates just after the replacement for the purloined pages indicates that the decision to include a record of an earlier civilization was part of the planning for the BoM remake. Ether was originally to have been a separate record apart from the *Book of Mormon*, i.e. following its conclusion with Mormon's Book of Mormon.

The basic point here is that this segmentation could have enabled two or more authors to work independently each on his own segment without serious contradiction. That is to say, when arranged to form ms𝒰, any contradictions that might emerge could be readily handled in the editorial process. In addition to storyline segmentation, the BoM features a high degree of geographical segmentation, further enabling multiple independent authorship.

Note too that the BoM text also features chronological segmentation. The standard ALJ dating (After Leaving Jerusalem) is interrupted at the end of Mosiah by the Reign of thr Judges. This enables Alma to begin with one YOJ (Year of the Judges), without any need to specify what this might be in the ALJ dating sequence. However, the commencement of Third Nephi pegs YOS to ALJ dating:

Table 61. Chronological Segmentation

Date	Reference
Beginning of Reign of the Judges	
590 ALJ (After Leaving Jerusalem)	Mosiah 29:46
Years of the Judges	
1 ALJ	Alma 1:1
39 YOJ (End of Alma)	Alma 63:16
40 YOJ (Beginning of Helaman)	Helaman 1:1
91 YOJ (=600 ALJ)	3 Nephi 1:1
100 YOJ (=609 ALJ)	3 Nephi 2:4-6
Years Since the Sign (that Jesus has been born) YOS: **BIRTH OF JESUS** (Gregorian Calendar Begins)	
Reckoning in YOS begins	3 Nephi 2:8
9 YOS	3 Nephi 2:8
34 YOS, 4th day of 1st month **CRUCIFIXION**	3 Nephi 8:5
360 YOS ("since the coming of Christ")	Mormon 3:4
400 YOS (AD) (Moroni writes after death of Mormon	Mormon 8:6
420 YOS (a date recorded by Moroni)	Moroni 10:1

Segmentation is threefold: storyline, geography, and chronology. It was most certainly developed purposefully. It served to facilitate multiple authorship. This is the

Multiple Authorship Issue

⟨decorative flourish⟩

< Chapter 28 >

Distribution of Word Preferences: <u>Style</u> versus <u>Context</u>

So far we have identified two fundamental considerations for research into the drafting of the BoM narrative. First, the most important source material is ms$\mathcal{O}$ (supplemented by ms$\mathcal{P}$ when necessary). These documents are absolutely contemporary with the process under examination, and contain important clues. They totally trump comments made years later by persons active in developing, defending or attacking the official history. Above all, the fact that ms$\mathcal{O}$ displays relatively few substantive edits requires the conclusion that it was produced by Joseph Smith reading from drafts (ms$\mathcal{U}$) for Oliver Cowdery (mostly) to write ms$\mathcal{O}$. The analysis of the division of Nephi and transition from 1 Nephi to 2 Nephi, and the reassignment to the replacement text of the original Chapter One of Mosiah (into parts of Omni and Words of Mormon), have shown that the underlying ms$\mathcal{U}$ draft(s), at least, were so finished that they had already been divided into numbered chapters.

The second fundamental consideration is the segmental character of the BoM narrative. The layout is made up of records of different recorders, producing books that are in some cases virtually stand-alone works. This feature is ideal for a degree of division of labor, and the possibility of two or more initial drafts being produced at roughly the same time. Supportive features include geographical and chronological segmentation that corresponds to the storyline segmentation.

Virtually all approaches to analyzing BoM genesis (such as the orthodox LDS position; the Spalding-Rigdon argument; and both the Nephi priority and Mosiah priority theories) have one thing in common. They assume that the production of the BoM books was done sequentially, one book after another in the order found in the published *Book of Mormon*. This sequential composition may have been rarely questioned because this is the way the BoM has come down to us, and how most researchers (LDS scholars and most BoM critics alike) have always seen it ever since Junior Sunday School. In practice, it is treated, perhaps subconsciously, as being axiomatic. Furthermore, apart from Hilton's wordprint results, the possibility of multiple drafters has been only rarely considered.

The Problem Posed by Differential Subject Matter

The issue of single vs multiple authorship was first tackled by Larsen, Rencher and Layton in 1978 at BYU. They were fully aware of the possibility that the differential subject matter (context) of the texts for comparison could influence the occurrence or nonoccurrence of the words that they might track from book to book. They undertook to control for this variable by studying the distribution of what they considered to be noncontextual words. John Hilton further refined this approach by using noncontextual *word patterns*. He contended that he could identify an author's *wordprint*, which, much like a fingerprint, persists in spite of efforts to change it. Also using noncontextual words, he felt that he could control for differential subject-matter contexts to isolate the author's style. His rather sophisticated statistical method produced a landmark conclusion: "these four high rejection tests …independently measure a statistical confidence of 999 greater than 99.5, 99.9, 99.99 and 99.997 probability that these texts from Nephi were written by a different author than wrote Alma." In his footnote, he states that the combined probability "is vanishingly small that Nephi and Alma could have had the same author."[475] Even so, he would attribute them to the Nephi and Alma in the *Book of Mormon*, as real historical persons. But, in the light of the archaeological verdict, secular research would attribute this authorship to a pair of early nineteenth century New England authors.

This chapter will present a totally different approach to produce independent results for comparison with Hilton's conclusion.

Controlling for Subject Matter: Synonymous-Pair Analysis

I initially undertook to replicate the Metcalfe study described in Chapter 26. For this purpose, I used an 1830 edition of the *Book of Mormon* that had been prepared in electronic format using the current LDS chapter-verse divisions.[476]

Although the data, so far presented, are somewhat striking, Metcalfe's procedure is flawed, largely because the BoM books vary so much in length, and the data were not standardized for this variable. Alma

---

[475] John L. Hilton, "On Verifying Wordprint Studies: *Book of Mormon* Author-ship," in *BYU Studies Quarterly* (vol 30 no 3, 1 July 1993), 99 and footnote 21.

[476] "The 1830 *Book of Mormon* Text," accessed at https://carm.org/1830-book-of-mormon on 12/02/2016. In addition to the current chapter-verse divisions, this text also has the original 1830 chapter divisions.

has 85,073 words, Moroni only 6,142 and Jarom 733.[477] The problem seems obvious, but can be exampled in this manner. Assume that it is claimed that more people are in church on Sunday in New York City than in Bountiful, Utah. Immediately one would protest that this is only because NY has such a huge population. But now let us state the issue in terms of the number of worshipers per 10,000 residents. Put this way, Bountiful would almost certainly come out on top.

A simple way to standardize for length is to calculate incidence per 5,000 words. But there is another factor. The major premise of the argument is that these word pairs are functional equivalents. So when the author needs a word with the function of *wherefore/therefore* or *whoso/whosoever*, which of the two synonyms does he choose?

For the tabulation of these pairs, only synonyms can be included. As it turns out, *wherefore* has two meanings. It occurs twice with interrogative meaning, once in 1 Nephi and once in 2 Nephi. Since these do not correspond semantically to *therefore*, they need to be omitted from the count.

1. Synonymous Pair Analysis: Therefore/Wherefore

The underlying assumption is that when the author wanted to express the meaning of either *therefore* or *wherefore*, he would have to choose one over the other. Each occurrence of either *therefore* or *wherefore* is actually the result of a synonym-choice opportunity, where the author chose *therefore* over *wherefore*, or vice versa. The aggregate of all occurrences of *therefore* and of *wherefore* is the total number of these choice opportunities in any given book. When we divide the occurrence of *therefore* by this total, we have the percent of times that the writer chose *therefore*. This procedure automatically controls for book size. The issue is no longer the total number of occurrences, which could conceivably be influenced by the subject matter of the book. Since the choice is being made between synonyms, either one will work in various subject matter contexts. Although the words may not be absolutely noncontextual, the

---

[477] To determine the book word totals, an MS Word file was created for each book. Then words not part of the text itself were laboriously deleted, including page headings, such as the "The *Book of Mormon*," the word "chapter" and any number accompanying it, and even verse designations, such as 7:32. The longer KJV inclusions were also deleted, but not the paraphrases. MS Word then provided the word count.

choice made between synonyms is highly independent of context. On the other hand, the number of occurrences per words in a book is a small fraction. It is then multiplied by 5,000, to produce the number per 5,000 words. Figure 22 shows these data both as controlled on a base of 5,000 words,[478] and as a percent that each synonym is chosen.

In both Figure 22 and Figure 23, the graph on the left is in Nephi priority order and the graph on the right is in Mosiah priority. As can be seen below, there is some observable similarity between 1 Nephi and Moroni. Based on this alone, the latter appears to belong to the Nephi group. But overall, the data do not evidence a gradual shift[479] in stylistic preference from *wherefore* to *therefore* in either order.

Figure 22. Distribution of *Therefore* versus *Wherefore*

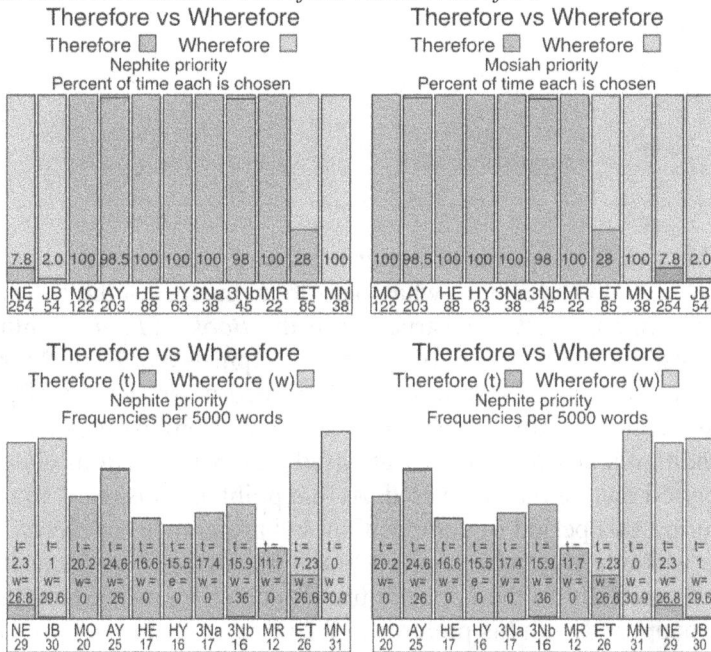

Therefore vs Wherefore
Therefore ▨   Wherefore ▨
Nephite priority
Percent of time each is chosen

7.8	2.0	100	98.5	100	100	100	98	100	28	100

NE	JB	MO	AY	HE	HY	3Na	3Nb	MR	ET	MN
254	54	122	203	88	63	38	45	22	85	38

Therefore vs Wherefore
Therefore ▨   Wherefore ▨
Mosiah priority
Percent of time each is chosen

100	98.5	100	100	100	98	100	28	100	7.8	2.0

MO	AY	HE	HY	3Na	3Nb	MR	ET	MN	NE	JB
122	203	88	63	38	45	22	85	38	254	54

Therefore vs Wherefore
Therefore (t)▨   Wherefore (w)▨
Nephite priority
Frequencies per 5000 words

t=	t=	t=	t=	t=	t=	t=	t=	t=	t=	t=
2.3	1	20.2	24.6	16.6	15.5	17.4	15.9	11.7	7.23	0
w=	w=	w=	w=	w=	e=	w=	w=	w=	w=	w=
26.8	29.6	0	.26	0	0	0	.36	0	26.6	30.9

NE	JB	MO	AY	HE	HY	3Na	3Nb	MR	ET	MN
29	30	20	25	17	16	17	16	12	26	31

Therefore vs Wherefore
Therefore (t)▨   Wherefore (w)▨
Nephite priority
Frequencies per 5000 words

t=	t=	t=	t=	t=	t=	t=	t=	t=	t=	t=
20.2	24.6	16.6	15.5	17.4	15.9	11.7	7.23	0	2.3	1
w=	w=	w=	e=	w=	w=	w=	w=	w=	w=	w=
0	.26	0	0	0	.36	0	26.6	30.9	26.8	29.6

MO	AY	HE	HY	3Na	3Nb	MR	ET	MN	NE	JB
20	25	17	16	17	16	12	26	31	29	30

Note too that the two Nephi books are combined since they were originally a single book. Instead of 1 Nephi and 2 Nephi, we have just Nephi.

---

[478] To standardize on a base of 5,000 words, the occurrence total is first divided by the number of words in the book, and then multiplied by 5,000.

[479] Metcalfe refers to this shift as "Smith's gradual transition from "therefore" to "wherefore." Metcalfe, "The Priority of Mosiah," 412.

2. Synonymous Pair Analysis: whoso/whosoever

In Figure 23 we see that Metcalfe's *whoso* and *whosoever* data also show no indication of a <u>gradual shift</u> in style. Note that this graph was constructed after correcting a major data error. In 3 Nephi, Metcalfe lists fifteen occurrences of *whosoever*, but the real number is only five. My data also differ slightly due to the inclusion of *whomsoever* in the tallies.

Figure 23. Distribution of *Whoso* versus *Whosoever*

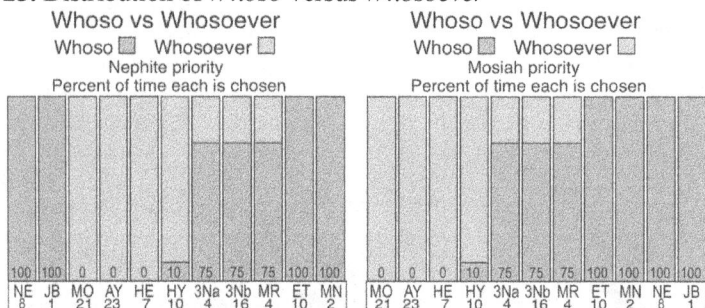

The Metcalf thesis posits that after it became necessary to replace the *Book of Lehi*, Smith had no idea what to do about the loss of the 116 pages. "The misplacement, theft or destruction of the *Book of Lehi*, eventually, [led] the despondent prophet to dictate 1 Nephi—Words of Mormon last..."[480] Not wanting to lose time, he continued where he left off, with Mosiah, and continued all the way to the end of Moroni, by which time he had the traditional answer worked out based on a parallel set of plates for the time period that *Lehi* had covered. At that point, he was ready to tackle Nephi. During this period of composition, his preference for *therefore* or *wherefore* was one way when Joseph Smith began work on Mosiah, but had shifted gradually to the opposite preference as his work progressed. The same happened with his preference for *whosoever* and *whoso*. Using gross numbers, his data fit his thesis a bit better. But when standardized for book size, we see that there is no gradual shift of style. The books Mosiah through Mormon show a virtually total preference for *therefore*, while the books Nephi through Jacob, plus Ether and Moroni, show a strong preference for *wherefore*. Overall, the data do not provide support for the Metcalfe thesis

---

[480] Metcalfe, "The Priority of Mosiah," 433.

This said, Metcalfe's study had a tremendous impact in *Book of Mormon* Studies, having been interpreted to be hard-data support for the Mosiah priority thesis. But when the data are standardized for book length, which is fundamental in such data analysis, the importance of both of these studies is reversed. Nephi and Alma are so different that these studies now must be seen to support the Hilton result, that Nephi and Alma were written by two different authors.

Synonymous Pair Analysis: Proposal for Insomuch/Inasmuch

Christopher C. Smith has studied this pair.[481] Although these two words can be synonymous, generally they are not. *Insomuch* stands between the main clause and an adverbial *that* clause, to indicate that the action or state in the main clause has obtained *to such an extent that* the result in the *that* clause has been produced. An example is "he did lust after it, insomuch [to such an extent] that he thrust us out, and sent his servants to slay us. [result]" (1 Nephi 3:25) Another example is "it began to be exceeding difficult, yea, insomuch [to such an extent], that we could obtain no food [result]." (1 Nephi 16:21)

By contrast, *inasmuch* is almost always *inasmuch as*. It has two quite different meanings: "because of the fact that" and "to the extent that, insofar as."[482] In the BoM, it is often used with this first meaning. It stands at the beginning of a statement, followed by the condition clause and then the consequence should the condition obtain. When used with a future verb, it resembles a conditional phrase. The action or state of the second clause might occur if the action or state of the first clause occurs sufficiently. A statement that examples this usage is: "inasmuch as [to the extent that, if] ye shall keep my commandments, ye shall prosper in the land." (Alma 9:13) When used with a past verb, it has a cause-and-consequence meaning: "inasmuch as [because of the fact that] the Lamanites have not kept the commandments of God, they have been cut off from the presence of the Lord." (Alma 9:14)

In 1 Nephi, there are five occurrences of *inasmuch as*. All have the consequence clause in the future, as a *possible* result. There are twenty-one occurrences of *insomuch*. In eighteen of these, insomuch is followed by an adverbial *that* clause in the past tense, a result of a past action in the main clause. In one case, it is followed by *as if* instead of *that*, but still

---

[481] Christopher C. Smith (post on 2012/11/15), "*Book of Mormon* Vocabulary and the Priority of Mosiah," retrieved on 08/18/2019 from *Worlds Without End: A Mormon Studies Roundtable* (worldswithend.org).

[482] The American Heritage Dictionary of the English Language (2011).

with a past verb. In one case, it is followed by a present verb, and in another by a future verb, but neither has any hint of conditionality. If ever one were to swap *insomuch* into a sentence for *inasmuch*, or vice versa, the syntax of the sentences would have to be changed, and the meaning would undergo a substantial change. These two words are not synonyms in the usage found in Nephi.

Even so, this study reveals one of a number of instances where Mosiah plays the maverick. 1 Nephi has 21 occurrences of *insomuch* and 5 of *inasmuch*, while AlmaY has 14 and 10 respectively, and HelamanY 46 to 2. In sharp contrast, *Mosiah has no occurrence of either*. For the distribution of insomuch, as a single variable study, see Figure 31.

A synonymous pair study also needs to be rejected due to an extreme paucity of cases of one member of the pair, as we see in the study of *on account of/because of*. This pair is interesting because there are ten cases of *on account of*, all in Alma. But, there are 557 occurrences of *because of*, including 148 in Alma. Note that AY and HE are combined into AL since HE has only one case. Even so, it is noteworthy that only Alma uses *on account of*.

Additional Synonymous Pairs Analyses

3. Synonymous Pair Analysis: behold (verb) versus see

We saw in Chapter 26 (Table 60) that *wherefore* was rarely used in the 1820s in New England, but somewhat more in the KJV (Genesis, Isaiah, Jeremiah, Ezekiel and especially Matthew). *Wherefore* was inserted consciously to create a distinct BoM style, not because it was ever part of Smith's personal style. As such, it was just one word for this purpose. Others include *behold*; *yea*; *and* (excessively); *thereof*; *and it came to pass*; and others.

Behold is one of the words used in the BoM to archaize its style. It occurs frequently as an interjection (e.g., Behold, the king is here! See Figure 31, *supra*.), but also verbally as a synonym for *see* ("they beheld those that had been delivered" (Mosiah 25:8. See Figure 24, *supra*.). This word's differential frequency can be one characteristic of differential style, from book to book.

Note that every time either *behold* (or its past tense, *beheld*) or *see* (or its temporal variations, *saw* or *have/had seen*) occurs, the author could just as well have chosen its synonym. The occurrence of either is a synonym-choice opportunity. Since they have the same denotation, the subject matter of the book has little or no influence. The choice, in this case, is influenced primarily by the extent that the author is comfortable using *behold* to archaize his text. Nephi is especially given to using *behold* verbally.

Figure 24. *behold/see, will/shall, unto/to & nevertheless/yet.*

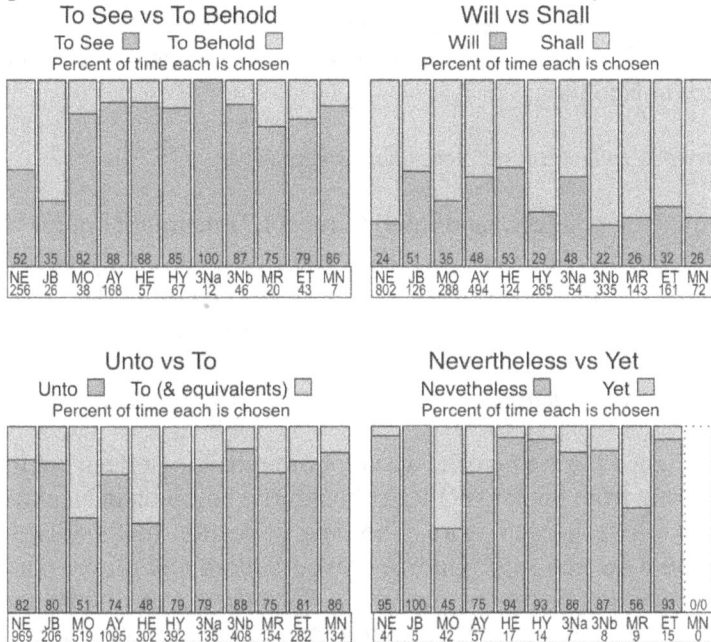

To See vs To Behold

To See ▨   To Behold ▨
Percent of time each is chosen

	NE	JB	MO	AY	HE	HY	3Na	3Nb	MR	ET	MN
%	52	35	82	88	68	85	100	87	75	79	86
	256	26	38	168	57	67	12	46	20	43	7

Will vs Shall

Will ▨   Shall ▨
Percent of time each is chosen

	NE	JB	MO	AY	HE	HY	3Na	3Nb	MR	ET	MN
%	24	51	35	48	53	29	48	22	26	32	26
	802	126	288	494	124	265	54	335	143	161	72

Unto vs To

Unto ▨   To (& equivalents) ▨
Percent of time each is chosen

	NE	JB	MO	AY	HE	HY	3Na	3Nb	MR	ET	MN
%	82	80	51	74	48	79	79	88	75	81	86
	969	206	519	1095	302	392	135	408	154	282	134

Nevertheless vs Yet

Nevetheless ▨   Yet ▨
Percent of time each is chosen

	NE	JB	MO	AY	HE	HY	3Na	3Nb	MR	ET	MN
%	95	100	45	75	94	93	86	87	56	93	0/0
	41	5	42	57	17	14	7	8	9	15	0

4. Synonymous Pair Analysis: will versus shall.

Shall and *will* have subtly different connotations, especially with respect to prescriptive grammar. These distinctions appear in the style of some writers more than in others. I have found it difficult to discover consistent differences in usage in the BoM text. This fluid situation allows room for considerable exercise of stylistic differences. Applying the rules of the so-called King's English may well have been beyond the BoM authors. Indeed, because *will* has become the dominant member of the pair, the choice of *shall* may simply have been perceived as a way to raise one's style to a more appropriate level for a sacred book. Although all books show this tendency, Nephi is especially apt to opt for *shall*.

5. Synonymous Pair Analysis: unto versus to (or an indirect object)

The marked tendency for the BoM to use *unto* rather than *to* is another example of archaization. It is important to note here that *to* is often not used when it is possible to use an indirect object. Instead of "He gave the book to me," one might choose "He gave me the book." Since our focus is the extent that *unto* has been used to archaize the text, the occurrence of *to* and of constructions using the indirect object are lumped together. The data therefore reflect the choice of *unto* rather than either *to* or an indirect object. Archaizing with the use of *unto* is clearly seen in all books, but especially in Nephi.

6. Synonymous Pair Analysis: nevertheless versus yet

Instead of "Nevertheless, he refused to repent," one might opt for "Yet, he refused to repent." For example, "they did not wear costly apparel, yet [nevertheless] they were neat and comely." (Alma1:27) The choice for *nevertheless* over *yet* is especially characteristic of Nephi.

7. Synonymous Pair Analysis: thereof versus (their, its, of it, of them)

Thereof (Figure 24) is a favorite word for its archaizing effect, but its usage varies sharply from book to book. Although it is common in Nephi, several other books love it even more. The data collection methodology needs explanation. One can say, "God destroyed Sodom and all the inhabitants thereof." But more commonly one says, "God destroyed Sodom and all its inhabitants." Thereof is useful, since it can replace *its, his, her, their, of him, of her, of them* or *of it*. A BoM case is: "great was the soreness thereof" [for: great was its soreness]. (1 Nephi 18:15) These alternatives were tallied and lumped together as "alternatives to *thereof*." The result shows the degree of preference for *thereof* over whatever alternative might have worked equally well in the sentence.

8. Synonymous Pair Analysis: pray unto versus cry unto

Cry unto (the Lord, the gods, etc.) is a common KJV expression, worked into the BoM narrative most probably solely for that reason. It seems to be stronger or more intense than *pray unto*, but in the BoM this distinction is not systematically respected. We often find it where there is no nuance distinction ruling out *pray unto*. As for data collection, throughout these studies, when the datum is a verb, it is necessary to collect all persons and tenses, such as to *cry, cries, crieth, criest, crying* and they *cry*. Not all of these yielded results. But the results for those that do occur were added together to produce the tally for *cry unto*. We again note the contrast between the results in Nephi and Alma.

Figure 25. *thereof/alternatives, pray unto/cry unto, and it came to pass*/elaborations of same & *must/must needs*.

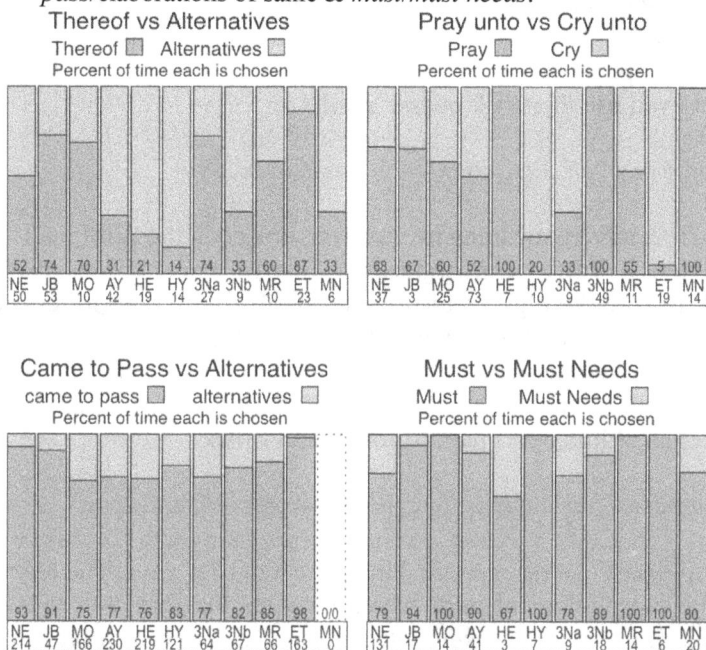

Thereof vs Alternatives	Pray unto vs Cry unto
Thereof ▨ Alternatives ▢	Pray ▨ Cry ▢
Percent of time each is chosen	Percent of time each is chosen

Thereof vs Alternatives:

NE	JB	MO	AY	HE	HY	3Na	3Nb	MR	ET	MN
52	74	70	31	21	14	74	33	60	87	33
50	53	10	42	19	14	27	9	10	23	6

Pray unto vs Cry unto:

NE	JB	MO	AY	HE	HY	3Na	3Nb	MR	ET	MN
63	67	60	52	100	20	33	100	55	5	100
37	3	25	73	7	10	9	49	11	19	14

Came to Pass vs Alternatives	Must vs Must Needs
came to pass ▨ alternatives ▢	Must ▨ Must Needs ▢
Percent of time each is chosen	Percent of time each is chosen

Came to Pass vs Alternatives:

NE	JB	MO	AY	HE	HY	3Na	3Nb	MR	ET	MN
93	91	75	77	76	83	77	82	85	98	0/0
214	47	166	230	219	121	64	67	66	163	0

Must vs Must Needs:

NE	JB	MO	AY	HE	HY	3Na	3Nb	MR	ET	MN
79	94	100	90	67	100	78	89	100	100	80
131	17	14	41	3	7	9	18	14	6	20

9. Synonymous Pair Analysis: And it came to pass versus modified versions

The most famous of the archaizing phrases in BoM style is "And it came to pass…" It sometimes repeats every few verses. This and the repetitive theology probably prompted Mark Twain to declare that the *Book of Mormon* is chloroform in print. Some BoM drafters also found it to be sufficiently tiresome that they sought to vary the wording at least a bit. The modifications found in the various BoM books include: For it came to pass; Wherefore it came to pass; Behold, it came to pass; For behold, it came to pass; And behold, it came to pass; Behold, now it came to pass; And behold now it came to pass; But behold, it came to pass; Now behold it came to pass; Now it came to pass; And now it came to pass; And thus it came to pass; But it came to pass; And it also came to pass; And again: It came to pass; Therefore it came to pass; and finally, Yea, and it came to pass. Even books with considerable usage of these modifications continued to allow the stock phrase, unchanged, to reign supreme. Data collection was a bit tedious. Individual searches had to be done on each version, including some not shown that differ only by punctuation, unimportant to us but essential for the search engine. All alternatives to the stock phrase were added together to learn the percentage of time the writer used the stock phrase and the percentage of time shear tedium drove him to resort to some modification. In the end, only Ether showed a greater tendency to opt for the stock phrase than Nephi. Moroni, the add-on book, does not even use the stock phrase at all.

10. Synonymous Pair Analysis: must versus must needs

Needs, as an adverb meaning *necessarily,* is used in the BoM with "must", as in 1 Nephi 19:21: "it must needs be that we know concerning them." Must is already the highest fortissimo possible regarding necessity. One either must do something or not. One does not think of it in terms of degrees. In this sense, *must needs* is pleonastic, and can be either added in, or not, at will. Interestingly, Nephi is guilty of this form of archaism less than Mosiah, Alma, Helaman, Mormon and Ether.

11. Synonymous Pair Analysis: morphological past versus *did* past

The simple past can be expressed in English in two ways. The oldest is by using the morphological past, which changes the form (*morph-*) of the verb: *speak, spoke* and *spoken, take, took* and *taken,* or *eat, ate* and *eaten.* In some cases there are only two forms: *think, thought* and *thought.* In other cases there is only one: *hit, hit* and *hit.* Probably emerging from some sort of English pigeon when many peoples of the Gaelic-Brythonic isles were struggling to cope with the complexity of the invaders' Anglo-Saxon verbal system, a simple past form came to the rescue with only *did* plus the infinitive: "I did go," instead of "I went." *Did* is invariable, and so one could speak properly without learning all of those morphological details. So, in the BoM, one finds both, sentences with the morphological past, that could have been constructed with the *did*+infinitive past, and vice versa. As seen in Figure 26, Nephi takes refuge in the *did*+infinitive version more than some, but less than Mosiah and Alma.

12. Synonymous Pair Analysis: yea versus yea, even

Even is added to *yea* for some stress (again, cf. *whosoever* and *must needs*). Nephi uses this less than Alma the Younger and Helaman.

13. Synonymous Pair Analysis: like versus like unto

This pair exhibits a significant centile difference between Nephi and both Mosiah and Alma, which are also separated from each other by a noteworthy difference.

14. Synonymous Pair Analysis : save versus except

The use of *save* with the meaning of *except* was rather rare in Smith's day (v. Table 60), but less so in the KJV Bible. It may have been used excessively in Nephi once again as an effort to give the text a more archaic or Biblical appearance.

The total number of cases in the BoM, and the number in each book, are sufficient to yield a meaningful study. The difference between Nephi and Alma supports Hilton's conclusion, that these two books cannot have been authored by the same person. Note too the difference between Mosiah and Alma.

Figure 26. morphological past/*did* past, *yea*/*yea, even,*
like/like unto & save/except, on account of/because of

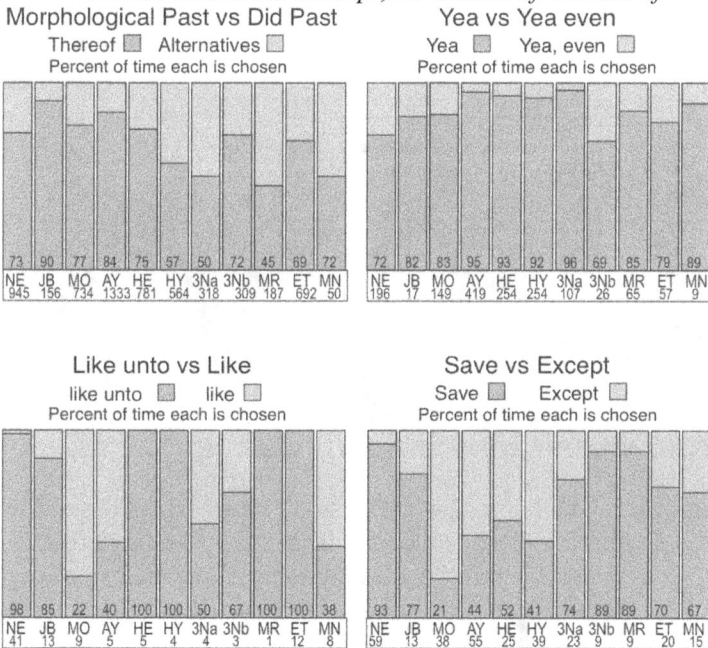

Morphological Past vs Did Past

Thereof ■ Alternatives □
Percent of time each is chosen

73	90	77	84	75	57	50	72	45	69	72
NE	JB	MO	AY	HE	HY	3Na	3Nb	MR	ET	MN
945	156	734	1333	781	564	318	309	187	692	50

Yea vs Yea even

Yea ■   Yea, even □
Percent of time each is chosen

72	82	83	95	93	92	96	69	85	79	89
NE	JB	MO	AY	HE	HY	3Na	3Nb	MR	ET	MN
196	17	149	419	254	254	107	26	65	57	9

Like unto vs Like

like unto ■   like □
Percent of time each is chosen

98	85	22	40	100	100	50	67	100	100	38
NE	JB	MO	AY	HE	HY	3Na	3Nb	MR	ET	MN
41	13	9	5	5	4	4	3	1	12	8

Save vs Except

Save ■   Except □
Percent of time each is chosen

93	77	21	44	52	41	74	89	89	70	67
NE	JB	MO	AY	HE	HY	3Na	3Nb	MR	ET	MN
59	13	38	55	25	39	23	9	9	20	15

In addition to controlling for differential book size, a major advantage of the percentage analysis of synonymous pairs is that one can compare results across books. If one synonym is A, then the percentage A in Nephi minus the percentage A in Mormon equals the difference in the preference for A between the two books, measured in centiles. The differences with respect to variable A for each pairing of books can be compared with the differences for each pairing of books for any other variable. First, we need to get all possible pairings of books.

Centile Analysis: Getting a Composite View

This is done using a pairing table, with all eleven books under study listed vertically (the left column), and all eleven listed horizontally (the top row). Thus every row represents a book, as does every column. Note that in Table 62, each cell on the diagonal is the intersect of each book with itself. We are not comparing a book with itself, so all cells on the diagonal are removed. Furthermore, all cells above the diagonal are duplicates of the cells below, but in reverse order, such as AB instead of BA. We are also not interested in this order, and all cells above the diagonal are superfluous and thrown out. The remaining cells, all those situated below the diagonal, represent all possible pairings of the eleven books included in our synonymous pair analysis.

Table 62. The Pairing Table for the Eleven Books in the Study

	A	B	C	D	E	F	G	H	I	J	K
A	AA	BA	CA	DA	EA	FA	GA	HA	IA	JA	KA
B	AB	BB	CB	DB	EB	FB	GB	HB	IB	JB	KB
C	AC	BC	CC	DC	EC	FC	GC	HC	IC	JC	KC
D	AD	BD	CD	DD	ED	FD	GD	HD	ID	JD	KD
E	AE	BE	CE	DE	EE	FE	GE	HE	IE	JE	KE
F	AF	BF	CF	DF	EF	FF	GF	HF	IF	JF	KF
G	AG	BG	CG	DG	EG	FG	GG	HG	IG	JG	KG
H	AH	BH	CH	DH	EH	FH	GH	HH	IH	JH	KH
I	AI	BI	CI	DI	EI	FI	GI	HI	II	JI	KI
J	AJ	BJ	CJ	DJ	EJ	FJ	GJ	HJ	IJ	JJ	KJ
K	AK	BK	CK	DK	EK	FK	GK	HK	IK	JK	KK
The total number of cells below the diagonal = (11-1)(11)/2 = 55.										

So if column A is Nephi and row D is AlmaY, then AD is the cell to record data when comparing these two books. The books will be indicated, and the difference between them in centiles for each of fourteen studies.

Table 63. Percentage Differences between Nephi & AlmaY in 14 Studies
(The superscripts correspond to the 14 numbered studies above.)

	AlmaY (row D above)				
Nephi	90.65^1	24.18^4	21.00^7	11.00^{10}	57.56^{13}
(column	100.00^2	8.00^5	15.52^8	10.28^{11}	49.58^{14}
A above)	35.66^3	19.68^6	16.00^9	23.30^{12}	

This centile difference is found by subtracting the percentage found in one book from the percentage in another book, for the same variable. So the percent *therefore* in Nephi is 7.87% while it is 98.52% in AlmaY. The difference, in centiles, is 90.65 centiles. Conversely, the percent *wherefore* in Nephi is 92.13% while it is 1.48% in AlmaY. Again, the difference is 90.65 centiles. Now we enlarge the AD cell, in order to write in it 90.65^1, where the superscript 1 indicates the first study, *therefore/wherefore*, and 90.65 is the centile difference for the two books represented by that cell, Nephi and AlmaY. Below this entry, but in the same cell, we can make an entry for *whoso/whosoever*. In Nephi, *whoso* is 100%, while Alma it is 0%. The difference is 100.00 centiles (100-0=100), as seen above. So the entry is 100.00^2, meaning for the second study, *whoso/whosoever*, the centile difference is 100.00. This is done for all fourteen studies and the data are entered in the cell corresponding to the intersect of Nephi and AlmaY. This example is our friend, the AD cell, but it now is the Nephi/AlmaY cell.

This is just one of 55 cells to be similarly recorded. As in this case, the studies are numbered in the order that they have been treated above. The centile differences can be validly compared across studies. These results show that Nephi and AlmaY are extremely different in style. Only one study produced a score under 10.01. Four are between 10.01 and 20.00, while eight are above 20.01. The centile-difference scores of two studies are above 90.01. These are the results we would expect if Nephi and AlmaY were authored by two individuals working independently.

So now, with the percentile differences between books calculated as above for all fourteen studies and all book pairs, we can enter them into yet another pairing table. For each of the 55 cells, we count all differences under 10.01 and enter the number into the corresponding cell. The result is seen in the following table.

Table 64. The Number of Studies Showing High Similarity between Books
(number of the 14 studies where the book pair centile difference was under 10.1)

Book	Nephi	Jacob	Mosiah	AlmaY	HelE	HelY	3Na	3Nb	Mormon	Ether	Mrn
Nephi											
Jacob	6										
Mosiah	2	4									
AlmaY	1	4	6								
HelE	3	2	7	9							
HelY	5	5	7	7	8						
3Na	3	4	3	6	5	6					
3Nb	6	3	4	5	5	6	5				
Mormon	6	3	7	4	4	7	5	5			
Ether	9	7	5	2	4	6	3	5	6		
Moroni	6	4	4	4	4	4	4	6	2	7	

Note that the cell in the top row and furthest to the left, i.e. the Nephi/Jacob cell contains the number 6, corresponding to two differences under 5.01 and four from 5.01 to 10.01. The remaining 55 cells have been done in the same way. We find in this table that the Nephi/AlmaY pair and Nephi/Mosiah pair show the fewest studies exhibiting minimal stylistic separation by the measure of this composite synonymous-pair result. These results show substantial systematic stylistic dissimilarity between Nephi and Alma. All in all, these studies, taken together, provide strong support for the conclusion of John Hilton's wordprint study: that Nephi and Alma were not drafted by the same person.

We also find that there is a region in the table with substantial systematic similarity, made up of where rows AlmaY, HelamanE and HelamanY intersect with columns Mosiah, AlmaY, HelamanE and HelamanY. A score of 6 also show strong stylistic similarity between Nephi and Moroni, although as we shall see, Moroni is a special case. The equally strong degree of similarity seen between Nephi and 3 NephiB will become important when we get to a similar analysis of the distribution of grammatical structures below.

When examining individual graphs, one will inevitably note that there are other books, not just Alma, that show even greater differences from Nephi, with respect to some particular study. The advantage of the composite procedure is that we can see if any of these other books exhibit a systematic pattern similar to what we find when comparing Nephi and Alma. The answer is that we do not. The only books that exhibit comparable *systematic* patterns are Nephi/Alma and Nephi/Mosiah.

The Distribution of Strategies and Habits of English Usage

So far we have results from two independent approaches, each based on its own rational for controlling for differential subject-matter context: wordprint distribution analysis done by Hilton, and synonymous pair distribution analysis presented in the foregoing section. Research has traditionally been based on words, those that one tracks and tallies from book to book, and those that make up the problematic contexts. This leads one to wonder what would happen if we used a methodology that does not even use words at all.

Because the *Book of Mormon* was written in English, the features of this language should give us some avenue to investigate Hilton's central issue: one author or more. The formation of English sentences can be highly complex. The simple sentence (Dick likes Jane), even amplified by a second clause with a coordinating conjunction (Dick likes Jane and she tolerates him), can be fleshed out with adjectives and adverbs. Additionally, meaning is added by the use of subordinating conjunctions. One website lists over 35. Although many occur in the *Book of Mormon*, by far the most common is *that*. In fact, if you open up 1 Nephi in MS Word and search on *that*, each match will be highlighted, and the page will light up like a Christmas tree. They number over 7,000 in the BoM. If this light show is not enough, search on *and*. Even though ancient Egyptian did not even have a word for *and*, the BoM is seriously addicted to this coordinating conjunction.

That is not only polysemous but multifunctional. It can be a simple pronoun (That is good), a demonstrative adjective (That man is my uncle), or a conjunctive relative pronoun (The man that you see is my uncle). It can introduce an adverbial subordinate clause, as in "The general sent a division to the river bank that the enemy might not cross." It indicates the objective or purpose of the action in the main clause, but it can also indicate degree or even consequence of an action. At times it is used with another word, such as *insomuch that*. Furthermore, it can introduce a noun clause, which is especially common as the direct object of a verb: "I know that it is true." The same clause can also function as the subject: "That it is true has not been questioned." Finally, it can serve as a type of predicate complement, as in "Should it be that you repent, then…"

In addition to clauses, English makes use of an arsenal of phrases. A direct object *that* clause can be replaced by a pronoun plus an infinitive phrase: "I know that it is a lie," or "I know it to be a lie." It can replace a *that* clause of objective, as in "He went to town to buy a pony," rather than "that he might buy a pony." BoM English tends to prefer the option with *that*. Perhaps the authors thought it sounded more formal.

A gerund (verbal noun) can replace an infinitive phrase, as in "To be or not to be" as opposed to "Being or not being, that is the question." (OK, I like Shakespeare's version better too.) The *–ing* ending has been very productive in English. In addition to what might be its primary function, to form the continuous tense ("John is riding his horse."), it can be a gerund phrase: "Bareback riding that horse is dangerous." It can also be a participial phrase of accompanying circumstance: "Yankee Doodle came to town, riding on a pony." In some books of the BoM it is used to introduce a main clause, at the head of a sentence: "Knowing your love for her, I did not repeat the rumor."

None of this is intended to teach English to my readers, who probably know the language better than I. This revue is intended to highlight the extent of English complexity, and the fact that it offers considerable choice in how to frame a sentence. This being the case we are led to wonder to what extent speakers develop individualized grammatical strategies and habits in both speaking and writing, and to what extent these preferences might be found in various BoM books. If so, is this lens capable of sufficient resolution to enable us to discriminate one author from another? Or is it too crude, leaving us peering through a glass darkly? The strategy of this chapter is to marshal English language features that can be clearly identified and therefore tallied by a computerized full-text search, to produce data sets for each book so we can inspect the resulting distributions for patterns and/or anomalies.

The Distribution of Participle, Infinitive and Gerund Phrases

In English, some of the basic phrases are participial phrases, infinitive phrases and gerund phrases. Without these, and subordinate clauses introduced by *that*, it is difficult to compose anything but the simplest text. The phrases can be used as an alternative to *that* clauses. An example of a participle phrase is, "Knowing him so well, I did not believe a word he said." An infinitive phrase can replace a direct object *that* clause, such as, "I know him to be just" instead of "I know that he is just." When such phrases occur, potentially a *that* clause could have been used. An example of a gerund phrase is, "Giving alms to the poor is commendable," instead of "It is commendable to give alms to the poor." Since these are among the most basic building blocks of the English language, they are amply represented in all of the books. The substantial magnitude of the data sets results in data stability.

Computer searches were performed to acquire virtually all of these phrases in the BoM text. A search on the preposition *to* not only turned up infinitive phrases, but resulted in many irrelevant "hits" that had to be waded through and weeded out, such as *together*, *today*, *unto*, and simply *to* used as a preposition. *To* is not part of the infinitive, and an infinitive with *to* is already an infinitive phrase, although nearly all included here have complements, such as "to give him compensation." An infinitive phrase in combination with a pronoun, can replace a direct-object *that* clause such as in "I know him to be reliable." It can also be a subject, such as in "To drive at night requires good night vision." It can replace an adverbial *that* clause of objective, such as in "the general sent a division to the river bank to prevent the enemy from crossing."

Both gerund and participle phrases were rounded up by searching on *-ing*. Once again it was necessary to wade through irrelevant hits, such as *king*, *sing* and *thing*. Every effort was made to be comprehensive. To be included, both had to have a complement. "Riding on a pony" can be an adverbial participle phrase with "on a pony" modifying "riding." Similarly, *blessing* would not be counted in the sentence "He gave her a blessing." But it would be counted when it has a complement, as in the sentence "Blessing the sick, he spoke these words."

As a gerund phrase, it would be counted in the sentence "Blessing the sick was typical of his ministry." Since it is the subject, it is *ipso facto* a verbal noun. Since it has a direct object, it is a phrase. However, gerunds that have become fully fledged nouns and were used as such were not included, such as *blessing*, or *killing*, as in "Five killings were reported." Nor were participles included when they were used to form the continuous tense, such as in "At that time, the king will be eating dinner." Past participial phrases were not included, as in "The books were provided with out cost." Exactly the same criteria were used in all books.

Once again we observe important differences between Nephi and Alma. Note Figure 27: (infinitive phrases as a verbal complement, infinitive phrases as potential that clauses, participial phrases and gerund phrases). These four phrase distributions are striking in that total frequencies range from 563 to 1,893, these being the total in the graphs, but also to the best of my ability the whole BoM text. In all four, the gap between Nephi and Alma is substantial. Alma is larger than Nephi by factors ranging 1.12, 1.7, 2.0 and 2.28. Of particular note is the fact that Helaman the Elder is quite a bit larger than any other book in the two infinitive distributions. What makes these centile differences important is the high frequencies making up these distributions. Because a review by inspection of all of these graphs is enough to make one's head swim, it helps to use a method that puts all four grammatical phrases into a single summary table that can reveal the salient patterns globally.

To do this, once again we will use the pairing table to create a table with the 55 cells for all possible pairs of the eleven BoM books in these four phrase studies. In the case of the synonymous pair studies, each pair member was a percentage of the two together, such as the percentage *therefore* and percentage *wherefore*. Conveniently, this percentage approach automatically controlled for differential book size. Contrasting with this, these grammatical structure studies have but a single variable, and are not amenable to this sort of percentage calculation.

Figure 27. Distribution of Infinitive and Participial Phrases

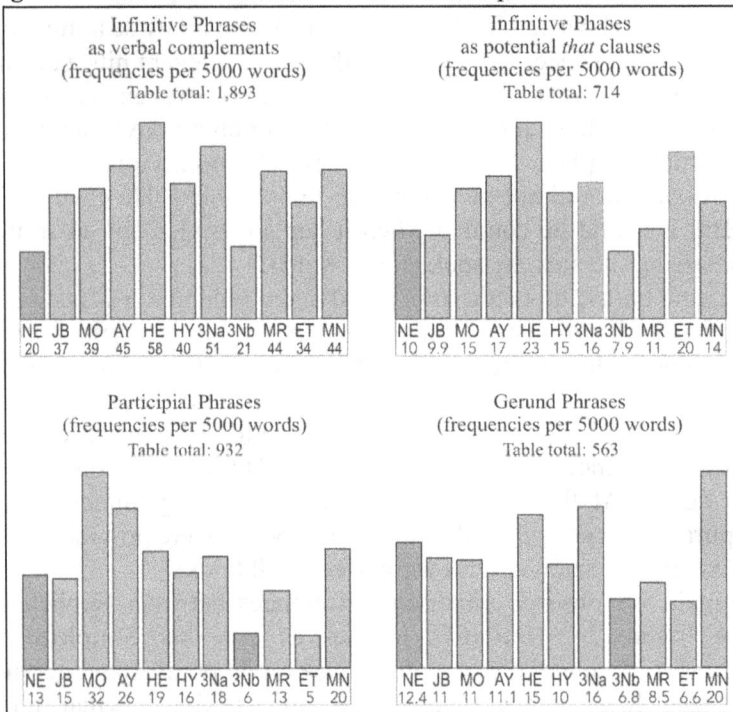

To control for differential book size, first we have to standardize the raw scores (each study's frequencies) on a base of 5,000 by dividing the raw scores of each book by the number of words in the book, and then multiplying each by 5,000. The result is referred to here as *standardized scores*. The participial phrase study will have eleven raw scores, one for each book. These eleven raw scores produce a distribution of eleven standardized scores.

For a given study, the eleven standardized scores, one for each book, are summed, yielding the total value in this *standardized distribution*. Then each standardized score of the study is divided by this total value (i.e. the sum of all eleven standardized scores in the study), to determine what percent of the standardized distribution is accounted for by this score. This is repeated for each standardized score in the study.

We are now analyzing these eleven percentages (for example for Nephi, for Mosiah, for Ether, etc.). Their sum is 100%. These percentages allow us to compare results between books. So, we can calculate the difference between the Nephi percent of the standardized distribution total and the percent in Mormon, for example. Smaller differences indicate greater similarity.

These percentages are fundamentally different from those in the synonymous pair studies. For example, *therefore* can occur 100% of the time in Mosiah, and *wherefore* 0% of the time. But in the grammatical structure analyses, if the adverbial clauses occurred 100% of the time in Nephi, for example, that would mean that the other books have none at all. In actual practice each book will hav at least some. It is for this reason that we find that the highest percent in any of the studies is 15.2103%. This means that the range is much smaller than in the synonymous pair studies. There, we were recording in the pairing table the scores that were 10% or less (i.e. c. 10% of a range of 100), as being book pairs with *minimal stylistic separation*. With this smaller range, for the grammatical structure studies, the comparable cutoff is 1.50 centiles or less (again c. 10% of the observed range). Table 65 displays the number of studies that produced this minimum separation. So for Nephi and Jacob, in three of the four studies these two books were minimally different. For Nephi and Alma, these books turned out to be this similar in only one study, and the other books turned in much larger scores (4.03, 5.39 and 7.30).

As we did in the case of the synonymous pair studies, we use a pairing table to get all book pairs, which number fifty five. Each table cell contains the differences corresponding to the column/row intersect. So the cell where Nephi and Alma intersect displays the Nephi/Alma differences for each of the four studies. Fifty-five cells times the four recorded differences in each equals 220 scores in the table. This table allows us to identify by inspection the score differences that are 1.5 or less. As in the case of the summary table for the synonymous pair studies, the results for Nephi, on the one hand, and AlmaY or Mosiah, on the other, reveal substantial separation, strongly supporting Hilton's result that Nephi and Alma cannot have been authored by the same person.

Table 65. The Number of Studies Showing High Similarity between Books

Book	NE	JB	MS	AL Y	HL E	HL Y	N3a	N3b	MR	ET	MN
Nephi											
Jacob	3										
Mosiah	1	2									
AlmaY	1	2	3								
HelamanE	0	0	0	0							
HelamanY	0	3	3	3	0						
Nephi 3a	0	0	1	2	3	2					
Nephi 3b	1	1	0	0	0	0	0				
Mormon	2	3	0	1	0	2	0	1			
Ether	0	1	1	0	0	1	0	2	1		
Moroni	0	0	2	1	1	2	3	0	1	0	

The Distribution of *That* Clauses

Figure 28. Direct Object That Clauses of Obligation

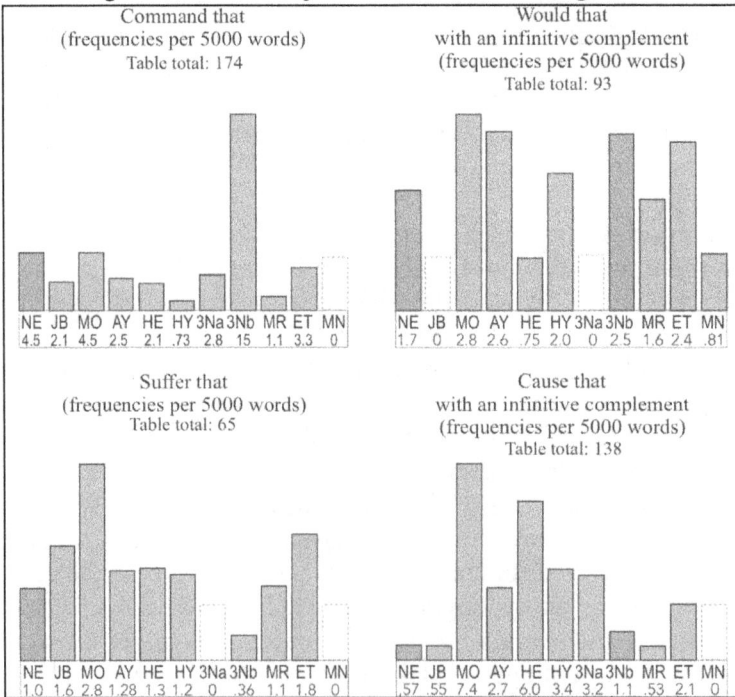

Command that
(frequencies per 5000 words)
Table total: 174

NE	JB	MO	AY	HE	HY	3Na	3Nb	MR	ET	MN
4.5	2.1	4.5	2.5	2.1	.73	2.8	15	1.1	3.3	0

Would that
with an infinitive complement
(frequencies per 5000 words)
Table total: 93

NE	JB	MO	AY	HE	HY	3Na	3Nb	MR	ET	MN
1.7	0	2.8	2.6	.75	2.0	0	2.5	1.6	2.4	.81

Suffer that
(frequencies per 5000 words)
Table total: 65

NE	JB	MO	AY	HE	HY	3Na	3Nb	MR	ET	MN
1.0	1.6	2.8	1.28	1.3	1.2	0	.36	1.1	1.8	0

Cause that
with an infinitive complement
(frequencies per 5000 words)
Table total: 138

NE	JB	MO	AY	HE	HY	3Na	3Nb	MR	ET	MN
.57	.55	7.4	2.7	6.0	3.4	3.2	1.1	.53	2.1	0

That Clauses: Direct Object Clauses as a Grammatical Structure
Before we examine direct object that clauses as a grammatical category, here are some illustrations with examples of specific verbs. Note that even though these are grammatical structures, since we are dividing the category according to the verbs in question, they are actually vocabulary items, and subject to influences from differential subject-matter context from book to book. In each case, the question "what?" is involved. "He commanded what?" "He commanded that…" "He would what?" "He would that…" "He shall not suffer what?" "He shall not suffer that…" "He supposes what?" "He supposes that…" Words such as *would that, suffer that* and *cause that* are as characteristic of BoM English as *behold, yea* and *it came to pass*. These results observed here are consistent with those of Hilton.

Figure 29. Direct Object That Clauses of Perception

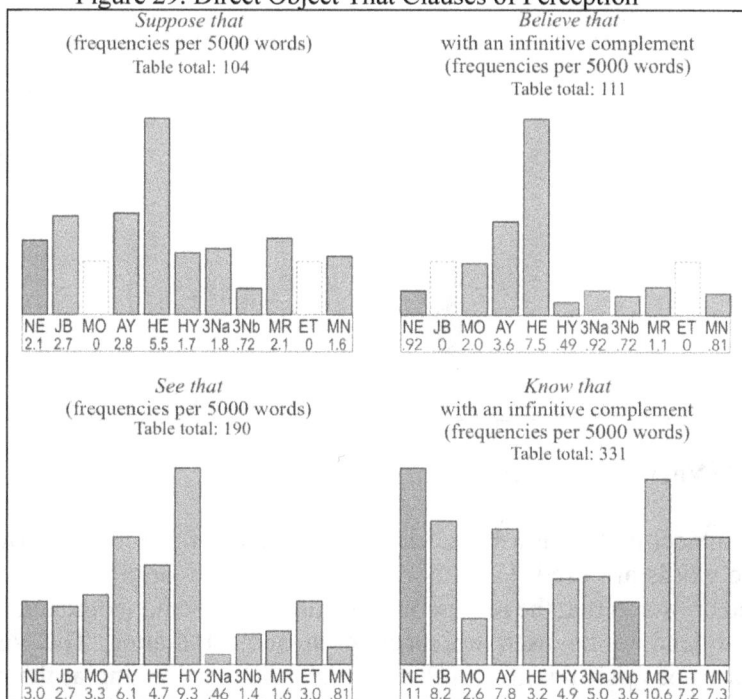

| *Suppose that* (frequencies per 5000 words) Table total: 104 | *Believe that* with an infinitive complement (frequencies per 5000 words) Table total: 111 |

NE	JB	MO	AY	HE	HY	3Na	3Nb	MR	ET	MN
2.1	2.7	0	2.8	5.5	1.7	1.8	.72	2.1	0	1.6

NE	JB	MO	AY	HE	HY	3Na	3Nb	MR	ET	MN
.92	0	2.0	3.6	7.5	.49	.92	.72	1.1	0	.81

| *See that* (frequencies per 5000 words) Table total: 190 | *Know that* with an infinitive complement (frequencies per 5000 words) Table total: 331 |

NE	JB	MO	AY	HE	HY	3Na	3Nb	MR	ET	MN
3.0	2.7	3.3	6.1	4.7	9.3	.46	1.4	1.6	3.0	.81

NE	JB	MO	AY	HE	HY	3Na	3Nb	MR	ET	MN
11	8.2	2.6	7.8	3.2	4.9	5.0	3.6	10.6	7.2	7.3

Distribution of Adverbial That Clauses
Adverbial *that* clauses indicate the objective, purpose, consequence, intent or degree of the action of the verb that it modifies. These are not items of vocabulary, and so are not subject to subject-matter context influences, unlike direct-object *that* clauses of specific verbs, such as *suppose, suffer*

and *know*. They can occur in a wide variety of contexts as a function of stylistic preference or grammatical usage habit. Considering the number of occurrences (1,395), and the high data stability that this would produce, the difference between Nephi and Alma is substantial.

Figure 30. Distribution of Adverbial & Direct Object *That* Clauses

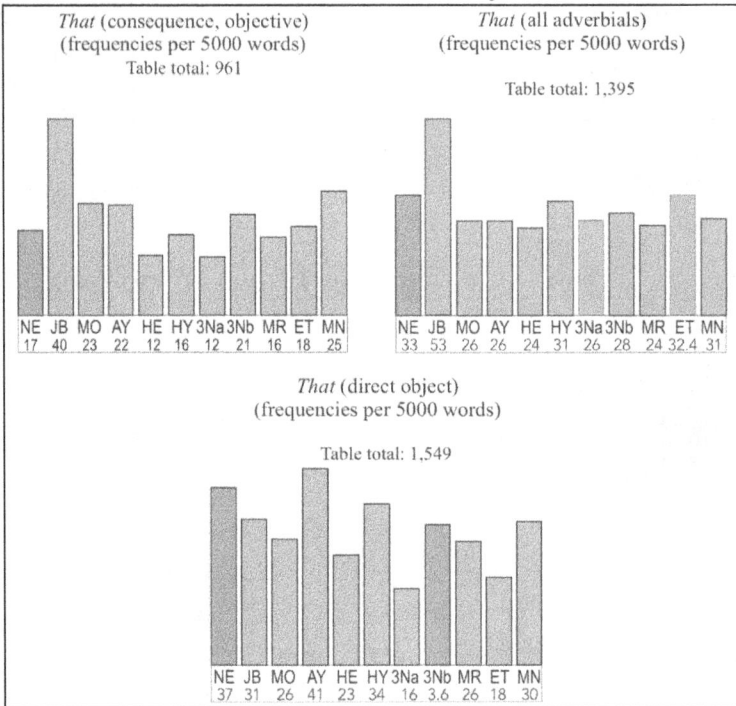

That (consequence, objective)
(frequencies per 5000 words)
Table total: 961

NE	JB	MO	AY	HE	HY	3Na	3Nb	MR	ET	MN
17	40	23	22	12	16	12	21	16	18	25

That (all adverbials)
(frequencies per 5000 words)
Table total: 1,395

NE	JB	MO	AY	HE	HY	3Na	3Nb	MR	ET	MN
33	53	26	26	24	31	26	28	24	32.4	31

That (direct object)
(frequencies per 5000 words)
Table total: 1,549

NE	JB	MO	AY	HE	HY	3Na	3Nb	MR	ET	MN
37	31	26	41	23	34	16	3.6	26	18	30

Single Variable Studies

The subject matter of a book has considerable influence over how often some words are used. For this reason, all of the wordprint studies were based on words that the researchers considered to be noncontextual. These would tend to be used irrespective of subject matter. The virtue of synonymous pair research is that one is no longer looking at the number of times that the synonyms occur. Rather, the studies are based on the percentage of times that one synonym is chosen over the other. Does this mean that we must eschew all single variable research? The position taken here is that some single variable studies can be valid, and make important contributions.

One of the issues of concern is the possibility of cherry picking. There are many words that occur quite often in all books. How does one select one for consideration, and not another? This issue did not arise with the synonymous pair research, for the simple reason that in spite of extensive assiduous investigation, I found only fourteen synonymous pairs with sufficient representation in the BoM to enable a valid study of their distribution. An example of a reject is *thereby/whereby*. The sum of both in the BoM is only 25. Although there is a major difference between Nephi on the one hand, and both Mosiah and Alma on the other (consistent with the above results), there are no occurrences in Jacob, HelamanE, 3 NephiA, Mormon and Moroni. This pair does not meet minimum criteria. Even so, two of the twelve pairs studied did not occur in one book, Moroni. These two studies are *"And it came to pas"* versus the alternatives and *nevertheless* versus *yet*. The first of these occurs 1,357 times in the BoM, and the second 215 times. After deciding to include both, the end result was that all known synonymous pairs were included. No cherry picking here.

In the case of single variable research, to minimize the problem posed by differential subject matter, several features were taken into consideration to minimize the cherry-picking issue. These are: words that were used for the purpose of archaizing the text or mimicking KJV usage, words that produce large data sets, and words that appear on their face to be largely noncontextual. When one or more of these features is lacking, the defect may be overcome when a data set has differences between books that are sufficiently large that the pattern observed cannot be simply due to a smaller than desired data set, or difference in book subject matter. Even so, these results are not as solid as those obtained from either the wordprint technique or synonymous pair analysis.

Single Variable Studies: and

The overuse of *and* is a major BoM hallmark. It is not clear whether its profusion is mostly due to bad English, or is at least partially deliberate in a perhaps misguided effort to archaize the text. *And* has been included in every wordprint project, being regarded as noncontextual.

The best way to control for differential book size is to express the total occurrence in each book as the number of occurrences per 5,000 words. This produces eleven standardized results, one for each book. The validity of a single variable study depends on two main factors apart from whatever degree of noncontextuality might exist. The first is the size of the data set, and the second is the size of the differences of the results observed between books. When the data set is extremely large, moderate differences can be considered quite valid. Smaller data sets require radical differences between books to merit our attention. A case in point is *and*, where the difference we observe between 1 Nephi and Alma is especially notable in view of the large number of occurrences: 12,650. The results for *that thereby* and *insomuch that* illustrate cases where inclusion in this project was due to the interesting difference between books in spite of the smallness of the data sets.

Figure 31. Single Variable Studies: *and, behold* (interjection), *insomuch*

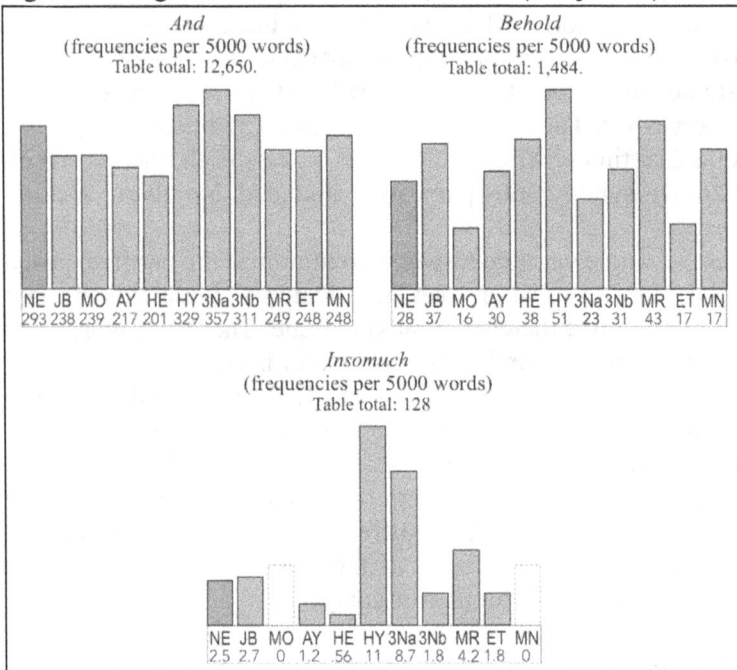

	And (frequencies per 5000 words) Table total: 12,650.										Behold (frequencies per 5000 words) Table total: 1,484.									
	NE	JB	MO	AY	HE	HY	3Na	3Nb	MR	ET	MN	NE	JB	MO	AY	HE	HY	3Na	3Nb	MR	ET	MN
	293	238	239	217	201	329	357	311	249	248	248	28	37	16	30	38	51	23	31	43	17	17

	Insomuch (frequencies per 5000 words) Table total: 128									
	NE	JB	MO	AY	HE	HY	3Na	3Nb	MR	ET	MN
	2.5	2.7	0	1.2	.56	11	8.7	1.8	4.2	1.8	0

Single Variable Studies: behold (as an interjection)

Behold is almost as characteristic of BoM English as "And it came to pass..." There are two very different usages. We have already studied the first of these, when it is used verbally, meaning *see*. The second, which we are studying here, is when it is used as an interjection. In this sense, it occurs a total of 1,484 times in the eleven books, a factor that provides good data stability. Although the difference between Nephi and Alma is notable, the most curious result is the value for Mosiah. We shall see that this book tends to be a maverick.

Superfluous *that* refers to cases where *that* is not needed, and even wrong. Perhaps it is added because the speaker feels that it is more formal. Or the writer feels that an adverb needs it to make it a subordinating adverb. *Before* can be used as an adverbial preposition, as in "I did it before the bell rang." *That* is erroneously added when used to introduce a subordinate clause, as in "I did it before that the bell rang."

Single Variable Studies: The Distribution of Superfluous That Phrases

There is a difference between using *that* too much in composition, and superfluous *that*. An example of the usage of this phrase is: "After that the king came, we attacked." The better sentence would be "After the king came, we attacked." My study lumps together the incidence of a number of such phrases, although my raw data list them individually. They are: *after that, before that, because that, for that, how that, since that* and *lest that* (Figure 32).

Figure 32. Single Variable Studies: Superfluous "that"

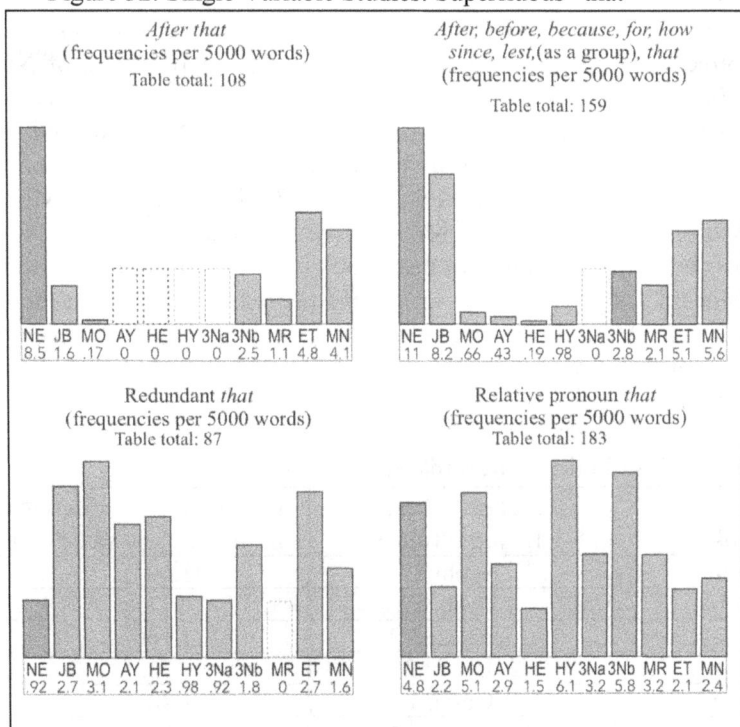

	NE	JB	MO	AY	HE	HY	3Na	3Nb	MR	ET	MN
After that (frequencies per 5000 words) Table total: 108	8.5	1.6	.17	0	0	0	0	2.5	1.1	4.8	4.1
After, before, because, for, how since, lest, (as a group), *that* (frequencies per 5000 words) Table total: 159	11	8.2	.66	.43	.19	.98	0	2.8	2.1	5.1	5.6
Redundant *that* (frequencies per 5000 words) Table total: 87	.92	2.7	3.1	2.1	2.3	.98	.92	1.8	0	2.7	1.6
Relative pronoun *that* (frequencies per 5000 words) Table total: 183	4.8	2.2	5.1	2.9	1.5	6.1	3.2	5.8	3.2	2.1	2.4

Although there is a somewhat acute difference between Moroni and Nephi, it is far more radical between Nephi and Mosiah through 3 NephiA. Here again, the results are consistent with the Hilton results indicating that Nephi and Alma were done by different authors. They are consistent as well with the study of Moon et al., which also found that Nephi and Mormon were done by two separate authors. Note again the difference within traditional 3 Nephi, between 3 NephiA and 3 NephiB. For this however, one must bear in mind the radical content difference of 3 NephiB (the ministry of Christ to the Nephites).

Single Variable Studies: "I, Nephi"

This is a study of recordkeeper introductions. How many times does Nephi say "I Nephi?" How many times does Jacob say, "I Jacob?" The same question is asked re each recordkeeper listed in column two. "I Nephi" (Nephi, son of Nephi, son of Helaman) does not occur in 3 Nephi. "I Nephi" (son of Lehi) occurs 87 times in Nephi (63 times in 1 Nephi and 24 times in 2 Nephi). Although this is the introduction of greatest occurrence, "I Mormon" occurs more per 5,000 words in Words of Mormon and the "Book of Mormon" combined. The names of other recordkeepers also have introductions in the small plates of Nephi (viz Jacob, Enos, Jarom and Omni.) There is no "I Mosiah," possibly lost in the shuffle of getting the original first chapter into Omni and Words of Mormon. This is not due to its being an abridgment by Mormon; Alma is as well, and "I Alma" occurs four times. Books attributed to Moroni have "I Moroni," in the Book of Moroni five times, and the Book of Ether ten times, in addition to once in the "Book of Mormon". The proliferation of "I Moroni" is possibly due to its unexpected occurrence in these books. The Nephi-Alma difference is seen here as well; "I, Alma" occurs only .2 times per 5,000 words in Alma, while "I, Nephi" occurs 13.4 times in 1 Nephi.

Table 66. Distribution of Recordkeeper Introductions

Book	occurrences: I, Nephi (etc.)	total words in the book	occurrences per 5,000 words
Nephi	I, Nephi:87	43,601	10.0
Jacob	I, Jacob: 12	9,127	6.6
Enos	I, Enos: 5	1,166	21.4
Jarom	I, Jarom: 2	733	13.6
Omni	I, Omni: 1	1,401	3.6
Words of M	I, Mormon: 3	857	17.5

Mosiah	I, Mosiah: 0	30,233	**0.0**
AlmaY	I, Alma: 4	58,519	**0.3**
Alma	I, Alma: 4	85,073	**0.2**
HelamanE	I, Helaman: 1	26,554	**0.2**
HelamanY	I, Helaman: 0	20,366	**0.0**
3 NephiA	I, Nephi: 0	10,895	**0.0**
3 NephiB	I, Nephi: 0	13,871	**0.0**
3 Nephi	I, Nephi: 0	24,766	**0.0**
4 Nephi	I, Nephi: 0	1,924	**0.0**
Mormon	I, Mormon: 8	9,420	4.2
	I, Moroni 1		0.5
Moroni	I, Moroni: 5	6142	4.1
Ether	I Moroni: 10	16,587	3.0

All in all, the results observed in this chapter, especially those of the synonymous pair studies, provide strong support for the John Hilton conclusion: that Nephi and Alma were not written by the same author.

Another interesting case is "the lamb of God", found thirty-five times in the BoM, thirty-two in Nephi, once in Alma and twice in Mormon.

Note: Verbs in Transition

The verb "to want" is not used with the meaning "to desire." The verb "to like" expressing positive affect is not used. The verb "will" in the present tense, expressing desire, is used rarely, as in 1 Nephi 18:10 ("we will not that…"). "I want you to…" is expressed either with the verb "to desire" or "I would that ye…" This is especially the case in Mosiah and Alma (Figure 28). To the extent that these verbs were in transition during the period of BoM composition with respect to semantic content and/or usage, their presence or absence in the BoM may reflect a preference for the older rather than the emerging "modern" usage. Or perhaps we are again witnessing attempts at archaization.

Nephi-Mosiah Simultaneity?

When considering a scenario of two or more authors, Smith and Cowdery come to mind. So it is important to note that on three occasions, when Cowdery was copying ms$O$ into ms$P$, he inadvertently wrote *whosoever*,[483] and then corrected it to *whoso*. Only one of these cases is present in the extant portion of MSO. It reads *whoso* (Ether 10:6). A

---

[483] Skousen, *History of the Text of the Book of Mormon.* II:1248-49.

second case must also have read *whoso* in MS𝒪, since it occurs in the same verse. This is evidence that the natural usage in his idiolect was *whosoever*. It is also the preference found in Mosiah through Helaman the Younger. Of the two, Smith and Cowdery, the latter may be to some degree associated with that group. An opposite scenario seems to have obtained in the case of *for to* (meaning *to*, i.e. *in order to*). In ms𝒫 there were 15 instances of *for to*, two in Mosiah, nine in Alma, two in Helaman, one in 3 Nephi and one in Ether. None occurs in the Nephi group. Joseph Smith marked nine for the deletion of *for* in ms𝒫 (*for̶ to*), removed four for the 1837 printing, and missed two. Apparently this usage may not have been prominent in Smith's idiolect.[484] Note that *therefore* occurs 15 times in the *Book of Abraham*, and *wherefore* not at all. *Therefore* also occurs 11 times in Smith's 1832 history, and *wherefore* only once. As for Cowdery, his text of the *Articles of the Church of Christ* has two instances of *therefore*.

It is virtually certain that Smith Jr. did the first draft of Nephi. First of all, in addition to the foregoing observation, he had already covered this ground in writing the *Book of Lehi*, so the basic outline would not have been new to him. Second, during all of his post-1830 life, he was determined to produce his inspired version of the Bible. This was an extension of the work he had already begun when producing the Isaiah inclusions for the Book of Nephi and his work on 3 NephiB. In addition to this, we have the evidence in BoC 3:1 (D&C 4:1, dated February 1829) and 1 Nephi 14:7:

a marvelous work is about to come forth among the children of men (BoC)

For the time cometh, saith the Lamb of God, that I will work a great and a marvelous work among the children of men (1 Nephi)

The similarity in wording cannot be coincidental: "a [great and] marvelous work," paired with "among the children of men." We are left only to wonder which came first. If it was Nephi, we would have to assume that at least 1 Nephi through chapter 14 was already drafted by the time of the visit of Smith's father and brother Samuel in February 1829. Equally probable (?), the revelation on the occasion of their visit came first, as a confirmation of the decision they had arrived at, to embark on a far grander project than the mission to the Lamanites mentioned in BoC 2 (D&C 3:19-20).

---

[484] Skousen, *History of the Text of the Book of Mormon.* I:310-13.

Mosiah-AlmaY Disparity

Although our results show an overall similarity between Mosiah and AlmaY, there are cases where the former differs radically, not only from AlmaY, but also from most if not all of the other books.

Figure 33. Mosiah-AlmaY Disparity

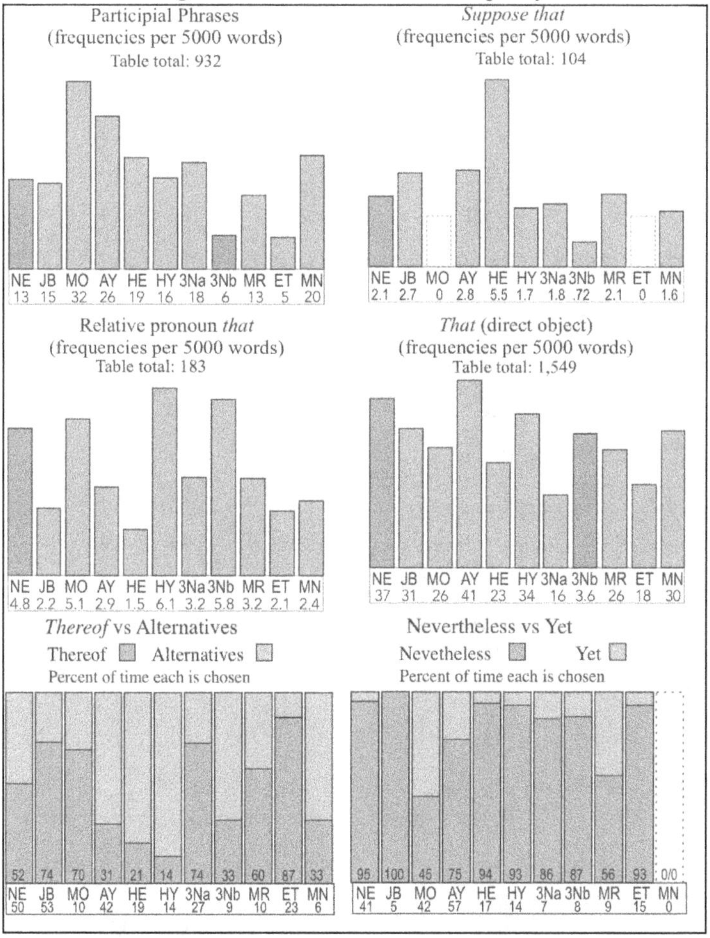

Participial Phrases
(frequencies per 5000 words)
Table total: 932
NE JB MO AY HE HY 3Na 3Nb MR ET MN
13 15 32 26 19 16 18 6 13 5 20
Suppose that
(frequencies per 5000 words)
Table total: 104
NE JB MO AY HE HY 3Na 3Nb MR ET MN
2.1 2.7 0 2.8 5.5 1.7 1.8 .72 2.1 0 1.6
Relative pronoun that
(frequencies per 5000 words)
Table total: 183
NE JB MO AY HE HY 3Na 3Nb MR ET MN
4.8 2.2 5.1 2.9 1.5 6.1 3.2 5.8 3.2 2.1 2.4
That (direct object)
(frequencies per 5000 words)
Table total: 1,549
NE JB MO AY HE HY 3Na 3Nb MR ET MN
37 31 26 41 23 34 16 3.6 26 18 30
Thereof vs Alternatives
Thereof Alternatives
Percent of time each is chosen
52 74 70 31 21 14 74 33 60 87 33
NE JB MO AY HE HY 3Na 3Nb MR ET MN
50 53 10 42 19 14 27 9 10 23 6
Nevertheless vs Yet
Nevetheless Yet
Percent of time each is chosen
95 100 45 75 94 93 86 87 56 93 0/0
NE JB MO AY HE HY 3Na 3Nb MR ET MN
41 5 42 57 17 14 7 8 9 15 0

In this context it is important to note that the word *curse*, as a verb and as a noun, occurs often in 1 Nephi and Alma, but not even once in Mosiah, even though there are ample contexts where a reference to the curse of the Lamanites would be fitting. Mosiah also lacks the pejorative usage of "dark skin," "loathsome" and "idle" in reference to the

Lamanites. If Mosiah was drafted by yet a third person, Hyrum Smith comes to mind. He was educated at Moore's Academy of Dartmouth College, which was established to teach Native Americans with the objective that some of them would bring the Gospel of Christ to their own people. Perhaps as a result of personal contact with these fellow students, he was no longer comfortable with this characterization of a people others called savages.

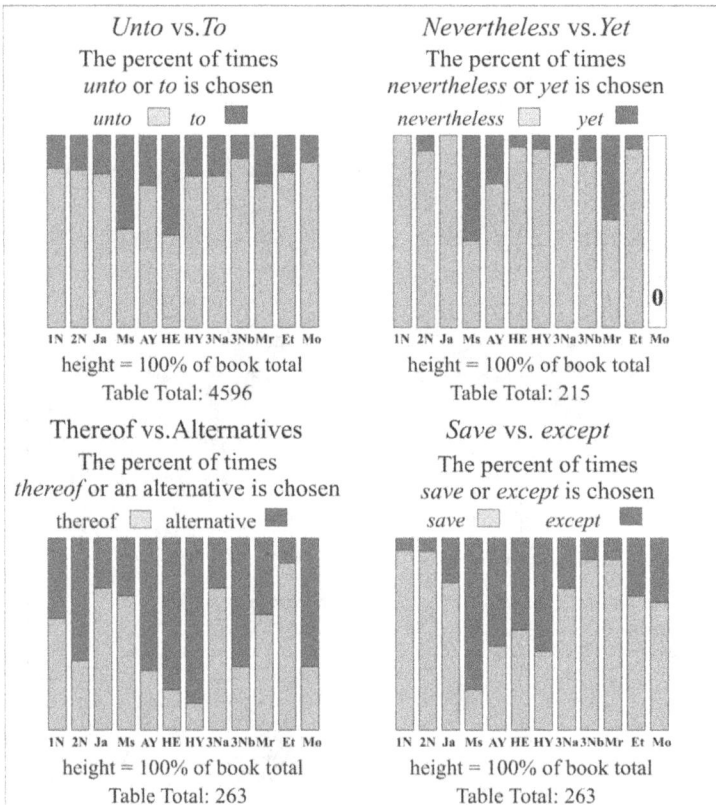

Unto vs. *To*
The percent of times
unto or *to* is chosen

unto ▢   to ■

1N 2N Ja Ms AY HE HY 3Na 3Nb Mr Et Mo
height = 100% of book total
Table Total: 4596

Nevertheless vs. *Yet*
The percent of times
nevertheless or *yet* is chosen

nevertheless ▢   yet ■

1N 2N Ja Ms AY HE HY 3Na 3Nb Mr Et Mo
height = 100% of book total
Table Total: 215

Thereof vs. Alternatives
The percent of times
thereof or an alternative is chosen

thereof ▢   alternative ■

1N 2N Ja Ms AY HE HY 3Na 3Nb Mr Et Mo
height = 100% of book total
Table Total: 263

Save vs. *except*
The percent of times
save or *except* is chosen

save ▢   except ■

1N 2N Ja Ms AY HE HY 3Na 3Nb Mr Et Mo
height = 100% of book total
Table Total: 263

Joseph-Oliver Collaboration

Once the Smiths and Cowdery had charted the recast of the gold record into a gold bible, Cowdery could have gone straight to work at father Smith's direction on a draft of Alma in Manchester. Someone else could have been drafting Mosiah, possibly Hyrum, keeping the work on these two key books close to home, i.e. father Smith. Joe Jr. would not have been broadsided in February. As early as the visit of his parents to Harmony in the September previous, father and son could have reviewed possibilities and arrived at initial options for a new course. During the February visit, Samuel assumed scrivener duty, with their father present. He is mentioned in David Hale's store ledger dated 20 March. Before Samuel's arrival, Emma provided scribal service perhaps as early as December 1, 1828. Some time in March, Smith issued a revelation that ordered him to stop (D&C 5:34), thereby dodging Harris' importuning; although this order came most probably from a previous agreement that at a certain point it would be advisable to wait for Cowdery's arrival to see what he would bring from Manchester. When these two got to work on April 7, their first task was to review each other's work, each making proposals for the other's writing, making notes directly on their drafts and adding, deleting and substituting pages. Eventually the had to collaborate on books not yet begun. This may have taken most of April and May before reading from the drafts for a scribe to copy into ms$\mathcal{O}$. Smith's sudden and irrepressible additions would make it impossible to determine before starting a new page in ms$\mathcal{O}$ how much of the draft might fit, and therefore what to write on the page content line before the page was completed. In other words, three separate authors may have drafted Nephi and Alma, and possibly even Mosiah, more or less simultaneously. Later books may reflect collaboration *ab initio*.

Indeed, if Cowdery arrived with a draft of Alma in hand, we can understand that he would initially expect to be cotranslator (coauthor).

The discussion so far presented gives rise to the following fundamental observations:

§ The fact that the extant portion of ms$\mathcal{O}$ is relatively free of substantive edits requires the conclusion that it was produced with Smith reading from ms$\mathcal{U}$ for Cowdery to write.

§ Numerous text copy errors in ms$\mathcal{O}$ have preserved fossilized elements of the ms$\mathcal{U}$ text, providing us with empirical evidence.

§ The chapter number confusion at the beginning of 2 Nephi and especially Mosiah (throughout, but including Omni and Words of Mormon) shows that the drafts at least for these two books were so highly developed that they already had numbered chapters.

§ The analysis of the distribution of Hilton's wordprint patterns; the analysis of the distribution of fourteen synonymous pairs; and also of some of the key grammatical building blocks of the English language, provide strong evidence that Nephi and Alma were not originally drafted by the same person. There is even substantial evidence for at least one other drafter, for Mosiah. Each of these three independent types of study is based on methodology to minimize the effect of differential subject-matter contexts. When three totally independent and fundamentally different methodologies produce the same result, they cannot be readily dismissed.

§ The layout of the BoM narrative was made up of highly segmental divisions, enabling two or more books to be drafted at the same time. Moreover, the initiation of a new calendar (years of the judges) at the end of Mosiah enabled the drafting of Alma to be done simultaneously with Mosiah, which used Nephi's ALJ (after leaving Jerusalem) calendar, without fear of any internal anachronism.

§ Evidence for multiple more-or-less simultaneous drafts liberates the analysis of the *Book of Mormon* production process from the time constraint of sequential composition.

Serious systematic textual analysis of the BoM, with special focus on the number of authors, began at BYU. Later, the foci increased, to include the authors' identity and the order of the production of the books. We now have unrelated methodologies that have yielded highly similar results, including the analysis of wordprints, of synonymous pairs and of grammatical structures. Minimally, they have shown that it is highly probable the Nephi and Alma were not authored by the same person. If there were two authors, they would most probably be Joseph Smith Jr. and Oliver Cowdery. There is evidence that there was also a third. The existence of substantial evidence that cannot be readily discounted is the

Authorship Issue

< Chapter 29 >

The Rough Road from Harmony to Church

The original BoM manuscript is a complex yet relatively clean document, with mostly various corrections of scribal copy errors and minimal minor substantive changes. It is not possible for anyone to have composed it extemporaneously while dictating to a scribe. In view of the historical and archaeological realities, which rule out supernatural assistance, the only viable alternative is that it was dictated from a draft or drafts (ms$\mathcal{U}$) that was later unceremoniously (yet sadly?) cremated in the family hearth.

According to Skousen, in at least two instances page numbers were written at the same time that the scribe wrote the page heading. This indicates that page numbers were not added after the whole ms had been completed.[485] Since the extant material begins with 1 Nephi 2:2, with only slightly more than the first chapter being missing, it is therefore clear that ms$\mathcal{O}$ began with Nephi in Fayette. (v. supra, p. 444-450 It would be wonderful if we had contemporary documents to study its development, but few relevant materials are available (v. Appendix 7). Most of the early history of the Mormon canon must be reconstructed from late and often secondary documents, some of them the product of early LDS leaders engaged in controlling the history of the movement, some others by pious believers, and many others produced by anti-Mormons fighting "heresy". Even though Joseph Smith's historical compositions are a good example of the first of these, he mentions a useful detail in his 1832 history. He wrote that prior to the coming of Oliver Cowdery to Harmony, on 5 April 1829, "now my wife had written some for me to translate and also my brother Samuel." [486] David Whitmer's estimate of eight months total would be December 1 to July 1, & according to Joseph Knight Sr., work was already under way at the first of winter, 1828 (c. December 1? See page 397.).

It became clear in the stylistic study of the BoM text that different authors must have drafted Nephi and Alma. Furthermore, the analysis of a number of distributions yielded evidence that yet a third person may have drafted Mosiah. It makes sense that Smith would be the drafter of Nephi.

---

[485] Skousen, *The Original Manuscript*, 33.
[486] Jessee, *Personal Writings of Joseph Smith*, 640, n14: "Neither the handwriting of Emma Hale Smith nor of Samuel H. Smith appears on the surviving pages of the original *Book of Mormon* manuscript.

He had already covered the same ground when he did the missing *Book of Lehi*. And his later extensive effort to produce a "corrected" version of the entire Bible is consistent with the work done to edit Isaiah for inclusion in Nephi. In the entire extant material of ms$O$, there are only two scribes apart from Cowdery, both in early 1 Nephi, and neither is Emma or Samuel. Smith's statement that Emma and Samuel had written for him prior to Oliver's arrival most probably refers to work on ms$U$, a draft, most probably of Nephi. Moreover, Alma addresses issues of church and court organization, separation of church and state, the legal profession and theological and legalistic disputation. All of this is consistent with Cowdery's interest in these issues, his later legal practice in two towns and efforts to enter politics.

From Initial Drafts to MsU, to MsO, to MsP

Two days after rodsman Cowdery's arrival he was made scryer Smith's scribe, even though according to statements made later by both, neither had ever laid eyes on the other before then. Not long after that, he was promoted to translator alongside Joseph Smith, making him coauthor. Although this rapid career progression is suspect, it could be that Smith's father had apprised his son of the advisability of this promotion during his visit to Harmony in February, especially if Oliver had already worked on drafts. It appears that this did not happen at Joseph's initiative, but Oliver's. "I [Jesus] grant unto you a gift if you desire of me." (D&C 6, dated April 1829) Later the same month, this status was revoked with a promise that he might translate other records at a future time. (D&C 9) This meteoric elevation would make sense if Cowdery had a justifiable claim to be a coauthor, one at once recognized by Smith, because in fact while in Manchester he had already begun to draft, most probably the Book of Alma the Younger. Also in Manchester, a third author may have been drafting Mosiah. This draft too could have been brought to Harmony by Cowdery, or if not, then by Hyrum who visited in May, ostensibly to check on how the work was coming. If Oliver and his friend Hyrum were drafting these two works, they could have conferred with each other to assure consistency and the transition from one to the other. Content-wise, they are almost totally independent works with respect to the text of Nephi through Jacob.

Table 67. The *Book of Mormon* Remake: Events and Dates

Date	Event
December 1827	Joseph and Emma Smith moved to Harmony; she began writing for him (beginning of the Book of Lehi).
01-thru-03 1828	Emma Smith and her brother Reuben Hale wrote for Smith.
February 1828	Harris took a transcription of characters to Anthon in NY.
12/04-14/06 1828	Harris assumed scrivener duty from Emma & Reuben. He wrote through p. 116 (possibly plus some retained pages).
06/1828	Martin Harris took the 116 pages to his farm.
15/06/1828	Date on the tombstone in Harmony of Joseph and Emma's son who died the day of his birth.
06/1828	The 116 pages in Harris' custody went missing.
Late 06/1828	Smith arrived in Manchester & learned of the loss of the 116 pages.
Mid 07/1828	Smith returned to Harmony, having stayed with his parents for a spell.
08/1828	Smith began farming to support his family.
c. late Aug. 1828	Joseph Sr. & Lucy stayed overnight at the Whitmer home.
c. mid July, 1828	Joseph Sr. and Lucy visited Joseph in Harmony.
C. 09/09/1828	Joseph Sr. and Lucy returned to Manchester to find Samuel Harrison Smith and his wife sick.
11/09/1828	Joseph Smith Sr. obtained medicine for Samuel ("Boy Harrison"), as recorded in doctor Robinsons's daybook, documenting the presence of Smith Sr. in Palmyra (and so Manchester). (Vogel, *Early Mormon Documents*, 3:439)
Late 09/1828	Lyman Cowdery visited Hyrum seeking a teaching position in Palmyra. A meeting of the school trustees agreed to hire him, but the next day Lyman presented Oliver to be hired in his place and this was accepted.
10/1828	Initially Oliver resided with the Smith elders. Shortly after beginning teaching he learned more about the BoM project. The date of his recruitment is unknown but it was possibly in mid fall.
Summer of 1828	David Whitmer "stops with" Cowdery.
Fall, 1828	Early winter Smith is again translating with Emma writing for him (Joseph Knight Sr.).
February, 1829	Joseph Sr. and Samuel visited Joseph Jr. and Emma in Harmony. Samuel served as scribe up to late of March. (He is listed in David Hale's daybook on March 20.).
Nov. 1828/March	For some unknown period, Emma wrote for her husband.
5/04/1829	Oliver Cowdery and Samuel Smith arrived in Harmony.
C. 7/04/1829	Oliver became Smith's scribe.
April, 1829	Oliver was made a translator (coauthor).
April, 1829	Oliver was demoted to just scribe.

May, 1829	Hyrum Smith visited Harmony.
c. 15 May 1829	Baptism of Joseph Smith and Oliver Cowdery, and the restoration of the priesthood. Cowdery said they sought it after reading the account of the ministry of Jesus to the Nephites in 3 Nephi (Letter of Cowdery to Phelps, 14 Sept. 1829). Presumably, Ms𝒰 had reached 3 Nephi by May 15.
May 1829	Samuel visited Harmony and was baptized. Then returned.
May 1829	Hyrum visited Harmony to check on progress.
May 1829	Joseph Knight Sr. came and brought them provisions.
C. 1 June 1829	David Whitmer arrived to take Joseph and Oliver to the home of his father, Peter Whitmer Sr. in Waterloo, Fayette, to complete the translation. Lucy reports that he drove his wagon 135 miles in 2 days. Whitmer states that translation was from June 1 to July 1. Smith indicates that the translation of the *Book of Mormon* was completed c. before the issuance of the copyright. Smith may have meant the abridgment of Mormon, while Whitmer may have included Ether as well.
Early June, 1829	Once the work had begun in the Whitmer home, John Whitmer also began writing for Joseph (plus one other Whitmer?).
June, 1829	Baptism of Hyrum Smith, David Whitmer and Peter Whitmer Jr.
c. June 7,1829?	Translation completion celebration in Whitmer home. (*Lucy's Book*)
c. 08/06/1829	*Book of Mormon* translation completed. (Smith's history, *Lucy's Book* & D&C 17)
c. 09/06/1829	An angel showed the plates to Oliver Cowdery, Martin Harris and David Whitmer with Joseph. Later, Joseph showed the plates to the eight witnesses.
c. 09/06/1829	Grandin asked Gilbert to estimate the cost of the proposed BoM printing project, and for that purpose, pages of the ms were brought to him. These would have to have been ms𝒪 pages. An estimate that there would be about 500 pages, based on ms𝒰.
11/06/1829	*Book of Mormon* Copyright was issued. (The text on the BoM title page appears on the copyright. Vogel, *Joseph Smith*, 3:461-63.)
June, 1829	Smith ordained Oliver an elder, & Oliver ordained Joseph.
Summer, 1829	Cowdery drafted a revelation (undated) he claimed to have received containing important church establishment passages. These were incorporated in 3 Nephi, Moroni & D&C 18.

June, 1829	Contract with Grandin to print 5000 copies for 3000 dollars.
26/06/1829	Grandin published the BoM copyright (for the Gold Bible).
Beginning of July	The whole Smith family moved into the log cabin, including Peter Whitmer Jr. and presumably Oliver Cowdery. (Lucy)
Mid August, 1829	Hyrum brought the first gathering of ms$P$ to Gilbert. Initially, Joseph collected it each night, but after a few days he trusted Gilbert with it.
25/08/1829	Harris mortgaged his farm as surety for the BoM printing.
02/09/1829	No. 1 of the old series of *The Reflector* appeared in Palmyra.
04/10/1829	Joseph Smith arrived back in Harmony. (Smith-Cowdery letter)
06/11/1829	Grandin's new type had not arrived, so the printing was going rather slowly. (Cowdery-Smith letter)
27/12/1829	The earliest Sunday that Hyrum and Oliver could have discovered Abner Cole publishing extracts from the *Book of Mormon*. (Vogel, Joseph Smith, 480)
28/12/1829	Cowdery-Smith letter alluding to the coming of Joseph Sr. [regarding Cole]. Lucy reports he went and came right back with his son in spite of the freezing weather.
End of December	Joseph Sr. in Harmony to fetch his son to deal with Cole?
02/01/1830	Abner Cole's *The Reflector* published the first installment of the *Book of Mormon* (1:1-2:3).
13/01/1830	Cole's second installment from the BoM.
16/01/1830	Agreement signed by Smith Sr. and witnessed by Cowdery re the compensation due to Harris for covering BoM printing. Joseph Jr. was probably in Harmony.
19/01/1830	Smith appeared in court in Pennsylvania over debt to Durfee.
22/01/1830	Cole's third installment from the BoM.
Late January 1830	Smith is in Manchester to deal with Cole. It appears that the dispute was eventually settled by some sort of arbitration. (*Lucy's Book*, 475) Possibly Grandin settled it.
Early 02/1830	Late sources say Smith received a revelation for a delegation to go to Kingston, Ontario, to sell the BoM copyright rights for Canada. Smith would have been in Manchester to set this up, & Whitmer recalled Smith was there when they returned. Lucy wrote he returned because Grandin had stopped printing fearing nonpayment. Gilbert later denied this.
19/03/1830	*Wayne Sentinel* announced the BoM would soon be ready.
26/03/1830	*Wayne Sentinel* announced the BoM was available.
26/03/1830	Smith was in Manchester when the book was published.

The production of the BoM drafts most probably resembled those of the *Book of Moses*, undertaken shortly after the 1830 publication of the new bible: "This included a complete rewriting of the early chapters of Genesis, which was then followed in the editorial process by a number of interlinear inserts and deletions. In some instances, additional material was written on small pieces of paper and pinned to the manuscript at places needing still further correction."[487] BoM drafting may have begun with some initial drafts, which already would have contained some edits, although relatively few, the emphasis having been on composition. Apart from possibly finishing up whatever drafts they had been working on, the first job of Smith and Cowdery was to review initial drafts and make corrections, additions and deletions. Collectively, these drafts are ms$\mathcal{U}$, the urtext. Once ms$\mathcal{U}$ emerged, the initial drafts no longer existed, just as upon the emergence of the adult, the youth no longer exists.

We have a good example of what ms$\mathcal{U}$ looked like in the extant highly edited drafts of the *Book of Moses*. At some point it became clear that it was so messy and cumbersome that a prospective printer would require a cleaned-up copy. Enter ms$\mathcal{O}$, initially undertaken to serve as the printer's copy. Ms$\mathcal{U}$ was completed shortly after Smith's arrival in early June, at the home of Peter Whitmer Sr. in Waterloo, NY. The identification of John Whitmer as unidentified scribe two (so designated by Royal Skousen) evidences both the date and the location of its commencement. Initially, only a few pages of ms$\mathcal{O}$ were needed to show the printer, according to typesetter Gilbert. As soon as ms$\mathcal{U}$ was done, Smith regarded the BoM to be completed, a fact that also agrees with Smith's early date in his timeline. The scribal service of the two Fayette scribes in 1 Nephi occasionally freed up Cowdery for other work. Their scrivener service ended at 1 Nephi 16:14. They became unavailable when Smith and Cowdery left the Whitmer home.

That we are dealing with dictation is clear, at least in much of the text, from errors, such as writing 'no' for 'know' (1 Nephi 10:8), an easy error for someone taking dictation. It is clear that there was a hierarchy among scribes. Cowdery might proof and correct a Fayette scribe, or one Fayette scribe might proof another. But only Cowdery proofed Cowdery's work. From Alma 10:31 on, Cowdery was the sole scribe, albeit with the exception of Alma 45:22, inexplicably in the hand of Joseph Smith Jr.

Approximately on June first, David Whitmer arrived in Harmony with a two-horse wagon and took Joseph and Oliver to the home of his

---

[487] Matthews, "How We Got the *Book of Moses*."

father, Peter Whitmer Sr.[488] Lucy Smith relates that to transport the gold plates he was instructed that, "he should commit them into the hands of an angel, for safety, and after arriving at Mr. Whitmer's, the angel would meet him in the garden, and deliver them up again into his hands."[489] She assures us that this worked just fine.

Cowdery's arrival on 5 April is generally taken to be a hard date, as well as May 15 when Smith and Cowdery were baptized. But the first documented hard date is 6 April 1829, the date of the contract for Smith to buy land from Isaac Hale, drawn up and witnessed by Oliver Cowdery. The next hard date is 11 June 1829 when the copyright was issued for the *Book of Mormon*. The requirement to obtain a copyright at that time was to provide the title of the work, and a description. This latter had to be printed, a task probably done by Grandin when Smith went to Palmyra to secure a printer. This accords with Smith's timeline. Once it was printed, Smith's contribution to the task of getting a copyright was done. Someone else, possibly Samuel or a Whitmer, undertook the trip to Utica, NY, with this printed copyright text and money for the fee. It was not required to submit the manuscript. The description submitted, which appears on the copyright document, is the same as the description that has always appeared on the title page of the published editions. The copyright was signed by R. R. Lansing, Clerk of the United States District Court, in Utica, for the Northern District of New York.[490]

Smith claimed that the title page text was "a literal translation, taken from the very last leaf, on the left hand side of the collection or book of plates…"[491] If the designation "left side" refers to its location when the last plate had been turned, i.e. the verso side, then it indicates that he visualized the plates, bound with rings, to turn from right to left like an English book, which would normally mean that he saw reformed Egyptian as being written from left to right. This is not impossible. Egyptians could write whichever way, including boustrophedon texts.

With the translation of ms$\mathcal{U}$ all but completed, Smith approached E. B. Grandin to publish the *Book of Mormon*. We learn from the printer/typesetter John H. Gilbert that Grandin press accepted only on their

---

[488] Smith, 1839 History, in Jessee, *Papers of Joseph Smith*, I:293-4; and in Vogel, *Early Mormon Documents*, I:79-80.

[489] Lucy Smith in Anderson, *Lucy's Book*, 450.

[490] Vogel, *Early Mormon Documents* (Salt Lake City: Signature Books, 2000), III:462-3.

[491] Smith, 1839 History, in Vogel, *Early Mormon Documents*, I:91.

second application.[492] On 26 June, Grandin published in the *Wayne Sentinel* a somewhat scornful account of the gold bible, and, *à contre cœur*, the copyright text. He did not say that Grandin Press would be the publisher.[493] This reflects the fact that all that Grandin had seen was those few first pages of ms$\mathcal{O}$. The first 24 pages of ms$\mathcal{P}$ (25 printed pages of 1 Nephi) were delivered to the printer, John H. Gilbert, who wrote that the printing was begun in August and completed in March, 1830.[494] Twenty-four pages are six sheets, folded in half to form gatherings (the equivalent of book signatures).

This completion date is further buttressed by a revelation dated June 1829 stating, "and he [Smith] has translated the book." (D&C 17:6) This is the revelation given just prior to the event of the three witnesses, which is just before Smith's trip to Palmyra to arrange for printing, and get the text printed for the copyright. Note too that Lucy Smith wrote that at the completion of the translation, the whole team had a completion celebration at Waterloo (Fayette). One can imagine that a libation or two was poured on that occasion; Joe Sr. is reported to have been a bit if a bibber. On that occasion, they also read some passages.[495] Her account also agrees with her son's timeline, since she indicated that the copyright was received after that. Smith's timeline indicates that after the trip to Palmyra, they focused more and more on proselyting.

The apparent discrepancy between David Whitmer's June dates, placing the translation completion closer to the end of June, and the completion date of Joseph and Lucy Smith placing the completion prior to the issuance of the copyright, is best understood by consulting the text of the copyright. This indicates that there would be two histories in the same volume, Mormon's abridgment of the records of the Nephites (viz the *Book of Mormon*), and Moroni's abridgment of the plates of Ether, i.e. the history of the Jaredites [the *Book of Ether*]. Smith was referring to the completion of Mormon's abridgment, the *Book of Mormon* proper, at which point Ether may have been still a work in progress. Whitmer's

---

[492] John H. Gilbert, "Memorandum, made by John H. Gilbert Esq., Sept 8th, 1892, Palmyra, N. Y.," Palmyra King's Daughters Free Library, Palmyra, NY; Vogel, *Early Mormon Documents*, II:542-8. It is in Wilfred C. Wood, *Joseph Smith Begins His Work. Book of Mormon 1830 First Edition, Reproduced from Uncut Sheets* (Salt Lake City: Deseret News Press, 1958).

[493] Dan Vogel, *Joseph Smith*, 469.

[494] John H. Gilbert, "Memorandum.

[495] Lucy Harris, Lucy's Book, 451-52.

dates refer to the completion of the text in his copy of the BoM that he had carried to Missouri, and the text in what he mistakenly thought was the original manuscript; actually it was the printer's manuscript. In other words, Whitmer included Ether, while Smith did not.

It is now that we encounter two very interesting phenomena. First, Smith had begun his career as a modern-day Moses with the first of his officially dated recorded revelations in July 1828. From February 1829 there ensued a flurry of recorded revelations, ending with the last one of 1829, dated in June.[496] With regard to recorded revelations, from July 1829 to March 1830, for eight months, silence reigned supreme. Second, Lucy reports that after the witnesses had viewed the plates, the contract was signed with Grandin Press and the copyright was received. She then skips to her son's return to Pennsylvania.[497] In a letter to Cowdery he wrote that he arrived in Harmony on 4 October 1829.[498] For three months, July-September, the translator and his scribe went off the radar.

It was apparently after closing up shop in Waterloo that Smith decided that it was necessary to produce an even cleaner copy of ms$O$, which was replacing ms$U$ and was being presented to the world as the "original" written by Cowdery while Smith dictated. This second copy would become ms$P$, the (new) printer's copy, which could also serve as a backup. He clearly remembered the fate of the purloined 116 pages. *Once bitten, twice shy.*

During these ninety days after the celebration party, Smith and Cowdery continued to copy U into O. This copy work was cut in half by two working on it. Smith would study through the next group of words and phrases in the edited mess, and dictate a brief passage as edited. Cowdery would write it. While he wrote, Smith would be figuring out in his mind the next group of words and phrases, and when Cowdery was ready he dictated that bit. If Cowdery were working alone, he would have had to do Smith's bit before writing. Working together, Cowdery wrote more or less nonstop. The principal obstacle to completing ms$O$ was the

---

[496] There are indications that Smith did claim to have had operational revelations that have never been printed. Lucy wrote that he received a commandment regarding the preparation of ms$P$ and associated issues. Lucy Smith, in Anderson, *Lucy's Book*, 459. Possibly in January of 1830 it appears that Smith claimed a revelation that the copyright could be sold in Canada for a large sum. See Marquardt, *Rise of Mormonism*, 93-94.

[497] *Ibid*, 451-59.

[498] Joseph Smith's letter to Oliver Cowdery of 22 October 1829, in the LDS Church Archives, reproduced in Vogel, *Early Mormon Documents*, I:7.

need now for Cowdery to work alone on copying it into ms𝒫 to get the first gathering, 24 pages, to the printer by late August.

Obviously there had been a sense of urgency to get the text done, as is seen by the fact that the period from Christ's departure, about year 34, to when Moroni buried the plates, about 421, was covered in only thirty-nine pages. This is only 8% of the BoM text (not counting the Jaredite account) to cover almost 40% of the *Book of Mormon* (Nephite) time span. This same period also has fewer people in the chain of transmission of Nephite records, i.e. the number of generations, thereby requiring radically longer generation spans, again showing haste. Likewise, few new personal and city names are introduced. A likely source of this urgency was largely to get on with the next stage of the project, i.e. the establishment of the Church. They may also have had some fear of getting behind the printer's schedule, even though printing was at that time slow, as we see in a letter from Cowdery to Smith dated 6 November 1829 when he wrote, "the printing goes rather slow yet as the type founder has been sick but we expect that the type will be in…"[499] Given Grandin's lack of sufficient type, it is probable that Cowdery did not have to provide the second gathering of ms𝒫 prior to mid October.

Apostle Cowdery's Revelation: Smith Is Just Primus inter Pares?

Sometime in mid 1829 Cowdery penned "A commandment from God unto Oliver [Cowdery] how he should build up his church & the manner thereof." He referred to it as the Articles of the Church of Christ. This and other Church history documents came into the possession of apostate elder Simonds Ryder, and were eventually donated to the Church by the Ryder family.[500]

The text is a collage of Church organization texts found in other LDS scriptures. It bears no specific date other than 1829. The phrase the "Church of Christ" occurs in Mosiah 18:17; 3 Nephi 26:21, 28:23; 4 Nephi 1:1, 26, 29; and Moroni 6:4. Around 70% of the text consists of passages found in 3 Nephi, Moroni and D&C 18. Some of these were relevant prior to the organization of the Church: a call to the world to repent (D&C 18:6, 9); procedures and the prayer for baptism (3 Nephi 11:23-27); the BoM

---

[499] Vogel, *Early Mormon Documents*, II:405-06.
[500] Scott H. Faulring, "An Examination of the 1829 Articles of the Church of Christ in Relation to Section 20 of the Doctrine and Covenants," in BYU Studies Quarterly, 43:4, p. 57.

monotheistic Trinity (3 Nephi 11:27), and that only the name of Jesus Christ can save (2 Nephi 25:20; 31:21; D&C 18:23-25). Others would be applicable (or more relevant) after Church organization: the procedures and prayer to ordain priests and teachers (Moroni 3:2-4); the procedures and blessing for the bread (Moroni 4:2-3); the procedures and blessing for the wine (Moroni 5:1-2); the order to not administer the sacrament to the unworthy, but to minister unto them (3 Nephi 18:28-33), frequent church meetings (3 Nephi 18:22); and speaking one to another regarding one's spiritual progress (Moroni 6:5). For example, the sacrament was first administered when the Church was established on April 6, 1830 (DHC 1:61-62).

Some LDS and even secular scholars have regarded this to be a Cowdery plagiarism. He simply rounded up all of these passages, cobbled them together, and attempted to foist them off as his own revelation.[501] This view gives us a simplistic, even a somewhat comical image of Cowdery the man. *Did he think that no one would notice?*

| *Vignette* | **Apostle Cowdery vs Moses Smith** |

In April of 1829 Cowdery managed to get a revelation through Smith making him cotranslator (coauthor; D&C 6). Smith quickly reversed himself, and reduced his ambitious collaborator to just a scribe (D&C 9). The two men were testing against each other regarding their authority in Church organization.

Smith was the self-styled prophet like unto Moses. As he emulated this OT hero, he too had to produce a book of the law given to his latter-day Israel.

At first, it was Cowdery who would essay to be a redactor by the command of God of a three-page work that he called the Articles of the Church of Christ. It was included in the earliest extant collection of revelations (Revelation Book 1). At some point, a postscript, or manifesto, was appended reading: "& now Ɨ if I have not authority to write these things Judge ye Behold ye shall know that I have authority when you & I shall be brought to stand before the Judgement seat of Christ now may the grace of God the Father & our Lord Jesus Christ be & abide with you all & finally save you eternally in his Kingdom through the infinite atonement which is in Jesus Christ amen Behold I am Oliver I am an Apostle of Jesus Christ by the will of God the Father & the Lord Jesus Christ Behold I have written the things which he hath commanded me for behold his word was unto me as a burning fire shut up in my bones & I was weary with forbearing & I could forbear no longer Amen—[cf. Jeremiah 20:9] Written in the yea[r] of our Lord & Saviour 1829——A true copy of the articles of the Church of Christ &c" The document is in Oliver Cowdery's hand.

---

[501] For a secular view quite different from my own, see Vogel, *Joseph Smith*, 406-7; Vogel, *Early Mormon Documents*, II:409-12.

Revelation Book 1, which is titled at the head of the first page: "A Book of Commandments and Revelations," is the earliest known collection, a precursor to the *Book of Commandments*, which would be supplanted by the 1835 edition of the *Doctrine and Covenants*. This initial collection was done largely by John Whitmer, with some Cowdery involvement.

Being thus assured that this Articles document was a true copy, one wonders how many other copies were made, and for what purpose? In E. B. Howe's *Mormonism Unvailed*, part of this postscript was quoted from Ezra Booth, another apostate elder, and a friend of Ryder. He may have had access to Ryder's copy.[502] Otherwise his would be yet a fourth copy. It seems that copies may have been made for elders as a sort of reference for performing the LDS ordinances.

A characterization of Articles, as a draft, can be found in the *Encyclopedia of Latter-day Saint History*, which states that "it appears from Cowdery's draft that Joseph Smith and Oliver Cowdery were formulating the documents [sections 20 & 22] throughout 1829."[503] In fact, Cowdery himself dated it succinctly: "in the yea[r] of our Lord & Saviour 1829."

Cowdery was not alone in thinking that apostles could receive revelation. Scribe William E. McLellin wrote: "I, as scribe, have written revelations from the mouth of both the Revelators, Joseph Smith and David Whitmer."

Initially, Smith's status among the founders was rooted in his person, as BoM translator and seer. The establishment of the Church would raise issues of the relationship between it and each believer's God. Cowdery and the Whitmers were suspicious of church organization, and saw the believer as answering directly to his or her Maker. This was to change in D&C 20:37, which required an applicant for baptism to "witness before the church" and pass a test of faith. Cowdery, initially supported by the Whitmers in Fayette, upbraided Smith sharply: "I command you in the name of God to erase those words that no priestcraft be amongst us." (JSH 1839, v. Vogel I:128) Smith asked him, "by what authority he took upon him to command me to alter, or erase, to add or diminish to or from a revelation or commandment from Almighty God."

The Smith/Cowdery relationship evolved in sacred writ. In D&C 18:9 the Lord says to Cowdery and Whitmer, "I speak unto you, even as unto Paul mine apostle, for you are called even with that same calling with which he was called." D&C 20:2-3, an overtly collaborative work that further elaborated aspects of the organization of the Church, comprises commandments "given to Joseph the seer who was called of God & ordained an Apostle of Jesus Christ an Elder of the Church & also to Oliver who was also called of God an Apostle of

---

[502] Howe, 303-04; Vogel, *Early Mormon Documents*, II:412.

[503] Arnold K. Garr, Donald Q. Cannon & Richard O. Cowan, "Articles and Covenants, The," *Encyclopedia of Latter-Day Saint History* (Salt Lake City: Deseret Book Company, 2000), 52.

Jesus Christ an Elder of the Church & ordained under his hand." Although this already gave pride of place to Smith over Cowdery, he was not satisfied with it. In the D&C version, Smith's, designation as "an elder" was changed to "the first elder," and Cowdery was changed to "the second elder."

We cannot know to what extent Cowdery continued to assert himself, but his defiant postscript must have been in reply to serious opposition, possibly on the part of Smith, who decided to further clarify and assert his status.

In D&C 28:2, the Lord admonishes Oliver Cowdery, saying: "no one shall be appointed to receive commandments and revelations in this church excepting my servant Joseph Smith, Jun., for he receiveth them even as Moses."

After the organization of the Church, Oliver Cowdery and David Whitmer were sent off to Missouri, to take the gospel to the Lamanites, and to take the first steps in the establishment of Zion. In the process, at Kirtland OH, they contributed to the recruitment of Parley P. Pratt and Sydney Rigdon, who would become the nemeses of these two partners of the original trio. Having them largely sidelined, Smith began work with a new team, and took the LDS faith in new and radically different directions.

What we know regarding Articles: 1) Cowdery writes that the Lord said "write the words which I shall command you concerning my Church." 2) Cowdery titles his work "Articles of the Church of Christ." 3) It contains the ordinance for baptism as found in 3 Nephi, and the ordinances for blessing the bread, blessing the wine, and ordaining priests and teachers as found in Moroni. 4) The bestowal of the Gift of the Holy Ghost is absent. 5) There is no mention of the ordinance to ordain elders, or to bestow the Melchizedek priesthood. 6) Smith, Cowdery & Whitmer relationship: see D&C 17, 18:4, 6 &9. 7) The ordinance for baptism is found in 3 Nephi without explanatory quotes. 8) The ordinance to ordain priests and teachers is found in Moroni without explanatory quotes. 9) The ordinances to bless the bread and wine are found in Moroni without explanatory quotes. 10) The requirement to assure the worthiness of participants to partake of the bread and wine, and to be baptized, are found in 3 Nephi 18:28-33. 11) The requirement to meet together often and to encourage each other's spiritual progress is found in paraphrase format in 3 Nephi 18:22 and Moroni 6:5. 12) The requirement to take upon oneself the name of Christ is found in D&C 18:23-25. 13) The commandment to live a sinless life is found in D&C 18:31. 14) We are assured that these words are of the Lord Jesus Christ, in D&C 18:34, 47. 15) At some point, Cowdery added a defiant postscript (v. *supra*). 15) The terminus ad quem for the innovation of the ordinance for the bestowal of the Gift of the Holy Ghost by laying on of hands is when Moroni was sent to the printer.

What we do not know: 1) We do not know when Cowdery added his postscript. 2) We do not know the meaning of "the things which you have written" in D&C 18:2. Possibilities include the whole BoM to date, the ordinance material in the BoM, the draft for Church establishment materials, or a draft of Articles as a resource for those building the Church in the field. 3) We do not know when the founding elders of the Church decided that the Gift of the Holy Ghost should be bestowed by the laying on of hands, rather than by a temporally proximate descent from heaven as happened with Jesus. 4) We do not know when it was decided that Church establishment material, including ordinances, should appear in the BoM rather than in latter-day revelations. In particular, we do not know why the prayers to bless the bread and wine were not inserted in 3 Nephi, where this is first mentioned, where it is highly relevant to Jesus' visit, and the commandment that none should partake unworthily.

In the view of many, D&C 18:2-5 *infra* refers to the church establishment materials in the BoM and D&C 18 and 20. They are "the things which you have written". The words "the foundation of my church, my gospel, and my rock" are found in Articles. The words "in them are all things written concerning the foundation of my church" (v. 4) cannot be comprehensive, since they fail to include the essential ordination for the Melchizedek priesthood and elders. They could well refer solely to the entire BoM through Mormon. "The establishment of my church" could have initially referred to just getting the Church legally organized in June, 1830, and not everything that would come through Smith's career.

Cowdery's Articles is a well-framed and properly written document. Even though *whoso* and *whosoever* both occur (one time each), *therefore* occurs twice, and both were originally *wherefore* and were changed to *therefore*. Accordingly, *wherefore* does not occur. Apart from a possible typo or coining of the word *covetiousness*, there is no misspelled word. By contrast, Smith in his 1832 history was even then unable to write a paragraph without several misspelled words. Since there are only two candidates, I have no hesitation accepting the authorship as Cowdery's.

D&C 20 seems to have been a work in progress from perhaps May 1829 to the end of the year, at least. The prefatory comment in the 2013 edition states: "Revelation on Church organization and government... Portions of this revelation may have been given as early as summer 1829." The complete revelation, known at the time as the Articles and Covenants, was likely recorded soon after April 6, 1830 (the day the Church was organized). The Prophet wrote, "We obtained of Him [Jesus Christ] the following, by the spirit of prophecy and revelation; which not only gave us much information, but also pointed out to us the precise day upon which, according to His will and commandment, we should proceed to organize His Church once more here upon the earth." Prior to the organization of the Church, the only Church ordinance in practice was baptism. The Lord's Supper (sacrament), the ordination of priests and teachers and the bestowal of the Gift of the Holy Ghost by the laying on of hands would be administered only after the official organization.

Cowdery's view of the true church (and that of the Whitmers) was apostolical, to wit, based on the authority of apostles. Of the Twelve Apostles, only Matthew makes Peter the rock upon which Jesus would build his church.(16:18) Among the Twelve, there was no papal figure, not even James the brother of Jesus who may have headed the Jerusalem church. The Gospels now in the canonical NT are attributed to four different apostles. With the church prior to "the great apostasy" as his model, Cowdery felt he had every right to be a revelator equal to Smith. If one could be like unto Moses, who alone received revelation for Israel, the other could be like unto Paul.

Smith responded to his colleague's use of the title "apostle" by extending it to David Whitmer as well, and putting them in charge of selecting the twelve, making it clear that they would be but two of a number of apostles. Although this commission may have already been included in what was to become D&C 18 as early as June 1829, at the time of the Church's first conference of June 9 1830, they had not yet made their selection. Quinn writes, "Eight days before the church's organization, evangelical preacher David Marks met the Whitmer witnesses to the *Book of Mormon* who 'further stated, that twelve apostles were to be appointed, who would soon confirm their mission by miracles.'"[504] At the time of this first conference, five had been specifically called apostles, Joseph Smith, Oliver Cowdery, David Whitmer, John Whitmer and Ziba Peterson. It seems clear that two others, Peter Whitmer and Samuel H. Smith, had the designation "apostle" included in their elder license.[505] The title was loosely used for other, charismatic apostles, and even evangelical apostles (missionaries). In 1835 Smith instructed the three witnesses (thereby adding Martin Harris) to select the Quorum of the Twelve. The selection did not include Joseph Smith, nor the three witnesses. The only Smith was

---

[504] Quinn, *The Mormon Hierarchy: Origins of Power* (Salt Lake City: Signature Books, 1994), 11. His source is David Marks statement, 29 Mar. 1830, in his *The Life of David Marks, To the 26th Year of His Age* (Limerick, ME: Office of the Morning Star, 1831), 340.

[505] Ibid, 11-13.

William. Since in June 1829 the Church was not even in existence, Smith's commission to Cowdery and Whitmer may have been primarily to indicate what was to come, and even Cowdery might have begun to wonder if it would be wise for every apostle, once selected, to be able to receive revelation for the Church just because he was an apostle.

One of the most basic cleavages in early Mormon practice was this conflict between Smith's tendency towards theocratic hierarchy on the one hand, and opposition to it by Cowdery, the Whitmers and their supporters. This conflict festered at first, but came to a head when these two were excommunicated, Rigdon's Salt Sermon was pronounced and they fled for their lives. That Cowdery's Articles of the Church of Christ played a role in the early period of this development can be seen by the fact that very late in 1833 or in 1834, LDS dissident Ezra Booth sent a letter to Eber D. Howe quoting from Cowdery's fiery defence of his authority to write his revelation.[506] At least to some degree, its text was in circulation, and now at least, armed with Cowdery's fiery declaration of authority. Perhaps this is why the extant text assures that it is a true copy. There may have been others.

Contentwise, the Articles of the Church of Christ may well have been intended to become nothing more than a convenient reference for those officiating in the Church, particularly elders, to have at hand the procedures and words to perform the principal ordinances of the new Church, once established. If so, its date may be somewhat later in 1829, in preparation for the establishment on April 6.

The Ordinances in Sacred Writ

Although there is a lot of "Thou shalt" and "Thou shalt not" in the Torah (the Pentateuch or Law of Moses), we do not find ordinance procedures spelled out, with what to do and what to say. Nor do we find this in the period of the tabernacle in the wilderness, nor in the books of the judges, nor even in the books of the prophets in the era of the first temple. When the authors of the BoM took the Bible as their model for how a new bible should look, it was natural for the ordinances of the Church to be absent. They could come later, as needed, probably in latter-day revelation.

This began to change when Smith and Cowdery became concerned with their own baptism, circa mid May. The result was the instructions for the ordinance of baptism in 3 Nephi. The established churches had

---

[506] Howe, *Mormonism Unvailed*, 303-04.

positions, rites and ordinances outlined. Converts might have expected no less in the Church of Christ.

It might have been appropriate for baptism and the ordinance for the gift of the Holy Ghost to co-occur with that for baptism, since these two are always paired. But this was not the case. Although the *Book of Mormon*, prior to Moroni, has 78 mentions of the Holy Ghost, the phrase "the gift of the Holy Ghost" occurs only three times, in 2 Nephi 28:26, Jacob 6:8 and Alma 9:2. It is important to note that the BoM, prior to Moroni but including 3 Nephi, treats the gift of the Holy Ghost as being a concomitant supplement to the baptism ordinance, a bit as it was in Jesus' case (referred to by Nephi[507]). Here we see the Nephite practice. In the original BoM (i.e. through Mormon):

> And it came to pass when they were all baptized and had come up out of the water, the Holy Ghost did fall upon them, and they were filled with the Holy Ghost and with fire. (3 Nephi 19:13)

Before Moroni, the BoM never mentions it as a separate ordinance by the laying on of hands. This is only found in Moroni in this full format. (2:2-3) But the gift of the Holy Ghost is also conspicuously absent from Articles. At the time of Articles' latest text, the Holy Ghost was thought to "fall upon" the person being baptized at the time of baptism, without a special ordinance, without the laying on of hands. For this reason, it was not possible to include a special ordinance for it. Moroni therefore seems to represent an instance of institutional innovation that is later than that in Articles.

Other ordinances that might have been appropriate in 3 Nephi are those for the Lord's supper, to bless the bread and wine. The idea that the basic ordinances should be in the new bible had not yet taken hold. Moreover, this ordinance would very closely follow the example of the last supper, found in Matthew (26:26), Mark (14:22) and Luke (22:19). At this point one may have felt that it would be inappropriate to try to improve on Jesus himself. The blessing for the bread and wine could easily follow this gospel model.

---

[507] 1 Nephi 11:27. See also 2 Nephi 31:8, 13-14; 3 Nephi 12:1, 18:37; 19:13; 26:17; Alma 6:1 & 9:21.

The Moroni Addition

The angel who delivered the gold plates to Smith was originally simply called a messenger, but eventually acquired the name Moroni, by the time of the copyright text, dated June 11, 1829. Even though the Book of Moroni mentions sealing them up (10:2), it does not mention hiding them up. However, both are mentioned in Ether. (See supra, p 473)

Somehow, this person had to be in possession of the gold plates to seal them, hide them up and reveal them to Smith. But the plates were in the possession of his father, Mormon. The *Book of Mormon* was just what the title says; early on it was envisaged that his own record, the "Book [record] of Mormon", would complete his abridgment of the record of the Nephites. In order to make it the last book of the overall work, and yet end up in the charge of his son, this great Nephite general and prophet was unexpectedly made to fall under the sword of the Lamanites. At this point, all prior BoM usage would lead us to expect the words "I Moroni, having received the sacred records of my father, shall proceed to engrave the account of the destruction of my people." (v. *supra* p 522) If in June of 1829 there was any plan for there to be a Book of Moroni, this would have been the moment for its inception. The course actually taken was to have Moroni write the completion of his father's record, thereby enabling that book to end the *Book of Mormon*, while at the same time enabling Moroni to seal the plates and hide them up.

With the printing nearing completion, it was belatedly decided that some church establishment material should be included in the new bible, which then could only be done by adding an additional book, even if it meant incongruously sandwiching a totally separate book, the record of the Jaredites, into the record of the Nephites. The copyright document clearly indicates that the *Book of Mormon* was to be two works published as companion works in one volume (v. p. 409).

When Gilbert worked to set the type for a gathering of ms$P$, he occasionally made *compositor's marks*, such as capitalization and punctuation. In addition, he made take marks, a sort of check mark to indicate where a stick of type left off so he could begin his next stick at that point. More rarely, he even cut pages apart to facilitate his work.

Skousen has informed us that four gatherings of P, numbers 16 through 19, lack all of these marks and cuts. The puzzle thickens when we learn that these marks are present on gatherings 14 through 16 of ms$O$. There is no evidence that Gilbert ever saw ms$P$ gatherings 16-19. Because some corresponding ms𝒪 gatherings do bear his marks, it is clear that they were provided to him instead of ms𝒫.

Skousen's explanation for this is that Cowdery had fallen behind in copying 𝒪 into 𝒫. His solution was a division of labor. Beginning with 3 Nephi 19:25 (just after the beginning of gathering 18), scribe number two copied ms𝒪 gatherings into 𝒫 as they came back from the printer. Thus freed up, Cowdery jumped ahead to copy Ether into 𝒫 beginning on the first page of a new gathering, number 20.

This is appropriate since *The Book of Ether* is an independent work. Mormon ends on the last page of ms𝒫 gathering 19, where it occupies only eleven lines. The remainder of the page (27 lines) was left *a blank gap*. This had never happened between books prior to this point. It is appropriate here because Mormon was the end of the *Book of Mormon*.[508] Gathering 20 seems to have been calculated to be sufficient for the Book of Ether, but it was not, and its last 18 verses had to begin gathering 21. These filled the first page and Moroni began at the top of page two. This explanation is perfect from the LDS perspective, which imposes the constraint of the traditional book sequence with Moroni at the end.

Table 68. 𝒪 Gatherings 13 through 18 & 𝒫 Gatherings 15 through 21[509]

BoM references follow the current LDS chapter-verse system. The segments are based on substantial albeit fragmentary evidence. Fragments are in curly brackets. (G = gathering, using Skousen's numbers, referenced *infra*. S = *scribe*.)					
G	S	BoM References	G	S	BoM References
13𝒪	C	Alma 61:11 –Helaman 13:36	15𝒫	?	Helaman 1:29–13:18
Ms𝒪 gatherings 14 through 16 were used by Gilbert to set type. Compositor marks appear in gatherings 14 & 16. MsP gatherings 16 through 19 were never seen by Gilbert. They totally lack compositor marks. The unknown scribe took over from Cowdery at 3 Nephi 19:21, & continued to the end of Mormon.					
14𝒪	C	{Helaman 13:36–3 Nephi 4:2}	16𝒫	C	Helaman 13:18–3 Nephi 11:8
15𝒪	C	3 Nephi 4:3–19:19	17𝒫	C	3 Nephi 11:8–18:30
16𝒪	C	{3 Nephi 19:26–27:7}	18𝒫	?	3 Nephi 18:30–Mormon 3:1
		Mormon in 16𝒪	19𝒫	?	Mormon 3:1–9:37
17𝒪	C	{Ether 3:9 to 15:17}	20𝒫	C	Ether 1–15:16
Because Cowdery did 20𝒫 (Ether), he must have had 17𝒪, not Gilbert.					

---

[508] Skousen, *Printer's Manuscript*, I:46. For photos of ms𝒫, see Ronald K. Esplin & Matthew J. Grow, gen. eds., *The Joseph Smith Papers*, vol. 3, pt. 2 (Salt Lake City: The Church Historian's Press, 2015).

[509] Skousen, *The Original Manuscript*: 14, 35-36; *The Printer's Manuscript*, I:9-10, 32-33.

18𝒪	C	? – end		21𝒫	Ether 15:16–Moroni 10:34

Mormon would mostly probably have ended in ms𝒪 16, thereby ending the *Book of Mormon*. If so, Ether would have begun a fresh gathering (ms𝒪 17) as an independent work. Skousen postulates the existence of ms𝒪 18 for Moroni, although no part of this gathering is extant. He estimates that it had six pages. In ms𝒫, Moroni occupies ten pages.

Because 19𝒫 (Mormon) has no compositor marks, clearly 16𝒪 (Mormon) was used. Because 20𝒫 (Ether) does have compositor marks throughout (beginning with Ether 1:1), clearly it was used instead. 17𝒪 contains mostly Ether and must have been in Cowdery's possession for him to prepare 20𝒫 (Ether). This implies that Mormon was concluded at the end of 16𝒪. If so, then in ms𝒪, Ether began a new gathering, just as it did in ms𝒫. Skousen postulates an additional gathering, 18𝒪, to accommodate Moroni, should it have already existed this early, although no part of this gathering is extant. When Cowdery jumped forward to copy Ether, if Moroni already existed, he could have jumped forward to it instead, to complete the *Book of Mormon* properly, copying Moroni on the last page of Mormon, before beginning a totally different work (i.e. Ether). He could not do so if Moroni was still being composed. This is a view that is fully consistent with the evidence.

The far more normal sequence would be for the *Book of Mormon* to be completed before Ether, a separate record of a different people. This would have been in accordance with the text of the copyright submission of June 11, which has subsequently appeared on the BoM title page. Ether is listed separately, even at the head of the second paragraph. It is highly incongruous for the Jaredite record to be sandwiched in between two books of the Nephite record. (See page 409 for the copyright text.)

After all, one does not sandwich the New Testament in between OT Zechariah and Malachi.

Cowdery could well have fallen behind in copying. Just as Smith had to return to Harmony to provide for his family, Cowdery too had to make a living. We have almost no information on what he did. It is possible that Grandin Press was in need of assistance. Lucy Smith wrote that at the time that "rabble, and a party of restless religionists" met to oppose work on the new bible, "Oliver and a young man by the name of Robinson were printing…"[510] We recall that in December 1829 he wrote to Smith, "it may look rather strange to you to find that I have so soon become a printer and

---

[510] Lucy Smith, in Anderson, *Lucy's Book*, 460.

you may cast in your mind what I shall become next."[511] Several years later he worked as a printer and was able to take on an apprentice. Perhaps this work slowed down his copying.

The foregoing textual evidence has to be analyzed in the context of the BoM narrative.

Clearly, the authors did not plan on Moroni recording very much of the Nephite record. It is the *Book of Mormon*, after all. When he took over briefly as a recordkeeper, referring to things his deceased father had written, he complained, "I would write it also if I had room upon the plates, but I have not; and ore [gold] I have none." (Mormon 8:5) Note that Mormon had taken all the records of the Nephites, plus those of Jared with their translation, plus the relics, from the hill Shim about 375 CE, and was killed in 400 CE. For all of this period he was the commander of all of the Nephite forces as they were driven from there to Cumorah, when, after a prolonged military retreat with occasional pitched battles, the Nephites suffered their final defeat. Remarkably, it is during this time that he did his entire share of the BoM narrative, from Lehi and Words of Mormon to Mormon 7:10. One can understand that the BoM authors would not also have had him abridge the plates of Jared. Rather, this was assigned to Moroni. We have to assume that he had calculated that there was still enough room on the gold plates for that.

The text of the end of Mormon, Chapter 9, clearly ends the *Book of Mormon*:

> 35. And these things are written that we may rid our garments of the blood of our brethren, who have dwindled in unbelief.
>
> 36. And behold, these things which we have desired concerning our brethren, yea, even their restoration to the knowledge of Christ, are according to the prayers of all the saints who have dwelt in the land.
>
> 37. And may the Lord Jesus Christ grant that their prayers may be answered according to their faith; and may God the Father remember the covenant which he hath made with the house of Israel; and may he bless them forever, through faith on the name of Jesus Christ. Amen.

It is accordingly late in the Jaredite narrative that we find Moroni's personal farewell speech to both the gentiles and his own people. He begins, "And now I, Moroni, bid farewell unto the Gentiles, yea, and also unto my brethren whom I love, until we shall meet before the judgment-seat of Christ..." (Ether 12:38)

---

[511] Oliver Cowdery, letter to Joseph Smith dated 28/12/1829, in Vogel, *Early Mormon Documents*, II:407

The BoM authors were well aware that Moroni had signed off, twice, when they decided to add an additional book to their work, and penned the first verse of Moroni. Although Moroni is portrayed as feeling awkward about this, his statements are crafted in view of possible reactions on the part of the reader.

> Now I, Moroni, after having made an end of abridging the account of the people of Jared, I had supposed not to have written more. (1:1)

He repeats,

> Wherefore, I write a few more things, contrary to that which I had supposed; for I had supposed not to have written any more. (1:4)

This evidence emphasizes that originally the *Book of Mormon* ended with Mormon. His death in 400 CE marked an even 1000 years after leaving Jerusalem in 600 BCE. This is the Nephite millennium. They intended the *Book of Ether* to be a separate record that would be a companion volume to the *Book of Mormon*. Then, as the completion of the printing was drawing nigh, they decided to add the Book of Moroni. But while it was still in the draft editorial stage, the printer finished Mormon. To avoid a delay it was necessary to provide him with gathering 20$\mathcal{P}$, Ether, unavoidably sandwiching it into the Nephite record.

Some ordinances would only be needed when the Church was actually established. It was decided to keep them all together in one tome, the *Book of Mormon*. Moroni has a lot in common with Words of Mormon. Each has a functional text that needed to be inserted, and each expanded it with additional material to disguise the real reason for the work. The second part of chapter one of the Mosiah draft was added to Words of Mormon, to disguise the real purpose of explaining the existence of the small plates of Nephi. In the case of Moroni, the functional material is the Church establishment verses, which needed to be expanded by the addition of three epistles of Mormon to his son, and then yet another farewell. Moroni specifically refers to his abridgment of Ether, indicating that he was following up on his Jaredite account. If Moroni had been completed by the end of summer, 1829, Moroni could have followed Mormon, and Cowdery's Articles, could have included an ordinance to bestow the gift of the Holy Ghost by the laying on of hands.

Getting the Job Done

From June on, events happened expeditiously. Martin Harris put up his farm as security for the contract with Grandin Press for publication. In a memorandum made by the printer and typesetter John H. Gilbert dated 8 September 1892 we read:

> When the printer was ready to commence work, Harris was notified, and Hyrum Smith brought the first installment of manuscript, of 24 pages, closely written on common foolscap paper—he had it under his vest, and coat closely buttoned over it...
>
> Martin Harris, Hyrum Smith and Oliver Cowdery were very frequent visitors to the office during the printing of the Mormon Bible.
>
> Names of persons and places were generally capitalized, but sentences had no end. The character for short &, was used almost invariably where the word and occurred, except at the end of a chapter. I punctuated it to make it read as I supposed the Author intended, but very little punctuation was altered. ...
>
> The work was commenced in August 1829, and finished in March 1830,— seven months...[512]

Steven Harding also reported on Smith's visit to the printer, placing him in Manchester in August.[513]

Meanwhile, in Palmyra, Abner Cole, the editor of *The Reflector*, was using Grandin press nights to print his paper. This gave him access to the printed pages of the BoM text printed so far. Around late December he promised his readers that his newspaper would print the new Gold Bible, giving them the chance to read some of it without buying a copy, and thereby avoiding putting money into the Smiths' coffers. On 2 January he published 1 Nephi 1:1-2:3. Two more installments appeared, on the 13th and 22nd. It is generally thought that Joseph Jr.'s return was delayed so that he could appear in court on 19 January regarding a debt owed to Lemuel Durfee.[514] If Smith departed Harmony the next day, he could have arrived at Manchester on 24 January. Apparently he was in Manchester in early February respecting a revelation to sell his Canadian rights to his copyright

---

[512] Gilbert, "Memorandum."

[513] Steven S. Harding, statement to Thomas Gregg, in Vogel, *Early Mormon Documents*, III:161.

[514] "Nathan Pierce Docket Book," in Vogel, *Early Mormon Documents*, III:491.

in Kingston, Ontario, Canada. This failed, but Whitmer recalled that Smith was in Manchester when the party arrived back. These events brought Smith back in touch with Cowdery, and at that time they could have arrived at agreement re the last book of the BoM, i.e. Moroni.

On 19 March 1830, the *Wayne Sentinel* announced that the BoM would be available the following week. It later confirmed that it was available at Palmyra's bookstore on 26 March. An old friend, Joseph Knight Sr. picked up Joseph Smith Jr. from Manchester to take him to Palmyra. Some books were ready but most still needed to be bound.[515] This segment of Joseph Smith's career was finished, and the business of building a community of believers was to begin.

The *Book of Mormon* has won a place in the history of the United States of America. It not only served well as a platform for a new world religion, but has been the backbone of its sustainability over time. Its community of believers went on to play an important role in settling the American West.

<hr>

[515] Vogel, *Joseph Smith*, 486.

< Chapter 30 >

Smith's "To Be" List, the Temple Text & the Converts

Long before having begun ms𝒫, Joseph Smith had assembled an all-star Biblical lineup to launch his career. His playbill left no room for doubt that God had saved the best for the last act. Now he must play to an enthusiastic house filling up with converts.

Agenda: Smith's "To be" list

He is that great seer, Joseph son of Joseph, foretold of old by that Joseph who was sold into Egypt, he who predicted the coming of a prophet like unto Moses. He is the High Priest after the order of Melchizedek, sent to prepare the restoration of all things for the advent of the Kingdom of the Redeemer.

Table 69. Origins of Joseph Smith's Authority

1829
But a seer will I raise up out of the fruit of thy loins; and unto him will I give power to bring forth my word unto the seed of thy loins (2 Nephi 3:11) [Words of Joseph son of Jacob, revealed in Lehi's blessing to his son Joseph].
• his name [0f "that seer," i.e. Joseph Smith] shall be called after me [Joseph, son of Jacob]; and it shall be after the name of his father [Joseph Smith Sr.]. And he shall be like unto me. (2 Nephi 3:15)
•And he shall be great like unto Moses (2 Nephi 3:9)
•Melchizedek, who was also a high priest after this same order...who also took upon him the high priesthood forever...
It was this same Melchizedek to whom Abraham paid tithes (Alma 13:14-15; cf. Genesis 14:17-20 & Psalms 110:4)
•And the Lord said: I will prepare unto my servant Gazelem, a stone, which shall shine forth in darkness unto light (Alma 37:23)
1835
• the duty of the President of the office of the High Priesthood is to preside over the whole church, and to be like unto Moses—(D&C 107:91)
•Behold, here is wisdom; yea, to be a seer, a revelator, a translator, and a prophet, having all the gifts of God which he bestows upon the head of the church. (D&C 107:92)

1841
> •...that my servant Hyrum may take the office of Priesthood and Patriarch, which was appointed unto him by his father, by blessing and also by right. (D&C 124:91)
>> •That from henceforth he shall hold the keys of the patriarchal blessings upon the heads of all my people (D&C 124:92)

1843
>> •I will give unto thee [Joseph Smith] the law of my Holy Priesthood, as was ordained by me and my Father before the world was. (D&C 132:28)
>> • Abraham received promises concerning his seed...from whose loins ye are, namely, my servant Joseph [Smith] (D&C 132:30)

It begins with the stick of Joseph in Ezekiel (37:15-17). The Old Testament is Judean, which the BoM identifies with the stick of Judah. In his blessing to his son Joseph, Lehi reveals the words of Joseph son of Jacob in the context of stressing that Lehi's group is descended from the tribe of Joseph. This ancient patriarch revealed that Joseph Smith has descended from his loins, and refers to him as a seer who will be great, like unto Moses. In Nephi, before the BoM was even published, the roles to which Smith aspired were given clear billing.

The BoM specifically linked only Joseph and Moses to Joseph Smith. In the D&C, blood descent from Abraham reaffirms the statement of Joseph son of Jacob, since the line of descent from Abraham would have to pass through him. Similarly, it is only in 1835 in the D&C that his priestly office reaches a pinnacle: the High Priest over the high priesthood according to the order of Melchizedek, to be "like unto Moses". The Abrahamic gift that Joseph did not appropriate to himself is the office of Church Patriarch, although it is kinship-based and so limited to males in the Smith family. The first Church Patriarch, Joseph Smith Sr., was followed by Hyrum (followed by William Smith, followed by John Smith). No comparable kinship tie is suggested with Moses or Melchizedek. The prediction makes it clear that he was chosen before his birth, and assures that he will magnify his calling. Smith Jr. aspired to be the culmination of all these great figures in the OT, having all of their authority and attributes.

Agenda: To Be Translator, Prophet, Seer, Revelator, High Priest

In March of 1829, Smith issued a self-imposed limitation on his powers, in which God addressed his gift to translate the gold plates, and said

> you have a gift to a translate the plates; and this is the first gift that I
> bestowed upon you; and I have commanded that you should pretend to no
> other gift until my purpose is fulfilled in this... (D&C 5:4)

An urgency was already developing to establish his true church and for the
Restoration of All Things. At the same time he understood that the chances
for success would be greatly enhanced if he undertook this ultimate project
with a handsomely bound copy of his new Nephite bible in hand. The gifts
that he associated with being a church-founding prophet would not be his
until then.

His eventual titles are often poorly defined, and definitions do at
times overlap. In general, a prophet tends to predict future events, but can
be used in the sense of a revelator of divine instructions, law or doctrine.
On some occasions, the revelation might express God's will for him
personally, while on other occasions, His will for instructions or law for
the Church. A seer is a person who sees with his spiritual eyes rather than
his natural (bodily) eyes. In this case, it is generally thought that spiritual
sight is superior (or more real) than natural vision. Moreover, a translator
is a seer. Smith's translation was done with a seer stone, so he was
claiming to receive the text by means of spiritual sight. In the case of the
first vision, and of the messenger guarding the gold plates, did the
instrumentality involve spiritual senses? It appears that the three and eight
witnesses had a spiritual experience, with spiritual senses, all the while
being willing to sign off on language implying bodily perception.

When predicting the coming of Joseph Smith in the latter days, the
BoM usually uses seer or prophet. As for which is higher:

> And Ammon said that a seer is a revelator and a prophet also; and a gift
> which is greater can no man have, except he should possess the power of
> God... (Mosiah 8:16)

This seems expected since scryer Smith was a proficient seerstone user.

Going beyond this, Smith began to consider himself to have a direct
blood lineage to Abraham the Patriarch.

Agenda: To Be High Priest, Church Font of All Priesthood

One usually associates the high priest with Melchizedek in both the OT,
and the BoM. Actually, the Hebrew text in Genesis is ambiguous regarding
just who paid tithing to whom (Abraham to Melchizedek, or vice versa).
Historical consensus has Abraham paying. For us, of greater interest is the
fact that Hyrum Smith had become a mason, where the office of high priest

is more similar to that office in early Mormon history, particularly with respect to the washing of the feet.[516] Joseph Smith had been restoring ancient scripture, and for him it appears that the Masonic text was a corrupted version of the sacred text of the rites in Solomon's temple. The restoration of all things would also require a more correct version. The first step was to restore the office of the high priest. In the Bible washings are not mentioned in connection with the priesthood, but in connection with washing clothes or utensils, or of a woman doing her washings. Hyrum would certainly have become familiar with the washings of the high priest in Masonic praxis.

Ultimately, Joseph Smith instituted more than one high priest, but he was the president of the high priesthood, and stood over every aspect of the Church.

Although not generally considered to be part of the LDS canon, it seems that Smith thought of the text of Solomon's temple as being a sacred text needing restoration.

Agenda: To Be the Temple Restorer, Not just a Masonic Imitator

The converts would soon learn that receiving the true baptism was not enough to achieve the highest degree of salvation in the hereafter. Other restored ordinances were necessary.

There is evidence that Cowdery's nemesis was Sidney Rigdon. Smith's attention now turned to establishing the rites of a new religion, in pursuit of his "to B" agenda. Rigdon, a former minister, would have ideas along these lines. Much of the *Doctrine and Covenants* was developed with a close Smith-Rigdon working relationship.

The announced mission for a latter-day prophet was the Restoration of All Things. The initial rites of the nascent church were largely limited to baptism by immersion, the gift of the Holy Ghost, the Sacrament (Holy Communion) and ordination to receive the priesthood by the laying on of hands. Added to these are the rites necessary for a temple endowment.

---

[516] W. Bro. B. David Shanas, WM, "The Many Washings of the High Priest" (Albion Lodge No. 109, PM, Queen's Lodge No. 578, GR Canada, Masonic Education Chair for Frontenac Masonic District); downloaded 2022/02/10, http://www.vermontlodgeofresearch.com/Publications/Masonic%20Interest/TH E%20MANY%20WASHINGS%20OF%20THE%20HIGH%20PRIEST.pdf.

Figure 34. A Lithograph of the Nauvoo Temple

Source: Mormons or Latter Day-Saints (London: Office of the National Illustrated Library, 1851.

The Nauvoo Temple was never fully completed. There were some distinctive features. Note the clock tower, and steeple surmounted by Moroni as a weathervane. In addition to salvation aspirations, it was designed to be useful in the here and now. The temple had been in use for less that three months, when it was burned down by arsonists at midnight on October 8-9, 1848.

1. Washings and Anointing. When the temple in Missouri had to be put on hold, near the end of 1832 a revelation commanded the saints in Kirtland to "establish a house, even a house of prayer, a house of fasting, a house of faith, a house of learning, a house of glory, a house of order, a house of God." (D&C 88:119) The founding of the School of the Prophets, commanded in a revelation 3 January 1833 (D&C 88:127), marked the beginning of ritual innovation. The first meeting, 23 January 1833, was in the upper room of the Newel K. Whitney store. Joseph Smith presided, and all present participated in the first practice of a ritual washing of the feet, also as commanded (D&C 88):

> 138. And ye shall not receive any among you in this school save he is clean from the blood of this generation;
> 139. And he shall be received by the ordinance of the washing of feet, for unto this end was the ordinance of the washing of feet instituted.
> 140. And again, the ordinance of washing feet is to be administered by the president, or presiding elder of the church.
> 141. It is to be commenced with prayer; and after partaking of bread and wine, he is to gird himself according to the pattern given in the thirteenth chapter of John's testimony concerning me. Amen.

The official account reads:

> On the 23rd of January, we again assembled in conference; when, after much speaking, singing, praying, and praising God, all in tongues, we proceeded to the washing of feet... Each Elder washed his own feet first, after which I girded myself with a towel and washed the feet of all of them, wiping them with the towel with which I was girded... Having continued all day in fasting and prayer, and ordinances, we closed by partaking of the Lord's supper. I blessed the bread and wine in the name of the Lord, when we all ate and drank, and were filled; then we sang a hymn, and the meeting adjourned.[517]

The Lord's Supper was described by Zebedee Coltrin:

> ... warm bread to break easy was provided, and broken into pieces as large as my fist, and each person had a glass of wine and sat and ate the bread and drank the wine; and Joseph said that was the way that Jesus and his disciples partook of the bread and wine; and this was the order of the church anciently...[518]

2. Sealing. One account refers to a consequence of the ordinance, saying, "they were cleansed and sealed up unto eternal life..."[519] The concept of sealing is at times very specific, indicating that whatever was bound on earth is sealed in the hereafter, for all eternity. The term is found in a *Book of Mormon* paraphrase (Helaman 10:7) of Matthew 16:19:

---

[517] Smith, *History of the Church*, 1:323.
[518] In David John Buerger, *The Mysteries of Godliness. A History of Mormon Temple Worship* (Salt Lake City: Signature Books, 1994), 9.
[519] Buerger, *Mysteries of Godliness*, 8.

Matthew: And I will give unto thee the keys of the kingdom of heaven: and whatsoever thou shalt bind on earth shall be bound in heaven: and whatsoever thou shalt loose on earth shall be loosed in heaven.
Helaman: Behold, I give unto you power, that whatsoever ye shall seal on earth shall be sealed in heaven; and whatsoever ye shall loose on earth shall be loosed in heaven;

Smith had promised a great blessing to come, the endowment (D&C 105; June 22, 1834):

12. For behold, I have prepared a great endowment and blessing to be poured out upon them [elders of the Lord].
33. Verily, I say unto you, it is expedient in me that the first elders of my church should receive their endowment from on high in my house, which I have commanded to be built unto my name in the land of Kirtland.

Smith became the President of the office of the High Priesthood in 1835. Anticipating the completion of the Kirtland Temple, on 21 January 1836 Smith and brethren met in the attic of the printing office. They washed their bodies in pure water and perfumed their bodies and heads. They then went to the unfinished temple where Joseph met with the Presidency and proceeded to anoint their heads with oil. They anointed the Patriarch (Joseph Smith Sr.) and invoked blessings upon him. Blessings were also invoked upon the Prophet. The Bishop of Kirtland and the Bishop of Zion (Missouri) were brought in with their counselors for their anointing, followed by the counselors of Kirtland and Zion. The next day more anointing ordinances were performed, for the Council of the Twelve, the Presidency of the Seventies, and members of the high councils of Kirtland and Missouri. The meeting was concluded with President Sidney Rigdon invoking the benediction of heaven upon the Lord's anointed. [520] When his benediction was done, he instructed all to shout: "Hosannah, Blessed be the name of the Most High God." These anointings were the first temple sealing ordinances.

The Kirtland Temple was dedicated on 27 March 1836. Each person coming for the event was asked to donate what he could to help pay the debts the Church had incurred. Joseph Smith gave the dedication prayer, followed by a short prayer by Sidney Rigdon. This time the whole congregation, apparently by instruction, raised both hands and shouted:

---

[520] Ibid, 12-17; Devery S. Anderson & Gary James Bergera, eds., *Joseph Smith's Quorum of the Anointed, 1842-1845, a Documentary History* (Salt Lake City: Signature Books, 2005), xvi-xvii.

"Hosannah! Hosannah! Hosannah to God and the Lamb. Amen! Amen." It was estimated that 1,000 attended and they contributed $963.[521] On 30 March 1836, about 300 of the Church's male elite came to the temple for a washing ordinance and solemn ceremony. Donations were again requested.

Due to intense persecution in Kirtland, serious financial difficulties, and considerable apostasy, the Saints abandoned this center of the Church, and moved out, first to Missouri, and then to Commerce, Illinois, the new LDS center renamed Nauvoo. John Taylor, a future President of the Church, converted only in 1836, stopped in Kirtland in late 1839 to get his endowment (17 November). By then, most Saints had gone west.

3. Temple Ceremony. In Nauvoo Smith undertook to go further in the Restoration of All Things, by restoring the ceremony in Solomon's temple. He had drawn from Biblical texts for much of his work so far. In this case, he needed to seek a text that did not make it into the Bible. Its only survival, as he might have seen it, was the Masonic ceremony. Smith's brother Hyrum had been a Mason. To get access to the ritual, Smith managed to get a Masonic lodge created in Nauvoo. It eventually became one of the largest lodges in the nation, all Mormon. Like any other enactment, the ceremony has a script. Smith and his colleagues apparently reasoned that like the Bible itself, it had been modified and corrupted. But it could serve as a base to arrive at a correct ceremony, with divine help.

On 16 February 1832, Joseph Smith and Sidney Rigdon received a vision in which heaven was clarified as being divided into three kingdoms. (D&C 76) The highest is the Celestial Kingdom, the lowest is the Telestial Kingdom, and in between is the Terrestrial Kingdom. Even the lowest is described in glowing terms, and the vast majority of mankind will go to one of these three. This vision is merged with Masonic lore to produce the Mormon temple ceremony. "On 4 and 5 May, forty-nine days after his Masonic initiation, Smith introduced the new endowment ceremony to trusted friends in the upper story of his Red Brick Store."[522]

The temple ceremony is enacted. First come the washing and anointing. A separate area for this existed for each gender. It appears that in the Nauvoo temple there were large basins to wash the entire body. Everyone donned a loose garment for modesty. Then came the anointings. When ready, the participants (later called patrons) went through the progress of mankind: creation (in the creation room), the Garden of Eden

---

[521] Marquardt, *Rise of Mormonism*, 253-54.
[522] Buerger, *Mysteries of Godliness*, 52.

and the fall of Adam and Eve (in the garden room) and the dreary world (in the Telestial room), where:

> ...after the man has proved himself faithful he receives the first signs and tokens of the Melchizedek priesthood and an additional charge. Here also he vouches for the conduct of his companion. They are then left to prove themselves faithful, after which they are admitted into the terrestrial kingdom, where at the alter (sic) they receive an additional charge and the second token of the Melchizedek Priesthood and also the key word on the five points of fellowship.

> There are words given with every token and the new name is given in the preparation room when they receive their washing and annointing (sic).

> After [having] received all the tokens and words and signs they are led to the vail (sic) where they give each to Eloheem through the vail (sic) and are then admitted into the Celestial Room...

> ...Heber C. Kimball acting as Eloheem, George A. Smith as Jehovah, Orson Hyde as Michael, W.W. Phelps as the serpent.[523]

The Masonic elements of the ceremony, and temple design, are:

> 1. The three Mormon hand grips correspond to the Masonic grip of the Entered Apprentice, the pass-grip of the Fellow Craft, and the pass-grip of the Master Mason.
> 2. The Mormon penalty enactments (one for having one's throat cut, one for having one's breast split open, and one for being disemboweled) are the Masonic sign and Due-Guard enactments.
> 3. Both have the five points of fellowship: inside of right foot of one to same of the other, knee to knee, chest to chest, and mouth to each other's right ear.
> 4. In the Mormon temple, this embrace through the veil is with the patron's left arm through the mark of the compass and the Lord's left arm through the mark of the square. The compass and square are the primary Masonic symbols.
> 5. The beehive, representing industriousness.
> 6. The all-seeing eye.

Although today's Saints are sometimes disturbed by the Masonic elements in the temple ceremony, this was not the case in Nauvoo, where so many

---

[523] William Clayton, in George D. Smith, ed., *An Intimate Chronicle: The Journals of William Clayton* (Salt Lake City: Signature Books, 1972), 205-208.

were Masons. Heber C. Kimball and Franklin D. Richards called the ceremony "true Masonry."[524]

Both ceremonies, Mormon and Masonic, have a strong emphasis on secrecy. This is the role of the penalties. For the first penalty, the officiator says "The execution of the penalty is represented by placing the thumb under the left ear, the palm of the hand down, and by drawing the thumb quickly across the throat to the right ear, and dropping the hand to the side." This enacts having one's throat cut. If John is the person going through the ritual, then he says, "I, John, covenant that I will never reveal the First Token of the Aaronic Priesthood, with its accompanying name, sign and penalty. Rather than do so, I would suffer [patrons all place right thumbs under left ears as described above] my life [patrons all draw thumbs across throats to right ears] to be taken [patrons all drop right hands down to sides]."

The second penalty, as described above, represents the chest being split apart. So John would say, "I, John, covenant that I will never reveal the Second Token of the Aaronic Priesthood, with its accompanying name, sign and penalty. Rather than do so, I would suffer [right hand to left breast] my life [draws hand across chest to right breast] to be taken [drops hands to side]." For the third penalty, representing being disemboweled, John would say, "I covenant in the name of the Son that I will never reveal the First Token of the Melchizedek Priesthood or Sign of the Nail, with its accompanying name, sign, and penalty. Rather than do so, I would suffer my life [patrons all draw the right thumb quickly across their body] to be taken [patrons all drop both hands to their sides]." Before passing through the veil into the Celestial Kingdom, the participants are instructed in the true order of prayer. As part of this, all again make the three signs, and the three penalties.

The temple ceremonies have evolved. They were updated in 1984, and again in 1990. These penalties have been disturbing to some members, and it was decided that they had outlived their usefulness. So in the 1990 revision, they were dropped.[525]

4. Baptism for the Dead. One application of the sealing power of the High (Melchizedek) Priesthood is baptism for the dead. This is a creative institution that addressed a vexing problem that had disturbed Christians

---

[524] See Buerger, *Mysteries of Godliness*, 56-58.

[525] Buerger, *The Mysteries of Godliness*, 120. For the temple ceremony c. 1980, see Chuck Sackett, *What's Going on in There? The Verbatim Text of the Mormon Temple Rituals Annotated and Explained by a Former Temple Worker* (Thousand Oaks, CA: Sword of the Shepherd Ministries, ND).

from the beginning. One of the NT red-letter passages (i.e., presumably stated by Jesus himself) declares, "Except a man be born of water and of the Spirit, he cannot enter into the kingdom of God." (John 3:5) This gave rise to speculation as to the eternal fate of infants who die without baptism, righteous persons who die having never heard the gospel message, and even pre-Christian prophets such as Abraham and Moses. For centuries, the Roman church held that such individuals go to a special place called limbo, sometimes located in Hell, and at times said to be an appendage on the fringe of Hell, between Heaven and Hell. This also led to infant baptism. Given the high rate of infant mortality, it was always advisable to have a priest on hand at childbirth to baptize the infant while it still breathed. In France, a young priest made the news for getting his girlfriend pregnant and when her condition became obvious, slitting her throat in a dark alleyway, ripping open her womb, baptizing the unborn infant, and then killing it. This shows how a deeply-rooted doctrine such as this can grip the mind of even the most deranged.

The Smith family was put into an extended mourning when Smith's elder brother Alvin died. The *Book of Mormon* states, "he that knoweth not good from evil is blameless..." (Alma 29:5) As early as September, 1830, a revelation stated (D&C 29:46-47):

> 46. But behold, I say unto you, that little children are redeemed from the foundation of the world through mine Only Begotten;
> 47. Wherefore, they cannot sin, for power is not given unto Satan to tempt little children until they begin to become accountable before me.

On 21 January 1836, on the occasion of the first washings in Kirtland, Smith reported a vision of which he said:

> I saw father Adam, and Abraham and Michael and my father and mother, my brother Alvin that has long since slept, and marveled how it was that he had obtained this an inheritance ‹in› that Kingdom, seeing that he had departed this life, before the Lord ‹had› set his hand to gather Israel ‹the second time› and had not been baptized for the remission of sins...[526]

An answer to this dilemma came from an interpretation of a verse by the Apostle Paul. Since Smith was so very collaborative, it is not possible to know who actually noticed this verse, but by this time, former minister Sidney Rigdon was Smith's most prominent collaborator in theological matters. Prior to his conversion to Mormonism, as a Campbellite he had

---

[526] Jessee, *Personal Writings of Joseph Smith*, 146.

been opposed to infant baptism. Arguing in defense of the doctrine of resurrection, Paul wrote, "Else what shall they do which are baptized for the dead, if the dead rise not at all? Why are they then baptized for the dead?" (1 Corinthians 15:29) A light went on in someone's head, and the answer came: Of course, baptism for the dead, by proxy. A major institution was born.

The ordinance was established by revelation on 19 January 1841 (D&C 124:29-35), but the practice was already under way. The first occurrence of this baptism was on 13 August 1840, when Smith baptized a widow, Jane Nyman, in the Mississippi River for her deceased son.[527] Once the Nauvoo temple was completed, baptism for the dead was to be limited to the temple, as directed in revelation.

After death, the spirits of the dead go to a spirit world where they have anthropomorphic spirit bodies, live in a social situation, subject to many concerns, opportunities to sin and many preaching various doctrines. Each person who has ever lived will get a meaningful opportunity to hear and accept or reject the true gospel of Christ, aka Mormonism. If the deceased is converted in this spirit world, and accepts his or her proxy baptism, then, and only then, is it validated. At the base of this practice is the doctrine that baptism cannot be done in the spirit world because it can only be done in the flesh.

5. Celestial Marriage and Polygamy. Celestial marriage also arises from a NT passage. In another red-letter verse, Jesus says, "For when they shall rise from the dead, they neither marry, nor are given in marriage; but are as the angels which are in heaven." (Mark 12:25) This might appear to mean that upon death, families are dissolved, not a happy thought for those who are very family oriented, nor for devoted couples. The LDS interpretation is that this is literally true in the case put to Jesus, but that a marriage performed and sealed for all time and eternity in a temple of God would be valid in the hereafter (D&C 132, recorded 12 July 1843). Marriages performed by a church minister, justice of the peace, by contracting parties in Islam or by a shaman, are all equally valid for this life. Only Mormon celestial marriages are forever.

This ordinance was revealed in the same revelation that established polygamy, dated July 12, 1843. (D&C 132:61-62) Marquardt has documented a list of 17 single women who were sealed to Joseph Smith. The oldest at the time of marriage was Rhoda Richards, 58. The youngest

---

[527] Garr, Cannon & Cowan, *Encyclopedia of Latter-day Saint History*, 76.

was Helen Mar Kimball, 14. Most were between 17 and 30 years of age. Although we do not know how much time passed between the receipt/drafting of the revelation and the date it was recorded, it is interesting to note that Louisa Beeman's sealing date was 5 April 1841, more than two years prior to the polygamy revelation. Two other sealings occurred a year before the recording date of the revelation. Three widows are also listed as sealed to Joseph Smith, two of them being in 1842. Whatever the actual date of the revelation, it is certain that the practice was kept secret for up to two years.[528]

In addition to these, Marquardt lists eight women, married to other men, who were sealed to Joseph Smith. Minimally, this means that they would be his in the next life. We have no way of knowing what contact Smith had with them in this life. Since a higher degree of glory in the Celestial Kingdom is possible to couples that are sealed than those who are not, this may be a matter of women deemed worthy of being sealed, but who are married to men who are not deemed worthy. These women may have sought an avenue to exaltation in the next life within the order of celestial marriage.

The practice of polygamy was from the start a point of major dissension among the Saints. Many if not most converts came from conservative Christian backgrounds. They would be aware of the *Book of Mormon*'s condemnation of both polygamy and concubinage (Ether 10:5& Jacob 1:15):

> *Ether.* And it came to pass that Riplakish did not do that which was right in the sight of the Lord, for he did have many wives and concubines, and did lay that upon men's shoulders which was grievous to be borne.
> *Jacob.* And now it came to pass that the people of Nephi, under the reign of the second king, began to grow hard in their hearts, and indulge themselves somewhat in wicked practices, such as like unto David of old desiring many wives and concubines, and also Solomon, his son.

For true believers, the answer to this was not hard to come by. Riplakish undoubtedly took many wives outside the "new and everlasting covenant." More probably, this condemnation of the practice probably represents the view of the scripture's authors earlier in their career.

In Utah, Brigham Young and his polygamous establishment put pressure on prominent men to take a second wife, partly to improve the image of the institution. In her famous and history-making book, *Tell It All, the Story of a Life's Experience in Mormonism* (1875), Fanny

---

[528] Marquardt, *Rise of Mormonism*, 342-3.

Stenhouse wrote of the pressure to take a second wife placed on her husband, Thomas. B. Stenhouse, a productive contributor to the *New York Herald* and, as editor of the *Salt Lake Telegraph*, a founder of real journalism in Utah (427, 430-31), who joined the Godbeites. Recounting what a trial it was for them both, and her own experience, she wrote (454):

> Brigham Young performed the ceremony. He sat at the end of the altar and we three knelt down—my husband on one side and Miss Pratt and myself on the other. Speaking to me, Brigham Young asked: "Are you willing to give this woman to your husband to be his lawful wife for time and for all eternity? If you are you will signify it by placing her right hand within the right hand of your husband.

> I did so; but what words can describe my feelings! The anguish of a whole lifetime was crowded into that one single moment. The painful meaning of those words, "for all eternity" withered my soul...

Ultimately, she and her husband left the Church. She wrote her book. Between 1874 and 1888, it was reprinted thirteen times, including once in Spanish. It has been republished numerous times ever since, including once in an American feminist series. After leaving the Church, she urged Congress to outlaw polygamy (already outlawed in most if not all states at the time), and the Federal law doing so was partly due to her efforts. This law has been challenged twice on grounds of being a violation of constitutionally protected freedom of religion, and the U. S. Supreme Court has upheld the law on grounds of being in the public interest.

Fanny Stenhouse wrote in her book about the observations young women would have growing up, [529]

> They would notice the neglect which wives endured even from good husbands; they would see a man leaving the wife of his youth, the mother of his children, and careless of the cruel wrong he did her, leave her in lonely sorrow while he was spending his time in love-making with some young girl who might have been his daughter. They would see a wife crushing out from her heart the holiest impulses which God had implanted there, striving to destroy all affection for him whose dearest treasure that affection should have been...

---

[529] Mrs. T. B. H. Stenhouse, *Tell It All: The Story of a Life's Experience in Mormonism. An Autobiography* (Hartford: Worthington & Co., 1874), 381.

Polygamy was practiced only through a temple sealing, which means that it had to be authorized. This gave the hierarchy power over access to women beyond one's first wife. If an elder took a second wife outside of the temple sealing framework, he could be tried for adultery.

Joseph Smith was accused of having two illicit relationships while in Kirtland. The first involved a young woman working in the Smith home. There is little information about this alleged affair. The second regards Fanny Alger. There is more information regarding this charge, but conflicting information. Whatever is the case, two things are certain. First, Smith had a strong penchant for women. Second, in his celestial marriage/polygamy revelation, the assertion of divine approval for concubinage was gratuitous, if it was not intended to further extend the license of a prophet. (See D&C 132:37-39: "in none of these things did he [Abraham] sin.")

Agenda: Be Like Unto Moses and Reveal the Fullness of the Gospel

Although the new scriptures and institutions of Mormonism examined thus far already set it apart as being unique within the Christian world, it is ultimately its theology that makes it truly a new religion, rather than just a further elaboration of a Christian faith that came over from Europe. What was to come is not obvious in the *Book of Mormon*. Like religionists in New England at the time, it argues against atheism (Alma 30:28) and agnosticism (Alma 30:48 & 54:21). About 47 BCE Alma urges his son: "cross yourself in all these things... Oh, remember, and take it upon you and cross yourself in these things." (Alma 39:9)

It is not altogether clear when the first vision story first contained the description of God the Father and the Son appearing to Joseph Smith, in human form, and as two separate divine beings, but this may be the earliest appearance of that doctrine. Perhaps it was after the *Book of Mormon* was written, which seems wedded to the doctrine that the Father and Son are one God. The Lord shows himself to the brother of Jared (at the time of the Tower of Babel), in full human form, and says (Ether 3):

> 14. Behold, I am he who was prepared from the foundation of the world to redeem my people. Behold, I am Jesus Chris. I am the father and the Son. In me shall all mankind have light, and that eternally, even they who shall believe on my name; and they shall become my sons and my daughters.
> 16. Behold, this body, which ye now behold, is the body of my spirit; and man have I created after the body of my spirit...

The Nephite prophet Abinadi says (Mosiah 15):

1. God himself shall come down among the children of men, and shall redeem his people,

 2. And because he dwelleth in flesh he shall be called the Son of God, and having subjected the flesh to the will of the Father, being the Father and the Son—

3. The Father, because he was conceived by the power of God; and the Son, because of the flesh; thus becoming the Father and Son—

4. And they are one God, yea, the very Eternal Father of heaven and of earth.

When adducing NT scriptural support for polytheism, LDS theology bases itself on the statement of Paul (1 Corinthians 8):

5. For though there be that are called gods, whether in heaven or in earth (as there be gods many, and lords many,)

6. But to us, there is but one God, the Father, of whom are all things, and we in him; and one Lord Jesus Christ, by whom are all things, and we by him.

On 20 March 1839, a revelation came, saying: "According to that which was ordained in the midst of the Council of the Eternal God of all other gods before this world was..." (D&C 121:32; March 20, 1839) An authoritative LDS reference, *Mormon Doctrine*, by Bruce R. McConkie, says:

Three separate personages—Father, Son, and Holy Ghost—comprise the Godhead. As each of these persons is a God, it is evident, from this standpoint alone, that a *plurality of Gods* exists. To us, speaking in the proper finite sense, these three are the only Gods we worship. But in addition there is an infinite number of holy personages, drawn from worlds without number, who have passed on to exaltation and are thus gods.[530] (v. p. 369)

Accordingly, Mormonism has the unique distinction of being the only polytheist Christian faith, historically, a clear oxymoron. The term polytheism is further delimited by the fact that these three are organized, along with all other gods that may be from this creation, and the angels, and the priesthood holders of the Church, in one priesthood, with God the Father at the head. The three are totally separate. Each of the two, God the Father and God the Son, has his own material anthropomorphic body. Yet while acting in the priesthood along with the Holy Ghost the three are functionally unitary. Admittedly this is a bit novel, but far easier to grasp than the mystery of the three-in-one Trinity. Mormons address all prayers

---

[530] McConkie, *Mormon Doctrine*, 576-77.

to Our Father or Our Father in Heaven, and close all prayers "In the name of Jesus Christ, Amen." They believe that Jesus, God the Son, died on the cross for the remission of the sins of mankind, and they commemorate this every Sunday with the rite of the sacrament, partaking of bread and water (rather than wine).

That LDS theology was in flux very early on is seen in the *Book of Moses*, where we read: "For I, the Lord God, created all things, of which I have spoken, spiritually, before they were naturally upon the face of the earth." Mormons believe that they lived in a preexistence prior to being born into a carnal body. Just as Jesus appeared to the brother of Jared as a spirit body, but of human form, humans also were of human form in the preexistence. There they had free will, and the capacity to do right and wrong. So each human being is born here already having an achievement record made in the preexistence.

Important principles of LDS theology are rooted in *The Book of Abraham*, guaranteeing its place in the canon. How to harmonize it with the Egyptian papyri is for Mormon scholars and apologists to figure out. In it, God speaks to Abraham, saying (Abraham 3):

> 18. …if there be two spirits, and one shall be more intelligent than the other, yet these two spirits, notwithstanding one is more intelligent than the other, have no beginning; they existed before, they shall have no end, they shall exist after, for they are gnolaum, or eternal.
> 19. …These two facts do exist, that there are two spirits, one being more intelligent than the others; there shall be another more intelligent than they; I am the Lord thy God, I am more intelligent than they all.
> 21. I dwell in the midst of them all... for I rule in the heavens above, and in the earth beneath, in all wisdom and prudence, over all the intelligences thine eyes have seen from the beginning; I came down in the beginning in the midst of all the intelligences thou has seen.
> 22. Now the Lord had shown unto me, Abraham, the intelligences that were organized before the world was; and among all these there were many of the noble and great ones;
> 3:23. And God saw these souls that they were good, and he stood in the midst of them, and said: These I will make my rulers; for he stood among those that were spirits, and he saw that they were good; and he said unto me: Abraham, thou art one of them; thou wast chosen before thou wast born.

This was anticipated, at least to some degree, in the Doctrine and Covenants (93):

> 29, Man was also in the beginning with God. Intelligence, or the light of truth, was not created or made, neither indeed can be.

30. All truth is independent in that sphere in which God has placed it, to act for itself, as all intelligence also; otherwise there is no existence.
31. Behold, here is the agency of man, and here is the condemnation of man; because that which was from the beginning is plainly manifest unto them, and they receive not the light.

The interpretation of these BoA verses separates the terms intelligences and souls or spirits. Verses 22-23, where Abraham saw that the intelligences had been organized, marks a transition from the intelligence stage to the spirit stage. This is generally taken to mean that the intelligences are coeternal with God, that they become clothed with a body of refined matter in human form to become spirits, and then acquire a corporeal body on earth, which will be the third component, in an incorruptible form, of the resurrected person. This is Mormonism's own three-in-one doctrine. Thus the problem of the origin of good and evil is partially solved. Since the intelligence was never created by God, He is not responsible for its evil. This does not solve the problem of why bad things happen to good people. Like some others, Mormons usually just say that it must be part of God's plan, somehow.

This is further explained in Mormon theology by the concept of the family unit in the hereafter. As we have seen, the LDS concept of Heaven is that it is tripartite, mirrored in the structure and ceremony of the temple. A Mormon couple that has been sealed together for time and eternity are eligible for the Celestial Kingdom. If judged worthy, they can enter on the path to become gods and goddesses. This most exalted status is not immediate. LDS theology has the concept of eternal progression. Over time they can progress to the point that they can achieve this degree of exaltation. A god-and-goddess couple produce spirit children. This is normally thought of as an increate intelligence entering into the spirit body as it develops. LDS who have a testimony of the truth of Mormonism but are not sufficiently valiant to be worthy of the Celestial Kingdom can be eligible for the Terrestrial Kingdom, as well as righteous persons who have not accepted the gospel in circumstances that would qualify for the Celestial Kingdom. Those who have failed to acquire a testimony or have denied a testimony once received have to go to the lowest, the Telestial Kingdom. Most who have ever lived will go there. This also includes murderers, thieves and all sorts of really bad guys, since Mormonism sends very few to Hell. Even so, persons in the Telestial Kingdom differ in glory. A Mormon worthy of the Celestial Kingdom, but who is not married, or whose spouse did not make it, can still go to that Kingdom, but would be an angel or servant (divine functionary) in that exalted place. All who do not make it to the Celestial Kingdom have their family ties severed. Family only exists in the Celestial Kingdom.

All of this leads to issues. Occasionally, in a gathering of Saints, two or three present might get into these issues and attempt to theorize. Others will shift nervously, until, often, someone will say, "Hey, don't you think we're going off the deep end here?" At least at this point, Mormonism does not have what one can truly call speculative theology. The normal position is that we have all the knowledge that is presently needed for our salvation, and if we need to know more, it will be revealed in due time.

Vignette   **Are Mormons Christians?**

This has been a vexing issue. Presidential candidate Mitt Romney attempted to finesse it. His statement was an example of LDS dissimulation. This is not to say that he lied, or that Mormons are not Christians. It simply means that one should tell the truth, but not necessarily the whole truth. Ultimately the issue is theological, which is the study of God. Theology defines the divine, it draws lines, and establishes cutoff points or boundaries.

If what is meant is "Do Mormons worship Jesus?" the answer is a resounding "Yes."

If what is meant is "Do Mormons accept Jesus as their personal Redeemer?" the answer is a resounding "Yes."

But is Jesus Christ in the traditional churches the same Jesus Christ in the LDS faith? In traditional Christian theology, Jesus is God. Father and Son are One God in the absolute sense. Even though their God can and did take on flesh, to better relate to His human creation, that was just a garment, not His essence or real being. For many if not all, this God is omnipotent, omniscient and omnipresent. For the Mormons, Jesus Christ is the Only Begotten Son of God, in the literal biological sense, in the flesh. They do not accept the doctrine of Virgin Birth, or even a Virginal Conception. God did not create all things, but organized them. He did not even create the ultimate beings within each of us, the intelligences, which are increate, and coeternal with God. LDS theological speculation is comfortable with the proposition that the law of eternal progression means that even the Supreme God, Elohim, is still progressing, at least in some sense. It is for each Christian faith to determine for itself where to draw the line. But there is a very strong logical case that the deity of traditional Christianity is not the LDS deity. Jesus is not God, but a god, and just the number-two god at that. Prayer is not offered to Jesus (much less the Virgin Mary). So it is quite reasonable to answer the question in the negative: strictly speaking, for the traditional churches, Mormons cannot be Christians.

It might be hoped that in this modern, ecumenical age, Christian charity can bridge this chasm. But if so, the LDS Church, and its Saints, have not led the way. In the *Book of Mormon*, all churches except the one true Church (Mormonism) are, collectively, the Whore of all the Earth mentioned in the *Book of Revelations* (although for John of Patmos, this phrase probably referred to the Roman Empire and its power establishment). There are variations in the wording of Joseph Smith's accounts of his first vision. But typical of his later characterizations of the churches of his day, the answer from Jesus was:

> I was answered that I must join none of them, for they were all wrong, and the Personage who addressed me said that all their Creeds were an abomination in his sight, that those professors were all corrupt, that "they draw near to me with their lips but their hearts are far from me; They teach for doctrines the commandments of men, having a form of Godliness but they deny the power thereof."[531]

Although the LDS position has remained essentially unchanged, the tone of its expression has softened. Ultimately, the Church and its Saints hold that all other churches are in error, and the Church of Jesus Christ of Latter-day Saints alone is recognized by God; it alone has the true priesthood, and can offer the valid baptism for the remission of sins, and salvation, and exaltation in the next life. This position is absolute, clear and foundational. The Church has remained aloof from ecumenism, and is not an appropriate participant in any serious ecumenical gathering.

Gathering: A Community of Belief in the Prophet's Scriptures

A scriptural canon without believers is an empty vessel. From the earliest days of his mission, Joseph Smith attracted a following, and after the establishment of his Church, he demonstrated an amazing ability to delegate authority. Within just ten months after baptism, individuals who would become early Mormon leaders were entrusted with important duties, and even sent off on distant missions to preach Mormonism.

This practice required controls. First, they were often sent off in groups of two or more. Second, they were, of course, preaching the *Book of Mormon*, which itself contained a message, and was ineluctably associated with Smith himself. Third, a document called the *Articles and Covenants* (D&C 20), developed during the summer of 1829, but read and unanimously accepted by the first conference of the Church on 9 June

---

[531] This is the 1938 account. For all three, and a study of them, see Backman, *Joseph Smith's First Vision*; and Jessee, *Early Accounts of Joseph Smith's First Vision*.

1830, served as a formal statement of beliefs, and a source that could be used for developing sermons. Fourth, a number of Biblical scriptures were identified that missionaries could use to bolster the claims of Mormonism. Proselyting by the general membership was strenuously promoted from the beginning.

In a sense, the first missionary work began when Smith recruited Martin Harris to work with him on a translation of the gold plates, and also when Joseph Smith Sr. recruited Oliver Cowdery to the cause, and they recruited David Whitmer. On 6 April 1830, Oliver Cowdery was designated "the first preacher of this church." (D&C 21:12) He preached in Fayette, New York, organized that branch of the Church, and baptized six converts. [532] Officially, the first missionary is said to have been Joseph's brother, Samuel H., who was sent, with copies of the *Book of Mormon*, to preach the Restoration. Subsequently he acquired a reputation for his missionary activities. On one mission, with Orson Hyde, he traveled on foot from Ohio to Maine. In 1830, almost immediately after the founding of the Church, Oliver Cowdery, Peter Whitmer Jr., Parley P. Pratt and Ziba Peterson were sent out to convert the Lamanites. Although they did not report Indian baptisms, in Kirtland, Ohio, on 29 October 1830, they baptized 127 people, according to Pratt.[533] Over time, this nucleus expanded, and their success may have led to the decision to locate the Church in Kirtland. In 1837, a delegation of the Quorum of the Twelve Apostles, including Orson Hyde and Heber C. Kimball, were sent to preach in England, where they met with considerable success. In 1843, Smith sent missionaries to the Society Islands in French Polynesia, presumably to convert the descendants of the Nephites taken there by Hagoth (Alma 63:5-8). In principle, every member is charged with a missionary responsibility with respect to their friends and acquaintances, and many early converts resulted from the efforts of ordinary members.

An examination of the conversion of some of the key early leaders of this new community shows that after Smith's early proselytism, he became primarily involved in the development of the Church, its organization, rites and theology. After 1831, spreading the message of the Restoration, also a top priority, had to be left largely to the missionaries, and other members.

---

[532] Marquardt, *The Rise of Mormonism*, 135.
[533] Parley P. Pratt, in Parley P. Pratt (Jr.), ed., *Autobiography of Parley P. Pratt* (Salt Lake City: Deseret Book Compa   `938 [1985]), 36.

Table 70. Who Converted Whom? (an incomplete list)

Convert	Instrumental Person	Comment
Martin Harris	Joseph Smith	Smith worked for him.
Joseph Knight Sr	Joseph Smith	Smith worked for him.
Oliver Cowdery	Joseph Smith Sr.	Cowdery roomed in Smith home.
David Whitmer	Cowdery & Smith Sr.	Cowdery had known him.
W. W. Phelps	P.P. Pratt (+Joseph Jr.)	Converted by reading the BoM.
Parley P. Pratt	Hyrum Smith	Hyrum Smith: baptized by Cowdery.
Sidney Rigdon	Pratt/Cowdery/others	Cowdery, missionary colleagues.
John Johnson	Baptized by Smith	Visited Smith in N.K. Whitney home
Luke S. Johnson	Baptized by Smith	Son of John Johnson
Lyman Johnson	Baptized by S. Rigdon	Son of John Johnson
John F. Boynton	Baptized by Smith	Disfellowshipped with Luke, Lyman
Titus Billings	Sidney Rigdon	Wife's brother was Isaac Morley
E. Partridge	Sidney Rigdon	Sought baptism after meeting Smith.
Isaac Morley	Pratt, Cowdery	Member of Rigdon's congregation.
Zebedee Coltrin	Baptized by S. Hancock	Confirmed by Lyman Wight
F. G. Williams	Cowdery & colleagues	Was Kirtland Justice of the Peace.
W. E. McLellin	D. Whitmer/Hyrum	First heard Whitmer preach.
John Corrill	Cowdery & colleagues	He gave the missionaries lodging.
Ziba Peterson	Baptized by Cowdery	Of Fayette, baptized in L. Seneca
Orson Hyde	Sidney Rigdon	Rigdon had known him earlier.
Willard Richards	Jos. & Brigham Young	They were cousins.
Phineas Young	Samuel H Smith	Samuel sold him a copy of the BoM
Brigham Young	Phineas, Joseph Smith	First contact was BoM from Phineas
Joseph Young	Brigham Young	Brigham was his younger brother.
John Taylor	P.P. Pratt & John's wife	Only LDS president born outside US
Amasa Lyman	Orson Pratt/L.Johnson	He sought to learn about the Church
N.K. Whitney	Sidney Rigdon	Daughter, a plural wife of Joseph Jr.
Kimball, Heber	Various Youngs	Friend of Phineas Young.

Smith's death resulted in a major succession crisis. On 8 August 1844, the Church voted to sustain the Quorum of the Twelve (apostles) to take the lead as guardians of the Church, assisted by Sidney Rigdon and Amasa Lyman as counselors, as they had been to the First Presidency. Brigham Young was effectively the leader of the Twelve, possibly even before Rigdon's exit from the scene. After a period of contention, and efforts of several claimants, on 27 December 1847, in Kanesville, Iowa, he, Willard Richards and Heber C. Kimball, were sustained as the new First Presidency, and Brigham Young was recognized as the new President, Prophet, Seer and Revelator.

The Smith family era was over. Emma Smith, with her son Joseph Smith III, remained in Illinois, and on 6 April 1860 he later became the head of the Reorganized Church of Jesus Christ of Latter Day Saints (RLDS, now the Community of Christ). On 14 January 1847, Brigham Young received his only revelation published in the *Doctrine and Covenants*, the plan of organization for the migration further west. Those who had the means were to load as much as possible into covered wagons and depart for a land not yet revealed. Lying sick in his wagon, on the outskirts of what is now Salt Lake City, he looked over the land lying at the foot of the Wasatch Mountains, and said, "This is the place."

A second group was to follow using handcarts. They could not arrange to depart until early fall, and requested that they be permitted to wait until spring. Young apparently feared that even more would join the ranks of the dissenters, and commanded that they depart immediately promising that the Lord would provide a mild winter for their journey. Unfortunately, the winter was hard, and many perished.

But once they had arrived, the Mormons finally occupied a land that was largely unpopulated and sufficiently remote that they would be able to develop their religion and society in security and splendid isolation.

This missionary work was oriented to more than just conversions. The members were urged to gather to the Church center, initially in Kirtland, Ohio, but which was eventually to be in Jackson County (Independence) Missouri, Zion, the place for the establishment of the New Jerusalem. As the converts increased the Mormon community in Missouri increased. Mormon determination to claim the land of their inheritance, their plans to convert the Indians, and fears that they supported abolitionist politics were threatening to the already established citizenry, who were also subject to motivations of bigotry. As a result, Missouri became the site of the most severe persecution. Following the destruction of the Phelps printing house, the Mormons continued to settle in Missouri, motivated by a desire to "gather to Zion." A non-Mormon, Jacob Hawn (Haun), established a mill on Shoal Creek, Haun's Mill. Although only a few Mormon families resided in this small settlement, over 750 LDS families resided in the adjoining area. On 30 October 1838, around 200 men attacked the settlement. Fifteen Latter-day Saints died as a result of this attack. Although it may be that this massacre was not a result of Governor Boggs' Mormon removal (extermination) order of October 27, violence and opposition to the Saints resulted in the expulsion of over 10,000 Mormons.

Gathering: Mobilizing Saints for Church Establishment Projects

To be like unto all his claimed forefathers, Smith must have a community of believers who sustain him as such. But, even a puppet master has to follow a script. Those who converted were persons interested in the message. They were religious people, seeking the truth, and the true baptism. Most already had a religious foundation to some degree, and of some sort. When they accepted the prophethood of Joseph Smith, they were prepared to give heed to the declaration:

> all [shall] be fulfilled, whether by mine own voice or by the voice of my servants, it is the same. (D&C 1: 38)

Even so, their submission to the voice of Smith's revelations was never absolute. They also came with expectations and temporal needs. Smith would have to make himself aware of these, and play his role well.

The missionaries had gone to many parts of the U.S. of his day, and even abroad. The converts were scattered about, beyond mountains, prairies, and even the sea. Smith's first step towards control to mobilize the believers was based on the concept of *gathering* (to Kirtland, to Zion). In December of 1830, Smith received a revelation that the whole church should gather to Ohio. (D&C 37:1-3) The decision to gather the Saints to this location was probably a response to the fact that, on 29 October, 1830, a group of missionaries sent to preach to the Indians in Missouri, journeyed by way of Kirtland, Ohio, where their efforts were more richly rewarded. There they preached and baptized numerous converts. These most notably included a major pillar of early Church development, Sidney Rigdon (8 Nov. 1830), and a number of his Baptist congregation, including another early Church leader, Parley P. Pratt (himself baptized c. 1 September 1830, in Seneca Lake, New York, by Oliver Cowdery). In January of 1831, Smith moved his family to Kirtland. Soon after his arrival, revelatory instructions were given regarding Church organization. Over half of the revelations in the *Book of Commandments* would be received there.

This plan was most effective from the prospective of effecting control. Recent converts, wherever they were, had to liquidate their property, leave family and friends, and move to Kirtland. This severed important ties and support of individuals and groups they had hitherto relied upon. There they had to get reestablished, including employment and a family residence. They were substantially dependent on assistance from the growing LDS community, and by extension, on its prophet, even as they began to weather persecution.

Gathering: Financial Bases to Build Temples & Other Projects

For much of Joseph Smith's career, his church was strapped for cash. Converts were generally not overly prosperous, and due to the call to gather, first to Kirtland, then to Missouri (Zion) and then to Nauvoo, they had to abandon or sell much of what they had, sometimes even an ancestral farm, and relocate, and relocate, and relocate, all the while facing persecution. We must always remember that there are two histories of Mormonism, the history of the founders and subsequent establishment, and the history of the membership, their trials and tribulations, and of their small triumphs and joys.

Money was a problem in early nineteenth-century America in general. By the end of 1780, the Continental bills, or continentals, were worth no more than one fortieth of their face value. Benjamin Franklin declared that they had in effect acted as a tax to pay for the war of secession from the British crown. The issuance of the United States dollar coin was in 1792, and the first one-dollar note was printed in 1863. Street-savvy Americans preferred coins to bills. A bill was by definition a promissory note. Paper money was issued by banks and private entities until 1861. It has been estimated that as many as 8,000 entities had issued paper instruments up to that point. Smith was not about to get his hands on coins in the quantities that he needed, and paper money was in any case not stable. This situation created ideal circumstances, or temptation, to create one's own money.

In 1836 Smith and some colleagues applied to the Ohio State Legislature for a charter to establish the Kirtland Society Bank. Sure of their success, Cowdery went to Philadelphia to get plates engraved for the notes. The plates arrived, but the charter was refused. After appealing, and failing, they organized a Stock Industrial Company, the Kirtland Safety Society Anti-Banking Company. Printing was commenced with the same plates, but with "anti-" printed before "BANK" and "ing co." after "BANK", in the little bit of space available. These notes were illegal, and rejected by creditors in New York, Pittsburgh and Cleveland, where large amounts of merchandise had been purchased on credit. The Kirtland Society failed, apparently in conjunction with a financial crisis in the country in general, although Smith promised that someday the notes would be as good as gold. Smith (Society cashier) and Rigdon (President) were arrested and in October 1837 were tried and convicted in a jury trial.[534]

---

[534] Sheridan L. McGarry, "Mormon Money," reprinted from *The Numismatist*, 1962, 3-4; Van Wagoner, *Sidney Rigdon*, 178-87.

They were each fined $1,000 plus court charges. After announcing their intention to appeal, they both fled the state.

Figure 35. The Kirtland Safety Society Anti-Bank ing Co. Note.

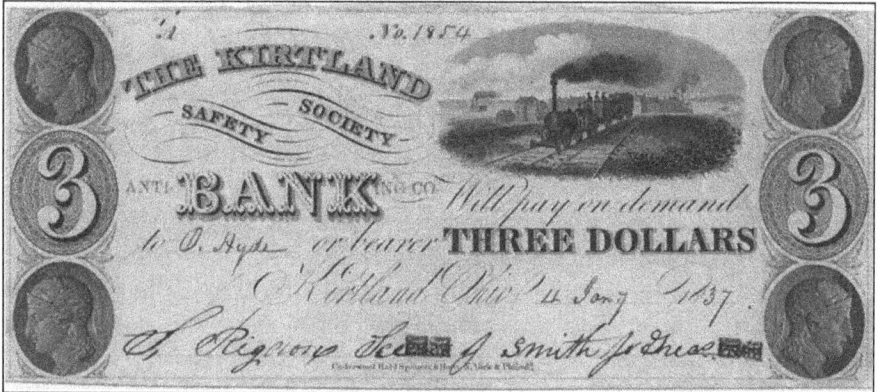

Source: A note (graded very fine) of PMG (Paper Money Guaranty), a paper money grading company, and member of the Certified Collectibles Group (CCG).

Also in Kirtland, the Church established a United Firm. This was a society for what the LDS more usually term the United Order, a voluntary society of members who would hold their property in common. But funds were desperately needed to construct the Kirtland Temple, and finance a paramilitary group called Zion's Camp. On 5 December 1833, Smith wrote "our means are already exhausted, and we are deeply in debt, and know of no means whereby we shall be able to extricate ourselves."[535] Although the United Firm was set up as a member's cooperative, it was used as collateral to raise funds. It is not certain to what extent the members had been apprised of this. On 11 January 1834, Smith and his associates prayed "that the Lord would provide, in the order of his Providence, the bishop of this Church with means sufficient to discharge every debt that the Firm owes, in due season, that the Church may not be braught (sic) into disrepute, and the saints be afflicted by the hands of their enemies."[536] The United Firm was dissolved in 1834. By 1835, the identities of the United Firm officers were obscured by pseudonyms. The 1835 edition of the Doctrine and Covenants reads:

---

[535] Smith, *History of the Church*, 1:450; Marquardt, *Rise of Mormonism*, 227.
[536] Joseph Smith, Journal, January 11, 1834, in Marquardt, *Rise of Mormonism*, 139.

And again, let my servant Ahashdah [Newel K. Whitney] have appointed unto him, the houses and lot where he now resides, and the lot and building on which the Ozondah [store] stands; and also the lot which is on the corner south of the Ozondah; and also the lot on which the Shule [ashery] is situated: And all this I [the Lord] have appointed unto my servant Ahashdah, for his stewardship, for a blessing upon him and his seed after him, for the benefit of the Ozondah of my order [Firm], which I have established for my stake in the land of Shinehah [Kirtland]; yea, verily this is the stewardship which I have appointed unto my servant Ahashdah; even this whole Ozondah establishment, him and his agent, and his seed after him...[537]

These maneuvers appear to have been to frustrate the Firm's creditors. Estimates of United Firm debts range from $102,300 (the more probable high end of the range) to as high as $150,000. When the Firm was dissolved, Rigdon received the home in which he was living, and a tannery for his future financial support.[538]

Along with the Firm, Smith and Rigdon's incomes came also from the Literary Firm, established to print the *Doctrine and Covenants*, *Book of Mormon* and several periodicals. There were plans also to publish Smith and Rigdon's revision of the Bible. Due to high operating expenses and low sales, the Firm collapsed, with debts, early in 1834.[539]

These financial failures, and legal difficulties, were the main reasons for the flight of Smith and Rigdon, but it was also due to rising mob violence, and perhaps the even sharper reaction of some unhappy members and apostates, some of whom had been thrown into financial ruin.

Once in Nauvoo, many ambitious projects were undertaken, including the new temple. Among the buildings undertaken was a hotel, the Nauvoo House. To cover this expense, the Mormons issued stock. The first series, a $50 certificate, was crudely printed. The second series, $50 and $100 certificates were much more professionally done. The first was transferrable by endorsement, and probably the second as well. In 1843, there was also a city scrip. In Smith's Journal History he recorded, "I burned twenty-three dollars of city scrip, and while it was burning, said, 'so may all unsound and uncurrent money go down!'"[540]

Once Brigham Young and the Saints were in Utah, financial institutions and instruments of exchange multiplied, much as they did

---

[537] D&C:98:7 (1835); see Marquardt, *Rise of Mormonism*, 256-57.

[538] Van Wagoner, *Sidney Rigdon*, 178-79.

[539] *ibid*, 177-78.

[540] *History of the Church*, 5:288; McGarry, "Mormon Money," 5-6.

across the United States, since the whole country was in need of stable instruments of exchange. Initially, and in practice for a large part of the second half of the nineteenth century, barter, payment in kind, was common. Brigham Young obtained authority to issue hand-written notes, but this turned out to be woefully inadequate. Certificates could be issued against goods in the Bishop's Storehouse that kept tithing. John Kay obtained the equipment needed to mint gold coins. Gold was procured from California, and Kay succeeded on his second attempt at minting. Young made a trip to the Mississippi and returned with a limited supply of U.S. coins, but they soon disappeared. Bad money drives out good. Gold obtained by the Church was used to back G.S.L. (Great Salt Lake) notes, which bore the private seal of the Twelve Apostles. Other notes were issued by The Drovers Bank, the Deseret Currency Association, Deseret University Bank, Holladay & Halsey, Great Salt Lake City Corporation, and The Salt Lake City National Bank of Utah. There were also merchandise-due bills issued by mercantile institutions, including the Zion's Cooperative Mercantile Institution. Currency issuance and minting ended in Utah as a ready supply of stable U.S. coins and currency became available.

There is no doubt that the Church, from the start, was struggling with an experimental and unstable monetary situation in the U.S. in general. It is also true that its projects far outstripped the real wealth available, and schemes to circumvent this problem were destined to doom, at the expense of many members. Although Mormonism was in principle a lay church, the burgeoning hierarchy meant a number of full-time personnel who needed an income, and it is safe to assume that higher officers expected a bit more. Funds were made available when needed, and land and business establishments were assigned to some. The situation at the top can be seen by the fact that one of the inheritance problems of Emma Smith, Joseph's legal widow, was the extreme commingling of Church finances with his own. In addition to all of the other causes for tension and even apostasy, Smith and Rigdon's financial schemes, especially in Kirtland, were a major irritant.

Although the LDS Church is a lay church, in "a 2014 memo from the Church's Presiding Bishopric (which handles all financial issues for the faith), the 'base living allowance' for all Mormon general authorities was being raised from \$116,400 to \$120,000."[541]

---

[541] Peggy Fletcher Stack *The Salt Lake Tribune*, published in sltrb.com in 2017, with the notice: "Ryan McKnight, a former Mormon in Las Vegas who posted the

As converts began to swell in numbers, the problems of control and mobilization became pressing. One approach, as we have seen, was to continually come up with new rites that one needed for the best possible hereafter, thereby keeping the saints spiritually off-balance.

Gathering: The Problems of Administration by Revelation: Missouri

On June 6 1831 a conference was held in Kirtland, when God revealed a fateful organizational decision that "the next conference shall be held in Missouri, upon the land which I will consecrate unto my people" (D&C 52:2).

Thus, the die was cast.

Smith and an exploratory party arrived in St. Louis, Missouri, on 1 July 1831, and on 20 July a revelation was received that a temple would be built west of Independence (D&C 57). The site for this temple was chosen, and on 3 August 1831, Smith laid a cornerstone as an expression of their determination that this building would be built. Plans for the city were developed, including a number of temples, for different purposes. In August of 1831, a commandment instructed Sidney Rigdon to write a description of this new land, a type of promotional prospectus to convince Saints to embrace it, and to donate funds for the temple (D&C 58).

These plans were overtaken by events on the ground. Many non-Mormon citizens of Missouri were bitterly opposed to the ever-growing Mormon population coming in and overrunning a land that they had settled. The events leading up to what has been called the Mormon-Missouri war are too complex to be examined here. The factors include: Religious clerical opposition, Cultural differences, rising LDS population, fear that eventually Mormons would control Missouri politics, concern among some that they would oppose slavery, the tendency for Mormons to buy only from Mormons as much as possible, no protection for the LDS against violent persecution and no redress from the courts. On 20 July 1833, citizens of Jackson County met at the courthouse in Independence and made a request for the Mormons to leave the county. This sounds like

---

documents to his new MormonLeaks website (formerly MormonWiki Leaks), stands by the numbers." Accessed on 02/13/2022 from https://archive. sltrib.com/ article.php?id=4800350&itype=CMSID.

a version of warning unwanted persons out of one's community, a common practice in New England, but quite unusual in Missouri. The Smith family themselves were warned out of Norwich, Vermont, in March 1816. When this request was refused, a mob destroyed Phelps' printing press. The LDS sought redress both in Missouri and in the U.S. Supreme Court. The latter rejected the petition citing states rights. Missouri had become a state in 1821.

On 1 June 1833, a revelation was received for the establishment of a temple in Kirtland, "which house I [the Lord] design to endow those whom I have chosen with power from on high..." (D&C 95:8) In a sense, for a while the Church would have two centers, one in Kirtland, Ohio, and the other in Missouri, where members of the Church continued to live in several counties, and later developed a center in a place that came to be called Far West, in a somewhat less inhabited area. The Missouri center has persisted for the church largely as an intention. This dream was forcibly put on hold when, in 1838, Missouri Governor Lilburn W. Boggs issued an executive order (the infamous removal/extermination order) for the removal of the Mormons from the state.

In May of 1839, the Saints made their first land purchases at Commerce, Illinois, on the east bank of the Mississippi River. In August, Smith reminted the new settlement Nauvoo, and in December the state of Illinois granted the Nauvoo Charter, which provided for the creation of a University of Nauvoo and the Nauvoo Legion. It grew rapidly and in only five years rivaled Chicago in population. Work began on the Nauvoo temple in March 1841, and in December Smith opened his Red Brick Store. On 15 March 1842 the Nauvoo Masonic Lodge was formed, and two days later a female Relief Society. Joseph Smith, President, Prophet, Seer and Revelator, became the Mayor of Nauvoo, and Lieutenant-General of the Nauvoo Legion. In August 1843 the Smith family moved into the Mansion House, which was partly an inn. Nauvoo was yet another place of gathering.

As the sole font of revealed doctrine, commands to the Church and priesthood authority, Joseph Smith had achieved his "To be" list. There now remained the challenge of surviving dangerous vortices. He had sown the wind, and risked reaping the whirlwind.

< Chapter 31 >

The Hubris of an Overreaching Prophet

Abraham represents head of the Patriarchal order, and Melchizedek head of the High Priesthood. Never did the twain merge. Joseph son of Jacob was never a Joshua, leading troops to secure Zion. Moses never sought to preside as the high priest of the tabernacle during the wandering of Israel in the wilderness, and certainly never sought to be the sum total of all of these. Joseph son of Joseph (Sr.) did, and succeeded within the narrow confines of his burgeoning gathering of converts. His successes gave birth to both opportunities and perils.

Theocracy: The Power to Coerce

Politically, the *Book of Mormon* strongly reflects concerns in the time of Joseph Smith in New England. "Nevertheless, the Nephites were inspired by a better cause for they were not fighting for monarchy, nor power but they were fighting for their home and their liberties..." (Alma 43:45) Some were called "king-men, for they were desirous that the law should be altered in a manner to overthrow the free government and to establish a king over the land." (Alma 51:5) Alma "selected a wise man who was among the elders of the church, and gave him power according to the voice of the people, that he might have power to enact laws according to the laws which had been given... Now Alma did not grant unto him the office of being high priest over the church, but he retained the office of high priest unto himself..." (Alma 4:16-18) "Now I would that ye should understand that the word of God was liberal unto all, that none were deprived of the privilege of assembling themselves together to hear the word of God." (Alma 6:5) "And whatsoever nation shall uphold such secret combinations, to get power and gain, until they shall spread over the nation, behold, they shall be destroyed..." (Ether 8:22)

In spite of this, theocracy seems to be inherent in Mormonism. It sees the Church as a precursor to the government of Christ on earth. Jesus will be King, authority will be priesthood, and raising one's hand will be to sustain and express allegiance. Of course no religion is a democracy. But the early history of the Church took place in situations where the functions of state tended to be performed, for a while, by the Church. And along with state power comes enforcement, the power to coerce.

Coercion does not necessarily mean the use of force. Ritual can be used to intimidate, as in the case of the Mormon temple marriage ceremony. Until the 1990 revision, married women receiving their endowments in the temple were required to take an oath of obedience to their husbands:

> *Elohim*: We will put the sisters under covenant to obey the law of their husbands. Sister, arise.
> [Female patrons stand as instructed.]
> *Elohim*: Each of you bring your right arm to the square. You and each of you solemnly covenant and promise before God, angels and these witnesses at this altar that you will each observe and keep the law of your husband, and abide by his council in righteousness. Each of you bow your head and say yes.
> *Women:* Yes

Similarly, regardless of whether Smith had any improper contact with the wives of other men whom he sealed to himself for time and eternity, this act must have been experienced by the other men as an exercise in male dominance. Compare this with the exercise of sexual privilege over the wives of male followers to establish dominance in some cults of the twentieth century, such as the Branch Dravidians.

Church councils could threaten disfellowship and excommunication, a threat that many took seriously, and could silence considerable criticism and opposition.

Violence was first encountered at the hands of persecuting mobs. Americans at the time, like now, often owned firearms. When mobs threatened one's home, it was wise to keep weapons close by. Mormons responded to defend themselves, and their forces acquired a role in internal enforcement as well. D. Michael Quinn has put together an impressive table of Mormon Security Forces, and their external and internal functions. Much of the following is based on his work.[542]

On 6 August 1833, "Smith announced a revelation authorizing Mormons to wage theocratic war when attacked by 'enemies' a fourth time." (D&C 98:39-48) On 4 November 1833, David Whitmer, presiding in Missouri, "led a counterattack against a Missouri mob, killing two anti-Mormons at the 'Battle of Blue River.' This was in response to the fourth attack, as allowed by the revelation."[543] A revelation was received on 24

---

[542] Quinn, *Mormon Hierarchy*, 467-478.
[543] *ibid*, 470.

February 1834 commanding "God's 'friends' to 'avenge me of mine enemies." [D&C 103] The Kirtland High Council appointed Smith as commander-in-chief of the "Armies of Israel." Within, dissenters are to "be 'cast out and trodden under the foot of men' by 'my friends.'"[544] Through 1834-37, Joseph Smith's "Lifeguards" provided internal and external security.[545]

In the fateful revelation, Smith promised the gathering to Zion in Independence Missouri, giving a date for the next conference to be there. To respond to the events of the summer of 1833, Smith organized the first Mormon military force in the summer of 1834, called Zion's Camp, and led it to Missouri to put this project back on track. He had to negotiate peace, without achieving his objectives. Zion's Camp became the basis for selecting the Quorum of the Twelve and the Seventy in 1835.[546]

On 24 September 1835, by revelation, the Kirtland High Council appointed Joseph Smith as "head" of the Church's "War Department."[547] The Ohio Army of Israel existed in Kirtland from 1835 into 1837. On 7 November 1836, an official ultimatum was issued by twelve general authorities, including the First Presidency, and fifty-nine others, warning out Kirtland's non-Mormon Justice-of-the-Peace to "depart forthwith out of Kirtland."[548] In December of 1837, Smith's Lifeguards went into apostasy, and Brigham Young carried weapons as an ad hoc bodyguard for the Prophet. On 22 December 1837, armed dissenters (former-Mormons) seized the temple and forced Brigham Young to flee the Kirtland headquarters for his life, followed three weeks later by the First Presidency. By December 1837, the Missouri Army of Israel was formed in Caldwell County, Missouri.[549]

During this period, the infamous Danites came into existence. They were drawn from members of Zion's Camp, Smith's Lifeguards, the Ohio Army of Israel and the Missouri Army of Israel. This group clearly felt that the problems of the Saints came from without *and* within. On 3 July 1837, the ground was broken for a temple at Far West. On 4 July 1838, Sidney Rigdon gave an oration in which he said:

> We therefore, take all men to record this day, that we proclaim our liberty on this day, as did our fathers. And we pledge this day to one another, our

---

[544] *Idem.*
[545] *Idem.*
[546] *Idem.*
[547] *Idem.*
[548] *ibid*, 471.
[549] *Idem.*

fortunes, our lives, and our sacred honors, to be delivered from the persecutions which we have had to endure, for the last nine years, or nearly that.[550]

George W. Robinson, that same month, wrote of the Danites:

> Thus far, according to the ‹Revelat[o]r› order of the Danites, we have a company of Danites in these times, to put to right physically that which is not right, and to cleanse the Church of verry (sic) great evils which hath hitherto existed among us inasmuch as they cannot be put to right by teachings & persuasyons (sic), This company or a part of them exhibited on the fourth day of July They come up to consecrate, by companies of tens, commanded by their captain over ten.[551]

One estimate of the eventual number of the Danites is 800-1,000. Quinn gives a list of many of them.[552] The formation of these forces to enable the Mormons to establish their Zion in Missouri caused great concern among the citizens of Missouri, and prompted Governor Boggs to issue his Mormon removal/extermination order.

With the collapse of LDS projects in Kirtland, the de facto center became Far West, Missouri. By this time, and with Smith preoccupied in Kirtland, a number of principal LDS leaders had developed a personal history in "Zion."

Their story began in October 1830, when Oliver Cowdery, Parley P. Pratt, Peter Whitmer, Jr., and Ziba Peterson were called to undertake a mission to the "Lamanites." They reached Independence, Missouri, early in the year 1831. Cowdery returned to Kirtland but in November 1831, he and John Whitmer were sent to Independence with the revelations to be published there by William W. Phelps. During Joseph Smith's second visit to Missouri (in 1832), Oliver was appointed one of the high priests to preside over the members in the gathering place. When conflict with Missourians developed in July of 1833, he was sent as a messenger to inform the First Presidency at Kirtland. When Smith marched with Zion's Camp to Missouri in May of 1834, Sidney Rigdon and Oliver were left in charge of the Church at Kirtland. By early 1838 he had returned to Far West, Missouri.

---

[550] Oration Delivered by Mr. S. Rigdon, on the 4th of July, 1838 (Far West: Printed at the Journal Office, 1838), 8, 12. See Marquardt, *Rise of Mormonism*, 284-85.

[551] *Scriptory Book of Joseph Smith*, 60-61, in Marquardt, *Rise of Mormonism*, 286-87.

[552] Quinn, *Mormon Hierarchy*, 479-85.

Theocracy: Incipient Church Organization and Control

Joseph Smith was successful in attracting many able, energetic and ambitious people, whom he appointed to serious positions in his Church. From the start, he was aware of the possibility that there could be an effort to wrest the movement away from him. His ace was, of course, his key connection to the founding scripture. Short of his untimely demise, or clear fall from grace as a fallen prophet, the *Book of Mormon* underpinned his position, at least to a large degree.

The three witnesses were apparently concerned to be listed as having seen the gold plates *by the power of God*, and not at the hand of Joseph Smith like the other eight witnesses, setting themselves apart as having a special connection with the divine. Oliver Cowdery revealed a desire to elevate his role when he tried to become a cotranslator along with Joseph. A revelation was received regarding Cowdery (April, 1829), wherein the Lord said, "And, behold, I grant unto you a gift, if you desire of me, to translate, even as my servant Joseph." (D&C6:25) A second revelation, also in April, says, "And that you may know the mysteries of God, and that you may translate and receive knowledge from all those ancient records which have been hid up, that are sacred;.." (D&C 8:11) But in a subsequent revelation, he was deprived of this power: "Be patient, my son, for it is wisdom in me, and it is not expedient that you should translate at this present time." Cowdery, claiming to be an apostle, also claimed to have received a command to write words for the establishment of the new church. Smith had to foil this effort to be on a par with the prophet. It is improbable that Cowdery's role in producing the *Book of Mormon* had changed. Rather, Smith understood that it was not in his interest for Cowdery to become, as it were, an equal to himself. And Cowdery was made to understand that the chance of the new scripture being accepted was far greater if there were no hint of collaboration in its composition. Potential converts should be left to conclude that Smith, farm boy that he had been, could never have written the *Book of Mormon*, just as Jesus is depicted as impressing the learned in the temple as a young boy, and Muhammad was always said to have been illiterate.

The first emergence of hierarchy was already there: Smith, who translated by the gift of God, Smith and Cowdery who received the priesthood from John the Baptist personally and became the first elders, David Whitmer and Martin Harris who were called to be shown the plates by the power of God, and those who were shown the plates by Joseph Smith. With the instruction given in D&C 20 for the selection of the twelve, the top of the hierarchy became Smith, and then Cowdery, with David Whitmer actually or nearly on the same level.

The express rational for the entire enterprise was the Restoration of All Things (D&C 27:6 & 86:10), prior to the coming of Christ. A minimal idea of what this would entail is already made clear in the *Book of Mormon*. The true church will bear the name of Christ. (3 Nephi 27:5-8) Nephi "did consecrate Jacob and Joseph, that they should be priests and teachers over the land of my people." (2 Nephi 5:26; cf. Jacob 1:18) A church was established by Alma at the waters of Mormon, "And they were called the church of God, or the church of Christ, from that time forward." (Mosiah 18:17) He established another "in the land of Sidom, and consecrated priests and teachers in the land, to baptize..." (Alma 15:13) He preached about the high priesthood of Melchizedek. (Alma 13:14-18) The procedures and prayer for baptism were given in 3 Nephi 11:23-27. The Book of Moroni makes a rather jarring break from the characteristic *Book of Mormon* style, and delineates church institutions and rites "that perhaps they may be of worth unto my brethren, the Lamanites, in some future day..." (Moroni 1:4) These passages were taken from the Articles of the Church of Christ by Oliver Cowdery in June and inserted into Moroni, which was added later on so they could appear as part of the BoM. They included the procedures and prayer for the ordination of priests and teachers, and the blessing of the Sacrament (Holy Communion). Moroni also adds the gift of the Holy Ghost, not found in Articles (Moroni 2:3). Even the wording of the prayers to bless the bread and wine is given. Although this did not yet constitute an ecclesiastical hierarchy, it shows that the issues of Church organization and rites were being thought out even before the new bible saw the light of day. The intention was clear: as soon as the *Book of Mormon* was printed, the foundation and rites of the new church could begin.

Theocracy: Controlling Information and Church History

The Church was organized on 6 April 1830 in the Fayette home of Peter Whitmer. A revelation received that day began with the words, "Behold, there shall be kept a record among you." (D&C 21:1) Oliver Cowdery was assigned to write the Church history, but after he was sent to Missouri, John Whitmer became the first historian in March of 1831. After Cowdery's return five months later, he, Whitmer and Phelps (Church printer) were assigned to prepare the Church revelations and print them in Missouri. The production of a Church history, which was at that point essentially the history of Joseph Smith, was considered so important that Smith himself put pen to paper and produced a personal account between 20 July and 27 November 1832.[553] He worked to produce another account in 1838-39.[554] On 1 March 1842, he provided a historical sketch, upon request, to a Chicago editor, John Wentworth.[555]

In 1834-35, in consultation with Joseph to some extent, Cowdery published a history of the Church in its publication, *Messenger and Advocate*. This account does not agree with the later official version in some important details.

Theocracy: Church & Community Management by Revelation

Smith's managerial style could be called *management by revelation*. For this reason, the collection of his revelations in the current *Doctrine and Covenants* contains considerable detail regarding Church history. As a result, God's word had to be carefully edited, and was subject to change over time. Cowdery worked with Smith on the preparation of the first publication of revelations, called the *Book of Commandments*. He was also either the editor, or on the editorial board, of early Church publications, such as the *Evening and the Morning Star*, the *Messenger and Advocate*, and the *Northern Times*. In this capacity he could also monitor the messages of the Church over time. An example of the problems that he could face is treated by Marquardt: "*The Evening and the Morning Star* [printed originally by Phelps in Missouri], printed in Kirtland between January and June 1835 under the title *Evening and Morning Star*, altered the texts, deleted previously published material, and inserted editorial comments by Cowdery."[556] An important Cowdery editorial comment reads: "On the revelations we merely say, that we were not a little surprised to find the previous print so different from the original."[557] In other words, the original used in Missouri for the *Book of Commandments* was not the original used in Kirtland for the D&C, and Cowdery feared he might be blamed.

For the occasion of the establishment meeting of the Church, a different sort of revelation was presented to the membership, a collaborative effort of Smith and Cowdery regarding details of church organization. In his 1839 history, Smith introduced it by saying, "We

---

[553] Dean C. Jessee, *Personal Writings of Joseph Smith*, 3-14.
[554] Jessee, *ibid*, 196-211.
[555] Jessee, *ibid*, 212-220.
[556] Marquardt, *Rise of Mormonism*, 175.
[557] *Idem.*

obtained of him [Jesus Christ] the following, by the spirit of prophecy and revelation..." [558] The text is not in the divine first person, but in the first person plural. Smith and Cowdery are referred to as "an Apostle of Jesus Christ an elder of the Church."[559] Smith was called of God and ordained, while Cowdery was just called of God. This is stated in the past tense, indicating that they claimed that they had already been called to that status. Perhaps Cowdery was ordained by Smith, since there is no other referent for the pronoun in the phrase "under his hand." It is interesting to note that in the later D&C version (20:3, 5), Smith became "the first elder of this Church," and Cowdery "the second elder of this church."

The revelation describes the manner of baptism (20:37); the duties of the elders, priests, teachers, deacons, and members of the church of Christ (20:38-67); and the duties of the members after they are received by baptism (20:68-84). Another revelation gives the position of Joseph Smith: "...thou shalt be called a seer, a translator, a prophet, an apostle of Jesus Christ, an elder of the church through the will of God the Father, and the grace of your Lord Jesus Christ." Oliver Cowdery was again called an apostle, and "the first preacher of this church unto the church, and before the world..." (21:10-12)

Another issue is the emergence of the status of apostle. It is no easy matter to separate the statuses of "apostle" and "elder" at this early date. The study of the evolution of the authority to receive revelation, and of various statuses and positions, has been difficult due to a lack of sufficient contemporary information, and statements made by those who left the Church, the dissenters. For men such as David Whitmer and William E. McLellin, these issues were points of contention in their war with Joseph Smith and the Mormon establishment.

Already prior to 6 April 1830, both Smith and Cowdery had been ordained to be apostles. Church tradition has held that this was under the hands of Peter, James and John, but early references to support this are not found (cf D&C 128:20). As for Smith's statuses indicated in his long title, the revelation states: "Wherefore it behooveth me that he shall be ordained by you, Oliver Cowdery mine apostle..." (D&C 21:10) Since the ordination by John the Baptist on 15 May 1829 was by the laying on of hands, and the ordination to be an apostle, and first and second elders, was "under his hand," it seems reasonable to conclude that Cowdery's ordination of Smith to be seer, translator, prophet, and apostle was also by

---

[558] Joseph Smith's 1839 history, in Vogel, *Early Mormon Documents*, I:90.
[559] D&C, 20:2-3; cf. the text in the Zebedee Coltrin Journal, in Marquardt, *Joseph Smith Revelations*, 63.

the laying on of hands. Cowdery and David Whitmer were called apostles in D&C 18 and the former is referred to as an apostle in his Articles in 1829.

Theocracy: Control over Revelation

Given the central role of revelation in the management of the church, establishing both doctrine and ritual, as well as the authority and power relations between the leaders of the Church, it quickly became obvious that the authority to receive revelation should be defined. In September of 1830, *Book of Mormon* witness Hiram Page claimed to have received revelations by means of his own seerstone pertaining to the "upbuilding of Zion." This set off alarms. A revelation came, addressing the issue (D&C 28):

> 1. Behold, I say unto thee, Oliver, that it shall be given unto thee that thou shalt be heard by the church in all things whatsoever thou shalt teach them by the Comforter, concerning the revelations and commandments which I have given.
> 2. But, behold, verily, verily, I say unto thee, no one shall be appointed to receive commandments and revelations in this church excepting my servant Joseph Smith, Jun., for he receiveth them even as Moses.
> 11. And again thou [Oliver] shalt take thy brother, Hiram Page, between him and thee alone, and tell him that those things which he hath written from that stone are not of me and that Satan deceiveth him...

Smith had taken two steps to counter this threat. First, he made it perfectly clear that although someone such as Cowdery could be guided by the Comforter to understand and teach what had already been received, only Smith could receive doctrine and commandments in the first instance, including directives, for the Church. Second, he used the talents of Cowdery to get Page to retract his revelation, while remaining in the faith.

This did not end there. A few months later a woman named Hubble claimed to be a prophetess, to have received a number of revelations, and to be a teacher to the Church.[560] After providing a number of examples of the problem, Elder George A. Smith said, "There was a prevalent spirit all through the early history of this church, which prompted the Elders to suppose that they knew more than the Prophet. Elders would tell you that

---

[560] *History of the Church,* 1:154n.

the Prophet was going wrong."[561] This situation prompted a second revelation, which went even further. Smith devised a strategy to undermine efforts to displace him (D&C 43):

> 3. And this ye shall know assuredly, that there is none other appointed unto you to receive commandments and revelations until he be taken, if he abide in me.
> 4. But verily, verily, I say unto you, that none else shall be appointed unto this gift except it be through him, for if it be taken from him, he shall not have power except to appoint another in his stead...

In other words, even if Joseph should be found to be a fallen prophet, he would have one remaining power: to designate his successor. This is not simply a matter of theology. It is a matter of authority, and ultimately power within the emerging organization. Smith did not establish the Church to stand idly by and allow recent converts, or even one of the eleven witnesses, arguably the least of them at that, to determine its organization or theology.

Theocracy: Establishing the Apostles of the Church

In the *Book of Mormon*, during the mission of Jesus Christ in the New World, he established his church, and selected twelve disciples. It is interesting that these were not called apostles. Most probably this was due to a concern that some latter-day converts may have felt that there could only be the twelve they were already familiar with. Apart from this change in title, their role was the same. By June14, 1829, a revelation commanded: "And now, behold, I give unto you Oliver Cowdery, and also unto David Whitmer, that you shall search out the Twelve who shall have the desires of which I have spoken" (D&C 18:37). Irrespective of title or role, it was decided already, long before the publication of the new scripture, that there would be twelve. This traditional number is already evident in Smith plus the eleven witnesses. During the first few years, sources refer to a number of persons as apostles, although it is not clear what is meant on each occasion.[562] The most we can say for sure is that with reference to apostleship as a fundamental component of Church organization, as early as 14 June 1829 there were to be twelve, and on 14 February 1835, in

---

[561] *Journal of Discourses*, (Liverpool: B. Young, 1867) 11:7. Edition cited, Photo Lithographic Reprint (Los Angeles: Gartner Printing & Litho Co., 1956).
[562] D. Michael Quinn, *Mormon Hierarchy*, 7-14.

Kirtland, Ohio, Cowdery, Whitmer and Harris, the original three witnesses, chose twelve men to be ordained as apostles.[563] These included: John F. Boynton, Orson Hyde, Luke S. Johnson, Lyman E. Johnson, Heber C. Kimball, Thomas B. Marsh, William E. McLellin, David W. Patten, Orson Pratt, Parley P. Pratt, William Smith and Brigham Young. William Smith is the only blood relative (brother) of Joseph Smith; and no witness to the *Book of Mormon* was included.

In the New Testament, the term "apostle" was not restricted to the twelve disciples of Christ. Those Twelve, however, became a special group very early in Christian custom and theology. However, they were scattered about, and were never able to function as a body. So too in Mormonism, even this Quorum of Twelve Apostles did not occupy the same position that they have today. Certainly Smith, the three witnesses, probably the eight as well, and other early leaders, such as Sidney Rigdon, did not see themselves as being reduced by their exclusion from the group.

The essence of authority in Mormonism is priesthood. The earliest printed reference to priesthood is in the *Book of Mormon* itself, which refers to Melchizedek as "having exercised mighty faith, and received the office of the high priesthood according to the holy order of God..." (Alma 13:18) The account of the visitation of John the Baptist to Smith and Cowdery does not find its way into print until Cowdery's October, 1834 history.[564] Baptisms were happening prior to the publication of the *Book of Mormon*, so it would appear that there was some event that served as the basis for this authority. Early references to priesthood refer to the high priesthood, probably taken from the *Book of Mormon* passage above. Two distinct priesthoods, the high priesthood (of Melchizedek) and the lesser priesthood (of Aaron, the Aaronic or Levitical priesthood) were explained on 22-23 September 1832: "Abraham received the Priesthood from Melchizedek... and the Lord confirmed a priesthood also upon Aaron and his seed..." Due to the sins of Israel, "therefore he [the Lord] took Moses out of their midst and the holy Priesthood also, and the lesser Priesthood continued, which Priesthood holdeth the keys of ministering of angels and the preparatory gospel,.. which [priesthood] the Lord caused to continue with the house of Aaron among the children of Israel..." (D&C 84:14, 18, 25-27)

Yet a third priesthood had emerged by 1834, the patriarchal priesthood, an appendage to the Aaronic priesthood, which came to be

---

[563] Kirtland Council Minute Book, 147, 149. See Marquardt, *Rise of Mormonism*, 231-32.

[564] Quinn, *Mormon Hierarchy*, 15.

limited to the bestowal and sealing of patriarchal blessings. A significant aspect is that it is by blood. Joseph Smith claimed to have it by birth (D&C 86:8-9).[565] No ordination or laying on of hands was needed. This implies that his bloodline goes back to the ancient patriarchs. In this sense, it served to add to Smith's status. In 1834, Joseph Smith Sr. was ordained Presiding Patriarch. Others are ordained to be patriarchs without having this hereditary priesthood. The duties of the Presiding Patriarch (Patriarch of the Church) have varied over time. Until 1942 he supervised, presided over, and sometimes ordained local patriarchs.[566]

Theocracy: The Keys, and Rigdon's Intrigue

Finally, the LDS doctrine of "keys" is an important adjunct to the concept of priesthood. The keys are powers to perform specific acts; they direct the use of priesthood. In current Mormon belief, Smith and Cowdery not only received the Melchizedek priesthood from Peter, James and John, but also the keys to the apostolic office. An account of events in the summer of 1832, told in an autobiographical work of Philo Dibble, is at least illustrative of the role of keys in the power struggle:

On invitation of Father [John] Johnson, of Hiram, Joseph removed his family to his home, to translate the New Testament. This was in the year 1831.

At this time Sidney Rigdon was left to preside at Kirtland and frequently preached to us. Upon one occasion he said the keys of the kingdom were taken from us. On hearing this, many of his hearers wept, and when some one undertook to dismiss the meeting by prayer he said praying would do them no good, and the meeting broke up in confusion.

Brother Hyrum [Smith] came to my house the next morning and told me all about it, and said it was false, and that the keys of the kingdom were still with us. He wanted my carriage and horses to go to the town of Hiram and bring Joseph. The word went abroad among the people immediately that Sidney [Rigdon] was going to expose "Mormonism."

Joseph came up to Kirtland a few days afterwards and held a meeting in a large barn. Nearly all the inhabitants of Kirtland turned out to hear him. The barn was filled with people, and others, unable to get inside, stood around

---

[565] *Ibid*, 32-34.
[566] Arnold K. Garr, Donald Q. Cannon & Richard O. Cowan, *Encyclopedia of Latter-day Saint History* (Salt Lake City: Deseret Book Company, 2011), 899.

the door as far as they could hear.

> Joseph arose in our midst and spoke in mighty power, saying: "I can contend with wicked men and devils--yes with angels. No power can pluck those keys from me, except the power that gave them to me; that was Peter, James and John. But for what Sidney [Rigdon] has done, the devil shall handle him as one man handles another."[567]

Smith had to act, but ever so carefully. Rigdon had brought with him into the church former members of his Baptist congregation who were loyal to him. Initially, he disfellowshipped Rigdon (6 July 1832), but on the next day he rebuked him again and stripped him of the high priesthood. After receiving an expression of repentance, Smith reordained him to the high priesthood (28 July 1832).[568]

Theocracy: Stakes & the Bishops: Law, Justice & Goods

The ecclesiastical administrative divisions in the Church developed slowly. Initially, Smith referred to Kirtland as a stake in Zion, a metaphor based on the stakes of a tent (cf. Isaiah 33:20 & 54:2). Another was the stake in Missouri. The Nauvoo stake was composed of wards. In modern Mormonism, these correspond roughly to a parish (ward) and a diocese (stake). In Nauvoo, the divisions were more administrative. Each ward, once established, was headed by a lay bishop, whose duties tended to be temporal, administering to the needs of the members, and mobilizing them for projects, such as work on the temple. Each stake was also headed by a bishop, initially Newel K. Whitney for Ohio, and Edward Partridge for Missouri (Zion). John Corrill and Isaac Morley were ordained as assistants to Bishop Partridge. Both were ordained to the position (1831), but the positions lacked definition. They were to collect donations, essentially for the poor, but the residue should be stored, and used to purchase land for the church or construction projects. They should also investigate those who sin, for if they do not repent they "shall be cast out of the church." (D&C 42:31-37) Jurisdictional issues arose, largely as Bishop Partridge interpreted his authority very broadly, to the point of challenging Smith's ecclesiastical supremacy. A revelation rebuked and warned Partridge. (D&C 58: 14-15)

In November of 1831 Smith issued a divine clarification:

---

[567] Philo Dibble in "Early Scenes in Church History," *Four Faith Promoting Classics* (Salt Lake City: Bookcraft, 1968), pp. 79-80.
[568] Quinn, *Mormon Hierarchy*, 42.

65. Wherefore, it must needs be that one be appointed, of the High Priesthood, to preside over the Priesthood; and he shall be called President of the High Priesthood of the Church.

66. Or in other words, the presiding High Priest over the High Priesthood of the Church.

67. From the same comes the administering of ordinances and blessings upon the church, by the laying on of the hands.

68. Wherefore, the office of a bishop is not equal unto it; for the office of a bishop is in administering all temporal things[569]

Five weeks after being ordained to that office by Sidney Rigdon, Smith chose counselors to assist him in the Presidency of the High Priesthood, later changed to the First Presidency of the Church. Out of this incident, Smith not only limited and defined the office of Bishop, but also added another title, making it perfectly clear that he presided over all priesthood in the Church.

When the First Presidency was established, Sidney Rigdon (a former minister), and Jesse Gause (a relatively recent convert), were chosen as Smith's counselors in this office. These selections were made under an unlucky star. Ordained 8 March 1832, Gause was excommunicated on 3 December 1832, following Smith's actions to reign in Sidney Rigdon. On 5 January 1833, Frederick G. Williams was appointed a counselor to Smith. Back in favor, Sidney Rigdon was made first counselor "to preside over the Church in the abscence (sic) of brother Joseph."[570] On 5 December 1834, Smith ordained Cowdery as Assistant President of the High Priesthood, placing him over Rigdon and Williams, administratively.

Having presented his mission as the Restoration of All Things, and not wanting to leave anything out, Smith established a quorum of seventies, like the seventy elders of Israel (Numbers 11:16) and the seventy to announce the gospel. (Luke 10:1-17) He began choosing them on 28 February 1835. Proselytism was the essence of their calling, but over time, the institution has been reinvented more than once. The fact that they are sometimes called apostles comes from their calling to travel out to preach (evangelical apostles), apostle originally meaning one who has been sent forth, an emissary. The Seventies, whether they actually numbered seventy or fewer, were presided over by seven drawn from their

---

[569] Received in a revelation of November 1831, but inserted into D&C 107:65-68. See Quinn, *Mormon Hierarchy*, 39-40 & 70-71.

[570] Dean C. Jessee, *Personal Writings of Joseph Smith*, 34.

midst. Beginning in 1835, the seven Presidents of the Seventy were included in the Church General Authorities.

Church hierarchy came to be the President of the Church, the two Counselors to the President (these three being the First Presidency), the Quorum of the Twelve Apostles, the Presidents of the Seventy, and the Presiding Bishopric.

Theocracy: Smith Sloughs off His Earliest Partners

As the role of Sydney Rigdon in the development of LDS theology and rites grew, Smith was enabled to reduce his reliance on his former partners, Oliver Cowdery and David Whitmer, who had been conveniently sidelined geographically.

Proliferation of positions and theological developments that marked more radical departure from Christian doctrines produced cleavage between two groups, those who had initially felt strongly that the churches had become far too bureaucratic and cherished the principle of a clear separation of church and state, and those who leaned toward hierarchy. In addition to the bureaucratic development in Mormonism, there emerged an inherent theocratic tendency. The Church was established as a precursor for the Second Coming, and Christ's reign on earth. That would be a world government, it would be totally theocratic under the Kingship of Christ, and church and state would be one and the same.

On July 7, 1834, Smith ordained Whitmer to be the president of the church in Missouri. He served in that capacity with his brother John Whitmer and William W. Phelps as his counsellors, from then until 1838. They and their fellows virtually founded the town of Far West.

In September of 1837, Smith personally announced that "Oliver Cowdery has been in transgression, but as he is now chosen as one of the presidents or counselors, I trust that he will humble himself and magnify his calling..."[571] The truth of the charge cannot be ascertained. But it is known that Cowdery had become increasingly interested in politics. Furthermore, he, David and John Whitmer, and W. W. Phelps sold their land in Missouri at a time when some prominent Saints felt that doing so showed a lack of faith in the prospects of Jackson County becoming the gathering place for Zion. They were seen by some to be property speculators.

On 30 January 1838, Cowdery, David and John Whitmer, W. W. Phelps, Frederick G. Williams, Jacob Whitmer and Lyman E. Johnson,

---

[571] Gunn, *Oliver Cowdery*, 141.

met in the home of Oliver Cowdery in Far West, to discuss the "state of said church and the manner in which some of the authorities of the same have for a time past, and are still endeavoring to unite ecclesiastical and civil authority, and force men under pretense of incurring the displeasure of heaven to use their earthly substance contrary to their own interest and privilege..."[572] The new presidency proceeded to try Cowdery and the Whitmers, and they were cut off from the Church. They and Cowdery protested that this council was illegitimate.

The Whitmers and Phelps were then the presidency in Missouri. They were replaced by Thomas B. Marsh and David W. Patten. The former gave an account in his autobiography.[573]

> Sometime in the winter, George M. Hinkle, John Murdock and some others came to my house, and suggested the importance of calling a meeting to take into consideration the manner that W. [William] W. Phelps and David and John Whitmer had disposed of the money which I had borrowed in the Tennessee and Kentucky Branches in 1836. Accordingly, a meeting was called February 5th, 1838, and the conduct of the Presidency in Zion investigated. The Church would not sustain said presidency, but appointed myself and Brother D. [David] W. Patten presidents, pro tem., until Joseph Smith would arrive. We also reorganized the Church in Zion, placing every officer in his proper place. Joseph arrived in Far West, March 14th, and approved of the course we had pursued.

On 14 March 1838, Smith arrived in Far West, but even with his presence things grew no better. Cowdery and the Whitmers openly confronted Smith regarding his failure to separate church and state. Cowdery accused Smith of immoral behavior. Nine formal charges were drawn up against Oliver Cowdery, including a charge that he had accused Joseph Smith of adultery. He was summoned, and when he failed (refused) to attend the hearing, he was excommunicated on 12 April 1838. David Whitmer was excommunicated the day after. John Whitmer had been excommunicated on 10 March, and William W. Phelps on 17 March. Since Martin Harris had joined the Kirtland apostates and the church of Warren Parrish, all of the Three Witnesses had left the Church, and all of the Eight Witnesses excepting the three Smiths. From September 1837 through May 1838, the excommunicated included two of the Church Presidency, the three of the Presidency at Far West, four of the Quorum of the Twelve

---

[572] Huntington Library Letters, no. 90, in Gunn, *Oliver Cowdery*, 149-50.
[573] Thomas B. Marsh, "History of Thomas Baldwin Marsh [by himself]," *The Latter-day Saints' Millennial Star* 26 (1864), 359-60, 375-76, 390- 92, 406.

Apostles and six of the *Book of Mormon* witnesses.[574] The purge left the Smiths and Rigdon in firm control. Joseph and his family had a whole new team. Again.

Excommunication was not sufficient. On 17 June 1838, Sidney Rigdon delivered his "salt" sermon, described by John Corrill as follows:

> President Rigden ⟨Rigdon⟩ delivered from the pulpit what I call the salt sermon; "If the salt have lost its savour, it is thenceforth good for nothing, but to be cast out and trodden under the feet of men," was his text, and although he did not call names in his sermon, yet it was plainly understood that he meant the dissenters, or those who denied the faith, ought to be cast out, and literally trodden under foot. He, indirectly, accused some of them with crime.[575]

Two days later, Oliver Cowdery, David Whitmer, John Whitmer, Apostle Lyman E. Johnson, and Mormon printer/editor William W. Phelps fled Missouri for their lives in response to a written death threat signed by eighty-three Saints, including the Danite chief Sampson Avard, two members of the First Presidency, and eight other Danites.[576] The letter reads as follows:

> …for out of the county you shall go, and no power shall save you. And you shall have three days after you receive this communication to you, including twenty-four hours in each day, for you to depart with your families peaceably; which you may do undisturbed by any person; but in that time, if you do not depart, we will use the means in our power to cause you to depart; for go you shall… and vengeance sleepeth not, neither does it slumber; and unless you heed us this time, and attend to our request, it will overtake you at an hour when you do not expect, and at a day when you do not look for it; and for you there shall be no escape; for there is but one decree for you, which is depart, depart, or a more fatal calamity shall befall you.[577]

Moses vs Apostles: Joseph Smith saw himself as a new Moses, while for Cowdery and the Whitmers, the appropriate model for the Church was

---

[574]Marquardt, *Rise of Mormonism*, 282.

[575] John Corrill, *A Brief History of the Church of Christ of Latter Day Saints*, 30; quoted in Marquardt, *Ibid*, 283.

[576] Marquardt, *ibid*; Quinn, *Mormon Hierarchy*, 472.

[577] *Document Containing the Correspondence, Orders &C. in Relation to the Disturbances with the Mormons; and the Evidence Given before the Hon. Austin A. King, Judge of the Fifth Judicial Circuit of the State of Missouri* (1841: Fayette, MO, Office of the Boob's Lick Democrat), 103.

Christ's Twelve Apostles with a high degree of autonomy in their revelation-guided ministries.

Joseph Smith and Criminal Justice in Missouri

The history of conflict between the Mormon settlers and Missouri residents tested Smith's judgment as a leader and statesman. The successful relocation to Commerce, Illinois, and its transformation to an impressive and viable community, shows that he had options. A simple revelation could have been received stating that because Satan had turned the hearts of enemies in Zion against the work of the Lord, and as in the case of Israel wandering in the desert, the plan of the Lord was for a temporary settlement in peace elsewhere until the time was ripe, thereby sparing innocent lives. The success of Brigham Young later to direct the Saints to undertake a massive move to the Rockies (D&C 136) also shows that alternatives existed. Perhaps inspired by the success of the holy warriors in the *Book of Mormon*, Joseph chose a less peaceful course.

During June to October 1838, the Mormon-Missourian conflict developed into what Missouri historians have dubbed the Mormon war. During this time, the Danites were "under the general command of Secretary of War Joseph Smith."[578]

On August 8: Smith led an armed group of over a hundred and surrounded the home of Justice of the Peace Adam Black, who had been elected Judge only two days earlier.

August 10: Based on a sworn statement from William P. Peniston, Judge King issued a warrant for the arrest of Smith and Lyman Wight.

August 28, Judge Black gave his sworn statement of the events. Sheriff William Morgan attempted to arrest Wight, but arrived at Wight's home only to find he was protected by an armed force of about 100 men.

Around August 16: Daviess County Sheriff Morgan, accompanied by Judge Josiah Morin, went to serve a warrant on Smith in Far West. Smith refused to return to Daviess County.

September 7: Judge Austin Augustus King conducted a hearing and found sufficient evidence to send the case to a grand jury. Smith was released on a $500 bond.

November 2: After the surrender of Mormon forces, Smith was surrendered to authorities, arrested and imprisoned in the jail at Liberty, Missouri.

---

[578] Quinn, *Mormon Hierarchy*, 472.

November 12: Judge King found "probable cause to believe that Joseph Smith, Jr., Lyman Wight, Hyrum Smith, Alexander McRay & Caleb Baldwin are guilty of Overt acts of Treason in Daviess County." Smith and other Mormons continued to be held at Liberty Jail (MO).

April 11, 1839: Smith was indicted by grand jury on the charge of treason.

April 16: Smith and his companions were permitted to escape while they were being escorted to Boone County. Smith fled across the border to Illinois.[579]

Security and Enforcement in Nauvoo

During 1839-1844, Joseph Smith's Lifeguards were in place in Nauvoo, with former Danites, including a former Danite captain.[580] During the period 1839-1843, ad hoc enforcers, former Danites, undertook internal and external security.

The Nauvoo Legion was organized for external security, but included former Danites and members of Smith's ceremonial Lifeguards.[581] The needs of internal and external security were also met by Nauvoo's constables, including a Danite officer. During 1843-46, the Nauvoo police undertook external and internal security duties, including acting as bodyguards for Joseph Smith until his murder in 1844, and for Brigham Young as of August, 1844. The officers were former Danites, and most policemen were Danites.[582] Even adolescents and preadolescents were organized into the Nauvoo Whistling & Whittling Brigade, primarily for non-Mormon targets.

On 7 June 1844, the *Nauvoo Expositor*, a four-page newspaper, was issued. Although expressing faith in the Bible and *Book of Mormon*, it criticized Joseph Smith. It contained a list of fifteen resolutions relating to Church abuses. The doctrines of spiritual wives and polytheism were rejected. At a time when Illinois was reviewing its decision to issue the Nauvoo Charter, it called for the repeal of the Charter. On June 8, the Nauvoo City Council met to discuss the *Expositor*. On June 10, Joseph Smith commanded the city marshal to destroy the press. William Clayton reported, "The City council passed a resolution declaring the Printing press on the hill a 'nuisance' and ordered it destroyed if not moved in 3 hours

---

[579] "Joseph Smith and the criminal justice system," *Wikipedia*, 20 October 2015.
[580] *Idem.*
[581] Quinn, *ibid*, 473.
[582] *ibid*, 474.

notice. The police gathered at the Temple about sundown and after organizing proceeded to the office and demolished the press & scattered the Type."[583]

Following Smith's death, there were various attempts against dissenters and traitors. In the period 1845-46, the Nauvoo Whistling & Whittling Brigade, now aged 17 to 56, targeted mainly dissidents. On 3 April 1845, Brigham Young praised the Nauvoo police for beating "a man almost to death in the Temple." On 14 September 1845, the Nauvoo police "had to flog" dissenters for trying to attend an open-air "business meeting" of the Church.[584]

Security and Enforcement in Brigham Young's Utah Territory

The main group of Mormons, with Brigham Young, arrived in the Salt Lake valley on 24 July 1847. Almost from the moment of their arrival, Brigham Young had undertaken to establish his own country in Utah Territory. Apparently anticipating Young's ambitions, three years later the U. S. Congress created the Utah Territory (9 September 1850). This act of Congress set up the territory political structure, including the office of Territorial Governor (appointed every four years), the Utah Territorial Assembly (representatives chosen annually), and a Utah judiciary, including a Supreme Court, District Courts, Probate Courts and a Justice of the Peace. On 9 February 1851, Brigham Young was inaugurated the first governor, and was appointed for two terms (appointed by Fillmore and Pierce). No sooner had the Mormons gotten across the plains and Rockies, and arrived in their new Zion, than the Federal government stepped in and, in a sense, took it over, created Federal institutions, and sent in Federal officers. The reaction on the part of some was violent. Shortly after Young's appointment, a number of Federal appointees left their posts, some claiming that they were fleeing for their lives. An Associate Justice, William W. Drummond was especially influential, and reported that the Mormons recognize no authority but the priesthood. Their reports convinced the White House that the Mormons were revolting against the United State government. Events led to the "Utah War." Alfred Cumming accompanied Albert Sidney Johnston's expedition to put down the rebellion. Brigham Young issued a call to arms:

---

[583] William Clayton Journal, entry for June 10, 1844; Marquardt, *Rise of Mormonism*, 387-89.
[584] Quinn, *ibid*, 476.

Proclamation by the Governor. "Citizens of Utah—We are invaded by a hostile force who are evidently assailing us to accomplish our overthrow and destruction ... Therefore I, Brigham Young, Governor and Superintendent for Indian Affairs for the Territory of Utah ... forbid all armed forces, of every description, from coming into this Territory under any pretence [sic] whatever ... That all the forces in said Territory hold themselves in readiness to march at a moment's notice, to repel any and all such invasion ... Martial law is hereby declared to exist in this Territory, from and after the Publication of this Proclamation...fifteenth day of September, A.D. Eighteen hundred and fifty seven..." [585]

Young was governing with an iron fist. "Ad hoc enforcers (former Danites, non-Danites and some trusted Mormon criminals on specific assignments against anti-Mormons and apostates)" continued activities, called variously "'minute Men,' 'Brigham's Boys' or 'Be'-boys,'."[586]

President James Buchanan decided to appoint a new governor. Initially, prospective appointees refused the honor. Finally, Alfred Cumming was appointed, and Buchanan sent a military force of 2,500 to create a post in Utah, in support of the governor. Cumming arrived in the territory in November, 1857. After considerable military developments on both sides, both decided that a peaceful settlement was the best option. Buchanan's terms were that the Mormons should submit to federal laws, and in exchange, amnesties were offered. Young accepted; but he was never again appointed governor. His loss of government office probably did not represent a significant decrease in his effective power and influence in Utah. Still, Utah was under *de facto* military occupation.

The times were changing, and eventually the Mormons sought statehood. In the process, the Utah territory was whittled down to a fraction of its maximum size, polygamy was outlawed, and Utah achieved statehood in 1896. The contrast between Utah, and its two neighbors, Wyoming and Colorado, is remarkable. While Utah was still practicing polygamy, Wyoming became the first state to give women the vote, and the first state to have a woman governor, while Colorado was the second.

---

[585] Text in an auction notice of Sotheby Park Bernet Inc.: *Highly Important American Historical Documents, Autograph Letters & Manuscripts. The Property of the Elsie O. & Philip D. Lang Foundation, Part Two* (New York: Cosmos Press, 1978), item 585.

[586] Quinn, *Mormon Hierarchy*, 477.

Joseph Smith: Loose Cannon, or Mission Accomplished?

After destroying the *Nauvoo Expositor*, Smith and a number of colleagues were charged at Carthage, Illinois, with instigating a riot in destroying the *Expositor*. Rather than submit to the sheriff who came to arrest them, he secured a writ from the Nauvoo court; he, Hyrum Smith, John Taylor, William W. Phelps and others were tried and acquitted on June 17 by Daniel H. Wells, a non-Mormon judge in Nauvoo, who was friendly to the Mormons. This provoked an angry reaction among his opponents, and thousands gathered to take up arms. On June 18, Smith called up the Nauvoo Legion, nearly 5,000 strong when in full force.

As the Saints were digging in, Governor Thomas Ford decided to visit the scene himself. At Carthage he found the forces against the Mormons to be formidable, and on 21 June he sent a letter to Smith asking that representatives come to Carthage to inform him. Smith immediately prepared statements which he sent to Ford with John M. Bernhisel and John Taylor. These delegates were given a message from Ford, in which he stated that the Mormons had violated freedom of the press, freedom from search and seizure without due process, and the division of powers, i.e., the legislative and judicial powers. He requested that Smith surrender for trial.

On 23 June, Joseph, Hyrum, Willard Richards and Orrin Porter Rockwell crossed the Mississippi to take refuge among friends. When word of his flight spread through Nauvoo, the reaction of the Mormons was confusion and dissension. Some accused him of cowardice, to flee in their hour of need. His wife Emma wrote a letter urging his return. When word of this reached Joseph, reportedly he said, "If my life is of no value to my friends, it is of none to myself," and he returned. Most probably he had had time to reflect. Missouri was full of people ready to hunt him down, even without the offer of a bounty. He must have realized that he had no chance on the run.

He returned, and upon the urging of Major General Jonathan Dunham he disbanded the Nauvoo Legion, and surrendered at Carthage. Those charged appeared at a hearing before Robert F. Smith, an anti-Mormon justice of the peace who was also Captain of the Carthage Greys. He charged them with riot in destroying the *Nauvoo Expositor,* released them on bond of five hundred dollars each to appear at the next term of the circuit court. That evening at their hotel they were served with a mittimus signed by Robert F. Smith to hold Joseph, Hyrum, and Apostles John Taylor and Willard Richards in jail until they could be tried for treason.

They protested this new charge, but to no avail. They were put in Carthage jail.

Joseph Smith had made serious miscalculations. The first was his response to the events in Missouri in the summer of 1833. He could have resorted to plan B, yet another location, with a metaphor of the children of Israel wandering in the wilderness, waiting for the time to be right to enter into the land of promise. Instead, he decided to pursue plan A with a military force, Zion's Camp, and to lead it to Missouri. Although a peaceful stalemate was arrived at in 1834, the military option had been prepared, and its use in response to subsequent persecution of Mormons contributed to the Mormon War in Missouri. Even when the court system falls short of justice, by any American law, then or now, raising a private military force to seek justice outside of the legal order, resulting in injury and death, has to lead to serious (probably capital) charges. Ohio, Illinois and Missouri were all long-since established states of the Union.

Following the serious events in Missouri, and having fled from the charge of treason against him there, Smith had become ensconced in Nauvoo, outside of Missouri jurisdiction, and protected by the Nauvoo legion, the Nauvoo police, his bodyguards and the Danites. His next miscalculation was the destruction of the *Nauvoo Expositor* press. He might rather have stood his ground theologically against his detractors, while possibly pursuing other legal action. As Ford put it to him, a legal response to the *Expositor* had to follow due process. Ignoring this enabled his enemies to press charges for violation of Illinois law, and gave them the opportunity to extricate him from Nauvoo.

Although the events of the arrest and assassination of Joseph and Hyrum Smith in Carthage Jail have not been fully clarified, the following seem to be noteworthy. First, Illinois Governor Ford was not a friend of the Mormons. Yet Smith relied on protection by Ford's two detachments. But once the accused were in custody, Ford sent them back home. His absence and the removal of his detachments created ideal circumstances for an anti-Mormon justice of the peace to prefer an outstanding Missouri charge of treason, and to jail them to await trial. Joseph and Hyrum Smith, John Taylor, and Willard Richards were arrested JP Robert F. Smith, who was also the captain of the Carthage Greys, an anti-Mormon government-authorized local militia. Next, Although doubted by some LDS scholars, it has been argued that Smith relied on rescue by the Nauvoo legion, by a command he sent to its major general Jonathan Dunham; but he failed to act.[587] At the time of the attack by the mob, the Carthage Greys stood

---

[587] Journal of Allen Joseph Stout. See Brodie, *No Man Knows My History*, 392.

down, although some few of them may have made a mock response, shooting over the heads of the mob.

His death on 27 June 1844 was totally traumatic to the Mormons in Nauvoo. Sidney Rigdon, having already attempted a failed effort to take over the movement, quickly played his cards, but was not accepted as the successor. He left to found his own church and was excommunicated. A second claimant, James Jesse Strang, claimed that Joseph had appointed him in a letter, but his claim was not accepted. He too left and established the "Strangites," and was excommunicated. At the urging of Apostle William E. McLellin, David Whitmer made his claim, but unsuccessfully. In 1847, Joseph's brother William announced that he was the legitimate successor by right of descent. His church lasted only a few years. On August 8, 1844, the Saints sustained the Quorum of the Twelve Apostles, with Brigham Young, as their leaders. Young then worked both with the Twelve and the Quorum of the Anointed, adding twenty new members to its rolls. He opened up the temple ceremony to all worthy members, which helped to weld the members into a cohesive community and prevent their scattering. By the time of the westward exodus, he had directed the endowment of some 5,615 Saints.[588] His succession was gradual. Having built a following among Church leaders and the general membership, he organized a new First Presidency and was sustained as President, Prophet, Seer and Revelator on 27 December 1847.

Joseph Smith apparently saw his mission in terms of family, and of creating a dynasty. More and more, it was family that he trusted. After the excommunication of Cowdery and the Whitmers, the only witnesses to the *Book of Mormon* left standing were the Smiths. By the time of his death, forty-four percent of the members of the Quorum of the Anointed were related to Smith, either by blood or marriage.[589] Although his virility is not in question, it may be that his interest in polygamy was largely due to a desire for progeny, or, as Mormons like to say, to build his kingdom.

Smith's priesthood doctrine follows suite. Judaism, Christianity and Islam trace themselves back to Abraham, and are called the Abrahamic religions by many scholars. Smith picked up on the fact that Abraham paid his tithing to Melchizedek. Surely he must have had a very high authority. The next towering figure is Moses. His revelation likens him to this leader, who spoke with God and received the Pentateuch, replete with laws and rituals, and instructions on who gets what. Smith clearly reasoned that it

---

[588] Garr, Cannon & Cowan, *Encyclopedia of Latter-day Saint History*, 1377.
[589] Anderson and Bergera, *Smith's Quorum of the Anointed* (Salt Lake City: Signature Books, 2005), xxx.

was not Moses who could not enter the Promised Land, but his priesthood, due to Israel's sin in worshipping the golden calf. The priesthood that did enter was that which became hereditary among the Levites, and must have come into the land of their inheritance with Aaron. Hence there were two, the Melchizedek and Aaronic (Levitical) priesthoods. But these had been restored by visitations, of John the Baptist and Peter, James and John. Surely, a hereditary priesthood would not need this. It would be by birth. Smith decided that this must be the Patriarchal priesthood, the highest of all. He and his family had it by birth. He made his father the Church Patriarch, and Joseph Smith Sr. was given a very special blessing in the first anointing in Kirtland. After his father's death, seven other members of the Smith family have held this office. With this strategy, Smith attempted to assure the continuance of his family in the top echelons of the Church.

      Smith had three main collaborators, each in a different sphere. Oliver Cowdery was essential for the production of the *Book of Mormon*, and the early elaboration of Church rites and hierarchy. Sidney Rigdon played his role in the development of ritual and theology. And according to some accounts, Smith's closest collaborator in celestial marriage and spiritual wives was Brigham Young. By 1845, Joseph Smith had been murdered, and his two principal associates, Oliver Cowdery and Sidney Rigdon, had been excommunicated. Harris and Cowdery eventually returned to the fold in their last years of life, sick and with nowhere else to go. For all practical purposes, the Mormons under Brigham Young for the first time had no one at the helm that had created the religion they believed in so firmly. Young began to pack the Quorum of the Anointed with polygamists, many of them spiritual wives.[590] He knew that his control over this privilege was a juicy plum to attract capable men, and cement their loyalty.

      For many, Joseph Smith had become a wildcard. His financial ventures had ruined many. His theology was getting more and more extreme, in the view of many. His personal life seemed out of control, although it was always rubber-stamped by the divine. And his conduct of external security affairs, and reliance on force inside and out, exposed the members to insecurity.[591]

      Joseph Smith all too often attempted to pursue his objectives acting as a law unto himself. He did this in well-settled states; Ohio achieved

---

[590] Quinn, *Mormon Hierarchy*, 176, 398-402.

[591] For a view of Joseph Smith that has not yielded to Mormon political correctness, see Joel Allred, *Mormonism under the Microscope. "Master, the Tempest is Raging."* (Salt Lake City: Mountain Press, 2015, 2016).

statehood in 1803, Illinois in 1818, and Missouri in 1821. In Ohio he attempted to trick the financial system and fled the state to avoid prosecution. He thought he could make a major part of Missouri into an inheritance for his Church, thus decreed in his revelations, in spite of a violent reaction on the part of the established citizenry. He first sought redress in the courts, and failing to get a judgment in his favor, he organized a military response. After some tragic deaths on both sides, again he had to flee justice, this time being charged with treason. When he got a charter for Nauvoo, including a militia, he became lieutenant general, and Mayor. All of this he did while branding the churches of his neighbors the church of the Devil, while promulgating his polytheist polygamist faith. He declared that their Bible had become corrupted, and promulgated his new bible. His financial activities in Kirtland had ruined some of his followers, producing the first breakaway dissenter groups. Combined with the suffering of many of his followers in Missouri, his polygamy and polytheism prompted many to consider him to be a fallen prophet. When he ordered the destruction of the Nauvoo Expositor press without due process, he again attempted to flee justice, but ultimately submitted.

Unlike Smith, whom he had faithfully supported, Brigham Young saw the wisdom in Nephi, and decided to lead his people to a land without inhabitants (or nearly so). Although his reputation in Utah for ruling with an iron fist seems well deserved, he realized that Mormonism had enough rites and theology, and adopted a policy of consolidation.

Partly because of Young's leadership, but mostly due to the abilities of Joseph Smith and his colleagues, the Mormon Canon has thrived. In 2030, the *Book of Mormon* will celebrate its 200th anniversary, and by 2045 the entire canon will be two centuries old.

< Appendices >

Appendix 1 Studies in LDS Apologetics

Secular Progress in Knowledge Relevant to LDS Claims

One dimension of insulation, with respect to one's beliefs, is the degree to which disconfirming information exists at all, and the degree that it can impinge upon the minds of individuals.[592]

The greater access to essential facts afforded by the ability to read ancient texts has had an impact among LDS information and scholarly elites. This has been seen in the case of the decipherment of Egyptian, which enabled LDS scholars to know that the so-called Abraham papyri are burial documents, and not the text of a scripture penned by Abraham. So too, the decipherment of the impressive Mayan writing system, and the translation of many monumental inscriptions, have enabled scholars to know that Mayan areas of Central America (Yucatan and Guatemala) cannot have been the setting for a Nephite/Lamanite civilization.

Mormon Apologetics

The word *apologist* does not mean *apologizing*. It comes from Greek, *apo* and *logos*, discourse in response to or against, in other words, a verbal defense, and in religious affairs, it is the defense of the faith: no apology needed, or intended, thank you very much.

LDS leadership are concerned about the exodus from the Church on the part of its best educated, its intelligentsia. If not stemmed, over the mid to long term, it can have a deleterious effect on the makeup of the Church, and on what it will become in the future, as it continues to reinvent itself.

A comment made in this regard by David A. Palmer has considerable poignancy: "The Church of Jesus Christ of Latter-day Saints has no official position on *Book of Mormon* geography. In fact, the Church sponsored New World Archaeological Foundation (NWAF), which for two decades has been conducting excavations in the state of Chiapas, Mexico, has steered away from direct *Book of Mormon* studies."[593] Many

---

[592] For a systematic study of these factors, see A. Chris Eccel, *Egypt, Islam and Social Change: Al-Azhar in Conflict and Accommodation* (Berlin: Schwartz Verlag, 1984).

[593] David A. Palmer, *In Search of Cumorah*, 19.

suspect that the real mission of the NWAF is to conduct valid research, so that the Church can point to its archaeologists and say, in effect, "See. They are experts, and they still believe."

This can be a powerful message, but the strategy can backfire. An example is that of self-taught archaeologist Thomas Stuart Ferguson, the principal founder and first president of the NWAF, coauthor (with Milton R. Hunter) of *Ancient America and the Book of Mormon*, author of *One Fold, One Shepherd* (1958), popular Mormon apologist lecturer, and occasional author of articles published in LDS periodicals. Posthumously, he is on the cover of *The Messiah in Ancient America*, along with Bruce W. Warren, although Ferguson's coauthorship has been challenged, and he has not spoken from the grave. A sympathetic account of his life journey has been written by Stan Larson, who details Ferguson's gradual loss of faith, and struggle with what to do about it.[594]

In 1961, the NWAF was reorganized, and a new Archaeological Committee was created to supervise it. The then Prophet, Seer, Revelator & President of the Church, David O. McKay appointed Howard W. Hunter, the youngest member of the Quorum of the Twelve Apostles of the Church as Chairman, while Ferguson was demoted to secretary. Presumably, it was at this point that it was decided, at the highest level, to erect a firewall between the *Book of Mormon* and New World archaeology. Ferguson knew that major breakthroughs were happening in New World, especially Mesoamerican, archaeology, in the form of more numerous and exhaustive excavations, but especially the decipherment of the Mayan glyphs. Initially he must have expected that the *Book of Mormon* would be vindicated, and, like the role of the Bible in the archaeology of Palestine, it would become a textual source that even non-LDS researchers would have to consult. When it turned out to be just the opposite, Ferguson was unable to repress his growing doubts. Larson analyzes Ferguson's correspondence, and finds that eventually he decided that God does not get involved in any of the religions. On 9 February 1976, he wrote to Harold W. Lawrence and his wife, who were also suffering a crisis of faith:

> Why not say the right things and keep your membership in the great fraternity [the LDS Church], enjoying the good things you like and discarding the ones you can't swallow (and keeping your mouths shut)? Hypocritical? Maybe. But perhaps a realistic way of dealing with a very

---

[594] Stan Larson, *Quest for the Gold Plates, Thomas Stuart Ferguson's Archaeological Search for the Book of Mormon* (Salt Lake City: Freethinker Press, 1996).

difficult problem. There is lots left in the Church to enjoy—and thousands of members have done, and are doing, what I suggest you consider doing.[595]

Over time, Church officials have adopted a systematic strategy. It can be illustrated in a study of its reaction to *The Book of Abraham* crisis. At first, it seemed to think that it could just simply acquire the papyri and let them disappear in the vaults at Brigham Young University. Their finder, Dr. Aziz Suryal Atiya, Founder and Director of the Middle East Studies Center at the University of Utah, made an announcement to the press regarding his find. This news hit like a thunderbolt among the Church leadership and intelligentsia. Among the latter were the editors of an unofficial periodical, *Dialogue a Journal of Mormon Thought*, who pressured the Church to enable scholarly access to the papyri. The Church responded with even better than that. It published them in large-format, full and clear photos, in its principal official organ the *Improvement Era*. *Dialogue* responded by getting top Egyptologists to analyze and translate them, within the context of their history since their acquisition by Joseph Smith, and Smith's *Egyptian Alphabet and Grammar*, as well.

Apologetics in the Official Church Organ. Prior to this event, the Church had used its official magazine, *The Improvement Era*, as a tool for apologetics, focusing primarily on what it considered to be material that supported the *Book of Mormon*. After acquiring the Joseph Smith (Abraham) papyri, the focus shifted almost entirely to *The Book of Abraham*. Figure 34 documents the Church's changing and initially uncertain approach to Church-wide apologetics.

The Improvement Era was the official magazine of the Church until January of 1971 (although other Church magazines were being published, for special audiences), when it was replaced by *Ensign*. As can be seen, from 1950 through 1966, an amazing amount of space was dedicated to support the *Book of Mormon*. Late in 1966 information was had that Dr. Aziz Atiyah, founder of the Middle East Center at the University of Utah, and an authority on the history of the Egyptian Coptic Christians, may have found the long lost Joseph Smith papyri. During the entire year of 1967, the *Era* did not publish a single thing on LDS apologetics. It is clear that this news had disrupted the normal conduct of information dissemination to the membership, as the LDS establishment attempted to determine what to make of this news, what positive or negative potential it might have, and in any case, who would handle the apologetics front, and how. In January of 1968, the Church announced the find in the *Era*,

---

[595] Larson, *Quest for the Gold Plates*, 161.

and in February it published the papyri in clear photos. The stance would be that *The Book of Abraham* had nothing to fear, and beginning with the January Issue, the LDS Apologist in Chief, Hugh Nibley, began a serialized work to address the issue: "A New Look at the *Pearl of Great Price*: Part 1, Challenge and Response." It is interesting that the title avoids a reference to *The Book of Abraham*, to give the impression that there is no need for a special focus on this *cause célèbre* that had all of Mormon intelligentsia asking the same question: Will this text translate into *The Book of Abraham*, and prove Joseph Smith to be a prophet, or will it turn out to be something quite other than what he and the Church had claimed.

Figure 36. Apologetics in the *Improvement Era* and *Ensign*

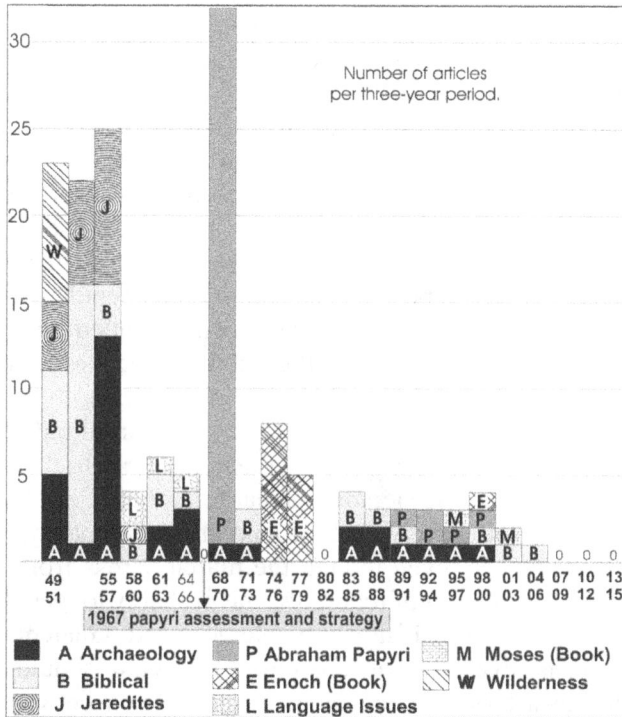

For a while, the Church published a number of articles about Abraham and the papyri. Then, silence, at which point the *Era* died. A coincidence? No way to know.

The *Ensign* would take a far different approach to apologetics. It had become clear to Church leadership that most members had no idea that a problem even existed, and that carrying on a defense in their official organs simply called attention re the problem to the great many who were living in blissful ignorance. From this time on, or to some extent even before, the Church was aware that it had a variety of audiences, and that its messages needed to be tailored for each one. It has since used its official organs more to educate regarding the cardinal points of the faith, and as faith-building tools. At the same time, it has established studies centers (the Religious Studies Center and the Neal A. Maxwell Institute for Religious Scholarship), and promotes apologetics by appropriate orthodox scholars. Individuals, who have become aware of the problems faced by Mormon scriptures, and/or controversial doctrines or events in Mormon history, can be discretely directed to these works. Figure 36 shows the abrupt change of policy, and the degree to which the *Ensign* was made largely into an exclusively devotional magazine to build the faith, and address daily issues of the Saints, including old age, temple marriage, unemployment and how to deal with a loved one "suffering" from "same-sex attraction."

The articles listed in the last three decades in the categories "archaeology" and "papyri" are mostly a diluted form of apologetics. For a while an occasional series was published to present a sort of survey of what BYU researchers were doing, and how their work supported Mormonism. Three or four research efforts were surveyed in a single short article, such that it was not possible to go into much detail. This approach was discontinued, but the items have been included in Figure 36, overstating the apologetics present in the last three decades covered. A list of all the articles gleaned for this graph is in Appendix 6.

John L. Sorenson has been one of the more ambitious apologists, whose magnum opus brings together the results of his life's work.[596] To his credit, he accepts the BoM geographical references for what they are, although he locates the narrow neck of land at Coatzacoalcos, across the Isthmus of Tehuantepec, even though the march across from sea to sea there would take a minimum of four days, and probably longer. This places virtually the entire BoM history in Mexico and Guatemala. Those interested in a massive effort to champion this view should study this work, but do beware of a certain point of contention between him and some of his colleagues. He locates the Cumorah, where Mormon, Moroni and the Nephite armies were finally destroyed, at Tuxtla in south-east Mexico, only about eighty miles north-west of Coatzacoalcos. Presumably Joseph Smith dug up his plates from a different Cumorah.

---

[596] Sorenson, *Mormon's Codex.*

The scientific validity of this work is not the issue. Its importance lies in its success in strengthening the faith of a believing readership. For us, it makes two contributions. First, it shows that after a lifetime of gathering information, he has not been able to successfully address the items in the archaeological item list. Finally, although he places the Nephites in the heartland of the Maya, Olmec, and others, he shows no sign of being aware of the biggest archaeological problem of all: the failure of the BoM narrative to mention any people other than its Jaredites, Nephites, Lamanites, Mulekites and Zoramites, all in an otherwise empty continent.

Archaeology: Just Horsing Around?

The articles designated under the rubric of "archaeology" in Figure 34 represents the situation but poorly. There are no excavation reports, or articles that analyze the finds of excavations, no attempt to label any site or artifact as being Nephite, or deriving from Nephite/Lamanite civilization. One example, however, invites us to exercise some caution regarding those articles labeled "Archaeology." In the 12/1955 issue of the *Improvement Era*, in a serialized work titled "Archaeology and the *Book of Mormon*," Milton R Hunter published a photo that he claimed to be an image of a horse carved in stone on a panel at Chichen Itza[597]:

Figure 37. The Temple of the Panels of Reliefs: Hunter vs Others[598]

Source: photo by Otto Done   Source: Church of Christ Temple Lot

---

[597] *Improvement Era*, December 1955.
[598] Otto Done (photographer), "Archaeology and the *Book of Mormon*, VII," *Improvement Era* (December, 1955), 899. Church of Christ Temple Lot, accessed online 19/04/2017 at: https://images.search.yahoo.com (photo sourced to http://www.cocsermons.net.

Hunter's photo on the left clearly has been heavily retouched. To me, this jollied-up version looks very much like a European. It is not clear who touched up the photo. A similar photo, also retouched, appeared in the book form of this series, in 1956.[599] Since it too was taken by Otto Done, both photos were probably taken on the same visit to the monument near the end of 1954. Several photos have appeared online, all resembling the photo on the right from the Church of Christ (Temple Lot). Hunter's project photographer is the likely candidate for the photo modification. Even so, Hunter himself, a member of the Church's Council of the Seventies, could not have not known that it had been done. We do not know why Hunter went back to an unretouched photo fifteen years later.[600] We do know that the site had become a must-see for LDS tourists to the "Land of Zarahemla" and BYU students on study tours. Hunter had possibly been made aware of their disappointment when they saw the real thing. In any case, these photos reveal the degree to which it was acceptable to someone in his position to enhance the evidence of the "truth" for the greater glory of the cause. This bas-relief has not survived in the artifact repertoire of later apologists.

As for the animal in the image, its identification is complicated by the fact that the images on this temple's panels feature a number of legendary animals. So a correct identification may be some animal that does not even exist. Note that the retouched photo made the feet look like the human is walking to the left, and the face was retouched from the back of the man's head gear. In the original, the human and animal are walking in the same direction. Also, the head of the animal has been modified, with a heftier lower jaw, making it resemble a horse a bit more. The head only comes up a bit higher than the human's navel. The neck does not rise up like that of a horse, but extends out like a big cat. Although the tail of a horse can extend out at full gallop, it hangs down when it is standing or walking. The tail is more appropriate for a big cat. My money is on some animal, perhaps real, perhaps mythical, of a more feline nature.

Hugh Winder Nibley, Apologist in Chief

The book that firmly established Nibley, and launched his career in LDS apologetics, was *Lehi in the Desert*, although the BoM narrative itself

---

[599] Milton R. Hunter, *Archaeology and the Book of Mormon* (Salt Lake City: Deseret Book Company, 1956), 6.
[600] Milton R. Hunter, *Great Civilizations and the Book of Mormon* (Salt Lake City: Bookcraft, 1970), 197.

states that Nephi's account of Lehi's travel in the wilderness lacks detail. His method can be illustrated by the following assertions: 1) Lehi possessed precious things not manufactured in Jerusalem (the BoM does not say this); 2) Lehi had close ties with Sidon (the BoM does not say this); 3) Lehi lived on an estate in the country (the BoM says he lived in Jerusalem all his days); and 4) Lehi was "something of an expert in vine, olive, fig and honey culture" (the BoM does not say this). He concludes, "so there can be little doubt of the nature of his business with Egypt." In fact, the BoM does not say that he had any business with Egypt. This whole sequence is fanciful and deliberately misleading. [601] In addition to effectively rewriting his only source for Lehi, i.e. the *Book of Mormon*, he searches a huge body of early, mostly out of date secondary literature about the Middle East to glean occasional statements, some of them paraphrased, to develop his analysis and to project erudition.

Nibley's works have not impressed the experts in any of the fields of Middle East scholarship, but they were not intended to do so. His elixir so expertly compounded is served to those whose great faith in the *Book of Mormon* is only matched by their great thirst for scholarly evidence to support it. Its success is virtually guaranteed.

Although Nibley had in the past defended *The Book of Abraham*, and its translation from the papyri, when the actual Egyptian document in question surfaced, he changed his argument. After providing the Egyptian text, transliteration and translation by Egyptologists, he states: "Though as correct and literal as we can make it, the translation in the preceding chapter is not a translation. It is nonsense."[602] He looks at the method of Joseph Smith in translating the gold plates, where phrases and sentences appeared before him, and, implying that something like that obtained in his translation of the papyri, he states: "Plainly, this peculiar type of translation depends on getting in the spirit and is not to be accomplished by intellectual effort alone."[603] It appears that his view is that while working on the papyri, the text of *The Book of Abraham* was revealed to him. He concludes: "If 'it mattereth not' by what imponderable method Joseph Smith produced his translations, as long as he came up with the right answers, it matters even less from what particular edition of what

---

[601] Hugh Nibley, *Lehi in the Desert & the World of the Jaredites* (Salt Lake City: Bookcraft, 1952/1980), 12.
[602] Hugh Nibley, *The Message of the Joseph Smith Papyri, An Egyptian Egyptian Endowment*. Second Edition, edited by John Gee & Michael D. Rhodes (Salt Lake City: Deseret Book Company, 2005), 52.
[603] Nibley, Message of the Joseph Smith Papyri, 58.

particular text he was translating. It is enough at present to know that the prophet was translating from real books of Abraham, Moses, Enoch, Mosiah and Zenos..."[604] This is a neat argument. But this effort to divorce *The Book of Abraham* from the papyrus ignores the fact that Abraham himself claims to have written the book. Writing in the first person, he refers to his own illustration, Facsimile Number 1 found in the Smith papyrus, which has actually turned out to be a Breathing Permit of the Book of the Dead.

Just when the Church was still engaged in the crisis caused by the discovery of the Joseph Smith papyri, Nibley began his series in *Ensign* on the *Book of Enoch*. The timing of the publication of this study served as a diversion from the Abraham issue. The *Book of Enoch* is a pseudepigraphic (falsely attributed) work, composed by various authors, some of it perhaps as early as 300 BCE, and some as late as the first century BCE. It is found in what appears to be its full text, at least as it existed by the first century CE, only in Geez (classical Ethiopic), and is recognized as canonical only in the Ethiopian Orthodox Church.

The details in Genesis make him an ideal figure to be a Pseudepigraphal author. His life lay between Adam and Noah, and the OT says that he walked with God, and then "he was not, for God took him." In view of the fact that there are so many apocryphal works, it would be strange if Enoch had been left out.

The *Book of Moses*, presented to the world by Joseph Smith, Oliver Cowdery and Sidney Rigdon about a year after the publication of the *Book of Mormon*, contains an elaborated account of Enoch. When I acquired Nibley's treatment,[605] I was already familiar with the Ethiopic text of *Enoch*, and fragments in Greek and Aramaic. So I was expecting to find a presentation in two columns, one having "the *Book of Moses* version says," and the other having "the Book of Enoch says." The conclusion would be that Smith and Cowdery did not have the *Book of Enoch*, and could not have produced these parallels. So the *Book of Moses* must have been received by revelation.

In Nibley's first comparison, the *Moses* Enoch weeps and is embittered by the vision of the destruction of man in the great deluge, but in the Ethiopic Enoch, the opposite happens, as it is Noah who cries out to his grandfather Enoch with a bitter voice, and Enoch consoles him. In the

---

[604] Nibley, Message of the Joseph Smith Papyri, 65.

[605] Hugh Nibley, *Enoch the Prophet* (Salt Lake City: Deseret Book Company, 1986). This volume contains two separate compositions: "Enoch the Prophet and His World," and "A Strange Thing in the Land."

second pairing, in the Enoch account of the *Book of Moses*, Methuselah prophesies that all the kingdoms of the earth shall spring from his own loins through Noah, while in a Greek fragment of Enoch 106:16 it is Enoch who speaks, simply foretelling that Noah and his three sons will be saved from the deluge. A couple of comparisons follow with considerable text and occasional similarities, all being predictable from the account given subsequently in the OT, including the divine promise to never again destroy the earth in a deluge.

Having hardly begun his book about Enoch, Nibley turns to making pairings mostly from other apocryphal books, including *Bet ham-Midrash*, *The Secrets of Enoch*, the Ethiopic *Book of Mysteries*, an Egyptian ritual text Papyrus Salt, The *Apocalypse of Abraham*, the *Combat of Adam and Eve*, the *Zohar*, the *Apocalypse of Adam*, the *Miracles of Jesus*, *Berayta*, the *Apocryphon of John*, the *Book of Adam*, the *Apocalypse of Elijah*, Origen, Clement of Alexandria, Jubilees, and post-Biblical materials. Even though not one of these works can be considered a sacred scripture, Nibley asserts that each one has its kernels of divine inspiration, or flashes of memory from a more ancient source. When gleaned and properly arrayed, one can glimpse a mosaic of a vision that is present as well in the *Book of Moses*, both drawn from the same Divine Source. Since Nibley's guide to separate the rare but precious kernels from the chaff is the *Book of Moses* itself, there is a degree of similarity, albeit vague, between it and the mosaic thus produced. No surprise here.

In *Lehi in the Desert* he took an assertive posture, attempting to present evidence for the authenticity of the *Book of Mormon*. When *The Book of Abraham* crisis happened, he was forced into a defensive posture. In both works, he took refuge in the hazy world of scholarly esoterica, never addressing the real issue, the archaeological verdict of the New World, for which, after all, the BoM narrative is supposed to be a historical record.

In Search of a Hebrew BoM Text

The hypothesis underlying Hebrew language arguments in the context of the BoM text is that BoM English displays certain peculiarities or abnormalities that can be explained by features, usually syntax, characteristic of Hebrew. The principal LDS researcher in this endeavor is my old friend and mission field colleague John Tvedtnes.[606]

The principal hurdle for this hypothesis is the hypothesis itself, inasmuch as the plates were supposed to have been written in reformed Egyptian, not Hebrew at all. So why should one even expect to find influences from a Hebrew text on the gold plates? Usually this problem is not mentioned, but, for the reader who might think of it independently, a solution is devised. Tvedtnes' solution is to suggest that we do not really know what language was on the plates, and that the phrase "reformed Egyptian" might simply mean that Hebrew was written with Egyptian characters, presumably logograms, to compress it, and thereby reduce the number of plates required, gold being in short supply (Mormon 9:32). In the very next verse, Mormon clearly states, "And if our plates had been sufficiently large we should have written in Hebrew…" Clearly, there was no Hebrew text on the gold plates, and the hypothesis is disconfirmed from the start. Still, giving Tvedtnes the benefit of the doubt, and assuming that somehow the influence of Hebrew morphology and syntax had found its way into Mormon's Egyptian, I will deal with his arguments on an "as though" basis.

One argument is that the BoM text uses phrases with *of* when normal English would prefer an adjectival noun.[607] He explains the Hebrew (and more broadly, the Semitic) construct state, as being two adjacent nouns, where the second is either possessive, or an adjectival modifier of the first, such as *house king* meaning *house of the king*, or *book brass* (my example), meaning *book of brass*. English would prefer *king's house* and *brass book* (a phrase used here, since it is not clear what word the OT might have used for *plates* to say *plates of brass*). In fact, English is perfectly at home with *house of the king* and even *plates of brass*.

Note that in the phrase *book brass* there is no word meaning *of*. In fact, the second noun is analogous to an adjective. Hebrew, like many other languages, prefers to place attributives after their noun, such as *man big* (*'îš gādōl*) instead of *big man*. In the adjectival construct state, the two nouns are better understood as being a primary noun followed by an attributive, in this case an adjectival noun, rather than reading *of* into the phrase when no such word is actually there.

An additional problem is that Hebrew actually has a word used to express the English preposition *of* in just such a context: *men* (usually

---

[606] John Tvedtnes, "Hebraisms in the *Book of Mormon*," transcript downloaded from the FARMS website.

[607] Tvedtnes, "Hebraisms," 3.

meaning *from* but also used to mean *of* much like *von* in German). Just as an English writer, wishing to stress the substance from which the book was made, might quite deliberately choose to say *book of brass*, Hebrew can say *sēfer men nəhošet* (*book of brass*) instead of *sēfer nəhošet*. So this argument falls, first because English is comfortable with the *of* phrases quoted by Tvedtnes, and because Hebrew can choose between an adjectival construct state comparable to *brass book* and a phrase using *men* directly equivalent to English *book of brass*.

A similar argument is made with regard to the phrase *of me* rather than *my*, or *of him* instead of *his*, both found in the BoM: "hear the words of me" (Jacob 5:2; cf. 2 Nephi 10:8) and "how unsearchable are the depths of the mysteries of him" (Jacob 4:8; cf. 2 Nephi 9:25 & Moroni 8:20). Here again we do not find in Hebrew any word meaning *of*. This is provided by Tvedtnes. When Hebrew affixes a pronoun to the end of a noun, it becomes a possessive pronoun. Here again, Hebrew syntax places an attributive after its noun. The suffixed pronoun means *my* and *his* respectively, and follows its noun. The BoM *of me* and *of him* is just quaint idiolectic English, having nothing to do with Hebrew. If we were really seeing a Hebrew influence here, we would also find such-and-such *of you* or *of them* as well.

Another example is what Tvedtnes calls a compound preposition, but is actually a preposition-noun phrase used in Hebrew, *by the hand of* or *by the mouth of* (the Lord, your enemies, etc.). An example is Mosiah 17:18, "Ye shall be taken by the hand of your enemies." Actually, such Hebrew phrases had entered into the English language, especially in religious writings, a phenomenon that produced a significant effect on the creation of modern English. Indeed, in the 1611 edition of the KJV, the translators wrote that they had completed it "through the good hand of the Lord upon us." Compare 1 Nephi 3:20 "spoken by the mouth of all the prophets" with "by the mouth of his true prophet Jeremiah" in the sermon "An Exhortation to Those Who Love Righteousness" by George Whitefield.

A true compound preposition is *mil-li-pnē* (*from+to* [before]+*face* [countenance, presence]). This phrase is translated literally: "from before," as in Exodus 14:19: "from before their face." A reader of the Bible would certainly know the phrase, and just add a noun complement ('presence,' etc.).

A certain amount of Hebrew influence in BoM English is expectable for two reasons: A) the English language in general has absorbed considerable Hebrew influence due to the influence of the very literal KJV translation, and B) a person who has read extensively in the Bible will have even more of these Hebrew expressions and syntax at his command. This is sufficient to explain the observations made by the proponents of this hypothesis, which is itself refuted by the BoM text cited above: the plates were not even in Hebrew.

BoM Names and LDS Apologetics

Make no mistake. The apologist studies BoM names with reference to Hebrew for only one reason: to find support for the authenticity of the *Book of Mormon*. It is hard work. My late friend, John Tvedtnes, spent much of his adult life honing his Hebrew and engaged in this quest.

Hebrew names, and Semitic names in general, often bear the name of a deity; they are *theophoric*. Sometimes the divine name is understood, such as in the name Joshua, which means "he (Yahweh) shall help." In very ancient times, the name Yahweh could be pronounced, but over time the Hebrews began to feel that it was too holy for human utterance. In English, it is sometimes called the pentagram, since it has five letters. But it still needed to be incorporated into names. To do this, the name was shortened, or otherwise modified. A longer form, almost Yahweh, is *–yahū* as in Netanyahu, "Yahweh has given." Note that Hebrew names are often sentences. Using *–yahū* instead of Yahweh is a bit like saying "Gosh!" rather than "God!" This can be further shortened to *–yah/-iah*. A totally different word can also do the trick. *Shem* is the ordinary word meaning *name*. But in some contexts, it means the divine name, Yahweh, and can be used with this meaning without incurring divine wrath. The shortening of a name, for example Jeff rather than Jeffrey, is called *hypocorism*, and such a name is a *hypocoristicon*. On the other hand, names that are not theophoric do exist, such as Deborah, honey bee. This does not mean 'honey bee of Yahweh.' Just honey bee.

Like all Semitic languages, Hebrew is based on triliteral roots, i.e. roots based on three consonants (triconsonantal). Each triad has a base meaning, and specific words are formed by configuring the root consonants, with vowels and prefixed, infixed and postfixed consonants, to produce standard forms. One cannot reconfigure at will for fun or effect. The very ability of the language to convey the desired meaning requires respecting the integrity of the forms. For this reason, all Semitic languages, after thousands of years of development, still have some of the same forms and have resisted change to a remarkable degree.

The study to be examined here is perhaps the principal one on the subject, coauthored by John Tvedtnes, John Gee and Matthew Roper (herein referred to as Tvedtnes et al.).[608] The central argument of the apologist is that a BoM name, not found in the OT, has been found in a Hebrew inscription. Joseph Smith et al. could not have known of this non-Biblical name, so its occurrence in the BoM text provides evidence that the *Book of Mormon* is a translation of an ancient record. The best evidence would be a BoM name that is not similar to any name in the OT, such as Shiz, or Zoram. Next to that would be a name that is similar to one that is found in the OT, but a distinguishing feature of the BoM name is present in the name in an inscription. The valid inclusion of a name actually found in the OT would require very special justification, and is even less impressive.

Table 71. Assertion that BoM Names Occur in Hebrew Inscriptions

Names Not Found in the Old Testament in Any Form
Abish (Claim: Abish is the name of a Lamanite woman. In ancient Hebrew inscriptions it is written *'bš'*. The final ' is an abbreviation of the theophoric element *'Yahweh'* found in other such names.) Comment: It is not certain that the final ' is a theophoric element for Yahweh since the root *'bš* does not exist in Hebrew, and therefore it is unlikely that it is the base for the hypocoristic ending. Avigad/Sas do not venture an interpretation, but they and Röllig suggest it is a variant of *'byšw'*.[609] As in similar names, the first element of two may be *'b* (*'by*, father). The fact that it also occurs in Egypt adds nothing to the issue. The meaning in the BoM is unknown. Note that Hebrew names do not begin with a vowel; in the initial position, a vowel can be preceded by either *aleph* (') or *'ayin* ('). As a result, BoM Abish could be *'abiš* or *'abiš*. Tvedtnes et al. fail to alert the reader to the fact that the inscription reads *'bš' ben Uri'el*, "Abisha son of Uri'el." It is a man's name, and inappropriate for a Lamanite woman.
Aha (Claim: This is *'ḥ'* from the root for brother with a hypocoristic ' standing for Yahweh, thereby meaning "brother of Yahweh," similar to the Biblical name *'aḥīyāh(u)*, of the same meaning.) Comment: The root for "brother" (*'ḥ*) has an alternative form (*'ḥy*) and the second is typically used to append suffixes. This is seen in *'aḥī-yāh(u)*. The final ' in the inscription is a Hebrew consonant that

[608] John Tvedtnes, John Gee and Matthew Roper, "*Book of Mormon* Names Attested in Ancient Hebrew Inscriptions," *Journal of Book of Mormon Studies*, 9/1/2000.

[609] Nahman Avigad, *Corpus of West Semitic Stamp Seals, revised and completed by Benjamin Sass*, herein referenced as Avigad/Sass (Jerusalem: Ketterpress, 1997), 66 & 476; Wolfgang Röllig, "Siegel und Gewichte," in Johannes Renz and Wofgang Röllig, *Handbuch der Althebräischen Epigraphik*, 4 vols. (Darmstadt: Wissenschftliche Buchgesellschaft, 1995 & 2003), II/2, 120.

is pronounced (as it still is in modern Arabic). We are invited to assume that the final *a* in Aha corresponds to this hypocoristic ending. Furthermore, the English letter *h* could be one of two letters in Hebrew: *h* and *ḥ*. In addition to its presence in some Hebrew inscriptions, it is also attested in a Moabite inscription written in Canaanite letters. In both of these languages, it is improbable that the final ' represents the Hebrew deity. Note too that Steve Smoot argues that this name is ancient Egyptian. It is not possible to know that BoM Aha is the same name attested in these inscriptions.

Himni (Claim: This is attested as *ḥmn* on two Hebrew seals. The final *i* of the BoM name is a gentilic ending: *of ḥmn*.) Comment: Again we are asked to believe that English *h* in Himni is Hebrew *ḥ* rather than Hebrew *h*. Avigad/Sass find it difficult to determine what the name might have been, proposing *'ḥmn* (with aphaeresis), or *ḥammon* (either a hypocoristicon or a noun meaning 'hot spring'). Furthermore, the so-called gentilic *i* is not attested in the inscription. There is no BoM toponym or personal name for which this could be a gentilic (such as *Hemen* [eg., *gezer*, a name of a place, Gezer, becoming *gizrī*, someone from Gezer]. It is not clear that Himni is even attested in an inscription.

Luram (Claim: A seal, dated c. 720 BCE, and found at Hamath, north Syria, bears the name *'dn lrm*, Lord of *lrm*.) Comment: The name hails from Hamath (Syria) at a time when it had been for some time an Aramaean center. It also had Hittite and Assyrian influences. The name also occurs on a brick at the same site followed by *skn byt mlkh* (steward of the king's house).[610] The terminal *h* on *mlk* is the Aramaic emphatic affix functioning in lieu of a definite article, and identifying this inscription as being Old Aramaic. Avigad/Sass vocalize the name *'adanluram* with no indication where it should be divided (i.e. *luram* may not be a unit). If *lrm* is a word, it is an unknown place name, not a personal name. Above all, there is no reason to assume that it is even Hebrew.

Names Similar to Old Testament Names

Ammonihah (Claim: The ending *-ihah* is a hypocoristicon for Yahweh, and therefore it is fair to claim that this name is attested as *'mnyhw* and *'mnwyhw*.) Comment: Only LDS apologists give *-ihah* this meaning. Doing so is ad hoc, and without merit since it does not readily work with other BoM names, such as Cumenihah, Moronihah, Mathonihah and Zemnariha. Ammon is in the OT, but Ammonihah is not attested in Hebrew.

Chemosh (Claim: The name has been found on seals as a personal name.) Comment: All of the occurrences are on Moabite seals, as the name of the

---

[610] Avigad/*Sass*, 285. For *skn byt mlkh* see J. Hoftijzer and K. Jongeling, *Dictionary of the North-West Semitic Inscriptions* (E.J. Brill: Leiden, 1995), 2:786.

Moabite deity Kemosh.[611] It is found in Numbers 21:29; Judges 11:24; 1 Kings 11:7, 33; 2 Kings 23:13; and Jeremiah 48:7, 13 and 46. The BoM authors simply changed the vowel. It is not surprising that it should show up in the BoM, which does occasionally switch good and evil, such as by making Noah a wicked king. No evidence for the BoM here.

Hagoth (Claim: It is attested in an Ammonite seal as *hgt*. The Ammonites wrote and spoke the same language as the Hebrews.) Comment: This is not a seal of the Hebrews. Although Hebrew and Ammonite are increasingly considered to be dialects, they are different cultures and have some different names. There is no Hebrew root *hgt* or *ḥgt*. Playing with possibilities, treating *h* as a preformative, or *t* as an affix, would be purely speculative. One notes that Tvedtnes et al. rigorously provide references, but strangely none is provided for this seal. I have not found it in the works edited by Aufrecht,[612] Renz/Röllig or Avigad/Sass. Furthermore, the BoM name could have been quite readily modified from Biblical Haggith (2 Samuel 3:4, etc.).

Isabel (Claim: It is now attested *yzbl* in an inscription that might be Phoenician.) Comment: It is not clear what this spelling has to do with the BoM name, since initial *i* would be preceded by aleph (' thereby reading *'zbl* or *'yzbl*), not *y*. In fact, Isabel is the proper rendition of Jezebel in the OT. Why not take credit for that? The seal has Egyptian influences, including a winged solar disk and a winged sphinx holding the ankh sign. The owner's gender is uncertain.[613] What is known is that the English name Isabel, derived from Elizabeth, has been extremely popular. It cannot have been a great leap to associate it with the Jezebel of the Bible. As such, it was appropriate that she be a harlot, a temptress, and of all places, at Siron (cf. the ancient Greek siren, temptress of sailors, and when borrowed in English, simply a temptress). Surely the extra-Biblical source for this name is clear. *Yzbl* is apparently Phoenician.

Jarom (Claim: The form *yrm* [rather than Biblical *ywrm*] is now attested. This is considered to be a hypocoristic form of Jeremiah). Comment: The name *yrm* is listed by Avigad/Sass and vocalized Yarim (*Yarīm*).[614] As a hypocoristic form of Jeremiah, it is not clear that it would be vocalized Jarom. The hypocoristicon *yrm* (from *rwm*: He [the deity] exalts, or is exalted) recurs in Phoenician. And since Joram occurs frequently in the OT, it is most probably the source of BoM Jarom. The relevance of this inscription is ambiguous.

---

[611] Avigad/Sass, 508.
[612] Walter E. Aufrecht, *A Corpus of Ammonite Inscriptions* (Lewiston, NY: The Edwin Mellen Press, 1989).
[613] Avigad/Sass, 375.
[614] Avigad/Sass, 112.

Josh (Claim: The form *y'š* has been attested. This should be vocalized *jōš* and considered to be the hypocoristic form of Josiah (*jōšiyyāhu*). Comment: Avigad/Sass indicate that the verbal root is *'wš*, and that the name should be vocalized *yo'aš* (Joash), a name that occurs many times in Judges and 1 and 2 Kings. The vocalization is not indicated in the inscription. The aleph (glottal stop) is a root letter, not a device to indicate a vowel. If it were, aleph would normally represent *ā*. In any case, Josh, as an English shorter form for Joshua, may be as far as we have to look for this BoM name.

Mathoni/Mathonihah (Claim: This is the BoM form for Mattaniah [Hebrew *mtnyhw*], with the theophoric hypocoristicon *-ihah* on the second one.) Comment: This is not possible, because the root is *ntn*, with a standard Hebrew preformative *m*:

m-vowel-**nt**-vowel-**n** (bolding the root) → m-vowel-tt-vowel-n (ie. mattān)

The consonant *n* is absolutely weak in Hebrew, Aramaic and even Akkadian. When directly before *t* (and many other consonants) as in this case, the first *n* of the root combines with *t*, in this case becoming *tt* (*Mantaniah ▶ Mattāniāh). The root means "to give" and the noun produced by this form (*mattān*) means "gift" (understood to be "gift of the deity"). *In this doubled form, t never aspirates*, i.e. *tt* cannot become *th*. Since Mattān and Mattāniah are both frequent in the OT, and are common Hebrew names, the fact that they are found at Lachish and Elephantine is superfluous. So why are these inscriptional sources referenced at all, when they occur so often in the OT? We can only speculate as to whether this name was derived by the BoM authors from Mattāniāh, or more probably from Matthew, since BoM Mathoni and Mathonihah were two of the twelve disciples (apostles) chosen by Jesus when he visited the Nephites after his resurrection. The th in Matthew developed in Greek.

Muloki (Claim: This appears on a bulla found in the City of David, as *mlky*. It is a hypocoristicon for *mlkyhw* [king Yahweh]. The objection that the vocalization of Mulok makes it inappropriate to be a hypocoristicon is not valid, since vowel changes do happen in such cases.) Comment: Vowel changes are not random changes. Tvedtnes et al. cite Baruch for Berechiah, Nahum for Nehemiah, Shallum for Shelmiah, and Zaccur for Zechariah. Note that in all of these cases, the *u* is in the second syllable. This is a standard form for passives. So Berechiah means "Yahweh has blessed," and Baruch means "blessed" (by Yahweh, understood). This makes sense as a short form, a hypocoristicon. Mulok is not even a Hebrew form at all and makes no sense as a base for a hypocoristicon. What can be said in a positive vein is that this inscription at least has terminal *y* that corresponds to the final *i* of Muloki. On the other hand, the BoM already has Mulek, which it claims to be a son of Zedekiah (while the OT says his sons were killed), and frequently makes modifications of existing names as a means of name generation. It occurs as Melech in 1 Chronicles 8:35, 9:41, etc. (*mlk*, where *ch* is aspirated *k*, a phenomenon in rabbinical Hebrew).

Sam (Claim: The name *šəmūʾēl* is comprised of *šem* ['name'] and *ʾēl* [(of) El], i.e. god. The name *šem* can be *śem* in inscriptional Hebrew, because the letters *š* and *ś* are written with the same character in the Hebrew of the inscriptions. In old Hebrew *ś* was pronounced variably, including *s*. So the name can be *sam*) Comment: It is implied that the first consonant of the name in the inscription was pronounced *s*. Evidence from Old South Arabian (OSA) and Hebrew indicates that there was an "extra" sibilant in Proto-Semitic, in addition to *s*, *z* and *š*. In Hebrew it is transliterated as *ś*. At some point, the pronunciation of *ś* was totally forgotten, and the convention developed to pronounce it the same as *s* as a matter of convenience. Since Hebrew already had a letter for *s* (*samech*), it is improbable that there would be two letters for the same sound. The assertion that *ś* was at an early date pronounced *s* is unevidenced.

In any case, this word, *šm* (not *śm*), occurs on a rather small signet seal. The surface is divided into upper and lower registers by a horizontal line. Above the line is the name of the signet owner, *ʾḥyhw* (*Aḥīyāhū*). Below the line we find *šm*.[615] It is common to place a patronymic below the line, such as "son of ..." Because space is lacking, the word *ben* (son of) was not written. So *šm* is Shem (son of Noah in Genesis). The name therefore is *Aḥīyāhū ben Shem*.

The assertion that *ʷ* is *ʷ*, and pronounced *s* is purely to argue that they have found Sam in inscriptional Hebrew, independent of the proper name "*šəmuʾēl*" (where *š* is *sh*). The objective is to counter the common observation that the BoM authors erroneously used the English nickname Sam, the English short form for Samuel, which should not be in the BoM.

Sariah (Claim: The name of the wife of Lehi has been found in an inscription as *śryh*. This is *śār* + the theophoric ending *–yā*, meaning "prince of Yahweh." It is attested at Elephantine as a woman's name.) Comment: The name in the OT is vocalized *śərāyā*, "one who contends for Yahweh, warrior of Yahweh" or "Yahweh has contended" (for his people). It is found in Jeremiah 36:26; 40:8; 51:59, 61; and 52:24; and 2 Samuel 8:17, spelled Seraiah in the KJV. There, *śərāyā* is a man's name. At Elephantine *śryh* is a woman's name. The experts on this, Porten and Lund, vocalize it also as *śərāyā*, KJV *serāiā* (*śərā* being the third person masculine of the root *śry*, "to contend") not *śaryā/saryā* (*śar* being a primitive noun meaning "person of note, commander, governor, prince).[616]

Lehi is to become the patriarch of a numerous people, much like Abraham, whose wife had two names, originally Sarai, and then Sarah. To enhance Lehi's persona as patriarch, his wife is given a name similar to that of Abraham,

---

[615] Avigad/Sass, 69.

[616] Bezalel Porten and Jerome A. Lund, *Aramaic Documents from Egypt: A Key-Word-in-Context Concordance* (Winona Lake: Eisenbrauns, 2002), p. 416.

combining the two, Sarai+Sarah=Sariah (pronounced in English Sarayah). When dictated to the scribe, *ay* was written with the letter *i* in keeping with the English convention. The English letter *i* is an abbreviation for *ay* (as in "Aye, aye, Sir!"). As a result, inadvertently, a name was given her that is phonologically nearly the same as Seraiah, a man's name. The very important vowel *a* distinguishes Sariah from Seraiah. It would be spelled in an unvocalized text the same as the OT name. If it is a blend of Sarai and Sarah, it is not the same name, and is not the name in the Elephantine inscription.

In any case, the Hebrew-origin residents in Elephantine, in the furthest south reaches of Egypt, apparently mercenaries, had unorthodox religious traditions and wrote Aramaic. If we grant that it is Seraiah, then at most the contribution only provides a case where it can be a woman's name.

Overall, this analysis finds that Tvedtnes et al. have not found any non-Biblical BoM names that are unambiguously attested in Hebrew inscriptional materials. Even if we admit that Sariah is an exception to this, it is a dictational version of a name common in one of the favorite books of the BoM authors, Jeremiah. This is by no means the end. Avigad/Sass, in a large folio-size book, and double columns, have 64 pages of West Semitic names. More material is being constantly discovered, and more names. More claims will be made of BoM names in Hebrew inscriptions. It's in the cards. Even so, the study analyzed here is a very successful work, in that the authors' apologist colleagues have cited it as strong evidence, if not proof for the authenticity of the *Book of Mormon*. Most Mormons never see the study itself, but just references to it.

Steve Smoot has made a substantially less impressive effort but relating Egyptian names to BoM names.[617]

Japanese in the BoM Narrative

The following comparisons are limited to BoM names:

Cumom	Kumon/Kumom	Mosiah	Masuyo
Cumorah	Kimura	Ogath	Ogata/Ogita
Himni	Hamano	Omer	Omori
Kib	Kaiba	Onidah	Onida
Kish	Kish[i]	Sam	Asami
Korihor	Kurihara	Shim/Shum	Shin
Kumen	Kimura	Shiz/shez	Shiz[u]/Shizuka
Minon	Mino	Shum	Shun

---

[617] See this in Arthur Chris Eccel, *Mormon Genesis*, 545-46.

Mocum	Megumi/Mikami

Of course there is no Japanese in the BoM. But a diligent search can make it appear to be the case.

The study of names is called onomastics. There are scholars who specialize in the onomastics of a particular language or dialect, such as Akkadian or Palmyrene Aramaic. Their results are often tentative. When comparing a noun, verb or adjective in one language to the same in another, usually there are two components, the phonological component, and the semantic component. Both are usually known in both languages. When the semantic component is not known, there is usually at least some context that can narrow it down. This is less true when the word occurs in a short inscription, such as those carved into stone in Arabia, which are at times not much more than "So-and-so did such-and-such." In the case of proper names in these short inscriptions, the semantic component is often not known, and at times not even the language. For these, the results of onomastic research are often especially tentative.

Chiasmus, *Parallelismus Membrorum, Māshal,* & Poetry

There has been a significant amount of LDS literary analysis of the *Book of Mormon*, partly to improve its reputation among those few in the world of literature who have actually read it, but mostly to find in it literary forms that could prove it to be an authentic translation of an ancient work of pre-Columbian Israelite origin. While tastes can and do vary, and good taste is at least significantly a reflection of cultural norms, it is clear that these scholars venerate the object of their study, and see it through the eyes of faith, as indeed the Church urges them to do.[618] Even so, there can be no doubt that it has a valid place in the history of religion. As a work of literature, I would suggest that it has a parallel in the history of art. Some museums of art have a collection of naïve art, where the word "naïve" is not intended as a pejorative. Some individuals have followed their creative inspirations totally without any formal training, and often without proper materials. Some worked in remote rural areas, and others in an urban ghetto. Yet they produced works that have museum-quality merit, within

---

[618] James T. Duke, *The Literary Masterpiece Called the Book of Mormon* (Springville, UT: Cedar Fort, 2003). Note too, Angela M. Crowell, *Hebrew Poetry in the Book of Mormon* (Zarahemla Research Foundation, published online, restoredcovenant.org)

their own genre. Similarly, even though the archaeological verdict is clear, the BoM is worthy of study for what it is.

Every culture has distinctive literary and public speaking patterns or devices. Take for example the classical drama of ancient Greece. The stichomythia (dialogue) with short statements, back and forth, in the language of the day in Attica, was balanced by periodical long passages sung/chanted by the chorus, in deliberately archaic forms and language. This is not found, to my knowledge, as an indigenous dramatic form, in other drama (barring imitations). More germane to our investigation is Old Testament poetry, and literary forms such as the *māšāl, parallelismus membrorum* and chiastic constructions.

Poetry

It is axiomatic that poetry was more important and generally more appreciated in the past than today. Ancient cultures of the circum-Mediterranean basin valued poetry. Perhaps the best of classical Arab literature was composed by the pre-Islamic poets. Tribes competed to recruit famous poets to their side, and feared that they would support the cause of an enemy tribe. Poetry competitions occurred in Arabia's Sūq 'Ukāz̧ and the ancient Greek Olympics. The poetry of the Old Testament shows that the Hebrews were not outdone by their neighbors.

Hebrew has both rhymed and unrhymed poetry. It often has accented-syllable rhythm much more than quantitative rhythm. Parallelism (*parallelismus membrorum*) is often used in poetry, but not always. Various genres exist. A common one is the dirge (*kinot*) comprising the entire Book of Lamentations. The rhythm of this form is marked by the fact that a longer line is followed by a shorter one. Another technique is anadiplosis, where the end of one phrase is the beginning of another:

> they came not to the help of the Lord,
> to the help of the Lord against the mighty (Judges 5:23)

> From whence shall my help come?
> My help cometh from the Lord (Psalm 121:1b-2a, R. V.).

Alphabetical acrostics are also found, where the first letter of each line occurs in the ordinary order of the alphabet. This has been found in the poetry of other cultures in the region. In addition to the dirge, we also find the psalm and the drama (Job). The Book of Ecclesiastes has a strong poetic quality. An oracle can come in poetry, as in the oracle of Balaam (Numbers 24).

Another distinct type is the taunt song. A shorter reference is in
Habakkuk 2:6:

> Shall not all these take up a parable against him,
> and a taunting riddle against him, and say:
> "Woe to him that increaseth that which is not his! how long?
> and that ladeth himself with many pledges!"

Many who have read the *Book of Mormon* many times will probably
say that it has no poetry. In fact, one can certainly identify passages that
remind one of the Bible, which it took as its model. The BoM authors were
not just imbued with Biblical material, but with the verses of numerous
Bible-inspired hymns. Poetic style was no stranger to them. BoM poetic
passages include Mosiah 2:13-17, Mormon 4:26, 1 Nephi 6:25-26 and
others. LDS writers have called one long passage the Psalm of Nephi (2
Nephi 4:15-35). An ambitious analysis of it is that of Stephen Sondrup,
my debate partner at East High in Salt Lake City, fellow graduate student
at Harvard, and later, a professor at BYU. He is as qualified as they come
in European-language comparative literature. In a footnote, he comments,
"Although Professor Sperry may be right in his unsubstantiated argument
that 'this is a true psalm in both form and ideas,' he seems to have
misunderstood the basic poetic structure of this passage, at least insofar as
his arrangement of lines and stanzas allows inference."[619] Sondrup adds,
"The question to be discussed with reference to these verses is not whether
they are a psalm in the biblical sense of the term but rather the nature and
extent of their poetic qualities…"

Parallelismus Membrorum

This technique has been discussed above, in the section on the Isaiah
inclusion in the *Book of Mormon*. An example adduced from the *Book of
Mormon* is:

> For his soul did rejoice,
> and his whole heart was filled. (1 Nephi 1:14)

This has been compared with:

---

[619] Stephen P. Sondrup, "The Psalm of Nephi: A Lyric Reading," *BYU Studies*
(Provo, UT: Brigham Young University, 21:3, 1981), 357. See page 358, &
footnote no. 4.

0 magnify the Lord with me,
and let us exalt his name together. (Psalm 34:3)

What is more distinctly characteristic of the Old Testament is when an actual series of these pairs is used. It is then that we have a fully developed pattern for a poetic work. An example is found in Isaiah in a taunt song (in this case, one of prophetic character, and hence tantamount to a curse) raised against the king of Babylon (Isaiah 14):

12. For the day of the Lord of hosts shall be upon
    every one that is **proud and lofty**
    and upon every one that is **lifted up** and he shall be made low:
13. And upon all the **cedars of Lebanon** that are high and lifted up
    and upon all the **oaks of Bāshan**
14. And upon all the **high mountains**
    and upon all the **hills that are lifted up**
15. And upon every **high tower**
    and upon every **fenced wall**

To be fair to Isaiah, we must add here that in some cases a single Hebrew word has been rendered by two or three English words, or even a subordinate clause, which disturbs the force of this device in translation. I am unaware of veritable taunt songs in the *Book of Mormon*, or of a series of paired verses using *parallelismus membrorum.* Note that just as the OT uses a specific term for dirge (*kinot*), it has a specific phrase for raising a taunt song against someone: *nāśā māšāl*: to raise up a similitude against... In this passage, the Lord commanded Isaiah to do so.

Chiasmus.

He used this rhetorical device to create the impression of logic,
To bestow the appearance of reason, he employed this figure of speech.

A simple form of a chiasmus is JFK's statement

Ask not what your country can do for you
But ask what you can do for your country.

The basic form has two members, each with two elements. The two in the second member must be essentially the same as the two in the first member, but in reverse order: AB-BA. In this one from JFK, they are "country" "you" – "you" "country". This can happen in ordinary speech without having any knowledge of rhetoric. It often happens that some A and some B will be repeated in the next breath, and one naturally mentions first the one that was mentioned last in the first member, simply because it is the most fresh in one's mind. But, at some point in cultural history, persons interested in using language to the best effect noticed that stating a sentence in this manner could be very effective. Some writers or speakers got the habit of doing it, it entered into the culture, and the Greeks gave it a name: *chiasmus*. For them, the ideal form could not repeat the same words, as in my own example above: "rhetorical device" "figure of speech" – "impression of logic" "appearance of reason". There are various types of chiasmus, and some are complex. But they should not be so complex that they escape the notice of the reader or listener. If it does, the effect would be lost. So, did JFK know about chiasmus, and use it deliberately, as a master of rhetoric? More likely, having heard it from time to time, he spontaneously produced a chiastic sentence as a result of his natural speaking ability. I once noticed an example in my college physics textbook, probably just because it sounded good to the author.

It has been asserted that ancient writers, among some ancient cultures, the Hebrews, Greeks and the Romans, used chiasmus more than modern English writers. This may well be the case. But to my knowledge, no one has ever done quantified research to prove that it is so. Some fun examples are:

> Your manuscript is both good and original;
>> but the part that is good is not original, and
>> the part that is original is not good.
>> (Samuel Johnson)

> Do I love you because you're beautiful?
> Or are you beautiful because I love you?
>> (Oscar Hammerstein II)

> You can take it out of the country,
> but you can't take the country out of it.
>> (slogan for Salem cigarettes, 1960s)

Someone once said that the difference between William James and Henry James was that:

the former was a psychologist who wrote like a novelist
while the latter was a novelist who wrote like a psychologist.
  (Archibald Henderson, "Aspects of Contemporary Fiction," *The Arena*, July 1906)

All of this is relevant inasmuch as some LDS apologists have claimed to have found a significant amount of chiasmus in the *Book of Mormon*, and argue that this shows that it is a translation of an ancient source, rather than a modern English composition. In particular, it would show that the BoM narrative was written by individuals schooled in a pre-Colombian Hebrew literary tradition.

Chiastic analysis necessarily poses the problem of how similar wording has to be, and how much one can delete whatever is deemed irrelevant, without being guilty of cherry-picking just that which fits. A good example of this issue in the study of Biblical chiasmus is a passage claimed to be chiastic in Joshua 1:5-9, where the proposed chiastic elements have been underlined:

A as I was with Moses, [so] I will be with thee: I will not fail thee, nor forsake thee.

 B Be strong and of a good courage: for unto this people shalt thou divide for an inheritance the land, which I sware unto their fathers to give them. Only be thou strong and very courageous,

  C that thou mayest observe to do according to all the law, which Moses my servant commanded thee: turn not from it [to] the right hand or [to] the left, that thou mayest prosper whithersoever thou goest.

   D This book of the law shall not depart out of thy mouth;

   D but thou shalt meditate therein day and night

  C that thou mayest observe to do according to all that is written therein: for then thou shalt make thy way prosperous, and then thou shalt have good success.

 B Have not I commanded thee? Be strong and of a good courage; be not afraid, neither be thou dismayed:

A for the LORD thy God [is] with thee whithersoever thou goest.

Calling this a true chiasmus is quite a stretch, but instances of chiasmus do occur in the BoM narrative (although matched elements repeat the same words). One is found in Jacob (3:12):

By the power of his word

man came upon the face of the <u>earth</u>;
which <u>earth</u> was created
By the power of his <u>word</u>.

Note also (1 Nephi 21:1):

A <u>Hearken,</u>
B <u>O ye house of Israel,</u>
C <u>All ye that are broken off and are driven out</u>
D Because of the wickedness of the pastors of my people;
C Yea, <u>all ye that are broken off, that are scattered abroad,</u>
B Who are of my people, <u>O house of Israel</u>.
A <u>Listen,</u> O isles, unto me, and <u>hearken</u> ye people from far

Here, D is not a pair. Furthermore, chapter 21 is an Isaiah inclusion (chapter 49) and the last line above is from Isaiah. The more verbiage in a long text, the more raw material one has at hand to "discover" a chiasmus. One proceeds to identify elements in a passage, and then scans down the page until roughly similar mates occur, but in reverse order. Consider for example the chiastic analysis of John Welch of Alma 26.[620] The bolded words are those that Welch extracts to construct his chiasmus. In other words, delete the words not bolded, and you will have his published chiasmus. He did not alert his reader to the large amount of text that had to be eliminated in the process. Instead, this is left for one to discover by reading Alma 26 for oneself (should you bother to do so). When thus displayed, A should equal A, B should equal B, and so on.

A **My son, give ear to my words**;
 B ~~for I swear unto you, that inasmuch as ye shall~~ **keep the commandments** ~~of God~~
 [and] ye shall prosper in the land.
  C ~~I would that ye should~~ **do as I have done,**
   D **in remembering the captivity of our fathers**; ~~for they were in~~ **bondage**,
    E ~~and none could deliver them except it was the God of Abraham, and the God of Isaac, and the God of Jacob; and~~ **he surely did deliver them** ~~in their afflictions~~.
     F ~~And now, O my son Helaman, behold, thou art in thy youth, and therefore, I beseech of thee that thou wilt hear my words and learn of me; for I do know that whosoever shall put their~~ **trust in God**
      G ~~shall be~~ **supported in their trials, and** ~~their~~ **troubles, and** ~~their~~ **afflictions,** ~~and shall be lifted up at the last day~~.

---

[620] John W. Welch, "Chiasmus in the *Book of Mormon*," in John W. Welch, ed., *Chiasmus in Antiquity* (Provo, UT: Research Press [The Foundation for Ancient Research and Mormon Studies—F.A.R.M.S.], 1981), 206. See also H. Clay Gorton, *A New Witness for Christ. Chiastic Structures in the Book of Mormon* (Bountiful, UT: Horizon Publishers, 1997).

H ~~And I would not that ye think that~~ **I know [this not] of myself** ~~— not of the temporal but of the spiritual, not of the carnal mind~~ **but of God**.

I ~~Now, behold, I say unto you,~~ if I had not been **born of God** ~~I should not have known these things; but God has, by the mouth of his holy angel, made these things known unto me, not of any worthiness of myself.~~

J ~~For I went about with the sons of Mosiah,~~ **seeking to destroy the church of God**; ~~but behold, God sent his holy angel to stop us by the way. And behold, he spake unto us, as it were the voice of thunder, and the whole earth did tremble beneath our feet; and we all fell to the earth, for the fear of the Lord came upon us. But behold, the voice said unto me: Arise. And I arose and stood up, and beheld the angel. And he said unto me: If thou wilt of thyself be destroyed, seek no more to destroy the church of God.~~

K. ~~And it came to pass that I fell to the earth; and it was for the space of three days and three nights that I could not open my mouth, neither had I the use of my limbs~~ **[my limbs were paralyzed]** ~~And the angel spake more things unto me, which were heard by my brethren, but I did not hear them; for when I heard the words — If thou wilt be destroyed of destroyed of Thyself, seek no more to destroy the church of God — of God — I was struck with such great fear and amazement lest perhaps I should be destroyed, that I fell to the earth and did hear no more. But I was racked with eternal torment, for my soul was harrowed up to the greatest degree and racked with all my sins. Yea, I did remember all my sins and iniquities, for which I was tormented with the pains of hell; yea, I saw that I had rebelled against my God, and that I had not kept his holy commandments.~~

L ~~Yea, and I had murdered many of his children, or rather led them away unto destruction; yea, and in fine so great had been my iniquities, that the very thought of coming into the presence of my God did rack my soul with inexpressible horror.~~ **[Fear of the PRESENCE OF GOD]** ~~Oh, thought I, that I could be banished and become extinct both soul and body, that I might not be brought to stand in the presence of my God, to be judged of my deeds.~~

M ~~And now, for three days and for three nights was I racked, even with the~~ **pains of a damned soul**. ~~And it came to pass that as I was thus racked with torment, while I was harrowed up by the memory of my many sins,~~

N ~~behold,~~ **I remembered** ~~also to have heard my father prophesy unto the people concerning the coming of~~ **one Jesus Christ, a Son of God**, ~~to atone for the sins of the world.~~

N ~~Now, as my mind caught hold upon this thought,~~ *I cried* ~~within my heart:~~ O **Jesus**, ~~thou~~ **Son of God**, ~~have mercy on me, who am in the gall of bitterness, and am encircled about by the everlasting chains of death.~~

M ~~And now, behold, when I thought this, I could remember my pains no more; yea, I was harrowed up by the memory of my sins no more. And oh, what joy, and what marvelous light I did behold; yea, my soul was filled with~~ **joy as exceeding as was my pain**! ~~Yea, I say unto you, my son, that there could be nothing so exquisite and so bitter as were my pains. Yea, and again I say unto you, my son, that on the other hand, there can be nothing so exquisite and sweet as was my joy.~~

L ~~Yea, methought [sic] I saw, even as our father Lehi saw, God sitting upon his throne, surrounded with numberless concourses of angels, in the attitude of singing and praising their God; yea, and my soul did long to be there.~~ **[Long to be in the PRESENCE OF GOD]**

K ~~But behold,~~ **my limbs did receive their strength again**, ~~and I stood upon my feet, and did manifest unto the people that I had been born of God.~~

J Yea, and from that time even until now, I have **labored** without ceasing, **that I might** **bring souls unto repentance**; that I might bring them to taste of the exceeding joy of which I did taste; that they might also be born of God, and be filled with the Holy Ghost. Yea, and now behold, O my son, the Lord doth give me exceedingly great joy in the fruit of my labors;

I For because of the word which he has imparted unto me, behold, many have Been **born of God**, and have tasted as I have tasted, and have seen eye to eye as I have seen;

H therefore they do know of these things of which I have spoken, as I do know; and **the** **knowledge which I have is of God**.

G And I have been **supported under trials and** **troubles** of every kind, yea, **and** in all manner of **afflictions**; yea, God has delivered me from prison, and from bonds, and from death;

F yea, and I do put my **trust in him,**

E **and he will still deliver me**.

D And I know that he will raise me up at the last day, to dwell with him in glory; yea, and I will praise him forever, for he has brought our fathers out of **Egypt**, and he has swallowed up the Egyptians in the Red Sea; and he led them by his power into the promised land; yea, and he has delivered them out of bondage and **captivity** from time to time. Yea, and he has also brought our fathers out of the land of Jerusalem; and he has also, by his everlasting power, delivered them out of bondage and captivity, from time to time even down to the present day; and I have always retained in remembrance their captivity; yea, and ye also ought to retain in remembrance, as I have done, their captivity.

C But behold, my son, this is not all; for ye ought to **know as I do know,**

B that inasmuch as ye shall **keep the commandments of God ye shall prosper in the** **land**; and ye ought to know also, that inasmuch as ye will not keep the commandments of God ye shall be cut off from his presence.

A **Now this is according to his word**.

He allows himself to call this "a rigorous chiastic pattern." [621] His extractions, displayed in chiastic format, may very well impress some. To me, it is obvious that he has picked the best of the low-hanging cherries from a very large tree to achieve his objective, viz to fabricate his very own chiasmus.

If you have to tease a chiastic structure from a forest of verbiage, its rhetorical efficacy for the listener or reader will be minimal or nonexistent. True chiasmus is a rhetorical tool. If it is lost in complexity, and cannot function as a chiasmus, it is just not a chiasmus. Note that occasionally he was unable to find the words he needed for the mates. So instead he matched passages with similar meaning, and inserted words in square

---

[621] Welch, Chiasmus in Antiquity, 206. See also Duane L. Christensen, *World Biblical Commentary* (Dallas, TX: Word Books, 1991), xli; and Yehuda Radday "Chiasmus in Hebrew Biblical Narrative", in John W. Welch, ed., *Chiasmus in Antiquity* (Provo, UT: Research Press [The Foundation for Ancient Research and Mormon Studies—F.A.R.M.S.], 1981), 50-76.,

brackets so his reader would not fail to notice them (as in the two "L" mates).

When faced with the fact that chiasmus occurs not only in English literature, but even in popular culture, we have to ask whether any of this rises to the level of passing the "So what?" test. It certainly cannot override the archaeological verdict, although it has been used effectively by apologists to buttress the faith of those ravenous for proof.

Lehi's Arabia

The study that most Mormons associate with this topic is *Lehi in the Desert* by Hugh Nibley.[622] This is the work that established his career in LDS apologetics. Various details in First Nephi were marshaled and claimed to be geographically or culturally correct, such as the fact that Lehi dwelled in a tent on route, or that when returning from the Red Sea to Jerusalem Nephi is said to go up to Jerusalem. This latter phrase is typical of Hebrew usage in reference to persons traveling from parts of Palestine, and especially from the Mediterranean, the Jordan river and the Dead Sea to Jerusalem, which is uphill. But it may be less applicable when traversing the varied terrain from the Red Sea, depending on the route. In any case, one can also say, in English, "Well, I went up to Chicago." This is not alien to English.

Others have referred to the Lihyani civilization as having been converted to the "true" Christian faith by Lehi, based on a superficial similarity between the names Lehi and Lihyani. This is a pure invention, being neither evidenced in archaeology nor mentioned in the BoM. Lihyan (also Dedan or Dadan) worshipped a number of pagan deities.[623]

Some have been impressed by the fact that when Ishmael died in the desert, he was buried in "the place which was called Nahom." In Hebrew, this could refer to "mourning" or "growling, groaning," depending on which h (h or $\d{h}$) one wishes to assign to it. There has been some LDS writing about it, in defense of the BoM text. Following BoM practice, we find that Lehi names a river after his eldest son, Laman (1 Nephi 2:8: "he called the name of the river Laman"). It flows in the Valley of Lemuel, clearly named after his second son. A camp site was also named by the party, (1 Nephi16:13): "we did call the name of the place Shazer"). The

---

[622] Hugh Nibley, "Lehi in the Desert" (*Improvement Era*, issues 1950/1-6, 9-10); Hugh Nibley, *Lehi in the Desert & the World of the Jaredites*.
[623] "The Divine Names at Dadan: a Philological Approach," in Siminar for Arabian Studies (Oxford: Archaeonpress, 2016), vol. 46, 125-135.

land where they dwelled to build their ship was also named by the group (1 Nephi 17:5: "the land which we called Bountiful"), as was the Indian Ocean (1 Nephi 17:5: "the Sea, which we called Irreantum, which being interpreted, is, many waters"). Contrary to this practice, Nahom is "the place which was called Nahom." The implication is that it already existed, and was not named because of mourning for Lehi. In any case, it is inevitable to find references to places, peoples, tribes or clans with a name with *n* at the beginning, *m* at the end, and one of three possible consonants in the middle, in Hebrew, Arabic, Old South Arabian (four languages) or considerable Arabian inscriptional material deriving from various languages. Moreover, it is not hard to get a general idea of where the BoM Nahom should be found. The party traveled southeast along the Red Sea, from Laman to Shazer, to the camp where Nephi broke his bow, to Nahom. There, they took a course to the east. Most probably this would be near Abha, or if further south, then it would be near Hudaydah in Yemen. On the other hand, this issue should not even arise, since most probably the BoM Nahom was taken from the KJV Book of Nahum.

Additional problems regarding the journey of Lehi include the forbidding distance from Jerusalem to the Red Sea requiring traveling 116 miles a day, and the absence of any river that could qualify as the River Laman. (See p. 98.)

Appendix 2 Additional Analysis of BoM-KJ Variants

Changes in Number

There are cases where a *Book of Mormon* variant finds agreement in the manuscripts, but, alas, no agreement of significance. A good example is the case where there is a change in number, such as "The men raised their hand" and "The men raised their hands." The number in these cases is optional. The following are the cases that found some agreement where there is a change from singular to plural (where the italics are original in the King James):

Variants in Number: singular to plural.

(Agreement is listed in parentheses: H=Hebrew; D=Dead Sea Scrolls; G=Greek; S=Syriac (Aramaic); T=Targumim (Aramaic); L=Latin; E=Ethiopic; C=Coptic; A=Arabic. The sources are listed in Eccel, *Mormon Genesis*, Bibliography 1.)

| Exodus 20:5: | visiting the iniquity of the fathers upon the children | (GSTY) |
| Mosiah 13:13 | visiting the iniquities of the fathers upon the children | |

| Exodus 20:5: | unto the third and fourth *generation* | (S) |
| Mosiah 13:13 | unto the third and fourth generations | |

| Isaiah 3:8: | their tongue and their doings *are* against the Lord | (GSC) |
| 2 Nephi 13:8: | their tongues and their doings are against the Lord | |

| Isaiah 3:9: | Woe unto their soul! | (LA) |
| 2 Nephi 13:9: | Woe unto their souls, | |

| Isaiah 5:24: | their blossom shall go up as dust | (A?) |
| 2 Nephi 15:24: | their blossoms shall go up as dust | |

| Isaiah 9:9: | the inhabitant of Samaria | (GSLC) |
| 2 Nephi 19:9: | the inhabitants of Samaria | |

| Isaiah 13:4: | the Lord of hosts mustereth the host of the battle | (S) |
| 2 Nephi 23:4: | the Lord of Hosts mustereth the hosts of the battle | |

| Isaiah 13:18 | their eye shall not spare children | (GSTCA) |
| 2 Nephi 23:18: | their eyes shall not spare children | |

| Isaiah 14:21; | for the iniquity of their fathers | (GTSCA) |
| 2 Nephi 24:21: | for the iniquities of their fathers | |

| Isaiah 14:32: | What shall *one* then answer the messengers of the nation? | (GSTLC) |
| 2 Nephi 24:32: | What shall then answer the messengers of the nations? | |

| Isaiah 29:13: | have removed their heart far from me | (A) |
| 2 Nephi 27:25: | have removed their hearts far from me | |

| Isaiah 49:6: | my salvation unto the end of the earth | (GSTA) |
| 1 Nephi 21:6: | my salvation unto the ends of the earth | |

| Isaiah 51:11: | *shall be* upon their head | (DSTL) |
| 2 Nephi 8:11: | shall be upon their heads | |

| Isaiah 53:6: | hath laid on him the iniquity of us all | (GST |
| Mosiah 14:6: | hath laid on him the iniquities of us all | LCA) |

| Isaiah 53:8: | for the transgression of my people | (GSLC) |
| Mosiah 14:8: | for the transgressions of my people | |

| Isaiah 53:12: | the sin of many | (DGS |
| Mosiah 14:12 | the sins of many | TLC) |

| Malachi 3:14: | we have kept his ordinance | (GSTLC) |
| 3 Nephi 24:14: | we have kept his ordinances | |

In Isaiah 49:6 above, the word for 'end' means the furthest point, not the end of times, and so here there is no difference in meaning.

In the legend for the table above, "H=Hebrew" was listed *pro forma*. As can be seen, there is no agreement in the original language, Hebrew. This is typical of agreement in general, when it happens. The other sources are translations, and so by definition, changed. As in all translation, some change happens either because the receiving language requires it grammatically, or prefers it. And in some cases, it is idiolectical, i.e., according to what the translator feels sounds better, his personal speech habit.

Variants in Number: plural to singular.

(Agreement is listed in parentheses: H=Hebrew; D=Dead Sea Scrolls; G=Greek; S=Syriac (Aramaic); T=Targumim (Aramaic); L=Latin; E=Ethiopic; C=Coptic; A=Arabic. The sources are listed in Eccel, *Mormon Genesis*, Bibliography 1.)

Exodus 20:3:	Thou shalt have no other gods before me.	(T)
Mosiah 12:35:	Thou shalt have no other God before me.	
Isaiah 13:22	her days shall not be prolonged	(T)
2 Nephi 23:22	her day shall not be prolonged	
Isaiah 48:18	O that thou hadst hearkened to my commandments	(S)
1 Nephi 20:18	O that thou hadst hearkened to my commandment	
Isaiah 51:5	mine arms shall judge the people	(GLSA)
2 Nephi 8:5	mine arm shall judge the people	
Isaiah 53:3	we hid as it were *our* faces from him	(H[?]GLA)
Mosiah 14:3	we hid as it were our face from him	
Matthew 3:10	the axe is laid unto the root of the trees	(SL)
Alma 5:52	the ax is laid at the root of the tree	

In the Isaiah 53:3 case, above, the agreement in Hebrew is marked with a question mark because the word for face in Hebrew is *pânîm*, which is plural in form, but most usually singular in meaning. Whether it is singular or plural in meaning is determined purely by context, as in this case, where the meaning is plural. But in English, it makes no difference.

In all other cases, the agreement occurs in translations of the original language, just as is the case in the group where the change was from singular to plural.

Variants Involving Verbs

The largest group is those that exhibit a change in tense:

Variants with a Change in Tense

(Agreement is listed in parentheses: H=Hebrew; D=Dead Sea Scrolls; G=Greek; S=Syriac (Aramaic); T=Targumim (Aramaic); L=Latin; E=Ethiopic; C=Coptic; A=Arabic. The sources are listed in Bibliography 1 of Eccel, *Mormon Genesis*.)

Isaiah 2:12	For the day of the Lord of Hosts shall be upon	(TA)
2 Nephi 12:12	For the day of the Lord of Hosts soon cometh upon	
Isaiah 3:6	a man shall take hold of his brother....*saying*	(A)
2 Nephi 13:6	a man shall take hold of his brother...and shall say	
Isaiah 9:7	Of the increase of *his* government and peace *there shall be* no end	(GSA)
2 Nephi 19:7	Of the increase of government and peace there is no end	
Isaiah 14:16	They that see thee shall narrowly look upon thee, and consider thee, saying	(GSA)
2 Nephi 24:16	They that see thee shall narrowly look upon thee, and shall consider the, and shall say	
Malachi 3:7	But ye said, Wherein shall we return?	(TCA3
Nephi 24:7	But ye say, Wherein shall we return?	
Matthew 3:10	every tree which bringeth not forth good fruit is hewn down	(SLCA)
Alma 5:52	every tree that bringeth not forth good fruit shall be hewn down	
Matthew 5:13	but if the salt have lost his savour	(SL)
3 Nephi 12:13	but if the salt shall lose its savor	
Matthew 5:25	and thou be cast into prison	(GL)
3 Nephi 12:25	and thou shalt be cast into prison	
Matthew 6:2	Therefore when thou doest *thine* alms	(LC)
3 Nephi 13:2	Therefore, when ye shall do your alms	

Minor Changes

Forty-five of the variants that find agreement in at least some ancient text are simply the addition of the word 'and.' In four cases, the word 'and' is deleted. In one verse, 'till' is substituted by 'and,' and in another 'but' is substituted by 'and.' In three cases 'that' (conjunction) is added, where it is optional. In one verse, 'according' is changed to 'according as' with no meaning change. Two variants enjoy agreement where 'wherefore' is changed from interrogative to declarative, but the punctuation was largely done by the typesetter. 'Behold' and 'yea' are deleted with slight meaning change, and find agreement in translations. In three verses, the deletion of optional repetitions of 'for' found agreement in some translations, and the addition of optional additions of 'with' also found some agreement, all being cases where there was no meaning change. In two cases, added prepositional phrases ('of them' and 'unto them') found some agreement in translations, but meaning was not changed. Optional, almost pleonastic, pronouns were added in two cases: 'that' changed to 'they that' and 'that' changed to 'she that.'

Appendix 3 Mistranslation in the KJ Version of Isaiah

Additional Mistranslations or Weak Translations in the KJ	
HM: the Hebrew Masoretic text Q: the Great Isaiah Scroll found at Qumran =Q designates orthographic differences to HM T: the Aramaic Targum of Jonathan (Yonatan, Sperber edition) S: the Greek Septuagint (edited by Rahlfs) Editions and dictionaries: All are listed in the bibliographies. Transliteration: In keeping with the early (pre-Rabbinical) date of Isaiah, b, g, d, k, p & t are not aspirated after vowels.	

Text at Issue with Chapter & Verse	Translation & Comments
2:6: they <u>please themselves</u> (in the children of strangers) HM: *yaśpîqû* (=Q) T: *b-nimūsēʸ ʿaməmayā ʾazlīn* S: τέκνα πολλὰ ἀλλόφυλα ἐγενήθη αὐτοῖς	HM: they <u>clap</u> (hands with the children of strangers; like us shaking hands, to make deals [the verb means "to clap"]) T: (you) have gone with the laws of the nations (gentiles) S: they have had many foreign children
2:19: to <u>shake</u> terribly the earth HM: *la-ʿᵃrôṣ hā-ʾāreṣ* (=Q) T: *lə-mitbar rašśîʿēʸ ʾîrʿā* S: θραῦσαι τὴν γῆν	HM: "to make the earth <u>tremble in fear</u>" The verb means "to fear" & "to terrify"; one might conjecture that it could mean "to tremble in fear". T: to shatter the wicked of the earth S: to shatter the earth
3:18: <u>round tires like the moon</u> HM: *šahᵃrônîm* (=Q) T: *sibkayā* S: μηνίσκους	HM: "<u>small crescent hair ornaments</u>" (the word is a diminutive form) T: net, hair net S: crescent-shaped ornament
3:19: <u>chains</u> HM: *nitîpôt* (Q reads *nṭpwt*) T: *ʿinqayā* S: κάθεμα	HM: "<u>pendants</u>" (possibly ear pendants (the variant in Q is orthographic) T: neck; neck ornament S: necklace
3:19: <u>muflers</u> HM: *raʿᵃlôt* (=Q) T: *hᵃnisnəsayā* S: τὸν κόσμον τοῦ προσώπου αὐτῶν	HM: <u>veils</u> (possibly with an eye slit) T: veils S: their face ornamentation

3:20: <u>bonnets</u>
HM: *pəʾērîm* (=Q) | HM: a <u>turban headwrap</u> worn by women
T: *kəlīlayā* | T: crown, bridal crown, women's head-dress
S: *τὴν σύνθεσιν τοῦ κόσμου τῆς* | S: the set of decoration of glory

3:20: <u>headbands</u>
HM: *qiššurîm* (=Q) | HM: women's bands or breast-<u>sashes</u>
T: *qūlmazməsayā* | T: hair ornament (or curling pins?)
S: *ἐμπλόκιον* | S: hair clasp (or wreath)

3:20: <u>tablets</u>
HM: *bottê han-nepeš* (=Q) | HM: "scent <u>bottles</u>" (houses of the spirit)
T: *qədāšayā* | T: ear or nose rings
S: *τοὺς δακτυλίους* | S: finger rings, signet rings

3:20: <u>earrings</u>
HM: *ləḥāšîm* (=Q) | HM: "<u>ornamental amulets</u>"
T: *ḥᵃlîṭāyā* | T: necklace
S: *ἐνώτια* | S: earrings (S has two items more than HM & T but this seems to match best)

3:23: <u>glasses</u>
HM: *gilyônîm* (Q reads: *glywnym)* | HM: either a fine garment, or <u>reflective decorations</u>, possibly sown into fabric
T: *maḥzəyātā* | T: mirrors
S: *βύσσινα* | S: fine linen (clothing)

3:23: <u>hoods</u>
HM: *ṣənîpôt* (=Q) | HM: "women's <u>turban</u>" (root means "to wind around")
T: *kitrayā* | T: crown, fine headdress
S: *βύσσον* | S: fine linen (with gold and blue interwoven)

3:24: <u>stomacher</u>
HM: *pətîgîl* (=Q) | HM: <u>fine robe</u> or chest band?
T: *məhalləkān bə-gēʸwāh* | T: (instead of) walking in pride
S: *τοῦ χιτῶνος τοῦ μεσοπορφύρου* | S: tunic mixed with purple

5:2: he <u>fenced</u> it
HM: *wa-yᶜazzēqahû* (=Q) | HM: "he <u>hoed it</u>", dug dug it up. Semitic evidence & post-Biblical Hebrew: "to dig up, hoe"
T: *qaddēʸštinūn* | T: I sanctified them (the translation here borders on exegisis)
S: *φραγμὸν περιέθηκα* | S: I set a hedge round about

5:5: shall be <u>eaten up</u>
HM: *lə-bāᶜēr* (=Q) | HM: "<u>for burning</u>, kindling". The root means "to burn". Hence, "it shall be for kindling (for firewood)" (or figuratively, "for plunder"?)
T: *lə-mîbazz* | T: for plundering
S: *εἰς διαρπαγήν* | S: for plunder

5:9: shall be <u>desolate</u> HM: *lə-šammâ yihyû* (=Q)	HM: "shall be <u>in ruins</u>" (laid waste, *šannâ*, used in passages of horrific destructionon/as a divine judgment)
T: *lə-ṣādū* S: εἰς ἔρημον	T: shall be for desolation S: shall be a desert, desolation
5:12: <u>harp</u> HM: *kinnôr* (Q: lacuna) T: *kinnār* S: κιθάρας	HM: <u>zither</u> T: a string instrument, lute, lyre S: cithora, lyre
5:12: <u>viol</u> HM: *nebel* (Q: lacuna) T: *nəbal qatrōs* S: ψαλτηρου	HM: <u>harp</u> T: a type of lute or lyre (*nebel* κιθάρας) S: a string instrument, lyre or harp
5:12: <u>pipe</u> HM: *ḥālîl* (Q unclear) T: *ᵓaᵇūbā* S: αὐλῶν	HM: <u>flute</u> T: reed; flute, pipe S: flute, pipe
5:14: <u>their</u> glory and <u>their</u> multitude and <u>their</u> <u>pomp</u> HM: *hᵃdārāh wa-hᵃmônāh û-šᵓônāh* (=Q) T: *yaqqīrēʸhōn w-sīgōyēʸhōn wə-ᵓitrəgōšāthōn* S: οἱ ἔνδοξοι καὶ οἱ μεγάλοι καὶ οἱ πλούσιοι καὶ οἱ λοιμοὶ αὐτῆς	HM: "<u>tumult</u> (roar, din)" The pronominal suffix is feminine singular for each noun, and seems to refer to Jerusalem;. T: their honorable (men), their multitudes and their tumultuous parties S: her honorable men, great men, rich men and destroyers (or plague-ridden)
5:24: the <u>flame consumeth the chaff</u> HM: *ḥᵃšaš lehābâ yirpe* Q: *w-ᵓš lwhbt yrph* T: *yitᵓakkəlūn kə-qaššā bə-ᵓeʸššātā* S: κανθήσεται καλάμη ὑπὸ ἄνθρακος πυρός	HM: "the <u>chaff</u> of [in] the flame withers" The verb means "to grow slack, wither" and is in the masculine, while "flame" is feminine. So the subject is chaff. Q: *ᵓš* is probably an error for *ḥᵃšaš* T: "they shall be consumed like chaff in the fire" S: straw is burned under the hot coals of fire
5:24: they have <u>cast away</u> the law of the <u>Lord</u> HM: *māᵓᵃsû ᵓēt tôrat yahwe* (=Q) T: *qaṣṣū bə-ᵓōrāytā də-ywy* S: οὐ γὰρ ἠθέλησαν τὸν νόμον κυρίου	 HM: the verb means to reject: "they have <u>rejected</u> the law of Yahweh" T: they have cut, destroyed, rejected the law of Yahweh S: they have not held to the law of the Lord

6:7: he <u>laid it upon</u> my mouth HM: *yaggaᶜ ᶜal* (Q: lacuna) *T:* *sədar bə-* *S:* ἥψατο	HM: "he <u>caused it to touch</u> my mouth" The verb means "to cause to touch" so: *T:* "he arranged it by/at my mouth" *S:* "he touched it to my mouth"
6:13: <u>teil tree</u> HM: *ʾēlâ* (=Q) *T:* *būṭmā* *S:* τερέβινθος	HM: <u>terebinth</u> (the KJ teil tree is a contemporary word for the linden tree (Latin *tilia*), which does not grow in the Mid East. It later became associated with the terebinth due to KJ mistranslation *T:* terebinth (cf. Arabic *buṭm*) *S:* terebinth
7:1: but could not <u>prevail</u> against it HM: *lō yākōl lə-hillāḥēm ᶜāleʸhā* (=Q) *T:* *lā yākēʸl la-ʾgāḥā ᶜalah* *S:* οὐκ ἠδυνήθησαν πολιορκῆσαι αὐτήν	HM: "<u>enter into battle</u>," "to wage war, fight". The verb is the infinitive of the "n" passive/middle, which is well known. The Assyrian army of Tiglath- pileser attacked Aram (Syria), forcing a dissolution of the Aramaean-Israelite coalition against Judah, so they were unable to enter into battle. *T:* "could not attack it" *S:* "could not besiege it"
7:4: for the fierce anger of Rēzin <u>with</u> Syria, and of the son of Remaliah HM: *bā-ḥᵒrî-ʾap rəṣîn wa-ʾᵃrām ū- ben-rəmalyāhū* (Q spelling: *ḥôrî*) *T:* *bi-tqōp rəgaz rəẓīn wa-ʾrām ū- bar rəmalyāh* *S:* this phrase is absent from S	HM: "for the fierce anger of Rezin <u>and</u> Aram (Syria) and the son of Remalyahu" ("with" in the KJ is not found) *T:* "for the strength of the anger of Rezin and Aram and the son of Remalyah" *S:*
7:19: <u>bushes</u> HM: *nahᵃlōlîm* (Q reads: *nhlylym*) *T:* *bātēʸ tūšbəḥātā* *S:* εἰς πᾶσαν ραγάδα καὶ ἐν παντὶ ξύλῳ	HM: "<u>watering holes</u>? wadis? pastures? " It is a hapax legomenon of uncertain meaning. (cf. Arabic *nhl*) *T:* houses of hymns of praise (i.e. of worship, or praised in song?) *S:* in every ravine and every tree

7:19: in the <u>desolate valleys</u> and in the holes of the rocks	
HM: *bə-naḥᵃlê hab-battôt ū-bi-nqîqê has-salāʿîm* (=Q)	HM: "in the <u>ravines of the cliffs</u> and the clefts of the rocks" *battôt* is a hapax legomenon, currently defined as "cliffs, precipices"; and *nəqîqê* means "clefts, cracks".
T: *bi-rḥōbēʸ qiryā u-bi-šqīpēʸ kēʸpayā*	T: "in the open area (town markets, squares) and in the clefts of rocks"
S: *ἐν ταῖς φάραγξι τῆς χώρας καὶ ἐν ταῖς τρώγλαις τῶν πετρῶν*	S: "in the ravines of the contryside and the caves of the rocks"
8:19: seek unto <u>them that have familiar spirits</u>	
HM: *hā-ʾōbôt* (=Q)	HM: "<u>seek unto returning spirits</u>". *ʾōbôt* (plural of *ʾōb*), is spirits of the dead that return to give an omen or prophecy. Note the story of Saul who consulted the "witch of Endor" (*baʿᵃlat ʾob*, a mistress of an *ʾōb*, i.e. a female necromancer).
T: *biddīn*	T: "lying oracles; conjuring" from a root meaning to invent, make things up.
S: *τοὺς ἀπὸ τῆς γῆς φθνοῦντας*	S: "those speaking from the earth" (i.e., the returning spirits)
8:19: <u>wizards</u>	
HM: *yiddəʿōnîm* (=Q)	HM: "<u>soothsayers</u>". *yiddəʿōnîm* comes from the common verb "to know". These are the knowers (by supernatural means); while wizards are practitioners of magic, sorcerers.
T: *zəkūrū*	T: "necromancy, necromantic apparition"
S: *ἐγγαστριμύθους*	S: "ventriloquists"
8:21: and <u>fret</u> themselves	
HM: *hitqaṣṣap* (=Q)	HM: "and <u>become enraged</u>". The base form of the verb means "to be angry" and this form means to be absorbed in anger
T: *w-īlōṭ wə-yibzē*	T: "he shall curse and despise"
S: *λυπηθήσεσθε*	S: "you shall be grieved, vexed"
9:11: <u>join</u> his enemies <u>together</u>	
HM: *ʾet ʾōyəbāʸw yəsaksēk* (=Q)	HM: "<u>incite</u> his enemies"
T: *yāt baʿalēʸ dəbābōhi yəʿārar*	T: "incite his enemies "
S: *τοὺς ἐχθροὺς αὐτῶν διασκεδάσει*	S: "shall scatter his enemies

9:10: we will <u>change them</u> into cedars HM: *wa-ʾᵃrāzîm naḥᵃlîp* (=Q) T: *wa-d-šappīrīn mi-hōn niqnēʸ* S: *ἐκκόψωμεν συκαμίνους καὶ κέδρους καὶ οἰκοδομήσωμεν ἑαυτοῖς πύργον*	HM: "We will <u>substitute</u> cedars ". The verb means to cause one thing to succeed another. T: " and we shall obtain more goodly ones than they" S: "We should cut down sycomores and cedars and build them a tower."
9:2: <u>shadow of death</u> HM: *ṣalmāwet* (=Q) T: *ṭūllēʸ mōtā* S: *ὀκια θανάτου EDIT A IN SKIA*	HM: "<u>gloom</u>". An ancient folk etymology separated this word into two pieces, *ṣēl* (shadow) and *māwet* (death), although it is always written as one word (*ṣalmôt*, even in Q) The meaning is "gloom, darkness." (cf. Arabic *ẓulm*) T: "shadow/s of death" S: "shadow of death"
9:4: <u>oppressor</u> HM: *nōgēś* (=Q) T: *da-hwā maplaḥ bēʸh* S: *ἀπαιτούντων*	HM: "<u>slave driver</u>"; It is the active participle of a verb meaning to spur on a beast of burden, or to use a rod to make slaves or forced labor to pull harder, etc. T: "by which he exacted forced labor" S: "exactors"
9:7: to <u>order it and to establish</u> it HM: *lə-hākîn ʾōtāh ū-l-saᶜᵃdāh* Q: .. *ʾôtô* .. *saᶜᵃdû* T: *lə-atqānā yātah u-l-mibnah* S: *κατορθῶσαι αὐτὴν καὶ ἀντιλαβέθαι αὐτῆς*	HM: "<u>to establish it and sustain it</u>" Q changes "it" from feminine to masculine, which does not agree grammatically T: "to establish it and build it" S: "to set it up and to take firm hold of it (support, help it)"
9:20: <u>snatch</u> on the right hand HM: *yigzōr ᶜāl-yāmîn* (=Q) T: *bazz min dārōmā* S: *ἐκκλινεῖ εἰς τὰ δεξιά*	HM: "shall <u>cut</u> on the right" (right hand). It means to cut. In Arabic it means "to cut, slaughter an animal, to butcher"). T: "he has plundered from the south" S: "he inclines (turn aside) to the right"
10:2: their <u>prey</u> HM: *šəlālām* (=Q) T: *ᶜᵃdāyhōn* S: *ἁρπαγὴν*	HM: "their <u>booty</u>" This is the normal word for booty. T: "their booty" S: "booty"

9:15: <u>ancient</u> HM: *zāqēn* (=Q)	HM: "<u>elder</u>" (This noun comes from a word meaning "beard" and can refer to a male old enough to grow a beard, but also means an elderly male, or an elder, as a leading elite of the community. Here, the verse refers to secular elites, "the elder and honorable man" and the religious elites, "the prophet", and the next verse lumps them together as "the leaders of this people" which indicates that here, *zāqēn* refers to more than just old men.)
T: *sāb* S: πρεσβύτην	T: "elder"; same comments as above S: "elder" (This word means old man, spokesman, and in the NT, bishop.)
10:1: that write grievousness <u>which</u> <u>they have prescribed</u> HM: *ū-mkattəbîm ʿāmāl kittēbû* T: *kətāb də-lēʸʾū kātəbīn* S: γράφοντεσ γὰρ πονηρίαν γράφουσιν	HM: "<u>writers who writ toil</u> (or burdensomness)" T: "who write writ of toil (or burdensomness)" S: "for writing (for when they write) they write wickedness"
10:31: Madmēnah <u>is removed</u> HM: *nādədâ madmēnâ* (=Q) T: *ʾiʸttabbarū ʾanāš madmēnā* S: ἐξέστη Μαδεβηνα	HM: "Madmēnah <u>has fled</u> (escaped, or is <u>wandering</u>)" T: "the people of Madmēnah are broken" S: "Madebēna is amazed"
10:31: <u>gather themselves</u> to flee HM: *hēʿîzû* (=Q) T: *gəlō* S: not present	HM: "bring (goods, flocks) to safety (or, <u>seek refuge</u>)" (root = "to take refuge") T: "have gone into exile [have fled]" S:
11:3: shall make him <u>of quick</u> <u>understanding</u> in the fear of the Lord HM: *hᵃrîhô bə-yirʾat yahweh* (=Q) T: *wə-yəqārbīnīnēʸh lə-daḥlətēʸh yahweh* S: ἐμπλήσει αὐτὸν πνεῦμα φόβου θεοῦ	HM: "he shall <u>inspire him</u> with fear of Yahweh"; where "inspire (*hᵃʾrîah*) would be denominated from *rûaḥ* (spirit) T: "he will bring him near to his fear of Yahweh" S: "he shall fill him with the spirit of the fear of God"

13:8: <u>sorrows</u> HM: ḥᵃbālîm (=Q) T: ḥᵃbālîm S: ὠδῖνες	HM: "<u>labor pains</u>", used here metaphorically. The context specifies pain, not sorrow. T: "labor pains" S: "labor pains"
13:21: <u>satyrs</u> HM: śᵃʿîrîm (=Q) T: šēʸdîn S: δαιμόνια	HM: <u>desert buck goat</u>? domon? satyr? Taken from the word for hair; v. Koehler & Baumgartner (p. 1341) T: "demons" S: "demons "
14:32: shall <u>trust</u> HM: yeḥᵉsû (=Q) T: yiḥdōn S: σωθήσονται	HM: "shall <u>take refuge</u>"; a common verb; cf. ḥāsût (refuge) T: "shall rejoice" S: "shall be saved"
48:3: I <u>shewed</u> them (also 48:6) HM: ʾašmîʿēm (=Q) T: bassartīnūn S: ἀκουστὸν ἐγένετο	HM: "I <u>made them heard</u>" T: "I announced them" S: "they were heard" (hence: known)
49:7: <u>whom man despiseth</u> HM: bᵉzōh nepeš (Q: bᵉzûy nepeš) T: not present S: τὸν φαυλίζοντα τὴν ψυχὴν αὐτοῦ	HM: "<u>despised of the soul</u>"; i.e., utterly despised? the Masoretic text is edited, usually to nibze ("despized"), but Q reads bᵉzûy (also "despised"); nepeš is the normal word for "spirit, soul" T: S: "him lowly valuing his own soul (life?)"
49:8: have I <u>heard</u> thee HM: ʿᵃnîtîkā Q: ʾeʿenkā T: mᵃqabbēʸl ṣᵃlōtkōn S: ἐπήκουσά σου	HM: "have I <u>answered</u> thee" Q: "shall I answer thee" T: "have received (accepted) your prayer" S: "have I listened to you"; with connotation of "heard you with favor"
49:9: <u>high</u> places HM: šᵉpāyîm (Q: špʾm) T: nigdîn S: τρίβοις	HM: "<u>wind-swept</u>" "<u>bare</u> places?" The root is špy, and has to do with being swept bare, wiped clean, polished, etc.; no word from this root has to do with being high. The word in Q (špʾm) is a possible variant spelling. T: " paths, wadis, water courses, steppe" S: "paths"

48:5: I <u>shewed</u> HM: *hišma'tîkā* (=Q) T: *bassartāk* S: ἀκουστόν σοι ἐποίησα	HM: "I caused you to hear" T: "I announced to you" S: "I made them heard unto you"
49:21: <u>am desolate, a captive and removing to and fro</u> HM: *galmûdâ gōlâ wə-sûrâ* (Q: ... *srh*) T: *yəḥîdā galyā u-məṭalṭəlā* S: ἄτεκνα καὶ χήρα	HM: "<u>barren, gone into exile and turned aside</u>" T: "alone, gone into exile and homeless" S: "childless and a widow"
49:24: <u>prey</u> HM: *malqôaḥ* (=Q) T: *'ᵃday* S: σκῦλα	HM: "<u>spoils</u>"; the passive imperfect and passive participle of the common verb "to take, seize" are used to say, literally, "shall that which has been seized be taken from the mighty (or, warrior)?" T: "spoil" S: "spoils"
51:11: <u>mourning</u> HM: *'ᵃnāḥâ* (=Q) T: *tînnaḥtā* S: στεναγμός	HM: "<u>sighing</u>" or groaning T: "sighing", groaning S: "sighing", groaning
51:17: <u>wrung *them out*</u> HM: *māṣît* (=Q) T: *'a'rît* S: ἐξεκένωσας	HM: "<u>drained</u> (it [the cup]]" The verb means "to drain" and it is conceptually hard to imagine the act of wringing out dregs. We find "drained" in T & S, and in Green, Clines, Koehler/Baumgartner. It is construed to mean "wring out" when used with fleece. T: "emptied [it] out, drained [it]" S: "emptied [it] out"
51:19: <u>desolation</u> HM: *šōd* (=Q) T: *bizzā* S: πτῶμα	HM: "<u>ruin</u>"; especially destruction through violent action. T: "ruin, spoiling" S: "fall (disaster)"
2:6: thou hast <u>foresaken</u> thy people HM: *nātaštâ* (=Q) T: *'ᵃrēy šəbaqtūn daḥlat taqqîpā da-hᵃwā pārîq lakōn* S: ἀνῆκεν	HM: thou hast <u>uprooted</u> thy people (literally, to pluck out, uproot; but here the implication is to uproot and cast out like a weed) T: you have forsaken the fear of the (All) Mighty, who was your redeemer S: he foresook

10:6: <u>prey</u> HM: *baz* (=Q) T: *ʿadāʾā* S: προνομήν	HM: "<u>booty</u>" T: "spoil" S: "booty"
13:2: <u>shake the hand</u> HM: *hānîpû yād* (=Q) T: *ʾanîpū yād* S: παρακαλεῖτε τῇ χειρί	HM: "<u>wave the hand</u>". The verb means to move a thing back and forth, and, in this case, to wave them through the gates of the nobles. The same verb is used for waving the wave-offering. T: "wave the hand"; same as above S: "call out with the hand"
13:11: <u>world</u> HM: *tēbēl* (=Q) T: *də-dāyrīn bə-tēbēl* S: οἰκομένη ὄλη (EDIT Ē)	HM: "<u>inhabited land</u>." *tēbēl* is often mentioned as only part of the world, and, hearkening back to Genesis, it may refer to the dry land, separated from the waters. It is best compared with Akkadian *tābalu*, dry land (derived from *ʾabālu*, "to dry up." While *tēbēl* seems to be derived from *ʾābal*, to dry up"; it is interesting to note that it never take the definite article, being a well established proper noun. It is not the "world." It is just the dry land, or the inhabited land. T: "those dwelling in the dry land, or inhabited land" *(tēbēl)* S: "the whole inhabitable land"
13:21: <u>wild beasts ... doleful creatures</u> HM: *ṣîyīm .. ʾōḥîm* (=Q) T: *tāmwʷān ... ʾōḥyān* S: θηρία... ἤχου	HM: "<u>desert animals</u>"? (related to *ṣîyâ*, a dry place); & "owl" (howling animals?) a name based on the sound made. T: "desert animals ... eagle owls" S: "wild animals ... sound (howling [beast])"?
14:23: <u>pools of water</u> HM: *ʾagmê māyim* (=Q) T: *bīṣīn də-mayīn* S: πήλου βάραθρον	HM: "<u>marshes</u>, reed pools" (cf. Syriac *ʾegmā* and Akkadian *agammu*) T: "marshes, swamps of water" [*biṣṣīn*] S: "mud pit"
14:29: <u>cockatrice</u> HM: *ṣepaʿ* (=Q) T: *məšîḥā* S: ἔκγονα ἀσπίδων	HM: "<u>poisonous snake</u>"; a hapax legomenon (v. 11:8) T: This translation is Messianic exegesis. S: "offspring of asps"

48:5: <u>from the beginning</u> HM: *mē-ʾāz* (=Q) T: *mib-ba-kēʸn* S: *πάλαι*	HM: "from then, <u>from of old</u>"; v. 48:3 T: "from of old" S: "of old"
49:2: <u>polished shaft</u> HM: *ḥēṣ bārûr* (=Q) T: *gīr bəhīr* S: *βέλος ἐκλεκτόν*	HM: "<u>sharpened arrow</u> or <u>select arrow</u>" T: "select arrow" S: "select arrow, dart"
51:14: captive <u>exile</u> HM: *ṣōʿe* (Q: ṣrh) T: *pōrʿānā* S: not present	HM: "captive" There is no word indicating exile. T: "vengeance" S:
51:22: <u>the Lord, thy Lord</u> HM: *ʾᵃdōnayik yahwe* (=Q) T: *rabbōnīk ywy* S: *κύριος ὁ θεὸς*	HM: "<u>thy Lord Yahweh</u> [Jehovah]" Rabbinical theology made it totally forbidden to pronounce Yahweh, as being too sacred for human lips, and the KJ follows this practice, translating Yahweh as Lord, even when it results in this ridiculous duplication. Since Mormons have no problem rendering it as Jehovah (Yahweh in English) "Thy Lord Jehovah" would be preferable here. T: "thy Lord Yahweh" Yahweh is not voweled, indicating that it should not be pronounced. S: "the Lord God", translating both words, but avoiding Yahweh
14:12: <u>Lucifer</u> HM: *hêlēl* (=Q:hylyl) T: *zēʸwtān bə-gō bənēʸ ʾᵃnāšā* S: *ἑωσφόρος*	HM: "<u>morning star</u>". The Hebrew verb from which it derives means "to shine." The following phrase, "son of the morning", confirms that it is the morning star. Here, Isaiah's curse mocks the king of Babylon, rather than the Christian head demon, the Prince of Darkness. The Latin Vulgate translation is *lucifer*, i.e., light bearer, which was personalized to serve theological needs. *hêlēl* is the king of Babylon. T: "resplendant among mankind, like the bright star (Venus) among the stars". S: "morning star"; bearer of the morning.

| 6:4: the <u>posts of the door</u>
HM: *ʾammôt has-sippîm* (=Q)

T: *ʾilwāt siᵞpēᵞ*

S: *ὑπέρθυρον* | HM: "<u>threshold pivots</u>"? *sippîm* is the threshold, i.e., a flat stone underlying and supporting the door frame. But the meaning of *ʾammôt* is still not resolved, except that they are a feature of, or a part associated with, the threshold, possibly the sockets into which the door pivots fit, or the door pivots, or door posts. In any case, the word "threshold" should be part of the translation.
T: meanings suggessted for *ʾilwāt* (*allātā/ʾalwātā*) include a piece of aloes wood, a wood span, branch, club, and door post; while meanings for *siᵞpēᵞ* (*sippēᵞ*) include a stone block, a course of stone blocks, door sill (threshold) and door post; so that put together one has "the door posts of the threshold" or "the posts of the lintel"
S: the door lintel |

Appendix 4 Scribe Details as per Manuscript Page of Ms𝒪

Scribe one is Cowdery, scribes two is John Whitmer, and scribe three is still unidentified. The Fayette scribes are listed here as scribe² and scribe³. The gatherings are numbered in the order of the page numbers. The ms𝒪 reference is the manuscript page number followed by the BoM chapter:verse. Line 0 is the page topic heading. The Ɲ designation refers to a note below. The outer sheet of gathering one is missing, with its four pages. The section covered by contributions from the Fayette scribes comprises 26 pages. Cowdery did only one full page, i.e. the first extant page.

Ms𝒪 Ref.	Scribe(s) & Lines	Ms𝒪 Ref.	Scribe(s) & Lines	Scribe Count 1 Nephi 1:1-16:14		
		1 Nephi				
		Gathering One		S¹	S²	S³
3||2:2-23	Cowdery (lines 0-54)	13||8:27-9:4	scribe³ (lines 0-53ᴺ)	1		1
4||2:23-3:18	Scribe³ (line 0) Cowdery (lines 1-13); Scribe² (lines 14-54)	14||9:4-10:11	scribe³ (lines 0-53ᴺ)		1	1
5||3:18-4:2	scribe³ (line 0); scribe² (lines 1-54)	15||10:11-11:1	scribe³ (lines 0-53ᴺ)		1	1
6||4:2-20	Cowdery (line 0); scribe² (lines 1-40); Cowdery (41-54)	16||11:1-18	scribe³ (lines 0-53ɴ)		1	1

7||4:20-37 scribe[3] (lines 0-53)	17||11:18-32 scribe[3] (lines 0-53)			2
8||4:38-5:14 scribe[3] (lines 0-53)	18||11:32-12:8 scribe[3] (lines 0-53[N])			2
9||5:14-7:3 scribe[3] (lines 0-53[N])	19||12:8-23 scribe[3] (lines 0-53)			2
10||7:3-17 scribe[3] (lines 0-53)	20||13:1-18 scribe[2] (lines 0-53)		1	1
11||7:17-8:11 scribe[3] (lines 0-53[N])	21||13:18-29 scribe[2] (lines 0-53[N])		1	1
12||8:11-27 scribe[3] (lines 0-53)	22||13:29-35 scribe[2] (lines 0-54)		1	1
Gathering Two				
25||14:11-16 scribe[2] (lines 0-21)	18:6-18 Cowdery (lines 1-39)	1		
26||14:23-29 scribe[2] (lines 0-21)	18:18-19:3 Cowdery (lines 0-39	1		
27||15:5-15 scribe[2] (lines 0-39)	19:3-12 Cowdery (lines 1-39)	1		
28||15:15-25 scribe[2] (lines 0-39)	19:12-20 Cowdery (lines 0-38[N])	1		
29||15:25-36 scribe[2] (lines 1-40[N])	20:1-20 Cowdery (lines 1-39)	1		
30||15:36-16:14 scribe[2] (lines 1-39[N])	20:20-21:14 Cowdery (lines 1-39)	1		
16:14-31 Cowdery (lines 1-40)	21:14-:22:4 Cowdery (lines 1-39[N])	TOTALS		
16:31-17:5 Cowdery (lines 1-39)	22:4-14 Cowdery (lines 1-39)	1	12	13
17:5-20 Cowdery (lines 1-39)	22:14-26 Cowdery (lines 1-39			
17:20-34 Cowdery (lines 1-39)	22:26-2 Nephi 1:7 Cowdery (lines 0-38[N])			
17:34-48 Cowdery (lines 1-39)	1:8-19 Cowdery (lines 1-39)			
17:48-18:6 Cowdery (lines 1-39)	1:19-30 Cowdery (lines 1-39)			
2 Nephi				
Gathering Three				
4:32-35 Cowdery (lines 22-31)	8:6-17 Cowdery (lines 13-35)			
5:12-16 Cowdery (lines 22-31)	9:1-2 Cowdery (lines 13-17)			
5:22-6:0 Cowdery (lines 13-34[N])	9:12-13 Cowdery (lines 13-17)			
6:6-12 Cowdery (lines 13-33)	Nephi 9:25-26 Cowdery (lines 13-18)			
6:18-7:9 Cowdery (lines 13-35[N])	9:41-42 Cowdery (lines 13-17)			
Gathering Four				
23:1-7 Cowdery (lines 29-39[N])	25:5-8 Cowdery (lines 29-39)			
23:22-24:4 Cowdery (lines 29-39)	25:16-18 Cowdery (lines 29-39)			
24:21-27 Cowdery (lines 29-39)	25:24-28 Cowdery (lines 29-39)			
2 Nephi-Jacob				
Gathering Five				
2 Nephi 33:4-9 Cowdery (lines 31-39)	Jacob 2:25-27 Cowdery (lines 27-29)			
Jacob 1:3-7 Cowdery (lines 31-39)	3:5 Cowdery (lines 26-29)			
1:18-2:2 Cowdery (lines 29-39)	4:3-5 Cowdery (lines 31-35)			
2:11-15 Cowdery (lines 28-39)	4:13-14 Cowdery (lines 31-36)			
Jacob-Enos				
Gathering Six				
5:46-48 Cowdery (lines 1-12)	6:11-7:6 Cowdery (lines 1-22[N])			
5:57-61 Cowdery (lines 1-12)	7:11-18 Cowdery (lines 0-22[N])			
5:69-70 Cowdery (lines 1-3)	7:24 Enos 1:1 Cowdery (lines 0-21[N])			
5:77-6:0 Cowdery (lines 1-3[N])	1:9-14 Cowdery (lines 0-21[N])			
Alma				
Gathering #?[1] (collected fragments)				
10:31-11:4 Cowdery (lines 6-28)	12:18-24) Cowdery (lines 5-28)			
11:13-23 Cowdery (lines 6-28)	12:26-32) Cowdery (lines 5-28)			

11:26-39	Cowdery (lines 5-28)	12:36-13:4	Cowdery (lines 5-27)
11:42-46)	Cowdery (lines 5-28)	13-7-16	Cowdery (lines 0-27)
Gathering #?[2] (collected fragments)			
19:3-11	Cowdery (lines 0-28)	19:29-36	Cowdery (lines 0-18)
19:13-19	Cowdery (lines 0-29)	20:5-8	Cowdery (lines 0-5)
19:21-25	Cowdery (lines 0-18)	20:19-22	Cowdery (lines 0-5)
Gathering #?[3]			
22:22-27	Cowdery (lines 14-32)	43:36-47	Cowdery (lines 0-35)
22:28-34	Cowdery (lines 4-32)	43:47-44:5	Cowdery (lines 0-35)
22:35-23:7	Cowdery (lines 1-31)	44:5-14	Cowdery (lines 0-35)
23:7-24:4	Cowdery (lines 0-35)	44:14-45:2	Cowdery (lines 0-35)
24:5-14	Cowdery (lines 0-35)	45:2-17	Cowdery (lines 0-35)
24:14-23	Cowdery (lines 0-35)	45:17-22	Cowdery (lines 0-17)
24:23-25:5	Cowdery (lines 0-35)	45:22	**Smith** (lines 17-19)
25:5-15	Cowdery (lines 0-35)	45:22	Cowdery (lines 19-35)
25:16-26:11	Cowdery (lines 0-35)	46:6-18	Cowdery (lines 0-35)
26:11-24	Cowdery (lines 0-35)	46:18-28	Cowdery (lines 0-35)
26:24-35	Cowdery (lines 0-35)	46:28-40	Cowdery (lines 0-35)
26:35-27:12	Cowdery (lines 0-35)	46:40-47:10	Cowdery (lines 0-35)
27:12-24	Cowdery (lines 0-35)	47:10-22	Cowdery (lines 0-35)
27:24-28:6	Cowdery (lines 0-35)	47:23-36	Cowdery (lines 0-35)
28:6-29:5	Cowdery (lines 0-35)	47:36-48:11	Cowdery (lines 0-35)
29:5-30:2	Cowdery (lines 0-35)	48:11-23	Cowdery (lines 0-35)
30:2-17	Cowdery (lines 0-35)	48:23-49:9	Cowdery (lines 0-35)
30:17-28	Cowdery (lines 0-35)	49:9-20	Cowdery (lines 0-35)
30:28-42	Cowdery (lines 0-35)	49:20-30	Cowdery (lines 0-35)
30:42-53	Cowdery (lines 0-35)	50:1:12	Cowdery (lines 0-35)
30:53-31:5	Cowdery (lines 0-35)	50:12-26	Cowdery (lines 0-35)
31:5-19	Cowdery (lines 0-35)	50:26-37	Cowdery (lines 0-35[N])
31:19-35	Cowdery (lines 0-35)	50:37-51:8	Cowdery (lines 0-35)
31:35-32:9	Cowdery (lines 0-35)	51:8-19	Cowdery (lines $0-35_N$)
32:10-24	Cowdery (lines 0-35)	51:19-31	Cowdery (lines 0-35)
32:24-36)	Cowdery (lines 0-35)	51:31-52:8:	Cowdery (lines 0-35)
32:37-33:5)	Cowdery (lines 0-35)	52:8-17	Cowdery (lines 0-35)
33:5-22)	Cowdery (lines 0-35)	52:17-28	Cowdery (lines 0-35)
33:22-34:12)	Cowdery (lines 0-35)	52:28-53:2	Cowdery (lines 0-35)
34:12-31)	Cowdery (lines 0-35)	53:2-10	Cowdery (lines 0-35)
34:31-41	Cowdery (lines 0-35)	53:10-22	Cowdery (lines 0-35)
35:1-14	Cowdery (lines 0-35)	53:22-54:11	Cowdery (lines 0-35)
35:14-36:10)	Cowdery (lines 0-35)	54:11-24	Cowdery (lines 0-35)
36:10-26	Cowdery (lines 0-35)	54:24-55:15	Cowdery (lines 0-35)
36:26-37:8	Cowdery (lines 0-35)	55:15-28	Cowdery (lines 0-35)
37:8-19	Cowdery (lines 0-35)	55:28-56:8	Cowdery (lines 0-35)
37:19-30	Cowdery (lines 0-35)	56:8-22	Cowdery (lines 0-35)
37:30-43	Cowdery (lines 0-35)	56:22-37	Cowdery (lines 0-35)
37:43-38:8	Cowdery (lines 0-35)	56:38-51	Cowdery (lines 0-35)
38:8-39:7	Cowdery (lines 0-35)	56:51-57:6	Cowdery (lines 0-35)
39:8-40:3	Cowdery (lines 0-35)	57:6-17	Cowdery (lines 0-35)
40:3-15	Cowdery (lines 0-35)	57:17-30	Cowdery (lines 0-35)

40:15-41:2	Cowdery (lines 0-35)	57:30-58:6	Cowdery (lines 0-35)	
41:2-14	Cowdery (lines 0-35)	58:6-18	Cowdery (lines 0-35)	
41:14-42:13	Cowdery (lines 0-35)	58:18-31	Cowdery (lines 0-35)	
42:13-29	Cowdery (lines 0-35)	58:31-59:3	Cowdery (lines 0-35)	
42:29-43:10	Cowdery (lines 0-35)	59:3-60:2	Cowdery (lines 0-35)	
43:10-22	Cowdery (lines 0-35)	60:5-13	Cowdery (lines 7-35)	
43:22-36	Cowdery (lines 0-35)	60:15-22	Cowdery (lines 7-35)	

Alma-Helaman	
Gathering #?[4]	

Alma		Helaman	
61:10-13	Cowdery (lines 11-14)	1:5-17	Cowdery (lines 0-35)
62:3:-5	Cowdery (lines 11-14)	1:17-27	Cowdery (lines 0-35)
62:17-18	Cowdery (lines 13-16)	1:27-2:8	Cowdery (lines 0-35)
62:30-31	Cowdery (lines 13-16)	2:8-3:8	Cowdery (lines 0-35)
62:36-49	Cowdery (lines 0-35)	3:8-21	Cowdery (lines 0-35)
62:49-63:11	Cowdery (lines 0-35)		
Alma-Helaman 63:11-17 &1:1-1:5	Cowdery (lines 0-35)		

Helaman-3 Nephi	
Gathering #?[5]	

Helaman		3 Nephi	
13:36-14:9	Cowdery (lines 11-35)	1:10-17	Cowdery (lines 16-35)
14:14-23	Cowdery (lines 11-35)	1:24-29	Cowdery (lines 15-35)
14:29-15:6	Cowdery (lines 11-35)	2:10-12	Cowdery (lines 25-35)
15:9-16:1	Cowdery (lines 11-35)	3:3-7	Cowdery (lines 25-35)
16:4-16	Cowdery (lines 10-35)	3:17-19	Cowdery (lines 32-35)
Helaman 16:20-25 & 3 Nephi 1:1-2	Cowdery (lines 10-35)	4:1-2	Cowdery (lines 32-35)

3 Nephi	
Gathering #?[6] (fragments with estimated line numbers)	

19:25-28	Cowdery (lines 1-6)	21:10-11	Cowdery (lines 2-5)
20:15-17	Cowdery (lines 1-6)	26:3-6	Cowdery (lines 1-8)
20:37-39	Cowdery (lines 2-5)	27:3-7	Cowdery (lines 1-8)

Ether	
Gathering #?[7] (fragments with estimated line numbers)	

3:9-10	Cowdery (lines 13-15)	10:30-11:6	Cowdery (lines 2-25)
4:4-5	Cowdery (lines 13-15)	11:20-12:7	Cowdery (lines 2-25)
5:1-6:3	Cowdery (lines 5-25)	12:21-29	Cowdery (lines 1-25)
6:18-27	Cowdery (lines 5-25)	12:41-13:8	Cowdery (lines 2-25)
7:18-24	Cowdery (lines 10-25)	13:20-14:1	Cowdery (lines 2-25)
8:13-19	Cowdery (lines 11-25)	14:15-27	Cowdery (lines 2-25)
9:3-11	Cowdery (lines 10-25)	15:8-17	Cowdery (lines 2-25)
9:26-10:7	Cowdery (lines 2-25)		

NOTES

1 Nephi 5:14-7:3	Line 22 reads "Chapter 2nd".
1 Nephi 7:17-8:11	Cowdery made supralinear edits, adding 'thee' to line 2 and 'me' to line 15.
1 Nephi 8:27-9:4	unidentified 2 made supralinear edits, adding 'are' to line 21 & 'to' to line 40.
1 Nephi 9:4-10:11	unidentified 2 made a supralinear edit in line 37, changing 'no' to 'know'
	Line 10 reads "Chapter 3rd".
1 Nephi 10:11-11:1	unidentified 2 made supralinear edits, adding 'ed' to 'scatter' in line 4, changing 'now' to 'know', adding 'to' to 'day' and changing 'co[r]ese' to 'coarse'.
1 Nephi 11:1-18	Cowdery made a supralinear edit, adding 'God' in line 14.
1 Nephi 11:32-12:8	Cowdery made supralinear edits, adding '& it fell' in line 16, and '&' and 'that they rent' in line 37,.
1 Nephi 13:18-29	Cowdery made a supralinear edit, adding 'seest' in line 43.
1 Nephi 15:25-36	Cowdery made supralinear edits, adding '&' in lines 9 & 33.
1 Nephi 15:36-16:14	Line 4 ends with "Chapter 5th".
1 Nephi 19:12-20	Line 24 reads "Chapter VI"
1 Nephi 21:14-:22:4	Line 28 ends with "Chapter VII".
1 Nephi 22:26-	
2 Nephi 1:7	Cowdery crossed out "Chapter VIII" in line 13 and added a supralinear edit "Chapter I" in line 14. Line 14-16 has the heading for currently found at the beginning of 2 Nephi.
2 Nephi 5:22-6:0	Line 34 ends: "Chapter V".
2 Nephi 7:1-9	Cowdery original to printer ms ( ) changes

wherefore when I came (come) there was no man
I make the (their) rivers a wilderness
They dieth (die) because of thirst
he wakeneth (waketh) morning by morning
he wakeneth (waketh) mine ear
the Lord God hath opened (appointed) mine ear

This is from a fragment of p. 59 or the "original".

2 Nephi 23:0-7	Line 29 reads "Chapter X".
Jacob 5:77-6:0	Line 3 reads "Chapter IIII"
Jacob 6:11-7:6	Line 5 ends with "Chapter (5)"
Jacob 7:11-18	Line 0 bears page number "112"
Jacob 7:24-Enos 1:1	Line 0 bears page number "113"
Enos 1:9-14	Line 0 bears page number "114"

Appendix 5 "That" Clause Methodology

The project presented here began by creating a key-word-in-context document for each BoM book. *That* is the key-word. Each book was copied into its own MS Word document, minus large Biblical inclusions if present (eg., *1 Nephi.docx*). The search function was used to manually examine every *that* in the book. Every one qualified for this project was copied into a key-word-in-context document for that book (eg., *that clauses 1 Nephi.docx*). In each case, *that* introduces a clause. Each entry begins with a chapter-verse identifier (e.g., 7:26). This is followed by the word *that* with enough text before and after it to provide context. On a second pass, each occurrence was assigned a code indicating the type of *that* clause. One category was when it introduces a direct object clause, in which case separate codes were used for each verb involved, such as "to know that" or "to expect that." Another code was used for a redundant *that*. In addition to the cases studied in the previous section, it sometimes occurs when the introduction "And it came to pass that…" is followed by a subordinate clause, followed by a second *that* to continue the sentence, as in "And it came to pass that, when the king came, that we greeted him." Delete the second *that*. When introducing an adverbial clause, the code indicates the nature of the clause. An example: "The general sent a division to the river bank that the enemy might not cross." In this case, the code would indicate an adverbial *that* clause, with the function of showing the objective of the action of the verb.

This work was done in such detail that the total number of codes came to 195. The detail was done to enhance the chance of discovering anything of interest, or perhaps even importance. This tedious work was done for the entire BoM. Searches were done for each code in each book to get its total incidence by type. It was found in the end that usually the most interesting results emerged when codes were grouped by meaningful criteria, and then the categories collapsed.

Appendix 6   Apologetics in the Improvement Era & Ensign

(Era: 1/1951-12/1970; Ensign 1/1971-12/2015)

Years 49-51
"Goldsmiths of Ancient Times," Levi Edgar Young, 49-04. "Anachronisms and the *Book of Mormon*," C. E. Moore, 49/10. "The Sensational Discovery of the Jerusalem Scrolls," Sidney B. Sperry, 49/10.
"Lehi in the Desert," Hugh Nibley, 50/1-6, 9-10. "Was Iron Known in Ancient America?" John A. Widtsoe, 50/3. "The World of the Jaredites," Hugh Nibley, 51/9-12, 52/1-5, 7. "Laman Found", Ariel L. Crowley, 51/2. "America's First Farmers", John Sherman Walker, 50/9.

Years 52-54: "The Anthon Transcript and the Maya Glyphs," Ariel L. Crowley, 52/9. "The Stick of Judah," Hugh Nibley, 53 1-5. "New Approaches to *Book of Mormon* Study," Nibley, 53/11-12, 54/1-3, 5-7. "Hebrew Idioms in *Book of Mormon* Study," Sidney B. Sperry, 54/10.

Years 55-57: "Archaeology and the *Book of Mormon*," Milton R. Hunter, 55/4-5, 7-10, 12. "Archaeology and the *Book of Mormon*," Milton R. Hunter, 56/1, 3-5. "There Were Jaredites," Hugh Nibley, 56/1, 3-5, 6, 9-10, 57/1, 59/7. "The Dead Sea Scrolls and Their Significance for Latter-day Saints," Sidney B Sperry, 57/12.

Years 58-60: "The Dead Sea Scrolls and Their Significance for Latter-day Saints," Sidney B Sperry, 58/1. "The Language of the *Book of Mormon*," James L. Barker, 60/6. "Charles Anthon and the Egyptian Language," Stanley H. Kimball, 60/10.

Years 61-63: "Hebrew Idioms in the Small Plates of Nephi," E. Craig Bramwell, 61/7. "Gold Plates and the *Book of Mormon*," Thomas Stuart Ferguson, 62/4. "The Dead Sea Scrolls" (the *Era*). "The Kinderhook Plates," Welby W. Ricks, 62/9. "The Prophet Said Silk," Maurice W. Cornell, 62/5.

Years 64-66: "Since Cumorah, New Voices from the Dust," Hugh Nibley, 64/10-12, 65/1, 3-4, 6, 8-9, 11, 65/1-4, 6-12. "Were the Golden Plates Made of Tumbaga?" Read H. Putnam, 66/9. "The Stone Box," Paul Cheesman, 66/10.

1967: No apologist articles the whole year, as LDS Church is occupied with the Abraham papyri.

68-70: "Ancient Land of Egypt," Doyl L Green, 68/1. "Egyptian Papyri Rediscovered," Jay M. Todd, 68/1. Publication of the Abraham papyri, 68/2. "A New Look at the Pearl of Great Price," Hugh Nibley, 68/1-12, 69/1-11, 70/1, 3-5. "Sketches on the Papyri Backings," Edgar Lyon, 68/5. "The Lebolo-Chandler Relationship," Jay M. Todd, 68/7. "Ancient Landings in America," John Lear, 70/10. "The *Book of Mormon* as a Mirror of the East," Hugh Nibley, 70/11.

Ensign **magazine debuts.**

Years 71-73
"Ancient Temples. What Do They Signify?" Hugh Nibley, 72/9.

Years 74-76: "A Strange Thing in the Land: The Return of the Book of Enoch," Hugh Nibley, 75/10, 12. "A Strange Thing in the Land: The Return of the Book of Enoch," Hugh Nibley, 76/2-4, 7, 10, 12.

Years 77-79: "A Strange Thing in the Land: The Return of the Book of Enoch," Hugh Nibley, 77/2-4, 6, 8.

Years 80-82

Years 83-85: "Digging into the *Book of Mormon*," 84/9-10.

Years 86-88: "The Mulekites," Garth A. Wilson, 87/3. "New Developments in *Book of Mormon* Research" (survey of LDS scholars) 88/2. "Chiasmus in Mayan Texts," Allen J. Christensen, 88/10.

Years 89-91: "Recent Research on BoM Studies," 89/06. "Hebrew Lit Patterns in BoM," Donald W. Parry, 89/10. "Where was Abraham's Ur?" Paul Y. Hoskisson, 91/07. Research BoM Update, *Era* feature, 92/04.

Years 92-94: Abraham in Ancient Egyptian, John Gee, 92/07. "News from Antiquity" (Re Abraham), 94/01.

Years 95-97: "The *Book of Mormon*, an Ancient Sacred Record" (Quiché tradition), 95/11. "Wonderful *Book of Moses*" (& Enoch), Richard D. Draper, 97/02. "*The Book of Abraham*, A Most Remarkable Book" (& papyri story), Andrew Skinner, 97/03.

Years 98-00: "The Abrahamic Covenant," S. Michael Wilcox, 98/01. "Enoch: What Modern Scripture Teaches," Richard D. Draper, 98-01. "The Flood and the Tower of Babel," Donald W. Parry, 98-01. "Mounting Evidence for the B00k of Mormon," Daniel C. Peterson, 00/01.

Years 01-03: "The Origin of Man," The First Presidency (Era, November, 1909), 02/02.

Years 04-06: "The Dead Sea Scrolls and Latter-day Truth," Andrew C. Skinner, 06-02.

Years 07-10: NONE

Years 11-13: NONE

Years 11-15: NONE

Appendix 7 **Some Documents Prior to 1830**

Historians in Mormon studies are unable to function without the use of documents written after the events they treat, sometime years and even decades after. Some information they contain reflects a strong orthodox bias due either to official efforts to control history, or due to the piety of the Saints. Other information reflects a strong anti-Mormon bias. I am not aware of any field of research that poses such difficult problems for professional historiography. For the events prior to 1830, ideally one would want primary documents, contemporary or real-time evidence, recorded at or near the time of the event(s) in question. As can be seen below, very little exists. For studies of the BoM text, the two most important primary documents are ms𝒪 and ms𝒫.

Brackets are used for the revelations of Joseph Smith because we have no document prior to 1830 to verify when they were actually composed. Even if we assume that all or most are in fact pre-1830, the actual year or time of the year is not documented prior to 1830. These have been culled from Marquardt, *The Joseph Smith Revelations*. Most other materials are from Vogel, *Early Mormon Documents*.

Date	Document
12/11/1799	members of the Anabaptist Society (which Joseph Smith?)
06/12/1797	Universalist Society (Joseph Smith Sr. signature)
15/03/1806	Teacher's note signed by Jos Smith (Joseph Smith Sr.?)
15/10/1807	Petition to Vermont Assembly (signature of Joseph Smith Sr.?)
15/03/1816	Smith Family Warning out of Norwich, VT
19/11/1823	Alvin Smith Gravestone
01/11/1825	Articles of Agreement
27/12/1825	*Wayne Sentinel*, many find treasure (from *Orleans Advocate*)
20/12/1825	County records, Durfy buys Smith farm; Smiths tenant-farm it
20/03/1826	Bainbridge (NY) Court records (Joseph Jr's examination) 1826 Albert Neely Bill of Costs 1826 Philip DeZeng Bill of Costs
17/10/1827	*Lyon's Advertiser*, Cowdery unclaimed letters, Arcadia
12/1827-02/1828	Joseph Smith's transcription of characters
(1827 & 1828)	1840 articles of John A. Clark re Harris & Smith (dates questionable)
1827-1828	Return of Mt. Moriah Lodge (04/06/1827-04/06/1828), listing Hyrum Smith, Mason
04/06/1828	Return of Mt. Moriah Lodge # 112, Hyrum, 1827-1828
05/06/1828	Joseph and Emma's deceased infant's gravestone (live birth, died same day)

11/07/1828	*Wayne Sentinel*, Lyman Cowdery unclaimed letters, Palmyra
[07/1828]	BC 2 (D&C 3) on the loss of the 116 pages
1828-1829	David Hale's Store Ledger
06/04/1829	Smith contract to buy land from Hale; Cowdery witness
[02/1829]	BC 3 (D&C 4), a marvelous work
[03/1829]	N. K. W Collection (cf. D&C 5), he hath a gift to translate
[04/1829]	BC 5 (D&C 6), Oliver's gift to translate
[04/1829]	LDS archives (cf. D&C 7), John will tarry until Christ comes
[04/1829]	BC 7 (cf. D&C 8), Cowdery's gift of the rod
[04/1829]	BC 8 (cf. D&C 9), gift to translate taken from Cowdery
[05/1829]	BC 9 (cf. D&C 10), Plates of Nephi, lost pages
[05/1829]	BC 10 (cf. D&C 11) Hyrum's gift
[05/1829]	BC 11 (cf. D&C 12) revelation for Joseph Knight
[early 06/1829]	Cowdery's revelation on church organization
early 06/1829	Title-page BoM description, also submitted for copyright
11/06/1829	*Book of Mormon* copyright
[06/1829]	BC 12 (D&C 14), revelation to David Whitmer
[06/1829]	BC 13 (D&C 15), revelation to John Whitmer
[06/1829]	BC 14 (cf. D&C 16), revelation to Peter Whitmer Jr.
[06/1829]	BC 15 (cf. D&C 18), Oliver & David ordained to ordain priests & instructed to select 12 disciples
[06/1829]	1835 D&C 42 (cf. D&C 17), the 3 witnesses selected
14/06/1829	letter of Oliver Cowdery to Hyrum Smith (begin outreach)
17/06/1829	letter of Jesse Smith to Hyrum Smith
26/06/1829	Wayne Sentinel article re re"gold bible" & its translation
c. 06/1829	Rochester (NY) The Gem article re Harris & "gold bible"
c. 06/1829?	Cowdery's revelation (Cowdery: I have written these things...)
c. 06/1829	Testimony of the witnesses
08/1829	*Book of Mormon* preface, prior to commencement of printing
11 08/1829	Palmyra Freeman article re "gold bible," translation completed and printing will begin (Jonathan Hadley, from Harris?)
27/08/1829	Niagara Courier article re "gold bible" & Smith's characters
29/08/1829	Rochester Dailey Advertiser re "gold bible"
02/09/1829	The Reflector, first BoM extracts printed by a newspaper
05/09/1829	Rochester (NY) Gem, "gold bible," Harris sought a printer
22/09/1829	Painesville Telegraph re "gold bible"
08/10/1829	Smith/Cowdery bible purchased by Cowdery from Grandin's
22/10/1829	letter of Joseph Smith letter to Oliver Cowdery
09/1829-01/1830	Palmyra Reflector notices re the "gold bible"
02/09/1829	Palmyra Reflector, "gold bible" is in press, will appear shortly
06/11/1829	letter of Oliver Cowdery to Joseph Smith (printing slow, type still awaited)
09/11/1829	Cowdery letter to Blatchly

28/12/1829	letter of Oliver Cowdery to Joseph Smith (I've become a printer)
[03/1830]	BC 16 (cf. D&C 19), revelation to Harris: "Pay the printer's debt."
02/01/1830	The Reflector (Abner Cole) begins installments of the BoM
13/01/1830	The Reflector publishes 2nd installment
22/01/1830	The Reflector publishes 3rd installment

< BIBLIOGRAPHIES >

Bibliography 1. Biblical Texts (Annotated)

An extensive bibliography can be found in *Mormon Genesis*.

Bibliography 2. Lexical and Linguistic Resources
Allen, James P. *Middle Egyptian. An Introduction to the Language and Culture of the Hieroglyphs* (Cambridge: Cambridge University Press, 2000)
Analytical Greek Lexicon, Harper Brothers, New York, n.d.
Aufrecht, Walter E. *A Corpus of Ammonite Inscriptions.* Lewiston, NY: The Edwin Mellen Press, 1989.
Avigad, Nahman. *Corpus of West Semitic Stamp Seals, revised and completed by Benjamin Sass.* Herein referenced as Avigad/Sass. Jerusalem: Ketterpress, 1997.
Brenton, Lancelot. *The Septuagint with Apocrypha: Greek and English* Peabody, MA: Hendrickson Publishers, 2015.
Clines, David J. A., ed. *The Dictionary of Classical Hebrew* (8 vols.). Sheffield: Sheffield Academic Press, 1993-2011.
Dalman, Gustav H., *Aramäisch-Neuhebräisches Handwörterbuch zu Targum, Talmud und Midrasch.* Hildesheim, Zürich: Georg Olms Verlag, 1997.
Gardiner, Alan. *Egyptian Grammar, Being an Introduction to the Study of Hieroglyphs.* London: Oxford University Press, 1973.
Gesenius, Wilhelm. *Handwörterbuch über das Alte Testament*, bearbeitet vom Dr. Frants Buhl. Leipzig: Verlag von F. C. W. Vogel, 1921.
Green, Jay P., editor & translator. *The Interlinear Bible, Hebrew-Greek-English.* London: Hendrickson Publishers, 2005.
Jastrow, Marcus. *A Dictionary of the Targumim, the Talmud Babli and Yerushalmi, and the Midrashic Literature.* (Two vols. in one, 1943.) Peabody, MA: Hendrickson Publishers, 2005 (4th printing).
Klein, Ernest, *A comprehensive Etymological Dictionary of the Hebrew Language for Readers of English.* Jerusalem: The University of Haifa, Carta, , 1987.
Knisley, Alvin. *Book of Mormon Dictionary.* Independence, MO: Ensign Publishing House, 1909.
Koehler, Ludwig, and Walter Baumgartner. *The Hebrew and Aramaic Lexicon of the Old Testament.* Leiden: E. J. Brill, 1994.
Levy, Jacob. *Wörterbuch über die Talmudim und Misraschim.* Berlin und Wien: Benjamin Harz Verlag, 1924
Lewis, Charlton T., and Charles Short, *A Latin Dictionary.* Oxford: at the Clarendon Press, 1966.
Liddell, Henry George, and Robert Scott, *A Greek-English Lexicon.* Oxford: at the Clarendon Press, 1961
Porten Bezalel, and Jerome A. Lund, *Aramaic Documents from Egypt: A Key-Word-in-Context Concordance.* Winona Lake: Eisenbrauns, 2002.
Renz, Johannes, & Wofgang Röllig. *Handbuch der Althebräischen Epigraphik*, 4 vols. Darmstadt: Wissenschftliche Buchgesellschaft, 1995 & 2003.
Lust, J, and E. Eynikel and K. Hauspie, *A Greek-English Lexicon of the Septuagint.* Stuttgart: Deutsche Bibelgesellschaft, 1992.
Sokoloff, Michael, *A Dictionary of Jewish Babylonian Aramaic of the Talmudic and Geonic Periods.* Ramat-Gan, Israel: Bar Ilan University Press, 2002.

————. *A Dictionary of Jewish Palestinian Aramaic*. Ramat-Gan, Israel: Bar Ilan University Press, 1990, 1992.

Stenning, J. F. *The Targum of Isaiah* [Targum Jonathan], *Edited with a translation*. Oxford : Clarendon Press, 1949.   661

Vogel, Dan. *Book of Abraham Apologetics. A Review and Critique*. Salt Lake City: Signature Books, 2021.

Bibliography 3. Book of Mormon Cartography

Allen Joseph Lovell, and Blake Joseph Allen, *Exploring the Lands of the Book of Mormon*, 2nd ed. Orem, UT: *Book of Mormon* Tours and Research Institute, Inc., 2008.

Aston, Duane R. *Return to Cumorah*. Sacramento, CA: American River Publications, 1998/2003.

Birrell, Verla. *The Book of Mormon Guide Book*. Salt Lake City: Stevens & Wallis, 1948.

Calderwood, David G. *Voices from the Dust. New Insights into Ancient America*. Austin TX: Historical Publications, Inc. [Print and Bind Direct], 2005.

Cheesman, Paul R. *Early America and the Book of Mormon, A photographic Essay of Ancient America*. Salt Lake City: Deseret Book Company, 1972.

————. *These Early Americans*. Salt Lake City: Deseret Book Company, 1974.

————. *The World of the Book of Mormon*. Salt Lake City: Deseret Book Co., 1978.

Cluff, Benjamin (1901). See Joseph Lovell Allen and Blake Joseph Allen, *Exploring the Lands of the Book of Mormon*, 2nd ed. (Orem, UT: *Book of Mormon* Tours and Research Institute, Inc., 2008), 382-83.

Comer, Heber, and Karl G. Maeser.1880. Map published in J. A. and J. N. Washburn, *An Approach to the Study of the Book of Mormon Geography*, Provo, Utah, 1939. 212.

Conway, Dayton E. *Where O Where is the Book of Mormon?* CreateSpace Independent Publishing Platform, 2012.

Coon, W. Vincent. *Choice above All Other Lands, Book of Mormon Covenant Lands According to the Best Sources* (Salt Lake City: Brit Publishing, 2009.

Curtis, Delbert W. *The Land of the Nephites*. Oren, UT: self-published, 1988.

Davila. "An Account of Our *Book of Mormon* Lands Tour." Provo, UT: BYU Library, Jan 27th to Feb 16th, 1961.

DeLong-Steede-Simmons model, *FRAA Newsletter* 23 (11 May 1986). "Proposed *Book of Mormon* Geographical Setting," Wikipedia, accessed 03/19/2017.

Dixon, Riley L. *Just One Cumorah*. Salt Lake city: Bookcraft, 1958.

Driggs, Jean R. *The Palestine of America*. Salt Lake City: no publisher, 1928.

Ellsworth, Robert B. "Lecture Notes on an Interpretation of a Map of Zarahemla and the Land Northward as Described in the *Book of Mormon*." Ogden, UT: 1980 (referenced in "Proposed Book of Mormon Geographical Setting," Wikipedia (accessed 25/02/2017).

Farnsworth, Dewey. *The Americas before Columbus*. El Paso, TX: Farnsworth Publishing Co., 1947.

Farnsworth, Dewey, and Edith Wood Farnsworth. *Book of Mormon Evidences*. Salt Lake City: Deseret Book Company, 1953.

Ferguson, Thomas Stuart. *Cumorah—Where?* Independence, MO: Press of Zion's Printing and Publishing, 1947, 14 & 55.

————. *One Fold and One Shepherd*. San Francisco: Books of California, 1958.

Hammond, Fletcher B. *Geography of the Book of Mormon*. Salt Lake City: Utah Printing Company, 1959.

Hansen. "*Book of Mormon* Geography," *Saints' Herald*, January 8, 1951. "Proposed *Book of Mormon* Geographical Setting," Wikipedia, accessed 03/19/2017.

Hansen, Vaughn E. *Discovering Book of Mormon Lands*. Springville, UT: Cedar Fort, 1997.

Hauck, F. Richard. *Deciphering the Geography of the Book of Mormon*. Salt Lake City: Deseret Book Company, 1988.

Hills, Louis Edward. *Geography of Mexico and Central America from from 2234 BC to 421 AD*. Independence, MO: 1917.

Holley, Vernal. *Book of Mormon Authorship: A Closer Look*. Ogden UT: Zenos Publications, 1983. Updated edition, Roy, UT: self published, 1992.

Holmes, Robert. *Geographical Sketches of the Book of Mormon*. LDS Historian's Office, 1903. "Proposed *Book of Mormon* Geographical Settings," Wikipedia, accessed 19/03/2017.

Hunter, Milton R. *Archaeology and the Book of Mormon*. Salt Lake City: Deseret Book Company, 1956.

———. *Great Civilizations and the Book of Mormon*. Salt Lake City: Deseret Book Company, 1970.

———. *Christ in Ancient America*. Salt Lake City: Deseret Book Company, 1972.

Jakeman, M. Wells. "The *Book of Mormon* Civilizations: Their Origins, and Their Development in Space and Time," in Ross T. Christensen, ed., *Progress in Archaeology and Anthropology*. Provo, UT: Brigham Young University, 1963.

Johnson, Daniel, Jared Cooper and Derek Gasser. *An LDS Guide to Mesoamerica*. (Springvile, UT: Cedar Fort, Inc., 2008).

Knisley, Alvin. *Dictionary of All Proper Names in the Book of Mormon*. Independence, MO: Ensign Publishing House, 1909.

Kocherhaus, Arthur J. *Lehi's Isle of Promise*. Fullerton, CA: Et Cetera Graphics and Printing, 1989.

Layton, Lynn C. "An 'Ideal' *Book of Mormon* Geography," *Improvement Era* 41 (July 1938), 394–395.

Le Poidevin, Cecil George. *Zion, Land of Promise. An Atlas Study of Book of Mormon Geography*. N.P.: by author, 1977.

Lund, John L. *MesoAmerica and the Book of Mormon*. Orem, UT: Granite Publishing & Distribution, 2007.

McGavin E. Cecil, & Willard Bean. *The Geography of the Book of Mormon* (Salt Lake City: Bookcraft, 1948.

Meldrum, Rod L. *Exploring the Book of Mormon Heartland Photobook*. New York: Digital Legend Press, 2011.

Neville, Jonathan, *Moroni's America: The North American Setting for the Book of Mormon* (Independent Publishing Platform, 2015)

Nielsen, Harold K. *Mapping the Action Found in the Book of Mormon*. Springville, UT: Cedar Fort, 1987.

Olive, Phyllis Carol. *The Lost Lands of the Book of Mormon*. Springville, UT: Bonneville Books, 2000.

Palfrey, Louise. *The Divinity of the Book of Mormon Proven by Archaeology*. Lamoni, IO: Zion's Religio-Literary Society at the Herald Publishing House, 1903.

Palmer, David A. *In Search of Cumorah. New Evidences for the Book of Mormon from Ancient Mexico*. Bountiful, UT: Horizon Publishers, 1981.

Peay, E. L. *The Lands of Zarahemla. A Book of Mormon Commentary*. (published by the author, 1993.

Potter, George, *Nephi in the Promised Land*, (Springvile, UT: Cedar Fort, Inc., 2009).

Pratt, Orson. "Nephite America—The Day of God's Power—The Shepherd of Israel" in *Journal of Discourses*. February 11, 1872, 14:324-31.

Priddis, Venice. *The Book and the Map, New Insights into Book of Mormon Geography.* Salt Lake City: Bookcraft, 1975.

Reynolds, George. *The Story of the Book of Mormon.* Salt Lake City: J. H. Parry, 1888.

Reynolds, George, and Janne M. Sjodahl. *Book of Mormon Geography. The Lands of the Nephites and Jaredites.* Salt Lake City, by author, dist. by Deseret Book Co., 1957.

Ricks, Joel. Only a mention by James E. Talmage in Joseph Trevor Antley, "The Talmage Journals: The *Book of Mormon* Geography Hearings, 1921," posted July 21, 2012 (withoutend.org/talmage-journals-book-mormon-geography-hearings-1921. See more at: http://www.withoutend.org/talmage-journals-book-mormon-geography-hearings-1921/#sthash.N5nCNQhL.dpuf 1921.

Roberts, B. H. (Brigham Henry). "*Book of Mormon* Difficulties, A Study" and "A *Book of Mormon* Study," both in Brigham D. Madsen, *Studies of the Book of Mormon. B. H. Roberts*, 2nd. Edition. Salt Lake City: Signature Books, 1992.

Shook, Chas. A. *Cumorah Revisited.* Cincinnati: Standard Publishing Company, 1910.

Smith, Joseph (?). He may have approved the article in *Times and Seasons*, volume 3, number 23 (1 October 1842).

Smith, Joseph (?). Douglas K. Christensen, "Moroni's 36 Year Trek to New York," (published on *Book of Mormon* Archaeological Forum: http//:www.Bmaf.org, accessed 24 March 2007). The map in this article is said to have a line of transmission going back to Joseph Smith.

Sorenson, John L. *An Ancient American Setting for the Book of Mormon.* Salt Lake City: Deseret Book Company, 1985.

———. *Mormon's Map* (Provo, UT: The Foundation for Ancient Research and Mormon Studies [F.A.R.M.S], 2000).

———. *Mormon's Codex, an Ancient American Book* (Salt Lake City: Deseret Books, 2013).

Stout, Richard M. *Harmony in Book of Mormon Geography.* Boulder City, NV: by author, 1950.

Sutton, Bruce S. *Lehi, Father of Polynesia. Polynesians Are Nephites.* Orem, UT: Hawaiki Publishing, 2001.

Washburn, J. A., and J. N. Washburn. *An Approach to the Study of the Book of Mormon.* Provo, Utah: New Era Publishing Company, 1939.

Washburn, J. Nile. *Book of Mormon Lands and Times.* Bountiful, UT: Horizon Publishers, 1974.

Welch, John W., and J. Gregory Welch. *Charting the Book of Mormon: Visual Aids for Personal Study and Teaching* (Provo, UT: Neal A. Maxwell Institute for Religious Scholarship, 1999).

Wilde, Orrin G. *Landmarks of Ancient American People.* N.P.: by author, 1947.

Wirth, Diane. *Decoding Ancient America: A Guide to the Archaeology of the Book of Mormon.* (Springvile, UT: Cedar Fort, Inc., 2007).

Bibliography 4. General References

Abbott, Benjamin. *The experience and gospel labours of the Rev. Benjamin Abbott: to which is annexed a narrative of his life and death, by John Ffirth*. Philadelphia: pr. by Solomon 1801., W. Conrad, for Ezekiel Cooper, 1801.

Adair, James. *The History of the American Indians* (1775). Edited and with an Introduction and Annotations by Kathryn E. Holland Braund. Tuscaloosa: University of Alabama Press, 2005.

Adams, Daniel, with H. (Hazen) Morse, engraver. *School Atlas to Adams Geography.* Boston: Lincoln and Edmonds, 1825.

Allport, Gordon, and Joseph Postman, *Psychology of Rumor.* New York: Henry Holt and Company, 1947.

Allred, Joel M., *Mormonism under the Microscope. "Master, the Tempest is Raging."* Salt Lake City: Mountain Press, 2015, 2016).

Andersen, Devery S., and Gary James Bergera, eds. *Joseph Smith's Quorum of the Anointed, 1842-1845, a Documentary History.* Salt Lake City: Signature Books, 2005.

Anderson, Lavina Fielding, ed. *Lucy's Book, A Critical Edition of Lucy Mack Smith's Family Memoir.* Salt Lake City: Signature Books, 2001.

Anderson, Richard Lloyd. *Investigating the Book of Mormon Witnesses*. Salt Lake City: Deseret Book Company, 1981.

Backman, Milton V. *Eyewitness Accounts of the Restoration.* Salt Lake City: Deseret Book Company, 1986.

————. *Joseph Smth's First Vision; Confirming Evidences and Contemporary Accounts, Second Edition.* Salt Lake City: Deseret Book, 1980.

Bates, Irene M. "Foreword. Lucy Mack Smith—First Mormon Mother," in Anderson, *Lucy's Book.*

Bell, Lanny. "The Ancient Egyptian 'Books of Breathings,' the Mormon 'Book of Abraham,' and the Development of Egyptology in America," in Stephen E. Thompson & Peter Der Manuelian, eds., *Egypt and Beyond, Essays Presented to Leonard H. Lesko upon his Retirement.* Providence, RI: Brown University, 2008.

Boudinot, Elias. *Star in the West or a Humble Attempt to Discover the Long Lost Ten Tribes of Israel Preparatory to Their Return to Their Beloved City Jerusalem.* Trenton, NJ: George Sherman, Printer, for D. Fenton, S. Hutchinson and J. Dunham, 1816.

Brennan, Michael, and Rachel Greenstadt, "Practical attacks against authorship recognition techniques," Association for the Advancement of Artificial Intelligence, 2009.

Brodie, Fawn. *No Man Knows My History. The Life of Joseph Smith.* Second edition, revised and enlarged (New York: Alfred A Knopf, 1986 [1945/1971]).

Buerger, David John. *The Mysteries of Godliness. A History of Mormon Temple Worship.* Salt Lake City: Signature Books, 1994.

Buttrick, George A. *The Interpreter's Bible.* New York: Abingdon Press, 1956.

Coe, Michael. *Breaking the Mayan Code.* London: Thames & Hudson, 1999.

Cogley, Richard W. *John Eliot's Mission to the Indians before King Philip's War.* Cambridge: Harvard University Press, 1999.

Cook, Lyndon W., ed. *David Whitmer Interviews: A Restoration Witness* (Orem, UT: Grandin Book Co.: 1991).

Crawford, Charles. *An Essay on the Propagation of the Gospel in Which There Are Numerous Facts and Arguments Adduced to Prove That Many of the Indians in America Are Descended from the Ten Tribes.* Philadelphia: James Humphreys, 1801.

Davis, William. "Reassessing Joseph Smith Jr.'s Formal Education," *Dialogue: A Journal of Mormon Thought* 49, no. 4 (Winter 2016).

Dirkmaat, Gerrit J., & Michael Hubbard MacKay, "Joseph Smith's Negotiations to Publish the *Book of Mormon*," in Dennis Largey, Andrew H. Hedges, John Hilton III & Kerry Hull, eds., *The Coming Forth of the* Book of Mormon. Salt Lake City, Deseret Book, 2015.

Duguid, Iain. *Ezekiel and the Leaders of Israel*. Leiden: Brill, 1994.

Eccel, A. Chris. *An Analysis of the Distribution of the BoM Variants*. Chicago: unpublished paper, 1972).

———. *Egypt, Islam and Social Change: Al-Azhar in Conflict and Accommodation*. Berlin: Schwartz Verlag, 1984.

———. *Mormon Genesis*. Hilo, HI: GP Touchstone, 2018.

Edgell, H. Stewart. *Arabian Deserts, Nature, Origin and Evolution*. New York: Springer Publishing, 2006.

Edwards, Jonathan. *Some Thoughts Concerning the Revival of Religion in New England*, Part II, Sect. II, "The latter-day glory, is probably to begin in America." Boston: Printed and sold by S. Kneeland and T. Green in Queen-street, 1742.

———. *The Works of Jonathan Edwards*. Edinburgh: The Banner of Truth Trust,1990.

Eerdmans Dictionary of the Bible. Grand Rapids: Eerdmans Publishing Company, 2000.

Esplin, Ronald K. & Matthew J. Grow, gen. eds. *The Joseph Smith Papers*, vol. 3, pt. 2. Salt Lake City: The Church Historian's Press, 2015.

Evans, Tripp, *Romancing the Maya, Mexican Antiquity in the American Imagination, 1820-1915*. Austin: University of Texas Press, 2004.

Fortier, John C. "Hobbes and a 'Discourse on Laws': The Perils of Wordprint Analysis," in *The Review of Politics*, vol. 59, no. 04, fall 1997.

Foster, Arthur Glen Jr. "The Plates of Jacob: An Analysis of the Replacement to the Lost Manuscript of the *Book of Mormon*," (privately circulated), 1983.

Fulton, Scott, and Sylvia Keochakian, "The conservation of tumbaga metals from Panama at the Peabody Museum, Harvard University," *Objects Specialty Group Postprints*, Volume Twelve (2005).

Garner, Bryan A. *A Dictionary of Modern American Usage*. Oxford: Oxford University Press, 1998.

Garr, Arnold K., Donald Q. Cannon & Richard O. Cowan, *Encyclopedia of Latter-day Saint History*. Salt Lake City: Deseret Book Company, 2011.

Gilbert, John H. Memorandum, made by John H. Gilbert Esq, Sept 8th, 1892, Palmyra, N. Y." Palmyra King's Daughters Free Library, Palmyra, NY. It is in Wilfred C. Wood, *Joseph Smith Begins His Work. Book of Mormon 1830 First Edition.*

Goodman, Felicitas D. *Speaking in Tongues: a Cross-cultural Study of Glossolalia*. Chicago: University of Chicago Press, 1972.

Gookin, Daniel. *Historical Collections of the Indians in New England*. Boston: At the Apollo Press, by Belknap & Hall, 1792. The copy cited is an exact replica from Book Renaissance.

Gunn, Stanley R. *Oliver Cowdery, Second Elder and Scribe*. Salt Lake City: Bookcraft, 1962.

Hale, David. "David Hale's Store Ledger. New Details about Joseph and Emma Smith, the Hale Family, and the Book of Mormon," *BYU Studies Quarterly* 53:3, 2014, 105, 111.

Hanke, Lewis. *Aristotle and the American Indians: A Study in Race Prejudice in the Modern World*. Mishawaka, IN: Better World Books, 1970.

Heimert, Alan, and Perry Miller, eds. *The Great Awakening*. Indianapolis and New York: The Bobbs-Merrill Company, Inc., 1967, 610.

Hilton, John L., "On Verifying Wordprint Studies: *Book of Mormon* Authorship," in *BYU Studies* 30, no. 3, 1990.

Holley, Vernal. *Book of Mormon Authorship: A Closer Look*. Ogden UT: Zenos Publications, 1983. Updated edition, Roy, UT: self published, 1992.

Holmes, D. I. "A Stylometric Analysis of Mormon Scripture and Related Texts," in the *Journal of the Royal Statistical Society. Series A (Statistics in Society)*, vol. 155, no. 1 (1992).

Howard, Richard P. *Restoration Scriptures*. Independence, MO: Herald House, 1969.

Howe, Eber D. *Mormonism Unvailed*. Salt Lake City: Signature Books, 2015.

Huddleston, Lee Eldridge. *Origins of the American Indians, European Concepts, 1492-1729*. Austin: The University of Texas Press, 1967.

Hunter, Milton R. *Archaeology and the Book of Mormon*. Salt Lake City: Deseret Book Company, 1956.

———. *Great Civilizations and the Book of Mormon*. Salt Lake City: Bookcraft, 1970.

Jessee, Dean C. *Papers of Joseph Smith*. Salt Lake City: Deseret Book Company, 1989.

———. *The Personal Writings of Joseph Smith*. Salt Lake City: Deseret Book, 1984.

———. *The Early Accounts of Joseph Smith's First Vision*. Sandy, UT: Mormon Miscellaneous [reprint series], 1984.

———. "The Early Accounts of Joseph Smith's First Vision," *BYU Studies 9 (3): 275–94*. Provo, Utah: Brigham Young University, 1969.

———. "The Original *Book of Mormon* Manuscript," in *BYU Studies* 10 (Spring, 1970).

Jockers, Matthew L., Daniela M. Witten and Craig S. Criddle, "Reassessing authorship of the *Book of Mormon* using delta and nearest shrunken centroid classification," *Literary and Linguistic Computing* Advance Access (17 February 2009).

Kimball, Helen Mar. *Helen Mar Kimball Autobiography*. March 30, 1881, LDS Church History Library.

King, Edward (Lord Kingsborough). *Antiquities of Mexico*. London: R. Havell and Colnaghi, Son & Company, 1831-48.

Kirkham, Francis W. *A New Witness for Christ in America, "The Book of Mormon."* Independence, MO: Press of Zion's Publishing Company, 1951.

Kohn, Hans. *The Idea of Nationalism, a Study in its Origins and Background*. New York: Macmillan, 1944.

Kunich, John C. "Multiply Exceedingly: *Book of Mormon* Population Sizes," in Metcalfe, ed., *New Approaches to the Book of Mormon. Explorations in Critical Methodology*. Salt Lake City: Signature Books, 1993.

Larsen, Wayne A., Alvin C. Rencher and Tim Layton, "Who Wrote the *Book of Mormon*? An Analysis of Wordprints," in Noel B. Reynolds, ed., *Book of Mormon Authorship*. Salt Lake City: Bookcraft, 1982.

Larson, Stan, *Quest for the Gold Plates, Thomas Stuart Ferguson's Archaeological Search for the Book of Mormon*. Salt Lake City: Freethinker Press, 1996.

LeSueur, Stephen C. *The 1838 Mormon War in Missouri*. Columbia, MO: University of Missouri Press, 1987.

Lindsay, John S. *The Mormons and the Theatre, or The History of Theatricals in Utah with Reminiscences and Comments, Humorous and Critical*. Salt Lake City: Century Printing, 1905.

Lipschits, Oded. *The Fall and Rise of Jerusalem. Judah under Babylonian Rule* (Winona Lake, IN: Eisenbrauns, 2005), 58, notes 81 & 82.

Love, Michael & Jonathan Kaplan, eds. *The Southern Maya in the Late Preclassic: The Rise and Fall of Early Mesoamerican Civilization.* Boulder, CO: University Press of Colorado, 2011.

MacKay, Charles. *Extraordinary Popular Delusions and the Madness of Crowds.* San Bernardino, CA: Pantianos Classics, 2017. First edition: London: Richard Bentley, 1841.

MacKay, Michael Hubbard, Gerrit J. Dirkmaat, and Robin Scott Jensen. "The 'Caractors' Document: New Light on an Early Transcription of the *Book of Mormon* Characters," *Mormon Historical Studies*, vol. 14, no. 1.

Madsen, Gordon A., Jeffrey N. Walker & John W. Welch, *Sustaining the Law, Joseph Smith's Legal Encounters* (Provo, UT: BYU Studies, 2014).

Marquardt, H. Michael. "Joseph Smith's Egyptian Papers: A History," in Robert K. Ritner, *The Joseph Smith Egyptian Papyri, A Complete Edition.* Salt Lake City: Signature Books, 2013, 11-68.

———. *The Joseph Smith Revelations, Text and Commentary.* Salt Lake City: Signature Books, 1999.

———. *The Rise of Mormonism: 1816-1844.* Second Edition, Revised and Enlarged. Maitland, FL: Xulon Press, 2013.

Marquardt, H. Michael, and Wesley P. Walters. *Inventing Mormonism. Tradition and the Historical Record.* Salt Lake City: Smith Research Associates, 1994.

Mather, Samuel. *An Attempt to Shew that America Must be Known to the Ancients.* Boston: J. Kneeland, 1773.

Matthews, Robert J. "How We Got the *Book of Moses*." Published online at lds.org, accessed 22/01/2017.

Mayhew, Henry. *The Mormons or Latter-day Saints, A Contemporary History.* London: Office of the National Illustrated Library, [1851?]

McConkie, Bruce R. *Mormon Doctrine.* Salt Lake City: Bookcraft, 1966.

McGarry, Sheridan L. "Mormon Money," reprinted from *The Numismatist*, 1962.

Metcalfe, Brent Lee. "The Priority of Mosiah: A Prelude to *Book of Mormon* Exegesis," in Brent Lee Metcalfe, ed., *New Approaches to the Book of Mormon. Explorations in Critical Methodology.*

Metcalfe, Brent Lee, ed. *New Approaches to the Book of Mormon. Explorations in Critical Methodology.* Salt Lake City: Signature Books, 1993.

Moon, Todd K., Peg Howland and Jacob H. Gunther, "Document author classification using Generalized Discriminant Analysis." Proc. Workshop on Text Mining, SIAM, 2006.

Morris, Larry E. "Oliver Cowdery's Vermont Years and the Origins of Mormonism." *BYU Studies* 39:1 (200).

Morton, A. Q., *Literary Detection: How to Prove Authorship and Fraud in Literature and Documents.* New York: Charles Scribner's Sons, 1978.

Nibley, Hugh. *Enoch the Prophet.* Salt Lake City: Deseret Book Company, 1986.

———. *Lehi in the Desert & the World of the Jaredites.* Salt Lake City: Bookcraft, 1952/1980.

———. *The Message of the Joseph Smith Papyri, An Egyptian Egyptian Endowment.* Second Edition, edited by John Gee & Michael D. Rhodes. Salt Lake City: Deseret Book Company, 2005.

Nickell, Joe. *Pen, Ink & Evidence, A Study of Writing and Written Materials for the Penman, Collector and Document Detective.* Lexington: The University of Kentudky, 1990.

Parker, Richard A., and Waldo H Dubberstein. *Babylonian Chronology: 626 B.C. - A.D. 75*. Providence, RI: Brown University Press, 1956.

Parkin, Max H. "A Preliminary Analysis of the Dating of Section 10." *The Seventh Annual Sidney B. Sperry Synposium: The Doctrine of Covenants*. Provo, UT: Brigham Young University, 1979.

Pearce, L. E. and C. Wunsch. *Documents of Judean Exiles and West Semites in Babylonia in the Collection of David Sofer*. Bethesda, MD: Cornell Univ. Studies in Assyriology and Sumerology 28, 201.

Petersen, Lamar. *Problems in Mormon Text*. Concord, CA: Pacific Publishing Co., no date.

Peterson, H. Donl. *The Story of* The Book of Abraham*, Mummies, Manuscripts and Mormonism*. Salt Lake City: Deseret Book Company, 1995.

Pratt, Orson. "Nephite America—The Day of God's Power—The Shepherd of Israel." *Journal of Discourses* (February 11, 1872).

Pratt, Parley P. *Autobiography of Parley P. Pratt*, edited by his son, Parley P. Pratt. Salt Lake City: Deseret Book Company, 1934 (edition quoted, 1994).

Priest, Josiah. *American Antiquities and Discoveries in the West being an Exhibition of the Evidence that an ancient population of partially civilized nations, differing entirely from those of the present Indians, peopled America, many centuries before its discovery by Columbus, and inquiries into their origin*. Albany, NY: Hoffman and White, 1833.

———. *The Wonders of Nature and Providence Displayed*. Albany: published by the author, 1826.

Purchas, Samuel. *Hakluytus Posthumus, or, Purchas his Pilgrimes (a Discourse on Virginia)*. Glasgow: James MacLehose & Sons, 1905.

Quinn, D. Michael. *The Mormon Hierarchy: Origins of Power*. Salt Lake City: Signature Books, 1994.

———. *Early Mormonism and the Magic World View*. Salt Lake City: Signature Books, 2nd ed., 1998.

Rafinesque, C. *Ancient History, or Annals of Kentucky; with a Survey of the Ancient Monuments of North America; and a Tabular View of the Principal Languages and Primitive Nations of the Whole Earth*. Frankfort in Kentucky: Printed by the author, 1824.

———. *Atlantic Journal and Friend of Knowledge*. Philadelphia: 1832-33.

———. *A C. S. Rafinesque Anthology*. Edited by Charles E. Boewe. Jefferson, NC: McFarland & Company, 2005.

Redford, Donald B. *The Wars in Syria and Palestine of Thutmose III*. Leiden: Brill, 2003.

Rensberger, David. "Elder," in *Eerdmans Dictionary of the Bible* (Grand Rapids: 2000).

Reynolds, Noel B., ed. *Book of Mormon Authorship*. Salt Lake City: Bookcraft, 1982.

Rigdon, John Wickliffe. "The Life and Testimony of Sidney Rigdon," *Dialogue: A Journal of Mormon Thought*, 1:4, 1966.

Ritner, Robert K. *The Joseph Smith Egyptian Papyri, A Complete Edition*. Salt Lake City: Signature Books, 2013.

Roediger III, H.L. "Reconstructive Memory, Psychology of," *International Encyclopedia of the Social & Behavioral Sciences*. Amsterdam: Elsevier B.V., 2001.

Sackett, Chuck. *What's Going on in There? The Verbatim Text of the Mormon Temple Rituals Annotated and Explained by a Former Temple Worker*. Thousand Oaks, CA: Sword of the Shepherd Ministries, ND.

Samarin, William J. *Tongues of Men and Angels: the Religious Language of Pentacostalism*. New York: Macmillan, 1972.

Schaalje, G. Bruce, John L. Hilton and John B. Archer. "Comparative Power of Three Author-Attribution Techniques for Differentiating Authors," *Journal of Book of Mormon Studies*, 6/1 (1997).

Schaalje, G. Bruce, Matthew Roper and Gregory L. Snow. "Extended nearest shrunken centroid classification: A new method for open-set authorship attribution of texts of varying sizes," *Literary and Linguistic Computing*, vol. 26, no. 1, 2011.

Scott, Patricia Bell. *The History of Agriculture in Susquehanna County from 1787.* By author? Lebanon Valley College, History 44, 1957-1958.

Selwyn, Lyndsie. "Corrosion Chemistry of Gilded Silver and Copper," in Terry Drayman-Weisser, *Gilded Metals, History, Technology & Conservation* (London: Archetype Publications, 2000).

Shalev, Eran. "'Revive, Renew, and Reestablish': Mordecai Noah's Ararat and the Limits of Biblical Imagination in the Early American Republic," posted on http//:www.americanjewisharchives.org (downloaded 25/03/2017).

Shipps, Jan. *Mormonism: The Story of a New Religious Tradition.* Urbana: University of Illinois Press, 1985.

Simon, Barbara Anne. *Hope of Israel: Presumptive Evidence that the Aborigines of the Western Hemisphere are Descended from the Ten Missing Tribes of Israel.* London: R. B. Seeley, 1829.

———. *The Ten Tribes of Israel Historically Identified with the Aborigines of the Western Hemisphere.* London: R. B. Seeley, 1836.

Skousen, Royal. *The History of the Text of the Book of Mormon. Part One, Grammatical Variation.* Provo, UT: The Foundation for Ancient Research and Mormon Studies, 2016.

———. *The History of the Text of the Book of Mormon. Part Two, Grammatical Variation.* Provo, UT: The Foundation for Ancient Research and Mormon Studies, 2016.

———. *The Original Manuscript of the Book of Mormon. Typographical Facsimile of the Extant Text.* Provo, UT: Foundation for Ancient Research and Mormon Studies, 2001.

———. *The Printer's Manuscript of the Book of Mormon: Typographical Facsimile of the Entire Text in Two Parts.* Provo, UT: Foundation for Ancient Research and Mormon Studies, 2001.

Skousen, Royal, & Robin Scott Jensen, , *Original Manuscript of the Book of Mormon, Facsimile Edition*, in *The Joseph Smith Papers*, volume 5. Salt Lake City: The Church Historian's Press, 2021.

Smith, Ethan. *View of the Hebrews, Exhibiting the Destruction of Jerusalem...* Poultney, VT: Smith & Shule, 1823.

———. *View of the Hebrews; or the Tribes of Israel in America. Second edition, improved and enlarged.* Poultney, VT: Smith & Shute, 1825 (Edition cited: Salt Lake City: Bookcraft for the Religious Studies Center at Brigham Young University, 1999.)

Smith, George D., ed. *An Intimate Chronicle: The Journals of William Clayton,* Salt Lake City: Signature Books, 1972.

Smith, Joseph. *History of the Church of Jesus Christ of Latter-day Saints.* Salt Lake City: Deseret News, 1902.

Smith, Lucy. *Biographical Sketches of Joseph Smith the Prophet and His Progenitors for Many Generations.* Lamoni, IA: Reorganized Church of Jesus Christ of Latter-day Saints, 1912.

Lucy Mack Smith, in Lavina Fielding Anderson, ed., *Lucy's Book, A Critical Edition of Lucy Mack Smith's Family Memoir.* Salt Lake City: Signature Books, 2001.

Sondrup, Stephen P. "The Psalm of Nephi: A Lyric Reading," *BYU Studies* (Provo, UT: Brigham Young University, 21:3, 1981),

Southerton, Simon G. *Losing a Lost Tribe. Native Americans, DNA and the Mormon Church.* Salt Lake City: Signature Books, 2004.

Spaulding [Spalding], Solomon. *The "Manuscript Found" or "Manuscript Story," of the Late Rev. Solomon Spaulding; from a Verbatim Copy of the Original Now in the Care of Pres. James H. Fairchild, of Oberlin College, Ohio, Including Correspondence Touching the Manuscript, Its Preservation and Transmission until It Came into the Hand of the Publisher.* Lamoni, Iowa: The Reorganized Church of Jesus Christ of Latter Day Saints, 1885); *Manuscript Found: The Complete Original.* Provo, UT: BYU Religious Studies Center, 1997.

Sperry, Sidney B. *Our Book of Mormon.* Salt Lake City: Bookcraft, 1950.

———."The 'Isaiah Problem' in the Book of Mormon," in Journal of Mormon Studies, 4:1 (1995), article 17.

Steindorff, George, & Keith C. Seele, *When Egypt Ruled the East.* Chicago: The University of Chicago Press, 1957.

Stenhouse, Mrs. T. B. H. *Tell It All: The Story of a Life's Experience in Mormonism. An Autobiography.* Hartford: Worthington & Co., 1874.

Stephens, John Lloyd. *Incidents of Travel in Central America, Chiapas and Yucatan.* 2 vols. Illustrations by Frederick Catherwood. New York: Harper, 1841.

Sweeney, Marvin A. "The Latter Prophets," in Steven L. McKenzie and M. Patrick Graham. *The Hebrew Bible Today: An Introduction to Critical Issues.* Westminster: John Knox Press, 1998.

Thorowgood, Thomas. (n.d.). *Jews in America, or Probabilities That the Americans Are of That Race.* London: T. Slater, 1650. (Edition cited: 1825 2nd Edition. Provo, UT: Bookcraft for the Religious Studies Center at Brigham Young University, 1996.)

Tvedtnes, John. "Hebraisms in the *Book of Mormon*," transcript downloaded from the FARMS website

———. "Isaiah Variants in the *Book of Mormon*" (1984), transcript accessed at http://publications.mi.byu.edu/people/john-a-tvedtnes/.

Tvedtnes, John, John Gee and Matthew Roper, "*Book of Mormon* Names Attested in Ancient Hebrew Inscriptions," *Journal of Book of Mormon Studies*, 9/1/2000.

Van Wagoner, Richard S. *Sidney Rigdon, A Portrait of Religious Excess.* Salt Lake City: Signature Books, 1994.

Vogel, Dan. *Early Mormon Documents.* Salt Lake City: Signature Books (5 vols.), 2007.

———. *Joseph Smith, The Making of a Prophet* .Salt Lake City: Signature Books, 2004.

———. "Preface" to *Mormonism Unvailed* by Eber D. Howe, and "Addenda" to the same. Salt Lake City: Signature Books, 2015.

Wadsworth, Nathaniel Hinckley. "Securing the *Book of Mormon* Copyright," in Gordon A. Madsen, Jeffrey N. Walker and John W. Welch, *Sustaining the Law. Joseph Smith's Legal Encounters.* Provo, UT: BYU Studies, 2014.

Walam Olum, or Red Score. The Migration Legend of the Lenni Lenape or Delaware Indians, including a transcription and ostensible translation of *Walam Olum* by C. (Constantine) S. (Samuel) Rafinesque, with studies by various authors. Indianapolis: Indiana Historical Society, 1954.

Walker, John. Walker's *Critical Pronouncing Dictionary, and Expositor of the English Language.* Abridged For the Use of Schools. To Which is Annexed, an Abridgment of Walker's Key to the Pronunciation of Greek, Latin, and Scripture Proper Names. Boston: Lincoln & Edmands, Samuel T. Armstrong, and Charles Ewer, 1823.

Watson, William C. *Dispensationalism before Darby. Seventeenth-Century and Eighteenth-Century English Apocalypticism.* Silverton, OR: Lampion Press, 2015.

Welch, John W. "Chiasmus in the *Book of Mormon,*" in John W. Welch, ed., *Chiasmus in Antiquity.* Provo, UT: Research Press [The Foundation for Ancient Research and Mormon Studies—F.A.R.M.S.], 1981.

Whitmer, David. *An Address to All Believers in Christ* (Richmond, MO: Snell's Printshop, 1887.

———. Lyndon W. Cook, ed., *David Whitmer Interviews: A Restoration Witness* (Orem, UT: Grandin Book Co., 1991).

Williams, Roger. (1643). *A Key into the Language of America.* London: Printed by Gregory Dexter, 1643. (Edition cited, reprint: Bedford, MA: Applewood Books, 1936.

Wood, Wilfred C. *Joseph Smith Begins His Work. Book of Mormon 1830 First Edition, Reproduced from Uncut Sheets.* Salt Lake City: Deseret News Press, 1958.

Worsley, Israel. (1828). *A View of the American Indians.* London: Printed for the author & sold by R. Hunter, 1828; Plymouth: W. W. Arliss. (edition cited: New York: Arno Press reprint, 1971.)

< Index >

This index is intended to complement the Table of Contents.

www.ingramcontent.com/pod-product-compliance
Lightning Source LLC
Chambersburg PA
CBHW050237270326
41914CB00034BA/1956/J